The Nurture Versus Biosocial Debate in Criminology

To my beautiful wife, Shonna, and
to my four children, Brooke, Jackson, Belle, and Blake.

—KMB

To Sara, without whom none of this would be worthwhile.
—JCB

To my family—Billy, Wanda, and Brett—your
support means everything; thank you so much.
—BBB

The Nurture Versus Biosocial Debate in Criminology

On the Origins of Criminal Behavior and Criminality

Kevin M. Beaver
Florida State University

J.C. Barnes
The University of Texas at Dallas

Brian B. Boutwell
Sam Houston State University

Editors

Los Angeles | London | New Delhi
Singapore | Washington DC

Los Angeles | London | New Delhi
Singapore | Washington DC

FOR INFORMATION:

SAGE Publications, Inc.
2455 Teller Road
Thousand Oaks, California 91320
E-mail: order@sagepub.com

SAGE Publications Ltd.
1 Oliver's Yard
55 City Road
London EC1Y 1SP
United Kingdom

SAGE Publications India Pvt. Ltd.
B 1/I 1 Mohan Cooperative Industrial Area
Mathura Road, New Delhi 110 044
India

SAGE Publications Asia-Pacific Pte. Ltd.
3 Church Street
#10-04 Samsung Hub
Singapore 049483

Acquisitions Editor: Jerry Westby
Editorial Assistant: MaryAnn Vail
Production Editor: David C. Felts
Copy Editor: Deanna Noga
Typesetter: C&M Digitals (P) Ltd.
Proofreader: Kristin Bergstad
Indexer: Scott Smiley
Cover Designer: Candice Harman
Marketing Manager: Terra Schultz

Printed in the United States of America

Library of Congress Cataloging-in-Publication Data

The nurture versus biosocial debate in criminology : on the origins of criminal behavior and criminality / Kevin M. Beaver, Florida State University, J.C. Barnes, The University of Texas at Dallas, Brian B. Boutwell, Sam Houston State University, editors.

pages cm
Includes index.

ISBN 978-1-4522-4225-5

1. Criminal behavior—Physiological aspects. 2. Criminal behavior—Genetic aspects. 3. Criminal psychology. 4. Criminology—Sociological aspects. I. Beaver, Kevin M. II. Barnes, James C. (James Christopher) III. Boutwell, Brian B.

HV6115.N87 2015
364.3—dc23 2013032278

This book is printed on acid-free paper.

14 15 16 17 18 10 9 8 7 6 5 4 3 2 1

Contents

Preface

One of the most heated academic debates that has cut across virtually every field of study is the nature versus nurture debate. The central focus of this debate focuses on whether human behaviors and traits are the result of environmental factors (nurture) or genetic factors (nature). Throughout much of the 1900s, the two sides were seen as mutually exclusive and incompatible. Advocates of each side to the debate vehemently defended their position and viewed the debate as a winner-takes-all approach where either nature accounted for everything or nurture accounted for everything. At different time periods and in different disciplines, both the nurture perspective and the nature perspective enjoyed dominance. As the 20th century progressed, the debate shifted from mere ideology and subjectivity to one that was grounded in empirical research and rigorous scholarly debate. The end result has been a declaration, in most disciplines, that the nature versus nurture debate is dead and that both environmental factors and genetic influences contribute to virtually every behavior and trait ever studied.

Most disciplines other than criminology were able to settle the nature versus nurture debate because of feuds that occurred in the literature and at academic conferences. Within criminology, however, there has not been a public nature versus nurture debate carried out by leading scholars. For the most part, the nurture side to the debate has been taken as fact, and virtually all theories, research, and curriculum focus almost entirely on nurture. In essence, the nature side of the debate was stamped out and excised from published criminological scholarship. Of course, nowadays no serious scholar believes in a purely nature explanation to human variability, but there are plenty of criminologists who adhere to a purely nurture explanation to human variability. As a result, the nature versus nurture debate is somewhat dead in criminology and has morphed into a newer debate: the nurture versus biosocial debate. The nurture side to the debate remains the same as always—that is, the environment is responsible for producing behaviors, traits, and other human characteristics. The biosocial side to the debate—which has effectively replaced the nature side—recognizes the importance of both the environmental and genetic factors.

The goal of the current book is to facilitate an open and honest debate between the more traditional criminologists who focus only on environmental factors and contemporary biosocial criminologists who examine the interplay between biology/genetics and environmental factors. For each topic, there are two chapters: one written by a renowned environmental criminologist and one written by a well-known biosocial criminologist. That way, readers will see both sides of the debate and can make their own informed decision about which one is a better explanation.

One of the more interesting aspects of the book that we encountered was during our recruitment of contributors. We had anticipated that it would be more difficult to find authors to write on the biosocial explanation and it would be rather easy to find authors willing to write on the sociological explanation. What we found out, however, was that many authors we contacted to write from the sociological perspective revealed to us (some publicly, some privately) that they actually believe more in the biosocial side but prefer to write and work from a sociological perspective. Some contributors have even noted in their chapters that they are writing the chapter from a purely sociological perspective, but that their own views fall more in line with a biosocial perspective. Seen in this way, the field of criminology may actually be going through the beginning stages of a shift away from a purely sociological perspective and more toward a biosocial perspective. Of course, in academia, scholars are judged by what they write, not what they silently believe. Hopefully, this book will help scholars revisit their own views and write more openly about what they believe when it comes to the causes and correlates to criminal involvement.

This book is divided into four sections, with each section including a number of topics. Briefly, the first section of the book focuses on key criminological correlates, including gender, race, and social class. The second section of the book focuses on theoretical perspectives, including learning theory, self-control theory, strain theory, and social bond theory. The third section of the book examines specific antisocial behaviors, including intimate partner violence, childhood antisocial behavior, and drug use and abuse. The last section of the book covers trends, current issues, and policy implications by examining the crime drop, the age-crime curve, and policies.

Our intent in developing this book is that it sparks debate, creates new opportunities for scholarship, and pushes the understanding of criminal behavior and criminality to a higher level. By bringing the nature versus biosocial debate to the forefront of criminology, our hope is that we are able to debate intelligently an issue that will likely have profound influence on the future of criminology.

Kevin M. Beaver
J.C. Barnes
Brian B. Boutwell

Introduction

Why We Need a Nature/ Nurture Book in Criminology

Does the world really need another rehashing of the age-old nature versus nurture debate? Is there anyone left who actually believes that genes or the environment play absolutely no part in the development of human behavior (Pinker, 2002)? Are there really naturalists who think that only biology and genetics are entirely deterministic of our every thought and action? Are there any prophets of sociology left to proselytize the power of nurture, the unending sway of parenting, the overarching omnipotence of culture? While it is hard to imagine any serious scholar taking one of these extreme positions, it is safe to say that the nature versus nurture debate has yet to be resolved among criminological thinkers and that certain theorists have, at times, espoused viewpoints strikingly similar to the embellished statements made above (Pinker, 2002).

In daily discourse with colleagues, it is not uncommon to hear off-the-cuff quips suggesting that no one *actually* doubts the importance of biology (Cohen, 1999). Yet, in many ways, actions speak louder than words. At the time this chapter was written, the flagship journal in the discipline, *Criminology,* had never published a peer-reviewed article with a measured gene included in the analysis. Why? Is there a shortage of good molecular genetics research examining the correlates of antisocial behavior? Surely not. In fact, entire journals with impact factors in the low to mid double digits publish such research in practically every issue (see, for example, *Molecular Psychiatry*).

So do we need another tome dealing with the issue of environment versus biology? We submit that the answer to this question is "yes." We need it now more than ever, because the field of criminology may be at a crossroads (Cullen, 2011). Down one path is the status quo. If we elect to travel this path, it means that we will continue to run multivariate models, conduct occasional experiments, publish studies, and convince ourselves that by ignoring the findings of other scientific fields they will somehow go away. Down the other path lie uncomfortable truths, many of which have direct implications for our understanding of human behavior. Truths like the fact that human beings are animals, no more or less special than any other animal on this otherwise nondescript planet. Humans are a product of evolution, everything we are has been shaped either directly or indirectly by a "blind watchmaker" (Dawkins, 1986) clumsily assembling our complexities from preexisting parts. Down this uncomfortable road, moreover, lies the very real possibility that many of the sacrosanct findings gleaned from decade upon decade of criminological research might be wrong. Indeed, these are possibilities brought about by a biosocial criminology.

The Biosocial Perspective

So what is biosocial criminology, exactly? You might be surprised to know that we do not conceive of biosocial criminology as a unique discipline, per se. From our vantage point, biosocial criminology is more accurately conceived of as an amalgamation of several perspectives, all of which biosocial researchers draw from to conduct their own research. Specifically, there are five perspectives that inform biosocial scholarship: behavior genetics, molecular genetics, neuroscience, biology, and evolutionary psychology. Now, we should note that presenting things in this manner necessarily oversimplifies much of the nuance that exists within biosocial scholarship. However, what should become clear in the chapters to follow is that practically all research mentioned by biosocial scholars will be classifiable in one (or several) of these domains. Moreover, we are not going to burden the reader with heavy citation at this point, much of that will come later. For now, we only want to present you the rationale of why these disciplines inform so much of what biosocial scholars do on a daily basis.

Let us begin with the perspective invented to explain the origin of individual differences, behavior genetics (BG). The history of BG research reaches back to Francis Galton (with roots also attributable to other great statisticians and mathematicians such as Karl Pearson, Sewell Wright, and Ronald Fisher, to mention only a few luminaries) (Plomin, DeFries, Knopik, & Neiderhiser, 2013). As you will see, BG research is capable of answering several key questions concerning biosocial research: (a) do genes influence a trait, (b) does the environment influence a trait, (c) which has the greater impact, genes or environment, and (d) how do the two coalesce to influence human development?[1] Doubtless, the reader can readily see why BG techniques are such a vital component of biosocial research. This particular set of tools helps answer a fundamental question: why are humans so different from one another? More specifically, why are some humans so much more violent, aggressive, antisocial, and delinquent than others? BG research allows biosocial scholars to begin unpacking the answers to these core questions.

Molecular genetics (MG) is the next logical component of biosocial research. If BG research tells us that genes matter, MG research helps us understand which genes, or more broadly which sections of DNA (including nonprotein coding regions, perhaps) are integral for understanding human variation. In the years following the completion of the human genome project, there has been a veritable glut of MG research examining a host of different outcomes ranging from disease to psychopathology, personality, and behavior. Because of MG research, current biosocial scholars are genuinely living through a "golden age" of science with the growing availability and accessibility of MG tools and analyses.

Travel up one more unit of analysis from MG research and you arrive in the arena of neuroscience. As Francis Crick (1994) so eloquently captured in his "astonishing hypothesis," all human mental life—our morality, our decision making, our feelings of love and affection, as well as anger and rage—all reside and originate in our brain. Pause for just a minute and ponder the nearly inexplicable idea that all of *who you are,* the entirety of your mental life (your hopes, dreams, memories, aspirations, everything that is you) resides in a three-pound physical organ sitting atop your spinal column. The brain is a product of the genome, insomuch as all of the capacity for building your brain comes preloaded in your DNA (Pinker, 2002). True, experience will help wire the brain in certain ways; brains do a fantastic job of importing and managing exterior information (i.e., learning) (Pinker, 2002). However, many of the genes analyzed in MG research are directly linked to structural and functional variation in the brain (Raine, 2008). As a result, neuroscience is an essential piece of the biosocial research agenda.

Our brains are not the only interesting component of our biology and physiology that might impact behavior. Broader still, biosocial research often examines additional biological markers (such as resting heart rate and skin conductance) that may act as proxies for various developmental traits such as low arousal (which might serve as a risk factor for impulsive and violent behavior). Hormone levels, as well, play a key role in social behaviors like bonding and feelings of aggression and more overt violent acts. As a result, biosocial research often makes use of measurements gleaned at the physiological and biological levels. Moreover, this line of inquiry has yielded much in the way of insight regarding the biological contributors to human behavior.

Finally, evolutionary psychology serves as an overarching meta-approach to the origins of human behavior (Pinker, 2002). Evolutionary psychology involves the simple recognition that if gradual modification through descent built all our internal and external structures—including the brain—then it must have exerted some influence over the development of human social behavior (Pinker, 2002). As we will see, evolutionary psychology offers a guiding framework for all that biosocial researchers do. If our theories fail to make sense in an evolutionary framework, then we should consider going back to the drawing board. Without the principles provided by Darwin and Russell-Wallace, there simply cannot be a thorough science of human (or any other animal) behavior.

Clearly, biosocial researchers draw heavily from many disciplines and perspectives. Even so, why wouldn't we conceive of biosocial criminology as representing its own discipline or subdiscipline? Our reasoning is simple. We view biosocial research as being indicative of the most viable and rigorous approach to studying human behavior. Unless we endorse creationism, mind-body dualism (in the sense that an immaterial soul, or "ghost in the machine" inhabits our corporeal bodies) (Pinker, 2002) or some other metaphysical explanation for behavior, our biology and our evolutionary past must matter in terms of our behavioral outcomes. What this means is that biosocial criminology is not some niche subfield, it is—or rather it should be considered—criminology.

Our Role in the Debate

As the editors of this volume, which was designed to inspire debate and dialogue, we faced an interesting scenario in which our role was to act as mediators (of sorts) for our colleagues writing on behalf of sociological and biosocial perspectives of human behavior. A perusal of any one of our research agendas will unveil all three of us as biosocial scholars. We have, nonetheless, great respect for those who contributed chapters concerning sociological explanations of human outcomes. Indeed, most of the contributors are friends, and all are valued colleagues. Yet, on many points and critical assumptions regarding the origins of human behavior, we hold alternative viewpoints. This is not to say that sociology—and nurture-based perspectives more broadly defined—have nothing to contribute to our understanding of antisocial behavior and crime. But we, as editors, should lay our cards fully on the table. From our vantage point, a purely sociological explanation for any human behavior is unlikely to be incorrect. Instead, an understanding of social and biological forces is essential to capturing the full breadth of the mosaic that is human behavioral variation. As readers work through the individual sections, the ways in which biosocial scholarship parts company with sociological scholarship should become quite apparent. Please allow us now to briefly elaborate and to tell you, the reader, why we feel this way and what led us to this point in our careers (prompting the compellation of this book).

Converts to the Biosocial Perspective

One of the key discussion points that repeatedly emerges when talking with biosocial scholars is how they converted to the biosocial perspective. Take, for example, the experiences of two of us (Boutwell and Barnes). Perhaps most fortuitous was that Beaver was a new faculty member—already deeply enmeshed in the biosocial perspective—when Brian Boutwell and J.C. Barnes arrived at Florida State University (FSU) for their graduate studies. Like most students, they entered into the program with very little background in biology, genetics, and evolutionary psychology. Boutwell completed his doctoral training in criminology. Barnes studied criminology and criminal justice, also receiving a doctorate in criminology. Our exposure, though, was to the same concepts, theories, and ideas that most of our colleagues experienced in their graduate and undergraduate training in various sociology, political science, and criminology/criminal justice programs. How, then, did we arrive at our current stance that biosocial research is perhaps the most appropriate method for studying human behavior?

Boutwell's conversion to biosocial science occurred during his first semester in graduate school at FSU. Many of the graduate students elected to enroll in a class known as *Proseminar.* In the course, a different faculty member would lecture each week regarding his or her particular substantive area of research, offering the students a broad overview of what the faculty as a whole was doing within the college. It was intended, in many ways, to jump start potential mentoring relationships between new students and current faculty. Each week, following the lecture, a group-based reaction paper was due, which included a general response to the topic of that week's presentation. Brian's group was assigned to write a reaction paper to the lecture given by Kevin Beaver. That week, Kevin discussed the broad strokes of biosocial research, offering a very general overview of the basic concepts and ideas. The reaction paper, interestingly enough, expressed concern and reservation regarding the dangers and moral questionability of biosocial research. On further reflection, however, Brian felt somewhat guilty about his incorrigible stance on a body of research that he knew nothing about; he sought Beaver out for a further conversation. That conversation blossomed into a broader discussion, which eventually led to collaboration, publication, and ultimately a mentoring relationship that continues to this day (Boutwell & Beaver, 2008).

Barnes's conversion to biosocial research involved far less resistance. He enrolled in FSU's doctoral program via the University of South Carolina's (USC) Master's program. Though he was not attending FSU with the intention of becoming a biosocial scholar, he was introduced to Kevin during his first semester and quickly developed a mentor-mentee relationship. Early discussions between Beaver and Barnes were not particularly "biosocial" but more broadly concerned current theoretical explanations of antisocial behavior. At some point, J.C. and Kevin conjured up a paper idea, which J.C. was to take the lead on. The paper required a brief discussion of genetic factors related to human behavior. J.C., recalling a lecture from his time at USC, pulled his notes from a filing cabinet and was surprised to find that he had taken extensive notes on the subject and had even written in the margins of several papers comments such as "this is the type of research I want to do."

Within a year of each other, Boutwell and Barnes became immersed in the work of behavior geneticists, psychiatrists, molecular geneticists, developmental psychologists, neuroscientists, and biologists. Terrie Moffitt and Avshalom Caspi's work, for instance, revealed the intimate connection between environment and genotype, and how ignoring either one produces an incomplete picture of human development. Richard Herrnstein and Charles Murray, along with other eminent scholars like Richard Lynn, Hans Eysenck, and Linda Gottfredson, revealed the far-reaching importance for traits like human intelligence on a host of outcomes that criminologists and sociologists spend a great deal of time trying to understand. The writing of Judith Rich Harris, perhaps one of the most important yet least appreciated child developmentalists ever, shook many of their closely guarded beliefs about the role of parenting in child development. And of course, the writings of Charles Darwin illustrated in a broad sense what true science should look like—unashamedly based in fact, carefully constructed, and logically assembled in a testable and falsifiable manner. The list could go on.

Ultimately, the evidence for Brian and J.C. became too overwhelming. Human behavior was a product of biology *and* the environment. In some cases, biology appeared to matter more, and in some cases it appeared to matter less. But in no instance was there a complete irrelevance for either biology or the environment when studying human behavior. Both are intimately intertwined and simply must be studied in all their interwoven complexity. For all three of us, there was no way around this fact. To operate in a void, only offering passing lip service to the importance of biology was simply not going to be good enough.

Oddly enough, however, it has recently become almost "fashionable" to do biosocial research. Indeed, one might argue that setting up a "debate" between sociology and biology is tantamount to erecting a straw man. As we have already mentioned, certain lines of research (like findings in molecular genetics) have yet to penetrate some of the top journals in criminology. More important, there are still areas that are staunchly off limits to biosocial scholars. Consider the experience of one of the editors while sitting in his office on campus. The door was open and a colleague entered to chat. The conversation was pleasant, until the visitor noticed a copy of Herrnstein and Murray's *The Bell Curve* (1994) lying on the desk. This realization prompted an odd look from the colleague followed by a very interesting question, which we paraphrase here: "Why would you read such a book. Don't you realize that it is a dangerous piece of literature?" You might have thought a rattlesnake lay curled on the desk. The idea had never entered the editor's mind that the book, or any of its ideas, was dangerous. The editor responded by asking whether the individual had read the book. The response was a resounding "no," why spend time reading something that simply had to be false?

Though it is a mere anecdote, the collegial conversation represents in a microcosm our experiences since converting to biosocial research. Indeed, there is evidence bearing on a larger trend in the field (Wright et al., 2008). A general rejection of biosocial research is clearly illustrated by Wright and colleagues' analysis of over 600 criminology/criminal justice faculty members across 33 doctoral granting programs in the discipline. Of those faculty members, 12 reported any type of training or interest in the incorporation and examination of biological factors in relation to overt forms of antisocial and aggressive human behavior. As Wright and colleagues note, that represents a whopping *2%* of the scholars who are responsible for training the next generation of criminological scientists. If one thinks that the field has moved past the need for a debate, perhaps one should reconsider.

The Prospects of a Biosocial Perspective

As academics, we are probably all familiar with the peer review process. An editor e-mails you, asks you to review a manuscript, and you gladly accept the honor. You open the document and begin reading, eventually arriving at the first table containing empirical results. In this case, the authors have constructed a wonderfully complex multivariate model, explained an acceptable amount of variance, and relayed their findings in a clear and cogent manner.

There is just one problem, and it is no trivial matter. The authors have omitted a key variable, indeed a lynchpin type measure that because it is not in the model makes their analysis virtually uninterruptable. It certainly looks like *X* influences *Y*, but *Z* is not in the analysis (and we know that *Z* is related to both *X* and *Y*), so where does that leave us? It leaves us in that dreaded zone feared by methodologists and theoreticians alike and known as a spurious result. In other words, the findings may be entirely illusory owing to unmeasured and omitted factors. As a reviewer, there are really only two options at this juncture: reject the manuscript or recommend revision if you believe the authors can somehow manage to include the measure they previously omitted from their analyses. Either way, the study would not be acceptable in its current form.

Now consider this in relation to the incorporation of biology into criminological research designs. For the sake of brevity, we are not going to review findings here (those are available in later chapters). Yet what will become clear is that the impact of biology on human behavior is ubiquitous. While the magnitude of the effect varies, the impact of biological factors (e.g., genes, evolution, etc.) is unlikely to ever be zero. Essentially, biology represents variable *Z* in the example above. Because variable *Z* was omitted from the study we were asked to review, we arrived at the conclusion that the paper was unacceptable. It was a basic methodological concern/issue. Was the study rigorous, did it account for all possible sources of bias? Our take on this in the example was no, it failed to meet a certain standard of rigor. Thus, we rejected the paper (or recommended sweeping changes). For some reason, though, criminologists have largely failed to take these same steps if variable *Z* represents a biological construct.

The issue at hand, then, is elementary. The reason that biosocial research is essential is because it represents a rigorous approach to studying human behavior allowing for the estimation of biological effects. Oddly enough, for example, behavior genetic methodologies (to illustrate the point) represent one of the most effective tools for studying the environment. Why? The answer is that behavior genetic methodologies allow the researcher to tease apart the influence of genes and the environment to isolate the effects that one might be interested in examining (e.g., the effect of peer group environments). Put differently, behavior genetic research allows the researcher to control for *Z* in order to examine the effects of *X* on *Y*. We are not suggesting that one should not study the environment, only that scholars in criminology should do it in a fashion that allows for the variance due to biological factors to be removed. This is not an exceptional or inflammatory request.

What to Expect Moving Forward

The idea for this book was born out of conversations among the editors lamenting the fact that criminologists and criminal justicians had yet to have an open and honest dialogue about the nature versus nurture issue. We wanted to offer a forum in which both sides of the debate could be heard from and have an opportunity to present their perspectives. One thing that readers can expect as they progress through each section is that they will encounter an expert in the given area writing about the topic in a very thorough and clear manner. Moreover, we hope that each chapter provides a natural contrast to its sister chapter in a way that gives readers the ability to examine the nature of a given topic from both a sociological and biosocial perspective. Ultimately, we hope this text compels scholars to open an objective discourse about these issues because discussion and testing of ideas is the only way we can move forward as a field. Thus, we offer the following text as a modest step toward such an open, objective discourse. Time will tell, and we will anxiously watch and continue to do our work.

As a final concluding thought, we should not forget that being a scientist is a high calling, not everyone has the luxury of being one. Moreover, the exercise of studying human behavior is no mere ivory tower exercise. Humans often do terrible and unspeakable things to one another. The questions we try to answer as criminologists are meaningful, and they have consequences that reverberate in the real world. It stands to reason, then, that we should utilize every tool available to us as scientists to ensure that answers to questions like "what causes crime" are correct. We leave you, the reader, to contemplate these issues as you enter the debate between social and biosocial scholars.

Note

1. By using the term *impact* we are misconstruing (although not entirely) the actual function of BG research. BG research functions to explain "variance" in a given trait. Thus, the reason that BG research is the science of individual differences is because it explains why humans vary so widely on various measures of physiology, personality, and behavior. Ultimately, the way in which BG research quantifies the sources of human variation is by decomposing trait variance into the components of heritability, shared environment, and nonshared environment, which are explained throughout the course of various biosocial chapters in this book.

References

Boutwell, B. B., & Beaver, K. M. (2008). A biosocial explanation of delinquency abstention. *Criminal Behavior and Mental Health, 18,* 59–74.

Cohen, D. B. (1999). *Stranger in the nest: Do parents really shape their child's personality, intelligence, or character?* New York, NY: Wiley.

Crick, F. H. C. (1994). *The astonishing hypothesis: The scientific search for the soul.* New York, NY: Touchstone.

Cullen, F. T. (2011). Beyond adolescence-limited criminology: choosing our future: The 2010 American Society of Criminology Sutherland address. *Criminology, 49,* 287–330.

Dawkins, R. (1986). *The blind watchmaker: Why the evidence of evolution reveals a universe without design.* New York, NY: W. W. Norton.

Herrnstein, R. J., & Murray, C. (1994). *The bell curve: Intelligence and class structure in American life.* New York, NY: Free Press.

Pinker, S. (2002). *The blank slate: The modern denial of human nature.* New York, NY: Viking.

Plomin, R., DeFries, J. C., Knopik, V. S., & Neiderhiser, J. M. (2013). *Behavioral genetics* (6th ed.). New York, NY: Worth.

Raine, A. (2008). From genes to brain to antisocial behavior. *Current Directions in Psychological Science, 17,* 323–328.

Wright, J. P., Beaver, K. M., DeLisi, M., Vaughn, M. G., Boisvert, D., & Vaske, J. (2008). Lombroso's legacy: The miseducation of criminologists. *Journal of Criminal Justice Education, 19,* 325–338.

PART I

KEY CRIMINOLOGICAL CORRELATES

1

Sociological Explanations of the Gender Gap in Offending

Abigail A. Fagan

University of Florida, Department of Sociology and Criminology & Law

Gender differences in the perpetration of illegal acts, with males much more likely to offend compared to females, are widely recognized in criminology. What is less clear is why this gender gap in offending exists. Biological, physiological, psychological, structural, and social factors have all been used to explain gender differences in offending. Although more investigation is needed to fully understand why males commit more crime than do females, this chapter contends that biological factors cannot adequately account for the gender gap in offending and that social factors influence males and females to engage in crime at different rates. After documenting the size and nature of the gender gap in offending, this chapter summarizes sociological explanations that have been put forth and tested in empirical research to explain this gap and identifies critical next steps needed to increase knowledge regarding gender differences in offending.

The Gender Gap in Offending

How large is the gender gap in offending? According to official records, in 2009, females accounted for 18% of all juvenile arrests for serious violent offenses and 38% of all arrests for serious property offenses (Puzzanchera & Adams, 2011). Of all the offenses tracked, females' rates exceeded males' for only two delinquent acts: prostitution (78% of all arrestees were female) and running away from home (55% of arrestees were female). Similar proportions are recorded for adults. The 2010 Uniform Crime Reports (UCR) indicated that women comprised 25% of all adults arrested for serious violent offenses and 38% of those arrested for property crimes; only 11% of homicide arrests involved women. Although official records indicate that the gender gap has been narrowing (Steffensmeier, Zhong, Ackerman, Schwartz, & Agha, 2006), males continue to be overrepresented in offending.

Given that not all crimes come to the attention of the criminal justice system and that there may be bias in determining who is arrested, it is also important to assess the gender gap using self-reported data. These sources also indicate that boys are more likely than girls to break the law and especially to engage in violence (Elliott, 1994; Jang & Krohn, 1995; Moffitt, Caspi, Rutter, & Silva, 2001; Peterson, Esbensen, Taylor, & Freng, 2007). According to over 15,000 12th-grade students participating in the Monitoring the Future national survey, in 2010, males reported more property crimes and more violent offenses compared to females (Bachman, Johnston, & O'Malley, 2010). Likewise, among high school students participating in the 2009 Youth Risk Behavioral Survey, males were more likely than females to report carrying a weapon (rates of 27% and 7%, respectively) and getting into fights (39% vs. 23%) (Centers for Disease Control and Prevention, 2010). According to adults interviewed in the National Crime Victimization Survey, only 17% of all those perpetrating simple and aggravated assaults from 1979 to 2003 were females (Steffensmeier et al., 2006).

Gender Similarities in Offending

Despite overwhelming evidence of a gender gap in offending, biological sex is typically not considered to "cause" crime. If this were the case, evidence would indicate that all males engage in crime and all females do not. Because this is clearly not true, gender is usually referred to as a "correlate" of crime—a variable showing an association with offending, but not a deterministic influence. That is, it is recognized that being male does not automatically lead to or necessarily cause an individual to break the law.

In fact, the disparity in offending between males and females is not uniform across all offenses or across all individuals, which suggests that biological differences between males and females cannot fully account for differences in crime rates. Official records uniformly report larger sex differences in offending than do self-reported data, suggesting that sex disparities may be due more to official and social responses to crime than to actual differences in behavior (Elliott, 1994; Steffensmeier et al., 2006). In addition, according to official and self-report statistics, the ratio of male to female offenders is larger for violent (about 3:1) than nonviolent (about 1.5:1) crime (Peterson et al., 2007). In fact, some property offenses show minimal gender differences. According to UCR data, the proportion of females arrested in 2010 for fraud (40%), larceny/theft (44%), and embezzlement (51%) approached that of males.

Even for violent offenses, the gender gap is largely nonexistent among some populations, particularly when comparing White males and African American females (Laub & McDermott, 1985) or high-risk females and low-risk males (e.g., female gang members and male non-gang members; see Kruttschnitt, Gartner, & Ferraro, 2002). In the National Youth Survey, in early adulthood when violent crimes peaked, about 25% of White males reported one or more serious violent offense compared to 20% of African American females (Elliott, 1994). Likewise, White males and African American females living in urban areas have been shown to have similar rates of arrest for some violent crimes (Chilton & Datesman, 1987; Sommers & Baskin, 1992). Geographical residence also seems to impact the gender gap. In a study of 5,935 8th-grade students from 11 communities, females living in each of two urban cities reported more violence than males living in the nine other rural or suburban locations (Peterson et al., 2007).

Gender similarities in offending are further demonstrated by evidence that trends in crime tend to be the same for males and females: when male offending rates are increasing, female rates are increasing, and vice versa. Patterns in offending are also similar. For both sexes, property offending far exceeds violent offending, and early antisocial behavior is associated with longer and more serious criminal careers. Last, the demographic characteristics of male and female offenders are similar; both groups are typically younger and from low-income and minority racial/ethnic groups (Kruttschnitt, 2001; Steffensmeier & Broidy, 2001).

Social Influences on Offending

Taken together, these data suggest that the gender gap is more "a difference in degree than in kind" (Lanctot & Le Blanc, 2002, p. 115) and further, that male overrepresentation in crime cannot be attributed solely to biological factors; social influences must play a significant role. This hypothesis is supported by evidence that rates of conduct disorder are similar for females and males during early childhood (ages 0–4). After this developmental period, there is a marked decline in behavioral problems for females compared to males (Keenan & Shaw, 1997; Zahn-Wexler, Shirtcliff, & Marceau, 2008). This stage of life coincides with children's entry into school and increased social interactions with peers, teachers, and other adults. According to feminist research, such interactions provide individuals with critical information on how to "do gender"; that is, how to display behaviors consistent with cultural stereotypes of femininity and masculinity (West & Zimmerman, 1987). Not coincidently, norms regarding acceptable male behavior stress attributes like rebelliousness and aggression, which may promote their involvement in crime, while norms regarding acceptable female behavior emphasize conformity and empathy, which may inhibit offending.

The remainder of this chapter reviews the principal sociological explanations that have been posited to account for gender differences in offending and summarizes how well these factors have been shown to account for the gender gap. This research evaluates macro-level political and social influences; peer, school, and family factors; and some individual attributes that are likely to be influenced by social interactions (e.g., attitudes regarding the acceptability of illegal behavior).

MACRO-LEVEL STRUCTURAL AND CULTURAL INFLUENCES

To date, much of the empirical research examining gender differences in offending has focused on psycho-social influences, such as parenting practices, exposure to delinquent peers, and academic achievement. Although some research has indicated that males are more likely to encounter such factors (Rowe, Vazsonyi, & Flannery, 1995; Smith & Paternoster, 1987), which could result in their overrepresentation as offenders, this work has typically left unanswered the question of why males would be differentially exposed to risk factors. Feminist criminologists have critiqued this exclusive focus on individual-level criminological influences and called for increased attention to macro-level power structures and social dynamics that may differentially affect male and female involvement in crime (Daly & Chesney-Lind, 1988). In particular, feminists emphasize the need to critically examine how patriarchy systematically constrains women and allows men greater power and control, and how these dynamics shape offending.

Following this perspective, some research contends that male and female offending is contingent on the opportunities each group has to engage in crime. In patriarchal societies, women are forced into the domestic sphere of society and are disproportionally responsible for child and family care, while males are more likely to be in the public (work) domain (Figueira-McDonough, 1992). This division of labor results in fewer opportunities for females to engage in crime. Data support this view. Violent offenses are disproportionately committed by males, who are also more likely to assault strangers and acquaintances, those encountered in public settings. When women engage in violence, they are more likely to attack family members (children and husbands). Males are also more likely to perpetrate sexual assault, which reflects their greater sexual power (Kruttschnitt, 2001).

While recognizing that females are underrepresented as offenders, current macro-level theories emphasize that when women do break the law their reasons for doing so are tied to their social and economic marginalization. Such work is in contrast to the "liberation hypotheses" proposed in the 1970s, which predicted that as women gained more social and economic equality their crime rates would increase and become more similar to men's (Adler, 1975; Simon, 1975). Liberation hypotheses have not been well supported. Instead, female poverty has been tied to female crime rates (Hunnicutt & Broidy, 2004; Parker & Reckdenwald, 2008), and official statistics indicate that incarcerated women are disproportionately from low socioeconomic backgrounds and racial/ethnic minority groups. The types of property crimes committed by women also reflect their marginalized position in society (Chesney-Lind, 1997). Women are most likely to be arrested for offenses such as embezzlement, shoplifting, passing bad checks, credit card theft, theft of services, and welfare fraud, consistent with their greater likelihood of being both consumers (i.e., shoppers) and single parents, as well as their overrepresentation in low-paying jobs and as welfare recipients (Steffensmeier, 1993). Interviews with female offenders often indicate that their crimes are committed out of economic necessity, particularly if they have children to support (Gilfus, 1992).

While this evidence suggests that female criminals are not economically liberated, there is some evidence that social equality could be associated with increased female offending. Consistent with the liberation hypothesis, some research suggests that girls who are less likely to endorse traditional views regarding gender (e.g., that females should be passive, accommodating, and empathetic, while males should be aggressive, dominant, and risk-seeking) are more likely to engage in delinquency (Heimer, 1996) and violence (Heimer & De Coster, 1999; Simpson & Ellis, 1995). However, other studies have shown the opposite: that female offenders are more likely to report traditional views of masculinity and femininity (Chesney-Lind, 1997; Hill & Crawford, 1990; Steffensmeier & Broidy, 2001). In addition, power control theory (Hagan, Gillis, & Simpson, 1987), which contends that both male and female delinquency will be fostered in more "liberated" and nontraditional (i.e., female-headed) homes, has not been well supported (Kruttschnitt, 2001; Lanctot & Le Blanc, 2002).

While macro-level explanations offer great potential for discovering the root causes that may give rise to gender differences in offending, these structural and cultural variables are difficult to operationalize and test empirically. Thus, a larger body of research has examined more proximal social influences on male and female offending, including family, peer, and school factors. Much of this research has focused on processes influencing the onset of offending during childhood and adolescence.

FAMILY INFLUENCES

Family factors have likely received the most attention in sociological explanations of the gender gap in offending. In particular, differences in how parents socialize their male and female children are thought to differentially impact their propensity for deviance. It has been posited that parents more closely monitor girls' behaviors, keep girls closer to home, and reinforce conformity and punish deviance more often for daughters than for sons (Keenan & Shaw, 1997). Conversely, boys are subject to less social control and monitoring, and parents are more likely to endorse (or passively accept) deviant behaviors in their male children. As a result, boys have more opportunities to engage in delinquency and receive fewer reprimands for doing so compared to girls. Some also assert that parents teach girls to place more importance on family relationships. Greater attachment to the family may serve as a protective factor, reducing the likelihood of female offending, and may also strengthen the effects of parental monitoring and other family factors (Chesney-Lind, 1997; Keenan & Shaw, 1997; Kroneman, Loeber, Hipwell, & Koot, 2009; Kruttschnitt & Giordano, 2009). Thus, even if boys and girls received similar levels of social control from parents, such practices would reduce delinquency more for girls than boys.

In fact, evidence of marked gender differences in parental socialization practices and in their effects on delinquency is mixed. Some studies have shown that girls are subject to more parental monitoring and control and have greater attachment to parents (Canter, 1982; Cernkovich & Giordano, 1987; Crosnoe, Erickson, & Dornbusch, 2002; Fagan, Van Horn, Hawkins, & Arthur, 2007; Jang & Krohn, 1995; Junger-Tas, Ribeaud, & Cruyff, 2004). Other research, however, has indicated that males and females receive similar levels of monitoring, discipline, and emotional support from parents (Daigle, Cullen, & Wright, 2007; Huebner & Betts, 2002; Rowe et al., 1995). Likewise, effects of family factors on delinquency often do not vary by sex (Daigle et al., 2007; Fergusson & Horwood, 2002; Hartman, Turner, Daigle, Exum, & Cullen, 2009; Hoeve et al., 2009; Rowe et al., 1995; Zahn, Hawkins, Chiancone, & Whitworth, 2008). In addition, while some research has shown that girls are more strongly influenced by parenting practices (Blitstein, Murray, Lytle, Birnbaum, & Perry, 2005; Bottcher, 1995), other studies have indicated that males are more affected (Canter, 1982; Cernkovich & Giordano, 1987; Fagan et al., 2007; Moffitt et al., 2001).

Heimer's research (Heimer, 1996; Heimer & De Coster, 1999) has identified more complex mechanisms linking gender, parenting practices, and delinquency. Consistent with a gendered socialization process, she contends that parenting practices produce differences in girls' and boys' endorsement of traditional gender roles and in their attitudes regarding the acceptability of deviant or violent behavior, and that these attitudes lead to different rates of offending. These hypotheses have been somewhat supported. In two studies using National Youth Survey data, girls from female-headed households were less likely to endorse traditional gender beliefs, and those who had closer emotional bonds to parents were less likely to approve of violence. These attitudes affected illegal behavior, with more delinquency among girls who rejected traditional gender roles and who had greater acceptance of violence (Heimer, 1996; Heimer & De Coster, 1999). For boys, support for traditional gender roles did not affect delinquency or violence, but attitudes favoring violence did increase reports of violent activities. Gender differences in the direct effects of parenting practices on offending were also found; parental supervision reduced violence more so for boys than girls, and attachment to parents reduced girls' violence more than boys' (Heimer & De Coster, 1999).

According to self-control theory, parents are responsible for establishing children's self-control; that is, their ability to regulate impulses and emotions, consider the long-term consequences of their actions, and tolerate frustration (Gottfredson & Hirschi, 1990). This theory posits that parents who monitor children's behavior, recognize deviant behavior, and effectively discipline children for acting out will help children establish strong, internal control. In turn, children with high self-control will be less likely to engage in crime. Although Gottfredson and Hirschi (1990) did not formally posit gender differences in these processes, they contend that the marked gender differences in offending are evidence that females have greater self-control than do males, which, in turn, must be the product of differences in parental socialization of daughters and sons.

In contrast to this claim, evidence that girls are more closely monitored by parents and more likely to be disciplined for deviant behaviors is not consistent. Moreover, empirical studies have produced somewhat mixed results in regard to gender differences in levels of self-control and in the effects of self-control on offending. A study of 2,000 Canadian teenagers found that females reported greater self-control on some indicators (impulsivity, risk-seeking, and being "present-oriented") but not all measures. In addition, higher self-control predicted less delinquency for both sexes, but impulsivity was most important for explaining male offending, while risk-seeking was most important for explaining female offending (La Grange & Silverman, 1999). Greater levels of self-control have also been reported by female versus male college students, but the effects of self-control on offending were similar for both sexes (Gibson, Ward, Wright, Beaver, & DeLisi, 2010). In adult samples, one study reported equal effects of self-control on crime for males and females (Tittle, Ward, & Grasmick, 2003), but a second showed that self-control influenced crime among women only when opportunities for criminal involvement were also present (Burton, Cullen, Evans, Alarid, & Dunaway, 1998). Finally, a meta-analysis of self-control research reported stronger effects on delinquency for females compared to males (effect sizes of 0.57 and 0.16, respectively), but this difference was not statistically significant (Pratt & Cullen, 2000). Overall, this research indicates that the impact of self-control on offending is similar for males and females, and while males may have lower self-control than females, it is unclear if differences in parenting practices account for this disparity.

Some feminist research has identified family experiences, specifically child sexual abuse, as producing a unique pathway to offending for females. According to this perspective, girls are more likely than boys to be sexually abused as children and many end up running away from home to escape the abuse. With few skills at their disposal, runaways engage in crimes such as prostitution and theft to support themselves (Belknap, 2001; Chesney-Lind, 1997; Zahn et al., 2008). General strain theory has similarly posited that girls are more likely than boys to experience family-related strains and to use criminal coping mechanisms to alleviate the stress produced by these events (Broidy & Agnew, 1997; Ness, 2004). Empirical studies provide mixed support for these claims. There is much evidence that girls are subject to higher levels of sexual abuse than boys and that these experiences increase the likelihood of female offending (Fagan, 2001; Zahn et al., 2008). However, child abuse and neglect have also been linked to increased offending among males, and a few studies have shown that the relationship between child maltreatment and crime is stronger for males versus females (Belknap & Holsinger, 2006; Fagan, 2005; Mersky & Reynolds, 2007; Topitzes, Mersky, & Reynolds, 2011; Widom, 1989).

Although feminists have critiqued mainstream criminology for failing to critically examine how gender affects criminal behavior (Daly & Chesney-Lind, 1988), this review of family influences suggests that progress is being made. Nonetheless, there are still limitations to be addressed. Many family-focused studies have utilized statistical models that separate male and female respondents, but have not evaluated if differences in effect sizes across these groups are statistically significant, which limits the ability to determine if family factors differentially affect boys and girls. This approach also precludes examination of the degree to which family influences explain the gender gap. If gender no longer predicts criminal involvement, or if its effect is significantly reduced once family influences are accounted for, there is stronger evidence that offending is attributable to family processes rather than biological sex.

Of the studies mentioned above, only a few have specifically tested the ability of family factors to explain the sex disparity in offending. In most cases, the impact of gender has been reduced but remained significant when all relevant family variables were included in statistical models; in these cases, males reported more crime than females regardless of how they were treated by parents (Alarid, Burton, & Cullen, 2000; La Grange & Silverman, 1999; Mersky & Reynolds, 2007). In contrast, Jang and Krohn (1995) found that when controlling for parental supervision, which was greater for females than males, the impact of gender on self-reported delinquency was nonsignificant when respondents were in Grades 7 through 9. Notably, the impact of supervision on delinquency waned as children aged, and correspondingly, the gender gap increased and became significant when children reached Grade 10. Heimer and De Coster (1999) reported that, controlling for family structure, supervision, and emotional support, 88% of the gender gap in violence was explained. Much of this effect operated via adolescents' attitudes regarding traditional gender roles and the acceptability of violence, both of which inhibited delinquency more so for girls than boys. Finally, Burton and colleagues (1998) reported that the effect of gender on crime became nonsignificant when assessing the impact of low self-control among adults. These studies provide greater support that differential parenting practices explain why males commit more crime than females.

PEER INFLUENCES

Although family influences have received the bulk of attention from those interested in gender differences in offending, many criminologists consider peer influences to be a stronger influence on delinquency (Akers, 1985; Elliott, Huizinga, & Ageton, 1985). Potential gender differences in peer influences have not been subject to much scrutiny, but two possibilities have been discussed. First, because males commit more crime than females, it follows that girls will be less likely to encounter delinquent peers and more likely to have prosocial friends, both of which should result in less offending by girls versus boys. Second, it has been posited that girls are socialized to be more empathetic and relationship-oriented than boys, which could result in their greater susceptibility to the attitudes, beliefs, and actions of their peers (Heimer, 1996; Zimmerman & Messner, 2010). Such influences could increase or decrease female involvement in crime, depending on how often their peers engage in delinquency.

There is empirical support for both of these assertions. Several investigations have demonstrated higher levels of exposure to delinquent peers for males compared to females (Crosnoe et al., 2002; Fagan et al., 2007; Liu & Kaplan, 1999; Mears, Ploeger, & Warr, 1998; Moffitt et al., 2001; Piquero, Gover, MacDonald, & Piquero, 2005; Zimmerman & Messner, 2010). In addition, Haynie, Steffensmeier, and Bell (2007) reported that exposure to peers of the opposite sex increased violence among girls but not boys, and that females' contact with males was only problematic when boys were engaging in violence. Some studies have demonstrated that females have greater attachment to their peers, which suggests that they may be more strongly influenced by their friends (Smith & Paternoster, 1987; Zimmerman & Messner, 2010). However, many studies have shown that the influence of delinquent peers is invariant across sex (Alarid et al., 2000; Moffitt et al., 2001; Rowe et al., 1995; Smith & Paternoster, 1987), and a few have reported that peer influences are stronger for males versus females (Crosnoe et al., 2002; Fagan et al., 2007; Mears et al., 1998). In the latter group, Mears and colleagues (1998) found that having delinquent peers was a stronger risk factor for boys than girls in large part because girls were more likely than boys to consider delinquency to be wrong, and these moral beliefs protected them against negative peer influences.

Although some studies have shown that males are more susceptible to peer influences during adolescence, there is some evidence that among adults women are more likely to be negatively impacted by romantic involvement with criminal partners. Two longitudinal studies showed that having a criminal spouse increased female offending more than male offending (Moffitt et al., 2001; Simons, Stewart, Gordon, Conger, & Elder, 2002). Similarly, Alarid and colleagues (2000) found that marriage was associated with increased rates of offending among women but had no effect on male offending, although other research has not indicated gender differences in the effects of marriage on crime (Giordano, Cernkovich, & Rudolph, 2002). Finally, Richie's (1996) qualitative study of battered women demonstrated that a substantial proportion of women were coerced into crimes like prostitution and drug selling by their abusive partners.

To summarize, research investigating gender differences in peer influences on offending tends to suggest that males are more likely to have delinquent peers but that such exposure has similar effects on offending for both sexes. In addition, peer influences do not appear to fully explain the gender gap in offending, because some studies have indicated that gender remains a significant predictor of illegal behavior controlling for exposure to delinquent peers (Liu & Kaplan, 1999; Mears et al., 1998; Piquero et al., 2005; Zimmerman & Messner, 2010). Whether or not gender differences in offending among adults can be explained by relationships with deviant spouses is less clear, because relatively few studies have examined this issue.

SCHOOL INFLUENCES

High academic achievement, commitment to education, and attachment to teachers and schools have all been found to reduce the likelihood of delinquency for both sexes (Blum, Ireland, & Blum, 2003; Cernkovich & Giordano, 1992; Crosnoe et al., 2002; Daigle et al., 2007; Fagan et al., 2007; Hartman et al., 2009; Payne, 2009; Resnick, Ireland, & Borowsky, 2004; Rowe et al., 1995; Zahn et al., 2008). Although a few studies indicate that attachment to school has a more protective effect on delinquency and drug use for girls versus boys (Payne, Gottfredson, & Kruttschnitt, 2009; Sale, Sambrano, Springer, & Turner, 2003), a greater number of studies have indicated that boys are exposed to more risk factors (e.g., poor academic performance) and fewer protective factors (e.g., attachment and commitment to school) in the school domain (Crosnoe et al., 2002; Daigle et al., 2007; Fagan et al., 2007; Junger-Tas et al., 2004; Liu & Kaplan, 1999; Rowe et al., 1995). In addition, much research indicates that the effects of school risk and protective factors are stronger for boys versus girls (Junger-Tas et al., 2004; Liu & Kaplan, 1999; Maguin & Loeber, 1996; Payne, 2009). For example, a meta-analysis reported mean effect sizes of academic performance on delinquency of –0.17 for males compared to –0.09 for females (Maguin & Loeber, 1996).

Although males may be more at risk for experiencing school problems and more influenced by such factors, school experiences do not appear to completely explain the gender gap in offending. Even with multiple school factors included in multivariate statistical models, the effect of gender on delinquency and/or drug use has remained significant in some studies, with boys more likely to report offending than girls (Junger-Tas et al., 2004; Liu & Kaplan, 1999; Payne, 2009). This conclusion is tentative, however, because few studies have assessed gender differences in the effects of school experiences, particularly environmental factors such as school climate, norms, and structure (Payne et al., 2009).

COMMUNITY INFLUENCES

Social influences on offending include not only family, peer, and school experiences, but also community characteristics such as residence in economically and socially disadvantaged neighborhoods (Sampson, Raudenbush, & Earls, 1997; Shaw & McKay, 1942). Compared to other domains, gender differences in community-level influences have been underexamined and often assumed not to exist (Kroneman, Loeber, & Hipwell, 2004; Zahn & Browne, 2009). However, some literature suggests that because boys receive less monitoring by parents and are more likely than girls to spend time in public places they will be more exposed to community risk and protective factors. Furthermore, because boys are perceived as more likely to engage in crime, they may be subject to more collective supervision by neighborhood residents, which could reduce their involvement in crime. It is also possible, however, that residents will view girls as in need of more protection and regulation, which could enhance community protective effects (Browning, Leventhal, & Brooks-Gunn, 2005).

The few empirical studies that have explored gender differences in the influence of neighborhood characteristics have produced mixed results. Some research has reported that economic disadvantage has equally small or nonsignificant effects on male and female offending (Beyers, Bates, Pettit, & Dodge, 2003; Jacob, 2006; Mrug & Windle, 2009; Simons, Johnson, Beaman, Conger, & Whitbeck, 1996) and that social processes like informal social control and collective efficacy have similar influences on both sexes (Karriker-Jaffe, Foshee, Ennett, & Suchindran, 2009; Molnar, Cerda, Roberts, & Buka, 2008; Mrug & Windle, 2009). In contrast, some studies have found that neighborhood poverty is more likely to increase violence among females than males (Karriker-Jaffe et al., 2009; Zimmerman & Messner, 2010), while others have reported that neighborhood affluence (Beyers et al., 2003) and collective efficacy (Meier, Slutske, Arndt, & Cadoret, 2008) are more protective for males. Finally, the Moving to Opportunities study (Kling, Ludwig, & Katz, 2005) found that girls who moved from highly disadvantaged communities to more affluent areas had fewer arrests for violent and property offending than girls who had not moved, while boys who moved were more likely to commit property offenses than nonrelocated boys.

Of these studies, only Zimmerman and Messner (2010) explicitly investigated whether or not the gender gap in offending could be accounted for by neighborhood factors, and they found that economic disadvantage could explain this differential. For adolescents living in Chicago neighborhoods classified at the mean level of disadvantage, males were 77% more likely to engage in violence compared to females; in neighborhoods one standard deviation above the mean, the odds were 45% greater, and gender differences became nonsignificant at 1.4 standard deviations above the mean of disadvantage. Additional analyses indicated that exposure to violent peers was greater in low-income neighborhoods, and the effect of such exposure was greater for females than males; thus, deviant peers mediated the effects of disadvantage on violence more so for girls than boys (Zimmerman & Messner, 2010).

Summary and Conclusions

Consistent with much criminological literature, this review suggests that many social factors influence involvement in crime and delinquency. By extension, it seems likely that the criminal behavior of both males and females, as well as the gender gap in offending, is best explained by multivariate models that can represent the complex mechanisms that lead to offending. Guided by this perspective, a few studies have investigated the degree to which the combined impact of multiple risk and protective factors can account for males' overrepresentation in offending. Surprisingly, much of this work demonstrates that even after accounting for some of the most robust social predictors of crime, gender differences in violence and delinquency persist (Hartman et al., 2009; Moffitt et al., 2001; Rowe et al., 1995; Stoddard, Zimmerman, & Bauermeister, 2012). Nonetheless, two studies reported that the gender gap was substantially reduced in multivariate models. Controlling for childhood, family, peer, and individual risk and protective factors, Moffitt and colleagues (2001) reported that 56% of the sex difference in antisocial behavior was explained, while Rowe and colleagues (1995) found that the relationship between sex and delinquency was reduced by two-thirds in models controlling for 18 risk and protective factors.

A few studies testing particular theories of crime found that the gender gap in offending disappeared when controlling for salient risk factors (Burton et al., 1998; Heimer & De Coster, 1999; Jang & Krohn, 1995; Zimmerman & Messner, 2010). However, more common is research indicating that gender differences persist. Such results can be interpreted in various ways. The ability of criminological research to explain offending in general tends to be modest. Similarly, a failure to adequately explain gender differences may simply reflect measurement error, lack of adequate theorizing regarding the causes of crime, or a failure of statistical models to account for all potential influences on offending. It is also possible that the gender gap in offending is due, at least in part, to individual or biological factors such as personality type or genetic predisposition. Although this review cannot rule out this potential, the ability of such factors to completely account for gender differences is unlikely, given evidence that social influences often differentially affect male and female criminality, and that, in some circumstances and among certain populations, rates of offending by females exceed those of males.

The gender gap in offending, while widely acknowledged, has only recently become the focus of dedicated empirical research. Much more investigation is needed to explain differences in offending between males and females, including studies that extend traditional theories of crime as well as research that relies on multivariate analyses and involves complex causal models. Studies should continue to assess factors that may uniquely affect offending by males and females and to conduct analyses separately for each sex when appropriate. Investigations are also needed that compare differences in effect sizes of particular variables across gender groups and that examine the degree to which the gender gap in offending is reduced or eliminated in such models. Such analyses have rarely been conducted, which impedes the ability to fully understand why males engage in illegal behavior more often than females.

References

Adler, F. (1975). *Sisters in crime: The rise of the new female criminal.* New York, NY: McGraw-Hill.

Akers, R. L. (1985). *Deviant behavior: A social learning approach* (3rd ed.). Belmont, CA: Wadsworth.

Alarid, L. F., Burton, V. S., Jr., & Cullen, F. T. (2000). Gender and crime among felony offenders: Assessing the generality of social control and differential association theories. *Journal of Research in Crime and Delinquency, 37,* 171–199.

Bachman, J. G., Johnston, L. D., & O'Malley, P. M. (2010). *Monitoring the Future: Questionnaire repsonses from the nation's high school seniors, 2010.* Ann Arbor, MI: Survey Research Center, Institute for Social Research, University of Michigan.

Belknap, J. (2001). *The invisible woman: Gender, crime, and criminal justice* (2nd ed.). Cincinnati, OH: Wadsworth.

Belknap, J., & Holsinger, K. (2006). The gendered nature of risk factors for delinquency. *Feminist Criminology, 1*(1), 48–71.

Beyers, J. M., Bates, J. E., Pettit, G. S., & Dodge, K. A. (2003). Neighborhood structure, parenting processes, and the development of youths' externalizing behaviors: A multilevel analysis. *American Journal of Community Psychology, 31*(1–2), 35–53.

Blitstein, J. L., Murray, D. M., Lytle, L. A., Birnbaum, A. S., & Perry, C. L. (2005). Predictors of violent behavior in an early adolescent cohort: Similarities and differences across genders. *Health Education and Behavior, 32*(2), 175–194.

Blum, J., Ireland, M., & Blum, R. W. (2003). Gender differences in youth violence: A report from Add Health. *Journal of Adolescent Health, 32,* 234–240.

Bottcher, J. (1995). Gender as social control: A qualitative study of incarcerated youths and their siblings in greater Sacramento. *Justice Quarterly, 12*(1), 33–57.

Broidy, L., & Agnew, R. (1997). Gender and crime: A general strain theory perspective. *Journal of Research in Crime and Delinquency, 34*(3), 275–306.

Browning, C. R., Leventhal, T., & Brooks-Gunn, J. (2005). Sexual initiation in early adolescence. *American Sociological Review, 70*(5), 758–778.

Burton, V. S., Jr., Cullen, F. T., Evans, T. D., Alarid, L. F., & Dunaway, R. G. (1998). Gender, self-control, and crime. *Journal of Research in Crime and Delinquency, 35*(2), 123–148.

Canter, R. J. (1982). Family correlates of male and female delinquency. *Criminology, 20*(2), 149–167.

Centers for Disease Control and Prevention. (2010). Youth risk behavior surveillance—United States, 2009. Surveillance summaries, June 4, 2010. *Morbidity and Mortality Weekly Report 59, SS-5.* Atlanta, GA: Office of Surveillance, Epidemiology, and Laboratory Services, Centers for Disease Control and Prevention (CDC), U.S. Department of Health and Human Services.

Cernkovich, S., & Giordano, P. C. (1987). Family relationships and delinquency. *Criminology, 25*(2), 295–319.

Cernkovich, S., & Giordano, P. C. (1992). School bonding, race, and delinquency. *Criminology, 30*(2), 261–291.

Chesney-Lind, M. (1997). *The female offender: Girls, women and crime.* Thousand Oaks, CA: Sage.

Chilton, R., & Datesman, S. K. (1987). Gender, race, and crime: An analysis of urban arrest trends, 1960–1980. *Gender and Society, 1*(2), 152–171.

Crosnoe, R., Erickson, K. G., & Dornbusch, S. M. (2002). Protective functions of family relationships and school factors on the deviant behavior of adolescent boys and girls: Reducing the impact of risky friendships. *Youth and Society, 33*(4), 515–544.

Daigle, L. E., Cullen, F. T., & Wright, J. P. (2007). Gender differences in the predictors of juvenile delinquency. *Youth Violence and Juvenile Justice, 5*(3), 254–286.

Daly, K., & Chesney-Lind, M. (1988). Feminism and criminology. *Justice Quarterly, 5*(4), 497–535.

Elliott, D. S. (1994). Serious violent offenders: Onset, developmental course, and termination—The American Society of Criminology 1993 Presidential Address. *Criminology, 32*(1), 1–21.

Elliott, D. S., Huizinga, D., & Ageton, S. S. (1985). *Explaining delinquency and drug use.* Beverly Hills, CA: Sage.

Fagan, A. A. (2001). The gendered cycle of violence: Comparing the effects of child abuse and neglect on criminal offending for males and females. *Violence and Victims, 16*(4), 457–474.

Fagan, A. A. (2005). The relationship between adolescent physical abuse and criminal offending: Support for an enduring and generalized cycle of violence. *Journal of Family Violence, 20*(5), 279–290.

Fagan, A. A., Van Horn, M. L., Hawkins, J. D., & Arthur, M. (2007). Gender similarities and differences in the association between risk and protective factors and self-reported serious delinquency. *Prevention Science, 8*(2), 115–124.

Fergusson, D. M., & Horwood, L. J. (2002). Male and female offending trajectories. *Development and Psychopathology, 14*(1), 159–177.

Figueira-McDonough, J. (1992). Community structure and female delinquency rates: A heuristic discussion. *Youth and Society, 24*(1), 3–30.

Gibson, C. L., Ward, J. T., Wright, J. P., Beaver, K. M., & DeLisi, M. (2010). Where does gender fit in the measurement of self-control? *Criminal Justice and Behavior, 37,* 883–903.

Gilfus, M. E. (1992). From victims to survivors to offenders: Women's routes of entry and immersion into street crime. *Women and Criminal Justice, 4,* 63–90.

Giordano, P. C., Cernkovich, S. A., & Rudolph, J. L. (2002). Gender, crime and desistance: Toward a theory of cognitive transformation. *American Journal of Sociology, 107*(4), 990–1064.

Gottfredson, M. R., & Hirschi, T. (1990). *A general theory of crime.* Stanford, CA: Stanford University Press.

Hagan, J., Gillis, A. R., & Simpson, J. (1987). Class in the household: A power-control theory of gender and delinquency. *American Journal of Sociology, 92*(4), 788–816.

Hartman, J. L., Turner, M. G., Daigle, L. E., Exum, M. L., & Cullen, F. T. (2009). Exploring the gender differences in protective factors: Implications for understanding resiliency. *International Journal of Offender Therapy and Comparative Criminology, 53,* 249–277.

Haynie, D., Steffensmeier, D., & Bell, K. E. (2007). Gender and serious violence: Untangling the role of friendship sex composition and peer violence. *Youth Violence and Juvenile Justice, 5*(3), 235–253.

Heimer, K. (1996). Gender, interaction, and delinquency: Testing a theory of differential social control. *Social Psychology Quarterly, 59*(1), 39–61.

Heimer, K., & De Coster, S. (1999). The gendering of violent delinquency. *Criminology, 37*(2), 277–318.

Hill, G. D., & Crawford, E. M. (1990). Women, race and crime. *Criminology, 28*(4), 601–623.

Hoeve, M., Dubas, J. S., Eichelsheim, V. I., Van der Laan, P. H., Smeenk, W., & Gerris, J. R. M. (2009). The relationship between parenting and delinquency: A meta-analysis. *Journal of Abnormal Child Psychology, 37,* 749–775.

Huebner, A. J., & Betts, S. C. (2002). Exploring the utility of social control theory for youth development: Issues of attachment, involvement, and gender. *Youth and Society, 34*(2), 123–145.

Hunnicutt, G., & Broidy, L. M. (2004). Liberation and economic marginalization: A reformulation and test of (formerly?) competing models. *Journal of Research in Crime and Delinquency, 41*(2), 130–155.

Jacob, J. C. (2006). Male and female youth crime in Canadian communities: Assessing the applicability of social disorganization theory. *Canadian Journal of Criminology and Criminal Justice, 48*(1), 31–60.

Jang, S. J., & Krohn, M. D. (1995). Developmental patterns of sex differences in delinquency among African American adolescents: A test of the sex-invariance hypothesis. *Journal of Quantitative Criminology, 11*(2), 195–222.

Junger-Tas, J., Ribeaud, D., & Cruyff, M. J. L. F. (2004). Juvenile delinquency and gender. *European Journal of Criminology, 1,* 333–375.

Karriker-Jaffe, K. J., Foshee, V. A., Ennett, S. T., & Suchindran, C. (2009). Sex differences in the effects of neighborhood socioeconomic disadvantage and social organization on rural adolescents' aggression trajectories. *American Journal of Community Psychology, 43,* 189–203.

Keenan, K., & Shaw, D. (1997). Developmental and social influences on young girls' early problem behavior. *Psychological Bulletin, 121*(1), 95–113.

Kling, J. R., Ludwig, J., & Katz, L. F. (2005). Neighborhood effects on crime for female and male youth: Evidence from a randomized housing voucher experiment. *Quarterly Journal of Economics, 120,* 87–130.

Kroneman, L., Loeber, R., & Hipwell, A. E. (2004). Is neighborhood context differently related to externalizing problems and delinquency for girls compared to boys? *Clinical Child and Family Psychology Review, 7*(2), 109–122.

Kroneman, L., Loeber, R., Hipwell, A. E., & Koot, H. M. (2009). Girls' disruptive behavior and its relationship to family functioning: A review. *Journal of Child and Family Studies, 18,* 259–273.

Kruttschnitt, C. (2001). Gender and violence. In C. M. Renzetti & L. Goodstein (Eds.), *Women, crime, and criminal justice: Original feminist readings* (pp. 77–92). Los Angeles, CA: Roxbury.

Kruttschnitt, C., Gartner, R., & Ferraro, K. (2002). Women's involvement in serious interpersonal violence. *Aggression and Violent Behavior, 7,* 529–565.

Kruttschnitt, C., & Giordano, P. C. (2009). Family influences on girls' delinquency. In M. A. Zahn (Ed.), *The delinquent girl* (pp. 107–126). Philadelphia, PA: Temple University Press.

La Grange, T. C., & Silverman, R. A. (1999). Low self-control and opportunity: Testing the general theory of crime as an explanation for gender differences in delinquency. *Criminology, 37*(1), 41–72.

Lanctot, N., & Le Blanc, M. (2002). Explaining deviance by adolescent females. *Crime and Justice, 29,* 113–202.

Laub, J. H., & McDermott, M. J. (1985). An analysis of serious crime by young Black women. *Criminology, 23*(1), 81–98.

Liu, X., & Kaplan, H. B. (1999). Explaining the gender difference in adolescent delinquent behavior: A longitudinal test of mediating mechanisms. *Criminology, 37*(1), 195–215.

Maguin, E., & Loeber, R. (1996). Academic performance and delinquency. *Crime and Justice, 20,* 145–264.

Mears, D. P., Ploeger, M., & Warr, M. (1998). Explaining the gender gap in delinquency: Peer influence and moral evaluations of behavior. *Journal of Research in Crime and Delinquency, 35*(3), 251–266.

Meier, M. H., Slutske, W. S., Arndt, S., & Cadoret, R. J. (2008). Impulsive and callous traits are more strongly associated with delinquent behavior in higher risk neighborhoods among boys and girls. *Journal of Abnormal Psychology, 117*(2), 377–385.

Mersky, J. P., & Reynolds, A. J. (2007). Child maltreatment and violent delinquency: Disentangling main effects and subgroup effects. *Child Maltreatment, 12,* 246–258.

Moffitt, T. E., Caspi, A., Rutter, M., & Silva, P. (2001). *Sex differences in antisocial behaviour: Conduct disorder, delinquency, and violence in the Dunedin Longitudinal Study.* Cambridge, UK: Cambridge University Press.

Molnar, B. E., Cerda, M., Roberts, A. L., & Buka, S. L. (2008). Effects of neighborhood resources on aggressive and delinquent behaviors among urban youths. *American Journal of Public Health, 98*(6), 1086–1093.

Mrug, S., & Windle, M. (2009). Mediators of neighborhood influences on externalizing behavior in preadolescent children. *Journal of Abnormal Child Psychology, 37,* 265–280.

Ness, C. D. (2004). Why girls fight: Female youth violence in the inner city. *The ANNALS of the American Academy of Political and Social Science, 595,* 32–48.

Parker, K. F., & Reckdenwald, A. (2008). Women and crime in context: Examining the linkages between patriarchy and female offending across space. *Feminist Criminology, 3*(1), 5–24.

Payne, A. A. (2009). Girls, boys, and schools: Gender differences in the relationships between school-related factors and student deviance. *Criminology, 47*(4), 1167–1200.

Payne, A. A., Gottfredson, D. C., & Kruttschnitt, C. (2009). Girls, schooling and delinquency. In M. A. Zahn (Ed.), *The delinquent girl* (pp. 146–163). Philadelphia, PA: Temple University Press.

Peterson, D., Esbensen, F.-A., Taylor, T. J., & Freng, A. (2007). Youth violence in context: The roles of sex, race, and community in offending. *Youth Violence and Juvenile Justice, 5*(4), 385–410.

Piquero, N. L., Gover, A. R., MacDonald, J. M., & Piquero, A. R. (2005). The influence of delinquent peers on delinquency: Does gender matter? *Youth and Society, 36*(3), 251–275.

Pratt, T. C., & Cullen, F. T. (2000). The empirical status of Gottfredson and Hirschi's general theory of crime: A meta-analysis. *Criminology, 38*(3), 931–964.

Puzzanchera, C., & Adams, B. (2011). *Juvenile arrests 2009.* Washington, DC: Office of Juvenile Justice and Delinquency Prevention.

Resnick, M. D., Ireland, M., & Borowsky, I. (2004). Youth violence perpetration: What protects? What predicts? Findings from the National Longitudinal Study of Adolescent Health. *Journal of Adolescent Health, 35,* 424.e1–424.e10.

Richie, B. E. (1996). *Compelled to crime: The gender entrapment of Black battered women.* New York, NY: Routledge.

Rowe, D. C., Vazsonyi, A. T., & Flannery, D. J. (1995). Sex differences in crime: Do means and within-sex variation have similar causes? *Journal of Research in Crime and Delinquency, 32,* 84–100.

Sale, E., Sambrano, S., Springer, J. F., & Turner, C. W. (2003). Risk, protection, and substance use in adolescents: A multi-site study. *Journal of Drug Education, 33*(1), 91–105.

Sampson, R. J., Raudenbush, S. W., & Earls, F. (1997). Neighborhoods and violent crime: A multilevel study of collective efficacy. *Science, 277,* 918–924.

Shaw, C. R., & McKay, H. D. (1942). *Juvenile delinquency and urban areas.* Chicago, IL: University of Chicago Press.

Simon, R. J. (1975). *Women and crime.* Lexington, MA: Lexington Books.

Simons, R. L., Johnson, C., Beaman, J., Conger, R., & Whitbeck, L. B. (1996). Parents and peer group as mediators of the effect of community structure on adolescent problem behavior. *American Journal of Community Psychology, 24*(1), 145–171.

Simons, R. L., Stewart, E., Gordon, L. C., Conger, R. D., & Elder, G. H. (2002). A test of life-course explanations for stability and change in antisocial behavior from adolescence to young adulthood. *Criminology, 40*(2), 401–434.

Simpson, S. S., & Ellis, L. (1995). Doing gender: Sorting out the caste and crime conundrum. *Criminology, 33*(1), 47–81.

Smith, D. A., & Paternoster, R. (1987). The gender gap in theories of deviance: Issues and evidence. *Journal of Research in Crime and Delinquency, 24*(2), 140–172.

Sommers, I., & Baskin, D. (1992). Sex, race, age, and violent offending. *Violence and Victims, 7*(3), 191–201.

Steffensmeier, D. (1993). National trends in female arrests, 1960–1990: Assessment and recommendations for research. *Journal of Quantitative Criminology, 9*(4), 411–441.

Steffensmeier, D., & Broidy, L. (2001). Explaining female offending. In C. M. Renzetti & L. Goodstein (Eds.), *Women, crime, and criminal justice: Original feminist readings* (pp. 111–132). Los Angeles, CA: Roxbury.

Steffensmeier, D., Zhong, H., Ackerman, J., Schwartz, J., & Agha, S. (2006). Gender gap trends for violent crimes, 1980 to 2003: A UCR-NCVS comparison. *Feminist Criminology, 1,* 72–98.

Stoddard, S. A., Zimmerman, M. A., & Bauermeister, J. A. (2012). A longitudinal analysis of cumulative risks, cumulative promotive factors, and adolescent violent behavior. *Journal of Adolescent Health, 22*(3), 542–555.

Tittle, C. R., Ward, D. A., & Grasmick, H. G. (2003). Self-control and crime/deviance: Cognitive vs. behavioral measures. *Journal of Quantitative Criminology, 19*(4), 333–365.

Topitzes, J., Mersky, J. P., & Reynolds, A. J. (2011). Child maltreatment and offending behavior: Gender-specific effects and pathways. *Criminal Justice and Behavior, 38*(5), 492–510.

West, C., & Zimmerman, D. H. (1987). Doing gender. *Journal of Women in Culture and Society, 1*(2), 125–151.

Widom, C. S. (1989). The cycle of violence. *Science, 244,* 160–166.

Zahn, M. A., & Browne, A. (2009). Gender differences in neighborhood effects and delinquency. In M. A. Zahn (Ed.), *The delinquent girl* (pp. 164–181). Philadelphia, PA: Temple University Press.

Zahn, M. A., Hawkins, S. R., Chiancone, J., & Whitworth, A. (2008). *The Girls Study Group: Charting the way to delinquency prevention for girls.* Washington, DC: U.S. Department of Justice.

Zahn-Wexler, C., Shirtcliff, E. A., & Marceau, K. (2008). Disorders of childhood and adolescence: Gender and psychopathology. *Annual Review of Clinical Psychology, 4,* 275–303.

Zimmerman, G. M., & Messner, S. F. (2010). Neighborhood context and the gender gap in adolescent violent crime. *American Sociological Review, 75*(6), 958–980.

2

A Biosocial Explanation for Male-Female Differences in Criminal Involvement

Kevin M. Beaver
Florida State University

Joseph L. Nedelec
University of Cincinnati

Criminological research has identified a long list of risk factors that are associated with involvement in criminal behaviors. These risk factors span virtually every level of analysis, touch on virtually every facet of life, and cover virtually every developmental time period. All these previously identified risk factors, however, are not equal. Some risk factors, for example, have been shown to be spurious, some have been shown to be methodological or statistical artifacts, and still others remain under close empirical scrutiny. But, for a small handful of risk factors, the evidence has been decidedly overwhelming in showing a connection with criminal behaviors. Of these risk factors, sex/gender[1] has emerged as perhaps the single most consistent predictor of crime, and while it has been one of the most studied correlates to crime, it also remains one of the least understood (Walsh, 2011a). The nexus between gender and crime is so well established that no serious scholar of crime can deny that there is a strong, consistent, and robust association between sex/gender and crime, wherein males are significantly more likely to engage in serious criminal acts than are females. What does remain as a matter of significant debate, however, are the underlying mechanisms that account for this association.

Much of this debate has swirled around whether the male-female difference in criminal offending is due largely to environmental factors or largely to biological and genetic factors. For the most part, biological explanations of the gender gap in offending have been purged from criminological theory and research, with virtually all scholarship focusing on potential environmental explanations. Although criminological research continues to center on environmental factors, in recent years the biological sciences have made great strides regarding uncovering biological factors that are able to explain, at least in part, male-female differences in virtually every trait, behavior, and characteristic. These studies have highlighted the importance of the brain, hormones, and even genetic factors as likely candidates that are at the heart of why males are much more criminal than are females (Beaver, 2009; Walsh, 2011a).

Identifying the causes of male-female differences in crime is more than just an academic exercise; rather, it has potential to prevent crime, treat criminals, and ensure the public safety of citizens. Against this backdrop, the current chapter examines the biosocial underpinnings of the male-female gap in offending behaviors. We begin by deconstructing arguments that only environmental factors are able to explain the male-female differences in crime and then move into a discussion of some of the biological/genetic factors that are likely responsible, at least in part, for why males have been found to be more violent and more criminal in virtually every society ever studied. In doing so, we draw attention to the very real likelihood that male over-involvement in crime is likely the result of a complex web of biological and social factors that work together in an interactive way.

Limitations of Environmental-Only Explanations

In January of 2005, Larry Summers made national headlines when he proclaimed that male-female differences in educational degrees and university positions at some of the most prestigious universities were the result of innate differences between males and females. Although Summers may have been somewhat callous in the way he packaged his statements about male-female differences, and failed to offer any qualifying comments regarding his position, his statements were grounded in empirical evidence generated from high-powered neuroscientific studies. Indeed, numerous scholars came to his defense and pointed out that the results of brain-imaging studies confirmed that there are both structural and functional differences in the brains of males and the brains of females. In many ways, the evidence did not matter because Summers had crossed over into politically incorrect territory and the "PC police" were out to get him. After being branded a sexist and a bigot, Summers was ultimately forced to resign from his position as President of Harvard University.

Two lessons can be garnered from the Larry Summers incident. The first lesson is that wandering into the politically incorrect world of biologically based differences between the sexes can have serious consequences, even if the statements are factually correct and are supported by mounds of research. The second lesson is that the general view held by the public and the guiding ideology of the social sciences is that all male-female differences in behavior and other outcomes are the result of differences in socialization/environmental experiences. Before we move into a discussion of the evidence regarding the biological differences between males and females, we begin by taking a close look at the argument that only environmental/socialization experiences matter in creating male-female differences.

Criminological theory and research focus almost exclusively on environmental/social explanations of delinquency, crime, and other forms of antisocial behaviors (Walsh, 2011b). These theories highlight the role of parents, peers, subcultures, and social-structural processes as being the etiological forces in the creation of criminal behaviors. This is especially true of theories and research that attempt to explain male-female differences in criminal involvement, wherein almost all criminological research identifies social and environmental factors as being the causal agents for why males are much more criminally violent than females. Although a wide array of environmental factors have been identified to explain the male-female gap in offending, two of the most common explanations that cut across multiple theoretical perspectives are those that center on cultures/subcultures and those that center on parental socialization.

Cultural explanations have been frequently employed to explain male-female differences in criminal and antisocial behaviors. These explanations are grounded in the assumption that the unique cultures of different societies, or even unique subcultures embedded within the same society, are able to shape and mold people in different ways. If, for example, a culture values aggression and violence, and the norms and values promote such behavior, then that culture will produce more violent behavior in comparison with other societies that value and reward passivity and compliance. Cultural explanations have been invoked to explain why crime rates vary significantly across different nations, such as the United States having high rates of crime while Sweden has comparatively lower levels of crime rates (Messner & Rosenfeld, 2007). Although there is some evidence indicating that differences in culture is part of the reason crime rates vary at the nation level, extending such explanations to explain male-female differences is not necessarily correct. One of the main reasons why such cultural explanations of male-female differences in crime may be incorrect is because in virtually every society ever studied males have been found to be much more violent and much more criminal than females. This finding has been detected even in societies where the culture is characterized as relatively egalitarian and in nations where policies have been implemented to promote gender equality in the workplace, including in large corporations (Ahern & Dittmar, 2011; Wright, Tibbetts, & Daigle, 2008). In short, male-female differences in criminal and violent behavior is a robust finding that has been detected in virtually every time period, in virtu-

ally every society, and in virtually every culture ever studied. So, while cultural factors may explain raw differences in crime rates across nations, descriptive data do not logically support the argument that cultures account for male-female differences in antisocial behaviors.

Despite the universal finding that males are more violent and more criminal than females, there remains a general assumption by social scientists that cultural-level factors are the main impetus behind male-female differences in crime. One of the primary reasons for the belief that male-female behavioral differences are the result of cultural forces is due to the research conducted by Margaret Mead. During the 1920s and 1930s, Mead was apparently deeply embedded in various cultures so as to explore, among other things, the role that culture had on behavioral patterns in males and females. In 1935, she published her findings in the widely acclaimed, widely cited, and ground-breaking book, *Sex and Temperament in Three Primitive Societies.* In this book, she detailed the various ways in which culture was able to shape males and females differently. For example, she noted that in one culture (i.e., Arapesh) both men and women were relatively passive and peaceful, while in another culture (i.e., Mundugumor), both men and women were relatively violent. Her analyses of different cultures seemed to lay waste to the belief that male-female differences in behavior and temperament were the result of any inborn, biological difference and supported the claim that these differences were sculpted by cultural factors.

Even though Mead's research is one of the very few pieces of scholarship to show that male-female behavioral patterns are highly variable and a reflection of culture, her analyses, findings, and interpretations of the data were largely accepted and spawned the growth of cultural anthropology and the emerging feminist perspective. One of the major problems with Mead's research is that it was not really held to the same level of critique as most other social science research. While there was some backlash against her findings and her interpretation of them, for the most part these criticisms just floated by as academics and laypersons alike championed the message that males and females were a product of their environments in general and their cultures in particular. And so Mead's research remained widely accepted as factual for decades by anthropologists, feminists, and other scholars until some critics began to publish major critiques of her work (Orans, 1996). One of the more outspoken of these critics was Derek Freeman.

Freeman (1983, 1999) published two major books that criticized Mead's research and called into question her conclusions. At the heart of his critique is that Mead did not fully understand Samoan culture (which formed the crux of her book, *Coming of Age in Samoa,* first published in 1928) and was not fluent in their native language. As a result, some of the "jokes" that the Samoan women would tell, Mead did not interpret as jokes, but rather as facts and incorporated them into her scholarship as pieces of empirical evidence. Although Freeman was quite critical of Mead, her research, and her interpretations, he did not believe that Mead intentionally misrepresented her observations, but rather was duped in what he called a "fateful hoaxing." Much of the criticism leveled against Mead by Freeman was directed at her research on Samoan culture, but his critiques spilled over to other lines of Mead's research and seriously called into question the integrity and validity of her entire body of research on culture, gender differences, and behaviors.

Consequently, advocates of purely social explanations of male-female differences in violence and aggression who rely on Mead's research are likely drawing heavily from a body of work that is fatally flawed.

An offshoot of the cultural explanation for male-female differences centers directly on the way in which the media socialize males to be aggressive and females to be passive and nonviolent. According to these media-based explanations, males and females are inundated with role models that underscore the ways in which males should act and the ways in which females should act. Over time, children and adolescents begin to adopt these gender-specific role types and act in ways that are in accordance with stereotypical male behaviors and stereotypical female behaviors. Explanations of the role that the media plays in creating male-female differences in antisocial behaviors also extend to differential exposure to certain types of media between males and females. Males, for example, are much more likely than females to view TV shows that promote aggression, such as violent movies and even highly aggressive athletic events, which ultimately have been shown to increase the use of aggression and violence in some studies (Bushman & Huesmann, 2006).

There are three key problems with explanations that center on the media to explain why males are much more violent than are females. First, males have been found to be more violent than females even in societies that lack any type of formal media or even electricity (Daly & Wilson, 1988), and the historical data indicate that males were always more violent than females across every time period (Wright et al., 2008). In virtually every society at every time in history, for instance, males accounted for all or nearly all the front-line soldiers in wars, and they were disproportionately the victims of violent, lethal encounters (Buss, 2005). So, even before media was invented and even in societies where it continues to be absent, males were and continue to be more violent than females. Second, research indicating that exposure to violence in movies, TV shows, or video games is related to increases in the use of aggression is far from established (Ferguson & Kilburn, 2009). Certainly there are studies supporting such an association, but there are plenty of other studies that do not show a linkage between media exposure to violence and subsequent antisocial/aggressive behavior. Even among those studies showing a statistically significant association, the study authors often concede that any association that does exist is likely small and thus could only account for a small percentage of the variance in violence and aggression (Ferguson & Kilburn, 2009). Third, while males may be more inclined to view violent media than females, this disparity reveals nothing about why this is the case. There is a very good possibility that males seek out violent TV shows to watch because they are more violently predisposed than females. In this case, any association between males' exposure to violence on TV and their over-involvement in aggressive behaviors could be entirely confounded by selection effects. Taken together, the available evidence suggests that even if the media contributes to violent and aggressive behavior, at best it could only account for a fraction of the male-female differences in antisocial behaviors that are observed around the world.

In addition to explanations that focus on cultural effects as shaping male-female patterns of antisocial behavior, perhaps the next most common explanation is socialization that takes place at the hands of parents. Virtually every single criminological theory, ranging from social bond theory to social learning theory to power-control theory to low self-control theory, integrates the role of parental socialization into its explanations. Most criminological theories are general theories, meaning they are designed to explain all types of crime at all times for all people (e.g., Gottfredson & Hirschi, 1990). At the same time, general theories also have to be able to account for the known correlates of crime and the known patterns of crime. If a general theory is to be taken seriously it would have to explain, at the very least, why males are more criminal than are females. One of the most common explanations used by criminological theories to explain male-female differences in crime is parental socialization. For parental socialization to be able to account for male-female differences in crime, two criteria must be fulfilled. First, empirical research must consistently reveal that parental socialization is related to criminal involvement in general. Second, empirical research must consistently reveal that males are differentially exposed to the types of parenting practices that increase criminal involvement whereas females must be exposed to the types of parenting practices that decrease criminal involvement. If either of these two criteria is not met, then the likelihood that parental socialization is causing males to be more criminal than females is unlikely to be true. Below we briefly review both these criteria to evaluate the merits of parental socialization explanations for the gender gap in offending behaviors.

There has been a good deal of criminological research examining the association between a variety of measures of parental socialization and a range of antisocial outcomes. The findings flowing from these criminological studies have revealed that measures of parental warmth, parental supervision/monitoring, and parental attachment, to name just a few, are related to delinquency, drug use, levels of self-control, and later-life criminal behavior (Ellis & Walsh, 2007). Much of the parental socialization literature focuses on the statistical significance of parental socialization measures and not on effect sizes. When the focus moves from statistical significance to substantive effect sizes, what becomes apparent is that parenting measures tend to have relatively small effects on antisocial and criminal behaviors. Moreover, most of the criminological research examining the effects of parenting on crime and delinquency is misspecified because it does not control for relevant confounding variables (especially genetic factors) and reciprocal effects (Beaver & Wright, 2007; Ge et al., 1996; Rowe, 1994; Rowe & Flannery, 1994; Wright & Beaver, 2005). Research that is more fully specified and that controls for genetic confounds and/or reciprocal effects typically reveals that the effect sizes of the parenting measures are either attenuated substantially or drop from statistical significance (Harris, 1998; Rowe, 1994; Wright & Beaver, 2005). In the best case scenario, then, parenting measures would only account for a small fraction of the variance in the male-female gap in offending and in the worst case scenario they would account for none of the variance in this gap. Either way, parental socialization is unlikely to be the main culprit in explaining why males are much more violent and criminal than females.

The second criterion that would have to be met for parental socialization to be able to explain differences in male and female behavioral patterns is for males and females to be exposed to different types of parental socialization techniques. Even if parenting does only have small effects on criminal behavior, it could be the case that males are exposed to criminogenic parenting tactics much more frequently than females. If that is the case, then small differences in main effects could still contribute, in part, to some of the observed male-female differences in serious violent offending, and the effects could become even larger via interactive effects. All this logic, however, hinges largely on differential exposure to parental socialization techniques. Lytton and Romney (1991) tackled this question head-on by conducting a meta-analysis of studies that had examined whether parents use different socialization patterns for their sons and daughters. This meta-analysis covered 172 studies and 19 different components/dimensions of parental socialization, including measures tapping discouragement of aggression, frequency of discipline, amount of interaction, and amount of warmth and nurturance provided to the child. Of these 19 different areas of parenting, only one—encouragement of sex-typed activities—was significantly different between boys and girls. Based on the available evidence, measures of parenting tend to (a) have small effects on antisocial behaviors and (b) be virtually identical for both boys and girls. When viewed against this backdrop, the available evidence strongly suggests that parental socialization can only account for a small part of the male-female gap in offending behaviors.

The preceding discussion is not meant to be an exhaustive review of all the environmental factors that have been posited to explain male-female differences in crime and delinquency, but rather to highlight some of the major limitations associated with some of the most widely employed criminological explanations for the gender gap in offending behaviors. If these common explanations are unable to account for much of the variance in criminal and delinquent involvement between males and females, then it is highly unlikely that some of the less commonly invoked explanations would be able to account for the remaining male-female differences that exist. Criminological explanations that focus purely on environmental factors and ignore biological factors, in short, appear to be inadequate when trying to explain the male-female gap in crime and delinquency. Below, we turn our attention to biological and genetic factors that might be involved in creating male-female differences in crime, delinquency, aggression, and violence.

Biological and Genetic Factors

Traditional criminological explanations of male-female offending patterns are grounded in the assumption that humans are born with a *tabula rasa*, wherein their minds are blank slates that are only molded and sculpted by salient environmental factors from birth onward (Pinker, 2002). According to this perspective, all healthy infants are born with relatively equal abilities, talents, traits, and propensities, and any differences that ultimately emerge later in life are the result of differential exposure to environmental factors. This same logic is employed to explain male-female differences in criminal behavior. What is rarely acknowledged by criminologists who study male-female differences in offending behaviors is that male-female differences are observed across a range of phenotypes, that they emerge very early in life, and that they are predictive of outcomes in adolescence and adulthood.

In a landmark study, for example, Connellan, Baron-Cohen, Wheelwright, Batki, and Ahluwalia (2000) examined the social behaviors in a sample of more than 100 neonates. To do so, they measured the amount of time that male and female infants stared at a social object (i.e., a human face) and a physical-mechanical object (i.e., a mobile). The results of their experiment revealed that female infants spent significantly more time looking at the social object whereas males spent significantly more time looking at the physical mechanical object. The study authors concluded that, "[a]t such an age, these sex differences cannot readily be attributed to postnatal experience, and are instead consistent with a biological cause, most likely neurogenetic and/or neuroendocrine in nature" (Connellan et al., 2000, pp. 116–117). While these findings might be viewed as interesting, they may also be viewed as a one-time aberration that would not be detected in other studies or with other types of behaviors; however, other research has revealed significant male-female differences in other types of behaviors during the very first few weeks of life (Wright et al., 2008).

Such early life differences might be downplayed with the argument that there is so much change from infancy to adulthood that any differences that surface early in life are meaningless to later behaviors, traits, and outcomes. Longitudinal research, however, has revealed a very different set of findings, wherein early life differences have been shown to be highly stable over the life course and predict a wide range of outcomes. To illustrate, personality traits at the age of 3, such as being under-controlled and inhibited, have been shown to predict aggression and negative emotionality in the late teenage years and early to mid-20s (Caspi et al., 2003). Far from being irrelevant to adolescence and adulthood, early life differences in certain traits and behaviors appear to forecast, at least in part, future behaviors and traits. What this necessarily means is that whatever causes variation in personality early in life remains salient up through adulthood. Purely environmental explanations are unable to account for such early life differences unless they take the untenable position that socialization has huge effects that take hold in some of the earliest moments after birth. Rather than ascribe to such a position, biosocial criminologists recognize that infants are born with their own unique suite of predispositions that ultimately unfold in the context of certain environments and certain developmental time periods. Given that male-female differences are evident around the time of birth, there has been a great deal of interest in examining brain development in utero to see if it offers some insight into male-female differences that exist at virtually every section of the life course.

The human brain is one of the most studied and most fascinating entities in existence, but it is also one of the least understood. Even so, during the past two decades a large body of research has been produced examining how the brain develops in utero, as well as postnatally. Although a full discussion of brain development is beyond the scope of this chapter, we focus attention on some of the developmental processes that differ between males and females and the developmental processes that have been found to "masculinize" the brain. These differences, as are discussed later, have been found to produce structural and functional differences between the brains of males and females, and these differences, in turn, have been found to explain some of the male-female differences that are observed in behaviors, personalities, and even talents and abilities.

From almost the moment of conception, the brain forms and begins to develop and will continue to develop well into the 20s. The organization of the brain, however, mainly occurs in utero, with processes such as neuronal migration and synaptogenesis. By default, the brain follows a female-developmental trajectory, and thus male brains and female brains are indistinguishable until around the 8th week of pregnancy. Around the 8th week of pregnancy, however, the SRY gene, which is located on the Y chromosome, is triggered on. Once activated, the SRY gene sets in motion a chain of events with the most important (for our purposes) being the production of testosterone. This production of testosterone leads to a minimum three-fold increase in exposure to prenatal testosterone (followed by a 10- to 20-fold increase in testosterone during puberty) for males (Ellis & Walsh, 2007). The saturation of the male brain in testosterone has organizing effects that, along with additional hormones, masculinize the brain, while other chemicals, such as Müllerian inhibiting substance (MIS), are ultimately responsible for defeminizing the male brain. The end result is a male brain that is quite different both structurally and functionally from the female brain (Brizendine, 2006, 2010).

Male-female differences in the structure of certain regions of the brain have been detected in many areas that are directly related to violence, aggression, risk-taking, and impulse control (Walsh, 2011a). For example, one region of the brain that has been found to be associated with violence and impulsive behaviors is the prefrontal cortex. In very general terms, the prefrontal cortex is responsible for judgment, the ability to anticipate the consequences of actions, emotional control, and other higher-order cognitive processes. Collectively, these operations of the prefrontal cortex are referred to as *executive functions*. Research has revealed that an underactive prefrontal cortex confers an increased risk to antisocial behaviors and that it is also related to a reduction in executive functions (Rowe, 2002). Neuroscience studies have revealed that the female prefrontal cortex is relatively larger and more active when compared against the male prefrontal cortex (Brizendine, 2006, 2010; Wright et al., 2008). These differences are observable very early in life, and thus they are unlikely to be the result of any type of socialization process or postnatal experience.

Another area of the brain that has been found to have relatively consistent effects on antisocial behaviors, as well as physical violence, is the limbic system. The limbic system consists of primitive brain structures, such as the amygdala and the hypothalamus, that are implicated in a range of different functions, including the generation of emotions. Given that intense emotions have been found to have a facilitative effect on antisocial behaviors, especially physical aggression, there has been some interest in examining whether the size and activity level of certain areas of the limbic system are related to aggression. The results of these studies have revealed that the hippocampus, striatum, and other areas of the limbic system are linked to various forms of antisocial behaviors, especially serious physical violence (Beaver, 2009; Brizendine, 2010; Wright et al., 2008). Perhaps the most studied and most consistent association with violence, however, is the amygdala. The amygdala has been found to be associated with psychopathic personality traits, violence, and even murder (for an overview see DeLisi, 2011). What is of particular interest is that neuroimaging studies have revealed that regions of the limbic system, including the amygdala and hypothalamus, tend to be larger and more active in males than in females (Brizendine, 2006, 2010); precisely what would be expected if the limbic system is partially responsible for male-female differences in violent, criminal acts (DeLisi, 2011).

Although a bit more complex than distilling all male-female differences in the brain to testosterone, prenatal exposure to testosterone is thought to be one of the key causal factors that produce anatomical differences in the brains of males and females (Baron-Cohen, 2003; Baron-Cohen, Lutchmaya, & Knickmeyer, 2004). As a direct result, there has been considerable interest in examining whether differential levels of prenatal testosterone are associated with different types of behaviors and traits that are more common or less common among either sex. There are three main lines of evidence that have directly examined whether prenatal levels of testosterone are associated with later-life antisocial behaviors: (1) evidence that comes from studies that directly measure prenatal testosterone levels, (2) evidence that comes from studies that indirectly measure prenatal testosterone levels, and (3) evidence that comes from studies that examine clinical samples where the subjects are afflicted with disorders that affect prenatal testosterone levels. Each of these lines of research is covered below.

The most accurate way to measure the effects that precise levels of prenatal testosterone have on outcomes later in life is by directly assaying testosterone levels from umbilical cord blood at birth, from maternal serum via venipuncture, and from amniotic fluid through an amniocentesis. Although directly measuring testosterone levels is perhaps the most reliable and valid way to study the effects of prenatal testosterone, there has been relatively little research using this measurement strategy. Furthermore, most of the studies that have been conducted do not focus on antisocial behaviors that occur later in life. Nonetheless, the available evidence tends to indicate that higher levels of prenatal testosterone are related to increases in male-like behaviors (Baron-Cohen et al., 2004). For example, studies have detected a positive relationship between prenatal testosterone levels and preference for boy-typical toys (e.g., cars and trucks) in samples of girls. In boys, higher levels of prenatal testosterone have been shown to be related to reductions in timidity. Later in life, direct measures of prenatal testosterone have been shown to be linked to sex-typed activities, Bem Sex Role Inventory, and male-like behaviors in general (Udry, 1994, 2000). Whether direct measures of prenatal testosterone would predict crime, violence, and aggression in adolescence and adulthood remains an open, empirical question awaiting future research.

Measuring prenatal testosterone directly (e.g., through amniotic fluid) is an invasive process, and trying to link prenatal testosterone levels to behaviors later in life is time-consuming and can take 15 to 20 years to wait for the infants to age into adolescents and young adults. As a result, researchers have employed indirect methods to measure exposure to prenatal testosterone. The most widely employed indirect method is the 2D:4D ratio, which measures the ratio between the length of the second finger (i.e., index finger or the second digit [2D]) and the fourth finger (i.e., the ring finger or the fourth digit [4D]). The 2D:4D ratio is known to be sexually dimorphic, and it remains relatively stable from around the 14th week of pregnancy throughout the remainder of the life course (Manning, 2002). Moreover, males tend to have a lower 2D:4D ratio in comparison with females. Empirical research has revealed evidence indicating that the 2D:4D ratio is correlated with the amount of exposure to testosterone in utero, where a lower 2D:4D ratio is an indicator of greater exposure to prenatal testosterone and a greater 2D:4D ratio is an indicator of lower exposure to prenatal testosterone (Manning, 2002). Although why there is a connection between prenatal testosterone and the 2D:4D ratio is not well understood, one explanation centers on the finding that the same genes (i.e., the HoxA and HoxD genes) that are related to the formation of the gonads are also known to affect the development of the fingers (Kondo, Zakany, Innis, & Duboule, 1997). Whatever the reason, the possibility that the 2D:4D ratio is a proxy indicator for prenatal exposure to testosterone allows for an examination of the association between the 2D:4D ratio and various types of behaviors, including antisocial behaviors.

A growing body of research has examined the association between the 2D:4D ratio and an array of different outcomes. Although the results have not always been consistent and replicated, there are studies showing an association between the 2D:4D ratio and autism, musical abilities, cognitive abilities, hyperactivity, and sexual orientation, to name a few (Manning, 2002; Manning, Baron-Cohen, Wheelwright, & Sanders, 2001; Manning & Taylor, 2001; Sluming & Manning, 2000). More germane to the current chapter, however, are studies that have examined whether the 2D:4D ratio is related to antisocial outcomes. Findings from both experimental and nonexperimental studies have detected that a lower 2D:4D ratio is associated with an increase in aggression, violence, and other behaviors that could translate into criminal behaviors in certain settings (Bailey & Hurd, 2005; Benderlioglu & Nelson, 2004; McIntyre, Barrett, McDermott, Johnson, & Rosen, 2007; Millet & Dewitte, 2007). These findings should be viewed cautiously because a recent meta-analysis failed to detect a significant relationship between the 2D:4D ratio and aggression across 15 studies (Hönekopp & Watson, 2011). Importantly, the question of whether the 2D:4D ratio is able to explain differences between males and females on antisocial behaviors remains relatively unknown because studies frequently examine males and females separately without exploring how much of the male-female gap in antisocial behaviors is explained by differences in the 2D:4D ratio.

The third main way to estimate the effect of prenatal testosterone on behavioral outcomes is by analyzing clinical samples. In these studies, researchers examine subjects who are afflicted with certain disorders or whose pregnant mothers were prescribed certain medications that are known to affect prenatal exposure to testosterone (Beaver, 2009). Perhaps the most widely studied group of clinical subjects that has been analyzed to estimate the effects of prenatal testosterone is females who are affected by congenital adrenal hyperplasia (CAH). CAH is a group of autosomal recessive disorders that results in an increased production of testosterone (and other androgens) in utero and continuing after birth. Females are thus exposed to levels of testosterone in utero that far exceed the normal range of variation. Females with CAH represent a naturally occurring experiment, wherein girls with CAH can be compared to girls without CAH. Any significant differences that exist between these two groups are usually attributed to differential exposure to testosterone in utero. Furthermore, if prenatal levels of testosterone are partially involved in the creation of antisocial phenotypes, then girls with CAH should display more "male-like" behaviors than girls without CAH.

A range of studies has employed samples of CAH subjects to examine whether girls afflicted with this disorder are behaviorally and cognitively different than girls without CAH. The results of these studies have documented some significant differences between CAH and non-CAH girls. For example, CAH girls have been found to engage in more rough-and-tumble behaviors in childhood, to be more likely to be labeled a tomboy, to be more likely to befriend boys, and to be more interested in boy toys, such as guns, trucks, and cars when compared to non-CAH girls (Berenbaum & Resnick, 1997; Hines, Brook, & Conway, 2004; Hines & Kaufman, 1994; Pasterski et al., 2005; Pasterski et al., 2007). The most straightforward interpretation of these findings is that exposure to high levels of testosterone in utero was a causal agent in producing such differences; however, critics of biological explanations invoke a different explanation. According to such critics, parents tend to socialize girls with and without CAH differently such that girls with CAH are socialized more like males. As a consequence, girls with CAH act more like boys not because of exposure to high levels of testosterone in utero, but because of the different socialization experiences (Beaver, 2009).

To address this criticism, Pasterski et al. (2005) examined toy preferences and toy play in samples of families with one girl who had CAH and her sister who did not have CAH. The sisters were presented with a series of toys and instructed to play with whatever toys they wanted. Their parents were also present to monitor their daughters and provide feedback to them. The results of the experiment revealed that girls with CAH were more likely to play with boy-typical toys when compared with their unaffected sisters. Of particular importance, however, was what the researchers found when they examined how the parents interacted with their daughters. Their analysis revealed that parents provided significantly greater positive feedback to their CAH daughters for playing with girl-typical toys than they did their non-CAH daughters. What this necessarily means is that CAH girls preferred to play with boy-typical toys more than their non-CAH sisters even though parents were more likely to encourage their CAH daughters more than their unaffected daughters to play with girl-typical toys.

The findings reviewed above provide some very strong evidence linking CAH to a range of boy-typical phenotypes. Behaviors like toy preference, however, might be viewed by some critics as being far removed from antisocial behaviors later in life, such as violence, aggression, and crime. A line of research has emerged examining the association between CAH and aggression later in life. Overall, the results of these studies have shown a statistically significant association between CAH and increased levels of aggressive personality traits and aggressive behaviors (Cohen-Bendahan, van de Beek, & Berenbaum, 2005). Some of the earliest research on this topic, though, was hampered by methodological shortcomings, but more recent research, which has overcome these limitations, has detected virtually identical findings. For example, in perhaps the most methodologically sound study to date, Pasterski and colleagues (2007) found that girls with CAH were significantly more aggressive than their non-CAH sisters. Interestingly, their study also revealed that boys without CAH were still more aggressive than girls with CAH. When pooled together, the available evidence suggests that boys (with and without CAH) are more aggressive than girls with CAH who, in turn, are more aggressive than girls without CAH. This general pattern of findings is consistent with explanations arguing that prenatal testosterone levels are partially responsible for producing antisocial behaviors. Whether prenatal testosterone levels are able to account for male-female differences in antisocial behaviors (especially violent and aggressive behaviors) remains undetermined and should be addressed in future research.

Biosocial Explanations of Male-Female Differences in Antisocial Behaviors

Thus far, we have discussed the limitations to purely environmental explanations for male-female differences in offending and, at the same time, focused on some of the key ways that biological factors may produce such disparities. This might seem like a throwback to the outdated nature versus nurture debate, but modern biosocial criminological theory and research actually moves far beyond arguments about whether genes/biology matter more than the environment. Instead, biosocial criminology focuses on the complex ways in which biological and genetic factors work in tandem with environmental factors to produce behavioral variation (Raine, 2002; Walsh, 2011b). Much of this research has been guided by the logic of interactions, wherein a biological risk factor only has effects when it is paired with an environmental liability. If the environmental liability is eliminated, then the biological risk factor will not exert an effect (or the effect will be attenuated substantially) on the behavioral phenotype. When viewed in this way, these types of interactions hold the potential to explain, in part, male-female differences in criminal behavior if males are differentially exposed to genetic/biological risk factors and/or environmental liabilities.

There has been a line of research that has revealed support in favor of the interaction between genes/biology and environmental factors in the production of antisocial behaviors (Beaver, 2009; Raine, 2002; Wright et al., 2008). In a classic study, for example, Caspi et al. (2002) were interested in examining why childhood maltreatment produces a wide array of heterogeneous outcomes. For the most part, children who are abused and maltreated tend to be relatively resilient and do not subsequently display any type of psychopathology. A small group of abused and maltreated children, however, tend to be quite vulnerable and suffer long-term negative outcomes, such as being depressed, engaging in externalizing behavioral problems, and even accruing a lengthy criminal history. Caspi and his colleagues posited that variation in outcomes was likely due in large part to differences in genetic factors. To test this assumption, they examined whether a genetic risk factor (i.e., a polymorphism in the promoter region of the monoamine oxidase A [MAOA] gene) moderated the effect of childhood maltreatment on antisocial and criminal behaviors. The results of their analysis indicated that MAOA only had an effect on antisocial phenotypes for males who were maltreated as children. MAOA did not have any effect on antisocial behaviors for males who were not maltreated as children. Numerous other studies have replicated this interaction effect (Edwards et al., 2010; Frazzetto et al., 2007; Kinnally et al., 2009) and, just as important, a line of additional research has revealed that MAOA has main effects (i.e., independent of the environment) on a swath of criminal outcomes (Beaver, DeLisi, Vaughn, & Barnes, 2010; Guo, Ou, Roettger, & Shih, 2008; Reif et al., 2007). MAOA, in short, has been found to be one of the most consistent genetic risk factors for antisocial and criminal behaviors.

One of the interesting aspects about the MAOA gene is that it is located on the X chromosome, which means that males have only one copy of this gene, but females have two copies of this gene. The available evidence tends to suggest that the MAOA gene is more strongly related to antisocial outcomes for males than females because if males have the risky version of this gene (i.e., the low MAOA activity allele), then they do not have another copy that compensates for it; females, in contrast, have two chances to inherit a copy of the gene that works efficiently (i.e., the high MAOA activity allele). And having just one efficient copy appears to be all that is needed to reduce the criminogenic effects associated with this gene (Beaver, 2009). There are likely other genes that are also located on the X chromosome that work in a similar fashion and that may also be able to explain male-female differences in antisocial behaviors. Taken together, the findings flowing from empirical research strongly hint at the possibility that part of the reason males are more criminal and antisocial than females is because they possess significantly greater genetic and biological risk factors than females (Vaske, Wright, Boisvert, & Beaver, 2011).

In addition to possessing more genetic risk factors, there is some research indicating that males are more likely to be affected by genetic risk factors than females. Known as the *polygenic multiple threshold model* (Carter, 1973), this model assumes that antisocial phenotypes are produced by the concentration of many different genetic factors and many different environmental pathogens. When the accumulation of these myriad risk factors reaches a certain threshold, antisocial and criminal behavior is likely to emerge. Although there is some evidence indicating that the polygenic multiple threshold model can explain male-female differences in criminal involvement, there is relatively little research examining how genetic risk factors might produce such differences. One of the main exceptions is a study by Vaske et al. (2011) that examined the distribution of genetic risk factors for both males and females. The study found that the threshold for criminal behavior for females was significantly greater than it was for males. In other words, females needed a significantly greater concentration of genetic risk than males for criminal behavior to surface. This differential threshold could be produced by other genetic/biological factors or by environmental factors. Regardless of the explanation for the unique thresholds, the results across studies suggest males possess more genetic risk than females and males are more likely than females to be affected by lower levels of genetic risk. This is a perfect genetic recipe for producing male-female differences in crime and other antisocial outcomes.

Conclusions

We conclude with a cautionary note. In 1965, identical twin brothers David (born as Bruce) and Brian Reimer were born, and during a routine circumcision, one of the boys (David) accidentally had his penis destroyed. Not knowing what to do, the boys' parents were put in touch with a psychologist, John Money. Money was a leading researcher on gender identity and believed, like most criminologists, that male-female differences are produced almost entirely by socialization patterns. He recommended that David undergo sex reassignment surgery and be raised as a girl. David was given a new name (Brenda) and was provided with psychological counseling by Money. Money monitored the boys over a span of about 10 years and published reports regarding the progression of the "experiment." Money concluded that David's case was a success in that he was very girlish, preferring to play with dolls and engage in girl-like behaviors, while his twin brother, Brian, was maturing in a normal male-like fashion, preferring to play with boy toys and engage in boy-like behaviors. These reports were largely welcomed by the academic and public communities and were added to the repertoire of propaganda used by social scientists to argue that any biological differences between males and females could be overcome by socialization.

The problem with Money's reports of the twin boys is that it was largely incorrect and fabricated. By all objective accounts, David was not making a smooth transition into being reared as a girl. He was often characterized as being a tomboy and as being quite rambunctious and preferring rough-and-tumble play in much the same way as his brother. As a teenager, David attempted to disguise his feminine characteristics in different ways and reported that he never felt as though he was a girl. Ultimately he would be informed of what had transpired and he reverted back to his original biological sex—that is, a male. The psychological consequences of trying to raise a biological male as a female, however, took their toll. Although he later married, he was never able to adjust to the torturous life he had been put through *after* the circumcision accident. Sadly, in 2004 he committed suicide. As for John Money, he continued to argue that male-female differences are largely the result of socialization factors. Believing so much in his cause, that in 1985, 20 years after the "experiment" with David, Money was told of another case where a boy had his penis destroyed. What did Money do? He recommended that the boy be raised as a girl (Colapinto, 2000).

The belief that male-female differences in antisocial behaviors are completely social creations may be politically correct, fall in line with the dominant ideology, and conform to commonsensical notions about human nature. However, the data do not support such a simplistic and monolithic explanation. Simply put, males and females are different and are born with many of these differences hardwired into their brains. As their lives unfold, these biological differences become accentuated and environmental factors likely exacerbate them. Unfortunately, the field of criminology has largely ignored the role of biology in creating male-female differences and instead has produced and adhered to a mythical reality that is devoid of empirical evidence, but is nonetheless politically correct. Denying, or even simply ignoring, biological differences is not only unscientific, but can also produce untold costs on society, destroy lives, and in some cases, ultimately lead to self-destructive behavior. Recognizing that boys and girls are born into this world differently and striving to understand how these differences are created should be the first steps in trying to unpack the mechanisms that ultimately account for male-female differences in criminal and antisocial behaviors.

Note

1. It is important to note that sex is a biological characteristic whereas gender is often considered a social construct. We use the terms "sex" and "gender" interchangeably throughout this chapter in recognition of our interdisciplinary perspective that male-female differences are created by both environmental forces and biological/genetic factors.

References

Ahern, K. R., & Dittmar, A. K. (2012). The changing of the boards: The impact of firm valuation of mandated female board representation. *Quarterly Journal of Economics, 127,* 137–197.

Bailey, A. A., & Hurd, P. L. (2005). Finger length ratio (2D:4D) correlates with physical aggression in men but not in women. *Biological Psychiatry, 46,* 558–564.

Baron-Cohen, S. (2003). *The essential difference: Male and female brains and the truth about autism.* New York, NY: Basic Books.

Baron-Cohen, S., Lutchmaya, S., & Knickmeyer, R. (2004). *Prenatal testosterone in mind: Amniotic fluid studies.* Cambridge, MA: MIT Press.

Beaver, K. M. (2008). Nonshared environmental influences on adolescent delinquent involvement and adult criminal behavior. *Criminology, 46,* 341–369.

Beaver, K. M. (2009). *Biosocial criminology: A primer.* Dubuque, IA: Kendall/Hunt.

Beaver, K. M., & Wright, J. P. (2007). A child effects explanation for the association between family risk and involvement in an antisocial lifestyle. *Journal of Adolescent Research, 22,* 640–664.

Beaver, K. M., DeLisi, M., Vaughn, M. G., & Barnes, J. C. (2010). Monoamine oxidase A genotype is associated with gang membership and weapon use. *Comprehensive Psychiatry, 51,* 130–134.

Benderlioglu, Z., & Nelson, R. J. (2004). Digit length ratios predict reactive aggression in women, but not in men. *Hormones and Behavior, 46,* 558–564.

Berenbaum, S. A., & Resnick, S. M. (1997). Early androgen effects on aggression in children and adults with congenital adrenal hyperplasia. *Psychoneuroendocrinology, 22*(7), 505–515.

Brizendine, L. (2006). *The female brain.* New York, NY: Broadway Books.

Brizendine, L. (2010). *The male brain: A breakthrough understanding of how men and boys think.* New York, NY: Broadway Books.

Bushman, B. J., & Huesmann, L. R. (2006). Short-term and long-term effects of violent media on aggression in children and adults. *Archives of Pediatrics and Adolescent Medicine, 160,* 348–352.

Buss, D. M. (2005). *The murderer next door: Why the mind is designed to kill.* New York, NY: Penguin.

Carter, C. O. (1973). Multifactorial genetic disease. In V. A. McKusick & R. Clairborne (Eds.), *Medical genetics* (pp. 199–208). New York, NY: HP.

Caspi, A., Harrington, H. L., Milne, B., Amell, J. W., Theodore, R. F., & Moffitt, T. E. (2003). Children's behavior styles at age 3 are linked to their adult personality traits at age 26. *Journal of Personality, 71,* 495–514.

Caspi, A., McClay, J., Moffitt, T. E., Mill, J., Martin, J., Craig, I. W., . . . Poulton, R. (2002). Role of genotype in the cycle of violence in maltreated children. *Science, 297,* 851–854.

Cohen-Bendahan, C. C. C., van de Beek, C., & Berenbaum, S. A. (2005). Prenatal sex hormone effects on child and sex-typed behavior: Methods and findings. *Neuroscience and Biobehavioral Reviews, 29,* 353–384.

Colapinto, J. (2000). *As nature made him: The boy who was raised as a girl.* New York, NY: HarperCollins.

Connellan, J., Baron-Cohen, S., Wheelwright, S., Batki, A., & Ahluwalia, J. (2000). Sex differences in human neonatal social perception. *Infant Behavior & Development, 23,* 113–118.

Daly, M., & Wilson, M. (1988). *Homicide.* New Brunswick, NJ: Transaction.

Edwards, A. C., Dodge, K. A., Latendresse, S. J., Lansford, J. E., Bates, J. E., Pettit, G. S., . . . Dick, D. M. (2010). MAOA-uVNTR and early physical discipline interact to influence delinquent behavior. *Journal of Child Psychology and Psychiatry, 51,* 679–687.

Ellis, L., & Walsh, A. (2007). *Criminology: An interdisciplinary approach.* Thousand Oaks, CA: Sage.

Ferguson, C. J., & Kilburn, J. (2009). The public health risks of media violence: A meta-analytic review. *Journal of Pediatrics, 154,* 759–763.

Frazzetto, G., Di Lorenzo, G., Carola, V., Proietti, L., Sokolowska, E., Siracusano, A., . . . Troisi, A. (2007). Early trauma and increased risk for physical aggression during adulthood: The moderating role of MAOA genotype. *PLoS ONE, 2*(5), e486, 1–6.

Freeman, D. (1983). *Margaret Mead and the heretic: The making and unmaking of an anthropological myth.* Los Angeles, CA: Penguin Books.

Freeman, D. (1999). *The fateful hoaxing of Margaret Mead: A historical analysis of her Samoan research.* Boulder, CO: Westview.

Ge, X., Conger, R. D., Cadoret, R. J., Neiderhiser, J. M., Yates, W., Troughton, E., & Stewart, M. A. (1996). The developmental interface between nature and nurture: A mutual influence model of child antisocial behavior and parent behaviors. *Developmental Psychology, 32,* 574–589.

Gottfredson, M. R., & Hirschi, T. (1990). *A general theory of crime.* Stanford, CA: Stanford University Press.

Guo, G., Ou, X. M., Roettger, M., & Shih, J. C. (2008). The VNTR 2 repeat in MAOA and delinquent behavior in adolescence and young adulthood: Associations and MAOA promoter activity. *European Journal of Human Genetics, 16,* 626–634.

Harris, J. R. (1998). *The nurture assumption: Why children turn out the way they do.* New York, NY: Touchstone.

Hines, M., Brook, C., & Conway, G. S. (2004). Androgen and psychosexual development: Core gender identity, sexual orientation and recalled childhood gender role behavior in women and men with congenital adrenal hyperplasia (CAH). *Journal of Sex Research, 41,* 75–81.

Hines, M., & Kaufman, F. R. (1994). Androgen and the development of human sex-typical behavior: Rough-and-tumble play and sex of preferred playmates in children with congenital adrenal hyperplasia (CAH). *Child Development, 65,* 1042–1053.

Hönekopp, J., & Watson, S. (2011). Meta-analysis of the relationship between digit-ratio 2D:4D and aggression. *Personality and Individual Differences, 51,* 381–386.

Kinnally, E. L., Huang, Y., Haverly, R., Burke, A. K., Galfalvy, H., Brent, D. P., . . . Mann, J. J. (2009). Parental care moderates the influence of MAOA-uVNTR genotype and childhood stressors on trait impulsivity and aggression in adult women. *Psychiatric Genetics, 19,* 126–133.

Kondo, T., Zakany, J., Innis, J. W., & Duboule, D. (1997). Of fingers, toes, and penises. *Nature, 390,* 29.

Lytton, H., & Romney, D. M. (1991). Parents' differential socialization of boys and girls: A meta-analysis. *Psychological Bulletin, 109,* 267–296.

Manning, J. T. (2002). *Digit ratio: A pointer to fertility, behavior, and health.* New Brunswick, NJ: Rutgers University Press.

Manning, J. T., Baron-Cohen, S., Wheelwright, S., & Sanders, G. (2001). The 2nd to 4th digit ratio and autism. *Developmental Medicine and Child Neurology, 43,* 160–164.

Manning, J. T., & Taylor, R. P. (2001). Second to fourth digit ratio and male ability in sport: Implications for sexual selection in humans. *Evolution and Human Behavior, 22,* 61–69.

McIntyre, M. H., Barrett, E. S., McDermott, R., Johnson, D. D. P., Cowden, J., & Rosen, S. (2007). Finger length ratio (2D:4D) and sex differences in aggression during a simulated war game. *Personality and Individual Differences, 42,* 755–764.

Mead, M. (1928). *Coming of age in Samoa: A psychological study of primitive youth for Western civilization.* New York, NY: HarperCollins.

Mead, M. (1935). *Sex and temperament in three primitive societies.* New York, NY: Morrow.

Messner, S. F., & Rosenfeld, R. (2007). *Crime and the American Dream* (4th ed.). Belmont, CA: Thomson/Wadsworth.

Millet, K., & Dewitte, S. (2007). Digit ratio (2D:4D) moderates the impact of an aggressive music video on aggression. *Personality and Individual Differences, 43,* 289–294.

Orans, M. (1996). *Not even wrong: Margaret Mead, Derek Freeman, and the Samoans.* Novato, CA: Chandler & Sharp Publishers.

Pasterski, V. L., Geffner, M. E., Brain, C., Hindmarsh, P., Brook, C., & Hines, M. (2005). Prenatal hormones and postnatal socialization by parents as determinants of male-typical toy play in girls with congenital adrenal hyperplasia. *Child Development, 76,* 264–278.

Pasterski, V., Hindmarsh, P., Geffner, M., Brook, C., Brain, C., & Hines, M. (2007). Increased aggression and activity level in 3- to 11-year-old girls with congenital adrenal hyperplasia (CAH). *Hormones and Behavior, 52,* 368–374.

Pinker, S. (2002). *The blank slate: The modern denial of human nature.* New York, NY: Viking.

Raine, A. (2002). Biosocial studies of antisocial and violent behavior in children and adults: A review. *Journal of Abnormal Child Psychology, 30,* 311–326.

Reif, A., Rösler, M., Freitag, C. M., Schneider, M., Eujen A., Kissling, C., . . . Retz, W. (2007). Nature and nurture predispose to violent behavior: Serotonergic genes and adverse childhood environment. *Neuropsychopharmacology, 32,* 2375–2383.

Rowe, D. C. (1994). *The limits of family influence: Genes, experiences, and behavior.* New York, NY: Guildford Press.

Rowe, D. C. (2002). *Biology and crime.* Los Angeles, CA: Roxbury.

Rowe, D. C., & Flannery, D. J. (1994). An examination of environmental and trait influences on adolescent delinquency. *Journal of Research in Crime and Delinquency, 31,* 374–389.

Sluming, V. A., & Manning, J. T. (2000). Second to fourth digit ratio in elite musicians: Evidence for musical ability as an honest signal of male fitness. *Evolution and Human Behavior, 21,* 1–9.

Udry, J. R. (1994). The nature of gender. *Demography, 31,* 561–573.

Udry, J. R. (2000). Biological limits of gender construction. *American Sociological Review, 65,* 443–457.

Vaske, J., Wright, J. P., Boisvert, D., & Beaver, K. M. (2011). Gender, genetic risk, and criminal behavior. *Psychiatry Research, 185,* 376–381.

Walsh, A. (2011a). *Feminist criminology through a biosocial lens.* Durham, NC: Carolina Academic Press.

Walsh, A. (2011b). *Social class and crime: A biosocial approach.* New York, NY: Routledge.

Wright, J. P., & Beaver, K. M. (2005). Do parents matter in creating self-control in their children? A genetically informed test of Gottfredson and Hirschi's theory of low self-control. *Criminology, 43,* 1169–1202.

Wright, J. P., Tibbetts, S. G., & Daigle, L. E. (2008). *Criminals in the making: Criminality across the life course.* Thousand Oaks, CA: Sage.

Discussion Questions

CHAPTERS 1 AND 2

1. Most research seems to indicate that males offend at a much higher rate than females. However, some studies have described circumstances in which male and female patterns of offending are quite similar to one another. Discuss these situations and describe some of the leading explanations for these observations.
2. For several decades, it has been believed that parents tend to socialize males and females differently, and such differences directly contribute to observed differences in rates of offending. Describe in detail these gender differences in socialization and how they may directly contribute to differences in criminal offending between males and females.
3. Social influences from sources other than parents have also been long believed to directly contribute to gender differences in offending. Describe how differences in socialization that occurs in peer groups and school may directly contribute to differences in criminal offending between males and females.
4. Most research examining gender differences in offending focuses exclusively on environmental factors such as parenting, peers, and neighborhoods in explaining such differences. Explain in detail the limitations of this approach.
5. Modern research has identified distinct biological differences between males and females. In addition, many of these differences have been directly linked to differences in criminal offending rates between males and females. Which specific biological differences have been found contribute to these differences in offending?
6. Explain in detail the benefit of taking a biosocial approach in attempting to understand differences in offending between males and females. How is this approach better than a purely sociological or biological approach?

3

Sociological Viewpoint on the Race-Crime Relationship

Nicole Leeper Piquero

The University of Texas at Dallas

Alex R. Piquero

The University of Texas at Dallas

Eric S. Stewart

Florida State University

Introduction

The relationship between race and crime is on the one hand very strong, at least when considered from the vantage point of official crime statistics. There is a consistency in the data in that minorities—primarily African Americans—are overrepresented in both (serious) offending and correctional statistics. The reason(s) underlying this overrepresentation, however, are neither well documented nor fully understood. The lack of a consensus has led some commentators to view the disparity as a function of (a) differential involvement in serious offending by minorities that brings them to the attention of formal criminal justice authorities, (b) differential enforcement by criminal justice personnel (including discriminatory practices and decisions), or (c) some combination of the two (see review in Piquero, 2008). On the other hand, and regardless of which explanation is most consistent with the data, the study of race and crime has been and continues to be both contentious and controversial (Kennedy, 1997; Sampson & Wilson, 1995; Walker, Spohn, & DeLone, 2011; Wilbanks, 1987).

This chapter focuses on the main sociological explanations of the race-crime relationship. In so doing, it neither discounts the relevance of nonsociological viewpoints—because these are covered elsewhere in this book—nor does it review any policy proscriptions associated with the race-crime relationship—also discussed in the book. Instead, two prominent sociological perspectives are considered along with how they attempt to understand and explain race differences in offending. Accordingly, this chapter focuses on social structures, social areas, and social contingencies including: (a) disadvantaged neighborhood environments (which are also characterized by disadvantaged family, school and health systems, and differential employment structures) and (b) differential cultural adaptations in urban communities. A few prominent empirical examples are highlighted that assess key aspects of the theories reviewed. Finally, the chapter concludes with an identification of three important directions for future research centered on: (1) the reason(s) underlying the overrepresentation of minorities in criminal justice statistics, (2) the development and empirical research needed on recent theoretical frameworks, and (3) data collection and ensuing research on the ethnicity-crime relationship, especially concerning Hispanics/Latinos and immigrants. Before we turn to the main portions of our chapter, we begin first with basic descriptive data on race and crime.

Race and Crime as Viewed Through Official Criminal Records

Although official criminal justice arrest and correctional data are subject to several limitations, they do offer one portrait of the race-crime relationship. Here, we review some of the most basic criminal justice data across race with primary focus distinguishing between Whites and Blacks, because most official data sources include informational breakdowns for these two demographic groups.

According to the most recent Federal Bureau of Investigation (FBI) data on arrests (2011, Table 43a), Whites comprised 69.2% of all persons arrested, while Blacks comprised 28.4%.[1] The percentage of Black arrests for specific crimes, such as murder/nonnegligent manslaughter (49.7%) and robbery (55.6%), was higher than the comparable percentage among Whites (48% and 43%, respectively). For both the violent and property crime rates, Whites had a higher percentage of arrests compared to Blacks. A particularly interesting finding emerged, however, when the arrest percentages by race are considered among juveniles (those persons under age 18; Table 43b). In this instance, although Whites have a higher percentage of arrests for the property crime rate compared to Blacks (62.4% vs. 35.0%), the opposite finding holds for the violent crime rate, where Black juveniles (51.4%) have a higher percentage than do Whites (47.0%). Among juveniles, the difference across race is most pronounced for robbery, where Black juveniles evidence a much higher percentage of arrests (68.5%) compared to White juveniles (30.4%). With respect to correctional statistics, recent prisoner data from the U.S. Department of Justice (Carson & Sabol, 2012, pp. 7–8) show that (a) imprisonment rates are about 0.5% of all White males, more than 3.0% of all Black males, and 1.2% of all Hispanic males; (b) Blacks and Hispanics were imprisoned at higher rates than Whites in all age groups for both male and female inmates; and (c) after excluding the youngest and oldest age groups (18–19, 65+), Black males were imprisoned at rates that ranged between 5 and 7 times the rates of White males.[2] Thus, after examining the official statistics, the need to understand race/ethnic disparities in offending, arrests, and imprisonment becomes even more paramount.

Next, we turn to a review of some of the more prominent theoretical frameworks that have been developed and/or applied to the sociological understanding of the race-crime relationship.

Theoretical Framework

SOCIAL DISORGANIZATION THEORY

Perhaps the best place to begin the review of the sociological understanding of the race-crime relationship is with Shaw and McKay's (1942) social disorganization theory. Briefly, these theorists were focused on community structures and (cultural) differences within and across a city that produced different rates of crime. Their explanation centered on how three key processes, low socioeconomic status, ethnic heterogeneity, and residential mobility, worked in concert to spur the disruption of community social organization and decrease informal social control mechanisms, which in turn created conditions that were ripe for delinquency and crime. One of the main and consistently reproduced findings of Shaw and McKay's arguments was that crime and other social ills were heavily concentrated in specific communities regardless of the population makeup. This led the theorists to deemphasize the importance of individual explanations and instead to emphasize community-level disadvantage and disorganization. Subsequent theoretical developments articulated after publication of Shaw and McKay's works paid closer attention to delinquent attitudes, status, subcultures, and opportunity structures (Cloward & Ohlin, 1960; Cohen, 1955; Miller, 1958).

Many of the modern-day versions of social disorganization theory devote specific attention to the role of concentrated disadvantage and in particular concentrations of racialized economic and residential isolation and segregation (see e.g., Massey & Denton, 1993; Wilson, 1987, 1996). One of the most prominent of these perspectives was developed by Sampson and Wilson. These theorists did much to advance the sociological viewpoint on race and crime by proposing a thesis that incorporates both cultural and structural arguments and in so doing "highlight[s] the very different ecological contexts that blacks and whites reside in—regardless of individual characteristics" (Sampson & Wilson, 1995, p. 38). As they note, "the basic thesis is that macro-social patterns of residential inequality give rise to the social isolation and ecological concentration of the truly disadvantaged, which in turn leads to structural barriers and cultural adaptations that undermine social organization and hence the control of crime" (p. 38).

Although their initial work was not designed to provide an empirical test of their theory, one key finding of their review of the existing data concerned the neighborhood context that African Americans reside in. Specifically, Sampson and Wilson observed that African Americans resided in extremely disadvantaged communities and that Whites could not be found to be living in the same kinds of disadvantaged neighborhoods and communities. As they note, "In not one city over 100,000 in the United States [in 1980] do blacks live in ecological equality with whites when it comes to these basic features of economic and family organization. Accordingly, racial differences in poverty and family disruption are so strong that the 'worst' urban contexts in which whites reside are considerably better than the average context of black communities (as cited in Sampson, 1987, p. 354)" (Sampson & Wilson, 1995, p. 42). Peterson and Krivo (2010) similarly observed that "white ghettos" do not exist—at least anywhere near the kind that exist among African American communities in general and over time in consecutive generations (Sharkey, 2008, p. 933).

Residence in severely distressed communities subsequently leads to Blacks being overly exposed to conditions that are conducive to criminal activity (and exposure to violence; see Zimmerman & Messner, 2013). Compared to Whites or Hispanics, a much higher proportion of Blacks live in inner-city communities that are characterized by severe economic distress and family disruption and are often isolated from adequate educational, employment, health, and recreation services. These effects are concentrated as well and thus increase the likelihood of a range of adverse outcomes regarding employment, access to well-performing schools, the availability of marriage partners, and exposure to conventional role models (Sampson & Wilson, 1995, p. 42). Thus, for Sampson and Wilson (p. 44, emphasis in original), "the most important determinant of the relationship between race and crime is the differential distribution of blacks in communities characterized by (1) *structural social disorganization* and (2) *cultural social isolation,* both of which stem from the concentration of poverty, family disruption, and residential stability." In addition to incorporating issues of political economy (i.e., municipal code enforcement, housing policies, etc.), their

> theoretical framework linking social-disorganization theory with research on urban poverty and political economy suggests that macro-social forces (e.g., segregation, migration, housing discrimination, structural transformation of the economy) interact with local community-level factors (e.g., residential turnover, concentrated poverty, family disruption) to impede social organization. This is a distinctly sociological viewpoint, for it focuses attention on the proximate structural characteristics and mediating processes of community social organization that help explain crime, while also recognizing the larger historical, social, and political forces shaping local communities. (p. 49)[3]

In sum, Sampson and Wilson highlight structural differences in economic and family organization as the underlying generators of differences in crime rates across race, especially with respect to serious crime.

It is important to note that further theoretical development of the social disorganization framework has been undertaken. One notable example is Bursik and Grasmick's (1993) merging of social disorganization and systemic theories. In short, these authors stress the importance of networks and associational ties for social control and in so doing highlight the importance of the broader political, social, and economic dynamics of urban systems. A prominent feature of their systemic approach to the study of neighborhoods and crime is the consideration of the ability of neighborhoods to exert local control by mobilizing various resources (e.g., schools, churches, and institutions) located outside the community. A second notable extension of the social disorganization framework is Sampson, Raudenbush, and Earls's (1997) notion of collective efficacy, which focuses on the mutual trust among neighbors combined with their willingness to intervene on behalf of the common good. Their findings from analyses of data from the Project on Human Development in Chicago Neighborhoods (PHDCN)[4] showed that neighborhoods scoring high on collective efficacy also tended to have significantly lower crime rates than neighborhoods scoring low on collective efficacy.

There is a rather sizable database exploring issues related to race and crime, and competent reviews of these studies exist elsewhere (see Hawkins & Kempf-Leonard, 2005; LaFree, Baumer, & O'Brien, 2010; Parker, 2008; Sampson & Lauritsen, 1997; Unnever & Gabbidon, 2011). Here, we highlight two specific studies that are exemplary in their approach to studying different aspects of the race-crime relationship using advanced methodology and a large array of variables.

In the first study, Sampson, Morenoff, and Raudenbush (2005) used three waves of data collected from the large-scale PHDCN data discussed above. In this research, Sampson and his colleagues examined the extent to which contextual explanations (focused on economic, family, and neighborhood context), as well as constitutional explanations (impulsivity and intelligence), were able to explain race/ethnic differences in violence. Results indicated that while violence was higher among Blacks compared to Whites (and Latino violence was lower), most of the Black-White gap and the entire Latino-White gap was explained largely by contextual factors—and especially neighborhood context, which was the most important source of the gap reduction (and constitutional differences being the least important). These results imply that race/ethnic differences in crime (especially violence) are largely attributable to the risk factors that different groups are exposed to, with Blacks being exposed to the most criminogenic of these, a finding that resonates well with the proscriptions from Sampson and Wilson's thesis described earlier.

In the second study, Zimmerman and Messner (2013) also used data from the PHDCN to examine the extent to which individual (e.g., lack of self-control, violent peers, verbal/reading ability), familial (e.g., family structure, family size, parental warmth), and neighborhood (e.g., concentrated disadvantage, residential stability, youth services, neighborhood violence) factors were able to explain the differential exposure to violence that is routinely observed across race/ethnicity. These authors found that (a) the odds of exposure to violence were extremely higher for Blacks (112%) and Hispanics (74%) compared to Whites; (b) 33% (Hispanic-White) and 53% (Black-White) of that differential exposure to violence was accounted for by familial, individual, and neighborhood factors; and (3) although Blacks and

Hispanics continued to have higher exposure to violence than Whites after controlling for demographic, neighborhood, familial, and individual variables, neighborhood context was "an appreciable source of the reduction in the racial/ethnic gaps in exposure to violence" (p. e7) because Black and Hispanic communities in the PHDCN are "characterized by high levels of concentrated disadvantage and a deficiency of youth services" (p. e7).

Although social disorganization theory stands as the most commonly applied framework for understanding race/ethnic differences in crime, specific features of distressed communities are worth highlighting. For example, research consistently documents the prevalence of African American family disruption—especially to include homes headed by single mothers, the lack of adequately performing schools, the lack of adequate health care and social service systems, and the lack of meaningful and gainful employment opportunities—which all compromise social control and supervision of youth and coalesce in economically isolated and distressed minority (mainly African American) inner-city communities (see review in Smelser, Wilson, & Mitchell, 2001).

Next, we review a theoretical framework that considers the role of culture and attitudes in severely distressed communities, especially those communities that are populated by high concentrations of poor, segregated, and marginalized African Americans, and how these attitudes in turn influence the likelihood of antisocial—especially violent—behavior.

ANDERSON'S CODE OF THE STREET

A key aspect of the social disorganization framework concerned the transmission of norms and values associated with antisocial behavior. Though Shaw and McKay did not discuss the development and effect that these norms and values had on antisocial behavior in great detail, a very important ethnographic contribution to the sociological understanding of crime by Elijah Anderson helped describe these specific attitudes, including their development and patterning in impoverished, inner-city minority communities. Integrating the macrostructural insights of disadvantage, racial inequality, social isolation, and limited economic opportunities that were empirically identified earlier in this chapter, Anderson (1994, 1999) argued that these "ghetto poverty" conditions combine to foster an oppositional street culture that is conducive to violence. This street culture fosters cynicism about societal rules that undermines mainstream conventional norms. Disadvantaged neighborhoods, therefore, help provide the context in which this street culture develops, attitudes conducive to violence form (i.e., the street code associated with "demanding respect," "espousing one's manhood," "being tough," "never backing down from a fight," and "saving face"), and such attitudes help guide and influence situational interactions and decision making, which, though primarily designed to deter victimization from others and negotiate respect on the street (Anderson, 1999, p. 10), increases the likelihood of aggression and antisocial behavior (see Fagan & Wilkinson, 1998; Wilkinson, 2001). This process, moreover, persists over time and within families in distressed neighborhoods that cannot organize against violence through the cultural transmission of values such that the "spatial arrangements of neighborhood codes of violence remain stable over time" (Matsueda, Drakulich, & Kubrin, 2006, p. 341). In sum, Anderson identified and distinguished between both a neighborhood "code of the street" as well as an individual's own adoption of "street code" values.[5]

It is also important to note that not all individuals nor do all families residing in economically distressed inner-city communities ascribe to and promote street code values. Specifically, he noted that there were two types of cultural orientations, "decent" and "street." The former embraces mainstream conventional values (education, employment, obedience to authority and the law), while the latter embodies an oppositional culture whose norms run counter to those of the more conventional, mainstream society. The problem in disorganized areas is that these two cultural orientations run up against one another, and while children from "decent" families may not necessarily espouse street code values, they nevertheless must have street knowledge to remain safe in disadvantaged communities (see Sharkey, 2006).

Anderson's characterization of street codes and their relationship to crime and violence was brought forth in vivid fashion throughout his observations and interviews in the City of Philadelphia. Aside from Anderson's own qualitative narratives, several empirical analyses of the street code thesis have emerged. Here, we highlight two of the more interesting ones.

In an elaboration of Anderson's thesis, Matsueda and his colleagues (2006) argued that the code of the street was an objective property that operated above and beyond individual-level assessments of the code among residents (p. 340). Then, using structural measures of disadvantage collected at census tracts throughout the City of Seattle and individual respondent data from the Seattle Neighborhoods and Crime Survey, a multilevel survey of about 5,000 households within 123 census tracts, these authors presented an empirical investigation of whether neighborhood codes of violence varied by structural characteristics and then whether areas with street codes conducive to violence mapped onto areas with high violent crime. A number of key features and findings of their analysis are worth highlighting.

After developing two separate measures for codes of violence—one centered around what residents thought about codes in their neighborhoods, and a second centered around their own personal street code attitudes—Matsueda and his colleagues (2006) found that (a) neighborhood codes of violence were predicted by several variables, including respondent's own individual codes, which operated in a consistent manner, as well as income and age, where older respondents as well as those reporting a higher income were less likely to hold perceived neighborhood codes of violence; (b) neighborhood codes of violence were disproportionately present in the most impoverished neighborhoods, but this effect disappeared after controlling for race—where, as expected, neighborhood codes were disproportionately present in neighborhoods with more African Americans as well as in neighborhoods with higher percentages of Latinos; and (c) violent crime was lower in neighborhoods that were characterized by lower neighborhood codes of violence (i.e., the northern half of the City of Seattle) whereas violent crime was higher in neighborhoods that were characterized by higher neighborhood codes of violence (i.e., the southern half of the City of Seattle). In sum, their analyses provided empirical support for the central tenets of Anderson's street code thesis: codes were more likely to be found in Black and Hispanic neighborhoods and in neighborhoods with high rates of violent crime.

In a second empirical study assessing Anderson's claims, Stewart and Simons (2010) used data from over 700 African American adolescents to examine the impact of neighborhood culture on violent delinquency. Not only did they find that neighborhood street culture was related to violent delinquency independent of one's own street code, but also that the effect of individual street code values on violence was magnified in neighborhoods where the street culture was widely endorsed.

This section has reviewed two of the most prominent theoretical frameworks that are nicely positioned to address the race-crime relationship from a sociological perspective. Recent extensions of Shaw and McKay's social disorganization theory have emphasized the concentration of poverty in African American (but not White) inner-city communities (Sampson & Wilson, 1995), the importance of neighborhood collective efficacy for preventing violence (Sampson et al., 1997), and the role that individual and neighborhood codes of violence constitute as part of a delinquent cultural tradition (Matsueda et al., 2006, p. 354). In the next section, we discuss some of the current issues involved in understanding the race-crime relationship.

Future Research on the Race-Crime Relationship

So far, this chapter has reviewed two of the more prominent theoretical frameworks that have shown promise in furthering the field's understanding of the race-crime relationship. Additionally, several empirical examples were highlighted that have assessed the race-crime relationship from the each of the respective theoretical models. Although important steps have been made in understanding the race-crime relationship, there remain several important issues that need theoretical and empirical attention. In this section, we discuss three of these in particular.

First and foremost, there remains a tension over the reason(s) why there is a race-crime relationship in the first place. Recall that at the outset of this chapter we made the observation, as have several researchers before us, that there is a disproportionality in official criminal records (especially in violent arrests) as well as in correctional populations among African Americans (and to a lesser extent Hispanics) when compared to Whites. Traditionally, researchers have taken one of two positions when attempting to attribute this overrepresentation. The first position is oriented around a differential involvement argument. This position argues that minorities (especially African Americans) are overrepresented in official crime statistics primarily because they offend at a disproportionately higher rate than do Whites, and more important that the nature of their offending is more violent or person-oriented criminal behavior (Blumstein, 1982). In contrast, a second position is oriented around a differential selection/processing argument. This position does not necessarily deny the existence of any potential differential offending involvement among minorities, but instead places the lion's share of the explanation regarding the overrepresentation of minorities in criminal statistics on agents of the criminal justice system. In particular, this argument contends that minorities are overrepresented in the criminal justice system because of the policies and decisions made by criminal justice actors and public policy officials (Chambliss, 1994; Tonry, 1994; Zimring & Hawkins, 1997). This would include, for example, differential police presence in certain (minority) neighborhoods, differential targeting of certain offenses that are committed largely by minorities, differential processing of criminal offenders—mainly in the form of police decisions to arrest, prosecutors' decision to charge (as well as the charges brought forward), and judge/jury decision making, and finally differential policy decision making that places undue and/or increased attention on minority communities and/or minority offending patterns, as was the case during the crack epidemic of the 1980s and 1990s (Blumstein, 1993).[6] And while there is a growing empirical knowledge base of individual-level and macro-level studies that have sought to assess the extent to which the two positions can explain the race-crime relationship, it is still unclear which position, absent a mixed perspective, is best apt to explain the race-crime relationship.

A second outstanding issue concerns the use of other sociological theories to explain the race-crime relationship. Some theories focus somewhat less on individual-level factors and instead place an emphasis on racism. As one example, Unnever and Gabbidon (2011) recently advanced a theory of African American offending, rooted in African Americans' "inimitable racial oppression" (p. 187), that focused on African Americans' unique worldview that has been shaped by racial injustices and a "peerless racialized daily experience" (p. 187; see also Hagan, Shedd, & Payne, 2005). Chief among these injustices are criminal justice injustices, various forms of racial discrimination, and the consequences of "being pejoratively stereotyped" (p. 167). How do these experiences and injustices relate to differential patterns of offending? According to Unnever and Gabbidon, "a cause of African American offending is their perceptions and experiences with criminal justice injustices" (p. 169). Because Unnever and Gabbidon's (2011, p. 172) theory holds as a key assumption that people are less likely to offend if they respect the legitimacy of the law, and because African Americans are more likely to perceive that laws and the criminal justice system systematically treat them differently because of their race, African Americans are more likely to react to perceived injustices with shame, anger, hostility, and aggression (p. 173). These emotional reactions, in turn, are believed to lead to a lower likelihood of obeying the law.

Two additional features of their theory are also important in their understanding of African American offending. The first concerns the notion of racial socialization, or the "specific verbal and non-verbal messages transmitted to younger generations for the development of values, attitudes, behaviors, and beliefs regarding the meaning and significance of race and racial stratification, intergroup and intragroup interactions, and personal and group identity" (Lesane-Brown, 2006, p. 400). According to Unnever and Gabbidon (2011, p. 183), individual differences in African American offending are also related to variations in racial socialization practices. To the extent that African Americans have positive racial socialization experiences, they are hypothesized to offend less—even if they perceive racial injustices. On the other hand, to the extent that racial socialization does not take shape, it may lead to youth adopting other identities, such as those favorable to a street code of honor and violence that can lead to various negative outcomes such as weak social bonds, school and employment failure, as well as criminal offending. The second additional point to be made concerns their recognition of the importance of place. Specifically, Unnever and Gabbidon (2011, p. 195) pay very close attention to "racially hypersegregated urban neighborhoods," arguing that residing in such an area "disproportionately exposes African Americans to racial discrimination, stereotypes that 'put them down,' and, most profoundly, criminal justice injustices" (p. 195). Moreover, and in addition to the presence of single-parent households, low-performing schools, and weak job prospects found in economically disadvantaged neighborhoods, these theorists also posit that there is a lower likelihood that families will racially socialize their children in areas of extreme disadvantage. This, in turn, is believed to increase the likelihood that African Americans will "more readily react to racial injustice with anger-defiance-depression, which in turn should increase their offending" (Unnever & Gabbidon, 2011, p. 200).[7] In short, Unnever and Gabbidon have outlined a unique theoretical framework designed to understand African American offending patterns, but because of the recency of their theory, a full empirical assessment has yet to be conducted but would be important to undertake.

A third area of needed research concerns an expansion of the race-crime relationship to consider the role of ethnicity. Due to data constraints, there has been a lack of empirical knowledge regarding offending patterns and criminal justice system responses among Hispanics/Latinos. And although this has been slowly changing with important theoretical, empirical, and policy-relevant research conducted at both the individual- and macro-levels of analyses (see, e.g., Maldonado-Molina, Piquero, Jennings, Bird, & Canino, 2009; Martinez, 2002; Stowell, Martinez, & Cancino, 2012), this demographic group remains an important and historically under-studied group in the race-crime area. Relatedly, there has been much public (policy) controversy surrounding the role of immigrants in criminal, especially violent, behavior. Among some of the general public and even a select few policy makers, the belief is that (primarily Mexican) immigrants are responsible for criminal—especially violent—behavior. It is important to note, however, that the empirical research does not find much support for this viewpoint, either at the individual- or macro-level of analysis (see Bersani, 2012; MacDonald & Sampson, 2012; Martinez & Valenzuela, 2006; Ousey & Kubrin, 2009; Sampson, 2008).

In short, the sociological perspective has much to offer to the study of the relationship between race and crime. It offers the promise of understanding how individuals are situated in areas and how these areas can influence cultural adaptations and structure situations. With the advent of continued expansions of data collection to move beyond the simple Black-White dichotomy, social scientists will be able to further develop explanations for disparities in criminal offending as well as the criminal justice system's response to such offending.

Notes

1. In this case the FBI arrest data contain information only for Whites, Blacks, American Indian or Alaskan Native, and Asian or Pacific Islander.

2. It will be noticed that our review of the criminal justice data comes from official record sources, mainly arrests and correctional data. Although we recognize that there are inherent problems with the use of official records to describe the race-crime relationship, we note here that many scholars point to precisely these data to make some arguments that the criminal justice system is somehow biased against minorities, especially African Americans. There does exist some self-reported offending data across demographic groups, but this literature is inconclusive with respect to race differences in the prevalence, frequency, and type of offending, mainly because of sampling limitations as well as customary limitations associated with self-report data (see Hawkins, Laub, & Lauritsen, 1998; Piquero & Brame, 2008; Piquero, Farrington, & Blumstein, 2003; Sampson & Lauritsen, 1997).

3. Sampson and Wilson also ascribe importance to the role of culture in distressed inner-city communities. In short, they argue that community contexts may shape ecologically structured norms, or "cognitive landscapes" that help govern appropriate conduct on the streets. We return to this theme shortly when we discuss Anderson's code of the street thesis.

4. Between 1995 and 2002, the PHDCN was a large interdisciplinary research project that combined an intensive study of Chicago neighborhoods as well as a series of coordinated longitudinal studies that followed over 6,000 randomly selected children, adolescents, and young adults to examine how families, schools, and neighborhoods affected child and adolescent development, including antisocial behavior.

5. Although Anderson's street code thesis is primarily concerned with inner-city African American males residing in severely distressed and isolated communities, other scholars before (Horowitz, 1983) and after (Bourgois, 1995, 1996) have considered similar cultural orientations and attitudes among Hispanic and Latino males.

6. A third position combines elements of the first two, differential involvement and differential enforcement.

7. To be sure, Unnever and Gabbidon (2011, p. 182–183) are mindful that their theory, like other theories of racial oppression and racial discrimination, can lead to an overprediction of African American offending. To help buttress against this potential problem, they argue that there is important individual variation among African Americans in the degree to which they experience racial injustices. Thus, among those African Americans who have more experience with injustice, the likelihood of their offending is believed to be higher than would be the case among those African Americans who have less experience with injustice.

References

Anderson, E. (1994). The code of the street. *Atlantic Monthly, 273*, 81–94.

Anderson, E. (1999). *Code of the street: Decency, violence, and the moral life of the inner city*. New York, NY: W. W. Norton.

Bersani, B. E. (2012). An examination of first and second generation immigrant offending trajectories. *Justice Quarterly*. doi:10.1080/07418825.2012.659200

Blumstein, A. (1982). On the racial disproportionality of United States' prison populations. *Journal of Criminal Law and Criminology, 73*, 1259–1281.

Blumstein, A. (1993). Racial disproportionality of U.S. prison populations revisited. *University of Colorado Law Review, 64*, 743–760.

Bourgois, P. (1995). *In search of respect: Selling crack in El Barrio*. Cambridge, UK: Cambridge University Press.

Bourgois, P. (1996). In search of masculinity: Violence, respect, and sexuality among Puerto Rican crack dealers in East Harlem. *British Journal of Criminology, 36*, 412–427.

Bursik, R. J., Jr., & Grasmick, H. G. (1993). *Neighborhoods and crime: The dimensions of effective community control*. New York, NY: Lexington Books.

Carson, E. A., & Sabol, W. J. (2012). *Prisoners in 2011*. Washington, DC: U.S. Department of Justice. Retrieved from http://bjs.ojp.usdoj.gov/content/pub/pdf/p11.pdf

Chambliss, W. J. (1994). Policing the ghetto underclass: The politics of law and law enforcement. *Social Problems, 41*, 177–194.

Cloward, R., & Ohlin, L. (1960). *Delinquency and opportunity: A theory of delinquent gangs*. Glencoe, IL: Free Press.

Cohen, A. K. (1955). *Delinquent boys: The culture of the gang*. Glencoe, IL: Free Press.

Fagan, J. A., & Wilkinson, D. L. (1998). Guns, youth violence and social identity in inner cities. In M. Tonry & M. Moore (Eds.), *Crime and justice: Annual review of research* (Vol. 24, pp. 105–188). Chicago, IL: University of Chicago Press.

Federal Bureau of Investigation. (2011). *Crime in the United States 2011*. Washington, DC: Federal Bureau of Investigation. Retrieved from http://www.fbi.gov/about-us/cjis/ucr/crime-in-the-u.s/2011/crime-in-the-u.s.-2011/tables/table-43

Hagan, J., Shedd, C., & Payne, M. R. (2005). Race, ethnicity, and youth perceptions of criminal injustice. *American Sociological Review, 70*, 381–407.

Hawkins, D. F., & Kempf-Leonard, K. (Eds.). (2005). *Our children, their children: Confronting racial and ethnic differences in American juvenile justice*. Chicago, IL: University of Chicago Press.

Hawkins, D. F., Laub, J. H., & Lauritsen, J. L. (1998). Race, ethnicity, and serious offending. In R. Loeber & D. P. Farrington (Eds.), *Serious and violent juvenile offenders: Risk factors and successful interventions* (pp. 30–46). Thousand Oaks, CA: Sage.

Horowitz, R. (1983). Honor and the American Dream: Culture and identity in a Chicano community. New Brunswick, NJ: Rutgers University Press.

Kennedy, R. L. (1997). *Race, crime, and the law*. New York, NY: Vintage Books.

LaFree, G., Baumer, E. P., & O'Brien, R. (2010). Still separate and unequal? A city-level analysis of the Black-White gap in homicide arrests since 1960. *American Sociological Review, 75*, 75–100.

Lesane-Brown, C. L. (2006). A review of race socialization within Black families. *Developmental Review, 26*, 400–426.

MacDonald, J., & Sampson, R. J. (Eds.). (2012). Immigration and the changing social fabric of American cities. *Annals of the American Academy of Political and Social Science, 641*.

Maldonado-Molina, M. M., Piquero, A. R., Jennings, W. G., Bird, H., & Canino, G. (2009). Trajectories of delinquency among Puerto Rican children and adolescents at two sites. *Journal of Research in Crime & Delinquency, 46*, 144–181.

Martinez, R., Jr. (2002). *Latino homicide: Immigration, violence, and community*. New York, NY: Routledge.

Martinez, R., Jr., & Valenzuela, A. (Eds.). (2006). *Immigration and crime: Race, ethnicity and violence*. New York: New York University Press.

Massey, D. S., & Denton, N. A. (1993). *American apartheid: Segregation and the making of the underclass*. Cambridge, MA: Harvard University Press.

Matsueda, R. L., Drakulich, K., & Kubrin, C. E. (2006). Race and neighborhood codes of the street. In R. D. Peterson, L. J. Krivo, & J. Hagan (Eds.), *The many colors of crime: Inequalities of race, ethnicity, and crime in America* (pp. 334–356). New York: New York University Press.

Miller, W. B. (1958). Lower class culture as a generating milieu of gang delinquency. *Journal of Social Issues, 14*, 5–19.

Ousey, G. C., & Kubrin, C. E. (2009). Exploring the connection between immigration and crime rates in U.S. cities, 1980–2000. *Social Problems, 56*, 447–473.

Parker, K. F. (2008). *Unequal crime decline: Theorizing race, urban inequality and criminal violence*. New York: New York University Press.

Peterson, R. D., & Krivo, L. J. (2010). *Divergent social worlds: Neighborhood crime and the racial-spatial divide*. New York, NY: Russell Sage Foundation.

Piquero, A. R. (2008). Disproportionate minority contact. *Future of Children, 18*, 59–79.

Piquero, A. R., & Brame, R. (2008). Assessing the race-/ethnicity-crime relationship in a sample of serious adolescent delinquents. *Crime & Delinquency, 54*, 390–422.

Piquero, A. R., Farrington, D. P., & Blumstein, A. (2003). The criminal career paradigm: Background and recent developments. In M. Tonry (Ed.), *Crime and justice: A review of research* (Vol. 30, pp. 359–506). Chicago, IL: University of Chicago Press.

Sampson, R. J. (2008). Rethinking crime and immigration. *Contexts, 7*, 28–33.

Sampson, R. J., & Lauritsen, J. L. (1997). Racial and ethnic disparities in crime and criminal justice in the United States. In M. Tonry (Ed.), *Crime and justice: An annual review of research* (Vol. 22, pp. 311–374). Chicago, IL: University of Chicago Press.

Sampson, R. J., Morenoff, J. D., & Raudenbush, S. (2005). Social anatomy of racial and ethnic disparities in violence. *American Journal of Public Health, 95*, 224–232.

Sampson, R. J., Raudenbush, S. W., & Earls, F. (1997). Neighborhoods and violence crime: A multilevel study of collective efficacy. *Science, 277*, 918–924.

Sampson, R. J., & Wilson, W. J. (1995). Toward a theory of race, crime, and urban inequality. In J. Hagan & R. D. Peterson (Eds.), *Crime and inequality* (pp. 37–54). Stanford, CA: Stanford University Press.

Sharkey, P. (2006). Navigating dangerous streets: The sources and consequences of street efficacy. *American Sociological Review, 71*, 826–846.

Sharkey, P. (2008). The intergenerational transmission of context. *American Journal of Sociology, 113*, 931–969.

Shaw, C., & McKay, H. (1942). *Delinquency in urban areas*. Chicago, IL: University of Chicago Press.

Smelser, N. J., Wilson, W. J., & Mitchell, F. (Eds.). (2001). *America becoming: Racial trends and their consequences* (Vols. 1–2). Washington, DC: National Academies Press.

Stewart, E. A., & Simons, R. L. (2010). Race, code of the street, and violent delinquency: A multilevel investigation of neighborhood street culture and individual norms of violence. *Criminology, 48*, 569–605.

Stowell, J. I., Martinez, R., Jr., & Cancino, J. (2012). Latino crime and Latinos in the criminal justice system: Trends, policy implications, and future research initiatives. *Race and Social Problems, 4*(1), pp. 31–40.

Tonry, M. (1994). *Malign neglect: Race, crime, and punishment in America*. New York, NY: Oxford University Press.

Unnever, J. D., & Gabbidon, S. L. (2011). *A theory of African American offending: Race, racism, and crime*. New York, NY: Routledge.

Walker, S., Spohn, C., & DeLone, M. (2011). *The color of justice: Race, ethnicity, and crime in America*. Belmont, CA: Cengage.

Wilbanks, W. (1987). *The myth of a racist criminal justice system*. Monterey, CA: Brooks/Cole.

Wilkinson, D. L. (2001). Violent events and social identity: Specifying the relationship between respect and masculinity in inner city youth violence. In D. Kinney (Ed.), *Sociological studies of children and youth* (Vol. 8, pp. 231–265). Bingley, UK: Emerald.

Wilson, W. J. (1987). *The truly disadvantaged: The inner city, the underclass, and public policy*. Chicago, IL: University of Chicago Press.

Wilson, W. J. (1996). *When work disappears*. New York, NY: Knopf.

Zimmerman, G. M., & Messner, S. F. (2013). Individual, family background, and contextual explanations of racial and ethnic disparities in youths' exposure to violence. *American Journal of Public Health, 103*(3), 435–442. doi: 10.2105/AJPH.2012.300931

Zimring, F. E., & Hawkins, G. (1997). *Crime is not the problem: Lethal violence in America*. Oxford, UK: Oxford University Press.

4

Human Biodiversity and the Egalitarian Fiction

John Paul Wright
University of Cincinnati

Mark Alden Morgan
University of Cincinnati

Biosocial criminology was born from a contrarian spirit. Deeply unsatisfied with traditional sociological explanations of crime, biosocial criminologists have pursued and reinvigorated lines of research that had been idle for decades (Wright & Boisvert, 2009). Indeed, with few and isolated exceptions (see Ellis & Walsh, 1997), biological criminology had essentially been relegated to the dustbin of history (Wright & Cullen, 2012). Not only had it been replaced by purely social explanations of crime, but it also became synonymous with racial prejudice. Indeed, it was just a few years ago that no mainstream criminologist would dare link genetic or biological forces to criminal behavior (Wright & Boisvert, 2009; Wright & Cullen, 2012). And for good reason: To do so invited public and private repudiation; it invited allegations of racism, sexism, or suspicions that the scholar was a conservative; or worse, it invited career death (Wright & Cullen, 2012). Against these real and perceived dangers, however, biosocial criminology has continued to grow. New studies are published almost daily and those once afraid to discuss the connections between human biology and behavior have now found their voice (Cullen, 2011).

What is missing from this account, however, are the values, principles, and personality traits that drove these scholars to risk their careers and reputations. We believe it fair to say that biosocial criminologists are a unique breed—no pun intended. As a group they are contrarian to the core. By this we mean they question every theory, every postulate, and every finding. It is more than Mertonian "organized skepticism"—because they often reject conclusions reached by a broad swath of scholars (Wright & Beaver, 2013). Contrarianism infuses their work, but it is backed by a rigid adherence to the scientific method and a rigid belief in science. Simply put, biosocial criminologists are skeptical of entire bodies of research in part because they believe much of it to be misspecified, or worse yet, infused with disciplinary or political bias (Cooper, Walsh, & Ellis, 2010; Wright & Beaver, 2013).

So it is here, at the crossroads between contrarianism, political bias, and science that we address the most controversial topic in the social sciences—that of race, biology, and behavior. In the spirit of contrarian science, we first address what we see as the core of a serious academic dispute. On one side of the dispute are powerful organizations that have issued major proclamations denying any biological basis for race. These organizations argue, with the full force and weight of their membership, that biological race does not exist, or in their language, that race is merely a "social construction." Many scholars, unfortunately, have taken this to mean that any conversation about biological race is inherently racist. Within these organizations we find serious-minded scholars who have reshaped the debate about race, who are highly respected by their peers, and who train future generations of academics. To be clear, these institutional and personal forces are formidable and intelligent, and they have made their voices heard.

On the other side of the dispute are a loose collection of scholars, some of whom belong to these powerful academic organizations, who have openly questioned these proclamations, and who have marshaled or imported empirical evidence showing that race is a useful biological concept (Risch, Burchard, Ziv, & Tang, 2002; Sarich & Miele, 2004). Some of these scholars are the most cited scientists in the world, but they have been largely ignored, neglected, or worse yet, ostracized because their work confronts deeply held beliefs about race and social equality. Nonetheless, against the full weight of large academic organizations and the zeal of some of their more vocal members, the few scholars who refute the mainstream account that race is merely a social construction remain a minority—a minority easily persecuted by more powerful interests.

Our chapter thus serves a dual role: We first tell a story of how science can sometimes be used for political purposes and how these political views can then become enshrined in scientific conversations. Nowhere, we believe, is this more obvious than in the "scientific" discussions of race, in discussions of aggregate differences between races, and in discussions concerning the race-crime link. While critics may dispute some of our renditions of this story, nobody in either camp can deny that race is unlike any other issue in the social sciences. Brilliant scientists have lost their jobs and seen their character assassinated because they dared say publically what many believe professionally (see, for example, Snyderman & Rothman, 1988). We tell this story, only in a condensed form, to show why biosocial criminologists remain unsettled with traditional accounts of race and biology and to show why those who question scientific dogma are neither racists nor unscrupulous.

Having told this story, we then cover the evidence of biological race. Unlike major academic organizations and their proclamations, we trust our readers to evaluate the evidence on their own and to arrive at their own conclusions. This evidence comes from studies conducted all over the world, from studies into genetic differences between groups of people, and from studies that reveal the complex interconnections between evolution and modern genotypes. To foreshadow our discussion, we argue that the scientific evidence indicates that race is both a biological construct and a social construct. While we argue that biological race is real, that it is measurable, and that it is socially meaningful, we make the very same argument about "social race." Indeed, we believe it misguided to argue that the realities of race and racism become neutral if people believe race to be a mere social construction.

Science and Politics: The Tribal Moral Community

At the 2011 meeting of the Society for Personality and Social Psychology, Jonathan Haidt brought to light, in dramatic fashion, the political biases present in the social sciences. After querying his audience of over 1,000 social psychologists about their political identity, Haidt calculated the ratio of liberal to conservative professors to be about 266:1, a "statistically impossible lack of diversity," he said. Haidt's talk was covered in the *New York Times* and the *Chronicle of Higher Education* and stimulated many conversations and discussions. But Haidt was not the first person to find that university faculty are extremely liberal—indeed, that was only a lead-in to his broader discussion of how political biases have materialized in the social sciences, and more important, how they have been enforced.

At the heart of Haidt's conversation, and his resulting book, was his idea that many social science disciplines have become "tribal moral communities." According to Haidt (2012), members of a tribal moral community share a set of sacred values. These values are deeply felt and internalized by members of the community, and because they represent deeply held convictions, they tend to "bind and blind." By this Haidt means that these values not only provide members a sense of belonging to a larger community, but that they also tend to create conditions where challenges to these values trigger unusually negative responses.

Just what are the sacred values identified by Haidt, the values that if challenged will cause backlash? Haidt argues that race, intelligence, class, sex, and nativism—the linking of biology to behavior—all serve as sacred values. To be clear, these values are moral viewpoints, or more accurately, are political viewpoints. They impose nonscientific standards on the discussions of these subjects, thereby shaping and creating conforming views despite evidence. As Haidt notes, tribal moral communities will "embrace science whenever it supports their sacred values," but that "they'll ditch it or distort it as soon as it threatens a sacred value" (Tierney, 2011, p. 1).

Haidt's work helps us understand why controversy erupts in the social sciences so frequently and why disputes can become so laden with rhetoric and invective.

Science is, to be sure, sometimes controversial. On occasion controversy erupts when scientific findings confront deeply held beliefs. Famous studies on human sexual behavior, for instance, caused social uproar when first published (Kinsey, Pomeroy, & Martin, 1948). On other occasions, controversy erupted when scientific methods of questionable ethics were used, such as the Tuskegee syphilis experiment or the Stanford prison experiment (Oakley, 2007). Today's controversies, however, stem not from the methodologies employed by social scientists or even from the social acceptance of some research findings. Instead, modern scientific controversy stems largely from the questionable objectivity of scientists—an objectivity that is compromised by open political activism and an adherence to sacred values. There is, unfortunately, good reason to question the objectivity of scientists, especially social scientists, as it relates to discussions of race.

A hallmark belief, or sacred value, of contemporary progressive ideology is that minority groups do not differ in their talents or abilities and thus that disparities found in the workplace, the educational arena, or even the criminal justice system, reflect bias and discrimination against these groups. Speaking specifically of intelligence differences between groups, Gottfredson (1994) refers to this sacred value as the "egalitarian fiction." More broadly, the egalitarian fiction provides liberal academics a script, or a narrative, from which they draw to interpret almost every racial disparity as the product of some form of racism. Differences between "races" in crime, for example, cannot occur because groups differ in their levels of conformity to the law, this narrative states, but because racism creates strain that results in crime (Jang & Johnson, 2003), or because laws are racially biased (Alexander, 2012), or because police racially profile (Rojek, Rosenfeld, & Decker, 2012).

The egalitarian fiction is a lynchpin for modern liberals and radicals. Perhaps unsurprisingly, litanies of studies reveal that university faculty are not just politically liberal, but that they are extremely liberal—especially when compared to the general public. Gross and Simmons (2007), for example, analyzed data from 1,471 university faculty members across 927 schools in the United States. They found that self-described politically conservative faculty composed less than 4% of faculty ranks in major research institutions. Gross and Simmons also found that politically conservative faculty constituted only 4.9% of all faculty in the social sciences and only 3.6% of faculty from humanities departments. Regarding political party membership, Gross and Simmons found that the ratio of Democrats to Republicans was 19.5:1 in sociology. Similarly, in a study of 1,678 university faculty, Klein and Stern (2004) found Democrat to Republican disparities of 30:1 in anthropology and 28:1 in sociology.

Clearly there exists, in academia, large disparities in the political leanings of faculty compared to the general population. Apologists are quick to argue that this disparity is unimportant, in part, because faculty are independently minded, objective analysts. This is undoubtedly true in some cases, but data show that the liberal bias in academia is not without consequence. First, Klein and Stern (2005) measured faculty support of various government intervention efforts. They found that liberal, Democratic professors (the majority of faculty members) strongly supported gun control, economic redistribution, government ownership over business, and minimum wage laws. Indeed, Klein and Stern found almost perfect correspondence between self-identified political orientation (being liberal) and support for a range of interventionist policies. So strong was the degree of association that Klein and Stern (2005) argued that the social sciences represent a one-party system that offers little in the way of ideological diversity.

Second, Klein and Stern's analysis also found that scholars within two academic disciplines were particularly liberal. Indeed, they state that the strongest predictor of political identification in their sample of university faculty was whether or not the scholar was a sociologist or an anthropologist. "There is something particularly left-wing," note Klein and Stern (2005) "about the disciplines of anthropology and sociology" (p. 289). Collectively, Klein and Stern's findings indicate that faculty political viewpoints can be almost perfectly predicted by which discipline they belong to. As we discuss later, we believe it no coincidence that these two disciplines, sociology and anthropology, have been the driving force in denying the biological foundation of race.

Third, it is impossible for academic disciplines to achieve, by chance, this level of ideological homophily. Until recently, however, no data existed regarding the mechanisms that produce ideological hegemony within the social sciences. Work by Yancey (2011) and by Inbar and Lammers (2012), however, sheds light on the ideological litmus tests now present in many fields, but especially in sociology and anthropology. Yancey, for example, found that applicants for academic positions were at a distinct disadvantage if they were religious or if they belonged to groups identified as "conservative" by other faculty, such as the National Rifle Association. Inbar and Lammers (2012), on the other hand, surveyed a large group of social psychologists. Almost 94% of respondents identified themselves as "liberal," compared to only 4% who identified themselves as "conservative." What was striking about their findings, however, was not the political disparity they detected, but the fact that liberal respondents freely admitted to a willingness to discriminate against conservatives. They wrote:

> The more conservative respondents were, the more they experienced a hostile climate, were reluctant to express their views to colleagues, and feared that they might be the victims of discrimination based on their political views. These fears are quite realistic: a sizeable portion of our (liberal) respondents indicated at least some willingness to discriminate against conservatives professionally. One in six respondents admitted that she or he would be somewhat inclined to discriminate against conservatives in inviting them for symposiums or reviewing their work. One in four would discriminate in reviewing their grants. And more than one in three would discriminate against conservatives when making hiring decisions. Thus, willingness to discriminate is not limited to small decisions. In fact, it is strongest when it comes to the most important decisions, such as grant proposals and hiring. *And the more liberal respondents were, the more willing they were to discriminate.* (emphasis added; p. 21)

We highlight this last point to show not only that ideological homophily exists in the social sciences, but that it is also sometimes enforced in ways that are not always obvious but that are no less insidious. Ideological homophily is created through the power scholars exercise in a tribal moral hierarchy. One unfortunate by-product of ideological homophily is that it easily allows scholars to also claim scientific consensus. Of course, scientific consensus occurs only after extensive research has been conducted by objective analysts, after prolonged debate, and after the results have been sufficiently vetted. This is not always possible, however, when political, moral, and scientific issues coalesce—as they do in discussions of race—or when scholars are afraid to speak candidly out of fear of violating the moral sensibilities of scholars higher up in the moral hierarchy (Felson, 2008).

Taken together, data from a wide range of studies reveal that university faculty are exceedingly left-leaning. This is especially true of sociology and anthropology where it is safe to say that little ideological diversity exists. It is also safe to say that the ideological hegemony found in these disciplines is supported by a strong belief in specific sacred values—especially belief in the egalitarian fiction. Yancy's and Inbar and Lammer's findings provide evidence that many (but not all) liberal professors in these fields serve not only as gatekeepers—keeping out individuals with different views—but also as enforcers of a moral or political code. Even so, critics might accuse us of injecting politics into an academic discussion of race. They would be missing the point: In academia virtually every discussion of race is a political discussion—a discussion held by individuals constrained not solely by scientific standards, but by a rigid adherence to sacred values (Haidt, 2012). Thus, our point is not to inject politics into the discussion of the biology of race, but to show that they are frequently one and the same.

AUTHORITARIAN SCIENCE: DENYING THE BIOLOGY OF RACE

The American Anthropological Association (AAA) and the American Sociological Association (ASA) have been the driving forces behind the mantra that biological race does not exist—issuing proclamations in 1998 and 2003, respectively. The 1998 AAA statement on race emerged out of a broader debate about race and intelligence, with the publication of *The Bell Curve* by Herrnstein and Murray (1994). They make their points clear not only about intelligence, but also about race:

- WHEREAS all human beings are members of one species, *Homo sapiens*, and
- WHEREAS, differentiating species into biologically defined "races" has proven meaningless and unscientific as a way of explaining variation (whether in intelligence or other traits),
- THEREFORE, the American Anthropological Association urges the academy, our political leaders and our communities to affirm, without distraction by mistaken claims of racially determined intelligence, the common stake in assuring equal opportunity, in respecting diversity and in securing a harmonious quality of life for all people. (AAA, 1994, para. 3)

In the 1998 AAA statement about race, Smedley writes that "race evolved as a worldview, a body of prejudgments that distorts our ideas about human differences and group behavior," and that "race as an ideology . . . became a strategy for dividing, ranking, and controlling colonized people used by colonial powers everywhere" (para. 8–9). Moreover, the ideology of "race" led to the "extermination of 11 million people of "inferior" races . . . and other unspeakable brutalities of the Holocaust" (AAA, 1998, para. 8). Framed this way, as an inherent moral evil, it should come as no surprise that Alan H. Goodman, a member of the committee responsible for the report and the President-elect of the AAA at the time, would go on to say that, "Race as an explanation for human biological variation is dead" (p. 1). He then went on to equate retaining the concept of race as akin to putting a gun in the hands of racists (Roylance, 2004).

The overt political connotations associated with the AAA statements are largely echoed in the ASA statement on race. "Respected voices from the fields of human molecular biology and physical anthropology . . ." argues the American Sociological Association (2003), "assert that the concept of race has no validity in their respective fields. Growing numbers of humanist scholars, social anthropologists, and political commentators have joined the chorus in urging the nation to rid itself of the concept of race" (p. 4).

Of course, the AAA and the ASA neither speak for all members of their respective organizations nor do they speak for all anthropologists and sociologists. Several studies, for example, show that while 40% to almost 70% of American anthropologists deny biological race, large majorities of eastern European, Polish, and Chinese anthropologists do not (Kaszycka & Strzałko, 2003; Kaszycka, Štrkalj, & Strzałko, 2009; Lieberman & Kirk, 2002). Addressing these differences, Kaszycka et al. (2009) argue that the acceptance of race as a biological construct reflects varying ideological influences more than it reflects scientific concordance. Indeed, we believe it important to note that the committees involved in creating these statements were not ideologically diverse and thus did not include views that were entirely objective. Instead, the composition of the committees reflected ideological homophily, where individuals with preconceived ideological views were tasked to provide a statement whose outcome could have easily been predicted. High ranking officials of the ASA, for example, were paid legal consultants who testified against corporations accused of racism in hiring in promotion. Others were avowed Marxists who advocated making science serve liberal political aims. Others had advanced highly controversial ideas about *white privilege*, *colonialism*, and *critical race theory*. An argument could be made, moreover, that the ASA committee was ideologically tame compared to the AAA committee, whose members were even less diverse and were even more politically active. Thus, instead of gathering a diverse array of neutral scholars to survey research findings and to arrive at a scientific consensus (see, for example, National Academy of Sciences, 2012) the outcomes of these committees were guaranteed from the outset.

What, in turn, has happened is that these statements have become reified in the academic community. They have taken on a special, scientifically authoritative status. Today, scholars and laypeople alike point to these statements as evidence that biological race does not exist. They use these statements to frame debates about race, to advocate for race-specific laws and social policies, and to repudiate those who offer different views. Forgotten are the motivations for creating these statements. Forgotten are the processes that created the ideologically pure committees, and forgotten are members of the committees who translated a singular political view into science. What has emerged from these statements is an authoritarian science, a science by fiat, a science by political will, and a science imposed by minority (Sesardic, 2010). As we discussed earlier, this is the science of a tribal moral community (Haidt, 2012).

Evidence Concerning Biological Race

To be certain, there does exist legitimate intellectual debate about the nature of biological race. This debate is complex because it involves the subtleties of imprecise definitions, the complexities of molecular genetics, and an understanding of human evolution. Below we outline the core points of those who argue that biological race does not exist.

- First, critics of biological race argue that there is only one race—the human race, or *Homo sapiens* (Hunley, Healy, & Long, 2009; Kitcher, 2007).
- Second, and relatedly, critics of biological race argue that no genetically discrete group of humans exists, thus invalidating taxonomic approaches (Gannett, 2004; Long & Kittles, 2003).
- Third, because *Homo sapiens* have not had sufficient time to evolve into distinct subpopulations, we are genetically more similar to each other than different (Gannett, 2004; Graves, 2010).
- Fourth, because we are genetically more similar than different, differences between groups (races) are trivial when compared to differences within groups (Maglo, 2011).

For a complete statement, see http://www.physanth.org/association/position-statements/biological-aspects-of-race.

THE DEFINITION OF RACE

First, we address the appealing notion that we all belong to a single race—appealing because it serves to remind us of our similarities while other definitions of race appeal to our differences. Moreover, it is also appealing because it converges with democratic views about human equality—views that are often cited as reasons to abandon the biological concept of race (Gould, 1996; Lewontin, 1972). Critics of biological race, however, often define *race* as a discontinuous, nonoverlapping, genetically dissimilar group (Graves, 2001; Zack, 2002). From this view, a "race" would include uniquely identifiable genes and phenotypes that are specific only to one racial category—that is, they could not be shared across racial categories. Of course, this definition imposes such an arbitrary constraint that is "so unrealistically demanding that . . . even the species concept would fail to pass muster" (Sesardic, 2010, p. 147). Sesardic's point is that if we applied the same criteria to other mammals, we would have to argue there are no differences between canines or no differences between whales, or dolphins, or chimpanzees.

Science has never detected a genetically "pure" race of humans, nor have any who view biological race as "real" defined race in terms of unique categories of human beings. As Walsh and Yun (2011) note, "Using purity as criterion of race is a semantic cheat that enables those who use it to correctly state that there is no such thing and, on that basis, to conclude that the concept lacks any scientific merit" (p. 1282). Instead, when race realists define race, they refer to "a population within a species that can be readily distinguished from other such populations on genetic grounds alone" (Sarich & Miele, 2004, p. 211), or they define race as a "distinct evolutionary lineage within a species" (Templeton, 1998, p. 646). All that is required for biological races to exist under these definitions is evidence of sufficient genetic differentiation—that is, evidence that gene frequencies vary significantly between groups (races) that have somewhat unique evolutionary pasts. Races do not reflect genetically distinct categories of people, but instead, reflect human variation that has been influenced by natural selection.

Critics of biological race often argue that biological race does not exist because human morphological traits fall along a continuum, because there is overlap across humans in these traits, and because there are fine gradations between these traits within any category of race. On closer inspection, however, virtually all physical, mental, and personality traits meet these same criteria—that is, they fall along a continuum, there exists overlap between groups, and they vary within each population grouping. The same can also be said of a variety of other characteristics. For example, we make meaningful distinctions between night and day. We have sunrise, midday, sunset, and night, and we treat these as distinct but related categories. In reality, however, they represent gradations based on visible light, which is related to the rotation of Earth around its axis and the sun. Should we say that sunrise has no intrinsic meaning because it simply represents a point along a continuous distribution? Humans recognize other meaningful categories found within distributions, too. In discussions of the life course, for example, we often speak of *infancy*, *childhood*, *adolescence*, and *adulthood* to discuss periods of developmental time. We can point to physical and mental differences at each point, we can juxtapose those differences, and we can also see continuity or similarity across each category. Is each period of developmental time a meaningless social construction devoid of any biological or physical reality? Of course not.

EVOLUTION AND RACE

The key to understanding biological race lies in understanding human evolution. Fortunately, modern science has made tremendous gains in accumulating evidence of not only our African origins, but also the processes that have led to human differentiation. First, modern humans first appeared in Africa approximately 250,000 years ago. About 50,000 years ago, small groups of humans began to migrate out of Africa (Wade, 2006). Evidence indicates that these groups migrated north, into Europe, and northeast into Asia. Migration appeared to create the conditions whereby natural selection would create unique anatomical and physiological differences between humans. Those who migrated north into Europe, for example, encountered a uniquely different climate, encountered different food supplies, and encountered different diseases compared to those who remained in Africa or those who migrated into Asia. As an example, white skin was likely an adaptation to vitamin D deficiency. Individuals living closer to the equator are exposed to more direct sunlight, which translates to relatively more vitamin D. The genes associated with white skin color are found in European populations significantly more often than in African populations.

Migration is one factor associated with human evolution. Another is isolation, both geographic and reproductive isolation. Isolation could occur for a variety of reasons. Humans, for example, are highly territorial and have traditionally killed or seriously injured those who encroached on their lands (Cochran & Harpending, 2009). Isolation could also occur when natural physical boundaries prevented humans from coming into contact with each other—boundaries such as large bodies of water, deserts, or mountain ranges. Geographic isolation likely led to reproductive isolation and thus to genetic adaptations to the local environment.

Migration and isolation worked in unison with natural selection. This is as true today as it was 50,000 years ago (Cochran & Harpending, 2009). Collectively, however, these forces acted on genes and the frequency with which genes were expressed in each population. Genes code for amino acids that then go on to affect cells and their regulation. When a genetic adaptation occurred—that is, when an allele, or a variant, of a gene emerged in the population—those adaptations that proved to enhance fitness and survival increased throughout the population over time. Sometimes new alleles spread rapidly across a population, such as the allele associated with language development (FOXP2) and brain mass (ASPM and CDK5RAP2), but sometimes genetic variants emerge in response to local selection pressures, such as the alleles that developed in response to malaria but that also cause sickle-cell anemia in individuals of African ancestry.

Natural selection thus worked not by creating entirely new genomes, as critics seem to infer, but by altering preexisting genes and the frequency and rate with which they spread through the population. Polymorphic genes come in two varieties: single nucleotide polymorphisms (SNPs), which are changes to a nucleotide base pair, and variable number tandem repeats (VNTRs), which reflect differences in the length of contiguous base pairs that are repeated a varying number of times (Walsh & Yun, 2011). Because of natural selection, geneticists are able to measure the frequency of polymorphic genes in a population, and they are able to compare these frequencies against those found in our closest genetic relatives—the great apes. This allows scientists to measure, with unparalleled precision, how much genetic variation exists between humans and apes, between human races, and between individuals.

Recall that critics argue that we are genetically similar and that there exists more genetic variation *within* races than *between* races. This is true, but only to an extent. For example, we share 97% of our DNA with gorillas. We share 99% of our DNA with chimpanzees. As should be readily apparent, very small differences in total genetic difference correspond to very large phenotypic differences. Nobody, for example, would say that humans are chimpanzees even though we are a derivative of a common ancestor and even though we differ genetically by only 1%. Moreover, when SNPs are used, estimates of human genetic variation reveal that individual humans are about 99.9% genetically similar. That apparently small 0.1% difference between individual humans corresponds to over 3,000,000 base pair differences. However, even greater genetic diversity between humans is found when copy number variants (CNVs) are used instead of SNPs. Redon et al.'s (2006) genetic analysis of 270 people with Asian, African, and European ancestry found that over 12% of the genes in the human genome, or about 2,900 genes, varied in the number of copy number variations. When geneticists add the genetic variation between humans because of CNVs, genetic similarity drops even further (Levy et al., 2007). Again, very small differences in gene frequency can result in substantial phenotypic differences.

EVIDENCE FOR BIOLOGICAL RACE

Geneticists have sampled DNA from individuals across the globe. Study after study has shown that clear patterns of genetic clustering emerge when only a handful of genes are examined. What is interesting is that these clusters correspond almost directly to "continentally based racial classification" (Shiao, Bode, Beyer, & Selvig, 2012, p. 71), or in other words, to African, European, and Asian races. Indeed, studies reveal that scientists can correctly classify an individual's race using loci from relatively few genes. Bamshad et al. (2003) correctly classified the race of 99% to 100% of the individuals in their sample using only 100 loci. Tang et al. (2005) correctly classified the race of 3,631 individuals out of 3,636—yes, only 5 were misclassified—using relatively few genes and the individual's self-reported race. In a follow-up study of over 50,000 Africans and European Americans, Bamshad and his colleagues found that 41% of the 3,931 genes they studied varied significantly between the two groups. They also found that 51% of haplotypes (genes inherited together) were shared between Africans and Europeans—49% were not. In short, then, geneticists can predict almost perfectly to which race or continent of origin a person belongs based on a few genetic markers. These predictions, moreover, correspond almost identically to one's self-reported race. We know of no other social classification scheme so accurate.

These findings are obviously difficult to reconcile with the idea that human races do not exist. Indeed, we believe it important to point out that the patterns of data revealing human races could not be produced by random variation, by sampling bias or even research methodology, or by contemporary environmental variation.

They were, instead, predicted by the science on human evolution. From an evolutionary point of view, given the relative time-frames involved, given human migration, and given the relative isolation and geographic distances between populations, human races almost had to emerge. How, after all, could genetic data reveal such strong and consistent patterns—patterns perfectly corroborated by self-reports of race?

But what about the criticism of greater within-race genetic variation than between-race variation? Wouldn't this invalidate the biological conception of race? Lewontin (1972) was the first to note this, and as Walsh and Yun (2011), Sesardic (2010), Shiao et al. (2012) and others (see, for example, Sarich & Miele, 2004) note, Lewontin's observation has been mindlessly rereported ever since. Nonetheless, A.W. F. Edwards (2003), the statistician responsible for the quantitative measures used by Lewontin, addressed what he called "Lewontin's Fallacy." In general, there is greater within-race genetic variation than between-race genetic variation. Modern estimates vary, but 70% to 85% of genetic variation is within a race, and between 6% and 20% occurs between races, depending on the type of genetic information analyzed (Melton et al., 2001). What Lewontin was referring to, however, was variation in a single loci, or a single point in a gene. One way of viewing this fallacy was offered by Walsh and Yun (2011). Imagine, they argue, combining the DNA of gorillas, chimpanzees, and modern humans. Analyses would review three separate races that share genes. There would also be greater genetic variation within gorillas, within chimpanzees, and within humans than between the groups (for another example, see Sesardic, 2010). Interestingly, Risch points out that greater genetic variation exists between the races than between the sexes. Moreover, Risch also notes that genetically based classification schemes, like those used to classify people based on their race, produce more errors in predicting self-reported sex than in predicting race (Gitschier, 2005, p. 14).

PHENOTYPIC DIFFERENCES BASED ON RACE

Phenotypic differences in humans are those characteristics that are visibly expressed in the individual. Applied to race, morphological differences are considered the most visually obvious set of characteristics that define race. Perhaps the most well-known phenotypic difference across racial groups is that of skin pigmentation. Other differences also exist, however, and were caused by selection pressures that affected the frequency of specific genes. Recent research by Kamberov et al. (2013), for example, has identified a mutation in the EDAR gene that is not found in individuals of African or European ancestry. Occurring approximately 30,000 years ago, this mutation is theorized to be responsible for the thicker hair, distinctive teeth, smaller breasts, and additional sweat glands found in East Asians. This genetic variant may have arisen as a result of sexual selection or in response to advantageous evolutionary benefits amid the warm and humid climate in what is now central China. Thus, natural selection produced visible and measurable differences between populations—differences that reflected the adaptation to local selection pressures. Morphological differences can also be used by forensic scientists and physical anthropologists to accurately predict the race of an individual. For example, Rushton and Rushton (2003) examined 37 separate morphological traits, including cranial shape, pelvic width, and knee joint surface area. They found that these characteristics not only differed across racial groups, but that they were also highly correlated ($r = .94$) with cranial capacity—that is, brain size.

Natural selection created morphological differences between humans—differences we use to classify ourselves and others by race. Few scholars would deny this. Yet they will deny the possibility that natural selection shaped or influenced other phenotypes, instead arguing that culture, geography, and economic inequality produced differences in intelligence, aggression, or specific personality factors. Nonetheless, it is entirely possible—if not entirely likely—that a wide variety of phenotypes have been under constant selection pressures that led to aggregate differences between groups.

Differences between racial groups are sometimes large, such as morphological differences, and sometimes small. However, even small differences between aggregate groups can be associated with large differences in social outcomes. Zeigler-Hill and Wallace (2011), for example, conducted three separate studies on narcissism involving hundreds of college students. Controlling for gender and self-esteem, they found that Black students reported significantly higher levels of narcissism than Whites. Similarly, Lynn (2002), in a comprehensive investigation of psychopathy, presents evidence that Native Americans, Blacks, and Hispanics score higher on the Minnesota Multiphasic Personality Inventory's (MMPI) Psychopathic Deviate scale compared to Whites, while East Asians score lower. Furthermore, Lynn argues that this racial trend extends to a host of related social outcome measures including childhood conduct disorder, ADHD, recklessness, aggression, criminality, the ability to delay gratification, marriage rates, and even moral understanding. Across the multitude of studies analyzed, a clear pattern emerges where Blacks score the worst on these measures, Whites intermediate, and Asians the best even when controlling for the effects of age and IQ.

As previously mentioned, one of the most obvious sources of maladjustment in society is the predilection toward crime and criminal behavior. According to Walsh (2004), one of the most consistent predictors of high crime rates is the number of Blacks living in an area. Although Blacks make up approximately 13% of the population in the United States, data from the Federal Bureau of Investigation (2011) shows that Black offenders are arrested for 38% of all violent crimes committed, including nearly 50% of all murders. Conversely, Whites, who constitute 78% of the population, are arrested for 59% of violent crimes and 48% of murders. Again, the aforementioned racial pattern begins to materialize from these data with Asians representing just 5% of the population, yet being arrested for only 1% of violent crimes and 1% of murders, a clear underrepresentation. Similar findings exist regarding arrests for property crimes with 30% for Blacks, 68% for Whites, and 1% for Asians. This stark disparity in Black offending leads Levin (2005) to note that if Black crimes were eliminated from statistical calculations in the United States the crime rates would be comparable to those found in Europe and Canada. In sum, Ellis (1988) states that after examining over 60 studies on race and crime a clear delineation appears with Blacks committing the most crimes, followed by Whites, and then Asians.

Biosocial Criminology and Race

We started this chapter with a discussion of the insidious politics found in the academy and how political concerns can influence, if not entirely shape, important academic debates. We explicitly linked liberal political notions of social equality to academic discussions on race generally, but drew special attention to the modern denial of biological race specifically. In true contrarian form, we called into question the conclusions of major academic societies, and we called into question the political motives of those who fashioned the conclusions.

Obviously, our concern with biological race is secondary to our concern about open scientific debate. To be direct, we have no vested interest in whether human races exist or do not exist. Their existence is an empirical question—a question we believe the evidence to date answers in the affirmative. Science, however, is often used to advance political agendas. In this instance, it appears that those who wish to deny biological race do so, in part, because they believe that is what the evidence indicates and, in part, because they believe that if we eliminate using the term *race* we help eliminate racism (AAA, 1998). Eliminating racism is an admirable goal and one that the United States has pursued with vigor since the 1960s. Yet eliminating racism, or *scientific racism* as some scholars refer to it, can easily infuse science with politics. Because of this, even the casual reader on the topic of biological race will likely come away more confused than informed.

The modern denial of biological race, however, also coincides with the historical denial of the role of human genetics and biology in a range of observable phenotypes—including criminal behavior, alcohol and drug addiction, and violence. For decades criminologists and other social scientists excluded the study of biological factors associated with crime, and they sanctioned those who pursued the subject. They did so for two reasons: First, they bought into the idea that biological theorizing was dangerous—that it inevitably brought about harsh, punitive state sanctions (Wright & Cullen, 2012). Until recently, almost every criminology textbook made a direct link between fascism and Nazism and biological theorizing (DeLisi, Wright, Vaughn, & Beaver, 2009; Wright et al., 2008). Even today, most textbooks still link biological theorizing to Lombroso, as though human science has not progressed since the Italian doctor measured the physical characteristics of inmates. In this sense, biosocial criminologists are keenly aware of how politics dressed up as science cuts off open inquiry and how it can bring harm to those who violate the sacred values of an academic discipline.

Second, and related, criminologists are accurately aware of racial differences in criminal behavior. These differences are large, geographically widespread, found in various institutions, and stable over time (Kalunta-Crumpton, 2006; Rushton, 1997; Trevethan & Rastin, 2004; Wortley, 2003). Given these facts, it is unlikely that racial differences in criminal behavior can be produced entirely by racial discrimination or racial animus. Yet discussions of racial patterns of offending always reflect a common narrative—that American society is racist; that the institutions within American society, such as the police, are racist; and that Blacks in America are the victims of widespread racial discrimination that amazingly accounts for disparities in health (Smedley & Stith, 2003; Williams, 2006), education (DeCuir & Dixson, 2004; Skiba, Michael, Nardo, & Peterson, 2002), behavior (Walsh & Ellis, 2003), and socioeconomic status (Thomas, 1993). The irony of such reductionism, a criticism almost always leveled at biological research, has never escaped us.

On the issue of race and offending, biosocial criminology has been largely agnostic. At one level, biosocial criminologists differ in their views on biological race and, to a greater extent, on the relevance of biological race to phenotypic variation. To date, no authoritative statement has been written summarizing the role of race in biosocial theorizing. At another level, it is fair to say that biosocial criminology at least offers room for biological race in explanations of offending and in explanations of offending differences by race. For example, as we discussed, certain phenotypes are expressed more frequently in Blacks than in other groups. Blacks, for example, tend to have significantly higher levels of self-esteem (Zeigler-Hill, 2007), more narcissistic traits (Zeigler-Hill & Wallace, 2011), and score significantly lower on measures of intelligence and intellectual functioning (Rushton & Jensen, 2005) than other groups. Each of these phenotypes is moderately to highly heritable across all races but appear expressed more often in Blacks. The possibility thus exists that certain evolved phenotypes are (a) somehow embedded in the genetic architecture of race, or (b) that these heritable phenotypes emerge under environmental conditions that Blacks are more likely to experience. Again, at this point, biosocial criminology remains agnostic on the possibility, but at a minimum it recognizes the possibility.

While we have argued that biological races exist, we also believe that critics of biological race have sufficiently documented how "social race" also exists (Smedley, 1998). Social race draws attention to how cultural images and beliefs about race can be used to structure a society or to regulate a society through law or through force. The "social construction of race" helps us understand how individuals and groups can intellectually justify unethical, undemocratic, and immoral treatment of other groups of humans, and it helps us understand how biases and preconceived notions influence perceptions and political beliefs. Prior to the United States' entry into World War II, for example, the Empire of Japan based much of its expansionist efforts on a racist ideology that viewed Koreans and Chinese as innately inferior. Japanese views of racial superiority were soon to be extended to Americans, as would their inhuman and brutal treatment. Unfortunately, any survey of world history will find that human beings have a long history of enslaving others and of justifying political subjugation based on a range of factors—including race.

There seems to be a belief, however, that if science establishes the existence of races that this will inevitably lead to harm to minority groups. We have to acknowledge the possibility that "biological race" could be used to justify harsh, punitive, state sanctions and to justify the withdrawal of social welfare assistance. Yet we also have to acknowledge the fact that the social construction of race can also easily justify the worst behaviors in humanity independent of any knowledge of biological race. Slavery, subjugation, and tyranny existed long before knowledge of Mendelian genetics and long before the decoding of the human genome. Thus, the existence of biological race is no more or less likely to incite racism than is the social construction of race—indeed, if race is truly socially constructed, then concern that biological race will somehow incite people to hatred seems misplaced. The social construction of race is what we should be more concerned about given the tendency of powerful politicians and academic societies to manipulate public opinions and views.

While academics debate the science behind biological race, write prolifically to warn against various incarnations of racism, and make broad proclamations concerning the "reality" of race, another unfortunate reality is played out daily on the streets of the United States. This reality involves the loss of life, the loss of opportunities, and the loss of innocence. It is a reality outside the view of most intellectuals but it is a reality that consumes and destroys those who participate in it—and it is a reality based on race. While we have drawn attention to the biological evidence on human races, we believe it also necessary to draw attention to the power of culture—especially to the power of the criminal subculture. To date, biosocial criminologists have not addressed how the criminal culture is influenced by genetic propensities, how the subculture influences criminal propensities, or how the subculture can override propensities and "attract" individuals who are otherwise normally functioning. This is an area, however, where criminology has excelled. Descriptive and vivid ethnographies exist that document the appeal of the criminal culture and how individuals embrace and make sense of their cultural identity and the harm they bring to others (Anderson, 2000; Copes, Hochstetler, & Williams, 2008; Wright & Decker, 1994, 1997).

The criminal subculture not only is nasty, brutish, and violent, but it also provides young men (predominately) with a sense of territory, with status, and with access to resources. The culture motivates criminal action, provides individuals with criminal rationalizations, and rewards antisocial and hedonistic conduct. The criminal subculture, moreover, is highly racist, with street and prison gangs usually constructed along racial lines. And while the criminal subculture exists in African Americans, Caucasians, and Asians, it is concerning African Americans where the manifestations of the criminal subculture are the most obvious and, some could argue, the most deleterious. Crime, victimization, disrepute, and incivility saturate inner cities populated primarily by Blacks—a fact it pains us to point out. Blacks are overrepresented in the criminal subculture, and because of this, they pay a hefty price for their participation. Incarceration, serious bodily injury, death, and a host of social penalties accompany involvement in the criminal subculture, and these penalties do not discriminate based on race.

Finally, we return to the point that research on race in American society is frequently tinged with political considerations. As we have shown, embedded in the American scholarly narrative of race is a fundamental belief in equality. By this we mean a belief that not only are individuals equal in talents, motivations, intelligence, and various traits, but so too are groups of individuals—groups that include races of people. Thus, aggregate differences between races, the narrative goes, must reflect some form of unjust bias if not some form of racial discrimination.

By any measure, however, groups differ along any number of dimensions. Professional athletes, for example, are, on average, more athletic than members of the general population. College professors likely know more about their respective fields than do laypeople. Clergy are likely less physically aggressive than are criminals. The point is that groups, including groups based on race, are likely to differ from each other. Sometimes these differences are trivial and other times they are not—but they do vary. And while overlap almost always exists between groups, important differences can still exist. Scholars, however, sometimes deny these differences. They deny the existence of socially or biologically derived groups, including sex and race-based groups, and they sometimes deny empirically verified differences between groups (Baumeister, 2010). In essence, they elevate the *egalitarian fiction*—that is, the belief that groups are fundamentally equal.

Human evolution can produce many unique adaptations. It has caused morphological differences across humans, disease resistance and disease susceptibility, and fundamental differences between the sexes. Although the forces of Darwinian evolution can produce many unique adaptations, they cannot produce equality within or between groups. And while we recognize that a variety of other factors outside of Darwinian evolution also influence individual and group differences, it remains an artful act to espouse a belief in evolutionary principles and to simultaneously deny the by-products of human evolution (Cochran & Harpending, 2009).

The academic wars that have erupted over the existence of biological race—not to mention the inclusion of evolutionary and genetic principles for understanding human behavior—have resembled tribal conflicts of the past. Territory is zealously guarded. Intruders are killed, at least symbolically, and dominance hierarchies emerge and exert control over others within the culture. This has been unfortunate. Unfortunate not only because it has infused political motives into science, nor because it has unjustly ruined the careers of important scholars, but because understanding individual and group differences can, and has, lead to important discoveries that have saved lives and that have reduced human suffering. Our hope is that biosocial criminology aids in bettering the lives of individuals through more scientifically informed treatments and that it reduces the suffering caused by criminal behavior. For biosocial criminology to do this, however, it must adhere to scientific principles so that it does not become yet another conduit for advancing any political agenda.

References

Alexander, M. (2012). *The new Jim Crow*. New York, NY: New Press.

American Anthropological Association. (1994). *Statement on race and intelligence*. Arlington, VA: American Anthropological Association. Retrieved from http://www.aaanet.org/stmts/race.htm

American Anthropological Association. (1998). *Statement on race*. Arlington, VA: American Anthropological Association. Retrieved from http://www.aaanet.org/stmts/racepp.htm

American Sociological Association. (2003). *The importance of collecting data and doing social scientific research on race*. Washington, DC: American Sociological Association. Retrieved from http://www2.asanet.org/media/asa_race_statement.pdf

Anderson, E. (2000). *Code of the street: Decency, violence, and the moral life of the inner city*. New York, NY: W. W. Norton.

Bamshad, M. J., Wooding, S., Watkins, W. S., Ostler, C. T., Batzer, M. A., & Jorde, L. B. (2003). Human population genetic structure and inference of group membership. *American Journal of Human Genetics, 72*(3), 578–589.

Baumeister, R. F. (2010). *Is there anything good about men? How cultures flourish by exploiting men.* New York, NY: Oxford University Press.

Cochran, G., & Harpending, H. (2009). *The 10,000 year explosion.* New York, NY: Basic Books.

Cooper, J. A., Walsh, A., & Ellis, L. (2010). Is criminology moving toward a paradigm shift? Evidence from a survey of the American Society of Criminology. *Journal of Criminal Justice Education, 21*(3), 332–347.

Copes, H., Hochstetler, A., & Williams, J. P. (2008). "We weren't like no regular dope fiends": Negotiating hustler and crackhead identities. *Social Problems, 55*(2), 254–270.

Cullen, F. T. (2011). Beyond adolescence-limited criminology: Choosing our future—The American Society of Criminology 2010 Sutherland Address. *Criminology, 49,* 287–330.

DeCuir, J. T., & Dixson, A. D. (2004). "So when it comes out, they aren't that surprised that it is there": Using critical race theory as a tool of analysis of race and racism in education. *Educational Researcher, 33*(5), 26–31.

DeLisi, M., Wright, J. P., Vaughn, M. G., & Beaver, K. (2009). Copernican criminology. *Criminologist, 34(1),* 14–16.

Edwards, A. W. F. (2003). Human genetic diversity: Lewontin's fallacy. *BioEssays, 25*(8), 798–801.

Ellis, L. (1988). The victimful-victimless crime distinction, and seven universal demographic correlates of victimful criminal behavior. *Personality and Individual Differences, 9*(3), 525–548.

Ellis, L., & Walsh, A. (1997). Gene-based evolutional theories in criminology. *Criminology, 35,* 229–276.

Federal Bureau of Investigation. (2011). "Arrests by race, 2011." Retrieved from http://www.fbi.gov/about-us/cjis/ucr/crime-in-the-u.s/2011/crime-in-the-u.s.-2011/tables/table-43

Felson, R. B. (2008). Barking up the right tree. *Criminologist, 33,* 1–3.

Gannett, L. (2004). The biological reification of race. *British Journal for the Philosophy of Science, 55*(2), 323–345.

Gitschier, J. (2005). The whole side of it—An interview with Neil Risch. *PLoS Genetics, 1*(1), e14.

Gottfredson, L. S. (1994). Egalitarian fiction and collective fraud. *Society, 31*(3), 53–59.

Gould, S. J. (1996). *The mismeasure of man.* New York, NY: W. W. Norton.

Graves, J. (2001). *The emperor's new clothes: Biological theories of race at the millennium.* New Brunswick, NJ: Rutgers University Press.

Graves, J. L. (2010). Biological v. social definitions of race: Implications for modern biomedical research. *Review of Black Political Economy, 37*(1), 43–60.

Gross, N., & Simmons, S. (2007). *The religiosity of American* college and university professors. *Social Science Research Council Web Forum.* doi:10.1093/socrel/srp026

Haidt, J. (2012). *The righteous mind: Why good people are divided by politics and religion.* New York, NY: Pantheon.

Herrnstein, R. J., & Murray, C. (1994). *The bell curve: Intelligence and class structure in American life.* New York, NY: Free Press.

Hunley, K. L., Healy, M. E., & Long, J. C. (2009). The global pattern of gene identity variation reveals a history of long-range migrations, bottlenecks, and local mate exchange: Implications for biological race. *American Journal of Physical Anthropology, 139*(1), 35–46.

Inbar, Y., & Lammers, J. (2012). Political diversity in social and personality psychology. *Perspectives in Psychological Science, 7,* 496–503.

Jang, S. J., & Johnson, B. R. (2003). Strain, negative emotions, and deviant coping among African Americans: A test of general strain theory. *Journal of Quantitative Criminology, 19*(1), 79–105.

Kalunta-Crumpton, A. (2006). A fair hearing? Ethnic minorities in the criminal court. *British Journal of Criminology, 46*(4), 774–776.

Kamberov, Y. G., Wang, S., Tan, J., Gerbault, P., Wark, A., Tan, L., . . . Sabeti, P. C. (2013). Modeling recent human evolution in mice by expression of a selected EDAR variant. *Cell, 152*(4), 691–702.

Kaszycka, K., & Strzałko, J. (2003). "Race"—still an issue for physical anthropology? Results from Polish studies seen in the light of U.S. findings. *American Anthropologist, 105,* 116–124.

Kaszycka, K., Štrkalj, G., & Strzałko, J. (2009). Current views of European anthropologists on race: The influence of education and ideological background. *American Anthropologist, 111,* 43–56.

Kinsey, A. C., Pomeroy, W. B., & Martin, C. E. (1948). *Sexual behavior in the human male.* Philadelphia, PA: W. B. Saunders.

Kitcher, P. (2007). Does "race" have a future? *Philosophy & Public Affairs, 35*(4), 293–317.

Klein, D. B., & Stern, C. (2004). Political diversity in six disciplines. *Academic Questions, 18*(1), 40–52.

Klein, D. B., & Stern, C. (2005). Professors and their politics: The policy views of social scientists. *Critical Review, 17*(3), 257–303.

Levin, M. (2005). *Why race matters: Race differences and what they mean.* Oakton, VA: New Century Foundation.

Levy, S., Sutton, G., Ng, P. C., Feuk, L., Halpern, A. L., Walenz, B. P., . . . Venter, J. C. (2007). The diploid genome sequence of an individual human. *PLoS Biology, 5*(10), e254.

Lewontin, R. (1972). The apportionment of human diversity. *Evolutionary Biology, 6,* 391–398.

Lieberman, L., & Kirk, R. (2002). The 1999 status of the race concept in physical anthropology: Two studies converge. *American Journal of Physical Anthropology, Suppl. 34,* 102.

Long, J., & Kittles, R. (2003). Human genetic diversity and the nonexistence of biological races. *Human Biology, 75*(4), 449–471.

Lynn, R. (2002). Racial and ethnic differences in psychopathic personality. *Personality and Individual Differences, 32*(2), 273–316.

Maglo, K. N. (2011). The case against biological realism about race: From Darwin to the post-genomic era. *Perspectives on Science, 19*(4), 361–390.

Melton, T., Clifford, S., Kayser, M., Nasidze, I., Batzer, M., & Stoneking, M. (2001). Diversity and heterogeneity in mitochondrial DNA of North American populations. *Journal of Forensic Sciences, 46*(1), 46–52.

National Academy of Sciences. (2012). *Current research not sufficient to assess deterrent effect of the death penalty* [Press release]. Retrieved from http://www8.nationalacademies.org/onpinews/newsitem.aspx?recordid=13363

Oakley, B. A. (2007). *Evil genes: Why Rome fell, Hitler rose, Enron failed and my sister stole my mother's boyfriend.* Amherst, NY: Prometheus Books.

Redon, R., Ishikawa, S., Fitch, K. R., Feuk, L., Perry, G. H., Andrews, T. D., . . . Hurles, M. E. (2006). Global variation in copy number in the human genome. *Nature, 444*(7118), 444–454.

Risch, N., Burchard, E., Ziv, E., & Tang, H. (2002). Categorization of humans in biomedical research: Genes, race and disease. *Genome Biology, 3*(7), 1–12

Rojek, J., Rosenfeld, R., & Decker, S. (2012). Policing race: The racial stratification of searchers in police traffic stops. *Criminology, 50,* 993–1024.

Roylance, F. D. (2004, October 10). New science undermines oldest notions about race. *Baltimore Sun,* 1–3. Retrieved from http://articles.baltimoresun.com/2004-10-10/news/0410100085_1_physical-anthropology-scientists-race

Rushton, J. P. (1997). *Race, evolution, and behavior: A life-history perspective.* New Brunswick, NJ: Transaction.

Rushton, J. P., & Jensen, A. R. (2005). Thirty years of research on race differences in cognitive ability. *Psychology, Public Policy, and Law, 11*(2), 235.

Rushton, J. P., & Rushton, E. W. (2003). Brain size, IQ, and racial-group differences: Evidence from musculoskeletal traits. *Intelligence, 31*(2), 139–155.

Sarich, V., & Miele, F. (2004). *Race: The reality of human differences.* Boulder, CO: Westview.

Sesardic, N. (2010). Race: A social destruction of a biological concept. *Biology & Philosophy, 25,* 143–162.

Shiao, J. L., Bode, T., Beyer, A., & Selvig, D. (2012). The genomic challenge to the social construction of race. *Sociological Theory, 30*(2), 67–88.

Skiba, R. J., Michael, R. S., Nardo, A. C., & Peterson, R. L. (2002). The color of discipline: Sources of racial and gender disproportionality in school punishment. *Urban Review,* 34, 317–342.

Smedley, A. (1998). *Race in North America: Origin and evolution of a worldview.* Boulder, CO: Westview.

Smedley, B. D., & Stith, A. Y. (2003). *Unequal treatment: Confronting racial and ethnic disparities in health care* (Vol. 1). Washington, DC: National Academies Press.

Snyderman, M., & Rothman, S. (1988). *The IQ controversy, the media and public policy.* New Brunswick, NJ: Transaction.

Tang, H., Quertermous, T., Rodriguez, B., Kardia, S., Zhu, X., Brown, A., . . . Risch, N. (2005). Genetic structure, self-identified race/ethnicity, and confounding in case-control association studies. *American Journal of Human Genetics, 76,* 268–75.

Templeton, A. R. (1998). Human races: A genetic and evolutionary perspective. *American Anthropologist, 100,* 632–650.

Thomas, M. E. (1993). Race, class, and personal income: An empirical test of the declining significance of race thesis, 1968–1988. *Social Problems, 40*(3), 328–342.

Tierney, J. (2011, February 7). Social scientist sees bias within. *New York Times,* 1. Retrieved from http://www.nytimes.com/2011/02/08/science/08tier.html

Trevethan, S., & Rastin, C. J. (2004). *A profile of visible minority offenders in the federal Canadian correctional system.* Ottawa, Ontario: Research Branch, Correctional Service of Canada.

Wade, N. (2006). *Before the dawn: Recovering the lost history of our ancestors.* New York, NY: Penguin.

Walsh, A. (2004). *Race and crime: A biosocial analysis.* New York, NY: Nova Science.

Walsh, A., & Ellis, L. (2003). *Biosocial criminology: Challenging environmentalism's supremacy.* New York, NY: Nova Science.

Walsh, A., & Yun, I. (2011). Race and criminology in the age of genomic science. *Social Science Quarterly, 92,* 1279–1296.

Williams, D. R. (2006). Race, socioeconomic status, and health: The added effects of racism and discrimination. *Annals of the New York Academy of Sciences, 896*(1), 173–188.

Wortley, S. (2003). Hidden intersections: Research on race, crime and criminal justice in Canada. *Canadian Ethnic Studies Journal, 35*(3), 99–117.

Wright, J. P., & Beaver, K. M. (2013). Do families matter? In P. Wilcox & F. T. Cullen (Eds.), *The Oxford handbook of criminological theory* (pp. 40–68). New York, NY: Oxford University Press.

Wright, J. P., & Boisvert, D. (2009). What biosocial criminology offers criminology. *Criminal Justice and Behavior, 36,* 1228–1240.

Wright, J. P., & Cullen, F. T. (2012). The future of biosocial criminology: Beyond scholars' professional ideology. *Journal of Contemporary Criminal Justice, 28*(3), 237–253.

Wright, J. P., Beaver, K. M., DeLisi, M., Vaughn, M. G., Boisvert, D., & Vaske, J. (2008). Lombroso's legacy: The miseducation of criminologists. *Journal of Criminal Justice Education, 19*(3), 325–338.

Wright, R. T., & Decker, S. H. (1994). *Burglars on the job: Streetlife and residential break-ins.* Boston, MA: Northeastern University Press.

Wright, R. T., & Decker, S. H. (1997). *Armed robbers in action: Stickups and street culture.* Boston, MA: Northeastern University Press.

Yancey, G. (2011). *Compromising scholarship: Religious and political bias in American higher education.* Waco, TX: Baylor University Press.

Zack, N. (2002). *Philosophy of science and race.* New York, NY: Routledge.

Zeigler-Hill, V. (2007). Contingent self-esteem and race: Implications for the Black self-esteem advantage. *Journal of Black Psychology, 35,* 51–74.

Zeigler-Hill, V., & Wallace, M. T. (2011). Racial differences in narcissistic tendencies. *Journal of Research in Personality, 45*(5), 456–467.

Discussion Questions

CHAPTERS 3 AND 4

1. Data have consistently revealed that minorities—primarily African Americans—are overrepresented in both serious offending and correctional statistics. What explanations do sociologists provide for this overrepresentation? What explanations does human evolution provide? How are they different?

2. Authoritarian science has argued that biological race does not exist and that race is better defined as a socially constructed concept. Discuss the scientific evidence related to biological race. For example, in what ways has natural selection worked to create differences between humans? How have phenotypic differences been used to classify individuals across race?

3. Findings from Shaw and McKay's (1942) social disorganization theory have led theorists to de-emphasize the importance of individual-level variables and to instead place importance on studying community-level disadvantage and disorganization to explain criminality. What role does human genetics and biology play in explaining criminal behaviors? Does research support the importance of individual characteristics?

4. Sociologists believe the most important determinate of the relationship between race and crime is the differential distribution of minorities in communities characterized by social disorganization and cultural social isolation. How can human evolution be used to explain distributions among groups?

5. As noted by Drs. Wright and Morgan, many social scientists believe the concept of biological race has no validity in their fields and will only breed racism. Describe the ways in which the social construction of race has been used to justify discriminating behaviors. Is there reason to believe the existence of biological race will only breed hatred?

6. How does the topic of race fit into Dr. Haidt's idea of "tribal moral communities"? Moving forward, do you believe race will remain a sacred value among social scientists?

5

A Sociological Analysis of Social Class

Karen F. Parker
University of Delaware

Thomas Mowen
University of Delaware

In this chapter we outline the role social class plays in the larger field of criminology. Like all good criminological investigations our chapter draws from existing theories and paradigms in the field. That is, we examine social class as a key correlate to crime by illustrating how this concept is embedded into criminological theories and thus commonly integrated into empirical work. Our review begins with an examination of micro theories of crime, followed by structural perspectives. The goal is not to provide a full investigation of any given theory, but rather demonstrate the central role social class plays in our theoretical understanding of crime.

Whereas macro-level theories seek to understand how large institutional-level polices and dynamics affect crime rates along socioeconomic status (SES) boundaries, micro-level theories seek to explore how individuals may be differentially motivated to engage in crime due to their location in the socioeconomic structure. The link between an individual's socioeconomic status and crime has garnished considerable attention and academic debate (Agnew, Matthews, Bucher, Welcher, & Keys, 2008; Gottfredson & Hirschi, 1990; Tittle, 1983; Tittle & Paternoster, 2000; Wright, Caspi, Moffitt, Miech, & Silva, 1999). At the core of the debate, at least historically, is that criminologists assume individuals of lower socioeconomic status have higher levels of criminal behavior (Tittle, 1983). This paradigmatic debate grew, and became more complicated, over time as a number of studies found little or no association between SES and crime (Clelland & Carter, 1980; Olena, Tittle, Botchkovar, & Kranidiotis, 2010; Tittle & Meier, 1990; Tittle & Villemez, 1976; Vazsonyi & Klanjsek, 2008), particularly when other characteristics, such as race, gender, and age, were accounted for (Agnew et al., 2008; Dunaway, Cullen, Burton, & Evans, 2000; Wright et al., 1999). Confounding the debate further, some scholars found a significant relationship between SES and crime when violent crime is the outcome (Heimer, 1997; Pratt & Lowenkamp, 2002). That is, scholars have argued that the SES-crime link may vary by the type of crime investigated (Elliott, Huizinga, & Menard, 1989; Grasmick, Jacobs, & McCollom, 1983; Heimer, 1997; Tittle & Paternoster, 2000).

It is not the purpose of this chapter to reconcile these academic debates; rather we consider how popular criminological theories address the SES-crime link and illustrate how these commonly used frameworks converge and diverge on these issues. To begin, we explore the micro theories of social control, differential association, self-control, and labeling. We also include a discussion of the developmental perspective regarding how the socioeconomic status and crime relationship may surface as a relevant predictor of crime over the life course.

Micro Theories of Crime

SOCIAL CONTROL THEORY

Social control theory, developed by Travis Hirschi (1969), has experienced a significant amount of attention from sociologists and criminologists alike in the study of individual-level crime and delinquency. Stressing the importance of ties to society and significant others in understanding whether an individual engages in criminal or deviant activities, Hirschi offers four bonds: *attachment* to others, *belief* in conventional values, *commitment* to those values, and *involvement* in prosocial activities. When these bonds are weakened or broken, crime can occur. This highlights the underlying assumption of this perspective; individuals are naturally inclined to engage in deviant activities, but bonds with others inhibit this natural behavior from occurring. For example, an individual who lacks attachment to friends and family, from this perspective, is more likely to engage in crime than an individual who is prosocially attached to significant others.

As with most micro-level theories of crime, social control theory does not directly deal with socioeconomic status; in fact, Hirschi (1969) does not address the role of SES as he theorizes that social control theory is invariant across all social characteristics. However, this does not mean researchers employing a social control perspective ignore the influence of socioeconomic status on crime. In fact, the majority of control theorists include social class in their empirical analyses

(Dunaway et al., 2000). As Dunaway and colleagues find, "level of education and income have been among the most common . . . indicators used to assess individual class position" (p. 596).

From this control perspective, one's socioeconomic status may strengthen or weaken social bonds to conventional society and significant others, ultimately contributing to criminal behavior. It follows, then, that the formation of social bonds is greatly impeded for individuals in lower SES brackets due to the structural disadvantage these individuals face (Piquero, Sullivan, & Farrington, 2011). Supporting this claim, a number of studies have found that delinquency among poorer individuals is much higher than delinquency among the middle and upper classes (Gainey, Catalano, Haggerty, & Hoppe, 1997; Hindelang, Hirschi, & Weis, 1979; Kreager, Rulison, & Moddy, 2011; Piquero et al., 2011; Simons, Simons, Burt, Broder, & Cutrona, 2005; Stattin & Kerr, 2000). However, adding caution, some criminologists suggest these findings could be due to misspecification of either socioeconomic status or social bonds.

In regard to the measurement of SES, Dunaway and colleagues (2000) find that when family income or the presence of employment are used as measures for SES, research more consistently finds a positive relationship between SES and crime. However, when criminologists consider SES as an individual's education or as a more gradient measure such as an individual's score of economic prestige, this relationship ceases to exist (see Wright et al., 1999). These findings suggest there is a disjuncture between the conceptual measurement of SES and the empirical assessment of SES.

Finally, criminologists and sociologists alike have discussed the relative difficultly in fully measuring social control. Although social control theory stresses four types of bonds (as described above), the tendency in most empirical studies is to focus on the element of attachment alone (Baker, 2010; Cernkovich & Giordano, 1987; Sampson & Laub, 1994). Considering both these issues—that is, the conceptual difficulty in assessing SES (and the correspondingly different findings regarding measurement of SES) and the relative difficulty in fully exploring all four types of social bonds—the result is an incomplete picture concerning the role social class plays in the formation of social bonds and thus within the control tradition. Specifically, while research suggests the formation of social bonds is more difficult for individuals from lower SES backgrounds, placing them at an increased risk of engaging in crime (Peguero, Popp, Latimore, Shekarkhar, & Koo, 2011), the understanding of exactly how these dynamics affect the relationship between social bonds and delinquency remains clouded (Dunaway et al., 2000; Peguero et al., 2011)

DIFFERENTIAL ASSOCIATION

Differential association is a theoretical framework concerned with delinquency and was introduced by Edwin Hardin Sutherland (1939). This perspective stresses the importance of the process in which a person learns how to become delinquent. According to Sutherland, the motivations for crime are purely individually based and occur through interactions within subcultures, such as peer groups or family. Through these groups, individuals learn the techniques, skills, knowledge, and attitudes toward acceptable behavior. Important to note, however, is differential association stresses that individuals not only learn conventional norms of the broader society, but that they also learn norms consistent with their subculture. Sometimes the conventional definitions for behavior clash with the norms of the subgroup, resulting in normative conflict. In cases where individuals experience an overabundance of definitions that are favorable for delinquent behavior, they are more likely to engage in delinquency as a result.

Unlike social control theory, differential association asserts that individuals only *learn to* become delinquent; the natural state of the individual is conformity. It is only through exposure to differential associates that one develops an overabundance to crime and delinquency. Thus, the assumption of differential association is that individuals with the most frequent and intense exposure to deviant associates will also experience the highest probability of engaging in criminal and delinquent behavior (Tittle, 1983). However, much like social control theory, differential association does not directly address the impact of socioeconomic status on crime and delinquency. As Tittle demonstrates, many scholars have operated under the assumption that lower SES subgroups are more likely to be comprised of individuals with more criminogenic tendencies than subgroups in higher SES brackets. Thus, differential association assumes lower-class individuals will be more likely to engage in criminality due to their learned behavior from differential associates, and there is research to support this indirect relationship.

A number of empirical studies have shown that socioeconomic factors indirectly affect peer association (Fergusson & Horwood, 2004; Matsueda, 1982), contributing to delinquency (Akers, Krohn, Lanza-Kaduze, & Radosevic, 1979). For example, adolescents from lower-SES families are more likely to become involved with gangs (Battin-Pearson, Thornberry, Hawkins, & Krohn, 1998) and more likely to learn attitudes and behaviors conducive to crime and delinquency. In this vein, many research projects have focused on the impact of parents on dissuading their child's association with delinquent peers. This focal point of study is important; parents who take a positive and active role in the life of their child generally have children who do not associate with delinquent peers. Thus, these children have been shown to have lower levels of delinquency (Patterson, DeBaryshe, & Ramsey, 1989; Vitaro, Brendgen, & Wanner, 2005).

Research has established that the common stressors among individuals in the lower-SES groups such as unemployment, income instability, higher rates of family violence, and neighborhood disadvantage greatly impact parents' ability to engage in positive parenting practices (Patterson et al., 1989), thereby increasing the risk that their child will become involved with delinquent associates (Barnes & Farrel, 1992). Comparatively, parents from the middle/upper classes have been found to take a more active role in managing their child's friends and peer networks (Simons, Chao, Conger, & Elder, 2001). Moreover, middle- and upper-class parents tend to choose which school their child attends and push their child to pursue conventional extracurricular activities such as sports or academic clubs

(Ladd, Profilet, & Hart, 1992). These types of strategies have been shown to mitigate the effects of deviant peers and have also been shown to reduce the involvement with deviant peer networks because the probability of interaction with deviant peers drops dramatically (Simons et al., 2001).

In sum, differential association stresses the importance of subgroups in exploring how criminality varies among individuals. From this perspective, SES does not directly relate to crime; instead, the conditions of the lower class increase the likelihood of involvement with delinquent peers such as gangs (Battin-Pearson et al., 1998). Projects exploring the link between differential association and class have focused on the relatively inhibited ability of parents from lower socioeconomic statuses ability to dissuade these relationships (Patterson et al., 1989).

SELF-CONTROL THEORY

Introduced in Gottfredson and Hirschi's (1990) book titled *A General Theory of Crime*, self-control theory is a theory of criminality that focuses on early childhood socialization. At the center of this perspective is the assumption that individuals develop differing levels of self-control as young children that determine their propensity for criminal activity over the life course; a trait called *self-control*. While self-control is on a spectrum, an individual with low self-control is characterized by immediate gratification, lack of diligence, thrill seeking, the preference for physical over mental activities, self-centeredness, and a low threshold for tolerance of frustration. Importantly, low self-control develops when there is little attachment between parent and child; in these cases, families may fail to recognize deviant behavior, or fail to correct for the deviant behavior. When individuals are predisposed to crime (low self-control) and the opportunity for criminal behavior is presented, they will engage in the crime. Contrastingly, an individual with high self-control and the opportunity to engage in crime will not.

As with previous theories outlined, self-control theory does not directly address socioeconomic status. In fact, Gottfredson and Hirschi (1990) argue that SES plays absolutely no role in explaining criminality and deviance from this perspective. At the same time, however, they also argue that there are differences along SES lines; that is, socioeconomic status continues to play an important role in the application of this theory. One of the primary concerns in exploring the link between SES and self-control is the conceptualization of both measures. First, there has been significant academic debate on how to properly measure self-control (Grasmick, Tittle, Bursik, & Arneklev, 1993; Pratt & Cullen, 2000). In an attempt to quantify self-control, Grasmick et al. (1993) develop a six-factor, 24-item scale based on Gottfredson and Hirschi's original conceptualization. This scale has received a significant amount of use from a number of criminologists (Arneklev, Cochran, Gainey, 1993; Romero, Gomez-Fraguela, Luengo, & Sobral, 2003; Tittle, Ward, & Grasmick, 2003); though not all criminologists agree Grasmick's scale adequately captures the multidimensional nature of self-control (Piquero, MacIntosh, & Hickman, 2000).

Second, the measurement of SES is also problematic. For example, because parenting is the primary avenue by which self-control is developed, scholars argue there is a lack of understanding of how the process of parental socialization is affected by structural dimensions, and thus a disjuncture over how structural location affects the development of self-control (Perrone, Sullivan, & Pratt, 2004; Pratt, Turner, & Piquero, 2004). In addition, many studies measure SES solely as income (Vazsonyi, Cleveland, & Wiebe, 2006), though SES is much more complex. While a number of studies on self-control utilize SES as a control variable in their model, because of the conceptual difficulties among these two concepts, to date only a few research projects have explicitly sought to explore how SES affects the development of self-control.

In one study, Lynam et al. (2000) found there were differences in levels of self-control around SES boundaries with individuals from lower SES groups exhibiting lower levels of self-control. However, a major limitation of the research design was the measure of self-control; due to data constraints, Lynam et al. (2000) measured self-control only through reported impulsivity. In addition, SES was measured only through neighborhood disadvantage. Limitations aside, the authors found impulsivity related to higher rates of offending in poor neighborhoods but not in more affluent neighborhoods. In stark contrast, Vazsonyi et al. (2006) found no difference in self-control and SES based on a representative sample of 20,000 male and female youth. Similarly to Lynam et al. (2000), Vazsonyi and colleagues conceptualize self-control only as a measure of impulsivity, not as self-control is fully conceptualized by Gottfredson and Hirschi (1990). Finally, in a test of self-control and SES, Vazsonyi and Klanjsek (2008) found no relationship between levels of self-control and SES.

Clearly, the relationship between criminality and socioeconomic status remains unclear from the perspective of self-control. While some studies find individuals from lower SES backgrounds may develop lower levels of self-control (Pratt et al., 2004), others find no difference between socioeconomic statuses (Vazsonyi & Klanjsek, 2008). As discussed, the major limitation of assessing this relationship is the disjuncture between the conceptualization of self-control and the empirical measurement, as well as the complex nature of SES. Taken together, there is little conclusive evidence to support the notion that individuals from lower SES groups have lower levels of self-control and are thus more likely to engage in crime.

LABELING THEORY

Originally introduced by Becker (1963), labeling theory, also referred to as *social reaction*, is concerned with understanding the process by which individuals become labeled as deviant or criminal and how criminality emerges because of that label. In sum, labeling theory describes the process by which individuals are labeled as deviant, come to internalize that label, and begin to behave in a manner that conforms to that label. For example, if an individual commits a crime, is prosecuted and convicted, his or her friends, families, and coworkers may view the person as criminal and treat the person accordingly. This could include resentment, mistrust, and ultimately, rejection (Lemert, 1967). In turn, the labeled individual will begin to internalize the label as criminal, and may begin to act accordingly.

When considering the relationship between labeling, criminality, and SES, there are two primary concepts to consider. First, theorists consider the differential probability of being labeled. The process of labeling and the probability that a successful label will be effectively applied coincides directly with an individual's ability to protect against the label (Tittle, 1983). Those individuals who lack the resources to reject the label, such as individuals from lower socioeconomic status groups, are more likely to be successfully labeled. Second, theorists consider the outcome of that label. Once a label has been applied, it comes with significant implications. For example, being labeled as a criminal inhibits the ability for that individual to engage in behaviors that fall outside the label because of the social response from others. In turn, the individual will begin to adopt a self-identity that corresponds to the label, which will eventually lead to more criminal acts.

When these two ideas are taken together, the relationship between socioeconomic status and crime begins to unfold. Unlike social control, self-control, and differential association, labeling theory begins with the assertion that everyone has an equal opportunity to engage in criminality; it is not the presence of peers (DA), bonds (social control), or inherent traits (self-control) that determine criminal predisposition; instead, it is the ability for an individual to reject the label as criminal that determines the relationship between SES and crime (Tittle, 1983). Because individuals who lack the resources to ward against the label are those who are disadvantaged (working class), they are more likely to be labeled than individuals in the middle/upper class. It follows, then, that lower SES individuals are then predisposed to higher rates of crime. However, this is purely an indirect relationship between crime and SES.

A number of research projects have found that individuals from lower socioeconomic status backgrounds are more likely to be labeled, and therefore more likely to engage in criminal acts (Hayes, 2010; Li & Moore 2001; Paternoster & Lee, 1989). This link, however, is purely indirect because the determining factor in the process of labeling is the ability to reject the label. Myriad research projects have shown that individuals from the middle/upper classes are more likely to be able to avoid the permanence of the label (Sharp, 2009). Overall, labeling theory suggests there is a link between SES and crime, but is solely meditated by access to resources; individuals from the lower SES are not predisposed to criminal tendencies, they merely lack the access to resources in the same capacity as the middle/upper class to overcome a criminal label if it is presented.

DEVELOPMENTAL CRIMINOLOGY: THE LIFE COURSE PERSPECTIVE

The life course perspective introduced by Sampson and Laub (1993) focuses on events over the life span of an individual that effect criminal offending. Overall, Sampson and Laub agreed with Hirschi's (1969) basic tenet that social bonds are the primary factors that inhibit individuals from engaging in crime. However, previous theories did not explain the crime-age relationship, and thus did not address fluctuations in criminal offending over the life span. Sampson and Laub (1993) argued that important events in an individual's life influenced criminality; strong bonds such as marriage and employment serve to promote desistance from crime. These events, referred to as *turning points,* include a number of social events such as marriage, birth of a child, incarceration, and reintegration (Laub & Sampson, 2003). Overall, the primary assumption of developmental theories is the idea that criminal activity and delinquency changes with age (Thornberry, 1997).

Unlike the previous theories outlined, life course perspective does not concentrate on a single concept in explaining crime. For example, while social control stresses attachment, differential association focuses on subgroups, self-control focuses on inherent traits, and labeling focuses on the process by which individuals internalize a criminal label, the life course perspective explores how turning points affect criminality over the life span. As such, there is no single explanation of how life course views the intersection of socioeconomic status and crime.

Laub and Sampson (1993) argue that changes in social bonds formally (such as employment) and informally (such as peer networks) can serve as turning points. For example, marriage has consistently been cited as an important bond formed in adulthood that inhibits crime from occurring (Laub & Sampson, 2003). However, just as a *good* marriage can serve as a positive turning point, a *bad* marriage has also been found to produce a turning point by which criminal desistance is weakened (Laub, Nagin, & Sampson, 1998). As such, a multitude of factors that affect offending over time are the focal point of analysis. Another aspect of life course that separates it distinctly from other theories of crime is the unique focus on intersectionality. The life course perspective explores how demographic and stratifying characteristics such as race, gender, age, and SES interact to influence criminal behavior. With the consideration of myriad social statuses, the role of each becomes correspondingly complex. Moreover, because life course perspective explores criminality over the life span, many researchers combine this framework with other theoretical orientations. For example, receiving a higher education generally leads to a higher paying job, which could increase bonding to others over the life course. However, if individuals lose their jobs, or drop out of school, they may experience a turning point that places them at a higher risk of criminal behavior. Regarding SES, higher education provides access to social capital, an increase of economic resources, stronger social relationships, and greater levels of social support (Ross & Van Willigen, 1997). Thus, from a life course perspective individuals from higher socioeconomic backgrounds may be more likely to develop stronger and greater numbers of social bonds over the life course, which would mean that middle-/upper-class individuals are more likely to desist and/or have shorter trajectories of offending compared to lower-class individuals.

Drawing on traditions in criminology (learning, control, strain, etc.), the above discussion illustrates the role of social class in a number of commonly used micro-level theories of crime: social control, differential association, self-control, and labeling. Furthermore, acknowledging the extant attention toward developmental processes, we also examine how social class could be integrated into a life course perspective, while also recognizing that the conception of social class will vary significantly in the life course literature as researchers attempt to account for the quality (rather than simply classification, such as poor/not poor) of one's experiences and life chances along socioeconomic lines. With that being said, our review suggests that although social class is rarely a core theoretical construct in micro theories of crime, it is often embedded in empirical examinations of these theories. For instance, we illustrate the considerable attention toward the role social class plays in the formation and maintenance of social bonds and/or how one's socioeconomic status may increase the exposure to delinquent peers. We also illustrate how one's SES status can impede important life events (social bonds, access to social capital) as one moves through the life course, thus impacting desistence from crime. We now turn to macro theories of crime.

Macro Theories of Crime

SOCIAL DISORGANIZATION

One of the most fundamental approaches to the macro study of crime emanates from the Chicago-school research of Shaw and McKay. In essence, Shaw and McKay (1942) argue that neighborhood dynamics lead to social disorganization in communities, which accounts for the variations in crime and delinquency. Here, *social disorganization* refers to the inability of a community structure to realize the common values of its residents and maintain effective social control (Bursik, 1988). Key to Shaw and McKay's social disorganization model is the assumption that structural barriers impede development of the formal and informal ties that promote the ability of the community to solve common problems. These structural barriers result when urban areas experience changes in their social and economic structures, which builds on Burgess's (1967) *zone of transition*. In this way, social and economic changes in a community shape structural conditions that impede group solidarity and contribute to the breakdown in social control.

Shaw and McKay (1942) identified three structural conditions—low economic status, ethnic heterogeneity, and residential mobility—as structural barriers that deteriorate community social organization. First, communities with low economic status lack adequate money and resources to generate the needed formal and informal controls necessary to reduce crime and delinquency. Second, racial and ethnic heterogeneity, which is often accompanied by fear and mistrust, impedes communication and patterns of interaction in a community. Third, residential mobility is said to disrupt a community's network of social relations by acting as a barrier to the development of extensive friendship networks, kinship bonds, and local social ties. Thus, unlike the micro theories reviewed above, economic conditions (poverty, unemployment) within the community are key theoretical constructs that lead to the breakdown in social control and thus higher crime rates within this structural perspective.

While social disorganization theory fell into disfavor throughout much of the 1970s, renewed interest in the theory has led to some important developments. First, researchers have extended the types of structural conditions in urban areas that impede social control, including population size, poverty, and family disruption (see Sampson, 1986; Sampson & Groves, 1989). Second, the mediating linkages between structural conditions, social control, and crime rates have been further articulated. While Shaw and McKay identified the capacity of the community to control group-level dynamics as a key mechanism linking community characteristics with crime rates, Sampson and Groves (1989) clarified the types of social networks in a community at both the informal (e.g., friendship ties) and formal (e.g., participation in community organizations) levels. They suggested that communities unable to: (a) control teenage groups through collective social control, (b) form informal local friendship networks, and (c) participate in local formal and voluntary organizations will experience high rates of crime and delinquency (Sampson & Groves, 1989).

A second development is the growing attention toward understanding the nature of community ties, including the inability of community residents to collectively display trust and deal with problems (such as disorderly teens or drugs) via *collective efficacy* (Sampson, Raudenbush, & Earls, 1997). Collective efficacy has been found to largely mediate the relationship between structural disadvantage and crime (Sampson et al., 1997; Sampson, Morenoff, & Earls, 1999), which is a discussion we return to in the conclusion section of this chapter. Finally, there is the work of Wilson (1987), who shifts our attention toward the economic marginalization of Blacks in the inner city as a result of spatial and industrial changes in the political economy. In *The Truly Disadvantaged,* he points to deindustrialization, coupled with racial residential segregation, as central to the rising concentration of poverty among inner-city residents. That is, the process of deindustrialization marks growing poverty levels and joblessness as manufacturing jobs move away from city boundaries (Kasarda, 1995). According to Massey and Denton (1993), Blacks remain spatially isolated and residentially segregated from Whites at all levels of economic status, while Wilson (1996) similarly argues that Blacks reside in areas of extreme poverty concentration, which is a reality not known to poor Whites. As a result, scholars not only acknowledge the persistent disadvantaged position of African Americans as a structural feature of urban areas, but they also have expanded on the ways they articulate the importance of economic conditions to crime rates, such as measuring the impact of joblessness, poverty concentration, and deindustrialization (Ousey, 1999; Parker & McCall, 1999; Peterson & Krivo, 1993, 1999). It is these recent efforts to expand on and extend social disorganization tradition that has made the case for its prominence as a leading community-level theory of crime (Sampson, 2012).

ANOMIE/RELATIVE DEPRIVATION

The idea that economic conditions contribute to crime has a long history in sociological theories, and Merton's theory of anomie is no exception. American culture places great emphasis on economic success, yet the social structure impedes group access to this cultural goal by placing barriers to the means that lead to success. The disjuncture between goals and legitimate means to achieving economic goals results in strain. Merton specifies a number of ways groups adapt to strain, some of which involve criminal innovation (Merton, 1938). The term *relative deprivation*, first elaborated by Merton (1947) and then Runciman (1966), exemplifies this process. Essentially, economic success is the carrot dangling in front of individuals who have hopes and aspirations of achieving it, only to find the avenues blocked and considerably limiting. The result is "intense pressure for deviation" (Merton, 1968, p. 199), which is quite clear in Runciman's early writings:

> **A** is relatively deprived of X when (1) he does not have X, (2) he sees some other person or persons, which may include himself at some previous or expected time, as having X (whether or not this is or will be in fact the case), (3) he wants X, and (4) he sees it as feasible that he should have X. . . . Given the presence of all four conditions, relative deprivation produces feelings of "envy and injustice." (1966, p. 10)

In this treatment of relative deprivation, then, it is not only that the legitimate means to economic success are blocked and unrewarding, but also that the blocked means are accompanied by feelings of injustice and resentment. As persons become aware of their blocked economic resources and grow resentful, the potential for crime is present. Thus, inequality suppresses the means to achieve material goals, contributing to feelings of frustration, which causes crime (Fowles & Merva, 1996; Messner & Tardiff, 1986). And similar to efforts within micro theories, scholars recognize that economic inequalities are closely associated with status groups, such as race, contributing to disparities in crime rates across these groups. That is, feelings of deprivation that contribute to crime are often accompanied by racial inequality. Here theorists attempt to explain the response of certain racial groups to unfulfilled promises of justice and equity by suggesting these racial groups are more likely to be blocked from economic resources.

More recent, Messner and Rosenfeld (2001) build on the anomie/strain tradition by further specifying the interconnections between culture and social institutions in American society. In their seminal work, *Crime and the American Dream,* they argue that the cultural emphasis on monetary success, which they refer to as *the American Dream*, is further complicated by the dominance of the economy over other major institutions in society, such as family, school, and polity. The devaluation of education and family, in comparison to economic success, only further glorifies material gain, contributing to higher crime rates in the United States relative to our counterparts. Furthermore, the imbalance of power between other institutions and the economy only perpetuates inequality by weakening these institutions as a means for success. Importantly, in Merton's classic work of anomie and Messner and Rosenfeld's recent articulation of institutional anomie theory, this tradition delineates specifically the connections between economic conditions, cultural adaptions, and crime within the United States. Whether economic success is blocked or imbalanced, the injustice and inequality that result lead to higher criminal offending.

CONFLICT THEORY

If the above two macro theories lead one to think the link between economic conditions and crime are bleak, might conflict theory offer a bit of optimism? By combining elements of social class with power, Marx describes how capitalism produces an ever-widening gap between the social classes. While Marx wrote only sporadically about crime, other scholars have more systematically spelled out the connection between capitalism and crime. Capitalism is the root cause of crime (Greenberg, 1993; Quinney, 1974) by promoting ruthless competition and the exploitation of others in the pursuit of profits (Bonger, 1916/1969). And much like the economic rulers pursue their own economic interests, they too work to ensure that government policies protect their advantageous position. As Reiman (1984) puts it, "the rich get richer and the poor get prison." Not only are laws shaped in such a way to promote the interest of the powerful (Chambliss & Seidman, 1980; Quinney, 1974; Turk, 1966), but criminal justice officials also are not above breaking the law, using such avenues as force and wrongful conviction (Chamlin, 1989; Holmes, 2000; Parker, Stults, & Rice, 2005).

Conflict criminologists tend to be divided on how best to conceptualize the economic conditions that result from a capitalist state. Essentially, it appears scholars differ regarding whether it is important to underline the relative economic differences by class or emphasize the more observable conditions of this inequality (poverty). In classic writings, Bonger (1916/1969) and Quinney (1974) focused on the exploitation of the poor, suggesting that poverty-stricken groups may engage in more crime as a result of these inequalities. Other conflict theorists argue that economic stratification perpetuates conflicts, thus it is the relative nature of the deprivation that affects crime rates. While the conflict paradigm has drawn from both absolute (poverty) and relative (income inequality) forms of economic deprivation as sources of crime, others see similarities in these constructs, at least empirically (Bailey, 1984; Messner, 1982; Peterson & Bailey, 1988). Despite conceptual differences, the solution to crime is a more equitable society. Both Bonger (1916/1969) and Quinney (1980) note the only end to this crisis is socialism. Even though the conflict approach offers an optimistic end, much of the literature tends to focus on the enduring consequences of economic deprivation, such as violent crime (Blau & Blau, 1982; Hagan, 1994: Hagan & Peterson, 1995; Messner, 1989; Short, 1997; William & Flewelling, 1988). Furthermore, like other structural approaches, the conflict perspective has also been applied to address racial disparities in arrest rates, regardless of the level of involvement in criminal behavior. Drawing on the position that crime control is an instrument used by the powerful groups to control groups who threaten their economic interests, Liska and Chamlin (1984) explain: "Conflict theory assumes that nonwhites have a substantially higher arrest rate than whites, because relative to whites, they are less able to resist arrest and because authorities share common stereotypes linking them to crime" (p. 384).

The significance of economic conditions is widely evident in each of these theories. Furthermore, each approach acknowledges that structural barriers (in the form of poverty, access to legitimate means, or economic inequality and capitalism) contribute to crime rates, and that these barriers are more pronounced among minority groups. Importantly, while race and ethnicity are acknowledged by many of these structural theories, nothing is stated within these theories that would suggest any one demographic group is inherently more disposed to violence. Rather, the underlining premise is that there are economic barriers and cultural elements in the geographical context that lead to crime, whether they operate through undermining community control, blocking opportunities, or creating power differentials and competition. These macro-level theories have been widely used in the study of crime and violence.

Conclusion

In this chapter, we illustrate the importance of social class to criminological studies by showing the role social class plays in both micro- and macro-level criminological theories. Whereas some macro-level theories, such as anomie and social disorganization, directly explore how economic disadvantage affects criminality, the primary micro-level theories explored here do not outline the role of socioeconomic status in predicting crime. Instead, researchers employ socioeconomic status in their analysis, and as such, the influence of SES on crime remains hotly debated (Dunaway et al., 2000; Gottfredson & Hirschi, 1990; Tittle, 1983; Tittle & Paternoster, 2000). Clearly, there is a disjuncture between micro- and macro-level theories on the role of social class in criminological work, whereby social class is central to the theoretical underpinnings of structural approaches but only integrated into investigations of micro theories as scholars attempt to test theoretical relationships.

As criminological theory moves forward, we wonder if this disjuncture may be remedied as researchers continue to build multilevel theory and examine contextual effects. Work by Sampson and colleagues (1997; Sampson et al., 1999) on collective efficacy serves as an example. Based on their social disorganization theory, Sampson and colleagues (1997) argued that the persistence of crime resulted from the breakdown of informal controls and collective solidarity of neighborhoods. That is, social organization was contingent on the trust and social support among residents of a given community combined with an orientation toward taking action. This collective efficacy of residents, they argued, mediated concentrated disadvantage and crime (Sampson et al., 1997). Collective efficacy, which consists of the two components of *social cohesion and trust* and *social control*, involves the micro processes of building trust between neighbors and a sense of solidarity, as well as the informal actions by residents to maintain order. In this literature, collective efficacy is often characterized as a macro-to-micro theory of community organization and crime rates because it delineates the mechanisms behind collective efficacy and illustrates how disadvantaged neighborhoods overcome structural barriers of poverty and residential instability to form the social capital needed to build collective efficacy. Clearly, this multilevel theory allows scholars to consider how linkages between economic disadvantage and crime are mediated through collective efficacy, addressing the level-of-explanation problem as it moves the theoretical focus on macro-to-micro transitions (see Matsueda, 2013).

The reconciliation of the micro/macro link is not unique to the field of criminology; rather, it is something all social sciences deal with. As shown by the theories we have outlined in this chapter, combining micro and macro theories into a unified perspective is no easy task. It requires attention given to both the macro- and micro-level context, as well as the macro- and micro-level outcome. Clearly, this is something most of the theories we have presented in this chapter are ill-equipped to do or, at least, something that is not entirely intuitive. However, using collective efficacy as an example, we demonstrate that it is possible to combine micro and macro elements into one perspective through multilevel modeling, thereby allowing researchers to consider both levels of measurement and theory concurrently.

References

Agnew, R., Matthews, S. K., Bucher, J., Welcher, A. N., & Keyes, C. (2008). Socioeconomic status, economic problems, and delinquency. *Youth & Society, 40,* 159–181.

Akers, R. L., Krohn, M. D., Lanza-Kaduze, L., & Radosevic, M. (1979). Social learning and deviant behavior: A specific test of a general theory. *American Sociological Review, 44,* 636–655.

Arneklev, B. J., Cochran, J. K., & Gainey, R. R. (1998). Testing Gottfredson and Hirschi's low self-control stability hypothesis: An exploratory study. *American Journal of Criminal Justice, 23,* 107–127.

Bailey, W. C. (1984). Poverty, inequality and city homicide rates. *Criminology, 22,* 531–550.

Baker, J. O. (2010). The expression of low self-control as problematic drinking in adolescents: An integrated control perspective. *Journal of Criminal Justice, 38,* 237–244.

Barnes, G., & Farrel, M. P. (1992). Parental support and control as predictors of adolescent drinking, delinquency, and related problem behaviors. *Journal of Marriage and the Family, 54,* 763–776.

Battin-Pearson, S. R., Thornberry, T. P., Hawkins, J. D., & Krohn, M. D. (1998). *Gang membership, delinquent peers, and delinquent behavior* (Juvenile Justice Bulletin). Washington, DC: U.S. Department of Justice.

Becker, H. (1963). *Outsiders: Studies in the sociology of deviance.* London, UK: Free Press.

Blau, J., & Blau, P. (1982). Metropolitan structure and violent crime. *American Sociological Review, 47,* 114–128.

Bonger, W. (1969). *Criminality and economic conditions.* (Abridged with an introduction by Austin T. Turk). Bloomington: Indiana University Press. (Original work published 1916)

Burgess, E. W. (1967). The growth of the city: An introduction to a research project. In R. Park, E. Burgess, & R. D. McKenzie (Eds.), *The city* (pp. 47–62). Chicago, IL: University of Chicago Press.

Bursik, R. J. (1988). Social disorganization and theories of crime and delinquency: Problems and prospects. *Criminology, 26,* 519–551.

Cernkovich, S. A., & Giordano, P. C. (1987). Family relationships and delinquency. *Criminology, 25,* 295–321.

Chambliss, W. J., & Seidman, R. (1980). *Law, order, and power.* Reading, MA: Addison-Wesley.

Chamlin, M. (1989). Conflict theory and police killings. *Deviant Behavior, 10*(4), 353–368.

Clelland, D., & Carter, T. J. (1980). The new myth of class and crime. *Criminology, 18,* 319–336.

Dunaway, R. G., Cullen, F. T., Burton, V. S., & Evans, T. D. (2000). The myth of social class and crime revisited: An examination of class and adult criminality. *Criminology, 38,* 589–632.

Elliott, D. S., Huizinga, D., & Menard, S. (1989). *Multiple problem youth: Delinquency, substance use and mental health problems.* New York, NY: Springer.

Fergusson, D., & Horwood, J. (2004). How does childhood economic disadvantage lead to crime? *Journal of Child Psychology and Psychiatry, 45,* 956–966.

Fowles, R., & Merva, M. (1996). Wage inequality and criminal activity: An extreme bounds analysis for the United States, 1975–1990. *Criminology, 34*(2), 163–182.

Gainey, R., Catalano, R., Haggerty, K., & Hoppe, M. (1997). Deviance among the children of heroin addicts in treatment: Impact of parents and peers. *Deviant Behavior, 18,* 143–159.

Gottfredson, M. R., & Hirschi, T. (1990). *A general theory of crime.* Stanford, CA: Stanford University Press.

Grasmick, H. G., Jacobs, D., & McCollom, C. B. (1983). Social class and social control: An application of deterrence theory. *Social Forces, 62,* 359–374.

Grasmick, H. G., Tittle, C. R., Bursik, R. J., & Arneklev, B. J. (1993). Testing the core empirical implications of Gottfredson and Hirschi's general theory of crime. *Journal of Research in Crime and Delinquency, 30,* 5–29.

Greenberg, D. (1993). Delinquency and the age structure in society. In D. Greenberg (Ed.), *Crime and capitalism: Readings in Marxist criminology* (pp. 334–356). Philadelphia, PA: Temple University Press.

Hagan, J. (1994). *Crime and disrepute.* Thousand Oaks, CA: Pine Forge Press.

Hagan, J., & Peterson, R. (1995). *Crime and inequality.* Stanford, CA: Stanford University Press.

Hayes, T. (2010). Labeling and the adoption of a deviant status. *Deviant Behavior, 31,* 274-302.

Heimer, K. (1997). Socioeconomic status, subcultural definitions, and violent delinquency. *Social Forces, 75,* 799–833.

Hindelang, M. J., Hirschi, T., & Weis, J. G. (1979). Correlations of delinquency: The illusion of discrepancy between self-report and official measures. *American Sociological Review, 44,* 995–1014.

Hirschi, T. (1969). *Causes of delinquency.* Berkeley: University of California Press.

Holmes, M. (2000). Minority threat and police brutality: Determinants of civil rights criminal complaints in U.S. municipalities. *Criminology, 38*(2), 343–367.

Kasarda, J. (1995). Industrial restructuring and the changing location of jobs. In R. Farley (Ed.), *State of the union: America in the 1990s* (pp. 215–267). New York, NY: Russell Sage Foundation.

Kreager, D. A., Rulison, K., & Moddy, J. (2011). Delinquency and the structure of adolescent peer groups. *Criminology, 49,* 95–127.

Ladd, G., Profilet, S., & Hart, C. (1992*). Parents' management of children's peer relationships: Facilitating and supervising children's acuities in peer culture.* Hillsdale, NJ: Erlbaum.

Laub, J. H., Nagin, D. S., & Sampson R. J. (1998). Trajectories of change in criminal offending: Good marriages and the desistence process. *American Sociological Review, 63*(2), 225–238.

Laub, J. H., & Sampson, R. J. (1993). Turning points in the life course: Why change matters to the study of crime. *Criminology, 31*(3), 301–325.

Laub, J. H., & Sampson, R. J. (2003). *Shared beginnings, divergent lives: Delinquent boys to age 70.* Cambridge, MA: Harvard University Press.

Lemert, E. (1967). *Human deviance, social problems and social control.* Englewood Cliffs, NJ: Prentice Hall.

Li, L., & Moore, D. (2001). Disability and illicit drug use: An application of labeling theory. *Deviant Behavior, 22,* 1–21.

Liska, A. E., & Chamlin, M. B. (1984). Social structure and crime control among macrosocial units. *American Journal of Sociology, 90,* 383–395.

Lynam, D. R., Caspi, A., Moffitt, T. E., Wikström, P. H., Loeber, R., & Novak, S. (2000). The interaction between impulsivity and neighborhood context on offending: The effects of impulsivity are stronger in poorer neighborhoods. *Journal of Abnormal Psychology, 109,* 563–574.

Massey, D. S., & Denton, N. A. (1993). *American apartheid: Segregation and the making of the underclass.* Cambridge, MA: Harvard University Press.

Matsueda, R. L. (1982). Testing control theory and differential association: A causal modeling approach. *American Sociological Review, 47,* 489–504.

Matsueda, R. L. (2013). The macro-micro problem in criminology revisited. *Criminologist, 38,* 2–7.

Merton, R. (1938). Social structure and anomie. *American Sociological Review, 3,* 672–682.

Merton, R. (1947). Selected problems of field work in the planned community. *American Sociological Review, 12*(3), 304–312.

Merton, R. (1968). *Social theory and social structure.* New York, NY: Free Press.

Messner, S. (1982). Poverty, inequality and the urban homicide rate. *Criminology, 20,* 103–115.

Messner, S. (1989). Economic discrimination and societal homicide rates: Further evidence of the cost of inequality. *American Sociological Review, 54,* 597–611.

Messner, S., & Rosenfeld, R. (2001). *Crime and the American Dream.* Belmont, CA: Wadsworth.

Messner, S., & Tardiff, K. (1986). Economic inequality and levels of homicide: An analysis of urban neighborhoods. *Criminology, 24*(2), 297–317.

Olena, A., Tittle, C. R., Botchkovar, E., & Kranidiotis, M. (2010). The correlates of crime and deviance: Additional evidence. *Journal of Research in Crime and Delinquency, 47,* 297–328.

Ousey, G. (1999). Homicide, structural factors, and the racial invariance assumption. *Criminology, 37,* 405–426.

Parker, K. F., & McCall, P. L. (1999). Structural conditions and racial homicide patterns: A look at the multiple disadvantages in urban areas. *Criminology, 37*(3), 447–473.

Parker, K. F., Stults, B., & Rice, S. (2005). Racial threat, concentrated disadvantage and social control: Considering the macro-level sources of variation in arrests. *Criminology, 43*(4), 1111–1134.

Paternoster, R., & Lee, I. A. (1989). The labeling perspective and delinquency: An elaboration of the theory and an assessment of the evidence. *Justice Quarterly, 6,* 359–394.

Patterson, G. R., DeBaryshe, B. D., & Ramsey, E. (1989). A developmental perspective on antisocial behavior. *American Psychologist, 44,* 329–335.

Peguero, A. A., Popp, A. M., Latimore, L. T., Shekarkhar, S., & Koo, D. J. (2011). Social control theory and school misbehavior: Examining the role of race and ethnicity. *Youth Violence and Juvenile Justice, 9,* 259–275.

Perrone, D., Sullivan, C., & Pratt, T. C. (2004). Parental efficacy, self-control, and delinquency: A test of a general theory of crime on a nationally representative sample of youth. *International Journal of Offender Therapy & Comparative Criminology, 48,* 298–312.

Peterson, R., & Bailey, W. C. (1988). Forcible rape, poverty and economic inequality in U.S. metropolitan communities. *Journal of Quantitative Criminology, 4,* 99–119.

Peterson, R., & Krivo, L. (1993). Racial segregation and Black urban homicide. *Social Forces, 71,* 1001–1026.

Peterson, R., & Krivo, L. (1999). Racial segregation, the concentration of disadvantage, and Black and White homicide victimization. *Sociological Forum, 14*(3), 465–493.

Piquero, A. K., MacIntosh, R., & Hickman, M. (2000). Does self-control affect survey response? Applying exploratory, confirmatory, and item response theory analysis to Grasmick et al.'s self-control scale. *Criminology, 38,* 897–929.

Piquero, A. R., Sullivan, C., & Farrington, D. P. (2011). Assessing differences among offenders who offend a lot over a short time period compared to offenders who offend a little over a long time period. *Criminal Justice & Behavior, 37,* 1309–1329

Pratt, T. C., & Cullen, F. T. (2000). The empirical status of Gottfredson and Hirschi's general theory of crime: A meta-analysis. *Criminology, 38,* 931–964.

Pratt, T. C., & Lowenkamp, C. T. (2002). Conflict theory, economic conditions, and homicide: A time series analysis. *Homicide Studies, 6,* 61–83.

Pratt, T. C., Turner, M. G., & Piquero, A. R. (2004). Parental socialization and community context: A longitudinal analysis of the structural sources of low self-control. *Journal of Research in Crime & Delinquency, 41,* 219–243.

Quinney, R. (1974). *Critique of the legal order: Crime control in capitalist society.* Boston, MA: Little, Brown.

Quinney, R. (1980). *Class, state and crime* (2nd ed.). New York, NY: Longman.

Reiman, J. (1984). *The rich get richer and the poor get prison: Ideology, class and criminal justice* (2nd ed.). New York, NY: Wiley.

Romero, E., Gomez-Fraguela, A. J., Luengo, A. M., & Sobral, J. (2003). The self-control construct in the general theory of crime: An investigation in terms of personality psychology. *Psychology, Crime and Law, 9,* 61–86.

Ross, C. E., & Van Willigen, M. (1997). Education and the subjective quality of life. *Journal of Health and Social Behavior, 38*(3), 275–297.

Runciman, W. G. (1966). *Relative deprivation and social Justice: A study of attitudes to social inequality in twentieth century England.* London, UK: Routledge & Kegan Paul.

Sampson, R. J. (1986). Crime in cities: The effects of formal and informal social control. In A. Reiss & M. Tonry (Eds.), *Crime and justice* (Vol. 8, pp. 271–311). Chicago, IL: University of Chicago Press.

Sampson, R. J. (2012). *Great American city.* Chicago, IL: University of Chicago Press.

Sampson, R. J., & Groves, W. B. (1989). Community structure and crime: Testing social-disorganization theory. *American Journal of Sociology, 94,* 774–802.

Sampson, R. J., & Laub, J. H. (1993). *Crime in the making: Pathways and turning points through life.* Cambridge, MA: Harvard University Press.

Sampson, R. J., & Laub, J. H. (1994). Urban poverty and the family context of delinquency: A new look at structure and process in a classic study. *Child Development, 66,* 523–540.

Sampson R. J., Morenoff, J., & Earls, F. (1999). Beyond social capital: Spatial dynamics of collective efficacy for children. *American Sociological Review, 64,* 633–660.

Sampson, R. J., Raudenbush, S. W., & Earls, F. (1997). Neighborhoods and violent crime: A multilevel study of collective efficacy. *Science, 227,* 916–924.

Sharp, S. (2009). Escaping symbolic entrapment: Maintaining social identities. *Social Problems, 56,* 267–284.

Shaw, C. R., & McKay, H. D. (1942). *Juvenile delinquency and urban areas: A study of rates of delinquents in relation to differential characteristics of local communities in American cities.* Chicago, IL: University of Chicago Press.

Short, J. (1997). *Poverty, ethnicity, and violent crime.* Boulder, CO: Westview.

Simons, R. L., Chao, W., Conger, R. D., & Elder. G. H. (2001). Quality of parenting as mediator of the effect of childhood defiance on adolescent friendship choices and delinquency: A growth curve analysis. *Journal of Marriage and Family, 63,* 63–79.

Simons, R., Simons, L., Burt, C., Broder, G., & Cutrona, C. (2005). Collective efficacy, authoritative parenting and delinquency: A longitudinal test of a model integrating community and family-level processes. *Criminology, 43,* 989–1029.

Stattin, H., & Kerr, M. (2000). Parental monitoring: A reinterpretation. *Child Development, 71,* 1072–1085.

Sutherland, E. H. (1939). *Principles of criminology.* Philadelphia, PA: J. B. Lippincott.

Thornberry, T. P. (Ed.). (1997). *Developmental theories of crime and delinquency.* New Brunswick, NJ: Transaction.

Tittle, C. R. (1980). *Sanctions and social deviance: The question of deterrence.* New York, NY: Praeger.

Tittle, C. R. (1983). Social class and criminal behavior. A critique of the theoretical foundation. In F. T. Cullen & V. S. Burton (Eds.), *Contemporary criminological theory* (pp. 225–251). New York: New York University Press.

Tittle, C. R., & Meier, R. F. (1990). Specifying the SES/delinquency relationship. *Criminology, 28,* 271–299.

Tittle, C. R., & Paternoster, R. (2000). *Social deviance and crime: An organizational and theoretical approach.* Los Angeles, CA: Roxbury.

Tittle, C. R., & Villemez, W. J. (1976). Category/continuum thought styles and survey research. *Sociological Focus, 9,* 1–10.

Tittle, C. R., Ward, D. A., & Grasmick, H. G. (2003). Self-control and crime/deviance: Cognitive vs. behavioral measures. *Journal of Quantitative Criminology, 19,* 333–365.

Turk, A. (1966). Conflict and criminality. *American Sociological Review, 31,* 338–352.

Vazsonyi, A. T., Cleveland, H. H., & Wiebe, R. P. (2006). Does the effect of impulsivity on delinquency vary by neighborhood disadvantage? *Criminal Justice and Behavior, 33,* 511–541.

Vazsonyi, A., & Klanjsek, R. (2008). A test of self-control theory across different socioeconomic strata. *Justice Quarterly, 25,* 101–131.

Vitaro, F., Brendgen, M., & Wanner, B. (2005). Patterns of affiliation with delinquent friends during late childhood and early adolescence: Correlates and consequences. *Social Development, 14,* 82–108.

William, K. R., & Flewelling, R. L. (1988). The social production of criminal homicide: A comparative study of disaggregated rates in U.S. cities. *American Sociological Review, 53,* 421–431.

Wilson, W. J. (1987). *The truly disadvantaged: The inner city, the underclass and public policy.* Chicago, IL: University of Chicago Press.

Wilson, W. J. (1996). *When work disappears: The world of the new urban poor.* New York, NY: Knopf.

Wright, B. R., Caspi, A., Moffitt, T. E., Miech, R. A., & Silva, P. A. (1999). Reconsidering the relationship between SES and delinquency: Causation but not correlation. *Criminology, 37,* 175–194.

6

The Role of Intelligence and Temperament in Interpreting the SES-Crime Relationship

Anthony Walsh
Boise State University

Charlene Y. Taylor
Boise State University

Ilhong Yun
Chosun University, South Korea

Socioeconomic Status and Crime

Twenty years ago, Theodore Kemper (1994) noted the importance of socioeconomic status (SES) for understanding social behavior: "Perhaps the fundamental social structure of society is the system of stratification. It so bluntly determines individual conduct, belief, and value preferences, on the one hand, and sheer biological fate on the other . . . it is the social structure par excellence worthy of close attention" (pp. 47–48). But he also notes that: "if sociology and biology have not been on speaking terms in general, sociological distain for the biological reaches its apogee when it comes to social stratification" (p. 48). If Kemper is correct, sociological disdain should reach stratospheric heights when it comes to linking biology, SES, *and* criminal behavior.

The relationship of SES to criminal behavior has been central to criminology since its inception. Almost all major theories predict a negative class-crime relationship. Of course, SES does not directly cause crime or anything else; it is a label conceptualized and measured in different ways and used to categorize people in order to compare them across various domains of interest. However, many criminologists posit that social class *causes* crime if class is seen in terms of a poverty/non-poverty dichotomy. Many mainstream criminological theories implicitly or explicitly indict society for crime and ignore the culpability of the flesh and blood creatures who commit it. For them poverty is not a function of individual character or ability, but rather a condition to be laid at the feet of society. Thus, the argument goes that because poverty causes crime and society causes poverty, it follows that society causes crime.

This proposition has served criminology for a long time, but some of its luminaries are now questioning it. Robert Sampson (2000) writes that "everyone believes that 'poverty causes crime' it seems; in fact, I have heard many a senior sociologist express frustration as to why criminologists would waste time with theories outside the poverty paradigm. The reason we do . . . is that the facts demand it" (p. 711). Frank Schmalleger (2004) also notes that sociologists assume that the "root causes" of crime are poverty and various social injustices, but notes further that "some now argue the inverse of the 'root causes' argument, saying that poverty and what appear to be social injustices are produced by crime, rather than the other way around" (p. 223).

Sampson and Schmalleger commit sociological heresy by diverting us from a variable that mainstream sociology considers "structural" to imply individual origins of poverty and crime. It is heretical because, as Rubenstein (1992,) tells us, "in structural sociology, there are no persons. That is, culture and personality, indeed everything that could distinguish one individual from another, either drop away entirely or are reduced to adaptive responses that have no autonomous power" (p. 9). Structural explanations are the egalitarian imperative and are adopted to avoid holding what Richard Felson (2001) calls "protected groups" responsible for their position in life or for their behavior. Apparently, the closer we get to human flesh, blood, and agency, the less structuralists like it. We get very cozy with these things in this chapter because it is becoming ever clearer that the traits and characteristics that place people at risk for being on the bottom rung of the SES ladder are the same as those associated with the risk of criminality.

The Indirect Causal Nature of Social Class

As noted earlier, social class does not *directly* cause anything, although we can certainly make many predictions based on it. We like to draw clear circles around nominated causes and straight arrows between them and their effects, but social class is one of those things that involves long chains of subcauses. This is not to say that the connection between low SES—particularly poverty—and criminality is spurious. It only means that once we take into account more specific factors associated with both SES and criminality and assess the variance in criminal behavior they account for independently there is little left over for the higher-order abstraction to explain. There should always be some residual, however, since we cannot capture every pertinent variable in our statistical models.

A large ($n = 1{,}265$) longitudinal study of a birth cohort conducted by Fergusson, Swain-Campbell, and Horwood (2004) illustrates this point. Their study is particularly informative because the majority of the information obtained from subjects, parents, and teachers was verified via multiple sources such as the police and other state agencies. Subjects were classified into six SES categories ranging from professional (Class 1) to the lowest income category, consisting primarily of children from father-absent homes (Class 6). Only comparisons between the highest and lowest SES categories are presented here. Outcomes were assessed when the cohort age was 10, 16, 18, and 21.

We note from Table 6.1 that the incidence rate ratios (IRR) for self-reported offending show that subjects from Class 6 self-reported a rate of offending 3.21 times greater than subjects from Class 1. However, the IRR for officially recorded convictions (at age 21) for Class 6 subjects was 25.82 times greater than for Class 1. The comparison of these two IRRs (3.21 and 25.82) supports the contention that the most seriously involved offenders are the least likely to honestly report the extent of their offending.

Although data from Classes 2, 3, 4, and 5 are omitted in the table, all variables showed almost a perfect monotonic increase in negative outcomes moving from Class 1 through Class 6. That is, with decreasing SES there are increases in family adversity, childhood adjustment problems, school problems, and affiliation with delinquent peers. This accumulation of stresses and strains often results in antisocial behavior and failure in the workforce. It is in this way that SES reproduces itself across the generations in the worst families in which all negative influences appear to coalesce.

The most salient point of this study is that it illustrates that SES per se contributes little independent variance to the prediction of criminal behavior once the effects of all other predictor variables are entered into negative binomial regression models. The IRR of 3.21 for self-reported offending reduces to 1.23, and the 25.82 for officially recorded convictions fell to 1.93 with all pertinent variables listed in the table in the equation. The remaining variance accounted for by SES would doubtless disappear with the inclusion of additional individual-level variables.

Determinants of Socioeconomic Status

The tendency among sociologists is to assume that the advantages and disadvantages of childhood SES largely determine adult SES. This status ascription position views SES as socially "inherited" and not requiring any further explanation. SES is included in almost all statistical models of criminal behavior as an independent variable, but we must come to terms with the fact that it is a dependent variable as well. Rank, Yoon, and Hirschl (2003), for instance, provide a laundry list of things said to cause poverty (and crime) including out of wedlock birth, dropping out of school, divorce, poor work record, and welfare dependence, and transform these individual choices into problems of "structural failure" (p. 8). The implication is that structural failure leads to poverty, and then poverty leads to crime. On the other hand, Michael Schwalbe and his colleagues (2000) allow the poor the dignity of agency by pointing out that the aforementioned "structural failures" are the personal choices of people who "acquire habits and create situations (drug addiction, lack of education, multiple dependents, criminal records) that are debilitating and risky, and diminish chances for mainstream success, even in the form of stable working-class employment" (p. 428).

Table 6.1 Crime-Related Factors in Highest and Lowest SES Categories

Crime-Related Factors		
Variable	**Highest Class (6) Percentage**	**Lowest Class (1) Percentage**
With parent with criminal history	3.3	34.5
Highest quartile of deviant peer affiliation	17.9	41.4
In highest quartile conduct problems+	7.4	45.8
IRR self-reported offending ^	1.0	3.21
IRR official record of conviction^	1.0	25.82
Individual, Family, School, and Peer-Related Factors		
Regular or severe physical punishment	3.6	15.9
Lowest quartile maternal care	13.5	40.3
Lowest quartile parental attachment	11.4	36.9
Highest quartile family change	8.8	44.7
Highest quartile school truancy	10.4	54.4
Ever suspended from school	4.2	22.8
Lowest quartile scholastic ability	5.3	49.3

Source: Adapted from Tables 2 and 4 in Fergusson, Swain-Campbell, and Horwood (2004). Classes 2, 3, 4, and 5 omitted.

Notes: All comparisons significant at < .0001. *Assessed at 21 years of age. + Assessed at 10 years of age. ^ IRR

No one denies that people are profoundly influenced by the environments they find themselves in, but neither can it be denied that people create their environments as surely as their environments create them. It is consistently found that genetics account for a fair amount of the variance in the family structures and practices that sociologists consider entirely structural (Beaver, Shutt, Vaughn, DeLisi, & Wright, 2012; Cleveland, Wiebe, van den Oord, & Rowe, 2000). A basic principle of ecology is the interrelationships of organisms and their environment; each affecting and being affected by the other. The Chicago school of human ecology made much of the effects of neighborhoods on individuals but neglected the other half of the whole. Neighborhoods are, after all, macro mirrors reflecting the combined micro images of all the individuals who live in them. As John Wright, Boisvert, Dietrich, & Ris (2009) explain:

> It should be expected that individuals with similar traits and abilities, who have made many of the same choices over their life-course, should tend to cluster together within economic and social spheres. In other words, a degree of homogeneity should exist within neighborhoods, within networks within those neighborhoods, and within families within those neighborhoods. (p. 148)

Certainly, a cultural ambience emerges from the combinations of individuals found in neighborhoods that is greater than the sum of their individual parts, but that is nevertheless predictable from the parts, as Wright and his colleagues aver. Choices people make are undeniably constrained by factors beyond their power to control. No one can do anything about the genes or rearing environment their parents provided for them, the fact that the factories have moved to safer areas, or that the people around them sell drugs and are not very nice. We can, however, decide to respond to the inevitable travails of life constructively or destructively within the limits of our abilities. This appeal to human agency is sadly missing in typical structural accounts of SES and crime in which criminals are mere pawns on the social chess board.

The Role of Intelligence in SES Attainment and Criminal Behavior

Contrary to the status ascription model, the status attainment model of SES maintains that regardless of childhood SES, cognitive ability and motivation (talent + effort) largely determine adult SES in modern meritocratic societies (Nielsen, 2006). Messner and Rosenfeld (2001) accept this model but nevertheless view it as unfair and criminogenic when they point out that the competition for economic success *requires* inequality of outcomes because "winning and losing have meaning only when rewards are distributed unequally" (p. 9). They also claim that far from being an aberration of the American Dream, inequality in the United States is an expression of it. Inequality is a natural outcome of competition, and so "high crime rates are intrinsic to American society. . . . [A]t all social levels, *America is organized for crime*" (p. 5). Sawhill and Morton (2007) also question the fairness of meritocracy, writing, "people are born with different genetic endowments and are raised in different families over which they have no control, raising fundamental questions about the fairness of even a perfectly functioning meritocracy" (p. 4).

The concept of fairness appeals to our moral sentiments because fairness is a process by which we expect to "make things right." With Sawhill and Morton, we cannot help feeling sorry for individuals burdened with environmental and genetic disabilities they did not create, and we would like to make it right for them. But fairness is an emotional issue saturated with contradictory notions; we all praise it but differ about when its promise is fulfilled. Conservatives tend to view fairness as an equal opportunity *process*—a nondiscriminatory chance to play the game—that governments can attempt to guarantee via law. In this view, unequal outcomes are fair if the process is fair, and the process is fair if everyone is subjected to the same rules and judged by the same standards. With the rules of the game and the standards of judgment held constant, the only things that vary are the qualities that individuals bring to it, and only God Almighty can be blamed for the diversity of human talents. Liberals, on the other hand, tend to view fairness as equality of *outcome*, which no power on earth can guarantee.

Intelligence, the quintessential human trait, is the primary key to success in modern complex societies. This is yet another sociological heresy. The sociological literature is famous for ignoring the role of intelligence in status attainment, and it is ignorant of decades of hard genetic and neuroscientific evidence for the biological underpinnings of human variation in intelligence as measured by IQ. Lee Ellis (1996) aptly states that "someday historians of social science will be astounded to find the word *intelligence* is usually not even mentioned in late-twentieth-century text books on social stratification" (p. 28). IQ tests were designed to be a class-neutral measure of aptitude that was supposed to turn schools into capacity-catching institutions by siphoning off the brightest children to provide an increasingly complex economy with competent workers (Pinker, 2002). Whatever a person's IQ score is, it is an indicator of the probability of being able to master intellectually demanding tasks; it is not an indicator of his or her innate inferiority, moral value, or social worthiness.

The correlation between parental SES and children's IQ is in the .30 to .40 range (Lubinski, 2004), and this has led some sociologists to claim that SES is the cause of IQ. If parental SES is the cause offspring SES, offspring IQ and offspring SES should be correlated roughly within the same range. But offsprings' own IQ is a considerably more powerful predictor of their adult SES than parental SES, with correlations between offspring IQ and attained SES in the .50 to .70 range (Lubinski, 2004).

A study of 60 years of data from males born between 1925 and 1932 found that parental SES was weakly but significantly related to their occupational status at age 25, but it dwindled to nonsignificance by age 65. The only two variables significantly related to occupational success by age 65 were IQ and years of education (DiRago & Vaillant, 2007). This study supports the behavior genetic "law" that states that as we age the effects of shared environment (in this case, childhood SES and all the baggage that comes with it) on many phenotypic traits fade to insignificance while genes and nonshared environments become more salient. The heritability of IQ, for instance, is around .52 at adolescence and about .80 in old age, with the remaining variance almost all accounted for by nonshared environment (Neubauer & Fink, 2009).

A longitudinal study of 4,298 British males found that individual meritocratic factors (IQ, motivation, and education) assessed when subjects were 11 and 16 years old accounted for 48% of the variance in occupational status at age 33 (Bond & Saunders, 1999). All measured background variables (parental SES, type of housing, type of school, and parents' aspirations) combined accounted for only 8% of the variance. Another British longitudinal study (Nettle, 2003) followed a cohort of all children born in one week in 1958 to the age of 42 found that childhood intellectual ability was associated with class mobility in adulthood uniformly across all social classes of origin. An IQ difference of 24.1 points separated those who attained professional status from those in the unskilled class, regardless of the class of origin. Parental SES independently accounted for only 3% of the variation in attained offspring SES. Nettle concluded that "intelligence is the strongest single factor causing class mobility in contemporary societies that has been identified" (p. 560).

An American behavior genetic study pitting the ascription thesis against the achievement thesis found strongly in favor of the latter (Nielsen, 2006). The variables examined were verbal IQ (VIQ), grade-point average (GPA), and college plans (CPL). The heritability coefficients were VIQ = .536, GPA = .669, and CPL = .600; the shared environment coefficients were VIQ = .137, GPA = .002, and CPL = .030, and the nonshared environmental variances were VIQ = .327, GPA = .329, and CPL =.370. Shared environment is everything shared by siblings as they grew up, including parental SES as well as other factors sociologists appeal to explain important life outcomes such as neighborhood and school characteristics and race/ethnicity. The proportions of variance accounted for by SES of origin in VIQ, GPA, and CPL are miniscule compared with the proportions explained by genes and nonshared environment.

Numerous other studies (see Walsh, 2011, for a review) document the weak effect of parental SES on offspring SES in modern open societies. This weak effect is considered almost a truism outside of sociology: "The net impact of measured family background on economic success is easy to summarize: very little. This conclusion holds across different data sets with different model specifications and measurements and applies to both occupational status and earnings" (Kingston, 2006, p. 121).

Claims of test bias and the assumed eugenic implications of IQ testing following World War II led to the virtual disappearance of IQ from the criminological literature until the 1980s. It has now reemerged, and a number of reviews of studies from around the world have characterized the IQ-crime relationship as robust (e.g., Ellis & Walsh, 2003). Then there is the National Longitudinal Study of Youth (NLSY) data showing that 93% of the males in the sample who had ever been interviewed in a correctional facility over a 10-year period had IQs in the bottom half of the

IQ distribution. Furthermore, the NLSY data showed that of those subjects located at the bottom 20% of the IQ distribution (IQ ≤ 87), 62% had been interviewed in jail or prison at some point over the study period compared with only 2% from the top 20% (IQ ≥ 113)—a ratio of 31:1 (Herrnstein & Murray, 1994, p. 376).

IQ may be related to crime and delinquency more strongly than suggested by a simple comparison of mean IQ levels of offenders and nonoffenders. Offenders' IQs are typically compared with the general population mean of 100, forgetting that the general population includes a fairly large number of offenders, as well as individuals with such low IQs that they are largely incapable of committing crimes. The difference in IQ between offenders and normally functioning nonoffenders (the mean of which is around 103–105) is actually greater than the 8 to 10 points typically reported.

A related problem is that many studies are conducted with delinquents rather than adult criminals. We know that almost all teenage boys commit some act that could get them into trouble with the law, and that most delinquents do not become adult criminals (Moffitt, 1993). Criminals who offend most frequently and most seriously tend to begin their antisocial careers prior to puberty and continue after the typical delinquent has desisted. Delinquents who desist in early adulthood have accrued enough social capital to allow them to do so, much of that by virtue of their cognitive abilities. It has been pointed out that the IQ difference between nonoffenders and adolescent limited offenders is typically only one IQ point, but the same comparison with life-course-persistent offenders reveals about a 17 point difference (Gatzke-Kopp, Raine, Loeber, Stouthamer-Loeber, & Steinhauer, 2002; Moffitt, 1993). Pooling these two very different groups obviously hides the magnitude of the IQ difference between nonoffenders and the most persistent and serious offenders, and thus the true strength of the relationship between IQ and criminality.

David Wechsler's (1958,) statement that "the most outstanding feature of the sociopath's test profile is the systematic high score on the performance as opposed to the verbal part of the scale" (p. 176) sparked interest in intellectual imbalance as a way of examining the relationship between IQ and antisocial behavior. IQ scores are typically rendered in terms of full-scale IQ (FIQ), which is obtained by summing verbal IQ (VIQ) and performance IQ (PIQ) scores and dividing by 2. Most people have closely matched VIQ and PIQ scores, with a population average of 100 on each subscale. Individuals who have either VIQ or PIQ scores significantly in excess of the other (VIQ>PIQ or PIQ>VIQ) are considered intellectually imbalanced. Offenders are almost always found to have significantly lower VIQ, but not lower PIQ, than nonoffenders (Walsh, 2003), which led L. Miller (1987) to conclude "this PIQ>VIQ relationship was found across studies, despite variations in age, sex, race, setting, and form of the Wechsler scale administered, as well in differences in criteria for delinquency" (p. 120).

A discrepancy of 12 points or more is considered a significant imbalance at $p < .01$ (Kaufman, 1976). VIQ>PIQ individuals are significantly *under*represented in criminal and delinquent populations, and PIQ>VIQ individuals are significantly *over*represented. Averaged across eight studies, V>P boys are underrepresented in delinquent populations by a factor of about 2.6, and P>V boys are overrepresented by a factor of about 2.2, rendering an odds ratio of about 5.7 (Walsh, 2003). A VIQ>PIQ profile appears to be a major predictor of prosocial behavior among adults. Barnett, Zimmer, and McCormack (1989) found that only 0.9% of prison inmates had such a profile compared to the 18% of the general male population; a 20-fold difference.

The Role of Temperament in SES Attainment and Criminal Behavior

Chamorro-Premuzic and Furnham (2005) inform us that temperament and intelligence are "the two great pillars of differential psychology" (p. 352). They add that these two constructs are vital to predicting all kinds of life outcomes, including social class attainment. *Temperament* is defined as "individual differences in emotional, motor, and attentional reactivity [that are] biologically based and linked to an individual's genetic endowment" (Rothbart, 2007, p. 207). The various components of temperament are highly heritable and exert their influence through the variation in autonomic nervous system and reticular formation arousal. People with temperamental problems find it difficult to form social bonds and to compete successfully in life because they evoke negative responses from parents, teachers, and peers (evocative gene-environment correlation—rGE) and find acceptance only among peers with similar dispositions (active rGE) (reviewed in Sanson, Hemphill, & Smart, 2004). Differences in temperament make children differentially responsive to socialization, which is exacerbated by the fact that temperaments of parents and children are typically positively correlated (passive rGE). That is, children temperamentally unresponsive to socialization will have parents who are inconsistent disciplinarians, irritable, and unstable, rendering them unable or unwilling to cope constructively with their children, thereby saddling their children with both a genetic and an environmental liability (Saudino, 2005).

Longitudinal studies typically find that children from low SES families are overrepresented at the "problematic end of temperament dimensions, especially those relating to child difficulty" (Sanson et al., 2004, p. 158). One such study identified males from middle-class families with or without a history of temper tantrums in childhood and traced them for 30 years (Caspi, Bem, & Elder, 1989). The majority of bad tempered boys ended up in lower status occupations than their fathers, had erratic work histories, and experienced more unemployment than other males with more placid temperaments and were more than twice as likely as other men to be divorced by age 40. This study illustrates the heterogeneity of negative outcomes that can arise from a single temperamental dimension.

Temperament provides the biological superstructure on which our personalities are built. Among the "big five" personality traits, the two most strongly associated with occupational success (positively) and criminal behavior (negatively) are conscientiousness and agreeableness. Conscientiousness is a composite of a number of subtraits that range from well-organized, disciplined, scrupulous, orderly, responsible, and reliable at one end of the continuum, and disorganized, careless, unreliable, irresponsible, and unscrupulous at the other (Lodi-Smith & Roberts, 2007). Conscientiousness is obviously of great importance to success in the workforce and climbing the class ladder. Behavior genetic studies of conscientiousness find a mean heritability of .49 (Bouchard et al., 2003).

Agreeableness is the tendency to be friendly, considerate, courteous, helpful, and cooperative with others. Agreeable persons tend to trust others, to compromise with them, to empathize with and aid them. This list of subtraits suggests a high degree of concern for prosocial conformity and social desirability. Disagreeable persons simply display the opposite characteristics, which suggest a lack of concern for prosocial conformity. A pooled heritability estimate of .48 for agreeableness is reported by Jang, McCrae, Angleitner, Riemann, and Livesley (1998). Conscientiousness and agreeableness are positively correlated but far from perfectly. A person can be conscientious at work but thoroughly disagreeable otherwise (think of the Machiavellian white-collar criminal), and one can be most agreeable socially but lackadaisical at work (think of Merton's happy-go-lucky anomic ritualist).

From a meta-analysis of personality and antisocial behavior, J. Miller and Lynam (2001) describe the personality of the typical criminal:

> Individuals who commit crimes tend to be hostile, self-centered, spiteful, jealous, and indifferent to others (i.e., low in Agreeableness). They tend to lack ambition, motivation, and perseverance, have difficulty controlling their impulses, and hold nontraditional and unconventional values and beliefs (i.e., are low in Conscientiousness). (p. 780)

J. Miller and Lynam's comparison of 29 prisoner/nonprisoner studies found a weighted mean effect size of −.41 and −.25 for antisocial behavior and agreeableness and conscientiousness, respectively. Another meta-analysis (Saulsman & Page, 2004) examining the relationship between the big five personality traits and each of the behavioral disorders listed in the *Diagnostic and Statistical Manual of Mental Disorders* (*DSM-IV*) found mean effect sizes for antisocial personality disorder over 15 studies of −.35 for agreeableness and −.26 for conscientiousness.

Employers doubtless favor high levels of conscientiousness in their employees and perspective employees because it "affects motivational states and stimulates goal setting and goal commitment" (Schmidt & Hunter, 2004, p. 169). An intergenerational study following subjects from early childhood to retirement, found that conscientiousness measured in childhood predicted adult occupational status ($r = .49$) and income ($r = .41$) in adulthood (Judge, Higgins, Thoresen, & Barrick, 1999). These correlations are slightly less than the correlations between *general mental ability* (GMA) and the same variables (.51 and .53, respectively). Schmidt and Hunter's (2004) analysis of the role GMA and personality variables play in attaining occupational success concluded that "the burden of prediction is borne almost entirely by GMA and conscientiousness" (p. 170).

Anomie, Class, and Criminal Behavior

Anomie/strain theory most clearly draws a straight arrow from social class to crime (Walsh, 2011). Cut to its bare bones, anomie/strain theory maintains that criminal and other antisocial behaviors are rational adaptations to a situation in which American culture exhorts all to achieve monetary success while at the same time its social structure denies access to legitimate means of attaining it to certain groups. The implication is that those who adopt a criminal adaptation are just as talented as those who do not, and would gladly enter the legitimate status game if allowed. The notion that criminal behavior is a rational response of talented people being denied opportunity has lost its cachet among many criminologists. As Vold, Bernard, and Snipes (1998) put it, "Rather, a good deal of research indicates that many delinquents and criminals are untalented individuals who cannot compete effectively in complex industrial societies" (p. 177).

While anomie/strain theory is unambiguously a class-based theory, it never asks what the precursors of social class are. The theory seems to view social class as *sui generis*, an uncaused first cause. This leads to "blaming society" for the emergence of an underclass and its behavior, even though the evidence is overwhelming that in an open society SES is attained by a combination of talent plus effort. To the extent that SES and criminal behavior are linked, both are "caused" by the individual traits and characteristics with which we all enter the status game. Some are advantaged and some disadvantaged by virtue of birth, but advantages can be disregarded and unappreciated, and disadvantages can be overcome by those who refuse to give in to the cult of victimhood so loudly touted by liberal social scientists.

There is still considerable occupational mobility in the United States for bright and ambitious individuals. Hurst's (1995) national intergenerational study found that 51% of sons of lower-manual status fathers achieved higher status, with 22.5% achieving "upper white-collar" status, and that 48% of sons of upper white-collar status fathers had lower status occupations than their fathers, with 17% falling all the way to lower-manual status. Another national study (Rettenmaier, 2003) found that 58% of sons of fathers in the bottom fifth moved up the ladder, with 5% making it to the top fifth, and that 63% of sons of fathers in the top SES fifth moved down the ladder, with 9% falling all the way to the bottom fifth.

There is still some "stickiness" to SES, however, because once a family attains an advantaged class position it is not happy to see its offspring generation relinquish it. As Saunders (2002) explains, "the main 'blockage' in social mobility has less to do with talented lower-class individuals failing to move up the system than with less talented higher-class individuals failing to move down it" (p. 561). While there are few barriers preventing talented children from the lower classes moving up the class ladder, less-than-talented children from the higher classes enjoy a number of safeguards against failure, such as parental support and encouragement and parental influence and contacts. This is surely a positive thing (more "losers" become "winners" than "winners" become "losers").

Still in the anomie/strain tradition, Robert Agnew has moved away from the implicit Mertonian notion that strain impacts individuals in the same social class in more or less similar ways. Agnew asserts that the presence of strain is less important than how one copes with it, which leads naturally to talk of individual traits. The traits that differentiate people who cope poorly from those who cope well include: "temperament, intelligence, creativity, problem-solving skills, interpersonal skills, self-efficacy, and self-esteem. These traits affect the selection of coping strategies by influencing the individual's sensitivity to objective strains and the ability to engage in cognitive, emotional, and behavioral coping" (Agnew, 1992, p. 71). These traits not only help determine how one copes with strain, but for obvious reasons they also help determine the SES level one ultimately achieves, as we have seen.

Agnew (2005) has more recently developed theory that penetrates the biosocial even deeper by integrating concepts from genetics, neuroscience, and evolutionary biology. In his theory, Agnew identifies five life domains—personality, family, school, peers, and work—that interact and feed back on one another across the life span. The theory avers that personality traits set individuals on a particular developmental trajectory that influences how other people in the various social domains react to them in rGE fashion. The theory shows how personality variables "condition" the effect of social variables on criminal behavior; that is, how different personality traits may lead their possessors to react to environment situations in radically different ways (gene × environment interaction).

Agnew identifies the traits of *low self-control* and *irritability* as phenotypic super traits, and which are composites of many endophenotypes such as sensation seeking, impulsivity, poor problem-solving skills, and low empathy. Both low self-control and irritability (a trait psychologists call negative emotionality) are underlain by low serotonergic functioning (Wright & Beaver, 2005) and by prefrontal cortex deficits (Friedman et al., 2008). People with low self-control and irritable temperaments are likely to evoke negative responses from family members, school teachers, peers, and workmates that feed back and exacerbate those tendencies.

This is the so-called multiplier effect in evocative rGE that magnifies (multiplies) what may have initially been an innately weak temperamental or cognitive characteristic into a strong one via social conditioning (Dickens & Flynn, 2001). As Agnew (2005) put it: "Biological factors have a direct affect on irritability/low self-control and an indirect affect on the other life domains through irritability/low self-control" (p. 213). We can readily see how such a personality type would render its possessors less than successful in their personal relationships and in their educational and work endeavors, and how that would result in an undesirable SES.

Regarding SES, Agnew (2005) states that "individuals from low-SES families may be more likely to inherit these traits, as these traits may be more common among low-SES individuals" (p. 143). Low-SES individuals may not only be more likely to inherit irritability/low self-control (or more correctly, the allelic polymorphisms underlying these traits), but are also more likely than higher SES individuals to suffer environmental insults that effect the biological mechanisms associated with these traits such as prenatal exposure to toxic substances, birth complications, and poor maternal health (Walsh & Bolen, 2012).

The Biological Effects of Childhood Poverty

Just as our biology influences the environments we expose ourselves to, our environments influence our biology. Due to space limitations we can only touch on some of these things here (see Walsh & Bolen, 2012, for more complete treatment).

Stress is a functional state of psychophysiological arousal because it focuses on and energizes us to confront the stressor, but toxic levels can lead to the dysregulation of stress mechanisms such as the hypothalamic-pituitary-adrenal (HPA) axis and the autonomic nervous system (Gunnar & Quevedo, 2007). Cortisol is the fuel that energizes our coping mechanisms by increasing vigilance and activity, and is therefore functional within the normal range. But frequent HPA axis arousal may lead to overproduction of cortisol, or *hyper*cortisolism, which leads to anxiety and depressive disorders and is most likely to be found in maltreated females (van Voorhees & Scarpa, 2004). Alternatively, *hypo*cortisolism, is a downward allostatic adjustment to chronic stress that leads to externalizing problems and is most likely to be found in maltreated males. Hypocortisolism signals a low level of anxiety and fear and has been linked to early onset of aggressive antisocial behavior (McBurnett, Lahey, Rathouz, & Loeber, 2000) and to criminal behavior in general (Ellis, 2005).

Exposure to teratogenic chemicals during the early process of brain development is another risk factor in low SES homes. The most common teratogen is alcohol. When pregnant women drink, they introduce their fetuses to neurotoxins that produce a number of neurological disorders, the most serious of which is fetal alcohol syndrome (FAS). FAS affects behavior via its effects on the frontal lobes, amygdala, hippocampus, hypothalamus, the serotonergic system, and the myelination process (Noble, Mayer-Proschel, & Miller, 2005). Because heavy drinking is most prevalent among low-SES women (Casswell, Pledger, & Hooper, 2003), FAS rates are higher in the lower classes. A review of numerous studies by the National Institute of Alcohol Abuse and Alcoholism (May & Gossage, 2008) found an average rate of FAS of about 0.26 per thousand for the middle class and about 3.4 per thousand for the lowest classes, which is about 13 times greater. Developmental deficits associated with FAS are low IQ, hyperactivity, impulsiveness, and poor social, emotional, and moral development, which are also independently related to criminal behavior.

Exposure to lead also has deleterious effects on children's brains, manifested most clearly in their IQs. The IQ decrement per 1 unit increase in μg/dl (micrograms per deciliter of blood) of lead is an average of 0.50 points (Koller, Brown, Spurfeon, & Levy, 2004). Low-SES neighborhoods contain the oldest houses, and the main source of lead exposure today is lead paint dust in older houses. An fMRI study found brain gray matter to be inversely correlated with mean childhood lead concentrations in young Black adults (Cecil et al., 2008). Although the gray matter lost to lead exposure was relatively small (about 1.2%), it was concentrated in the frontal lobes and the anterior cingulate cortex, which are vital behavior moderating areas responsible for executive functioning and mood regulation. Another study examined the relationship between childhood blood lead and verified criminal arrests. The main finding of this study was that after adjusting for relevant covariates, for every 5 μg/dl lead increase there was an increase in the probability of arrest for a violent crime of about 50% (Wright et al., 2008).

Prolonged breastfeeding has many benefits, and increased IQ appears to be one of the most important. In a study of 13,889 Belarusian breastfeeding mothers, a random half of whom were given incentives to encourage prolonged breastfeeding while the half were not, it was found that the children breastfed for 6 months or more had a mean IQ almost 6 points higher than the control group children and received higher academic ratings from teachers (Kramer et al., 2008). The experimental design allowed researchers to measure breastfeeding effects on IQ without any biasing confounds such as the positive relationship between mothers' IQ and the probability of prolonged breastfeeding.

The literature consistently shows a marked downward gradient in the rates of breastfeeding as IQ, income, education, and occupational status fall. Children of lower-class women are thus more likely to be deprived of important evolutionarily experience-expected input. A random sample of 10,519 mothers in California found that the odds of breastfeeding for the women in the highest income category was 3.65 times the odds of the women in the lowest income category (Heck, Braveman, Cubbin, Chavez, & Kelly, 2006).

Conclusion

We have examined the class-crime relationship through a biosocial lens; a lens that allows a magnification factor far more powerful than the structural failure → low SES → crime model favored by traditional criminology. One may sympathize with the sociological notion that society "sets the stage for crime," but crime is committed by flesh and blood human beings with brains, genes, hormones, and an evolutionary history. By integrating robust findings from the hard sciences, we criminologists gain far more insight into human behavior than we do by treating humans as empty vessels into which society pours its prescriptions and proscriptions. Douglas Massey (2004), ex-President of the American Sociological Association, maintains that biosocial analyses are just what the doctor ordered for liberal sociology:

> [B]y understanding and modeling the interaction between social structure and allostasis [hyper- and hypo-cortisolism is an example of the process of allostasis—the achievement of physiological stability through change] social scientists should be able to discredit explanations of racial differences in terms of pure heredity. In an era when scientific understanding is advancing rapidly through interdisciplinary efforts, social scientists in general—and sociologists in particular—must abandon the hostility to biological science and incorporate its knowledge and understanding into their work. (p. 22)

Social scientists have worried themselves silly over the supposed fixity and determinism of biology. This view is bogus and can be rectified by learning something about human biology. A number of natural scientists have made the claim that it is our biology that guarantees our human freedom and agency (e.g., Badcock, 2000). After all, our genes are *our* genes, making us uniquely ourselves and resistant to influences that grate against our natures while constantly extracting information from the environment and manufacturing the proteins we need to navigate it. Rather than viewing biology as a threat to criminology we should welcome it as a very robust ally. The history of physical and natural science demonstrates that the cross-fertilization of concepts, methods, and theories from the more fundamental sciences breed hybrid vigor into their offspring (Walsh, 1997).

References

Agnew, R. (1992). Foundations for a general strain theory of crime and delinquency. *Criminology, 30,* 47–87.

Agnew, R. (2005). *Why do criminals offend? A general theory of crime and delinquency*. Los Angeles, CA: Roxbury.

Badcock, C. (2000). *Evolutionary psychology: A critical introduction*. Cambridge, UK: Polity Press.

Barnett, R., Zimmer, L., & McCormack, J. (1989). P>V sign and personality profiles. *Corrective and Social Psychiatry and Journal of Behavior Technology Methods and Therapy, 35*(1), 18–20.

Beaver, K., Shutt, J., Vaughn, M., DeLisi, M., & Wright, J. (2012). Genetic influences on measures of parental negativity and childhood maltreatment: An exploratory study testing for gene × environment correlations. *Journal of Contemporary Criminal Justice, 28,* 273–292.

Bond, R., & Saunders, P. (1999). Routes of success: Influences on the occupational attainment of young British males. *British Journal of Sociology, 50,* 217–240.

Bouchard, T., Segal, N., Tellegen, A., McGue, M., Keyes, M., & Krueger, R. (2003). Evidence for the construct validity and heritability of the Wilson-Patterson conservatism scale: A reared-apart twins study of social attitudes. *Personality and Individual Differences, 34,* 959–969.

Caspi, A., Bem, D., & Elder, G. (1989). Continuities and consequences of interaction styles across the lifecourse. *Journal of Personality, 57,* 375–406.

Casswell, S., Pledger, M., & Hooper, R. (2003). Socioeconomic status and drinking patterns in young adults. *Addiction, 98,* 601–610.

Cecil K., Brubaker, C., Adler, C., Dietrich, K., Altaye, M., Egelhoff, J., Wessel, S., . . . Lanphear, B. (2008). Decreased brain volume in adults with childhood lead exposure. *PLoS Medicine, 5,* 742–750.

Chamorro-Premuzic, T., & Furnham, A. (2005). Intellectual competence. *Psychologist, 18,* 352–354.

Cleveland, H., Wiebe, R., van den Oord, E., & Rowe, D. (2000). Behavior problems among children from different family structures: The influence of genetic self-selection. *Child Development, 71,* 733–751.

Dickens, W., & Flynn, J. (2001). Heritability estimates versus large environmental effects: The IQ paradox resolved. *Psychological Review, 108*(2), 346–349.

DiRago, A., & Vaillant, G. (2007). Resilience in inner city youth: Childhood predictors of occupational status across the lifespan. *Journal of Youth and Adolescence, 36,* 61–70.

Ellis, L. (1996). A discipline in peril: Sociology's future hinges on curing its biophobia. *American Sociologist, 27,* 21–41.

Ellis, L. (2005). A theory explaining biological correlates of criminality. *European Journal of Criminology, 2,* 287–315.

Ellis, L., & Walsh, A. (2003). Crime, delinquency and intelligence: A review of the worldwide literature. In H. Nyborg (Ed.), *The scientific study of general intelligence* (pp. 343-365). Amsterdam, Holland: Pergamon.

Felson, R. (2001). Blame analysis: Accounting for the behavior of protected groups. In S. Cole (Ed.), *What's wrong with sociology?* (pp. 223–245). New Brunswick, NJ: Transaction.

Fergusson, D., Swain-Campbell, N., & Horwood, J. (2004). How does childhood economic disadvantage lead to crime? *Journal of Child Psychology and Psychiatry, 45,* 956–966.

Friedman, N., Miyake, A., Young, S., DeFries, J., Corely, R., & Hewitt, J. (2008). Individual differences in executive functions are almost entirely genetic in origin. *Journal of Experimental Psychology, 137,* 201–225.

Gatzke-Kopp, L. Raine, A., Loeber, R., Stouthamer-Loeber, M., & Steinhauer, S. (2002). Serious delinquent behavior, sensation seeking, and electrodermal arousal. *Journal of Abnormal Child Psychology, 30,* 477–486.

Gunnar, M., & Quevedo, K. (2007). The neurobiology of stress and development. *Annual Review of Psychology, 58,* 145–173.

Heck, K., Braveman, P., Cubbin, C., Chavez, G., & Kelly, J. (2006). Socioeconomic status and breastfeeding initiation among California mothers. *Public Health Reports, 121,* 51–59.

Herrnstein, R., & Murray, C. (1994). *The bell curve: Intelligence and class structure in American society*. New York, NY: Free Press.

Hurst, C. (1995). *Social inequality: Forms, causes, and consequences*. Boston, MA: Allyn & Bacon.

Jang, K., McCrae, R., Angleitner, A., Riemann, R., & Livesley, W. (1998). Heritability of facet-level traits in a cross-cultural twin sample: Support for a hierarchical model of personality. *Journal of Personality and Social Psychology, 74,* 1556–1565.

Judge, T., Higgins, C., Thoresen, C., & Barrick, M. (1999). The big five personality traits, general mental ability, and career success across the life span. *Personnel Psychology, 52,* 621–652.

Kaufman, A. (1976). Verbal-performance IQ discrepancies on the WISC-R. *Journal of Counseling and Clinical Psychology, 44,* 739–744.

Kemper, T. (1994). Social stratification, testosterone, and male sexuality. In L. Ellis (Ed.), *Social stratification and socioeconomic inequality: Reproductive and interpersonal aspects of dominance and status* (Vol. 2, pp. 47–61). Westport, CT: Greenwood.

Kingston, P. (2006). How meritocratic is the United States? *Research in Social Stratification and Mobility, 24,* 111–130.

Koller, K., Brown, T., Spurfeon, A., & Levy, L. (2004). Recent developments in low-level lead exposure and intellectual impairment in children. *Environmental Health Perspectives, 112,* 987–994.

Kramer, M., Aboud, F., Mironova, E., Vanilovich, I., Platt, R., Matush, L., Igumnov, S., . . . Shapiro, S., for the Promotion of Breastfeeding Intervention Trial (PROBIT) Study Group. (2008). Breastfeeding and child cognitive development: New evidence from a large randomized trial. *Archives of General Psychiatry, 65,* 578–584.

Lodi-Smith, J., & Roberts, B. (2007). Social investment and personality: A meta-analytic analysis of the relationship of personality traits to investment in work, family, religion, and volunteerism. *Personality and Social Psychology Review, 11,* 68–86.

Lubinski, D. (2004). Introduction to the special section on cognitive abilities: 100 years after Spearman's (1904) 'General intelligence,' objectively determined and measured. *Journal of Personality and Social Psychology, 86,* 96–111.

Massey, D. (2004). Segregation and stratification: A biosocial perspective. *Du Bois Review, 1,* 7–25.

May, P., & Gossage, P. (2008). *Estimating the prevalence of fetal alcohol syndrome: A summary.* National Institute of Alcohol Abuse and Alcoholism. National Institute of Health. Retrieved from http://pubs.niaaa.nih.gov/publications/arh25-3/159-167.htm

McBurnett, K., Lahey, B., Rathouz, P., & Loeber, R. (2000). Low salivary cortisol and persistent aggression in boys referred for disruptive behavior. *Archives of General Psychiatry, 57,* 38–43.

Messner, S., & Rosenfeld, R. (2001). *Crime and the American Dream* (3rd ed.). Belmont, CA: Wadsworth.

Miller, J., & Lynam, D. (2001). Structural models of personality and their relation to antisocial behavior: A meta-analytic review. *Criminology, 39,* 765–798.

Miller, L. (1987). Neuropsychology of the aggressive psychopath: An integrative review. *Aggressive Behavior, 13,* 119–140.

Moffitt, T. (1993). Adolescent-limited and life-course-persistent antisocial behavior: A developmental taxonomy. *Psychological Review, 100,* 674–701.

Nettle, D. (2003). Intelligence and class mobility in the British population. *British Journal of Psychology, 94,* 551–561.

Neubauer, A., & Fink, A. (2009). Intelligence and neural efficiency. *Neuroscience and Biobehavioral* Reviews, *33,* 1004–1023.

Nielsen, F. (2006). Achievement and ascription in educational attainment: Genetic and environmental influences on adolescent schooling. *Social Forces, 85,* 193–216.

Noble, M., Mayer-Proschel, M., & Miller, R. (2005). The oligodendrocyte. In M. Rao, & M. Jacobson (Eds.), *Developmental neurobiology* (pp. 151–196). New York, NY: Kluwer/Plenum.

Pinker, S. (2002). *The blank slate: The modern denial of human nature.* New York, NY: Viking.

Rank, M., Yoon, H., & Hirschl, T. (2003). American poverty as a structural failing: Evidence and arguments. *Journal of Sociology and Social Welfare, 30,* 3–29.

Rettenmaier, A. (2003). *Economic mobility.* Dallas, TX: National Center for Policy Analysis.

Rothbart, M. (2007). Temperament, development, and personality. *Current Directions in Psychological Science, 16,* 207–212.

Rubenstein, D. (1992). Structural explanation in sociology: The egalitarian imperative. *American Sociologist, 23,* 5–19.

Sampson, R. (2000). Whither the sociological study of crime? *Annual Review of Sociology, 26,* 711–714.

Sanson, A., Hemphill, S., & Smart, D. (2004). Connections between temperament and social development: A review. *Social Development, 13,* 142–170.

Saudino, K. (2005). Behavioral genetics and child temperament. *Journal of Developmental and Behavioral Pediatrics, 26,* 214–223.

Saulsman, L., & Page, A. (2004). The five-factor model and personality disorder empirical literature: A meta-analytic review. *Clinical Psychology Review, 23,* 1055–1085.

Saunders, P. (2002). Reflections on the meritocratic debate in Britain in response to Richard Breen and John Goldthorpe. *British Journal of Sociology, 53,* 559–574.

Sawhill, I., & Morton, J. (2007). *Economic mobility: Is the American Dream alive and well?* Washington, DC: The Economic Mobility Project/Pew Charity Trusts.

Schmalleger, F. (2004). *Criminology today.* Upper Saddle River, NJ: Prentice Hall.

Schmidt, F., & Hunter, K. (2004). General mental ability in the world of work: Occupational attainment and job performance. *Journal of Personality and Social Psychology, 86,* 162–173.

Schwalbe, M., Goodwin, S., Holden, D., Schrock, D., Thompson, S., & Wolkomer, M. (2000). Generic processes in the reproduction of inequality: An interactionist analysis. *Social Forces, 79,* 419–452.

van Voorhees, E., & Scarpa, A. (2004). The effects of child maltreatment on the hypothalamic-pituitary-adrenal axis. *Trauma, Violence, and Abuse, 5,* 333–352.

Vold, G., Bernard, T., & Snipes, J. (1998). *Theoretical criminology.* New York, NY: Oxford University Press.

Walsh, A. (1997). Methodological individualism and vertical integration in the social sciences. *Behavior and Philosophy, 25,* 121–136.

Walsh, A. (2003). Intelligence and antisocial behavior. In A. Walsh & L. Ellis (Eds.), *Biosocial criminology: Challenging environmentalism's supremacy* (pp. 105–124). Hauppauge, NY: Nova Science.

Walsh, A. (2011). *Social class and crime: A biosocial approach.* New York, NY: Routledge.

Walsh, A., & Bolen, J. (2012). *The neurobiology of criminal behavior: Gene-brain-culture interaction.* Farnham, UK: Ashgate.

Wechsler, D. (1958). *The measurement and appraisal of adult intelligence.* Baltimore, MD: Williams and Wilkin.

Wright, J., & Beaver, K. (2005). Do parents matter in creating self-control in their children? A genetically informed test of Gottfredson and Hirschi's theory of low self-control. *Criminology, 43,* 1169–1202.

Wright, J., Boisvert, D., Dietrich, K., & Ris, M. (2009). The ghost in the machine and criminal behavior: Criminology for the 21st century. In A. Walsh & K. Beaver (Eds.), *Biosocial criminology: New directions in theory and research* (pp. 73–89). New York, NY: Routledge.

Wright, J., Dietrich, K., Ris, M., Hornung, R., Wessel, S., & Lanphear, B. (2008). Association of prenatal and childhood blood lead concentrations with criminal arrests in early childhood. *PLoS Medicine, 5,* 732–740.

Discussion Questions

CHAPTERS 5 AND 6

1. Criminologists recognize social class as a key correlate to crime, as evident in the field's theoretical and empirical work. How does criminological theory link social class to crime? Are individual characteristics considered when explaining the SES-crime relationship? Does research support a "purely" sociological explanation for the relationship between social class and crime?
2. Individual SES has traditionally been predicted by family income in criminological research. Describe the downfalls to using parental SES for predicting individual SES. Can IQ be used as a valid measure to predict SES? What does the available evidence indicate about the relationship between IQ and social class?
3. As noted by Drs. Walsh, Taylor, and Yun, individuals with temperament problems find it difficult to form social bonds. However, social control theorists suggest low SES directly influences social bond formation. What does the available research indicate about the relationship between temperament and SES? In other words, once we take into account more specific factors associated with both SES and criminality, does the SES-crime correlation disappear?
4. Some criminologists have argued that aspects of SES are influential for creating criminality, such as impeding important life events that influence later involvement in crime. Discuss the ways in which childhood poverty may influence biology and thus lead to criminal behavior. Which environmental factors yield the strongest effects on biology?
5. Traditional anomie/strain theorists believe inequality contributes to feelings of strain, thus leading to criminal behavior. Describe some of the traits that differentiate people who cope poorly or well with feelings of strain. In your opinion, are these traits important for explaining criminal behavior?
6. Discuss the limitations of assuming "social injustices" to be the cause of crime. Given the available research, can we completely rule out the role of the individual when studying crime causation? In the future, do you envision a change in the climate surrounding the study of the SES-crime relationship?

PART II

THEORETICAL PERSPECTIVES

7

Learning Theories of Crime

Promises and Potential

Jonathan R. Brauer
University of Nebraska at Omaha

Jonathan D. Bolen
University of Nebraska at Omaha

A Brief History of Learning Theories of Crime

In 1939, Edwin Sutherland advanced criminological theory by presenting an explicit statement of differential association theory in the third edition of his *Principles of Criminology* textbook. Dissatisfied with the fragmented multiple factor explanations that were common in American criminology at the time, Sutherland developed the principles of differential association with the goal of providing a general theory that promised to explain all known patterns of crime (Sutherland, 1973). The basic premise was attractively simple; he posited that criminal behavior, like all human behavior, is learned via communication and interaction within social groups. Differential association theory was not the first general social theory to depict crime as learned behavior—in the late 19th century, French sociologist Gabriel Tarde (1903/1962) postulated that criminal behaviors are learned through a general process of behavioral imitation (see also Rafter, 2011). However, the original statement of differential association theory and its later refinements (e.g., Sutherland, 1947, 1973; Sutherland & Cressey, 1966) now constitute one of the most well-known, oft-tested, and widely supported theories of crime (Akers, 2009; Matsueda, 1988).

Differential association theory (DAT) assumes that societies contain conflicting normative codes and that individuals learn specific values primarily though frequent interactions within salient social groups. The theory posits that the likelihood of an individual engaging in criminal and deviant behaviors depends on the relative exposure to social patterns that are favorable versus unfavorable to law violating behavior. Associations with criminal patterns are expected to result in the learning of specific techniques and skills necessary to engage in crime and in learning crime-favorable cognitive definitions, which include motives, drives, or rationalizations that define crime as appropriate in certain situations. Individuals who commit crime, then, presumably have learned requisite techniques and an excess of definitions marking criminal behavior as appropriate in certain situations, through frequent exposure to salient criminal patterns (Sutherland & Cressey, 1966).

Robert Burgess and Ronald Akers (1966) later developed a differential association-reinforcement theory by integrating Sutherland's nine principles with operant learning mechanisms found in behavioral psychology. Their efforts embraced Sutherland's primary theoretical contributions while also addressing criticisms that DAT failed to specify the precise mechanisms underlying the learning of definitions (Burgess & Akers, 1966; see also Akers, 2009, pp. 6–12; Sutherland & Cressey, 1966, pp. 93–94). This work marked another significant advancement in criminological theory, as Akers's continued efforts to refine and test the theory over the next few decades ultimately culminated in the formal development of a general social learning theory of crime and deviance (Akers, 1973, 2009). Today, Akers's social learning theory is one of the most frequently cited by scholars as their favored theory in criminology (Cooper, Walsh, & Ellis, 2010), and it appears to be as oft-tested and as widely supported as its predecessor (Akers, 2009, pp. 110–117; Akers & Jensen, 2006).

Like DAT, social learning theory (SLT) asserts that individuals are more likely to commit crime when they associate with criminal patterns and when they learn cognitive definitions favorable to crime. However, SLT expanded on DAT's nebulous specification of learning mechanisms by claiming that individuals learn through a process of differential reinforcement. Differential reinforcement learning involves experiencing direct and vicarious punishments and rewards as consequences for a given behavior. Subsequently, accumulated experience with rewards and punishments for specific behaviors (e.g., crimes) results in the formation of cognitive definitions. These definitions represent the cognitive "residues of past reinforcements" (Bandura, 1995, p. 179; see also Brauer, 2009) and serve to cue potential behaviors as rewarding or punishing, thereby aiding individuals in discriminating among the potential consequences of various action alternatives and in generalizing past consequences to similar behavioral alternatives (Akers, 2009, pp. 84–87). Thus, SLT posits that future criminal behavior is selected based primarily on the history of direct and vicarious experiences with consequences for crime and, derivatively, on the cognitive perception and evaluation of potential consequences associated with various action alternatives.

Specifying Linkages Between Social Relationships and Crime

The basic premises found in learning theories of crime are supported by decades of research that documents robust empirical linkages between one's own criminal behaviors and those of one's intimate associates (for reviews, see Akers, 2009; Akers & Jensen, 2006, pp. 37–76; Brauer & Tittle, 2012; Pratt et al., 2010). However, recent research on social relationships and crime raises intriguing questions and challenges about whether the real or perceived behaviors of intimate associates actually do influence individuals' law violating behaviors, and if they do, precisely why and how.

BEYOND SALIENCY AND INTERCHANGEABILITY OF PARENTS AND PEERS

Early work on socialization and crime focused almost exclusively on establishing an empirical connection between adolescent behaviors and the attitudes or behaviors of parents and peers (e.g., Jensen, 1972; Matsueda, 1982; Warr, 1993, 2002). Contemporary scholarship turned attention to the relative importance of these social domains, with numerous scholars investigating whether parents' or peers' behaviors are more salient in influencing adolescent delinquency (Aseltine, 1995; Bao, Has, Chen, & Pi, 2012; Huizinga, Weiher, Espiritu, & Esbensen, 2003; Johnson & Menard, 2012). Recently, scholars have begun to challenge implicit assumptions about the interchangeability of various sources of social influence in prior literature (Brauer & De Coster, 2012; Giordano, 2003; Lonardo, Giordano, Longmore, & Manning, 2009). For instance, some scholars have suggested that parental and peer relationships are fundamentally different and, as a result, may influence youths' delinquency in qualitatively different ways (Brauer & De Coster, 2012; Giordano, 2003). In addition, a growing body of work has documented the importance of considering romantic partners as a unique source of social influence during adolescence and of conceptualizing specific influences (e.g., parents, peers, and partners) as part of larger social networks characterized by varying degrees of normative heterogeneity within which adolescents are enmeshed (Giordano, 2003; Haynie, 2002; Haynie, Giordano, Manning, & Longmore, 2005; Lonardo et al., 2009).

Taken together, these studies highlight the importance of carefully examining not only *who* is influencing whom, but also *how* and *under what conditions* when investigating socialization processes. In addition, they provide models for expanding on the typical conceptualization and operationalization of social influence processes. Finally, they demonstrate the utility of attempting to capture an individual's entire social network when measuring differential associations. The latter contribution is particularly noteworthy given that most work cited as supportive of social learning theory focuses solely on associations with delinquent peers, while failing to capture other relevant associations (Brauer & Tittle, 2012; Pratt et al., 2010).

TRANSCENDING THE SELECTION VERSUS SOCIALIZATION DEBATE

The overwhelming focus on peer influence processes is not surprising given the vast body of work marking criminal peer associations as one of the strongest correlates of individual criminality. However, many scholars have called into question whether this correlation reflects the processes outlined in learning theories or, instead, reflects alternative theoretical processes (e.g., Agnew, 1995; Gottfredson & Hirschi, 1990; Warr, 2002, pp. 45–89). For instance, Haynie and Osgood (2005) suggest that the empirical linkage between criminal peer associations and individual crime instead might reflect increased opportunities resulting from unstructured socializing. They contend that even associating with nondelinquent peers, if occurring frequently in unsupervised contexts, may promote individual criminal behavior by increasing experiences with situations conducive to delinquency (see also Osgood & Anderson, 2004). Alternatively, correlations between criminal peer associations and individual offending may reflect general group homophily processes (Kandel, 1978) or other social selection processes, such as individuals seeking out delinquent subcultures in an attempt to cope with outside stress or manage stigmatization (Braithwaite, 1989; Hagan, 1997).

Most scholarly attention on this topic has focused on the selection versus socialization debate. Akers (1999) has aptly characterized this debate as one of "dueling folk sayings" (p. 480), in which scholars aim to determine whether similarities between peers' behaviors and one's own behaviors reflect "birds of a feather flocking together" (selection) or, instead, are due to individuals "laying down with dogs and getting up with fleas" (socialization). Furthermore, this debate often is framed as a competition between learning theories and rival control theories that advocate for selection arguments (e.g., Knecht, Snijders, Baerveldt, Steglich, & Raub, 2010). For instance, Gottfredson and Hirschi (1990) suggest that the oft-cited link between delinquent peer association and individual crime is likely due to "faulty measurement and the tendency of people to seek the company of others like themselves" (p. 156). They also assert that peers only broaden the abilities of already delinquent individuals by enabling criminal behaviors that would be "too difficult or dangerous to do alone" (p. 159), thus denying associates any initial causal power over an individual's own delinquency.

Research on this topic primarily consists of attempts to decompose empirical correlations between peer associations and individual criminality into group selection or social influence processes. Overall, research findings on this topic are mixed, with most studies concluding that both selection and socialization processes are at work (e.g., Baerveldt, Völker, & Van Rossem, 2008; Gordon et al., 2004; Kandel, 1978; Matsueda & Anderson, 1998; but see Knecht et al., 2010; Weerman, 2011). Also, several scholars have documented important ways that parents influence their children's friendship selections (Kandel, 1996; Snyder, Dishion, & Patterson, 1986; Warr, 1993), and some find evidence that delinquent group formation might by triggered by labeling processes that accompany formal sanctioning (Bernburg, Krohn, & Rivera, 2006). Still others point out that delinquent group formation may occur from proximity selection and other general mechanisms occurring in social networks (Weerman, 2011).

Akers notes that extant research findings on this topic are consistent with social learning theory's premises, because the theory accounts for dynamic and reciprocal relationships between peers' and individuals' behaviors (Akers, 2009, pp. 53–6, 117–126). Even so, we believe that learning theories would benefit from focused efforts to specify and integrate the precise mechanisms by which individuals select into delinquent peer groups, including those suggested by Hagan (1997), Braithwaite (1989), and others (e.g., Bernburg et al., 2006; Weerman, 2011). In addition, efforts should be devoted to examining alternative social influence processes that might account for empirical linkages between criminal associations and individual behavior and, where appropriate, toward systematically integrating new insights within the general learning theory framework. For example, Haynie and Osgood's (2005) contention that unstructured socializing promotes delinquency by increasing situational opportunities seems consistent with discussions of opportunity's role in DAT (e.g., Sutherland, 1973, pp. 13–29) and with the peer influence processes outlined in SLT (Akers & Jensen, 2006, pp. 44–45). Put simply, in measuring time spent in "unstructured socializing" with peers, researchers might be parsimoniously capturing the frequency of youth's experiences with situations in which opportunities for delinquency abound, in which few potentially punishing constraints on behavior exist, and in which criminal behaviors are most likely to be modeled and socially rewarded. The power of their insights, then, may not rest in providing an alternative theory but instead in providing a crucial impetus for directly measuring alternative theoretical mechanisms (e.g., learning vs. opportunity mechanisms) and for specifying the precise conditions under which peer associations are most likely to result in criminal behavior.

PERCEPTIONS AND THE (MIS)MEASUREMENT OF OTHERS

While numerous scholars have charged learning theories with offering inadequate explanations for group selection processes (e.g., Glueck & Glueck, 1950, p. 164; Gottfredson & Hirschi, 1990, pp. 154–159; Hirschi, 1969, pp. 136–137), these critiques have resurfaced with renewed vigor amid accumulated findings from social network research examining links between differential peer association and delinquency. Specifically, an emerging body of network research suggests that widespread reliance on self-reports to measure the criminality of one's associates in tests of learning theories may have resulted in frequent overestimation of socialization effects due to respondents' tendencies to misperceive or misreport the delinquency of peers (e.g., Aseltine, 1995; Boman, Krohn, Gibson, & Stogner, 2012; Haynie & Osgood, 2005; Young, Barnes, Meldrum, &Weerman, 2011). Such findings were presaged by symbolic interaction theorists who recognized the power found in (mis)perception, parsimoniously summarized by Thomas and Thomas's (1928) well-known theorem: "If men define situations as real, they are real in their consequences" (p. 572). Drawing from symbolic interactionism, learning theories assert that perceptions of others' behaviors should be expected to be more influential than associates' actual behaviors in explaining crime. For instance, Akers (2009) points to research in the areas of deterrence and strain to bolster claims that behavior matches subjective perceptions of legal consequences and blocked opportunities more closely than objective reality (p. 119). Thus, perception is at the theoretical core of SLT, and inaccurate as perceptions may be, personal accounts of the behavior of associates remain crucially informative in understanding individuals' decisions to engage in or refrain from crime.

Nonetheless, the emerging scholarship on misperceptions (e.g., Boman et al., 2012; Young et al., 2011) holds great promise for advancing learning theories. Methodologically, research on this topic may be able to specify the conditions under which self-reports might be used as accurate proxies for peers' actual behaviors. Theoretically, this line of inquiry may prove useful in illuminating the processes underlying the formation of cognitive perceptions. As we discuss in more detail in the next section, the question of how individuals develop cognitive perceptions concerning crime is essential to the theorizing of both Sutherland and Akers, and it remains highly relevant to the future development of learning theories.

Clarifying the Nature and Function of Cognitions

By reserving a central role for perception and cognition in the genesis of crime, sociological learning theories portray criminal offenders, like all humans, as thinking beings who actively consider whether to refrain from or engage in law violation. Cognitions, or cognitive "definitions," are more than epiphenomenal remnants of the products of a history of interactions with social and nonsocial environments; they also presumably allow individuals to self-regulate behavior by evaluating, defining, or cuing criminal behavior as acceptable or unacceptable, as appropriate or inappropriate, or as rewarding or punishing, in general and in specific situations (Akers, 2009, pp. 77–87; Sutherland, 1973, p. 23). Furthermore, the emphasis on cognition and human agency in sociological learning theories of crime is rooted in insights from symbolic interactionism and is primarily what distinguishes these theories from early mechanistic versions of classical and operant behaviorism in psychology (Akers, 2009, pp. 85–87; see also Akers, 1990; Bandura, 1989).

ALTERNATIVE INTERPRETATIONS OF COGNITIVE DEFINITIONS

Numerous studies find that the empirical relationship between criminal peer association and individual law violation is mediated at least partly by definitions favorable to crime, supporting the assertion that cognitive definitions are learned via differential associations and that they subsequently influence offending decisions (e.g., Heimer & De Coster, 1999; Jensen, 1972; Matsueda, 1982; Tittle, Burke, & Jackson, 1986; Warr & Stafford, 1991). However, learning theories are not alone in staking claim to supportive research on cognitive definitions. For instance, some scholars posit that definitions of the wrongfulness of criminal behavior play a causal role in law violation by acting as situational neutralizations that temporarily free an individual from the moral constraints of conventional norms (Sykes & Matza, 1957), or as moral rules that preclude crimes from consideration as action alternatives (Wikström, 2006). Others downplay any potential causal role of cognitive definitions, instead suggesting that they reflect post hoc rationalizations or accounts of behavior (Scott & Lyman, 1968), or that they merely serve as indicators of an individual's bond to society by tapping the strength of beliefs in the moral validity of the law (Hirschi, 1969).

Akers's (2009) conceptualization of cognitive definitions in social learning theory appears to encompass all these meanings and functions, while he further stipulates that cognitive definitions also operate as discriminative stimuli cuing certain behaviors as rewarding or punishing (pp. 77–87). However, it remains unclear whether, or under what conditions, cognitive definitions should *cause* individual behavior as suggested by learning theories, rather than spuriously reflect post hoc interpretations of behavior or other processes (e.g., Heimer & Matsueda, 1994; Sampson, 1999, p. 440; Scott & Lyman, 1968; Tittle et al., 1986, p. 425). Further, if cognitive definitions cause crime, it is unclear whether, or under what conditions, they do so by temporarily allowing otherwise morally constrained behavior (Sykes & Matza, 1957), by limiting action alternatives (Wikström, 2006), or by motivating or signaling behavior as appropriate or rewarding (Akers, 2009; Sutherland, 1947).

Thus, although breadth is often viewed as a strength of theory (Tittle, 1995), in this case, a broad conceptualization of cognitive definitions seems to be bought at the price of theoretical precision. We believe that additional theoretical clarification concerning the precise nature and function of various cognitive definitions is required to advance learning theory's predictive and explanatory utility. Fortunately, scholarship in motivational psychology, cognitive and behavioral psychology, and criminology offers a springboard for such efforts.

NORMATIVE INTERNALIZATION AND SELF-REGULATED CONFORMITY

Social theorists long have presumed that individual actions are influenced by internalized social norms or an internal moral conscience (e.g., Campbell, 1964;

Durkheim, 1961; Etzioni, 1988, 2000; Parsons, 1951; Wrong, 1961). Akers' formulation of SLT extended prior theorizing by identifying precise mechanisms through which internalization or moral socialization presumably occurs. Specifically, SLT contends that normative values and moral rules represent cognitive definitions that "are developed through imitation and differential reinforcement" (Akers, 2009, p. 84). Furthermore, cognitive definitions frequently are described as discriminative stimuli cuing behaviors as rewarding or punishing, or as an additional internal reward or cost attached to behavior (e.g., Akers, 2009, pp. 50, 62, 80, 84–85, 98–100). Few direct tests of these propositions have been conducted in criminology (Brauer & Tittle, 2012), though there is some evidence supporting the contention that cognitive definitions concerning crime are developed through a process of differential reinforcement (Tittle, Antonaccio, & Botchkovar, 2012).

However, SLT's implication that human cognition and action largely reflect instrumental learning processes is only partially congruent with recent perspectives in psychology concerning intrinsic motivation and human development. For instance, consistent with SLT, self-determination theorists (Deci & Ryan, 1985, 1987, 2000; Grolnick, 2003) agree that reinforcement and punishment contingencies are effective in controlling behavior in the short term and that these operant conditioning processes often form the basis for internalized values and subsequent autonomous self-regulation. However, these theorists warn that attempting to control individual behavior by altering reward and punishment contingencies results in a form of contingency-dependent, controlled compliance that is unlikely to be maintained in the absence of anticipated rewards or punishments. They also caution that manipulating rewards and costs in an attempt to control behavior may result in unintended consequences. For instance, such behavioral control attempts may be perceived as a challenge to autonomy and therefore may be met with defiance. Additionally, reliance on rewards and punishments to control behavior may undermine one's inner motivation or capacity for autonomous self-regulation. In contrast, self-regulated behavioral conformity is not posited as contingent on anticipated external consequences of behavior; rather, it is presumably motivated by an internalized desire to conform that should continue to be present even in contexts where anticipated rewards for deviance are salient and expected punishments are scarce (Deci & Ryan, 1987).

Self-determination theory, which enjoys much empirical support (for reviews, see Deci & Ryan, 1987; Grolnick, 2003; Ryan, Deci, Grolnick, & LaGuardia, 2006), challenges the strict instrumental depictions of human cognition found in operant and cognitive learning theories. The theory portrays individuals' decisions to conform as reflecting more than a hedonic calculus in which each individual weighs that which he or she stands to lose or to gain—rather, long-term conformity (unlike short-term compliance) also presumably reflects one's identity or one's sense of self. In fact, behaviors regulated by reward and punishment contingencies may even rely on different neural mechanisms than those governing self-regulation via internalized norms or self-identity (Ryan & Deci, 2006).

Interestingly, self-determination theory's descriptions of internalization and autonomous self-regulation processes are consistent with earlier sociological depictions of cognitive definitions as reflecting internalized social norms that constitute a central part of the self (Campbell, 1964; Etzioni, 1988; Grasmick & Green, 1980, pp. 327–328; Wrong, 1961, pp. 186). Further, the theory's contention that reward and punishment contingencies may be less important to human behavior after the successful internalization of normative values also is compatible with recent developments in cognitive and behavioral psychology, which depict human behavior as governed largely by cognitions or "verbal rules" rather than as directly controlled by operant contingencies (e.g., Hayes, Blackledge, & Barnes-Holmes, 2001; Stewart, Barnes-Holmes, Barnes-Holmes, Bond, & Hayes, 2006). That is, cognitive rules, once learned, presumably continue to shape behaviors despite later changes in reinforcement contingencies (see also Brauer, 2009, p. 957).

Thus, current advancements in psychology seem to suggest that cognitive definitions are more than epiphenomenal remnants of differential reinforcement histories or subjective evaluations of the expected utility of action alternatives. Rather, cognitions also appear to tap an individual's relatively stable sense of self. It is important to note that these insights are compatible with sociology's symbolic interaction paradigm (for summaries, see Matsueda, 1992; Matsueda & Heimer, 1997), and with learning theories as well, since symbolic interactionism was central to both Sutherland's and Akers's theoretical formulations (see Akers, 2009, pp. 10–11, 43–44, 85–86). However, DAT offers ambiguous statements about the processes by which internalization occurs and about the nature and function of cognitions. In contrast, SLT provides thorough discussions of cognitions as reflecting instrumental learning processes, yet offers relatively little theoretical development concerning potential noninstrumental processes governing normative internalization and conforming behavior.

SLT's emphasis on instrumental rationality in explaining human cognition and action may have emerged in response to criticisms charging learning theories with portraying human action as an unthinking product of perfect socialization, and thereby with denying human agency (see Akers, 2009, pp. 90–106). Alternatively, instrumental interpretations of human cognition may be a logical inevitability of granting a central role to operant conditioning processes (Akers, 1990). Interestingly, Akers (2009) notes that in developing SLT over the years, he has shifted farther away from strict operant interpretations while simultaneously giving a greater role "to direct cognitive processes more in line with symbolic interactionism in sociology and the social behaviorism of Bandura and others in psychology" (p. 11). We argue that additional theoretical elaboration and a greater shift in emphasis may be necessary—farther away from the instrumental interpretations of human cognition found in operant behaviorism, and toward interpretations of internalization processes found in symbolic interactionism and in classical sociological theorizing on the development of morality. In the following sections, we offer some suggestions concerning how this might be done.

COGNITIONS MARKING MORALITY AND EXPECTED UTILITY

Several theorists assert that moral beliefs and instrumental concerns affect behavior in qualitatively different ways, with moral beliefs taking primacy by dominating considerations of relative utility or by limiting which action alternatives enter into cognitive deliberation (e.g., Etzioni, 1988; Tyler, 2010; Wikström, 2006). Also, recent research corroborates these claims that cognitions tapping morality and expected utility influence individuals' criminal offending decisions in unique ways (Kroneberg, Heintze, & Mehlkop, 2010; Tittle, Antonacio, Botchkovar, & Kranidioti, 2010). Since adequate clarification of the precise nature and function of various cognitions is a daunting task for learning theorists, we believe that a useful first step might be to formally distinguish between *moral definitions*, or evaluations of the wrongfulness of criminal behaviors, and *instrumental definitions*, or anticipated consequences of criminal behaviors (for a similar argument, see Tittle et al., 2012, p. 881; see also Campbell's [1964] distinction between cognitions reflecting internalization vs. identification processes).

After formalizing this distinction, elaboration on the potential causal linkages between definitions marking morality and definitions summarizing subjective expected utility, and among these cognitive constructs and the other concepts in the theory, will be required. Furthermore, learning theories would be enriched by explicit consideration of the potentially unique cognitive processes governing morally based actions, instrumentally guided actions, and other types of social actions (e.g., Weber, 1978, pp. 22–26). For instance, integrating insights from self-determination theory, moral definitions might be more closely linked to long-term conformity because these cognitions presumably reflect a process of reflexive deliberation and willful assent to social rules. Alternatively, instrumental definitions might be a better predictor of short-term "controlled" compliance, while perhaps cuing normative defiance under some conditions (e.g., when control structures are perceived as coercive or illegitimate), and particularly when instrumental cognitions conflict with one's moral beliefs.

TOWARD AN ADEQUATE THEORY OF THE SELF

While distinguishing between qualitatively different types of definitions might be a useful first step, we believe a coherent theory of the self is required before sociological learning theories can adequately clarify the roles that cognitions play in governing criminal actions. Giordano and colleagues' (Giordano, Cernkovich, & Holland, 2003; Giordano, Cernkovich, & Rudolph, 2002; Giordano, Cernkovich, & Schroeder, 2007) symbolic interaction perspectives on crime might prove useful in shifting from piecemeal depictions of the learned or internalized content of actors' cognitions and toward the development of a more complete theoretical model of the cognitive and emotional "self." These authors describe an actor-centered process of cognitive transformation in which one works to change one's life by purposively abandoning previous habits and perspectives in favor of new ones. They note how "hooks for change" (Giordano et al., 2002, p. 992) act as cues to an individual for a fundamental departure from a previous version of self, not merely a recalibration of potential punishments and rewards. Furthermore, Giordano and colleagues' (2007) work offers insights into how broader structural arrangements might influence cognitive and emotional transformation and, likewise, criminal maintenance and desistance processes.

Our suggestion to develop a more sophisticated theory of the self is compatible with earlier attempts to expand on the learning theory framework through systematic integration of insights from symbolic interactionism (Glaser, 1956; Matsueda, 1992; Matsueda & Heimer, 1997). In addition, this suggestion overlaps with other recent efforts to improve criminology's self-control theory (E. Silver & Ulmer, 2012) and to enrich network sociology (D. Silver & Lee, 2012). At the very least, discussions of various symbolic concepts in these works, such as "future selves" or "idealized selves," "feared selves," "identification," and "reflected appraisals," might be useful in rekindling critical dialogue about whether and how to substitute common *behavioral* interpretations of self-reported cognitive "learning" measures, including personal evaluations of behaviors and anticipated social reactions, with *cognitive* interpretations of these common measures. We view such dialogue as especially important given recent trends in criminology to eschew "subjective" perceptual, and hence cognitive or symbolic, measures in favor of "objective" (or, perhaps more accurately, "intersubjective" other-reported) behavioral measures (e.g., Boman et al., 2012; Haynie & Osgood, 2005).

Furthermore, these works could motivate much-needed elaboration on the linkages between social structural arrangements and individual-level learning processes. Scholarship on the structural implications of learning theory is relatively scarce, yet recent findings appear promising for the theory (e.g., Kobayashi, Akers, & Sharp, 2011; Lanza-Kaduce & Capece, 2003; Tittle et al., 2012; but see Orcutt & Schwabe, 2012). However, Giordano and colleagues' (2007) work among many others not reviewed here (cf., discussions of the development of *social schemas:* Simons & Burt, 2011; *defiant individualism:* Sanchez-Jankowski, 1991; *code of the street:* Anderson, 1999) provides useful insights into how specific structural arrangements, such as poverty, concentrated disadvantage, coercion, and chronic victimization, might result in the formation of identities, patterned cognitions, or worldviews that promote crime. Finally, we hope that systematic integration of insights from these various works might imbue sociological learning theories with a more complete portrait of the self—one that recognizes human actors' differential—and structurally shaped—abilities to reflexively monitor and evaluate their own actions, relationships, and life trajectories, envisaging themselves as different people, with different reward and punishment regimens, different goals and purposes, and different environments and social networks, and at times making laborious cognitive and emotional choices toward these new identities.

Conclusion: Moving From Promises to Potential

Sociological learning theories of crime have witnessed significant growth over the past century, offering comprehensive and dynamic explanations for crime that potentially account for stability and change in individual offending and for structural variations in rates of crime. These theories have been tested extensively in various contexts, accumulated much empirical support, and produced countless practical insights concerning the nature and causes of criminal behavior. In this chapter, we argue that these theories boast more potential for growth that can be realized through focused theoretical refinement and empirical attention.

We contend that learning theories can be strengthened by clarifying and expanding on the hypothesized mechanisms through which social interactions presumably influence criminal behaviors. Specifically, we suggest that scholars move beyond simple explorations of the similarities between individuals' behaviors and those of parents and peers. Rather, additional efforts geared toward investigating the potential uniqueness of various social relationships, exploring the consequences of being embedded in (or isolated from) diverse social networks, and identifying specific social selection processes might improve theoretical precision and outline important scope conditions for the theory. Additionally, expanding on recent efforts to identify the extent of (mis)match between individual perceptions of others' offending behaviors and others' own self-reported criminal involvement might lead to greater elucidation of the processes by which cognitive perceptions are formed and subsequently influence behavior.

We also maintain that learning theories would benefit from further theoretical clarification concerning the nature and function of cognitive definitions. Formal distinctions between potentially unique types, including moral versus instrumental definitions, may prove useful as an initial step. However, we contend that learning theories ultimately will require a more inclusive theoretical vision of the self if they are to adequately portray the importance of human cognition to criminal offending. To these ends, we have pointed to insights from modern psychology, classical sociology, and symbolic interactionism that may prove useful for elaborating on the instrumental and noninstrumental mechanisms governing normative internalization and behavioral conformity.

Our recommendations above are offered in the spirit of further advancing a titan in the criminological world, and they can be accomplished not by abandonment of the central premises of the theory, but by focusing attention on underexamined, ambiguous, or forgotten components. In this way, our suggestions should be viewed as supplementary to other recent calls for attention to—and empirical tests of—social learning theory's underexamined differential reinforcement hypotheses (e.g., Brauer, 2009; Brauer & Tittle, 2012; Rebellon, 2006; Tittle et al., 2012). Our hope is that these recommendations will modestly improve learning theory's already impressive ability to provide precise predictions, to boast convincing empirical support, and to offer intellectually satisfying explanations for criminal behavior.

References

Agnew, R. (1995). Testing the leading crime theories: An alternative strategy focusing on motivational processes. *Journal of Research in Crime and Delinquency, 32,* 363–398.

Akers, R. L. (1973). *Deviant behavior: A social learning approach.* Belmont, CA: Wadsworth.

Akers, R. L. (1990). Rational choice, deterrence, and social learning theory in criminology: The path not taken. *Journal of Criminal Law and Criminology, 81,* 653–676.

Akers, R. L. (1999). Social learning and social structure: Reply to Sampson, Morash, and Krohn. *Theoretical Criminology, 3,* 477–493.

Akers, R. L. (2009). *Social learning and social structure: A general theory of crime and deviance*. New Brunswick, NJ: Transaction.

Akers, R. L., & Jensen, G. F. (2006). The empirical status of social learning theory of crime and deviance: The past, present, and future. In F. T. Cullen, J. P. Wright, & K. R. Blevins (Eds.), *Advances in Criminological Theory Series: Vol. 15. Taking stock: The status of criminological theory* (pp. 37–76). pp. 37–76). New Brunswick, NJ: Transaction.

Anderson, E. (1999). *Code of the street*. New York, NY: W. W. Norton.

Aseltine, R. H., Jr. (1995). A reconsideration of parental and peer influences on adolescent deviance. *Journal of Health and Social Behavior, 36,* 103–121.

Baerveldt, C., Völker, B., & Van Rossem, R. (2008). Revisiting selection and influence: An inquiry into the friendship networks of high school students and their association with delinquency. *Canadian Journal of Criminology & Criminal Justice, 50,* 559–587.

Bandura, A. (1989). Social cognitive theory. In R. Vasta (Ed.), *Annals of child development: Six theories of child development* (Vol. 6, pp. 1–60). Greenwich, CT: JAI Press.

Bandura, A. (1995). *Self-efficacy in changing societies*. Cambridge, UK: Cambridge University Press.

Bao, W.-N., Haas, A., Chen, X., & Pi, Y. (2012). Repeated strains, social control, social learning, and delinquency: Testing an integrated model of general strain theory in China. *Youth and Society*. doi:10.1177/0044118X11436189

Bernburg, J. G., Krohn, M. D., & Rivera, C. J. (2006). Official labeling, criminal embeddedness, and subsequent delinquency: A longitudinal test of labeling theory. *Journal of Research in Crime and Delinquency, 43,* 67–88.

Boman, J. H., IV, Krohn, M. D., Gibson, C. L., & Stogner, J. M. (2012). Investigating friendship quality: An exploration of self-control and social control theories' friendship hypotheses. *Journal of Youth and Adolescence, 41,* 1526–1540.

Braithwaite, J. (1989). *Crime, shame and reintegration*. New York, NY: Cambridge University Press.

Brauer, J. R. (2009). Testing social learning theory using reinforcement's residue: A multilevel analysis of self-reported theft and marijuana use in the National Youth Survey. *Criminology, 47,* 929–970.

Brauer, J. R., & De Coster, S. (2012). Social relationships and delinquency: Revisiting parent and peer influence during adolescence. *Youth and Society*. doi:10.1177/0044118X12467655

Brauer, J. R., & Tittle, C. R. (2012). Social learning theory and human reinforcement. *Sociological Spectrum, 32,* 157–177.

Burgess, R. L., & Akers, R. L. (1966). A differential association-reinforcement theory of criminal behavior. *Social Problems, 14,* 128–147.

Campbell, E. Q. (1964). The internalization of social norms. *Sociometry, 27,* 391–412.

Cooper, J. A, Walsh, A., & Ellis, L. (2010). Is criminology moving toward a paradigm shift?: Evidence from a survey of the American Society of Criminology. *Journal of Criminal Justice Education, 21,* 332–347.

Deci, E. L., & Ryan, R. M. (1985). *Intrinsic motivation and self-determination in human behavior*. New York, NY: Plenum.

Deci, E. L., & Ryan, R. M. (1987). The support of autonomy and the control of behavior. *Journal of Personality and Social Psychology, 53,* 1024–1037.

Deci, E. L., & Ryan, R. M. (2000). The "what" and "why" of goal pursuits: Human needs and the self-determination of behavior. *Psychological Inquiry, 11,* 227–268.

Durkheim, E. (1961). *Moral education*. New York, NY: Free Press.

Etzioni, A. (1988). *The moral dimension: Toward a new economics*. New York, NY: Free Press.

Etzioni, A. (2000). Social norms: Internalization, persuasion, and history. *Law and Society Review, 34,* 157–178.

Giordano, P. C. (2003). Relationships in adolescence. *Annual Review of Sociology, 29,* 257–281.

Giordano, P. C., Cernkovich, S. A., & Holland, D. D. (2003). Changes in friendship relations over the life-course: Implications for desistance from crime. *Criminology, 41,* 293–328.

Giordano, P. C., Cernkovich, S. A., & Rudolph, J. L. (2002). Gender, crime, and desistance: Toward a theory of cognitive transformation. *American Journal of Sociology, 107,* 990–1064.

Giordano, P. C., Cernkovich, S. A., & Schroeder, R. D. (2007). Emotions and crime over the life-course: A neo-median perspective on criminal continuity and change. *American Journal of Sociology, 112,* 1603–1661.

Glaser, D. (1956). Criminality theories and behavioral images. *American Journal of Sociology, 61,* 433–444.

Glueck, S., & Glueck, E. (1950). *Unraveling juvenile delinquency*. New York, NY: Commonwealth Fund.

Gordon, R. A., Lahey, B. B., Kawai, E., Loeber, R., Stouthamer-Loeber, M., & Farrington, D. P. (2004). Antisocial behavior and youth gang membership: Selection and socialization. *Criminology, 42,* 55–87.

Gottfredson, M. R., & Hirschi, T. (1990). *A general theory of crime*. Stanford, CA: Stanford University Press.

Grasmick, H. G., & Green, D. E. (1980). Legal punishment, social disapproval and internalization as inhibitors of illegal behavior. *Journal of Criminal Law and Criminology, 71,* 325–335.

Grolnick, W. S. (2003). *The psychology of parental control: How well-meaning parenting backfires*. Upper Saddle River, NJ: Erlbaum.

Hagan, J. (1997). Defiance and despair: Subcultural and structural linkages between delinquency and despair in the life-course. *Social Forces, 76,* 119–134.

Hayes, S. C., Blackledge, J. T., & Barnes-Holmes, D. (2001). Language and cognition: Constructing an alternative approach within the behavioral tradition. In S. C. Hayes, D. Barnes-Holmes, & B. Roche (Eds.), *Relational frame theory: A post-Skinnerian account of human language and cognition* (pp. 3–20). New York, NY: Kluwer Academic/Plenum.

Haynie, D. L. (2002). Friendship networks and delinquency: The relative nature of peer delinquency. *Journal of Quantitative Criminology, 18,* 99–134.

Haynie, D. L., Giordano, P., Manning, W., & Longmore, M. (2005). Adolescent romantic relationships and delinquency involvement. *Criminology, 43,* 177–210.

Haynie, D. L., & Osgood, D. W. (2005). Reconsidering peers and delinquency: How do peers matter? *Social Forces, 84,* 1109–1130.

Heimer, K., & De Coster, S. (1999). The gendering of violent delinquency. *Criminology, 37,* 277–317.

Heimer, K., & Matsueda, R. (1994). Role-taking, role commitment, and delinquency: A theory of differential social control. *American Sociological Review, 59,* 365–390.

Hirschi, T. (1969). *Causes of delinquency*. Berkeley: University of California Press.

Huizinga, D., Weiher, A. W., Espiritu, R. C., & Esbensen, F. A. (2003). Delinquency and crime: Some highlights from the

Denver Youth Survey. In T. B. Thornberry & M. Krohn (Eds.), *Taking stock: An overview of findings from contemporary longitudinal studies* (pp. 47–91). New York, NY: Plenum Press.

Jensen, G. F. (1972). Parents, peers, and delinquent action: A test of the differential association perspective. *American Journal of Sociology, 78,* 562–575.

Johnson, M. C., & Menard, S. (2012). A longitudinal study of delinquency abstention. *Youth Violence and Juvenile Justice, 10,* 278–291.

Kandel, D. B. (1978). Homophily, selection, and socialization in adolescent friendships. *American Journal of Sociology, 84,* 427–436.

Kandel, D. B. (1996). The parental and peer contexts of adolescent deviance: An algebra of interpersonal influences. *Journal of Drug Issues, 26,* 289–315.

Knecht, A., Snijders, T. A. B., Baerveldt, C., Steglich, C. E. G., & Raub, W. (2010). Friendship and delinquency: Selection and influence processes in early adolescence. *Social Development, 19,* 494–514.

Kobayashi, E., Akers, R. L., & Sharp, S. F. (2011). Attitude transference and deviant behavior: A comparative study in Japan and the U.S. *Deviant Behavior, 32,* 405–440.

Kroneberg, C., Heintze, I., & Mehlkop, G. (2010). The interplay of moral norms and instrumental incentives in crime causation. *Criminology, 48,* 259–294.

Lanza-Kaduce, L., & Capece, M. (2003). A specific test of an integrated general theory. In R. L. Akers & G. F. Jensen (Eds.), *Social learning theory and the explanation of crime: A guide for the new century. Advances in criminological theory* (Vol. 11, pp. 179–196). Newark, NJ: Transaction.

Lonardo, R. A., Giordano, P.C., Longmore, M. A., & Manning, W. D. (2009). Parents, friends, and romantic partners: Enmeshment in deviant networks and adolescent delinquency involvement. *Journal of Youth and Adolescence, 38,* 367–383.

Matsueda, R. L. (1982). Testing control theory and differential association: A causal modeling approach. *American Sociological Review, 47,* 489–504.

Matsueda, R. L. (1988). The current state of differential association theory. *Crime and Delinquency, 34,* 277–306.

Matsueda, R. L. (1992). Reflected appraisals, parental labeling, and delinquent behavior: Specifying a symbolic interactionist theory. *American Journal of Sociology, 97,* 1577–1611.

Matsueda, R. L., & Anderson, K. (1998). The dynamics of delinquent peers and delinquent behavior. *Criminology, 36,* 269–308.

Matsueda, R. L., & Heimer, K. (1997). A symbolic interactionist theory of role transitions, role commitments, and delinquency. In T. P. Thornberry (Ed.), *Developmental theories of crime and delinquency: Advances in criminological theory* (Vol. 7, pp. 163–213). New Brunswick, NJ: Transaction.

Orcutt, J. D., & Schwabe, A. M. (2012).Gender, race/ethnicity, and deviant drinking: A longitudinal application of social structure and social learning theory. *Sociological Spectrum, 32,* 20–36.

Osgood, D. W., & Anderson, A. L. (2004). Unstructured socializing and rates of delinquency. *Criminology, 42,* 519–549.

Parsons, T. (1951). *The social system*. New York, NY: Routledge.

Pratt, T. C., Cullen, F. T., Sellers, C. S., Winfree, L. T., Jr., Madensen, T. D., Daigle, L. E., . . . Gau, J. M. (2010). The empirical status of social learning theory: A meta-analysis. *Justice Quarterly, 27,* 765–802.

Rafter, N. (2011). Origins of criminology. In M. Bosworth & C. Hoyle (Eds.), *What is criminology?* (pp. 143–156). New York, NY: Oxford University Press.

Rebellon, C. J. (2006). Do adolescents engage in delinquency to attract the social attention of peers? An extension and longitudinal test of the social reinforcement hypothesis. *Journal of Research in Crime and Delinquency, 43,* 387–411.

Ryan, R. M., & Deci, E. L. (2006). Self-regulation and the problem of human autonomy: Does psychology need choice, self-determination, and will? *Journal of Personality, 74,* 1557–1586.

Ryan, R. M., Deci, E. L., Grolnick, W. S., & LaGuardia, J. G. (2006). The significance of autonomy and autonomy support in psychological development and psychopathology. In D. Cicchetti & D. J. Cohen (Eds.), *Developmental psychopathology: Theory and method* (Vol. 1, pp. 795–850). Hoboken, NJ: Wiley.

Sampson, R. J. (1999). Techniques of research neutralization. *Theoretical Criminology, 3,* 438–451.

Sanchez-Jankowski, M. (1991). *Islands in the street: Gangs and American urban society*. Berkeley: University of California Press.

Scott, M. B., & Lyman, S. M. (1968). Accounts. *American Sociological Review, 33,* 46–62.

Silver, D., & Lee, M. (2012). Self-relations in social relations. *Sociological Theory, 30,* 207–237.

Silver, E., & Ulmer, J. T. (2012). Future selves and self-control motivation. *Deviant Behavior, 33,* 699–714.

Simons, R. L., & Burt, C. H. (2011). Learning to be bad: Adverse social conditions, social schemas, and crime. *Criminology, 49,* 553–598.

Snyder, J., Dishion, T. J., & Patterson, G. R. (1986). Determinants and consequences of associating with deviant peers during preadolescence and adolescence. *Journal of Early Adolescence, 6,* 29–43.

Stewart, I., Barnes-Holmes, D., Barnes-Holmes, Y., Bond, F. W., & Hayes, S. C. (2006). Relational frame theory and industrial/organizational psychology. *Journal of Organizational and Behavioral Management, 26,* 55–90.

Sutherland, E. H. (1939). *Principles of criminology* (3rd ed.). Philadelphia, PA: J. B. Lippincott.

Sutherland, E. H. (1947). *Principles of criminology* (4th ed.). Philadelphia, PA: J. B. Lippincott.

Sutherland, E. H. (1973). Development of the theory. In S. Schuessler (Ed.), *On analyzing crime* (pp. 13–29). Chicago, IL: Chicago University Press.

Sutherland, E. H., & Cressey, D. R. (1966). *Principles of criminology* (7th ed.). Philadelphia, PA: J. B. Lippincott.

Sykes, G. M., & Matza, D. (1957). Techniques of neutralization. *American Sociological Review, 22,* 667–669.

Tarde, G. (1962). *The laws of imitation* (P. Smith, Trans.). New York, NY: Henry Holt. (Original work published 1903)

Thomas, W. I., & Thomas, D. S. (1928). *The child in America: Behavior problems and programs*. New York, NY: Knopf.

Tittle, C. R. (1995). *Control balance: Toward a general theory of deviance*. Boulder, CO: Westview.

Tittle, C. R., Antonaccio, O., & Botchkovar, E. (2012). Social learning, reinforcement and crime: Evidence from three European cities. *Social Forces, 90,* 863–890.

Tittle, C. R., Antonaccio, O., Botchkovar, E., & Kranidioti, M. (2010). Expected utility, self-control, morality, and criminal probability. *Social Science Research, 39,* 1029–1046.

Tittle, C. R., Burke, M. J., & Jackson, E. F. (1986). Modeling Sutherland's theory of differential association: Toward an empirical clarification. *Social Forces, 65*, 405–432.

Tyler, T. R. (2010). *Why people cooperate: The role of social motivations*. Princeton, NJ: Princeton University Press.

Warr, M. (1993). Parents, peers, and delinquency. *Social Forces, 72*, 247–264.

Warr, M. (2002). *Companions in crime*. Cambridge, UK: Cambridge University Press.

Warr, M., & Stafford, M. (1991). The influence of delinquent peers: What they think or what they do? *Criminology, 29*, 851–866.

Weber, M. (1978). *Economy and society* (Vol. 1) (G. Roth, & C. Wittich, Eds.). Berkeley: University of California Press.

Weerman, F. M. (2011). Delinquent peers in context: A longitudinal network analysis of selection and influence effects. *Criminology, 49*, 253–286.

Wikström, P.-O. H. (2006). Individuals, settings and acts of crime: Situational mechanisms and the explanation of crime. In P.-O. H. Wikström & R. J. Sampson (Eds.), *The explanation of crime: Contexts, mechanisms and development* (pp. 61–107). Cambridge, UK: Cambridge University Press.

Wrong, D. H. (1961). The oversocialized conception of man in modern sociology. *American Sociological Review, 26*, 183–193.

Young, J. T. N., Barnes, J. C., Meldrum, R. C., & Weerman, F. M. (2011). Assessing and explaining misperceptions of peer delinquency. *Criminology, 49*, 599–630.

8

The Integration of Biological and Genetic Factors Into Social Learning Theory

Jamie Vaske

Western Carolina University

Social learning theory has traditionally been a criminological theory that is grounded in sociology and behavioral psychology. Edwin Sutherland (1939), a sociologist by training, argued that people engage in crime because they have been taught to engage in crime. Specifically, he noted that criminal behavior and attitudes favorable to crime are learned through social interaction with others. Social interaction that is frequent, occurs early in life, is of long duration, and is emotionally relevant will have the greatest effect on behavior. Also, individuals will engage in criminal behavior when their attitudes favoring criminal behavior outweigh their attitudes favoring prosocial behavior. While Sutherland's theory of differential association provided a foundation of social learning theory, it did not fully describe what was considered "attitudes favorable to crime" or explain the precise mechanisms through which individuals learned criminal behavior and attitudes.

Later theorists, such as Sykes and Matza (1957), explain the specific content of procrime attitudes in their description of the techniques of neutralization. Sykes and Matza argued that people will try to rationalize their antisocial behavior or neutralize the harm of their actions by denying responsibility for the event, denying that their actions caused injury, casting the victim as the wrong-doer, condemning those who judge their antisocial behavior, or by stating that their behavior is in accordance with higher group interests (i.e., religious doctrine, gang codes). These techniques of neutralization may be considered before a person engages in crime, or they may be invoked after one has committed a crime to neutralize one's feeling or attitudes that the behavior is wrong. Sykes and Matza extended Sutherland's theory by describing the specific content of antisocial attitudes, but other theorists (such as Burgess and Akers) also expanded on the original differential association theory in different ways.

In line with Sutherland's theory, Akers's social learning theory argues that (a) individuals learn criminal attitudes and behaviors from associating with antisocial others (i.e., differential association), (b) people may imitate the techniques and behavioral styles of offenders when committing crime (i.e., imitation), and (c) individuals may learn attitudes that are both positive toward criminal behavior as well as attitudes that neutralize the harm of their behaviors (i.e., definitions). Burgess and Akers (1966), however, expanded on Sutherland's theory by describing how individuals acquire and develop their antisocial attitudes and behaviors. Drawing from behavioral psychology's notion of operant conditioning, Akers argued that individuals internalize criminal behaviors and norms through differential reinforcement processes. Differential reinforcement refers to the process of using rewards and consequences to shape one's attitudes and behaviors.

Reinforcement can be either positive or negative in nature. Positive reinforcement occurs when individuals receive a reward or something pleasurable in response to their behavior or attitude, while negative reinforcement refers to situations when an individual avoids or escapes negative consequences (i.e., avoiding arrest). Both positive and negative reinforcement increase the likelihood that individuals will continue to engage in antisocial behavior or will retain their antisocial attitudes. Punishment, on the other hand, is when an individual receives a painful consequence or when a positive/rewarding consequence is withheld. Punishment increases the probability that a person will stop offending or will discard his or her attitudes favorable to criminal behavior (Figure 8.1).

Akers's social learning theory integrated and expanded on previous social learning theories, making it one of the most comprehensive social learning theories in criminology. The breadth of the theory has appealed to many criminological researchers, and it is one of the most tested theories in the criminology field. While Akers's social learning theory is a cornerstone in the explanation of criminal and antisocial behavior, Akers did not elucidate the biological processes that facilitate social learning or the biological changes that occur in response to social learning.

Without understanding the biological factors that are involved in social learning, scholars will have a limited view of human nature and the learning process. For instance, two individuals may be exposed to the same behavior and receive the same reinforcement for imitating the behavior, yet only one of the individuals may repeat the behavior in the future. In this example, both people are equally exposed to the social learning process as described by Akers, but the theory fails to explain why one individual continues the behavior while the other person does not.

Furthermore, failing to understand the biological mechanisms that underlie the learning process completely ignores one level of explanation in the etiology of

Figure 8.1 Illustration of Social Learning Theory

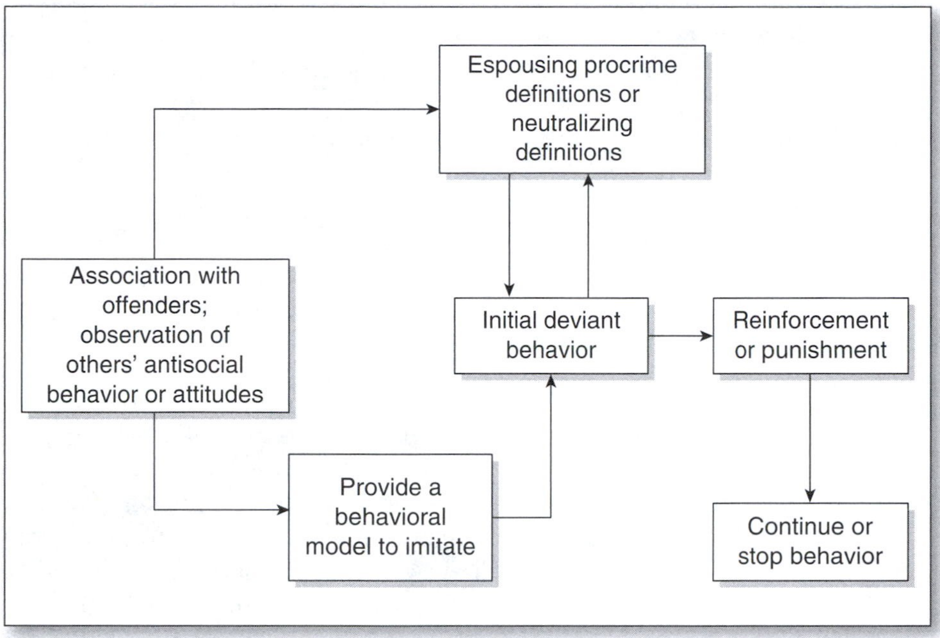

criminal behavior, and it subsequently knifes off the possibility of biologically informed interventions. For example, neuropsychologists have identified the brain regions that are linked to depression, and medical practitioners have used pharmacological treatments and transcranial magnetic stimulation on these brain regions to reduce depressive symptoms among patients who were not helped by other depression treatments (Pascual-Leone, Rubio, Pallardó, & Catalá, 1996; Schutter, 2009). If scholars did not understand the biological processes of depression, practitioners would be limited to only one form of treatment (i.e., cognitive, behavioral, or interpersonal interventions) rather than having access to pharmacological and other biologically based interventions. Understanding the biological mechanisms of social learning theory may also help researchers identify the brain regions that should be activated by therapies that are grounded in social learning theory. If researchers understand the brain regions that are active during social learning tasks, they may begin to understand why some therapy approaches are more effective than others. Having such knowledge can empower practitioners and researchers to build better interventions and to maximize the effectiveness of cognitive and behavioral therapies (Vaske, Galyean, & Cullen, 2011). Thus, understanding the biological factors involved in the social learning process is important at both a theoretical and a practical level.

In light of these concerns, this chapter describes the neurobiological processes that underlie the social learning process. More specifically, it discusses changes in genetic expression, brain structure and functioning, and neurotransmitter activity that occur during the social learning process (as shown in Figure 8.1). The next section begins by reviewing the neurobiological changes that occur after the general social learning process concludes, and then the following section discusses the neurobiological factors that are specific to each stage of the social learning process. For instance, some brain regions and neurotransmitters are more relevant to the reinforcement of one's own behavior, while other regions are important to the imitation portion of the process. Finally, the chapter discusses the neurobiological factors that condition or moderate the effects of social learning components on behavior.

The Neurobiological Correlates of the Social Learning Process

GENERAL CHANGES

Research has established that learning through operant conditioning processes may actually lead to changes in the expression of genes and in the growth of brain cells (Kelly & Deadwyler, 2002; Rapanelli, Lew, Frick, & Zanutto, 2010). Typically, studies find that learning increases the expression of genes that are related to the growth of new neurons and stronger connections between brain cells, especially in the hippocampus and frontal cortex (Bertaina-Anglade, Tramu, & Destrade, 2000). For instance, Rapanelli, Frick, and Zanutto (2009) found that animals that completed an operant conditioning task had a higher expression of six genes (*BDNF, Synapsin I, CREB, Arc, c-fos,* and *c-jun*) in the hippocampus than animals that were not exposed to the operant conditioning task. These genes are related to synaptic plasticity, or the growth of connections between brain cells. Interestingly, the researchers found that expression of the six genes was highest during the initial phases of learning, and that the expression levels decreased as the animals mastered the task. A follow-up study by Rapanelli, Frick, and Zanutto (2011) also showed that the birth, maturation, survival, and proliferation of neurons (and astrocytes) in the medial prefrontal cortex and hippocampus increased during the initial learning stages, and then began to decrease once the task was fully learned. These results show that learning through rewards and punishments triggers the growth of new brain cells, new connections between brain cells, and increases the expression of genetic variants that are crucial to brain plasticity, especially in the beginning stages of learning.

While research has assessed the neurobiological changes in the brain that occur after the entire learning process is complete, other areas of research have examined the neurobiological changes that are specific to certain components of the social learning process. For instance, some researchers have examined the brain regions that are activated during the neutralization process, while other researchers have investigated the neural substrates that are relevant to behavioral reinforcement. The next section discusses the neurobiological factors that are related to specific components of the social learning process. The specific components of the social learning process include: (1) observation of others' behavior and the consequences of their behavior, (2) formation of one's own attitudes based on others' actions or attitudes, (3) attitudes that precede or motivate behavior, (4) changing one's own attitudes to be in line with one's own behavior (i.e., neutralizations), and (5) reinforcement or punishment for one's behavior.

It is important to note that the current social learning theories within psychology and neuropsychology differ from the social learning theories of criminology in various ways. For instance, current psychological theories of social learning argue that individuals learn when there is a difference between the expected rewards and the actual rewards (i.e., prediction error), while criminological social learning theories merely state that individuals learn when they are rewarded (or punished) for their behavior. Also, the neuropsychological tasks employed in the brain imaging studies rarely parallel the behaviors or activities discussed in the criminological social learning theories. As an example, studies that examine the effects of peer pressure frequently use individuals' consensus on the ratings of music choices or the attractiveness of faces as a measure of peer pressure; neither of these topics may be particularly relevant to criminal behavior unless one is studying the theft of music or perhaps the assault of others. Thus, the neurobiological changes shown in neuropsychological social learning studies may differ from the changes experienced in criminological social learning paradigms. Future criminological biosocial research should examine whether the biological changes are similar to those found from neuropsychological social learning studies.

NEUROBIOLOGICAL CHANGES BY SOCIAL LEARNING COMPONENT

Observation of Others' Behavior and the Consequences of Their Behavior

Social learning theorists argue that individuals may primarily learn antisocial behaviors by observing others' deviant behavior. For instance, Warr and Stafford's (1991) analysis of the National Youth Survey data suggested that peers' delinquent behavior had a stronger effect on youths' delinquency than peers' antisocial attitudes. Thus, youths engaged in delinquent behavior because they observed their peers engaging in delinquent behavior (and they imitated their peers' behavior) rather than their peers' attitudes justifying or approving of antisocial behavior. Warr and Stafford's analyses confirm that youths learn delinquent behavior primarily through observational learning processes rather than through attitude transference.

Part of the observational learning process is the ability to monitor others' behavior, create a cognitive representation of the behavior, and evaluate the utility of others' behavior (Bandura, 1979). The ability to anticipate outcomes and monitor the errors of others allows one to adjust one's own behaviors accordingly to avoid committing similar errors in the future. Shane, Stevens, Harenski, and Kiehl (2008) investigated the neural correlates of watching others perform a task and commit a series of errors during the task. In their fMRI study, they found that the anterior cingulate cortex (ACC), orbitofrontal cortex (OFC), thalamus, medial temporal cortex, and parts of the parietal cortex were activated when the participant watched another person make an error in the go/no-go task. Other studies have also found that these regions are activated when watching others make a mistake during a task (Kang, Hirsch, & Chasteen, 2010; Koban, Pourtois, Vocat, & Vuilleumier, 2010).

Researchers posit that these areas are relevant to the observational learning process because these areas mentally represent others' actions and the outcomes of those actions. For instance, portions of the parietal cortex are responsible for providing cognitive representations of physical movements. Other regions, such as the ACC and OFC, are critical to identifying errors and outcomes. Specifically, the ACC is responsible for monitoring individuals' performance during a task and signaling when a mistake occurs, while the OFC is said to be activated when one is expecting a punishment or reward. Together, these regions are activated during observational learning because they encode mental representations of others' behavior, anticipate the outcomes of that behavior, and monitor the errors committed during a task.

Effects of Others on Our Attitudes

Delinquent peers may not only have an effect on one's behavior, but they may also influence a person's attitude toward criminal and prosocial behavior. Cognitive neuroscience has begun to investigate the neural mechanisms that explain how others' attitudes influence our own attitudes. Research has revealed that brain regions associated with anxiety and pain are activated when one does not agree or conform with peers' opinions, while areas associated with reward and pleasure are activated when an individual conforms to the group's opinion (Klucharev, Munneke, Smidts, & Fernández, 2011). More specifically, Berns and colleagues (Berns, Chappelow, Zink, Pagnoni, Martin-Skurski, & Richards, 2005; Berns, Capra, Moore, & Noussair, 2010) have found that individuals who did not agree with others in a judgment task had increased activity in the amygdala, insula, and ACC and decreased activity in the ventral striatum. The authors explain these activation patterns by positing that the amygdala is responsible for generating negative emotional signals, and the insula is thought to project these signals to higher processing areas (such as the ACC and frontal cortex) where they are consciously evaluated and integrated into decision making. The ACC monitors conflicts between emotional and cognitive signals and makes one aware that the conflict exists. Decreased activity in the ventral striatum may reflect the loss of "reward" that comes from disagreeing with others. Thus, holding attitudes that are not in line with others' attitudes produces a negative emotional signal and reduces positive signals within the brain.

When our attitudes are consistent with those of the group, our brains produce positive emotional signals that reinforce our attitudes. Studies have found that activity in the striatum significantly increases when an individual's attitude or opinion matches others' attitudes (Berns et al., 2010; Campbell-Meiklejohn, Bach, Roepstorff, Dolan, & Frith, 2010). The striatum is a subcortical structure within the brain that is rich in dopamine and glutamate neurons, and this region has been highly implicated in drug use and addiction. Thus, agreeing with others activates the same reward centers that are activated when we engage in other highly pleasurable activities (Morgan & Laland, 2012). These studies may provide the neurobiological mechanism for Warr's (2002) statement on peer group consensus that people tend to equate liking or positive feelings with being in agreement with others.

Other brain regions may also be sensitive to the influence of others' attitudes and opinions. Campbell-Meiklejohn et al. (2010) found that individuals who were more susceptible to peer influence had higher levels of activity in the right temporoparietal junction (TPJ), lateral prefrontal cortex, anterior cingulate cortex, and insula. The TPJ is believed to be responsible for detecting and processing social cues, and the lateral prefrontal cortex has been implicated in managing one's reputation. Overall, the empirical findings suggest that it is beneficial from a neurobiological point of view to agree with others because we are intrinsically rewarded when doing so, and we avoid the negative emotions associated with disagreement (Falk, Way, & Jasinska, 2012).

Attitudes That Precede or Motivate Behavior

Attitudes and cognitions may motivate us to engage in certain behaviors, or they may also instruct us in how to perform a certain behavior. The brain regions involved in processing attitudes that motivate behavior partially overlap with the regions that are activated when we recall how to perform a behavior. For instance, the cingulate cortex has been implicated in psychological tasks that motivate or trigger someone to engage in an action, as well as tasks that require participants to retrieve information from memory. Other regions, such as the frontal cortex, may also be similarly activated during both tasks. While there are some similarities in the neural correlates that motivate behavior and regions that guide behavior, there are also a host of differences in the activation patterns.

Before proceeding into the discussion of the neural correlates of attitudes, it is important to note that psychology has differentiated between two types of attitudes: implicit attitudes and explicit attitudes. *Implicit cognitive tasks* refer to attitudes and memories that are predominantly unconscious, emerge quickly, and frequently have an emotional component. *Explicit cognitive tasks*, in contrast, refer to attitudes and memories that are conscious, deliberate, and require the retrieval of information. These two types of attitudes may activate similar neural structures, such as the frontal cortex, and they also correspond to distinct regions as discussed below.

Research has shown that implicit attitudes are associated with greater activity in the amygdala, insula, ACC, OFC, sensory cortex, and dorsolateral prefrontal cortex (DLPFC) (Cunningham, Raye, & Johnson, 2004; Forbes & Grafman, 2010). The amygdala is believed to be responsible for crude or automatic emotional evaluations of stimuli. The insula relays the emotional signals from the amygdala to the ACC where the signals are detected (i.e., come into consciousness), and then the signals are passed to the OFC and DLPFC where they are monitored and regulated, respectively (Stanley, Phelps, & Banaji, 2008). Thus, attitudes that subconsciously motivate one to engage in criminal or antisocial behavior may have an emotional component (i.e., vengeance, sneaky thrills) that originates in the amygdala and limbic system, and then these signals are sent to higher-order areas for processing and regulation. Deficits in the processing and regulation areas, such as the frontal cortex, may allow one to act based on unchecked emotional signals.

Explicit attitudes involve slower, more deliberate cognitive processes where individuals may make moral judgments (i.e., "It is morally wrong to break the law"), evaluate and attribute the intentions of others (i.e., "The police stopped you because of your race"), and/or engage in social categorization processes (i.e., "It's you against the police"). Research has revealed that portions of the frontal cortex are predominantly activated during explicit attitude tasks. More specifically, explicit attitudes are associated with activation in the ventromedial prefrontal cortex (VMPFC), DLPFC, OFC, medial prefrontal cortex (MPFC), and the ACC (Cunningham et al., 2004; Forbes & Grafman, 2010). The VMPFC has been implicated in perspective taking, evaluating the intentions of others, and processing social stereotypes or categories. Other areas, such as the DLPFC, are believed to be responsible for regulating the influence of social stereotypes on behavior. Finally, the ACC, OFC, VMPFC, MPFC, and the TPJ have been linked to moral reasoning and judgments (Greene & Haidt, 2002). These frontal cortex regions, therefore, may be implicated in a wide range of explicit antisocial attitudes.

Finally, attitudes or cognitions may instruct us on how to perform a certain type of criminal behavior. The specific regions that are activated during this process will differ based on the type of memory systems that one is retrieving information from to perform the behavior. For instance, action-based memory (i.e., motor movement memory) has been associated with activity in the dorsal premotor cortex, inferior parietal lobe, and intraparietal sulcus, while functional memory (i.e., memory related to the function of an object and the context that is associated with the object) is linked to the cingulate cortex and inferotemporal cortex (Canessa et al., 2008). Explicit memory related to the linguistic skills has been associated with the posterior cingulate cortex, anterior medial prefrontal cortex, and bilateral parietal cortex (Schott et al., 2005). These studies suggest that various regions of the frontal and parietal cortices are activated when attitudes motivate behavior and when they guide our performance of behaviors, but the specific areas may vary based on the types of memory one is invoking during the process.

Neutralization Processes

Social learning theory states that relatively prosocial people, who generally do not support antisocial behavior, may espouse antisocial attitudes *after* they engage in criminal behavior as a way to neutralize the harm or negative consequences of the criminal behavior. Psychologists note that individuals tend to experience negative feelings or cognitive dissonance after they behave in a way that conflicts with their attitudes, and thus they will subsequently change their attitudes to be consistent with their behavior in order to neutralize any discomfort. Researchers have begun to investigate the brain regions that are associated with the negative feelings of cognitive dissonance and the subsequent attitude change. Studies have shown that the negative feelings of dissonance are related to increased activations in the insula, cingulate cortex, and DLPFC (Izuma et al., 2010; van Veen, Krug, Schooler, & Carter, 2009). As previously discussed, the insula may pass along signals from subcortical areas to higher level areas such as the cingulate cortex. The cingulate cortex is believed to detect conflict between attitudes, emotions, and behavior, and then this conflict signal is sent to the DLPFC where it is regulated. The DLPFC may also be important for helping resolve conflicts between the attitudes and behaviors (Izuma et al., 2010). Together, these regions are part of the cognitive dissonance process where individuals feel tension or discomfort when their behavior conflicts with their attitudes.

The subsequent attitude change that comes from experiencing the discomfort of cognitive dissonance may invoke regions in the frontal cortex. Jarcho, Berkman, and Lieberman's (2011) fMRI study of adults revealed that attitude change during a cognitive dissonance task was associated with increased activity in the inferior frontal gyrus, the frontoparietal region, and the ventral striatum, and decreased activity in the insula. The researchers explained that the inferior frontal gyrus may be responsible for downregulating activity in the insula, a region that has been implicated in anxiety (Paulus & Stein, 2006). The increased activity in the frontoparietal region may reflect the idea that attitude change is most likely to happen when one's behavior conflicts with his or her core concept of self; thus, the more the behavior is "not like him or her," the greater the activation of the frontoparietal region. Finally, the ventral striatum is a region that is highly active during reward processes, and greater activation of the striatum during attitude change may reflect the intrinsic reward or relief that occurs when one resolves a conflict between attitudes and behavior.

The above studies and those showing the effects of others on our attitudes indicate that it is internally rewarding for people to hold attitudes that are similar to others' attitudes and to hold attitudes that are consistent with our behaviors. These studies provide neurobiological evidence for why the effects of antisocial peers and the techniques of neutralizations are so salient and have such a significant effect on antisocial behavior. That is, agreement with antisocial peers and successful use of the techniques of neutralization may stimulate the reward centers of the brain, the same regions that are activated when individuals use drugs, have sex, or engage in other pleasurable activities. Disagreement with others and with our concept of self produces negative emotional signals within the brain, such as the feelings of tension, anxiety, and discomfort. Thus, agreeing with others and effectively using the techniques of neutralization reinforces our behaviors, while disagreeing with peers activates the "punishment" regions of our brains. The next section expands on the neurobiological factors that are relevant to both the reinforcement and punishment processes.

Reinforcement and Punishment

Akers extended on Sutherland's differential association theory by stating that individuals learn behaviors in social interactions through operant conditioning processes. That is, individuals continue to engage in antisocial behavior when they are rewarded for such behavior, and people cease to offend when they are punished for antisocial behavior. Neuroimaging studies have found that there is some overlap in the circuits that process reward and punishment, but there are also specific regions that are relevant to each process. For instance, the insula, thalamus, amygdala, and medial prefrontal cortex (including the ventromedial prefrontal cortex and orbitofrontal cortex) are activated during both reward and punishment processes (Falk et al., 2012; Knutson & Greer, 2008; Schoenbaum, Chiba, & Gallagher, 1998; Shane et al., 2008). These regions are believed to be important for processing psychophysiological responses (i.e., changes in heart rate, skin conductance) to both reward and punishing outcomes. Conversely, the striatum and nucleus accumbens are particularly relevant to rewarding processes, while the anterior cingulate may be more important to the processing of punishment and pain than rewards (Schultz, Dayan, & Montague, 1997; Singer et al., 2004).

Aside from these regions merely being activated when receiving a reward or punishment, studies have also shown that activity in the insula, thalamus, striatum, orbitofrontal cortex, and anterior cingulate is associated with positive changes in behavior. Wrase and colleagues (2007) found that activity in the dorsal striatum, insula, thalamus, orbitofrontal cortex, and anterior cingulate cortex was associated with improvements in performance on a decision-making task. Wrase et al.'s results, together with previous studies' findings, suggests that these regions are not only responsive to rewarding and punishing outcomes, but that they also help motivate individuals to change their behavior to be more advantageous.

Before proceeding to the next section, one additional comment should be made about the role of reward and punishment in shaping behavior. Current psychological learning theories propose that individuals learn when the actual rewards or punishments differ from the expected rewards or punishments. This difference in expected and actual outcomes is referred to as *prediction error*. Studies have consistently shown that the ventral striatum is highly active when processing both reward and punishment prediction errors (Burke, Tobler, Baddeley, & Schultz, 2010; Wrase et al., 2007), with other regions (such as the OFC and ACC) being activated when prediction errors occur in a social learning context (Behrens, Hunt, Woolrich, & Rushworth, 2008; Bellebaum, Jokisch, Gizewski, Forsting, & Daum, 2012). It is important to note that these regions, especially the striatum, house neurons that process dopamine and glutamate. These neurotransmitters have been linked to the processing of reward and motivation. Current research suggests that dopamine initially is released in response to a reward, but that over time it codes for the difference between expected and actual rewards rather than in response to an outcome (Guerra & Silva, 2010; Schultz et al., 1997). These studies indicate that current criminological social learning theories may be advanced by considering the difference between expected and actual outcomes and the timing of "reward," rather than solely focusing on the deliverance of outcomes.

NEUROBIOLOGICAL MODERATORS OF THE SOCIAL LEARNING PROCESS

Gene × Environment Interactions Involving Peer Association

While the social learning process may be related to changes in brain activity and neurotransmission, research has shown that there is significant interindividual variation in the effects of peers and reinforcement on behavior. That is, some people may be more sensitive to the influence of peers, rewards, or punishments on antisocial behavior than other people. Interindividual variation in the effects of the social learning process may partially be due to individual differences in biological or genetic factors. For instance, data from twin studies have shown that genetic factors moderate the influence of deviant peer association on antisocial behavior (Brendgen, 2012). Harden, Hill, Turkheimer, and Emery's (2008) analysis of data from the National Longitudinal Study of Adolescent Health (Add Health) revealed that genetic factors exacerbated the effects of substance using peers on youths' own substance use (i.e., a gene × environment interaction). Adolescents who were genetically at risk for substance use had a higher rate of substance use when they associated with substance using peers, compared to at-risk youths who did not associate with substance using peers. Very similar results regarding deviant peers have been garnered from other behavioral genetic studies (Agrawal et al., 2010; Guo, Elder, Cai, & Hamilton, 2009; van Lier et al., 2007). Studies have also shown a significant interaction between genetic factors and prosocial peers on antisocial behavior, with genetic effects on antisocial behavior being stronger for youths with low levels of prosocial peer association than youths with a high number of prosocial peers (Burt & Klump, 2013).

Aside from the behavioral genetic studies showing a general moderating effect of genetic factors, molecular genetic studies have identified specific genetic variants that condition the effects of peers on antisocial behavior. A recent study of Caucasian males revealed that deviant peer association had a stronger impact on overt antisocial behavior among males who carried the high activity allele of the monoamine oxidase A (MAOA) genetic polymorphism, compared to males who carried the low activity allele (Lee, 2011). The MAOA gene codes for the monoamine oxidase enzyme that degrades catecholamines (i.e., dopamine, norepinephrine) during neurotransmission processes. The MAOA gene has a 30 base pair variable sequence that produces a low activity variant and a high activity variant or allele. The low activity allele is presumed to result in less MAOA enzyme and higher catecholamines, while the high activity allele is believed to lead to high MAOA enzyme activity and deficits in catecholamines. Thus, Lee's (2011) study suggested that adolescent and young adult males who carried the high activity allele (and presumably had lower catecholamine activity) were more sensitive to the criminogenic effects of deviant peer association than males with the low activity allele.

Other studies have also reported that genetic factors may increase youths' sensitivity to the effects of deviant peers. Latendresse and colleague's (2011) analysis of 378 Caucasian youths showed that peer delinquent behavior moderated the effects of the muscarinic acetylcholine receptor M2 gene (CHRM2) on externalizing behavior trajectories. Growth mixture models revealed that externalizing behavior from ages 12 to 22 is characterized by three trajectories (stable high, decreasing low, and decreasing moderate). The authors found that six polymorphisms in the CHRM2 gene differentiated between externalizing trajectories (decreasing low vs. stable high) for youths with high delinquent peer involvement, compared to youths with low delinquent peer involvement. These results showed that genetic factors may interact with delinquent peer association to influence the development of antisocial behavior from adolescence into emerging adulthood.

Experimental research also shows that genetic factors may exacerbate the effects of deviant peers on antisocial behavior. Larsen and colleagues (2010) conducted an experiment where respondents were invited to a laboratory bar, and they were exposed to confederates who drank either two sodas (control condition), one alcoholic drink and one soda (light drinking condition), or three to four alcoholic drinks (heavy drinking condition). The authors then recorded the number of drinks each respondent consumed and examined whether a genetic variant in the D4 dopamine receptor (DRD4) gene moderated the effects of peers' alcohol use on respondents' alcohol consumption. Results revealed that exposure to heavy drinking peers increased the number of drinks consumed by respondents, especially for participants who carried one or more copies of the 7R allele of the DRD4 gene. In fact, respondents who carried one or more copies of the 7R allele and who were exposed to heavy drinking peers consumed twice as many alcoholic drinks as respondents who were exposed to heavy drinking peers but did not carry a copy of the 7R allele. The 7R allele of the DRD4 48 base pair polymorphism is believed to result in weaker dopaminergic signaling, and so it is expected that youths with hypodopaminergic functioning may be especially sensitive to the effects of substance using peers. This interpretation is in line with the findings from Lee's (2011) study, which found that youths with the high activity allele of MAOA (and presumably lower dopamine functioning) were most influenced by deviant peers.

The previous studies suggest that genetic factors may interact with peer processes to influence substance use and antisocial behavior. This ultimately leads to the question: *How* or *why* do genetic factors moderate the effects of peers on antisocial behavior? Research has typically invoked findings from animal studies to explain these associations. That is, researchers have cited animal studies that show that genetic factors influence the production of proteins and neurotransmitters, and then authors hypothesize that these processes (gleaned from animal studies) provide the mechanisms for the interactive associations. Other researchers, however, have integrated molecular genetics with brain imaging techniques to show that genetic factors may interact with reward and social punishment processes to influence brain activity, and these changes in brain activity then lead to interindividual differences in behavior. This research area, referred to as *imaging genetics*, has been applied to components of the social learning process and is the subject of the next section.

Imaging Genetics Involving Social Learning Processes

Imaging genetics research suggests that some individuals may be more sensitive to the effects of rewards and social punishments because genetic variants influence how the brain processes those stimuli. Specifically, genetic variants influence the functioning of brain regions so that individuals with certain variants exhibit more activity in response to social learning processes than individuals without those variants. Subsequently, individuals with certain variants (and greater activity in a brain region) may be more likely to engage in certain behaviors or to have certain traits (i.e., genetic variant → greater activity in brain region [in response to social learning component] → behavior or trait).

Studies have shown that genetic variants related to the dopamine system (DRD2, DAT1, DRD4, COMT) may influence how individuals process reward-related information in the ventral striatum and in the prefrontal cortex (Hahn et al., 2011; Nikolova, Ferrell, Manuck, & Hariri, 2011). For instance, Forbes and colleagues (2009) reported that variants in the DRD2, DRD4, and DAT1 genes explained 9% to 12% of the variation in ventral striatum activity in response to receiving rewards during a card guessing task, with carriers of the 9R DAT1 allele, –141C Del DRD2 allele, and 7R+ DRD4 allele showing greater ventral striatal responses to the presentation of rewards. These genetic variants are believed to lead to higher levels of dopamine availability in the brain. Other studies have revealed that carriers of the Met/Met COMT allele and the 9R DAT1 allele have greater activation of the ventral striatum when they are anticipating rewards and greater activation of the prefrontal cortex when rewards are actually delivered (Aarts et al., 2010; Dreher, Kohn, Kolachana, Weinberger, & Berman, 2009). Interactions between the COMT gene and DAT1 gene have also been linked to the anticipation and the processing of rewards (Dreher et al., 2009; Yacubian et al., 2007). In sum, genetic variants that result in greater extracellular dopamine availability (9R DAT1 and Met/Met COMT), fewer dopamine receptors (–141C Del DRD2), and weaker intracellular processing of dopamine (7R+ DRD4) may lead to greater ventral striatal reactivity in the anticipation of reward related outcomes and greater activity in the prefrontal cortex in processing reward outcomes. These imaging genetic results suggest that individuals with genetic variants related to increased dopamine availability are more sensitive to the effects of rewards, and thus individuals who have such genetic attributes may be more likely to continue their socially learned behavior than individuals who do not carry such genetic variants (i.e., Genetic variants in DAT1, DRD2, DRD4, and COMT → greater reactivity in the ventral striatum and prefrontal cortex in response to reward → continue behavior that triggered the reward).

In addition to investigating the molecular genetic and neural correlates of reward processes, researchers have also examined how genetic variants condition the brain's responses to social punishment processes, such as social exclusion and rejection. Way, Taylor, and Eisenberger (2009) examined whether a genetic variant in the μ-opioid receptor gene (OPRM1) was related to activity in the dorsal anterior cingulate (dACC) and insula when individuals were excluded from a social activity. The authors found that participants with the G allele of the OPRM1 gene had greater activity in the dACC and insula during the social exclusion task than A allele carriers, and that G allele carriers reported higher levels of self-reported trait sensitivity toward rejection. The study also found that activity in the dACC (i.e., a biological state-like measure of sensitivity to rejection) mediated the effects of the G allele on trait sensitivity. This study showed that individuals with the G allele of OPRM1 may be more sensitive to rejection in general because they have greater activity in brain regions associated with pain when they are socially excluded.

Aside from the OPRM1 gene, researchers have also shown that variants in the MAOA gene are associated with how people process thoughts and emotions related to social rejection or exclusion (Sebastian et al., 2010). A study of healthy adults showed that individuals who carried the low activity allele of the MAOA gene reported higher levels of trait aggression and trait interpersonal hypersensitivity in a self-report survey. Eisenberger, Way, Taylor, Welch, and Lieberman's (2007) findings also revealed that activity in the dACC mediated the association between MAOA and trait aggression, suggesting that low activity allele carriers engage in higher levels of aggression because they exhibit greater activity in the dorsal anterior cingulate when processing social exclusion. Thus, low activity allele carriers may be more aggressive than high activity allele carriers because their dACC—a region implicated in pain processing and detection of negative emotions—is more reactive to social exclusion.

In conclusion, the results from the gene × environment studies suggest that genetic factors can increase individuals' sensitivity to the effects of deviant peers. One reason why some individuals are hypersensitive to the effects of deviant peers may be because these genetic variants increase individuals' biological sensitivity to the rewarding aspects of peers and sensitivity to the negative aspects of being socially excluded or rejected. Thus, individuals with a genetic sensitivity to reward and punishment may be more likely to value associations with deviant peers and those peers' attitudes, especially if failure to associate with such peers will result in negative feelings.

Conclusion

Social learning and differential association theories are considered as some of the most relevant theories of crime, with researchers stating that "peer variables can help to explain some of the most fundamental features of delinquent behavior" (Warr, 2002, p. 91). Although social learning and differential association theories have been shown to be empirically valid and have undergone some refinement over the years, researchers have not explicated the neurobiological mechanisms that underlie the social learning process. Without these mechanisms, readers and students are left with questions such as *how* or *why* others' opinions and attitudes have such a salient effect on our attitudes, and *why* are people so quick to change their attitudes when their behavior conflicts with their deeply held value systems. Some of these answers are addressed in neurobiological research studies that show that agreement with others and with our own value systems activates intrinsic reward systems of our brain, while disagreement activates areas associated with pain, grief, and guilt.

The goal of this chapter was to review the neurobiological factors that relate to the main aspects of Akers's social learning theory. As can be seen throughout the chapter, each component may have its own distinct neural activation pattern, but there is a host of brain regions that are similarly activated for all components of social learning theory. For instance, the insula, anterior cingulate cortex, striatum, and portions of the medial prefrontal cortex (including the VMPFC, OFC, and DLPFC) seem to be activated in the majority of components. These regions may be important to the social learning process and behavior in general because they relay information from lower-order systems to higher-order systems (insula); detect emotional signals, errors in performance, and conflict between cognitions and/or emotions (ACC); process reinforcement-related information (OFC and striatum); evaluate the intentions, attitudes, beliefs, and behavior of others (VMPFC); and regulate brain signals and activity (DLPFC).

While these regions are similarly activated by various components of social learning theory, research has also shown that some individuals' brain regions are more reactive to social learning components than other individuals'. Part of this individual variation in response may be due to genetic factors. There is a growing body of research that shows that genetic factors related to neurotransmission moderate individuals' neuropsychological responses to social learning components and subsequently lead to individual differences in behavior. Specifically, research has shown that genetic factors related to the dopamine system (DRD2, DRD4, DAT1), acetylcholine system (CHRM2), opioid system (OPRM1), and degradation enzymes (MAOA, COMT) condition how individuals respond to deviant peers, rewards, and social rejection or exclusion. Thus, genetic factors may influence how individuals perceive social learning components and ultimately influence the decisions they make regarding antisocial behavior, as exemplified in Larsen et al.'s (2010) study.

Social learning theory in criminology is predominantly a sociological paradigm that integrates some aspects of behavioral psychology into the explanations for stability of behavior. Although the theory is sociological in its roots and origins, a new avenue for criminological social learning theory is to investigate how biological factors can be integrated into the theory. Integrating biology into the theory will provide greater insight into why peer association is such a salient risk factor for antisocial behavior, and how individuals vary in their responses to peers, rewards, and punishments. Without consideration of these issues, social learning theorists are left without a rich explanation for the salience of social learning variables and the interindividual variation in responses to social learning processes.

References

Aarts, E., Roelofs, A., Franke, B., Rijpkema, M., Fernández, G., Helmich, R. C., & Cools, R. (2010). Striatal dopamine mediates the interface between motivational and cognitive control in humans: Evidence from genetic imaging. *Neuropsychopharmacology, 35,* 1943–1951.

Agrawal, A., Balasubramanian, S., Smith, E. K., Madden, P. A. F., Bucholz, K. K., Heath, A. C., & Lynskey, M. T. (2010). Peer substance involvement modifies genetic influences on regular substance involvement in young women. *Addiction, 105,* 1844–1853.

Bandura, A. (1979). The social learning perspective: Mechanisms of aggression. In H. Toch (Ed.), *Psychology of crime and criminal justice* (p. 198–236). New York, NY: Holt, Reinhart & Winston.

Behrens, T. E. J., Hunt, L. T., Woolrich, M. W., & Rushworth, M. F. S. (2008). Associative learning of social value. *Nature, 456,* 245–249.

Bellebaum, C., Jokisch, D., Gizewski, E. R., Forsting, M., & Daum, I. (2012). The neural coding of expected and unexpected monetary performance outcomes: Dissociations between active and observational learning. *Behavioural Brain Research, 227,* 241–251.

Berns, G. S., Capra, C. M., Moore, S., & Noussair, C. (2010). Neural mechanisms of the influence of popularity on adolescent ratings of music. *Neuroimage, 49,* 2687–2696.

Berns, G. S., Chappelow, J., Zink, C. F., Pagnoni, G., Martin-Skurski, M. E., & Richards, J. (2005). Neurobiological correlates of social conformity and independence during mental rotation. *Biological Psychiatry, 58,* 245–253.

Bertaina-Anglade, V., Tramu, G., & Destrade, C. (2000). Differential learning-stage dependent patterns of c-Fos protein expression in brain regions during the acquisition and memory consolidation of an operant task in mice. *European Journal of Neuroscience, 12,* 3803–3812.

Brendgen, M. (2012). Genetics and peer relations: A review. *Journal of Research on Adolescence, 22,* 419–437.

Burgess, R. L., & Akers, R. L. (1966). A differential association-reinforcement theory of criminal behavior. *Social Problems, 14,* 128–147.

Burke, C. J., Tobler, P. N., Baddeley, M., & Schultz, W. (2010). Neural mechanisms of observational learning. *Proceedings of the National Academy of Sciences, 107,* 14431–14436.

Burt, S. A., & Klump, K. L. (2013). Prosocial peer affiliation suppresses genetic influences on non-aggressive antisocial behaviors during childhood. *Psychological Medicine, 10,* 1–10.

Campbell-Meiklejohn, D. K., Bach, D. R., Roepstorff, A., Dolan, R. J., & Frith, C. D. (2010). How the opinion of others affects our valuation of objects. *Current Biology, 20,* 1165–1170.

Canessa, N., Borgo, F., Cappa, S. F., Perani, D., Falini, A., Buccino, G., . . . Shallice, T. (2008). The different neural correlates of action and functional knowledge in semantic memory: An fMRI study. *Cerebral Cortex, 18,* 740–751.

Cunningham, W. A., Raye, C. L., & Johnson, M. K. (2004). Implicit and explicit evaluation: fMRI correlates of valence, emotional intensity, and control in the processing of attitudes. *Journal of Cognitive Neuroscience, 16,* 1–13.

Dreher, J. C., Kohn, P., Kolachana, B., Weinberger, D. R., & Berman, K. F. (2009). Variation in dopamine genes influences responsivity of the human reward system. *Proceedings of the National Academy of Sciences, 106,* 617–622.

Eisenberger, N. I., Way, B. M., Taylor, S. E., Welch, W. T., & Lieberman, M. D. (2007). Understanding genetic risk for aggression: Clues from the brain's response to social exclusion. *Biological Psychiatry, 61,* 1100–1008.

Falk, E. B., Way, B. M., & Jasinska, A. J. (2012). An imaging genetics approach to understanding social influence. *Frontiers in Human Neuroscience, 6,* 1–13.

Forbes, C. E., & Grafman, J. (2010). The role of the human prefrontal cortex in social cognition and moral judgment. *Annual Review of Neuroscience, 33,* 299–324.

Forbes, E. E., Brown, S. M., Kimak, M., Ferrell, R. E., Manuck, S. B., & Hariri, A. R. (2009). Genetic variation in components of dopamine neurotransmission impacts ventral striatal reactivity associated with impulsivity. *Molecular Psychiatry, 14,* 60–70.

Greene, J., & Haidt, J. (2002). How (and where) does moral judgment work? *Trends in Cognitive Sciences, 6,* 517–523.

Guerra, L. G. G. C., & Silva, M. T. A. (2010). Learning processes and the neural analysis of conditioning. *Psychology & Neuroscience, 3,* 195–208.

Guo, G., Elder, G. H., Cai, T., & Hamilton, N. (2009). Gene-environment interactions: Peers' alcohol use moderates genetic contribution to adolescent drinking behavior. *Social Science Research, 38,* 213–224.

Hahn, T., Heinzel, S., Dresler, T., Plichta, M. M., Renner, T. J., Markulin, F., . . . Fallgatter, A. J. (2011). Association between reward-related activation in the ventral striatum and trait reward sensitivity is moderated by dopamine transporter genotype. *Human Brain Mapping, 32,* 1557–1565.

Harden, K. P. H., Hill, J. E., Turkheimer, E., & Emery, R. E. (2008). Gene-environment correlation and interaction in peer effects on adolescent alcohol and tobacco use. *Behavior Genetics, 38,* 339–347.

Izuma, K., Matsumoto, M., Murayama, K., Samejima, K., Sadato, N., & Matsumoto, K. (2010). Neural correlates of cognitive dissonance and choice-induced preference change. *Proceedings of the National Academy of Sciences, 107,* 22014–22019.

Jarcho, J. M., Berkman, E. T., & Lieberman, M. D. (2011). The neural basis of rationalization: Cognitive dissonance reduction during decision-making. *SCAN, 6,* 460–467.

Kang, S. K., Hirsch, J. B., & Chasteen, A. L. (2010). Your mistakes are mine: Self-other overlap predicts neural response to observed errors. *Journal of Experimental Social Psychology, 46,* 229–232.

Kelly, M. P., & Deadwyler, S. A. (2002). Acquisition of a novel behavior induces higher levels of Arc mRNA than does overtrained performance. *Neuroscience, 110,* 617–626.

Klucharev, V., Munneke, M. A. M., Smidts, A., & Fernández, G. (2011). Downregulation of the posterior medial frontal cortex prevents social conformity. *Journal of Neuroscience, 31,* 11934–11940.

Knutson, B., & Greer, S. M. (2008). Anticipator affect: Neural correlates and consequences for choice. *Philosophical Transactions of the Royal Society B, 363,* 3771–3786.

Koban, L., Pourtois, G., Vocat, R., & Vuilleumier, P. (2010). When your errors make me lose or win: Event-related potentials to observed errors of cooperators and competitors. *Social Neuroscience, 5,* 360–374.

Larsen, H., van der Zwaluw, C. S., Overbeek, G., Granic, I., Franke, B., & Engels, R. C. M. E. (2010). A variable number of tandem repeats polymorphism in the dopamine D4 receptor gene affects social adaptation of alcohol use: Investigation of a gene-environment interaction. *Psychological Science, 21,* 1064–1068.

Latendresse, S. J., Bates, J. E., Goodnight, J. A., Lansford, J. E., Budde, J. P., Goate, A., . . . Dick, D. M. (2011). Differential susceptibility to adolescent externalizing trajectories: Examining the interplay between CHRM2 and peer group antisocial behavior. *Child Development, 82,* 1797–1814.

Lee, S. S. (2011). Deviant peer affiliation and antisocial behavior: Interaction with monoamine oxidase A genotype. *Journal of Abnormal Child Psychology, 39,* 321–332.

Morgan, T. J. H., & Laland, K. N. (2012). The biological bases of conformity. *Frontiers in Neuroscience, 6,* 1–7.

Nikolova, Y. S., Ferrell, R. E., Manuck, S. B., & Hariri, A. R. (2011). Multilocus genetic profile for dopamine signaling predicts ventral striatum reactivity. *Neuropsychopharmacology, 36,* 1940–1947.

Pascual-Leone, A., Rubio, B., Pallardó, F., & Catalá, M. D. (1996). Rapid-rate transcranial magnetic stimulation of left dorsolateral prefrontal cortex in drug-resistant depression. *Lancet, 348,* 233–237.

Paulus, M. P., & Stein, M. B. (2006). An insular view of anxiety. *Biological Psychiatry, 60,* 383–387.

Rapanelli, M., Frick, L. R., & Zanutto, B. S. (2009). Differential gene expression in the rat hippocampus during learning of an operant conditioning task. *Neuroscience, 163,* 1031–1038.

Rapanelli, M., Frick, L. R., & Zanutto, B. S. (2011). Learning an operant conditioning task differentially induces gliogenesis in the medial prefrontal cortex and neurogenesis in the hippocampus. *PLoS One, 6,* e14713.

Rapanelli, M., Lew, S. E., Frick, L. R., & Zanutto, B. S. (2010). Plasticity in the rat prefrontal cortex: Linking gene expression and an operant learning with a computational theory. *PLoS One, 5,* e8656.

Schoenbaum, G., Chiba, A. A., & Gallagher, M. (1998). Orbitofrontal cortex and basolateral amygdala encode expected outcomes during learning. *Nature Neuroscience, 1,* 155–159.

Schott, B. H., Henson, R. N., Richardson-Klavehn, A., Becker, C., Thoma, V., Heinze, H.-J., & Düzel, E. (2005). Redefining implicit and explicit memory: The functional neuroanatomy of priming, remembering, and control of retrieval. *Proceedings of the National Academy of Sciences, 102,* 1257–1262.

Schultz, W., Dayan, P., & Montague, P. R. (1997). The neural substrate of prediction and reward. *Science, 275,* 1593–1599.

Schutter, D. J. L. G. (2009). Antidepressant efficacy of high-frequency transcranial magnetic stimulation over the left dorsolateral prefrontal cortex in double-blind sham-controlled designs: A meta-analysis. *Psychological Medicine, 39,* 65–75.

Sebastian, C. L., Roiser, J. P., Tan, G. C. Y., Viding, E., Wood, N. W., & Blakemore, S. J. (2010). Effects of age and MAOA genotype on the neural processing of social rejection. *Genes, Brain and Behavior, 9,* 628–637.

Shane, M. S., Stevens, M., Harenski, C. L., & Kiehl, K. A. (2008). Neural correlates of the processing of another's mistakes: A possible underpinning for social and observational learning. *Neuroimage, 42,* 450–459.

Singer, T., Seymour, B., O'Doherty, J., Kaube, H., Dolan, R. J., & Frith, C. D. (2004). Empathy for pain involves the affective but not sensory components of pain. *Science, 303,* 1157–1162.

Stanley, D., Phelps, E., & Banaji, M. (2008). The neural basis of implicit attitudes. *Current Directions in Psychological Science, 17,* 164–170.

Sutherland, E. H. (1939). *Principles of criminology* (3rd ed.). Philadelphia, PA: J. B. Lippincott.

Sykes, G. M., & Matza, D. (1957). Techniques of neutralization. *American Sociological Review, 22,* 664–670.

van Lier, P., Boivin, M., Dionne, G., Vitaro, F., Brendgen, M., Koot, H., . . . Pérusse, D. (2007). Kindergarten children's genetic vulnerabilities interact with friends' aggression to promote children's own aggression. *Journal of the American Academy of Child and Adolescent Psychiatry, 46,* 1080–1087.

van Veen, V., Krug, M. K., Schooler, J. W., & Carter, C. S. (2009). Neural activity predicts attitude change in cognitive dissonance. *Nature Neuroscience, 12,* 1469–1475.

Vaske, J., Galyean, K., & Cullen, F. T. (2011). Toward a biosocial theory of offender rehabilitation: Why does cognitive-behavioral therapy work? *Journal of Criminal Justice, 39,* 90–102.

Warr, M. (2002). *Companions in crime: The social aspects of criminal conduct.* Cambridge, UK: Cambridge University Press.

Warr, M., & Stafford, M. (1991). The influence of delinquent peers: What they think or what they do? *Criminology, 29,* 851–866.

Way, B. M., Taylor, S. E., & Eisenberger, N. I. (2009). Variation in the μ-opioid receptor gene (OPRM1) is associated with dispositional and neural sensitivity to social rejection. *Proceedings of the National Academy of Sciences, 106,* 15079–15084.

Wrase, J., Kahnt, T., Schlagenhauf, F., Beck, A., Cohen, M. X., Knutson, B., & Heinz, A. (2007). Different neural systems adjust motor behavior in response to reward and punishment. *NeuroImage, 36,* 1253–1262.

Yacubian, J., Sommer, T., Schroeder, K., Gläscher, J., Kalisch, R., Leuenberger, B., . . . Büchel, C. (2007). Gene-gene interaction associated with neural reward sensitivity. *Proceedings of the National Academy of Sciences, 104,* 8125–8130.

Discussion Questions

CHAPTERS 7 AND 8

1. Akers's social learning theory argues that individuals learn behaviors through the process of differential reinforcement. However, as noted by Dr. Vaske, social learning theory does not take into account the biological processes that facilitate social learning. What biological mechanisms underlie the social learning process, and how do they contribute to variations in behavior between individuals?
2. Discuss the ways social learning theories within psychology and neuropsychology differ from the social learning theories of criminology. Can these two viewpoints be reconciled?
3. Criminological research suggests the socialization process with delinquent peers is instrumental in producing criminal behaviors. Cognitive neuroscience has also addressed the ways peers influence behaviors. In your opinion, which research findings are the most compelling for explaining the underlying mechanisms of the socialization process?
4. Discuss the differences and similarities between implicit attitudes and explicit attitudes as well as the neural structures associated with each. How do these cognitions differ from the cognitive definitions described in traditional social learning theories of crime?
5. Behavioral genetic research reveals interindividual variation in the effects of peers and reinforcement on behavior. How do genetic factors work to moderate the relationship between antisocial peers and delinquent behaviors? Additionally, which genetic variants have been identified to condition the effects of peers on antisocial behavior?
6. Discuss the benefits of integrating neurobiological research into social learning theories. For example, how could the integration of the two be used to inform intervention efforts?

9

Self-Control and Crime

A Sociological Perspective

Callie H. Burt

Arizona State University

Self-control has attracted an incredible amount of attention across scientific disciplines. Exercising self-control (not eating that second piece of chocolate cake) and failing to exercise self-control (eating that first piece of cake when on a diet) are part of being human. In this chapter, this author focuses on the link between self-control and crime from a *sociological* perspective. At present, the governing sociological view of self-control is contained in Gottfredson and Hirschi's (1990) self-control theory, which this author refers to as SCT. This theory also goes by the name "the general theory of crime," but since other theories of crime claim to be general ones as well, this author sticks to SCT.

In the following pages, this author discusses self-control and crime from the perspective of SCT. First, this author discusses the development of the theory, highlighting its sociological basis and elements, then discusses research on the theory, noting what studies suggest about its accuracy, and concludes by describing a modified version of the theory (modified in light of research). Before moving on, this author wants to issue a disclaimer. In this chapter, this author writes from the position of Gottfredson and Hirschi's theory. This is neither a personal endorsement of the theory or its ideas nor of the superiority of sociological perspectives on self-control. Instead, this chapter is a description of SCT—the foremost social theory of self-control and crime, including its assumptions, arguments, implications, and research.

Self-Control Theory (SCT)

THEORETICAL BACKGROUND

Boldly proclaiming an explanation of all crime at all times, Gottfredson and Hirschi (1990; hereafter G&H for short), presented their self-control theory. The first thing the theorists did was to define what they are trying to explain: crime. Rejecting a strictly legal definition of crime that can vary across time and place (e.g., the different legal status of smoking marijuana in Colorado vs. Alabama in 2013), G&H defined *crime* as "acts of force or fraud undertaken in the pursuit of self-interest" (p. 15). G&H argued that the vast majority of crimes are trivial and involve little or no planning, little loss, and even less gain. Certainly, most of us appreciate the fact that most acts of force and fraud are not the elaborate bank heists engaged in by (quite good looking) males as depicted in popular films (e.g., *Ocean's Eleven, Twelve, Thirteen*—thankfully they stopped at 13). Instead, G&H stress that most crimes are petty and unplanned, but—and this is key—have benefits that are *immediate* and costs are that are largely *delayed*. This author returns to this vital point shortly.

All theories rest on a number of assumptions that form the foundation for their ideas and propositions. For example, some theories assume that people are naturally prosocial and cooperative, even altruistic, and only behave badly when pushed to do so by abnormal conditions. Self-control theory does not adopt this benevolent view of human nature—quite the opposite. As a control theory, SCT is based in a set of assumptions known as the *classical view*, which assumes that humans are naturally selfish and pleasure seeking (or hedonistic). G&H explain: "In this view, all human conduct can be understood as the self-interested pursuit of pleasure or the avoidance of pain" (p. 5). Thus, SCT assumes that we all want to please ourselves, regardless of consequences to others, in the most gratifying way (which happens to be the quickest, easiest way possible). To use one of G&H's examples, we all want "money without work, sex without courtship, revenge without court delays" (p. 89).

The theory also assumes we are *rational* pleasure-maximizers. In other words, we weigh costs and benefits and choose the action that our calculations reveal will bring us the most pleasure (called *hedonistic calculus*). We eat one piece of chocolate cake, for example, after thinking about the consequences and determining that the pleasure from the one piece outweighs the costs (e.g., will not violate our diet), but stop after one piece realizing that the fullness would be uncomfortable and two pieces would violate our diet. The opposite of the rational actor would be the nonrational actor who does not follow his or her hedonistic calculations; he or she would thus weigh the costs and benefits, realize that an act risks more pain than pleasure, and still choose that act. If we were not rational, then we would not be bound by our hedonistic calculation. According to SCT, we are rational, so we choose the act that our calculations suggest will bring us the most pleasure and the least pain.

Notably, different preferences, tastes, or the like have no role in SCT. Instead, the theory assumes that we are all (highly) motivated to the immediate benefits of crime. According to SCT, we all want to take a television without paying; we all want to shoot the dog that constantly barks his head off; and we all want to ease our mental anguish by getting high rather than by going to therapy, meditating, or exercising. We are all motivated to the short-term benefits of crimes because they provide immediate pleasure or gratification of desires with little effort (pain). If behavior had no long-term consequences, presumably we would all commit crimes. So why don't we? Why do most of us most of the time pay for our televisions, talk to the neighbors about their barking dog or ignore it, and use other forms of coping rather than getting high? The answer is found in the reality—unfortunate for the caught offender—that criminal behaviors do have long-term negative consequences.

G&H highlight four categories of pains or punishments that follow from crimes, drawing on the classical scholar Jeremy Bentham (1823/2007). The most obvious is legal or political penalties. Legally specified penalties attached to most acts of crimes are much greater than the rewards to be gained by them. That is, of course, the whole idea of deterrence and a basis for modern day criminal justice systems. If the penalty for stealing a $1,000 television was a $20 fine, the threat of this legal punishment would not sway us against offending. Even so, most of us would still not steal a television even if the fine was this paltry because of penalties or potential long-term negative consequences from other sanctioning systems. Perhaps the most influential is social penalties. Potential social consequences for getting caught offending are important influences on behavior. Getting caught offending disappoints others, threatens relationships, and damages reputations for most people. Most of us would not steal a television even if the penalty were only $20 if there was a chance of being caught (which there always is) in part because we would recognize how others would view us or change their relationships with us if they found out. Thus, offending carries with it the risk of painful delayed social consequences.

The two other sanctioning systems G&H recognize are religious and physical. Many individuals are kept in line, so to speak, because they believe in a higher power(s) who sees their force or fraud, and they believe they will be punished by this higher power(s) for such behavior (especially in an afterlife, a punishment that is particularly delayed). A final category of potential negative consequences of crime is physical punishment or pains. Drawing on Bentham, G&H describe physical sanctions as those "consequences of behavior that follow naturally from it and require no active intervention by others" (p. 6) "It turns out," G&H state, "that many criminal or deviant acts are sufficiently risky or inherently difficult that they are, at least to some extent, naturally limited" (p. 6). The theorists use the example of intravenous drug use that "apparently produces great pleasure, but also carries with it a large increase in the risk of accident, infection, permanent physiological damage, and death" (p. 6). Victims may also be a source of physical pain, because people can react violently to threats or attacks to life and limb or even property. Moreover, physical pain has also been associated with imprisonment, for example by attacks from other inmates. One study of prisons across four Midwestern states found that about 20% of male inmates reported a pressured or forced sex incident while incarcerated. Roughly 9% reported that they had been raped (Struckman-Johnson & Struckman-Johnson, 2000). Many crimes risk delayed physical pains or punishments.

To summarize the discussion thus far, SCT assumes that the motivation for the immediate gains of crime is universal. We are all motivated to the ends of crime but are restrained by potential consequences, the most important ones being social. Crimes risk long-term consequences that for most crimes far exceed any benefits to be gained from the pleasurable act. Therefore, as rational, hedonistic beings, we should all forgo crime because crime objectively risks more pain than gain. G&H (1990) argue: "the balance of the total control structure favors conformity, even among offenders" (p. 86). How, then, do we explain individuals' commission of crime given that we are rational and pleasure-maximizing? Hirschi and Gottfredson (1994) raise this question explicitly: "The mystery is, rather, how some people can ignore or misapprehend the automatic consequences of their behavior, both positive and negative, and thus continue to act as though these consequences did not exist" (p. 4).

THE CONCEPT OF SELF-CONTROL

To rephrase the above question somewhat awkwardly (you're welcome): How can we explain this objectively nonpleasure maximizing choice (crime) given a model that assumes we are both rational and pleasure-maximizing when making choices? The answer, according to SCT, lies in individuals' time horizons at the point of decision making. According to G&H, although we all see the immediate consequences of behavior (how good that cake will taste), but how far into the future we extend our consequence considerations varies across individuals. This size of the window of time we consider affects the factors we consider when making our cost-benefit calculations, as many behavioral consequences are quite delayed. G&H (1990) summarize their position thusly:

> The object of the offense is clearly pleasurable and universally so. Engaging in the act, however, entails some risk of social, legal, and/or natural sanctions. Whereas the pleasure attained by the act is direct, obvious, and immediate, the pains risked by it are not obvious, or direct, and are in any event at greater remove from it. It follows that, though there will be little variability among people in their ability to see the pleasures of crime, there will be considerable variability in their ability to calculate potential pains. . . . So, the dimensions of self-control are, in our view, factors affecting calculation of the consequences of one's acts. (p. 95)

According to SCT, this variable—time perspective at the point of decision making—is a continuum. At the one end are individuals who consider potential consequences over a long time range. To use the cake example (which you are probably tired of by now), these individuals would consider how they will feel after eating the cake, the next hour, for the rest of the day, how it will influence their diet across the week, and so on. At the other end of the spectrum are individuals who are myopic, or have short time horizons. These individuals consider only the immediate consequences of their behavior. Thus, they would choose to eat cake when the immediate benefits outweigh the immediate costs, because they do not even consider the delayed benefits or costs in their calculations. According to SCT, this variable—time perspective in cost-benefit calculations—accounts for between-individual variation in perceptions of pleasures and pains, and thus the choice of crime or noncrime.

People who lack self-control are not constrained from crime by the potential long-term consequences of crime because they do not consider these consequences when making decisions. Individuals with high self-control are able to forgo the immediate benefits that crimes offer because they extend their considerations into the future and recognize that such benefits risk much more painful delayed consequences.

Time perspectives at the point of decision making are the key individual variable accounting for individual differences in the propensity to commit crime and are called *self-control.* Low self-control is defined by G&H (1990) as "the tendency of individuals to pursue short-term gratification without consideration of the long-term consequences of their acts" (p. 177) or "the tendency to . . . ignore the long-term consequences of one's acts" (Hirschi & Gottfredson, 1993a, p. 49). To answer the question raised earlier by G&H, the mystery of how some people can continue to act as though delayed consequences do not exist: because they do not see these consequences when making decisions. These long-term consequences actually do not exist in the mind's eye for individuals with low self-control. To reiterate, having low self-control is equivalent to having a short time perspective, such that cost-benefit calculations and decisions are based only on immediate consequences, whereas individuals with high self-control consider a range of consequences that extend out past immediate pains and pleasures.

According to G&H, self-control is the sole variable responsible for individual differences in the propensity to offend. Self-control is "the individual characteristic relevant to the commission of criminal acts" (G&H, 1990, p. 88). As, such low self-control is equivalent to *criminality*, which is a term referring to individuals' propensities to offend. Since self-control is the primary variable accounting for differential propensities to commit crimes, what is not relevant to individual's criminality is, ta-da: everything else. This includes differential motivations, which we have already discussed, and beliefs about the legitimacy of rules or norms. According to SCT, offenders believe just as strongly in the value or moral sway of rules as nonoffenders. It also excludes variation in the tendency to feel moral emotions (such as shame, guilt, sympathy, empathy, love); therefore, offenders should feel just as guilty as anyone else after committing their offenses. Ability to satisfy wants or needs legitimately is also unrelated to individual offending according to the theory. In other words, whether you can buy the television or not has no effect on your likelihood of stealing the television. Since self-control is the only significant individual factor that distinguishes criminals from law-abiders, the offender is "just as forgiving, as unarmed, as lacking in nefarious plans, or as remorseful and self-critical as non-offenders" (Felson & Osgood, 2008, p. 163).

DEVELOPMENT OF SELF-CONTROL

What is the source of criminality, a.k.a. low self-control? Consistent with the theory's assumptions about our naturally selfish, pleasure-maximizing nature, SCT asserts that we are born with low self-control. Spend time with an infant, and you will probably wholeheartedly agree with this idea. Short-term rationality is humans' natural disposition. The lack of self-control, or criminality, requires no special learning, pressures, or pains—its causes are "negative rather than positive" (G&H, 1990, p. 95). Instead, (high) self-control is *learned*, and this is a key sociological component of the theory.

According to SCT, effective parenting during the first 6 to 8 years of life inculcates (high) self-control. Fortunately, given the importance of self-control according to the theory, effective parenting is not rocket science (duh, it's parenting). Driven largely by affection for the child, effective parenting includes three minimum conditions: monitoring, recognition of deviance, and punishment of deviance. Regarding parental monitoring, G&H (1990) note, "such supervision presumably prevents criminal or analogous acts and at the same time *trains* the child to avoid them on his own" (p. 99, emphasis added). "In order for supervision to have an impact on self-control, the supervisor must perceive deviant behavior when it occurs. . . . Some parents allow the child to do pretty much as he pleases without interference. Extensive television watching is one modern example, as is the failure to require completion of homework" (G&H, 1990, p. 99).

Noting that "disapproval by people one cares about is one of the most powerful of sanctions," G&H (1990) suggest that effective punishment "usually entails nothing more than explicit disapproval of unwanted behavior" (pp. 99–100). They do remark, however, that not all parents punish effectively, with some being too harsh and others being too lenient. Moreover, consistent with their model, they note, "rewarding good behavior cannot compensate for failure to correct deviant behavior" (p. 100).

The idea is that parents who supervise their children, recognize inappropriate behavior, and punish the child for bad behavior instill in the child the ability to recognize that many pleasurable behaviors (especially deviant ones) have negative consequences that are neither immediate nor directly tied to the qualities inherent in the acts themselves (including punishment and parental anger, disappointment, and frustration). G&H also describe the situation where self-control is not developed.

> When we seek the causes of low self-control, we ask where this system can go wrong. Obviously parents do not prefer their children to be unsocialized in the terms described. We can therefore rule out in advance the possibility of positive socialization

> to unsocialized behavior . . . the system can go wrong at any one of four places. First, the parents may not care for the child (in which case none of the other conditions would be met); second, the parents, even if they care, may not have the time or energy to monitor the child's behavior; third the parents, even if they care and monitor, may not see anything wrong with the child's behavior; finally, even if everything else is in place, the parents may not have the inclination or the means to punish the child. So, what may appear at first glance to be non-problematic turns out to be problematic indeed. Many things can go wrong. (p. 98)

As sociological theorists, G&H do not get into the underlying processes of *how* effective parenting shapes time perspective. The important thing is that these parenting practices teach children to consider the more distant consequences of behavior and ingrain the ability to appreciate that the immediate pleasures from many behaviors (crimes and analogous behaviors) are outweighed by painful consequences that are delayed. As the theorists note, "Socialization, in this sense, may be seen as a process of educating individuals about the consequences of their behavior" (1994, p. 4), and "[t]rouble is likely unless something is done to train the child to forego immediate gratification in the interests of long-term benefits" (1990, p. 269).

STABILITY OF SELF-CONTROL

Perhaps the most controversial aspect of SCT is the stability proposition. The theory postulates that after childhood (around ages 8–10), between-individual levels of self-control are fixed. Either individuals develop self-control largely as a result of effective parenting during these formative years, or they do not, in which case they will suffer from low self-control and its many negative manifestations across the life course. In the words of Hirschi and Gottfredson (2001): "The differences observed at ages 8 to 10 tend to persist. . . . Good children remain good. Not so good children remain a source of concern to their parents, teachers, and eventually to the criminal justice system. These facts lead to the conclusion that low self-control is natural and that self-control is acquired in the early years of life" (p. 90).

According to SCT, then, the first decade of life is a crucial window of opportunity for the development of self-control. The social influence on self-control is limited to the formative years. After this time, while a cohort's overall level of self-control likely increases as socialization continues throughout life, between-individual levels of self-control are crystallized and impervious to change. "Our theory asserts that following childhood the population can be meaningfully ranked in terms of self-control, the tendency to consider or ignore the long-term consequences of one's acts" (Hirschi & Gottfredson, 1995, p. 137). Notably, this is a distinction between *absolute* and *relative* stability. While self-control levels will likely increase slowly for all individuals in a particular age group (cohort) over time as socialization continues through the life course (absolute increases in self-control), relative levels of self-control should remain fixed. Thus, if Bob has more self-control than Billy at age 10, then Bob should be less likely to commit crimes given greater time perspective than Billy throughout the life course, even though both Bob's and Billy's self-control likely increases in absolute terms over time (and regardless of what happens in their lives).

Presumably, SCT implies that decision-making habits, neural pathways, or other unspecified cognitive mechanisms responsible for the degree to which individuals consider long-term consequences of actions when calculating pleasures and pains are cemented in late childhood. (Such neuropsychological processes are outside the concern of this social theory.) SCT proposes that those individuals who were not fortunate enough to be effectively parented and, therefore, failed to develop self-control, will make myopic decisions—those promising immediate gratification with delayed costly outcomes—across the life course. The first decade of life is the window of opportunity to develop self-control (or not).

ALTERNATIVE (NON)SOURCES OR INFLUENCES ON SELF-CONTROL

There are, of course, a multitude of other possible sources of self-control. G&H address, and largely dismiss, several of these in their theoretical monograph. The first of these they focus on is the school. G&H (1990) remark: "Those not socialized sufficiently by the family may eventually learn self-control through the operation of other social institutions. The institution given principal responsibility for this task in modern society is the school" (p. 105). They argue, however, that despite its potential for inculcating self-control among children who were not effectively parented, the school is largely unable to compensate for lack of training in the home. The primary reason for this lack of success of the school in teaching self-control is that the school relies on parents' cooperation and support. Making sure that the child does his or her homework, is well fed and rested, and arrives at school on time (or at all) are all essential for the school to be an effective socializing institution (acts that require monitoring, recognition of deviance, and punishment). Unfortunately, those ineffective parents are not likely to be cooperating with and supportive of the school's mission. Thus, noting that the "net effect of the school must be positive" (p. 106), G&H reiterate that self-control differences are primarily attributable to parenting practices.

G&H also address the potential role of biology in criminality. Indeed, they devote an entire chapter to "biological positivism." Here they attack both the approach and its assumptions, but for our purposes, the important idea is found in their interpretation of the findings from existing research (recall that this book was published in 1990). They concluded, based on their reading of the results, that the magnitude of "the true genetic effect on the likelihood of criminal behavior . . . is minimal" (p. 58) and "near zero" (p. 60). They note, however, that this "should not be interpreted as showing that biology has *nothing* to do with crime," but that its effect is "substantively trivial" (pp. 60–61).

In other words, G&H grant the possibility that biology plays some role in human propensities and behaviors, such as self-control and crime. However, its role is minimal; regardless of inborn temperaments, effective parenting is needed to instill self-control. Although some children may be easier to socialize than others based on these small, in-born differences, G&H assert that effective parenting is still the major source of individual differences. Thus, SCT is a theory of intergenerational transmission of criminality through effective parenting rather than genes.

Obviously, since self-control is fixed by age 10 according to SCT, experiences that occur after this time should have no effect on self-control. What the stability proposition implies is that many factors that have been identified as influencing the change in criminal propensity across the life course, such as employment, marriage, having children, incarceration, and deviant peers, do not influence individuals' levels of self-control. Instead, G&H argue these are social consequences of self-control. Individuals select themselves into these experiences based on their levels of self-control, thus making it appear that there is a causal relationship between these factors. In other words, the link between employment, marriage, and peers with crime is spurious. Levels of self-control cause both crime and negative social consequences.

Take the example of deviant peers, which has been identified as the strongest correlate of individual offending. While other theories (e.g., Sutherland's [1947] differential association and Akers's [1973] social learning) propose that delinquent peers have a causal influence on individual offending through definitions conducive to crime, G&H argue that it is not so. Instead, they use the old adage, "birds of a feather flock together." They maintain that individuals with low self-control select themselves into peer groups that have low self-control as well. This is due to several factors, including the fact that their common myopia will lead to a shared interest in immediate gratification. On the other hand, individuals with higher self-control select themselves into groups that have shared interests based in part on their longer time perspective, such as persisting at school work for a shared college goal, involvement in athletic training that reaps athletic rewards in the future, or a disinclination to (illegal) behaviors, such as drinking and substance use, which threaten long-term goals.

This same explanation applies to other social factors. Individuals with low self-control select themselves out of well-paying, meaningful jobs; it is not the absence of the job that leads to their continuing crime, but their levels of self-control that create both their joblessness and their offending. Likewise for marriage. Stable, satisfying relationships, which sometimes end in marriage, require individuals to delay gratification and foresee potential consequences of various actions (cheating, working toward mutual goals, etc.) for the sake of their partner and relationship. Individuals with low self-control are thus unlikely to end up in such stable relationships, which have been linked to reduced offending. According to G&H, then, it is not marriage or a steady relationship that is responsible for less offending, but rather the underlying levels of self-control that influences both. As such, SCT is a social theory, but the influence of society on individual differences in offending is limited to the first decade of life. After this time, because self-control is already set in stone, positive interventions, life events, or the like will have no influence on criminality. Instead, these later social factors are social consequences of self-control.

SELF-CONTROL AND "ANALOGOUS" BEHAVIORS

"Crimes result from the pursuit of immediate, certain, easy benefits. Some noncriminal events appear to result from pursuit of the same kinds of benefits. As a result, these noncriminal events are correlated with crime" (G&H, 1990, p. 42). These acts similar to crimes that are also manifestations of low self-control, according to SCT, are known as "noncriminal acts analogous to crime" (p. 91).

G&H identify a number of analogous acts that stem from low self-control. In fact, they note that low self-control has many manifestations, crime being only one of them. The first class of acts that they identify is accidents. While at first blush accidents may not seem to result from pursuit of immediate gratification, G&H (1990) point out that accidents often are the result of myopia: "For example, motor vehicle accidents tend to be associated with speed, drinking, tail-gating, inattention, risk-taking, defective equipment, and young males. House fires tend to be associated with smoking, drinking, number of children, and defective equipment" (p. 42). Certainly regularly checking equipment, such as fire alarms and preparing the house appropriately with fire extinguishers, does not provide immediate gratification but the failure to do so could have really severe consequences. (This author may or may not have just checked her smoke detectors after writing this.)

Other noncriminal acts analogous to crime that G&H identify are smoking, drinking, and other drug use. Each of these acts (ostensibly) provides immediate pleasure and/or the attenuating of current pains (especially for those addicted to such substances), but threatens severe delayed punishments/pains. Smoking is an excellent example. While providing immediate benefits (nicotine fix, looking "cool" or "adult like," etc.), we are all well aware of the long-term consequences of smoking. For those with low self-control, these delayed consequences never enter their cost-benefit calculations, and thus they may choose to smoke. Binge drinking is another example; while many people enjoy the immediate consequences of being quite intoxicated, the delayed consequences can be severe, including terrible hangovers, missed or impaired school/work, involvement in behaviors that may threaten relationships due to intoxication, and even more long-term, irreversible damage to the liver or other internal organs (brain). Drinking responsibly rather than getting wasted is generally due in large part to the recognition of the delayed costs of getting really drunk. Thus, SCT predicts that those with low self-control are more likely to smoke, drink, use drugs, get in accidents, and farther down the line suffer from diseases. In that sense, G&H (1990) note, "[t]he 'costs' of low self-control for the individual may far exceed the costs of his criminal acts" (p. 94).

CRIMINALITY (SELF-CONTROL) AND CRIME

Essential to SCT is the distinction between crime and criminality. Crimes are acts, or "short-term circumscribed events that presuppose a peculiar set of necessary conditions (e.g., activity, opportunity, adversaries, victims, goods)" (G&H, 1990, p. 137). Criminality, which as you recall is tantamount to low self-control in SCT, refers to individual propensities to commit criminal acts. The idea inherent in the concept of criminality is that, all else equal, individuals with higher levels of criminality should be more likely to engage in acts of crime. However, G&H (1990) note on several occasions that low self-control does not require crime due to the variable effect of opportunity (another social influence).

According to SCT, criminal events occur when individuals with low self-control encounter opportunities for offending. Inherent in the notion of opportunities is not only the availability of goods, victims, and so on, but also conditions facilitating immediate gratification through illegal acts without immediate pains. Thus, if an underage individual has surreptitious possession of alcohol but is under the supervision of her or his parents or other authorities, we would not consider that an opportunity. The opportunity for theft is present when goods are available to be stolen without monitoring (electronic devices, salespersons). Similarly, the opportunity for rape would be present when individuals are in situations where the potential victim is weakened and/or isolated from monitoring by individuals who would intervene or alert the authorities.

To repeat, then, crime results when individuals with low self-control encounter opportunities for offending. G&H (1990) note, "Self-control is only one element in the causal configuration leading to a criminal act, and criminal acts are, at best, imperfect measures of self-control" (p. 137). SCT proposes that crime is not an automatic consequence of self-control, because it depends on opportunities, and that many acts analogous to crimes, such as smoking, drinking, and accidents, are also manifestations of low self-control.

At this point the social emphasis of the theory should be quite apparent. Individuals are born with low self-control, and it is the role of society, specifically caregivers, to socialize individuals to be functioning members of the social body. Socialization enables individuals to foresee the long-term consequences of their acts for themselves and others thereby allowing cooperation, pursuit of goals, and overall the continuance of the orderly(ish) society that we live in. When things go wrong—when parents do not adequately socialize their children—behavior is still shaped by social factors: opportunities. There is no place or need to recognize biological or psychological factors in this theory. Make no mistake, G&H do not argue that biological differences do not exist or psychological processes are not at play. Instead, they contend that such differences are unnecessary for the theory. If parenting and opportunities determine differences in individuals' crime and criminality, then delving into these other factors is superfluous at best and misguided at worst.

SCT AND PROMINENT CORRELATES OF OFFENDING

The distinction between crime and criminality is key to understanding other facets of the theory, such as the theory's position on offender specialization versus versatility. By versatility, G&H (1990) mean that "offenders commit a wide variety of criminal acts, with no strong inclination to pursue a specific criminal act or a pattern of criminal acts to the exclusion of others" (p. 91). G&H's "image therefore implies that no specific act, type of crime, or form of deviance is uniquely required by the absence of self-control" (p. 91). SCT does propose that the class of crime and analogous acts will be engaged in at a relatively high rate by people with low self-control. Within the domain of crime, however, there will be much versatility in the criminals acts in which individuals engage. In short, SCT proposes that individuals with low self-control will be likely to engage in the opportunity for crime, regardless of type, because crimes provide immediate gratification. Therefore, SCT predicts that offenders will be versatile and will not specialize in particular offenses.

The crime-criminality distinction is also essential for understanding the theory's position on age and crime. Several years prior to the publication of their book, Hirschi and Gottfredson (1983) published a rather famous and controversial piece in the *American Journal of Sociology* where they begin explicating their view on the connection between age and crime. In their theoretical monograph, they further develop their view of the relationship between age and crime, which they call "age theory."

The age theory rests on a number of theoretical assertions and empirical interpretations. First, drawing on evidence at different times and places, G&H concluded that the age crime curve is invariant across cultural and social conditions (i.e., found everywhere) (Note: The "age crime curve" refers to the inverted J pattern of offending that rises after late childhood, reaching a peak around age 16 years, and then steadily declines thereafter.) Going through existing social scientific explanations of the age-crime curve, the authors found them lacking and inconsistent with available evidence. For example, Sutherland's differential association theory would argue that the decline in crime with age is due to the decreased affiliation with criminal individuals and, therefore, a change in individuals' definitions toward crime. However, they noted that research shows that "even with equal exposure to criminal influences, propensity toward crime diminishes as one grows older" (Rowe & Tittle, 1977, p. 229).

In contrast to the prevailing view that adequate theories must be able to explain the age-crime connection, G&H argued that this inability to explain the age effect does not invalidate a theory. Instead, they took the unusual position of saying that the age-crime curve is inexplicable with social scientific explanations. G&H (1990) conclude, in a rather interesting bit of reasoning, that crime declines with age *independent of criminality* "due to the inexorable aging of the organism" (p. 141). In other words, although self-control remains stable, individuals' involvement in criminal events declines for reasons beyond the concern of social theories. "The distinction between crime and self-control thus provides a device for solving one of the major empirical dilemmas of criminology: the fact that crime everywhere declines with age while differences in 'crime' tendency across individuals remain relatively stable over the life course" (G&H, 1990, p. 145). To be clear, because the age effect is invariant, both high and low rate offenders will decrease their offending with age, even though their levels of self-control remain fairly stable across the life course.

Like age, sex differences in offending appear to be ubiquitous. "Men are always and everywhere more likely than women to commit criminal acts" (G&H, 1990, p. 145). Moreover, G&H note, sex differences in behaviors analogous to crimes are similar to those for criminal acts. For example, G&H point to evidence that shows that males are more likely to get in accidents (traffic accidents and otherwise) as well as abuse alcohol and drugs. The theorists also note that sex differences in crime and analogous acts are established early in life and persist throughout life, a fact that implies differences in the stable trait of self-control.

As social theorists, G&H do not theorize about possible biological differences between the sexes that could influence their offending patterns. Instead, they look to social factors. After reviewing research showing gender differences in patterns of child rearing, the theorists conclude, consistent with SCT, that sex differences in offending are largely due to sex differences in parenting. G&H argue that females are often subject to higher levels of monitoring, recognition of deviance, and punishment, which translates into higher levels of stable self-control across the life course. We are all aware of the phrase "boys will be boys," which can be applied to young boys' fighting, risk-taking, and the like. There is no adage "girls will be girls" that fits risk-taking or physically aggressive behavior. Indeed, G&H point to research suggesting not only that females are monitored more closely, but that their deviant behavior is also more likely to be recognized as such and punished than that of males.

In addition to differences in self-control, G&H (1990) also argue that differences in opportunities (that "peculiar set of necessary conditions" [p. 137] for crime) should also play a role in the higher rates of male offending. The role of direct supervision by parents and other social institutions plays a large part in shaping opportunities. They note that historically girls have been supervised more closely than boys, a situation that continues to the present day, albeit at diminished levels. This greater supervision of females was not due, as G&H point out, to the presumed higher levels on criminality among females, but rather to "the fact that most forms of delinquency are more costly to females than to males . . . [for example] sexual misbehavior could result in pregnancy and reduced opportunities for a successful marriage. In general, the connection between good behavior and life chances was so much stronger for females than for males that their life chances could be damaged by all sorts of misbehavior that would have little impact on the life chances of males" (p. 148).

G&H thus conclude that differences in both criminality and opportunity play a role in the gender gap, with opportunity being less important. The theorists, however, leave the door open for other factors, stating: "It is beyond the scope of this work (and beyond the reach of any available set of empirical data) to attempt to identify all of the elements responsible for gender differences in crime" (1990, p. 149). Thus, while levels of self-control should play a major role in explicating gender differences, other factors are at play and more research is needed.

Theories of crime should also be able to explain or shed light on racial-ethnic disparities in offending. Although official statistics are biased to some (unknown) degree by racial discrimination in the criminal justice system, self-report and victimization studies provide further evidence that rates of offending vary across racial and ethnic groups. G&H note that these differences are large and fairly stable over time. As with gender, the theorists remark that differences in crime rates across racial-ethnic groups are likely due to differences in both self-control and opportunity, with self-control having a stronger influence. G&H (1990) state that "there are differences among racial ethnic groups (as there are between the sexes) in levels of direct supervision by the family," and that "research on racial differences should focus on differential child-rearing practices" (p. 153).

Notably, this does not imply that factors such as economic or family stress do not play a role in explaining racial-ethnic differences in crime rates. To the contrary, these factors almost certainly do play a role *but through their effects on parenting*. The economically stressed parent, on average, according to G&H, is less able to effectively parent than the economically secure parent, as is the single parent, the working parent, and the parent of many children. This explanation does, however, discard cultural explanations for racial-ethnic differences. "Unfortunately for the cultural view of criminality," G&H (1990) remark, "the empirical evidence supports virtually none of its assumptions" (p. 151).

G&H also address cross-cultural differences in crime and explanations for these differences. Not surprisingly, they take a different tact than most others: "Our approach therefore rejects the conventional wisdom of comparative criminology. It assumes instead that cultural variability is *not* important in the causation of crime, that we should look for constancy rather than variability in the definition and causes of crime, and that a single theory of crime can encompass the reality of cross cultural differences in crime rates" (G&H, 1990, pp. 174–175; emphasis in original). That constancy they identify is, of course, consistent with their theory and suggests to them that self-control is the primary cause of crime regardless of the cultural context. As with other correlates, they ascribe a smaller role to opportunities as "crimes have minimal elements over and above their benefits to the individual . . . that do vary from time to time and place to place" (G&H, 1990, p. 177).

In sum, G&H argue that differences in crime rates across the sexes, racial-ethnic groups, and cultures are due in large part to differences in self-control. These self-control differences, in turn, are due to differences in effective parenting across groups. Differences in opportunities play a less important role, and the theorists open the door to other influences, citing the need for more research. Nonetheless, the key to understanding these differences, according to SCT, is found in differential child-rearing practices that produce different levels of criminality. Gibbs and Giever (1995) articulately describe the portrait of the offender according to SCT:

> The picture of the personality with low self-control that emerges from Gottfredson and Hirschi's theory is not flattering. The owner of such a personality is the product of parental disinterest, who has developed into a rather dull and inept creature unfettered by conventional concerns but tethered to the pursuit of momentary pleasure. Throughout life, this person engages in a variety of criminal and analogous acts when the opportunity for pleasure arises. His or her chances for success in conventional terms (e.g., employment, education, relationships), or in unconventional terms, for that matter (e.g., a successful criminal career), are circumscribed by a lack of self-control. This person has not acquired the persistence and the time perspective required to succeed in just about any long-term endeavor. (pp. 233–234)

Policy Implications of SCT

A theory's public policy recommendations can basically be understood as the procedures that should be instituted to reduce or control crime *assuming that the theory is correct.* Theories are useful both for evaluating existing criminal justice policies as well as suggesting changes. Regarding the adequacy of existing policies, G&H (1990) are quite frank: "Clearly, the general thrust of the public policy implications of our theory is counter to the prevailing view that modifications of the criminal justice system hold promise for major reductions in criminal activity" (p. 255).

G&H highlight four facets of their theory that undergird their claim of a weak effect of the criminal justice system. First, SCT emphasizes the stability of individual differences in criminality (low self-control), differences that are established in the crucial first decade of life. These fixed levels of self-control are "highly resistant to the less powerful inhibiting forces of later life, especially the relatively weak forces of the criminal justice system" (1990, p. 255). Second, SCT emphasizes the diversity among crime and analogous acts, sharing a common etiology (low self-control + opportunity). Since the causes of truancy are the same as those for drug use and violence, they argue: "It follows that the criminal justice system is at best a weak cause of any of them" (1990, p. 256). Furthermore, they argue that targeting any one of the acts as a cause of another (e.g., drug use as a cause for theft) is unlikely to be successful, because self-control is the primary cause of both. Third, because they assume that the motivation to commit crime is high for all, G&H (1990) criticize those policies that seek to curb crime by the "satisfaction of theoretically derived wants (e.g., equality, adequate housing, good jobs, self-esteem)" (p. 256). Finally, the theory recognizes the inexplicable age effect, whereby crime declines with age for all persons. Thus, the natural crime decline with age may be wrongly interpreted as support for programs that follow individuals across this natural crime decline.

Because they occur after the crucial time period of the first decade of life, criminal justice interventions are unlikely to be effective. Therefore, prison rehabilitation programs, drug treatment programs, and the like are a waste of money because they have insignificant influence on individuals' criminality. The current dominant policy in our system at present—incapacitation—is ineffective for several reasons. First, it is a response after crime has occurred, because we have no means for identifying chronic offenders with high degrees of accuracy prior to the commission of their crimes, according to G&H. While incapacitation does prevent individuals behind bars from victimizing others outside prison walls, it is incredibly costly (cost-ineffective) to reduce crime by warehousing. Finally, given the age effect, for incapacitation to be maximally effective, it should be focused on the age period prior to the peak years of crime, which would be around 13 or 14 years of age. As G&H note, the ethical issues around such a policy preclude further discussion or investigation of its potential effects.

Attempting to reduce crime by modifying policing is also unlikely to be successful according to G&H. The notion of specialized police divisions to deal with the specialized offender is contrary to their view of the versatile offender. Similarly, increasing the number of police is unlikely to have much of an effect because "[i]n the bulk of these offenses, the offender does not know or does not care about the probability of being observed by the police" (G&H, 1990, p. 270). Their view of "sting" operations is similarly unfavorable: "The common result of such expensive and time-consuming operations is the capture of a number of ordinary 'losers,' many of whom may have very low self-control but few of whom, if accurately described by the police in media representations, would engender public support for such programs" (p. 270).

In sum, G&H (1990) state,

> Contemporary crime policies, from criminal-career programs to modifications in policing, from selective incapacitation to the drug-crime connection, all have their roots in positivistic conceptions of the offender. According to the theory of self-control, none of these programs is likely to have much of an impact on the crime problem. (p. 274)

Although not as lengthy as their criticisms of current policies, G&H do offer suggestions for interventions to reduce and prevent crime. In particular, SCT implies that "[e]ffective and efficient crime prevention that produces enduring consequences would thus focus on parents or adults with responsibilities for child-rearing" (1990, p. 269). According to SCT, "all that is required to reduce the crime problem to manageable proportions is to teach people early in life that they will be better off in the long run if they pay attention to the eventual consequences of their current behavior" (Hirschi & Gottfredson, 1993b, p. 271). Thus, SCT proposes parenting interventions to teach caregivers how to effectively parent (monitor, recognize deviance, and punish deviance) so that they will instill in their children high self-control that will last throughout the life course. Unlike most criminal justice interventions, an effective parenting intervention would occur before crime is committed and before the age at which levels of self-control are fixed. Such a program would be cost-effective, according to G&H (1990), and "few serious objections can be raised to it on justice grounds" (p. 269).

In other words, since parenting is the major cause of self-control, which is the source of individual differences in criminality, to prevent and thereby reduce crime, a society should focus on teaching caregivers how to effectively parent their children. Of course, there is the nagging issue raised earlier by G&H that parents who have low self-control themselves are unlikely to have the patience and persistence to engage in effective parenting given its delayed benefits. Thus, taking this into consideration, its seems as though the positive effect of parenting interventions will be greater among parents with intermediate levels of self-control and less effective among those most at risk—kids whose parents have really low self-control. Even so, parenting is an extraordinarily complex undertaking without an instruction manual, thus teaching parents how to engage in better parenting should be useful even if not always applied evenly or consistently. "Apart from the limited benefits that can be achieved by making specific criminal acts more difficult, policies directed towards enhancement of the ability of familial institutions to socialize children are the only realistic long-term state policies with potential for substantial reduction" (G&H, 1990, pp. 272–273).

SCT is a social theory of crime. Although self-control is an internal characteristic, it is produced by a social factor—effective parenting—and relatively stable after the formative years. According to the theory, criminal events result when individuals with low self-control encounter the opportunity for crime, which is a function of the social circumstances encountered by the person. SCT posits social conditioning, social effects, and social consequences. The propositions are clear. What does research say about their accuracy?

TESTING SCT

The central thesis of SCT is that low self-control is the major source of individual differences in offending; low self-control is "for all intents and purposes, *the* individual level cause of crime" (G&H, 1990, p. 232, emphasis in original). This can be tested by examining whether levels of self-control are inversely related to offending; do individuals who offend have lower self-control, on average; and those who do not offend have higher self-control? To test this proposition, researchers will need a measure of self-control. Unfortunately for scholars endeavoring to test SCT (and maybe fortunately for the rest of us), we have not yet advanced to a level where we can actually observe the window of time individuals consider when calculating the consequences of their actions. This is an unobservable cognitive aspect of decision making. This is not unusual, because a number of social science theories of crime rely on indirect measures of their central construct. In contrast to other theories, however, G&H did not provide general guidance for how to measure self-control (e.g., Barlow, 1991; Marcus, 2004). Scholars have dealt with this issue by developing indirect measures of self-control. These can be broadly classified into attitudinal/personality measures and behavioral measures. Each has limitations and is discussed in turn.

Attitudinal or personality measures of self-control are based largely on a section titled "Elements of Self-Control" in G&H's monograph. In this section, G&H describe observable characteristics of persons with low self-control or, in other words, characteristics that people with low self-control are more likely to have or display. G&H (1990) identify six elements, including: (1) a "here and now orientation" or an inability to delay gratification; (2) preference for easy or simple pleasures as well as a lack of "diligence, tenacity, or persistence in a course of action"; (3) preference for adventure versus caution (risk-taking); (4) preference for physical activity over mental or cognitive activity; (5) self-centeredness and indifference or insensitivity to the needs and suffering of others; and (6) "minimal tolerance for frustration and little ability to respond to conflict through verbal rather than physical means" (pp. 89–90). "In sum," G&H argue, "people who lack self-control will tend to be impulsive, insensitive, physical (as opposed to mental), risk-taking, short-sighted, and nonverbal, and they will tend therefore to engage in criminal and analogous acts" (p. 90).

The idea is, then, that because these characteristics are manifestations of an underlying myopia, they tend to cluster in individuals with low self-control and therefore can be used to measure an individual's underlying level of self-control. Scholars have taken this list of personality characteristics of individuals with low self-control and created survey questions that tap into each of these elements. The best known is the Grasmick, Tittle, Bursik, and Arneklev (1993) scale, which consists of 24 questionnaire items, four for each of the identified elements, such as "I often act on the spur of the moment without stopping to think" (impulsivity), "I frequently try to avoid projects that I know will be difficult" (simple tasks), and "Sometimes I will take a risk just for the fun of it." Although the Grasmick scale is the most widely used, other scholars have developed similar ones based on this list of characteristics of persons with low self-control (e.g., Burton, Cullen, Evans, Alarid, & Dunaway, 1998; Gibbs & Giever, 1995).

A second, and less common, approach to measuring self-control is through an assessment of behaviors. Perhaps surprising given the cognitive nature of their construct, G&H advocate for behavioral measures. Behavioral measures rest on the link between self-control and the behaviors being measured, as scholars are assuming that self-control differences between individuals produce the between-individual differences in the behavioral measures. This assumption has led some scholars to argue that behavioral measures are ultimately a tautology, which means that they rest on circular reasoning or are true by definition. Behavioral measures assume that self-control is the cause of some behaviors that are then used to test whether self-control is related to another behavior (crime; e.g., Akers, 1991). Some find this measurement strategy particularly unsatisfying because it assumes the very thing it is trying to demonstrate (that low self-control increases "bad" behavior; Akers, 1991; Geis, 2000; Meier, 1995). Other scholars argue that behavioral measures of self-control are superior (e.g., Hirschi & Gottfredson, 1993a; Marcus, 2004). This tautology debate continues to the present, with some scholars seeing this as a critical issue and others not so much (see Piquero, 2008).

Hirschi and Gottfredson (1993a) argue that the best measures of self-control are the acts the theory is intended to explain, and they propose several behaviors that could be used as indicators of self-control. "With respect to crime, we have proposed such items as whining, pushing, and shoving (as a child); smoking and drinking and excessive television watching and accident frequency (as a teenager); difficulties in interpersonal relations, employment instability, automobile accidents, drinking, and smoking (as an adult)" (Hirschi & Gottfredson, 1993a, p. 53). Scholars have used these and similar items to develop measures of self-control based on behaviors that the individual admits to engaging in (Marcus, 2004; Tittle, Ward, & Grasmick, 2003b) or others (teachers, parents) report that the individual has engaged in (Chapple, 2005; Hay & Forrest, 2006; Ward, Gibson, Boman, & Leite,). Notably, research comparing the predictive ability of behavioral and attitudinal measures did not find that they were significantly different in magnitude in predicting crime and delinquency (e.g., Pratt & Cullen, 2000; but see Benda, 2005), but the trend is toward behavioral measures having a stronger relationship to offending than cognitive/attitudinal ones (e.g., Tittle et al., 2003b).

The indirect nature of these two measures has led scholars in recent years to focus more directly on decision making and individuals' thinking (or lack thereof) at the point of decision making.

This third, and more recent, way of measuring individuals' self-control seeks to tap more directly into individual time perspective at the point of decision making. For example, Burt and Simons (2013) assess the extent to which individuals consider (or would consider) the possible negative consequences the first time they considered drinking alcohol, using drugs like crack or cocaine, or driving after drinking. These items were combined with three additional ones that tap into the individuals' deliberation at the point of decision making; respondents were asked to indicate on one end that they carefully weighed the pros and cons of an act before deciding what to do and on the other end whether they just did what feels right. A different approach, but one also focusing on decision-making considerations, was taken by Piquero and Bouffard (2007) and Higgins, Wolf, and Marcum (2008). In these studies, they asked respondents to indicate the perceived costs and benefits of crime as well as the importance of these costs and benefits in vignette scenarios (hypothetical situations where respondents would indicate their likelihood of offending in such situations). Interestingly, all three of these studies find that the self-control measure focused on decision making reduces offending (or the hypothetical intention), but the personality scales (e.g., Grasmick scale) remain significant predictors.

The clearest conclusion that can be drawn from work on self-control measures is unsatisfying but true: more research is needed to assess the relationship among the different measures and refinements on what these measures are capturing (if not solely self-control). It remains the case that until we can actually observe by some fancy technology individuals' actual cognitive decision making, we will have to make do with these indirect measures, each imperfect in its own way.

Research (Is SCT True?)

Not surprisingly, given the bold presentation of SCT as well as its grand and controversial claims (e.g., to explain all crime at all times), empirical assessments of the theory are plentiful. Hundreds of studies have tested SCT since its arrival on the criminological scene in 1990, making it the most frequently tested theory of crime at present. Most aspects of the theory have now received enough research attention that they can be assessed with a body of evidence. G&H's (1990) book had been cited more than 5,300 times at the time of this writing (Google Scholar, 01/2013). Below, this author samples some of the research findings; this review is necessarily limited, because covering all the research on SCT would take a tome. This author limits the discussion to research explicitly testing SCT (and even within this restricted scope, this is only a sample of this large body of work).

Support for the central premise of the theory, that low self-control is strongly related to increased offending, is consistent (e.g., Pratt & Cullen, 2000). Many studies have found that low self-control is linked to increased general crime and deviance, measured cross-sectionally and longitudinally, using both self-reports and official criminal records (see Pratt & Cullen, 2000, for a review). Low self-control has also been linked to "analogous behaviors," including binge drinking (Gibson, Schreck, & Miller, 2004), cutting classes (Gibbs & Giever, 1995), risky driving (Jones & Quisenberry, 2004), counterproductive work behavior (Marcus & Schuler, 2004), risky sex (Jones & Quisenberry, 2004), smoking (Arneklev, Grasmick, Tittle, & Bursik, 1993), and even eating disorder symptoms (Harrison, Jones, & Sullivan, 2007). In their meta-analysis, which is a statistical summary of studies, Pratt and Cullen (2000) noted that the effect size of self-control qualifies it as "one of the strongest known correlates of crime" (p. 952) and the consistently strong support among studies of youth has led scholars to conclude that "[self-control's] relationship to delinquent involvement is a fact" (Unnever, Cullen, & Pratt, 2003, p. 483).

Research has also tested the generality of self-control by examining its ability to explain offending across different groups and cultures. Evidence suggests that low self-control predicts crime and deviance across different age groups (Burton, Evans, Cullen, Olivares, & Dunaway, 1999), and ethnicities (H. V. Miller, Jennings, Alvarez-Rivera, & Lanza-Kaduce, 2009; Shekarkhar & Gibson, 2011; Vazsonyi & Crosswhite, 2004), and for both males and females (e.g., LaGrange & Silverman, 1999; Tittle, Ward, & Grasmick, 2003a). Furthermore, SCT appears to shed light on offending in different cultural contexts, as research shows that low self-control is associated with increased deviance in non-U.S. contexts, such as Canada (Forde & Kennedy, 1997), Japan (Vazsonyi, Clifford Wittekind, Belliston, & Van Loh, 2004), and Russia (Tittle & Botchkovar, 2005). In their comparison across several nations, Vazsonyi, Pickering, Junger, and Hessing (2001) concluded that "different aspects of self-control operate in a similar fashion in all national contexts; there do not appear to be unique or culture-specific relationships and patterns of association" (p. 120).

Research is not, however, uniformly supportive of the central proposition of SCT. First, research clearly shows that self-control is not the sole individual difference factor responsible for crime. Studies show that factors identified by rival theories (e.g., delinquent peers, social learning theory [Akers, 1973]; strain (general strain theory [Agnew, 1992] continue to influence the likelihood of offending after accounting for levels of self-control (e.g., Pratt & Cullen, 2000). In addition, studies indicate that self-control does not explain differences in offending among different groups. Given that low self-control is the main cause of crime according to SCT, statistically controlling for self-control should largely explain the link between group membership and crime. Research does not support this strong claim. Although self-control does explain some of the differences in offending between groups and across cultures, it does not fully explain sex differences (e.g., Blackwell & Piquero, 2005; Chapple, Vaske, & Hope, 2010; LaGrange & Silverman, 1999) or racial ethnic ones (e.g., Pratt, Turner, & Piquero, 2004). Indeed, Pratt and colleagues (2004) found that while there were racial differences in levels of monitoring and supervision, with non-Whites having lower levels than Whites, there were no significant differences in levels of self-control. Furthermore, while research has indicated that self-control does influence crime in different cultural and national contexts, at least one study focusing on crime in Nigeria noted that self-control did not fare well in that context, in part because it contains "unacknowledged value assumptions" that "undermine its claim to universality" (Marenin & Reisig, 1995, p. 501).

Such findings are not completely at odds with the theory, because G&H do not argue that the link between social factors such as race and crime are fully explained by self-control, and opportunity factors do play a role in the genesis of criminal events. Yet such findings do undermine the theory's claim that self-control is the major source of individual differences in offending.

In addition, some research questions the generality of self-control, or its claim to explain "all crimes, at all times" without a complex of factors. In particular, scholars have questioned the ability of SCT to explain white-collar crimes, especially those committed by individuals in high ranks within a corporation or occupation, in part because rising to such a position requires a fair bit of self-control (e.g., Benson & Moore, 1992; Reed & Yeager, 1996; Steffensmeier, 1989). After reviewing evidence on white-collar crime from the perspective of SCT, Friedrichs and Schwartz (2008) concluded: "Rather than accepting Gottfredson and Hirschi's argument that we can explain criminality by means of a single factor, we should recognize that accounting for crime entails a multitude of factors, that we are highly unlikely to realize a comprehensive explanation of crime, and that the complex of factors explaining different forms of white collar crime is not the same complex of factors that can be invoked to explain the different forms of conventional crime" (p. 158). Similar critiques have been leveled at SCT's explanation of violence (Felson & Osgood, 2008), sexual assaults and violence against women (Iovanni & Miller, 2008; S. L. Miller & Burack, 1993), property crime (Swatt & Meier, 2008), and substance use (Goode, 2008). In sum, this work suggests that while levels of self-control may contribute to these different types of behaviors, again is it not the only individual-level factor that contributes, and its influence may depend on the type of crime in question.

Is self-control *the* major source of individual differences in crime? The answer to this point is no. The evidence does suggest that low self-control is *a* major cause of individual differences in the likelihood of offending. Being a major cause of crime is no small feat, yet, as this author has noted, G&H set their aims quite high, and, it appears, too high.

A second line of research has examined the influence of parenting on self-control. Recall, G&H (1990) maintain that effective parenting during the first 6 to 8 years of life is needed to produce self-control in children. Is effective parenting the main cause of individual differences in self-control? Again, the answer appears to be not exactly. Research does suggest that effective parenting (monitoring, recognition of deviance, and punishment of deviance) is associated with higher levels of self-control (e.g., Feldman & Weinberger, 1994; Hay, 2001; Polakowski, 1994). Studies also suggest, however, that a broader conceptualization of parenting, which includes both the monitoring and punishment aspects identified by G&H (demandingness) as well as the context of this parenting—such as warmth, support, and positive reinforcement (responsiveness)—does a better job at explaining levels of self-control (e.g., Burt, Simons, & Simons, 2006; Hay, 2001).

More damaging for SCT's parenting thesis are findings that other factors shape individuals' levels of self-control. These include both social factors, such as community (Pratt et al., 2004; Simons & Burt, 2011), school (Beaver, Wright, & Maume, 2008; Meldrum, 2008; Turner, Piquero, & Pratt, 2005), and peer (Burt et al., 2006; Meldrum, 2008; Meldrum & Hay, 2011) influences as well as genetic and/or biological factors (J. P. Wright & Beaver, 2005; J. P. Wright, Beaver, DeLisi, & Vaughn, 2008), including maternal smoking during pregnancy (Turner, Livecchi, Beaver, & Booth, 2011). In short, this research suggests that while effective parenting is related to individual levels of self-control it is not the only source of self-control.

One of the most contentious aspects of SCT, and one that distinguishes it most sharply from other social theories of crime, is the stability proposition. Recall, this postulate asserts that self-control rankings between individuals remain stable after early childhood (after ages 8–10).

Although research on the stability of self-control was slower to emerge, in recent years a number of studies have put SCT's stability proposition to a test. This research has tested the stability of self-control rankings between individuals in samples of undergraduates across a few months (Arneklev et al., 1993), between offenders and nonoffenders across a few years (Turner & Piquero, 2002), and in community (Burt et al., 2006) and nationally representative samples of youth (Hay & Forrest, 2006) that span several years and waves of data (see also Higgins, Jennings, Tewksbury, & Gibson, 2009; Winfree, Taylor, He, & Esbensen, 2006). In general, these studies find that self-control is only moderately stable, with correlations ranging usually from about .4 to .6 (whereas SCT would predict that the correlations would be near 1). Notably, stability estimates are higher when the follow-up times are shorter, which is not surprising, and are higher when other-reporters (e.g., teacher or mother) are used instead of self-reports.

Although research points to moderate stability, studies have not found just slight reshuffling among individuals. Although most individuals are roughly stable in their self-control rankings after late childhood (moderate reshuffling), there is also evidence of drastic changes in self-control, with individuals moving from among the lowest to highest levels and vice versa (Burt et al., 2006; Hay & Forrest, 2006). Hay and Forrest (2006), for example, found that more than 10% of their sample fit into a trajectory of declining self-control across adolescence. This latter finding, of drastic decreases in self-control, is particularly inconsistent with SCT, because self-control has been thought of as a skill that once gained is never lost (Hay & Forrest, 2006). In sum, research evidence to date is inconsistent with the strict stability proposition of SCT, suggesting instead that between-individual levels of self-control are moderately stable for most, and really unstable for a notable minority.

Some scholars, including G&H, would argue that these findings of instability are really errors in measurement. In other words, rather than being real or meaningful changes, different moods, recollections, and mistakes in responding to surveys and the like are responsible for the changes observed. A recent study, however, suggested that this is not the case. Using a large sample of youth from Baltimore, Na and Paternoster (2012) estimated fancy statistical models that account for measurement error and demonstrated that these changes are not merely attributable to errors in measurement or a particular statistical model. Furthermore, two studies have demonstrated that changes in self-control are related as expected to changes in offending, a pattern that would not be observed if the changes were meaningless errors (Burt et al., 2006; Hay, Meldrum, Forrest, & Ciaravolo, 2010).

Given this evidence of instability, researchers have begun examining factors that may contribute to self-control changes after the first decade of life. Thus far, research has identified several factors that are linked to increases and decreases in self-control. Factors associated with deteriorations in self-control include associating with deviant peers (Burt et al., 2006) and victimization (Agnew et al., 2011), while improvements in parenting, increased association with prosocial peers, and increased attachment to teachers/school have been linked to improvements in self-control over time (Burt et al., 2006; Hay & Forrest, 2006). Criminal justice and/or therapeutic interventions also deserve a second look in this modified version. As Greenberg (2008) notes, "The proposition that rehabilitation programs do nothing to prevent further crimes is out of date. Evaluations show that some programs do reduce return to crime for some juvenile and adult law violators" (p. 42). Furthermore, Hay and colleagues (2010) found that a parenting intervention designed to improve parenting practices (after the first decade of life) was associated with increased self-control among youth.

Evidence is mixed regarding the theory's versatility proposition. Although much research indicates that some offenders are highly versatile (e.g., Brame, Paternoster, & Bushway, 2004; DeLisi, 2003; Piquero, 2008), research also indicates that some offenders specialize and/or limit their offending to certain groups of offenses (e.g., Farrington, Snyder, & Finnegan, 1988; Lussier, LeBlanc, & Proulx, 2005; Osgood & Schreck, 2007; Shover, 1996). Other studies suggest that the versatility-stability issue is more complex than previously thought, with offenders displaying stability over a shorter time period and versatility over the long term (e.g., Deane, Armstrong, & Felson, 2005; Sullivan, McGloin, Pratt, & Piquero, 2006). Consistent with SCT arguments about the role of opportunities in the genesis of criminal events, research suggests that the short-term specialization in individual offending is due to "local life circumstances," which shape opportunities toward specific acts (e.g., McGloin, Sullivan, Piquero, & Pratt, 2007).

Articulately summarizing the body of research on SCT, Matsueda (2008) stated,

> Perhaps a judicious evaluation of Gottfredson and Hirschi's (1990) theory of self-control would state that it has effectively challenged the criminological community, contains important insights, arguments, and findings but also makes strong assumptions that are questionable in light of research results, and derives equally strong implications that are questionable given faulty assumptions. The assumptions are that there is constant motivation to deviate, that self-control is a stable trait and explains crime, and that the age-crime curve is invariant. Implications are that life course events have no effect, delinquent peer effects are an artifact, crime is never learned, and crime is not organized. (p. 123)

Given the sweeping claims of the theory—to explain individual differences in the propensity to force and fraud with a single variable—it is not surprising that research has failed to support the grand claims of SCT. It does seem to be clear that self-control is a major cause of individual differences in crime, parenting does shape individual levels of self-control, and levels remain relatively stable after childhood for a substantial majority. Nonetheless, the contrary evidence for the general theory suggests that it needs to be modified in light of the evidence. What would the theory look like if we left the major assumptions intact but provided a better fit with empirical reality, and therefore a better explanation of offending?

Modifying the Theory to Fit the Facts

Social scientific theories are works in progress, which can (and should) be modified in response to new facts and evidence. Clearly, a considerable amount of research has tested SCT, and while much of this work is consistent with the general thrust of the theory, this work also suggests various ways the theory can be modified to better fit with reality. Modifications can (and should) be made while retaining core assumptions of the theory and its social emphasis. In the following paragraphs, this author describes this modified version of SCT.

This modified version of the theory has to start somewhere so this author starts at the same place G&H did: with what the theory is trying to explain. Although self-control is likely related in some degree to most crimes, there are certain offense categories that do not fit into SCT's formula. As G&H admit, their theory was designed to explain the typical acts of crime. Indeed, the theorists note that those crimes that are "rare," "complex," and "difficult" are "an inadequate basis for theory and policy" (p. 119). As Geis (2008) states, however: "There obviously are numerous criminal activities, such as antitrust conspiracies, that are long-term and quite complex" (p. 207), such as Enron and Bernie Madoff's Ponzi scheme. Political crimes and organized crimes are also largely inexplicable with the theory because they are both complex and/or require long-term planning. The theory cannot claim to be general (explaining all crimes) while also dismissing crimes that it cannot explain as being too rare to be worthy of explanation, particularly given evidence that these types of crimes are not particularly rare at all (Kane & Wall, 2006; Sutherland, 1940). A theory does a greater service to science by accurately simplifying a smaller portion of reality than it does by inaccurately oversimplifying a larger portion. As such, SCT should restrict its scope to be an explanation of street crimes, which include most acts of force and many acts of fraud committed by individuals, as well as analogous acts like substance use.

Evidence also suggests that the theory's equal motivation assumption is an oversimplification of a more complex reality. Individuals *do* differ in their tastes, preferences, and aversions, and these differences *do* influence motivation to various behaviors such as crime (e.g., Tittle & Botchkovar, 2005; Tittle, Ward, & Grasmick, 2004). Take the example of illicit drugs. Some people enjoy using illicit drugs and some do not, and within those who do, some enjoy certain drugs but not others. Two individuals with equivalent time perspectives (levels of self-control) may be differentially attracted to LSD, marijuana, 'shrooms, or cocaine given the opportunity, and, thus, partake in those substances at different levels for reasons other than their self-control. Moreover, crimes are inherently risky, and individuals differ in the extent to which they are attracted to (enjoy) risk taking (e.g., Felson & Osgood, 2008).

The extent to which individuals can achieve immediate gratification without resorting to illegal behavior is also likely a motivating factor to crime. For someone with a full bank account, the ability to satisfy the desire for a new flat screen television is as easy as swiping a credit card, whereas those with an empty bank account and weak credit must steal such a television if they want to own it immediately. As Geis (2008) notes, "It is likely a great deal easier to be self-controlled if you have what you desire." Although recognizing that motivation varies across individuals both in general and toward specific crimes will make the theory less parsimonious, such a change is necessary for the theory to fit with the facts. Theories founded on erroneous assumptions will eventually collapse.

Changes to the propositions are also necessary. Effective parenting as defined by SCT is not the only source of self-control. As noted above, levels of self-control are influenced by both parental demandingness (monitoring, punishment) and responsiveness (warmth, support). Moreover, school, community, and peer factors also influence individuals' levels of self-control.

Regarding the stability of self-control, while self-control is roughly stable for a majority of the sample, it continues to develop into early adulthood, remaining responsive to changes in social factors. Current research suggests that while individuals may be more responsive to changes in the formative years, there is no "window of opportunity" after which interventions play no role. Thus, SCT should be modified to take account of other social factors in individuals' levels of self-control and the instability of self-control and its responsiveness to social changes after the formative years.

In part as a consequence of self-control's malleability past the first decade of life, social factors are not merely "social consequences of self-control." While birds of a feather (birds with low self-control) may flock together, they also influence one another (Akers, 1991). As Akers (2008) notes, citing Benjamin Franklin, "If you lie down with dogs, you get up with fleas" (p. 85). The influence of many (or most) social factors is reciprocal—it goes both ways. Levels of self-control not only likely influence whether individuals get good jobs, find stable partners, and the like, but it is also the case that these social relationships and transitions influence behavior and perhaps self-control as well (B. R. E. Wright, Caspi, Moffitt, & Silva, 1999). It is not necessary for self-control to fully account for all other social variables, which is fortunate because it does not do so. Thus, the theory should be modified to take account of both selection and socialization across the life course.

Since the genesis of SCT, scholars have noted its potential to shed light on age-offending patterns, and commented that the "age theory" is unnecessary for the theory (e.g., Greenberg, 2008). This modified version of SCT should not throw in the towel over trying to explain the age-crime curve. Instead, the theory should attempt to explain the association between age and crime the same way it explains the link between other ubiquitous social facts (e.g., the link between sex/gender and crime) by drawing on the link between age, levels of self-control, and opportunity.

The rise in crime during adolescence could be partially explained by a combination of a still developing level of self-control with a sudden increase in opportunities brought about by decreased supervision and the like. Moreover, many of the same acts that are immediately gratifying and legal for adults are illegal for youth (drinking, driving, smoking, etc.). Thus, there is a perfect storm of still relatively low levels of self-control for a large portion of adolescents, combined with an increase in opportunities for behaviors, many of which are criminalized. To be sure, this is just a potential explanation; the important point is that SCT should try to explain the age-crime curve rather than deem it inexplicable.

Additionally, while levels of self-control do appear to explain some of the differences between groups, such as racial/ethnic, sex/gender, and socioeconomic class, self-control is not the only factor that contributes to the different rates of offending across groups. Self-control provides a partial explanation, but not a complete one. While research is ongoing as to what other factors contribute to offending in concert with levels of self-control, some possible answers have already been suggested by research, some this author has mentioned, such as attitudes toward risk, violence (harming others), and the like. It is not the purpose of this modification to add numerous factors or contingencies to the theory, however, but rather to correct the oversimplifications of the current version. It should be noted that several scholarly efforts to combine self-control with other concepts as part of a broader (and more complex) explanation of crime have been proposed (see, e.g., Agnew, 2005; Simons & Burt, 2011; Wikström & Treiber, 2007). SCT can better contribute to the knowledge of crime and its explanation as an independent theory *if* modifications are made. One is acknowledging that self-control is only one individual-level factor responsible for offending.

Conclusion

> *As the limits of the general theory are revealed—as occurs with all prominent theories—a rigid fidelity to the original statement of the general theory is likely to ensure its staleness if not decline . . . it appears that the time has come for the general theory to broaden its horizons so as to confront criminological realities that now rest beyond its boundaries*
>
> —Cullen, Unnever, Wright, & Beaver, 2008, p. 74

SCT is a grand theory of crime. Grand in the sense that it has pushed the field forward in a significant way, is striking in size and what it claims to encompass, and is definitely intended to impress. In the more than 20 years since its inception, it has come to occupy a major place in criminological thought, challenging many beliefs, inspiring an incredible amount of research, and providing further spark to debates on stability, versatility, public policy, and the causes of crime. For these reasons alone, the theory always holds a key position in criminological textbooks and thought with new generations of criminology students becoming familiar with its ideas and implications.

Yet for a theory to remain at the forefront of criminological thought it has to remain consistent with facts, especially those that directly speak to its propositions. Some of the stances the theory takes are clearly misguided. Thus, for SCT to remain a dominant theory as we move further into the 21st century, it will need to undergo some changes. Some sociological ones have been described; further interdisciplinary acknowledgments or restrictions in scope will need to be addressed. Denying biological and genetic influences on human behavior is no longer a defensible position. Even so, the influence of social factors, such as parenting, should not be downplayed. Here, too, the evidence is overwhelming.

References

Ackers, R. L. (2008). Self-control and social learning theory. In E. Goode (Ed.), *Out of control: Assessing the general theory of crime* (pp. 77–89). Stanford, CA: Stanford University Press.

Agnew, R. (1992). Foundation for a general strain theory of delinquency. *Criminology, 30*, 47–87.

Agnew, R. (2005). *Why do criminals offend? A general theory of crime and delinquency*. New York, NY: Oxford University Press.

Agnew, R., Scheuerman, H., Grosholz, J., Isom, D., Watson, L., & Thaxton, S. (2011). Does victimization reduce self-control? A longitudinal analysis. *Journal of Criminal Justice, 39*(2), 169–174.

Akers, R. L. (1973). *Deviant behavior: A social learning approach*. Belmont, CA: Wadsworth.

Akers, R. L. (1991). Self-control as a general theory of crime. *Journal of Quantitative Criminology, 7*, 201–211.

Arneklev, B., Grasmick, H. G., Tittle, C. R., & Bursik, R. J. (1993). Low self-control and imprudent behavior. *Journal of Quantitative Criminology, 9*, 225–247.

Barlow, H. D. (1991). Review essay: Explaining crimes and analogous acts, or the unrestrained will grab at pleasure whenever they can. *Journal of Criminal Law and Criminology, 82*, 229–242.

Beaver, K. M., Wright, J. P., & Maume, M. O. (2008). The effect of school classroom characteristics on low self-control: A multilevel analysis. *Journal of Criminal Justice, 36*, 174–181.

Benda, B. B. (2005). The robustness of self-control in relation to form of delinquency. *Youth & Society, 36*, 418–444.

Benson, M. L., & Moore, E. (1992). Are white-collar and common crime the same? An empirical and theoretical critique of a recently proposed general theory of crime. *Journal of Research in Crime and Delinquency, 29*, 251–272.

Bentham, J. (2007). *An introduction to the principles and morals of legislation*. Mineola, NY: Dover. (Original work published 1823)

Blackwell, B. S., & Piquero, A.R. (2005). On the relationship between gender, power control, self-control, and crime. *Journal of Criminal Justice, 33*, 1–17.

Brame, R., Paternoster, R., & Bushway, S. D. (2004). Criminal offending frequency and offense switching. *Journal of Contemporary Criminal Justice, 20*, 201–214.

Burt, C. H., & Simons, R. L. (2013). Self-control, thrill seeking, and crime: Motivation Matters. *Criminal Justice and Behavior, 40*(11), 1326–1348.

Burt, C. H., Simons, R. L., & Simons, L. G. (2006). A longitudinal test of the effects of parenting and the stability of self-control: Negative evidence for the general theory of crime. *Criminology, 44*, 353–396.

Burton, V. S., Cullen, F., Evans, T. D., Alarid, L., & Dunaway, R. G. (1998). Gender, self-control, and crime. *Journal of Research in Crime and Delinquency, 35*, 123–147.

Burton, V. S., Evans, T. D., Cullen, F., Olivares, K. M., & Dunaway, R. G. (1999). Age, self-control, and adults' offending behaviors: A research note assessing a general theory of crime. *Journal of Criminal Justice, 27*, 45–54.

Chapple, C. L. (2005). Self-control, peer relations, and delinquency. *Justice Quarterly, 22*, 89–106.

Chapple, C. L., Vaske, J., & Hope, T. (2010). Sex differences in the causes of self-control: An analysis of mediation, moderation and gendered etiologies. *Journal of Criminal Justice, 38*, 1122–1131.

Cullen, F. T., Unnever, J. D., Wright, J. P., & Beaver, K. M. (2008). Parenting and self-control. In E. Goode (Ed.), *Out of control: Assessing the general theory of crime* (pp. 61–74). Stanford, CA: Stanford University Press.

Deane, G., Armstrong, D. P., & Felson, R. B. (2005). An examination of offense specialization using marginal logit models. *Criminology, 43*, 955–988.

DeLisi, M. (2003). The imprisoned non-violent drug offender: Specialized martyr or versatile career criminal? *American Journal of Criminal Justice, 27*, 167–182.

Farrington, D. P., Snyder, H. N., & Finnegan, T. A. (1988). Specialization in juvenile court careers. *Criminology, 26*, 461–485.

Feldman, S. S., & Weinberger, D. A. (1994). Self-restraint as a mediator of family influences on boys' delinquent behavior: A longitudinal study. *Child Development, 65*, 195–211.

Felson, R. B., & Osgood, D. W. (2008). Violent crime. In E. Goode (Ed.), *Out of control: Assessing the general theory of crime* (pp. 160–172). Stanford, CA: Stanford University Press.

Forde, D. R., & Kennedy, L. W. (1997). Risky lifestyles, routine activities, and the general theory of crime. *Justice Quarterly, 14*, 265–288.

Friedrichs, D. O., & Schwartz, M. D. (2008). Low self-control and high organizational control: The paradoxes of white-collar crime. In E. Goode (Ed.), *Out of control: Assessing the general theory of crime* (pp. 145–159). Stanford, CA: Stanford University Press.

Geis, G. (2000). On the absence of self-control as the basis for a general theory of crime: A critique. *Theoretical Criminology, 4*, 35–53.

Geis, G. (2008). Self-control: A hypercritical assessment. In E. Goode (Ed.), *Out of control: Assessing the general theory of crime* (pp. 203–216). Stanford, CA: Stanford University Press.

Gibbs, J., & Giever, D. (1995). Self-control and its manifestations among university students: An empirical test of Gottfredson and Hirschi's general theory. *Justice Quarterly, 12*, 231.

Gibson, C., Schreck, C. J., & Miller, J. M. (2004). Binge drinking and negative alcohol-related behaviors: A test of self-control theory. *Journal of Criminal Justice, 32*, 411–420.

Goode, E. (2008). Drug use and criminal behavior. In E. Goode (Ed.), *Out of control: Assessing the general theory of crime* (pp. 185–199). Stanford, CA: Stanford University Press.

Gottfredson, M., & Hirschi, T. (1990). *A general theory of crime*. Stanford, CA: Stanford University Press.

Grasmick, H., Tittle, C., Bursik, R., & Arneklev, B. (1993). Testing the core empirical implications of Gottfredson and Hirschi's general theory of crime. *Journal of Research in Crime and Delinquency, 30*, 5–29.

Greenberg, D. F. (2008). Age, sex, and racial distributions in crime. In E. Goode (Ed.), *Out of control: Assessing the general theory of crime* (pp. 38–48). Stanford, CA: Stanford University Press.

Harrison, M. L., Jones, S., & Sullivan, C. (2007). The gendered expressions of self-control: Manifestations of noncriminal deviance among females. *Deviant Behavior, 29*, 18–42.

Hay, C. (2001). Parenting, self-control, and delinquency: A test of self-control theory. *Criminology, 39*, 707–736.

Hay, C., & Forrest, W. (2006). The development of self-control: Examining self-control's stability thesis. *Criminology, 44*, 739–774.

Hay, C., Meldrum, R., Forrest, W., & Ciaravolo, E. (2010). Stability and change in risk seeking: Investigating the effects of an intervention program. *Youth Violence and Juvenile Justice, 8*, 91–106.

Higgins, G. E., Jennings, W. G., Tewksbury, R., & Gibson, C. L. (2009). Exploring the link between low self-control and violent victimization trajectories in adolescents. *Criminal Justice and Behavior, 36*, 1070–1084.

Higgins, G. E., Wolf, S. E., & Marcum, C. D. (2008). Digital piracy: An examination of three measures of self-control. *Deviant Behavior, 29*, 440–460.

Hirschi, T., & Gottfredson, M. (1983). Age and the explanation of crime. *American Journal of Sociology, 89*, 552–611.

Hirschi, T., & Gottfredson, M. (1993a). Commentary: Testing the general theory of crime. *Journal of Research in Crime and Delinquency, 30*, 47–54.

Hirschi, T., & Gottfredson, M. (1993b). Rethinking the juvenile justice system. *Journal of Research in Crime and Delinquency, 30*, 47–54.

Hirschi, T., & Gottfredson, M. (1994). The generality of deviance. In T. Hirschi & M. Gottfredson (Eds.), *The generality of deviance* (pp. 1–22). New Brunswick, NJ: Transaction.

Hirschi, T., & Gottfredson, M. (1995). Control theory and the life course perspective. *Studies on Crime and Crime Prevention, 4*, 131–142.

Hirschi, T., & Gottfredson, M. (2001). Self-control theory. In R. Paternoster & R. Bachman (Eds.), *Explaining criminals and crime* (pp. 81–96). Los Angeles, CA: Roxbury.

Iovanni, L. A., & Miller, S. L. (2008). A feminist consideration of gender and crime. In E. Goode (Ed.), *Out of control: Assessing the general theory of crime* (pp. 127–141). Stanford, CA: Stanford University Press.

Jones, S., & Quisenberry, N. (2004). The general theory of crime: How general is it? *Deviant Behavior, 25*, 401–426.

Kane, J., & Wall, A. D. (2006). *The 2005 National Public Survey on White Collar Crime*. Fairmont, WV: National White Collar Crime Center.

LaGrange, T. C., & Silverman, R. A. (1999). Low self-control and opportunity: Testing the general theory of crime as an explanation for gender differences in delinquency. *Criminology, 37*, 41–72.

Lussier, P., LeBlanc, M., & Proulx, J. (2005). The generality of criminal behavior: A confirmatory factor analysis of the criminal activity of sex offenders in adulthood. *Journal of Criminal Justice, 33*, 177–189.

Marcus, B. (2004). Self-control in the general theory of crime: Theoretical implications of a measurement problem. *Theoretical Criminology, 8*, 33–55.

Marcus, B., & Schuler, H. (2004). Antecedents of counterproductive behavior at work: A general perspective. *Journal of Applied Psychology, 89*, 647–706.

Marenin, O., & Reisig, M. D. (1995). A general theory of crime and patterns of crime in Nigeria: An exploration of methodological assumptions. *Journal of Criminal Justice, 23*, 501–518.

Matsueda, R. L. (2008). On the compatibility of social disorganization and self-control. In E. Goode (Ed.), *Out of control: Assessing the general theory of crime* (pp. 102–126). Stanford, CA: Stanford University Press.

McGloin, J. M., Sullivan, C. J., Piquero, A. R., & Pratt, T. C. (2007). Local life circumstances and offending specialization/versatility: Comparing opportunity and propensity models. *Journal of Research in Crime and Delinquency, 44*, 321–346.

Meier, R. F. (1995). Book review. *Social Forces, 73*, 1627–1629.

Meldrum, R. C. (2008). Beyond parenting: An examination of the etiology of self-control. *Journal of Criminal Justice, 36*, 244–251.

Meldrum, R. C., & Hay, C. (2011). Do peers matter in the development of self-control? Evidence from a longitudinal study of youth. *Journal of Youth and Adolescence, 41*, 691–703.

Miller, H. V., Jennings, W. G., Alvarez-Rivera, L. L., Lanza-Kaduce, L. (2009). Self-control, attachment, and deviance among Hispanic adolescents. *Journal of Criminal Justice, 37*, 77–84.

Miller, S. L., & Burack, C. (1993). A critique of Gottfredson and Hirschi's general theory of crime: Selective (in)attention to gender and power positions. *Women and Criminal Justice, 4*, 115–134.

Na, C., & Paternoster, R. (2012). Can self-control change substantially over time? Rethinking the relationship between self- and social control. *Criminology, 50*, 427–462.

Osgood, D. W. , & Schreck, C. J. (2007). A new method of studying the extent, stability, and predictors of individual specialization in violence. *Criminology, 45*, 272–312.

Piquero, A. R. (2008). Measuring self-control. In E. Goode (Ed.), *Out of control: Assessing the general theory of crime* (pp. 26–37). Stanford, CA: Stanford University Press.

Piquero, A. R., & Bouffard, J. A. (2007). Something old, something new: A preliminary investigation of Hirschi's redefined self-control. *Justice Quarterly, 24*, 1–27.

Polakowski, M. (1994). Linking self- and social control with deviance: Illuminating the structure underlying a general theory of crime and its relation to deviant activity. *Journal of Quantitative Criminology, 10*, 41–78.

Pratt, T. C., & Cullen, F. T. (2000). The empirical status of Gottfredson and Hirschi's general theory of crime: A meta-analysis. *Criminology, 38*, 931–964.

Pratt, T. C., Turner, M. G., & Piquero, A. R. (2004). Parental socialization and community context: A longitudinal analysis of the structural sources of low self-control. *Journal of Research in Crime and Delinquency, 41*, 219–243.

Reed, G. E., & Yeager, P. C. (1996). Organizational offending and neoclassical criminology: Challenging the reach of a general theory of crime. *Criminology, 34*, 357–377.

Rowe, A. R., & Tittle, C. R. (1977). Life-cycle changes and criminal propensity. *Sociological Quarterly, 18*, 223–236.

Shekarkhar, Z., & Gibson, C. L. (2011). Gender, self-control, and offending behaviors among Latino youth. *Journal of Contemporary Criminal Justice, 27*, 63–80.

Shover, N. (1996). *Great pretenders: Pursuits and careers of persistent thieves.* Boulder, CO: Westview.

Simons, R. L., & Burt, C. H. (2011). Learning to be bad: Adverse social conditions, social schemas, and crime. *Criminology, 49*, 553–598.

Steffensmeier, D. J. (1989). On the causes of "white-collar" crime. *Criminology, 27*, 359–372.

Struckman-Johnson, C., & Struckman-Johnson, D. (2000). Sexual coercion rates in seven Midwestern prison facilities for men. *Prison Journal, 80*, 379–390.

Sullivan, C. J., McGloin, J. M., Pratt, T. C., & Piquero, A. R. (2006). Rethinking the "norm" of offender generality: Investigating specialization in the short-term. *Criminology, 44*, 199–233.

Sutherland, E. H. (1940). White-collar criminality. *American Sociological Review, 5*, 2–10.

Sutherland, E. H. (1947). *Principles of criminology* (4th ed.). Philadelphia, PA: L. B. Lippincott.

Swatt, M. L., & Meier, R. F. (2008). Property crimes. In E. Goode (Ed.), *Out of control: Assessing the general theory of crime* (pp. 173–184). Stanford, CA: Stanford University Press.

Tittle, C. R., & Botchkovar, E. V. (2005). Self-control, criminal motivation and deterrence: An investigation using Russian respondents. *Criminology, 43*, 307–354.

Tittle, C. R., Ward, D. A., & Grasmick, H. G. (2003a). Gender, age, and crime/deviance: A challenge to self-control theory. *Journal of Research in Crime and Delinquency, 40*, 426–453.

Tittle, C. R., Ward, D. A., & Grasmick, H. G. (2003b). Self-control and crime/deviance. Cognitive vs. behavioral measures. *Journal of Quantitative Criminology, 19*, 333–365.

Tittle, C. R., Ward, D. A., & Grasmick, H. G. (2004). Capacity for self-control and individuals' interest in exercising self-control. *Journal of Quantitative Criminology, 20*, 143–172.

Turner, M. G., & Piquero, A. R. (2002). The stability of self-control. *Journal of Criminal Justice, 30*, 457–471.

Turner, M. G., Livecchi, C. M., Beaver, K. M., & Booth, J. (2011). Moving beyond socialization hypothesis: The effects of maternal smoking during pregnancy on the development of self-control. *Journal of Criminal Justice, 39*, 120–127.

Turner, M. G., Piquero, A. R., & Pratt, T. C. (2005). The school context as a source of self-control. *Journal of Criminal Justice, 33*, 327–339.

Unnever, J. D., Cullen, F. T., & Pratt, T. C. (2003). Parental management, ADHD, and delinquent involvement: Reassessing Gottfredson and Hirschi's general theory. *Justice Quarterly, 20*, 471–500.

Vazsonyi, A. T., Clifford Wittekind, J. E., Belliston, L. M., & Van Loh, T. D. (2004). Extending the general theory of crime to "the East": Low self-control in Japanese late adolescents. *Journal of Quantitative Criminology, 20*, 189–216.

Vazsonyi, A. T., & Crosswhite, J. M. (2004). A test of Gottfredson and Hirschi's general theory of crime in African American adolescents. *Journal of Research in Crime and Delinquency, 41*, 407–432.

Vazsonyi, A. T., Pickering, L. E., Junger, M., & Hessing, D. (2001). An empirical test of a general theory of crime: A four-nation comparative study of self-control and the prediction of deviance. *Journal of Research in Crime and Delinquency, 38*, 91–131.

Ward, J. T., Gibson, C. L., Boman, J., & Leite, W. L. (2010). Assessing the validity of the Retrospective Behavioral Self-Control Scale: Is the general theory of crime stronger than the evidence suggests? *Criminal Justice and Behavior, 37*, 336–357.

Wikström, P. O., & Treiber, K. (2007). The role of self-control in crime. *European Journal of Criminology, 4*, 237–264.

Winfree, L. T., Taylor, T. J., He, N., & Esbensen, F. A. (2006). Self-control and variability over time: Multivariate results using a 5-year, multisite panel of youth. *Crime & Delinquency, 52*, 253–286.

Wright, B. R. E., Caspi, A., Moffitt, T. E., & Silva, P. A. (1999). Low self-control, social bonds, and crime: Social causation, social selection, or both? *Criminology, 37*, 479–514.

Wright, J. P., & Beaver, K. M. (2005). Do parents matter in creating self-control in their children? A genetically informed test of Gottfredson and Hirschi's theory of low self-control. *Criminology, 43*, 1169–1202.

Wright, J. P., Beaver, K. M., DeLisi, M., & Vaughn, M. (2008). Evidence of negligible parenting influences on self-control, delinquent peers, and delinquency in a sample of twins. *Justice Quarterly, 25*, 544–569.

10

Low Self-Control Is a Brain-Based Disorder

Matt DeLisi

Iowa State University

The underlying biological basis of constraint is believed to be located in attentional networks in the brain.

—Hampson, 2012, p. 327

The heightened risk-taking and impulsivity observed in adolescence has been partly attributed to the slow development of the brain regions necessary for cognitive control, subsuming response selection, top-down control and inhibitory processes, and including prefrontal cortex (PFC).

—Blakemore & Robbins, 2012, p. 1184

Introduction

It is difficult to overestimate the importance of self-control for leading a happy, healthy, and productive life. Self-control, which is the basic capacity to regulate one's thoughts, emotions, and behaviors in the face of external demands, is a necessary and essential ingredient to function in society. Although it is a continuously distributed construct, individuals who are generally low in their self-control suffer mightily compared to their peers with higher self-control. Low self-control makes more difficult the likelihood of getting along with others, performing well in school, maintaining and sustaining relationships and work commitments, and engaging in healthy lifestyle habits. When an individual's self-control is significantly discrepant from others', the result is a disorganized, chaotic life of impulsively living from moment to moment. Because self-control is so importantly related to life, it has intrigued humans since time immemorial. As Heatherton and Baumeister (1996, p. 90) noted, "The human capacity for self-control has been an enduring theme in philosophy, poetry, politics, and theology throughout history."

Self-control is also a big deal in criminology and criminal justice, thanks to the seminal theory by Gottfredson and Hirschi (1990). In their landmark book, *A General Theory of Crime,* Gottfredson and Hirschi suggested that ineffective parental socialization inculcated low self-control characterized by temper/aggression, self-centeredness, action-orientation, impulsivity, preference for immediate gratification, and the like by late childhood. This single, global construct in turn was theorized to be predictive of not only delinquent and criminal behaviors, but also imprudent and other maladaptive behaviors. The empirical support linking self-control to conduct problems and crime is substantial (Buker, 2011; de Ridder, Lensvelt-Mulders, Finkenauer, Stok, & Baumeister, 2012), so much so that the theory and its construct have been colorfully likened to the larger-than-life dinosaur *Tyrannosaurus rex* (DeLisi, 2011). In many respects, low self-control is without peer as a correlate and cause of crime.

But there is an irony about the success of self-control as a potent predictor of crime. In Gottfredson and Hirschi's theory, self-control is differentially produced by parental management techniques during the socialization processes of childhood. It is not, from this perspective, something that is congenital, neurogenetic, or brain-based. Here, this author argues the exact opposite. This chapter highlights theory and research that indicates that low self-control is primarily a brain-based disorder. The chapter draws on scholarship from a range of fields in the social and behavioral sciences, explores phenotypes (behavioral manifestations) that are associated with deficits in self-control, and examines research using genetically sensitive data to study self-control. The chapter concludes with a self-control interpretation of the famous Phineas Gage case and implications for the neurological basis of low self-control.

Conceptual Frameworks

Although the human brain denotes sublime interaction between its various regions, neuropsychologists have paid particular attention to the frontal or cortical areas because they involve the areas that set humans apart from our animal relatives. As Duckworth (2011) suggested, "It seems the less-evolved species are not tortured in the same way as we humans, who struggle to stay on diets, kick smoking habits, stop biting our nails, put an end to procrastinating, control our tempers, and otherwise, follow through on resolutions we know will improve our overall well-being"

(p. 2639). The prefrontal cortex is comprised of the orbitofrontal region, dorsolateral prefrontal region, and medial frontal/anterior cingulate region. Of these, the orbitofrontal region or cortex is relevant for self-control, and as a consequence, relevant for understanding crime. Cummings and Miller (2007) summarized its role in the following way:

> The orbitofrontal cortex, particularly the right-hemispheric orbitofrontal regions, mediates the rules of social convention. Patients with orbitofrontal lesions are socially disabled, manifesting interpersonal disinhibition, poor social judgment, impulsive decision making, lack of consideration for the impact of their behavior, absence of an appreciation for the effect of their behavior or comments on others, and lack of empathy for others. (p. 15)

At a basic level, the frontal or cortical regions of the brain serve to modulate instinctual and emotionally laden impulses emanating from subcortical regions. What this means is that individuals with better frontal control (sometimes referred to as executive control or executive governance) are better equipped to stifle and appropriately handle emotions, thoughts, and motivations that could be socially problematic. This is essential for functioning in daily life. For instance, as Baumeister and Alquist (2009) assessed, "[t]he need to be able to alter behavior to accord with standards has figured prominently in human social life because of the proliferation of standards: laws, distant goals, social norms, religious ideals, moral and ethical principles, traditions and customs, and more" (p. 115).

Across disciplinary perspectives, a variety of conceptual frameworks articulate the neurological basis of self-control. Michael Posner (2012) and Mary Rothbart (2011) have utilized an approach that combines research from the neurosciences and the study of temperament to illustrate the ways that self-regulation develops across childhood. According to both Posner and Rothbart, self-regulation/control in early infancy is accomplished by attentional control, which is the ability to focus on environmental demands in the face of distractions, irrelevant information, and habitual or over-learned behaviors. Attentional control involves brain networks from the frontal and parietal lobes. By about age 3 to 4 years, however, there is shift in self-regulation where effortful control or the ability to subordinate a dominant or prepotent impulse in favor of a subdominant but socially appropriate one develops. Effortful control involves the frontal lobe or the executive attention system (Posner, 2012; Rothbart, 2011; Posner, Rothbart, Sheese, & Voelker, 2012), specifically the lateral prefrontal cortex and anterior cingulate regions. Regarding neurotransmission, this shift also characterizes a shift from the cholinergic system to the dopaminergic system.

In psychiatry, there is overlapping evidence that neurobehavioral disorders are importantly caused by brain-based deficits in self-control. In Moffitt's (1993) influential developmental taxonomy, pathological criminal offenders are theorized to develop from interactions between life-course-persistent offenders' global neuropsychological deficits and adverse environments in which they are raised. Neuropsychological deficits create a suite of deficits for these offenders, but central among them is low self-control—a behavioral tendency that paves the road from temperamental difficultness, to conduct problems, to delinquency, to crime, and ultimately to criminal justice system penalties.

In a series of works, Séguin and his colleagues (e.g., Séguin, Arsenault, & Tremblay, 2007; Séguin, Nagin, Assaad, & Tremblay, 2004; Séguin, Pihl, Harden, Tremblay, & Boulerice, 1995) have shown that neuropsychological deficits generally and deficits that specifically relate to self-regulation are pronounced among children who are the most aggressive and impulsive. Comings (2003) suggested that defects in the dorsolateral prefrontal lobes produce symptoms that are essentially those of Attention-Deficit/Hyperactivity Disorder (ADHD). These include inattention, impulsivity, distractibility, disinhibition, impaired planning, poor organization, absence of motivation, and poor abstract reasoning. In addition, Comings suggested that deficits in the orbitofrontal prefrontal lobes produce symptoms that are essentially those of conduct disorder (when observed in children and adolescents) and antisocial personality disorder (when observed in adults). These characteristics include affective disorders, aggression, poor self-control, emotional outbursts, and lack of guilt, remorse, and/or empathy. In short, the nadir of common neurobehavioral disorders occurs in brain networks associated with self-control.

Personality neuroscience is a broad conceptual framework that studies the neurogenetic bases of personality to understand the etiology of behavior. Recently, investigators conducted a neuroimaging study of the personality using resting-state functional connectivity, which can detect brain activation patterns without relying on specific tasks (Adelstein et al., 2011). There were significant findings for all personality features, but of particular relevance for the current chapter were the findings for conscientiousness, the personality domain that is most directly associated with self-control. Conscientiousness predicted resting-state functional connectivity in frontal or executive areas associated with planning, self-discipline, industriousness, carefulness, and organization.

Within criminology and criminal justice, the Biosocial Criminology Research Group, which includes Kevin Beaver, Matt DeLisi, Michael Vaughn, John Paul Wright, and their colleagues, has translated self-control theory (Gottfredson & Hirschi, 1990) into an explicitly neurological explanatory model. In an empirical study, for example, Beaver, Wright, and DeLisi (2007) suggested that the set of characteristics that embodies low self-control, such as impulsivity; poor temper, which suggests deficits at inhibitory control; preference for action as opposed to intellectual pursuits, which suggests cognitive deficits; and short time horizon actually comports with executive functioning. Executive functions are the higher-order cognitive abilities that pertain to self-regulation. Thus from their theoretical vantage, low self-control as Gottfredson and Hirschi have articulated is actually shorthand for the cluster of neurocognitive or executive deficits that are systematically associated with externalizing behaviors (see Moffitt, 1990, 1993).

Within this biosocial framework, there is growing evidence that self-control is mostly neurogenetic regarding its etiology. Based on twin data selected from the National Longitudinal Study of Adolescent Health, Beaver, Wright, DeLisi, and Vaughn (2008) reported that between 52% and 64% of variance in self-control is heritable. Moreover, at Wave 1, heritability estimates for self-control approached 80%, and were about 50% at Wave 4. In addition, 82% of the stability of self-control over time is attributable to genetic factors.

There is also evidence that self-control is definitely not caused by parenting. Drawing on data from the Fragile Families and Child Wellbeing Study, Boutwell and Beaver (2010) conducted a propensity score matching design to examine the effects of broken homes/parenting on self-control. After rigorously controlling for selection effects, they found zero evidence that any of six measures of being reared in a broken home were associated with self-control. Using data from the National Survey of Children, Ratchford and Beaver (2009) found that neuropsychological deficits predicted parent and teacher reports of self-control and a composite measure despite the competing effects of birth complications, low birth weight, parental punishment, family rules, neighborhood disadvantage, gender, race, and age.

In sum, several conceptual approaches draw on self-control and allied constructs as an essential ingredient for behavioral competence. Although environmental factors such as parenting and peers are widely acknowledged, these conceptual models also assert the primarily brain-basis of self-control. The next section examines some of the behavioral phenotypes associated with low self-control.

Phenotypes

There is voluminous evidence that self-regulation/control and its cognate constructs relating to attentional control, focusing, planning, attention shifting, effortful control, and others are significantly associated with externalizing behavior problems (Garstein, Bridgett, Young, Panksepp, & Power, 2013; Garstein, Putnam, & Rothbart, 2012), emotional regulation (Braungart-Rieker, Hill-Soderlund, & Karrass, 2010; Kochanska, Murray, & Harlan, 2000), aggression (DeWall, Finkel, & Denson, 2011), conduct problems (Moffitt & Caspi, 2001; Vaughn, DeLisi, Beaver, & Wright, 2009), delinquency (Vaughn, Beaver, & DeLisi, 2009), criminal violence (Finkel, DeWall, Slotter, Oaten, & Foshee, 2009; Vaughn, Beaver, & DeLisi, 2009), and diverse forms of noncompliance with the criminal justice system (DeLisi, 2011). In some cases, low self-control produces very negative social consequences. For example, DeLisi and Vaughn (2008) examined the relationship between self-control and career criminality among a large sample of institutionalized juvenile delinquents. They found that youth who scored one standard deviation above the mean on a low self-control scale were nearly 450% more likely to become career criminals. Since career criminals account for more than half the crime in society (DeLisi, 2005), a substantial amount of variance in the crime problem relates to low self-control. Similarly, a recent study of the linkages between self-control and criminal justice system interaction found that persons who are at the high end of the low self-control distribution have a probability of criminal conviction that is 7 times greater than persons who score at the low end of the low self-control distribution (Beaver, DeLisi, Mears, & Stewart, 2009).

The obverse is also true: high self-control is almost without exception linked to positive, adaptive phenotypes. To illustrate, Tangney, Baumeister, and Boone (2004) studied an undergraduate sample and found that high self-control was associated with earning higher grades, experiencing higher self-esteem, having fewer psychiatric symptoms, drinking less alcohol, having better eating habits, having better interpersonal skills, enjoying better relationships, and being more emotionally healthy. In fact, there was no evidence of a negative outcome among individuals with high self-control.

Self-control phenotypes emerge early. A universal sign of low self-control during early childhood is the temper tantrum. Temper dysregulation is a normative and usually short-lived response to a frustrating or upsetting event. At a clinical level, temper tantrums are characterized by long-lasting emotional and behavioral upset, spontaneous or unexplained onset, and occurrence across multiple settings with diverse adults. In a recent study of nearly 1,500 preschoolers, it was found that nearly 85% of preschool children have a tantrum sometimes. However, 8.6% of children had daily tantrums that were significantly indicative of self-control problems (Wakschlag et al., 2012). In addition, this subgroup was also characterized by extreme scores on aggression, impulsivity, and hyperactivity.

Nationally representative data sources have been marshaled to demonstrate that the neurogenetic bases of low self-control produce a cascade of negative social and behavioral consequences. Drawing on data from a nationally representative sample of kindergarteners in the United States, Vaughn, DeLisi, and colleagues (2009) conducted a latent class analysis and reported evidence of a severely impaired subgroup that comprised 9.3% of kindergarteners. One of the most glaring differences between these children and their peers (some of whom had moderate behavioral problems) were cognitive/executive problems that compromised their self-control. Children in the severe group had worse fine motor skills, worse gross motor skills, more externalizing behaviors, worse interpersonal skills, poorer social interaction, more barriers to learning, and worse classroom behavior. They were reared in households characterized by greater levels of parental stress, fewer family rules, more physical punishment, and less parental affection.

In a study utilizing data from the E-Risk Longitudinal Twin Study, which tracks the development of a nationally representative birth cohort of 2,232 British children, Houts, Caspi, Pianta, Arsenault, and Moffitt (2010) tracked 7 years of development between ages 5 and 12 to examine the effects of early emerging dispositional features on classroom conduct. They found that children with low self-control/self-regulation characterized by hyperactivity, impulsivity, negative affect, and challenging behaviors caused a disproportionate amount of difficulty in classroom settings that required teacher effort. The disruptive behavior of children with low self-control required disproportionate attention from the teacher—attention that was consistently diverted from well self-regulated children.

Drawing on birth cohort data from the Dunedin Multidisciplinary Health and Development Study, Moffitt and her colleagues (2011) recently evaluated the predictive validity of childhood self-control on a range of life outcomes during adulthood. The findings were startling. Persons who displayed low self-control during childhood reported a range of difficulties at age 32. These included worse physical health, greater depression, higher likelihood of drug dependence, lower socioeconomic status, lower income, greater likelihood of single-parenthood, worse financial planning, more financial struggles, and most important for a criminological audience, more criminal convictions. Indeed, 45% of participants with low self-control during childhood had criminal convictions at age 32, a level that is nearly fourfold higher than the prevalence of criminal convictions for persons who had high childhood self-control.

The particular importance of these findings based on Dunedin data is the role of neurocognitive factors in producing self-control. For example, White, Moffitt, Earls, Robins, and Silva (1990) found that preschool self-regulation/behavior problems occurring at age 3 were the best predictor of conduct problems at age 11. Preschool neurocognitive ability was among the strongest predictor of conduct problems at age 11. Indeed, preschool predictors such as neurocognitive ability and externalizing behaviors correctly classified 81% of youth who were antisocial at age 11 and 66% of youth who were antisocial at age 15.

In sum, there is tremendous evidence that antisocial phenotypes are associated with deficits in self-control and impressive evidence that phenotypes associated with success, health, and happiness are in part caused by high self-control. Central to this research area is that intact neuropsychological functioning is essential for effective self-governance. Because more than half of all human genes are expressed in the brain, the next section examines molecular genetic association studies that have linked various genes to self-control.

Genotypes

Given the neurological basis of low self-control, it is understood that a significant amount of variance in it is attributable to genetic factors. A host of scholars in the social and behavioral sciences have examined associations between specific genes, self-control, and other related phenotypes. For example, researchers have shown that the 7-repeat allele of the dopamine receptor D4 gene (DRD4) has significant pleiotropic effects on multiple constructs relating to self-control. A variable number tandem repeat (VNTR) located in the third exon of the gene codes for the receptor protein. The 7-repeat allele exhibits decreased signal efficiency for neural circuits that are associated with effortful control (Smith et al., 2012).

Several gene × environment interactions have been found in studies using this allele. For instance, Sheese, Rothbart, Voelker, and Posner (2012) reported an interaction between the DRD4 7-repeat allele and parenting quality in the prediction of effortful control among a sample of children ages 3 to 4 years. An independent study of the same DRD4 7-repeat allele reported an interaction with negative parenting in the prediction of effortful control among children age 3 years (Smith et al., 2012). There is also evidence that the DRD4 exon III polymorphism is associated with behavioral examples of low self-control, such as binge drinking (Vaughn, Beaver, DeLisi, Howard, & Perron, 2009). Indeed, the latter study found that DRD4 was nearly as strong a predictor of binge drinking as low self-control (which itself was significant).

Identifying genes that code for neural substrates is critical for understanding the neurogenetic framework of self-control. Protein phosphatase 2, regulatory subunit B, gamma (PPP2R2C) encodes a protein that is associated with cell division that is part of neurodevelopmental networks. Geneticists recently discovered that the major G allele of the single nucleotide polymorphisms (SNP) rs 16838844 significantly increased risk for ADHD. In addition, the rs16838698 (SNP) was associated with temperamental features that are associated with externalizing behaviors, such as openness to experience, extraversion, and novelty seeking (Jacob et al., 2012). In other words, PPP2R2C is a potential neurobiological risk factor for a constellation of personality and temperament constructs that compromise self-regulation.

Various neurotransmitter systems are associated with self-regulation. Kochanska, Philibert, and Barry (2009) examined the polymorphism in the serotonin transporter gene (5HTTLPR) and its interaction with maternal attachment at age 15 months on self-regulation among children at 25, 38, and 52 months. Among children at genetic risk, which is indicated by the short ss/sl allele of 5HTTLPR, who were insecurely attached had poor regulatory capacities; children at genetic risk but with secure attachment had normal self-regulatory capacity.

Catechol-o-methyltransferase (COMT) is an enzyme that metabolizes dopamine and norepinephrine in the frontal areas of the brain and is implicated in the modulation of aggressive impulses. Polymorphisms in the COMT gene have been linked to disorders of self-regulation/control, including ADHD. Geneticists recently linked the rs6269 SNP with childhood-onset aggressive behavior and provided suggestive evidence that rs6269 and rs4818 SNPs were associated with callous and unemotional traits among children who scored at or exceeding the 90th percentile on a parent-report of aggression (Hirata, Zai, Nowrouzi, Beitchman, & Kennedy, 2013).

Finally, there is also molecular genetic evidence linking various genes to self-control as it is contemporarily understood in criminology and criminal justice (Gottfredson & Hirschi, 1990). For example, Beaver, DeLisi, Vaughn, and Wright (2010) examined the interrelations between the monoamine oxidase A gene (MAOA) and neuropsychological deficits in the prediction of low self-control. They found significant effects for an interaction between neuropsychological deficits and low-activity alleles of MAOA that predicted low self-control. These relationships were found across two waves of data. Investigators have shown that the serotonin transporter gene (5HTTLPR) interacts with delinquent peers to predict variation in self-control during adolescence and adulthood (Beaver, Ratchford, & Ferguson, 2009). To summarize, it is understood that what criminologists for decades believed to be social constructs are actually multifactorial constructs that are often strongly heritable. Criminologists will therefore continue to explore genetic factors to understand their role in producing self-control.

Conclusion

Nearly 150 years before the publication of *A General Theory of Crime,* on September 13, 1848, Phineas Gage was injured in a railroad accident where a tamping iron blasted through his face, skull, and brain and exited his head. The accident caused a personality transformation of Gage from a responsible, intelligent, prudent, and socially well-adjusted person to an irreverent, capricious, bellicose, irresponsible person whose life devolved into that of a drifter. This amazing case was immortalized by John Harlow in 1868 in perhaps the most interestingly titled academic paper ever: "Recovery From the Passage of an Iron Bar Through the Head." Gage had been transformed from a man of self-control to a man of low self-control.

In 1994, Hanna Damasio and her colleagues resurrected the case and examined Gage's skull with modern neuroimaging techniques to ascertain the brain areas that affected Gage's decision making and emotional processing (Damasio, Grabowski, Frank, Galaburda, & Damasio, 1994). They determined the affected areas were the anterior half of the orbital frontal cortex, the polar and anterior mesial frontal cortices, and the anterior-most sector of the anterior cingulate gyrus in the left hemisphere. In the right hemisphere, Gage's lesion included the anterior and mesial orbital region, the mesial and polar frontal cortices, and the anterior segment of the anterior cingulate gyrus. Overall, frontal lobe white matter damage was more extensive in the left hemisphere than in the right. Damasio and her colleagues advised that Gage's injuries were consistent with persons with similar injuries who evince similar impairments in rational decision making, emotional processing, or simply, self-control.

To the casual reader, understanding the brain-basis of low self-control is potentially disconcerting from a policy perspective. But like many brain-based disorders, low self-control can be targeted for treatment. For example, a recent self-control experiment required participants to use their nondominant hand between 8am and 6pm to perform a variety of tasks over a period of 2 weeks (Denson, Capper, Oaten, Friese, & Schofield, 2011). These tasks included brushing their teeth, opening doors, operating a computer mouse, carrying items, holding cups and cutlery, and others. Participants were informed that the treatment condition was intended to investigate using one's nondominant hand for individuals recovering from a stroke. At the end of the 2 weeks, participants were insulted and given the opportunity to retaliate by administering a blast of white noise. Compared to controls, those who received self-control training exhibited reduced aggression and reduced anger. Moreover, the aggression reductions were only seen among those with the highest levels of trait aggression. There is also meta-analytic evidence that self-control programs improve self-regulation in children and adolescents that in turn can reduce delinquency (Piquero, Jennings, & Farrington, 2010). Of course, environmental moderators such as family and peer relationships are also important for modulating self-control.

In the end, the brain-basis of low self-control is mostly good news. Despite occasional forgetfulness, despite occasional lapses in judgment, despite sometimes failing to pay attention, and despite a lack of perseverance in exercise programs and diets, most people function and function well in society despite what nature provided in the area of self-control. For a smaller proportion of fortunate souls whose self-regulation is so extraordinary that they are almost machine-like, life is characterized by multiple, overlapping positive outcomes. And for another small proportion of the self-control distribution, the opposite is true: Life is a series of bad decisions, wrong choices, and accidents just waiting to happen. They too have nature to thank.

References

Adelstein, J. S., Shehzad, Z., Mennes, M., DeYoung, C. G., Zuo, X-N., Kelly, C., . . . Milham, M. (2011). Personality is reflected in the brain's intrinsic functional architecture. *PLoS ONE, 6,* e27633. doi:10.1371/journal.pone.0027633

Baumeister, R. F., & Alquist, J. L. (2009). Is there a downside to good self-control? *Self and Identity, 8,* 115–130.

Beaver, K. M., DeLisi, M., Mears, D. P., & Stewart, E. (2009). Low self-control and contact with the criminal justice system in a nationally representative sample of males. *Justice Quarterly, 26,* 695–715.

Beaver, K. M., DeLisi, M., Vaughn, M. G., & Wright, J. P. (2010). The intersection of genes and neuropsychological deficits in the prediction of adolescent delinquency and self-control. *International Journal of Offender Therapy and Comparative Criminology, 54,* 22–42.

Beaver, K. M., Ratchford, M., & Ferguson, C. J. (2009). Evidence of genetic and environmental effects on the development of low self-control. *Criminal Justice and Behavior, 36,* 1148–1162.

Beaver, K. M., Wright, J. P., & DeLisi, M. (2007). Self-control as an executive function: Reformulating Gottfredson and Hirschi's parental socialization thesis. *Criminal Justice and Behavior, 34,* 1345–1361.

Beaver, K. M., Wright, J. P., DeLisi, M., & Vaughn, M. G. (2008). Genetic influences on the stability of low self-control: Results from a longitudinal sample of twins. *Journal of Criminal Justice, 36,* 478–485.

Blakemore, S. J., & Robbins, T. W. (2012). Decision-making in the adolescent brain. *Nature Neuroscience, 15,* 1184–1191.

Boutwell, B. B., & Beaver, K. M. (2010). The role of broken homes in the development of self-control: A propensity score matching approach. *Journal of Criminal Justice, 38,* 489–495.

Braungart-Rieker, J. M., Hill-Soderlund, A. L., & Karrass, J. (2010). Fear and anger reactivity trajectories from 4 to 16 months: The roles of temperament, regulation, and maternal sensitivity. *Developmental Psychology, 46,* 791–804.

Buker, H. (2011). Formation of self-control: Gottfredson and Hirschi's general theory of crime and beyond. *Aggression and Violent Behavior, 16,* 265–276.

Comings, D. E. (2003). Conduct disorder: A genetic, orbitofrontal lobe disorder that is the major predictor of adult antisocial behavior. In A. Walsh & L. Ellis (Eds.), *Biosocial criminology: Challenging environmentalism's supremacy* (pp. 145-164). New York, NY: Nova Science.

Cummings, J. L., & Miller, B. L. (2007). Conceptual and clinical aspects of the frontal lobes. In B. L. Miller & J. L. Cummings (Eds.), *The human frontal lobes: Functions and disorders* (2nd ed., pp. 12–24). New York, NY: Guilford Press.

Damasio, H., Grabowski, T., Frank, R., Galaburda, A. M., & Damasio, A. R. (1994). The return of Phineas Gage: Clues about the brain from the skull of a famous patient. *Science, 264,* 1102–1105.

DeLisi, M. (2005). *Career criminals in society.* Thousand Oaks, CA: Sage.

DeLisi, M. (2011). Self-control theory: The *Tyrannosaurus rex* of criminology is poised to devour criminal justice. *Journal of Criminal Justice, 39,* 103–105.

DeLisi, M., & Vaughn, M. G. (2008). The Gottfredson-Hirschi critiques revisited: Reconciling self-control theory, criminal careers, and career criminals. *International Journal of Offender Therapy and Comparative Criminology, 52,* 520–537.

Denson, T. F., Capper, M. M., Oaten, M., Friese, M., & Schofield, T. P. (2011). Self-control training decreases aggression in response to provocation in aggressive individuals. *Journal of Research in Personality, 45,* 252–256.

de Ridder, D. T. D., Lensvelt-Mulders, G., Finkenauer, C., Stok, M., & Baumeister, R. F. (2012). Taking stock of self-control: A meta-analysis of how trait self-control relates to a wide range of behaviors. *Personality and Social Psychology Review, 16,* 76–99.

DeWall, C. N., Finkel, E. J., & Denson, T. F. (2011). Self-control inhibits aggression. *Social and Personality Psychology Compass, 5/7,* 458–472.

Duckworth, A. L. (2011). The significance of self-control. *Proceedings of the National Academy of Sciences of the United States of America, 108,* 2639–2640.

Finkel, E. J., DeWall, C. N., Slotter, E. B., Oaten, M., & Foshee, V. A. (2009). Self-regulatory failure and intimate partner violence perpetration. *Journal of Personality and Social Psychology, 97,* 483–499.

Garstein, M. A., Bridgett, D. J., Young, B. N., Panksepp, J., & Power, T. (2013). Origins of effortful control: Infant and parent contributions. *Infancy, 18,* 149–183.

Garstein, M. A., Putnam, S. P., & Rothbart, M. K. (2012). Etiology of preschool behavior problems: Contributions of temperament attributes in early childhood. *Infant Mental Health Journal, 33,* 197–211.

Gottfredson, M. R., & Hirschi, T. (1990). *A general theory of crime.* Stanford, CA: Stanford University Press.

Hampson, S. E. (2012). Personality processes: Mechanisms by which personality traits "get outside the skin." *Annual Review of Psychology, 63,* 315–339.

Harlow, J. M. (1868). Recovery from the passage of an iron bar through the head. *Publication of the Massachusetts Medical Society, 2,* 327–334.

Heatherton, T. F., & Baumeister, R. F. (1996). Self-regulation failure: Past, present, and future. *Psychological Inquiry, 7,* 90–98.

Hirata, Y., Zai, C. C., Nowrouzi, B., Beitchman, J. H., & Kennedy, J. L. (2013). Study of the catechol-o-methyltransferase (COMT) gene with high aggression in children. *Aggressive Behavior, 39,* 45–51.

Houts, R. M., Caspi, A., Pianta, R. C., Arsenault, L., & Moffitt, T. E. (2010). The challenging pupil in the classroom: The effect of the child on the teacher. *Psychological Science, 21,* 1802–1810.

Jacob, C., Nguyen, T. T., Weißflog, L., Herrmann, M., Liedel, S., Zamzow, K., . . . Reif, A. (2012). PPP2R2C as a candidate gene of a temperament and character trait-based endophenotype of ADHD. *Attention Deficit Hyperactivity Disorders, 4,* 145–152.

Kochanska, G., Murray, K. T., & Harlan, E. T. (2000). Effortful control in early childhood: Continuity and change, antecedents, and implications for social development. *Developmental Psychology, 36,* 220–232.

Kochanska, G., Philibert, R. A., & Barry, R. A. (2009). Interplay of genes and early mother-child relationship in the development of self-regulation from toddler to preschool age. *Journal of Child Psychology and Psychiatry, 50,* 1331–1338.

Moffitt, T. E. (1990). The neuropsychology of juvenile delinquency: A critical review. In N. Morris & M. Tonry (Eds.), *Crime and justice: An annual review of research* (Vol. 12, pp. 99–169). Chicago, IL: University of Chicago Press.

Moffitt, T. E. (1993). Adolescence-limited and life-course-persistent antisocial behavior: A developmental taxonomy. *Psychological Review, 100,* 674–701.

Moffitt, T. E., Arsenault, L., Belsky, D., Dickson, N., Hancox, R. J., Harrington, H., . . . Caspi, A. (2011). A gradient of childhood self-control predicts health, wealth, and public safety. *Proceedings of the National Academy of Sciences of the United States of America, 108,* 2693–2698.

Moffitt, T. E., & Caspi, A. (2001). Childhood predictors differentiate life-course persistent and adolescence-limited antisocial pathways among males and females. *Development and Psychopathology, 13,* 355–375.

Piquero, A. R., Jennings, W. G., & Farrington, D. P. (2010). On the malleability of self-control: Theoretical and policy implications regarding a general theory of crime. *Justice Quarterly, 27,* 803–834.

Posner, M. I. (2012). *Attention in a social world.* New York, NY: Oxford University Press.

Posner, M. I., Rothbart, M. K., Sheese, B. E., & Voelker, P. (2012). Control networks and neuromodulators of early development. *Developmental Psychology, 48,* 827–835.

Ratchford, M., & Beaver, K. M. (2009). Neuropsychological deficits, low self-control, and delinquent involvement: Toward a biosocial explanation of delinquency. *Criminal Justice and Behavior, 36,* 147–162.

Rothbart, M. K. (2011). *Becoming who we are: Temperament and personality in development.* New York, NY: Guilford Press.

Séguin, J. R., Arsenault, L., & Tremblay, R. E. (2007). The contribution of "cool" and "hot" components of decision-making in adolescence: Implications for developmental psychopathology. *Cognitive Development, 22,* 530–543.

Séguin, J. R., Nagin, D., Assaad, J. M., & Tremblay, R. E. (2004). Cognitive-neuropsychological function in chronic physical aggression and hyperactivity. *Journal of Abnormal Psychology, 113,* 603–613.

Séguin, J. R., Pihl, R. O., Harden, P. W., Tremblay, R. E., & Boulerice, B. (1995). Cognitive and neuropsychological characteristics of physically aggressive boys. *Journal of Abnormal Psychology, 104,* 614–624.

Sheese, B. E., Rothbart, M. K., Voelker, P. M., & Posner, M. I. (2012). The dopamine receptor D4 gene 7-repeat allele interacts with parenting quality to predict effortful control in four-year old children. *Child Development Research.* doi:10.1155/2012/863242

Smith, H. J., Sheikh, H. I., Dyson, M. W., Olino, T. M., Laptook, R. S., Durbin, C. E., . . . Klein, D. N. (2012). Parenting and child DRD4 genotype interact to predict children's early emerging effortful control. *Child Development, 83*(6), 1932–1944. doi:10.1111/j.1467-8624.2012.01818.x

Tangney, J. P., Baumeister, R. F., & Boone, A. L. (2004). High self-control predicts good adjustment, less pathology, better grades, and interpersonal success. *Journal of Personality, 72,* 271–324.

Vaughn, M. G., Beaver, K. M., & DeLisi, M. (2009). A general biosocial paradigm of antisocial behavior: A preliminary test in a sample of adolescents. *Youth Violence and Juvenile Justice, 7,* 279–298.

Vaughn, M. G., Beaver, K. M., DeLisi, M., Howard, M. O., & Perron, B. E. (2009). Dopamine D4 receptor gene exon III polymorphism associated with binge drinking attitudinal phenotype. *Alcohol, 43,* 179–184.

Vaughn, M. G., DeLisi, M., Beaver, K. M., & Wright, J. P. (2009). Identifying latent classes of behavioral risk based on early childhood manifestations of self-control. *Youth Violence and Juvenile Justice, 7,* 16–31.

Wakschlag, L. S., Choi, S. W., Carter, A. S., Hullsiek, H., Burns, J., McCarthy, K., . . . Briggs-Gowan, M. J. (2012). Defining the developmental parameters of temper loss in early childhood: Implication for developmental psychopathology. *Journal of Child Psychology and Psychiatry, 53,* 1099–1108.

White, J. L., Moffitt, T. E., Earls, F., Robins, L., & Silva, P. A. (1990). How early can we tell? Predictors of childhood conduct disorder and adolescent delinquency? *Criminology, 28,* 507–533.

Discussion Questions

CHAPTERS 9 AND 10

1. Gottfredson and Hirschi argue that by the age of 8 or 10, individual levels of self-control are fixed and result from sufficient socialization. Neuroscientific research reveals support for the development of self-regulation across childhood involving specific brain regions. Discuss some of the brain regions involved in the development of self-regulation. Does the evidence support a "purely" social role in the development of self-control?
2. There is variation in the definition of self-control between Gottfredson and Hirschi's theory and neuroscientific research. Discuss the differences between the two perspectives. For example, what type of outcomes result from having low self-control? Which perspective highlights sociological outcomes rather than characteristic outcomes?
3. As noted in Dr. Burt's chapter, parents are believed to be responsible for producing self-control in their children. As a result, better parenting practices are encouraged to reduce antisocial behavior in children. What, in your opinion, does the available evidence indicate about the link between poor parenting and low self-control? Does the evidence support it?
4. When addressing the role of biology in criminality, Gottfredson and Hirschi concluded the genetic effect to be "minimal" or "near zero." Discuss the genetic factors that have been found to be associated with low self-control. In your opinion, do genetic factors account for a large amount of variance in self-control?
5. Sociologists continue to argue that proper socialization will lead to high levels of self-control. When thinking about the case of Phineas Gage, are the accusations of sociologists supported? What resulted from Gage's accident, and how did it influence his self-control?
6. Proponents of self-control theory believe focusing on parent, school, and peer influences is beneficial for treating low self-control. However, programs based on brain research have also been used to treat low self-control. In your opinion, should sociological-based or biological-based preventions be used to treat low self-control? Beyond the ideas provided by Dr. DeLisi, describe how low self-control might be targeted for treatment.

11

The Role of the Social Environment in General Strain Theory

Robert Agnew
Emory University

General strain theory (GST) states that certain strains or stressors increase the likelihood of crime (Agnew, 2007). Examples of criminogenic strains include the inability to achieve monetary success, harsh parental discipline, peer abuse, and discrimination. These strains lead to negative emotions such as anger and frustration, which create pressure for corrective action. And crime is one possible response. Crime is a means to reduce or escape from strains; for example, individuals may steal the money they desire or run away from abusive parents. Crime may be used to obtain revenge against the source of strain or related targets; for example, juveniles may assault the peers who are bullying them. And crime may be used to alleviate the negative emotions associated with strains, as when juveniles use illicit drugs to feel better.

This chapter examines the role of the social environment in GST. After providing a brief overview of GST, this author describes how the social environment influences (a) the creation of strains, (b) the exposure to strains, (c) the emotional and cognitive response to strains, and (d) whether individuals cope with strains and their effects in a criminal manner. The focus is on both the immediate (face-to-face) and the larger social environment. For example, at the immediate level the exposure to strains is a largely a function of how individuals are treated by others such as parents, peers, teachers, coworkers, and neighbors. Such treatment, however, is strongly influenced by the larger groups and collectivities to which individuals belong (e.g., communities, societies), as well as individuals' social position in these groups—as indexed by such things as their social class, gender, race/ethnicity, and age.

Not surprisingly, the social environment plays a major role in GST. The classic strain theories that inspired GST were developed by sociologists, who stated that strain is caused by both cultural and structural factors (Cloward & Ohlin, 1960; Cohen, 1955; Merton, 1938). The cultural system, in particular, leads individuals to place much emphasis on monetary success or the somewhat broader goal of middle-class status. The stratification system, however, prevents many individuals from achieving such success through legitimate channels. This is especially true of lower-class individuals, who are less well prepared for school by their parents, attend inferior schools, and lack the means to pursue a higher education or start their own business. Whether individuals respond to this monetary strain with crime, however, is said to depend on such things as whether they were socialized to accept conventional norms and they belong to criminal groups.

GST is more social psychological in nature than classic strain theory, and so focuses on the immediate environment—particularly the family, peer, school, and work environments. But GST also considers the larger social environment in a series of publications focusing on communities (Agnew, 1999), societies (Agnew, 2007; Maier, Mears, & Bernard, 2009), gender (Broidy & Agnew, 1997), race/ethnicity (Kaufman, Rebellon, Thaxton, & Agnew, 2008), age stratification (Agnew, 1997), and economic status (Agnew, 2013). These environments are said to influence the creation of, exposure to, and reaction to strains. One can appreciate the enormous importance of the social environment by considering two similar individuals, one born into severe poverty in a depressed inner-city community and the other born into a wealthy suburban family. The first individual is much more likely to experience the criminogenic strains listed in GST and to cope with them in a criminal manner—for reasons indicated below.

This focus on the social environment, however, is not meant to imply that biological and psychological forces play a small role in GST. They in fact play a central role, as demonstrated in much recent work on GST. For example, Agnew, Brezina, Wright, and Cullen (2002) discuss the critical role played by two major dimensions of personality with strong biological foundations: low constraint and negative emotionality. In popular terms, individuals with these traits are "out of control" and "quick to anger." These traits influence the likelihood that individuals will define certain events and conditions as strains. For example, individuals with these traits are more likely to dislike school, partly because they have trouble getting good grades and following rules. Such individuals are also more likely to be exposed to strains. They have trouble achieving their goals and elicit negative reactions from others (e.g., they upset their parents, who respond in a harsh manner). Further, they sort themselves or are sorted into environments where the likelihood of negative treatment is high (e.g., delinquent peer groups, bad jobs). Finally, they are more likely to react to strains with anger and cope in a criminal manner.

Still others have discussed the key role that biological and psychological factors play in GST and in the stress process more generally (e.g., Belsky, Bakermans-Kranenburg, & van Ijzendoorn, 2007; Carber & Connor-Smith, 2010; Eitle & Taylor, 2011; Jackson, 2012; Johnson & Kercher, 2007; McCaffery, 2011; Schroeder, Hill, Hoskins Haynes, & Bradley, 2011; Simons et al., 2011; Southwick, Vythilingam, & Charney, 2005; Stogner & Gibson, 2010; Wachs, 2006; Walsh, 2000; Williams, Smith, Gunn, & Uchino, 2011). A companion chapter in this volume focuses explicitly on this topic. And this author frequently *notes* the major role played by biological and psychological factors in this chapter. So there is little doubt that GST needs to take account of social, psychological, *and* biological factors if it is to adequately explain crime. All play central roles in the creation of, exposure to, and response to strain. Further, they interact in their effects. Most notably, crime is most likely when individuals with certain bio-psychological characteristics are in environments where strain is common (e.g., Belsky et al., 2007; Simons et al., 2011). But, being a sociologist and given the assignment by the editor, this author focuses on the role of the social environment in this chapter.

An Overview of General Strain Theory

Strains refer to disliked events and conditions (Agnew, 2007). Most strains involve negative treatment by others, with such treatment falling into three general categories. Others prevent the individual from achieving valued goals, such as monetary and status goals. Others take or threaten to take things that the individual values; for example, others steal valued possessions or kill a close friend. And others treat the individual in an aversive manner; for example, they verbally or physically abuse the individual. A distinction is made between "objective" and "subjective" strains. *Objective strains* refer to events and conditions disliked by most people in a given group, while *subjective strains* refer to events and conditions disliked by the people experiencing them. People often differ in their subjective reaction to the same objective strain. For example, some people may be devastated by their divorce, while others may view their divorce as a cause for celebration.

Strains lead to a range of negative emotions, such as anger, frustration, and depression. These negative emotions create pressure for corrective action, and crime is one possible response. Anger is especially conducive to crime, since it energizes the individual for action, reduces concern over the consequences of one's behavior, and creates a desire for revenge. As indicated above, crime may be used to reduce or escape from strains, retaliate against the source of strain or related targets, or alleviate negative emotions. Strains may also have an indirect effect on crime. Strains may reduce social control. For example, parental abuse may reduce the juvenile's emotional bond to his or her parents. And chronic unemployment may lower one's "stake in conformity." Strains may also foster the social learning of crime. For example, strained individuals often develop beliefs that justify or excuse crime. So individuals who are bullied by peers may come to view violence as a justifiable response to abuse. And strained individuals sometimes form or join gangs as a way to cope with their strains. Gangs, for example, may provide them with the status and respect they cannot get through legitimate channels. Finally, the chronic exposure to strains contributes to personality traits conducive to delinquency, such as negative emotionality and low constraint (see Agnew, 2007; Colvin, 2000).

GST states that some types of strain are more likely than others to lead to crime (Agnew, 2007). Such strains lead to strong negative emotions, reduce the ability to cope in a legal manner, and have the other criminogenic effects described above. The most criminogenic strains are high in magnitude. That is, they are high in degree (e.g., a serious vs. minor assault), long in duration, frequent, expected to continue into the future, and high in centrality (they threaten core goals, needs, values, activities, and/or identities). Criminogenic strains are also perceived as unjust, with perceptions of injustice being especially conducive to anger. In addition, criminogenic strains are associated with low social control. Parental rejection, for example, is associated with a weak bond to parents. Finally, criminogenic strains create some pressure or incentive for criminal coping. For example, they are easily resolved through crime—as is the case with monetary strain. The specific strains that increase crime are listed further below.

GST also states that some people are more likely than others to cope with strains through crime (Agnew, 2007). Those most likely to engage in criminal coping have poor coping skills and resources. For example, they have poor social and problem-solving skills, as well as limited financial resources. They are low in conventional social support, having few people they can turn to for emotional support and assistance in coping. They are low in social control, such that the costs of criminal coping are low. For example, they are poorly supervised by parents and are doing poorly in school. They associate with criminal others, who reinforce, model, and otherwise encourage criminal coping. They have beliefs that approve of, justify, and/or excuse criminal coping. For example, they believe that violence is a justifiable response to disrespectful treatment (Anderson, 1999). And they are in situations where the costs of criminal coping are low and the benefits are high.

As discussed below, the social environment has a fundamental impact on all the above areas, including the creation of, exposure to, and reaction to strains.

The Creation of Strains

Strains refer to disliked events and conditions, but *why* are certain events and conditions disliked? There is good reason to believe that individuals are biologically predisposed to dislike many events/conditions, including those that involve physical injury; inadequate food, water, and shelter; the lack of respect/status among members of their group; rejection by certain others, including parents and caregivers; the failure of others to reciprocate in an equitable manner; and—related to this—being treated in an "unfair" manner (Agnew, 2011). Certain possibly universal notions of unfairness are emerging; for example, individuals believe they have been treated unfairly when they are treated differently than similar others and when they have no voice in the decisions that affect them (Agnew, 2007). Many of the strains described in GST involve events and conditions with one or more of these characteristics, including criminal victimization; the inability to achieve monetary and status goals; parental rejection; and verbal and physical abuse by family, peers, teachers, employers, and others.

At the same time, the social environment also plays a critical role in influencing the events and conditions that are disliked. The social environment helps specify the above dislikes. For example, while individuals desire to be treated in a respectful manner, social groups help define what constitutes "respectful" treatment, such as what constitutes a respectful (or disrespectful) form of address. Related to this, the social environment leads individuals to dislike other events and conditions. For example, individuals are not born with a biological predisposition to dislike low grades. But individuals in some groups are taught to strongly dislike such grades. The specification of dislikes and the creation of new dislikes occur in three ways.

The first is through the process of conditioning, especially operant conditioning. In this case, an event or condition is followed by something that is intrinsically reinforcing or punishing. For example, the receipt of low grades is followed by spanking, the loss of parental affection, and reduced status among peers. As a result, low grades soon come to be strongly disliked. To give another example, wearing "stylish" clothes results in social approval and status. As a result, individuals develop a strong desire for such clothes, and the inability to obtain them is disliked.

Individuals also specify and develop new dislikes by observing others, making note of what is reinforced and punished. Children in market-oriented societies, for example, quickly observe that money results in status/respect, the ability to purchase a range of desirable objects and services, and the ability to avoid much of what is viewed as undesirable. Partly as a consequence, the inability to obtain money through legal channels is strongly disliked by most people in such societies.

Finally, individuals learn through instruction, being taught that certain goals, values, identities, roles, possessions, and acts are desirable or undesirable. And this too influences what they like and dislike, particularly when their instruction corresponds to their experiences and observations about what is reinforced and punished. Males, for example, may be taught that they should have a particular type of masculine identity, one emphasizing toughness, independence, and heterosexuality. And they may find and observe that acting on the basis of this identity is differentially reinforced. Acts that challenge this identity will therefore be disliked.

It is important to note that the above learning processes have a strong biological basis. Individuals are generally self-interested, and so are very responsive to reinforcement and punishment. And individuals have a strong desire to observe and imitate others, especially close others whose acts are reinforced. But the social environment influences the content of learning, so individuals in different environments may learn to dislike different things. Some individuals, for example, may learn to strongly dislike even minor slights, especially those that challenge their masculine identity, while others may care little about such slights. This is, in fact, a central theme of most subcultural deviance theories of crime. Such theories do not state that individuals learn to generally approve of violence or other crimes, but rather learn that certain acts are serious affronts, requiring or justifying a violent response (e.g., Anderson, 1999; Baron, Forde, & Kennedy, 2001; Bernard, 1990).

There is of course the larger question of why different groups dislike different things. A full answer is beyond the scope of this chapter, involving a detailed consideration of both the history and current circumstances of groups. But at a general level, it is commonly argued that groups like those things that serve their interests and dislike those that threaten their interests (Agnew, 2011). These interests are often material in nature. So business owners are more inclined to dislike unions and government regulations than are workers, since these things threaten business profits. These interests may also be symbolic in nature. So Whites may dislike civil rights initiatives since they threaten their status relative to Blacks.

The Exposure to Strains

THE IMMEDIATE SOCIAL ENVIRONMENT

Some individuals are more likely than others to be in environments where they are subject to strain or mistreatment. This mistreatment most often occurs at the interpersonal level, and so the strains described in GST focus on mistreatment by family, school officials, peers, employers, and neighbors. Those strains most conducive to crime include:

- Parental rejection.
- Parental supervision and discipline that are erratic, excessive, and/or harsh. This includes the use of humiliation, insults, screaming, physical threats, and/or physical punishment.
- Child abuse and neglect.
- Negative secondary school experiences, including low grades, negative relations with teachers (e.g., teachers are unfair, belittling), and the experience of school as boring and a waste of time.
- Abusive peer relations, including insults, gossip, threats, attempts to coerce, and physical violence.
- Work in the secondary labor market, where jobs are poorly paid; have little prestige, few benefits, and limited opportunities for advancement; are unpleasant; provide little autonomy; and employ coercive methods of control.

- Chronic unemployment.
- Marital problems, including frequent conflicts and verbal and physical abuse.
- The failure to achieve certain goals, including thrills/excitement, high levels of autonomy, masculine status, and monetary success.
- Economic problems, such as the inability to pay bills and purchase needed items.
- Criminal victimization.
- Homelessness.
- Discrimination based on race/ethnicity, gender, sexual orientation, and/or religion.

There is of course the question of why some individuals are more likely to be mistreated than others. This depends partly on the characteristics of individuals. As noted above, it depends on their personality traits, which are in part biologically based. It also depends on their resources, including financial resources and social and problem-solving skills. Individuals with such resources are less likely to elicit negative reactions from others or to sort themselves into environments where the likelihood of negative treatment is high. Also, they are better able to resist and escape from negative treatment. Individuals with much money, for example, can more easily change schools, jobs, or neighborhoods if they are mistreated in these environments. And, as discussed below, it depends on their social position.

The likelihood of mistreatment also depends on the characteristics of those one interacts with. For example, children are more likely to be mistreated by parents with certain characteristics (Agnew & Brezina, 2012). Mistreatment is more likely when parents are high in negative emotionality and low in constraint. (So once more, the likelihood of negative treatment is influenced by factors that are in part biologically based.) Mistreatment is more likely among parents who lack knowledge of good parenting practices. This lack of knowledge most often stems from the fact that the parents were not exposed to good parenting practices when they were children. Mistreatment is more likely when parents are strained or stressed, with strained parents being more likely to reject and abuse their children. Finally, mistreatment is more likely among socially isolated parents who lack support from others and are less likely to be sanctioned when they engage in mistreatment.

Many of the same factors help explain peer abuse. Individuals are more likely to suffer such abuse when they interact with peers high in negative emotionality and low in constraint. Abuse is also more likely when peers are low in social control. For example, abuse is more likely when peers frequently engage in unsupervised activities and they attend schools that fail to set clear rules forbidding abuse, closely monitor student behavior, and consistently sanction abuse. Further, abuse is more likely when peers hold values favorable to abuse, regularly model abusive behavior, and reinforce one another for such behavior. Finally, abuse is higher when peer groups are in conflict with one another, such as youth groups in a community.

THE LARGER SOCIAL ENVIRONMENT: COMMUNITIES AND SOCIETIES

Strain is also more common in certain types of communities, particularly those with high levels of economic deprivation and inequality. There are several reasons for this. Such communities are more likely to attract and retain strained individuals, particularly those experiencing economic problems. And such communities are lower in social control, for reasons described by social disorganization theory (Agnew & Brezina, 2012). As such, they are less able to exclude or control the behavior of individuals who mistreat others. Beyond that, such communities directly foster strain in the following ways (see Agnew, 1999, 2007).

First, residents have more trouble achieving their economic and status goals, since they have less access to jobs, especially jobs in the primary sector that pay a decent wage. This is because such jobs are often located outside such communities, inaccessible to the many poor who lack automobiles. Also, relatively few people in the community have job contacts or information. In addition, residents are less able to teach and model those skills and attitudes necessary for successful job performance. Further, the schools in such communities suffer from a host of problems, including a lack of experienced teachers, meager resources, and poorly prepared students. As such, they are less effective in preparing students for such jobs. Consequently, unemployment is high, as is work in the secondary labor market. The low economic standing of individuals and the larger community, in turn, contribute to the inability of residents to obtain status through legitimate channels. Further, the perceived magnitude and injustice of these economic and status strains are exacerbated by high levels of inequality—with residents often surrounded by more advantaged others.

Second, these economic and status strains contribute to most of the criminogenic strains described by GST, including family, school, and peer-related strains. The stresses associated with low economic status contribute to family disruption and a range of family problems, such as parental conflict, parental rejection of children, and the use of harsh/erratic discipline. Economic and family problems contribute to school strains, such as school failure and negative relations with teachers. Among other things, parents are less able to adequately prepare their children for school, monitor their school performance, and assist them when necessary. And delinquent peer groups and gangs are more common in such communities, with such groups emerging partly to cope with status and economic strains. Gangs, for example, are a source of status and often provide access to illegitimate methods of obtaining money, such as drug selling.

Finally, individuals in these communities are not only more likely to experience the above strains, but they are also more likely to have confrontations with other strained, angry individuals. This is partly because these communities contain more strained individuals, both because they select for such individuals and contribute to strain. Also, factors such as high rates of unemployment, a lack of transportation, and density contribute to frequent interaction in public settings—making confrontations more likely. Data confirm these arguments. For example, Warner and

Fowler (2003) found that the residents of deprived communities are more likely to report that they or someone in their household had received verbal threats or insults, felt cheated by someone, and been harassed by police. Further, the rates of criminal victimization are much higher in such communities.

Likewise, individuals are more likely to be exposed to strains in some societies than in others, particularly what Currie (1997) calls "market societies—those in which the pursuit of private gain becomes the dominant organizing principle of social and economic life" (p. 147; see also Messner & Rosenfeld, 2007). Such societies are characterized by intense competition, little concern for those who fare poorly in the competitive process, and little support for noneconomic institutions. Poverty and inequality are high in such societies, and institutions such as the family and school are placed under great stress—with their functioning impaired. Many parents, for example, must work long hours for low wages and, consequently, cannot provide adequate care for their children.

Relatedly, strain is more common in societies characterized by high levels of group conflict. Conflict occurs between groups with conflicting interests and/or values, and may be structured along class, race/ethnic, gender, religious, and/or other lines. Typically, more advantaged groups seek to maintain their privileged position by oppressing other groups (Agnew, 2007, 2011). This oppression may take a variety of forms, which all result in increased exposure to strain on the part of those in the less advantaged groups. Those in more advantaged groups may deliberately harm others in the pursuit of their interests and values. This may involve physical and emotional abuse; the theft and destruction of property; and restricting access to education, good jobs, and other valued resources. For example, males may employ physical intimidation and emotional abuse to induce obedience in females. Also, those in advantaged groups may pursue their interests and values in a reckless manner, with little regard for the harm they cause those in less advantaged groups. For example, corporate officials may pursue high profits with little regard for the strain created by low wages, unsafe working conditions, and environmental pollution.

SOCIAL POSITION

As suggested above, one's social position in the larger society has a major impact on the exposure to strains. Social position is important because it influences all aspects of social life, including the roles that people play (e.g., wife, child); the goals, values, and identities they are taught; the norms they are subject to; the extent and nature of their social control; the types of settings they encounter; and how people view and treat them in those settings—including the discrimination they experience. As such, the occupants of some social positions are much more likely than others to be exposed to criminogenic strains, although the relationship between social position and strain varies somewhat over time and across groups.

To illustrate, GST states that lower-class individuals are more exposed to the criminogenic strains listed above (Agnew, 2007, 2013). The effect of class is often direct and obvious. For example, lower-class individuals are almost by definition more likely to be chronically unemployed or work in the secondary labor market. Similarly, lower-class individuals are more likely to be homeless. In other cases, the effect is indirect. For example, lower-class parents are less likely to provide their children with cognitive stimulation (e.g., have lots of books in the home, regularly read to their children). This lack of cognitive simulation impairs the intellectual development of the children, who in turn are more likely to do poorly in school—with negative school performance being a major strain. It should be noted, however, that upper-class individuals do experience certain strains, such as threats to corporate profits and more generally to their privileged position, with these strains being conducive to certain white-collar and state crimes (Agnew, 2011; Agnew, Piquero, & Cullen, 2009).

Likewise, gender affects exposure to strains (Agnew, 2007; Broidy & Agnew, 1997). GST states that males engage in more crime than females partly because they are more likely to experience most criminogenic strains, including harsh parental discipline, negative secondary school experiences, abusive peer relations, criminal victimization, and homelessness. Further, males are more likely to attach high relative and absolute importance to several goals conducive to crime, including autonomy, thrills/excitement, masculine status, and monetary success. It is important to note, however, that females do experience many strains more often than males. Of these, certain strains, such as sexual abuse and gender discrimination, are conducive to crime. Others, however, are not conducive to other-directed crime. These include strains such as close supervision by family members and the burdens associated with the care of conventional others, such as children and spouses. One might argue that gender differences in exposure to strains are in part biologically based. For example, males are more likely to be victimized because they are more competitive/aggressive in nature. But it is clear that these differences are also strongly tied to the social environment. The degree of gender discrimination, for example, varies a good deal over time and across societies (Agnew, 2011).

GST also explains race differences in offending partly by differences in exposure to strains (e.g., Hoskin, 2011; Jang & Johnson, 2003; Kaufman et al., 2008; Piquero & Sealock, 2010; Unnever & Gabbidon, 2011). African Americans, for example, are more likely to experience most strains conducive to crime, such as abuse, chronic unemployment, work in the secondary labor market, criminal victimization, and discrimination. The main reason for this is that African Americans are more likely to be poor and to live in high poverty communities than Whites. And this in turn is due to the effects of past and present discrimination.

Finally, age differences in crime are linked to differences in the exposure to strains (Agnew, 1997, 2007; Greenberg, 1997). Adolescents have higher rates of offending partly because they are more exposed to criminogenic strains. This greater exposure is influenced by the biological characteristics of adolescents, including their tendency to be more impulsive and risk-seeking than adults—due to such things as hormonal surges during puberty and a still-developing brain (see Walsh, 2000). But the difference in exposure is also due to the social circumstances of adolescents. Adolescents spend much time interacting with peers in unstructured, unsupervised settings, which dramatically increases opportunities for mistreatment. Also, adolescents come to desire many of the privileges of adulthood, such as autonomy and status, but are prevented from achieving them through legitimate channels. In fact, they are accorded little status and are subject to strict control in school. As such, goal blockage is more common among adolescents.

THE EMOTIONAL AND COGNITIVE REACTION TO STRAINS

The social environment also influences the emotional and cognitive reaction to strains (Agnew, 2007). While strains refer to disliked events and conditions, people differ regarding how much they dislike strains, whether strains are seen as unjust, the particular emotions they elicit, and the strength of these emotions. Such differences are critical, influencing both the likelihood and nature of crime. Intense anger, for example, is more likely to result in violent crime than is mild depression. The emotional and cognitive reaction to strains is influenced by traits that are in part biologically based. Those high in negative emotionality, for example, are more likely to perceive strains as severe and unjust and to react with intense anger. But at the same time, the social environment is also critical.

As suggested above, the nature of the strain or mistreatment has a large impact on emotions and cognitions. Strains that are high in magnitude are more likely to be strongly disliked and elicit strong emotional reactions. To give an obvious example, a serious physical assault will be disliked more than a mild verbal insult. Strains with certain other characteristics are more likely to be perceived as unjust and elicit anger, with the literatures on procedural and interactional justice describing such characteristics (Agnew, 2007). For example, being arrested by the police is more likely to be seen as unjust and generate anger when the police do not allow the arrestee to tell his or her version of events and are disrespectful. And still other characteristics contribute to emotions such as depression, fear, and frustration (Ganem, 2010). The reaction to strain, however, is also a function of how individuals are socialized, varied other features of their social environment, and the social context of the particular strain.

Socialization affects a range of individual characteristics, which in turn affect the reaction to strains. To illustrate, young men in deprived communities are sometimes socialized to develop a type of masculine identity that places much emphasis on such things as toughness, independence, and hypersexuality. Not surprisingly, individuals with this identity view threats to their masculinity as much more severe than others. To give another example, research on emotional socialization suggests that individuals are taught what emotions they should experience and display in response to particular stimuli, including strains. While this socialization does not supplant the biological foundations of emotion, it does modify the experience and especially the display of emotion. Further, one's social position influences the nature of emotional socialization. GST researchers have drawn on this work to argue that females are more likely than males to respond to strains with emotions such as depression, guilt, and anxiety, and that when females do experience anger, they are less likely to express or display it (e.g., Broidy & Agnew, 1997; De Coster & Zito, 2010; Sigfusdottir & Silver, 2009). These gendered differences in emotion are used to partly account for gender differences in crime.

Many additional features of the social environment also influence the emotional and cognitive reaction to strains (Agnew, 2007). Some of these features, such as social support and association with criminal peers, are described in the next section since they also influence the likelihood of criminal coping. One feature of special interest is the degree of strain in the individual's past and current social environments. Recent research suggests that individuals who have previously experienced moderate levels of strain are better able to cope with current strains, partly because these strains seem less severe (Seery, Holman, & Silver, 2010). But prior and current experiences with high levels of strain impede coping. Among other things, high levels of strain contribute to traits such as negative emotionality—making current strains seem more severe and unjust. This is a central theme of several bodies of work, including Anderson's (1999) "code of the street," where the many stressors of inner-city life cause individuals to develop a "short fuse," or tendency to react with anger at even minor irritations. Bernard (1990) makes a similar point in his theory of angry aggression, as does Colvin (2000) in his discussion of the negative impact of erratic coercion controls.

Finally, the social context in which particular strains are experienced also has a large impact on the reaction to them (Agnew, 1992, 2007; Cohen, 1965). Individuals frequently look to others when deciding how to react to strains, especially strains of an ambiguous nature. An individual teased by peers, for example, may be uncertain how to interpret such teasing. The response of other individuals, particularly those who witness the teasing, can go a long way toward determining whether the individual responds with laughter or anger. To give another example, a key social process influencing the reaction to strain is social comparison. Individuals compare the events and conditions they experience to those experienced by others, particularly others similar to them on relevant characteristics. For example, individuals compare their pay to that of others with similar work credentials in similar jobs. If they make less than these others, they will likely feel severely deprived and unjustly treated (see Bernburg, Thorlindsson, & Sigfusdottir, 2009, for an excellent study on relative deprivation).

COPING WITH STRAIN

Finally, the social environment has a large influence over whether individuals cope with strains and their effects in a criminal manner (Agnew, 2007). The social environment affects coping skills and resources. As noted above, for example, the social environment has a large impact on the education and income of individuals. Individuals with these resources are in a much better position to legally avoid, escape from, or reduce the strains they face. Imagine, for example, a well-educated individual with substantial savings who is being harassed by a coworker. Compared to a poorly educated person with no savings, this individual is better able to negotiate with the coworker and her supervisor, file a formal complaint with the police or others, hire an attorney and seek the assistance of other professionals, and—if necessary—quit her job and seek other employment. To give another example, some individuals are more likely than others to be taught effective coping skills—such as problem-solving and social skills. These individuals, for example, are taught how to be assertive without being aggressive, as well as how to cope with particular strains, such as being stopped by the police.

The social environment also affects the individual's level of conventional social support. Some individuals are in environments where they are much more likely than others to receive support from family, friends, school officials, employers, religious figures, neighbors, and government agencies, among others. The support received depends on such factors as the strength of their ties to these others and the resources possessed by these others, including financial resources and knowledge. To illustrate, data suggest that conventional social support is lower in deprived communities, partly because individuals in such communities have weaker ties to their neighbors and fewer resources (Agnew & Brezina, 2012). But programs have been created to provide support where it is lacking, such as mentoring programs, and they show some success at reducing crime (Agnew, 2007; Agnew & Brezina, 2012).

Further, the social environment affects the individual's level of social control, with control being higher in some environments than others. Such control includes the individual's emotional bond to conventional others and institutions, such as parents and school. It includes the level of supervision provided by parents, school officials, neighbors, police, and others. It includes the individual's investment in conventional institutions, including school and work, with this investment reflected by such things as grades, educational and occupational expectations, and income. And it includes the extent to which individuals have internalized conventional norms and values, particularly those that condemn crime.

The extent to which individuals associate with criminal peers is another critical feature of the social environment. Criminal peers create a strong disposition for criminal coping by modeling such coping, reinforcing such coping, and teaching beliefs favorable to criminal coping. Finally, criminal coping is more likely when strained individuals are in situations where the costs of crime are low and the benefits are high. The routine activities perspective describes such situations, which involve exposure to attractive targets for crime in the absence of capable guardians (see Agnew & Brezina, 2012, for an overview). So the nature of the environment has a large effect on the likelihood of criminal coping.

Once more, these arguments should not be taken to mean that biopsychological factors are unimportant in the coping process. They too play a critical role. For example, the ability and disposition to cope in a legal manner is enhanced by traits such as intelligence, creativity, and high constraint, which all have some biological (as well as social) basis. And, again, biopsychological factors affect the types of environments that individuals are exposed to. Individuals with traits such as low constraint and negative emotionality, for example, are less likely to be in environments where social control is high. Among other things, they are less likely to form strong bonds with conventional others and do well in conventional endeavors, such as school. They are also more likely to be sorted or sort themselves into environments where control is low, such as bad jobs and deprived communities. And since these traits have a genetic component, such individuals are more likely to have parents who lack the ability to establish effective controls.

Conclusion

In sum, the social environment influences the definition of, exposure to, and reaction to strains. As suggested above, virtually every aspect of the social environment has implications for these processes. At the micro-level, this includes the roles people play, the social control they are subject to, their socialization by parents and others, the social support they receive, the groups they belong to, and their social position in these groups. At the macro-level, this includes both cultural and structural factors, including the goals and values that are emphasized; the nature of the stratification system; the strength of social institutions—such as the family, school, and economy; and—more generally—the extent and nature of group conflict.

At the same time, it is clear that biopsychological factors also influence the definition of, exposure to, and reaction to strain. Further, biopsychological and social factors are intimately related. Biopsychological factors influence the environments individuals are exposed to and their reaction to these environments, and the social environment influences biopsychological factors. Individuals in deprived families and communities, for example, are more likely to be exposed to "biological harms" that affect their psychological development, such as maternal drug use during pregnancy and exposure to toxic substances such as lead, and head injury (Agnew & Brezina, 2012). Further, it is becoming increasingly clear that biopsychological and social factors interact in their effect on the definition of, exposure to, and reaction to strains. Given the complex relationship between biopsychological and social factors it is difficult to assess their relative importance, except to say that both are quite important and must be considered together if we are to fully explain crime. And, hopefully, the next edition of this volume will have only one chapter on strain theory, focusing on the interdependent effects of biopsychological and social factors on strain.

References

Agnew, R. (1992). Foundation for a general strain theory of crime and delinquency. *Criminology, 39*(1), 47–87.

Agnew, R. (1997). Stability and change in crime over the life course: A strain theory explanation. In T. P. Thornberry (Ed.), *Developmental theories of crime and delinquency* (pp. 101–132). New Brunswick, NJ: Transaction.

Agnew, R. (1999). A general strain theory of community differences in crime rates. *Journal of Research in Crime and Delinquency, 36*(2), 123–155.

Agnew, R. (2007). Pressured into crime: An overview of general strain theory. New York, NY: Oxford University Press.

Agnew, R. (2011). *Toward a unified criminology.* New York: New York University Press.

Agnew, R. (2013). Strain, economic status, and crime. In A. Piquero (Ed.), *Handbook of criminological theory.* Hoboken, NJ: Wiley-Blackwell.

Agnew, R., & Brezina, T. (2012). *Juvenile delinquency: Causes and control.* New York, NY: Oxford University Press.

Agnew, R., Brezina, T., Wright, J. P., & Cullen, F. T. (2002). Strain, personality traits, and delinquency: Extending general strain theory. *Criminology, 40*(1), 43–72.

Agnew, R., Piquero, N. L., & Cullen, F. T. (2009). General strain theory and white-collar crime. In S. S. Simpson & D. Weisburd (Eds.), *The criminology of white-collar crime* (pp. 35–60). New York, NY: Springer.

Anderson, E. (1999). *Code of the street: Decency, violence, and the moral life of the inner city*. New York, NY: W. W. Norton.

Baron, S. W., Forde, D. R., & Kennedy, L. W. (2001). Rough justice: Street youth and violence. *Journal of Interpersonal Violence, 16*(7), 662–678.

Belsky, J., Bakermans-Kranenburg, M. J., & van Ijzendoorn, M. H. (2007). For better and for worse. *Current Directions in Psychological Science, 16*(6), 300–304.

Bernard, T. J. (1990). Angry aggression among the "truly disadvantaged." *Criminology, 28*(1), 73–96.

Bernburg, J. G., Thorlindsson, T., & Sigfusdottir, I. D. (2009). Relative deprivation and adolescent outcomes in Iceland. *Social Forces, 87*(3), 1223–1250.

Broidy, L. M., & Agnew, R. (1997). Gender and crime: A general strain theory perspective. *Journal of Research in Crime and Delinquency, 34*(3), 275–306.

Carber, C. S., & Connor-Smith, J. (2010). Personality and coping. *Annual Review of Psychology, 61*, 679–704.

Cloward, R., & Ohlin, L. (1960). *Delinquency and opportunity*. Glencoe, IL: Free Press.

Cohen, A. K. (1955). *Delinquent boys*. Glencoe, IL: Free Press.

Cohen, A. K. (1965). The sociology of the deviant act: Anomie theory and beyond. *American Sociological Review, 30*(1), 5–14.

Colvin, M. (2000). *Crime and coercion*. New York, NY: St. Martin's Press.

Currie, E. (1997). Market, crime and community. *Theoretical Criminology, 1*(2), 147–172.

De Coster, S., & Zito, R. C. (2010). Gender and general strain theory: The gendering of emotional experiences. *Journal of Contemporary Criminal Justice, 26*(2), 224–245.

Eitle, D., & Taylor, J. (2011). General strain theory, BIS/BAS levels, and gambling behavior. *Deviant Behavior, 32*(1), 1–37.

Ganem, N. M. (2010). The role of negative emotion in general strain theory. *Journal of Contemporary Criminal Justice, 26*(2), 167–185.

Greenberg, D. (1977). Delinquency and the age structure of society. *Contemporary Crises, 1*, 189–223.

Hoskin, A. (2011). Explaining the link between race and violence with general strain theory. *Journal of Ethnicity in Criminal Justice, 9*(1), 56–73.

Jackson, D. B. (2012). The role of early pubertal development in the relationship between general strain and juvenile crime. *Youth Violence and Juvenile Justice, 10*(3), 292–310.

Jang, S. J., & Johnson, B. R. (2003). Strain, negative emotions, and deviant coping among African Americans: A test of general strain theory. *Journal of Quantitative Criminology, 19*(1), 79–105.

Johnson, M. C., & Kercher, G. A. (2007). ADHD, strain, and criminal behavior: A test of general strain theory. *Deviant Behavior, 28*, 131–152.

Kaufman, J. M., Rebellon, C., Thaxton, S., & Agnew, R. (2008). A general strain theory of the racial differences in criminal offending. *Australian and New Zealand Journal of Criminology, 41*, 421–437.

Maier, D., Mears, D. P., & Bernard, T. J. (2009). Toward a criminology of crimes against humanity. *Theoretical Criminology, 13*(2), 227–255.

McCaffery, J. M. (2011). Genetic epidemiology of stress and gene by stress interaction. In R. J. Contrada & A. Baum (Eds.), *Handbook of stress science* (pp. 77–85). New York, NY: Springer.

Merton, R. K. (1938). Social structure and anomie. *American Sociological Review, 3*, 672–682.

Messner, S. F., & Rosenfeld, R. (2007). *Crime and the American Dream*. Belmont, CA: Wadsworth.

Piquero, N. L., & Sealock, M. D. (2010). Race, strain, and general strain theory. *Youth Violence and Juvenile Justice, 8*(3), 170–186.

Schroeder, R. D., Hill, T. D., Hoskins Haynes, S., & Bradley, C. (2011). Physical health and crime among low-income urban women: An application of general strain theory. *Journal of Criminal Justice, 39*(1), 21–29.

Seery, M. D., Holman, E. A., & Silver, R. C. (2010). Whatever does not kill us: Cumulative lifetime adversity, vulnerability, and resilience. *Journal of Personality and Social Psychology, 99*(6), 1025–1041.

Sigfusdottir, I., & Silver, E. (2009). Emotional reactions to stress among adolescent boys and girls. *Youth & Society, 40*(4), 571–590.

Simons, R. L., Lei, M. K., Beach, S. R. H., Brody, G. H., Philibert, R. A., & Gibbons, F. X. (2011). Social environment variation, genes, and aggression: Evidence supporting the differential susecpitibily perspective. *American Sociological Review, 76*(6), 883–912.

Southwick, S. M., Vythilingam, M., & Charney, D. S. (2005). The psychobiology of depression and resilience to stress: Implications for prevention and treatment. *Annual Review of Clinical Psychology, 1*, 255–291.

Stogner, J., & Gibson, C. L. (2010). Healthy, wealthy, and wise: Incorporating health issues as a source of strain in Agnew's general strain theory. *Journal of Criminal Justice, 38*(6), 1150–1159.

Unnever, J. D., & Gabbidon, S. L. (2011). *A theory of African American offending: Race, racism, and crime*. New York, NY: Routledge.

Wachs, T. D. (2006). Contributions of temperament to buffering and sensitization processes in children's development. *Annals of the New York Academy of Sciences, 1094*, 28–39.

Walsh, A. (2000). Behavior genetics and anomie/strain theory. *Criminology, 38*(4), 1075–1107.

Warner, B. D., & Fowler, S. K. (2003). Strain and violence: Testing a general strain theory model of community violence. *Journal of Criminal Justice, 31*, 511–521.

Williams, P. G., Smith, T. W., Gunn, H. E., & Uchino, B. N. (2011). Personality and stress. In R. J. Contrada & A. Baum (Eds.), *Handbook of stress science* (pp. 231–245). New York, NY: Springer.

12

General Strain Theory and Biosocial Criminology

Pathways to Successful Theoretical Integration

John M. Stogner

University of North Carolina at Charlotte

Introduction

Perhaps none of the major theoretical models in the field of criminology have the potential to be as intricately and effectively linked to biosocial research as Agnew's (1992, 2006) general strain theory (GST). Though the following pages will show that general strain theory has the potential to become a solid sociological segment within an integrated and influential explication of crime and deviance, strain theorization and research typically omits biological influences. This has not been without consequence; once a leading perspective in the field, strain theories have recently been relegated to second-tier status with the field intently focusing on peer influences, neighborhood or community factors, and crime over the life course. The weaknesses of strain theory that have led to its devaluation, however, may not be a deficiency of the broader perspective, but instead the result of the theory and its tests excluding factors intimately related to both stress and deviant outcomes. The correlation between stress and deviance that is the focus of Agnew's (1992, 2006) work cannot be unraveled without removing the "sociological blinders" that restrict our vision (Walsh, 2000) and directing some focus onto biological structure and physiology.

Such a task is far easier to introduce than to accomplish. As recently as a decade ago, the field of criminology was reticent to accept biosocial research due to ethical issues with early biological studies on crime, misconceptions about several policy implications, and a lack of training and information (Raine, 1993; Ellis & Walsh, 2004). Though biosocial criminology is rapidly developing and has gained a solid foothold in the field, concrete theoretical integration remains elusive. Despite research that demonstrates that biology underpins variation in some of the most core theoretical constructs (for example, Wright and Beaver's [2005] study on low self-control), academic discussion revolves around biological considerations augmenting or being tangential to sociological factors as opposed to complete, complex, and appropriately balanced integration. Even leading biosocial criminologists often use language that places biological variation into a secondary or subservient role. They often suggest that biology "complements" (Walsh, 2009), can be "incorporated" with (Wright & Boisvert, 2009), or can "supplement and add clarity to existing criminological theories" (Ratchford & Beaver, 2009, p. 157) rather than discussing full theoretical integration. Though this may simply be an issue of semantics and words carefully chosen to increase the likelihood of publication in a field largely comprised of sociologically trained reviewers, it suggests that the idea of fully integrated biosocial theories of crime has not gained mainstream acceptance.

These concerns should not intimidate academics from making attempts to integrate biology with sociology. As Wright and Boisvert (2009) note, underexplored areas are the most exciting and rewarding for curious academics to study, and biosocial criminology potentially offers the best opportunity for truly improving our understanding of the etiology of deviance. That being said, the following pages offer several suggestions for curious academics looking to better intertwine the strain perspective with our understanding of the human mind and body. Rather than offering a single, detailed integrated theory within this chapter, three distinct ways in which both biology and stress may be related to deviant behavior are discussed separately in hopes that each encourages the development of thorough yet parsimonious, testable theories. This author first briefly discusses GST noting both its strengths and weaknesses and suggests that genetic variation may account for differing reactions to strain. The author then proposes that genetic influences on deviance may operate through their effect on stressful situations and environments. Next, this author suggests that many of those strains central to Agnew's theory may largely operate through altering the neural development of children. Finally, the author reviews previous attempts, including his own "biosocially informed general strain theory" (BIGST), to create an integrated biosocial strain theory.

General Strain Theory and Its Empirical Support

In its simplest form, Agnew's (1992, 2006) GST argues that *strains*, defined as events or situations disliked by people, cause them to experience negative emotions that in turn create pressure to alleviate those emotions through coping or action. Agnew suggests that there are three distinct sources of strain that have the potential to lead to crime. He (1992) claims that strain can result from not being able to achieve a positively valued goal, from the removal of positively valued stimuli, or the addition of noxious stimuli. In response to Jensen's (1995) and others' challenges that GST's breadth made it impossible to falsify and therefore a problematic theory, Agnew (2001) further specified four characteristics of the type of strains that are most likely to result in criminal behavior. He argues that strains that are seen as higher in magnitude, perceived as unjust, are associated with low social control, and those that create an incentive for delinquent coping are most likely to drive deviant behavior. He (2006) additionally created a list of 13 sources of strain that fit these criteria: parental rejection; punishment that is erratic, harsh, or excessive; abusive peers; abusive or neglectful parents; negative school experiences such as poor grades or conflict with instructors; discrimination; homelessness; victimization; living in a bad neighborhood; failure to achieve the goals of autonomy, masculinity, financial success or happiness; marital stress; unemployment; and employment in a menial, low paying, or repetitive job.

Agnew (1992) argues that strains operate through negative emotions. Because individuals do not like experiencing negative emotions, the emotions create pressure for their resolution or elimination. In other words, people feel the need to make themselves feel better. Crime is one way that individuals may try to deal with their negative emotions; however, most strains and negative emotions do not lead to crime. While they create pressure for resolution, they can be resolved in both deviant and legitimate ways. Agnew (2006) argues that strains make crime more likely and that strains lead to crime when an individual lacks the appropriate cognitive, emotional, or coping skills. When faced with the same problem, different individuals respond differently because due to their education, social network, background, and other resources they have differing options for remedying the issue. Those who have exhausted their options or do not possess legitimate means to cope with strains and negative emotions often choose illicit means of reacting.

Much support has been found for GST's core proposition that strain has an effect on delinquency (Agnew, 2001; Agnew & White, 1992; Aseltine, Gore, & Gordon, 2000; Baron, 2004, 2009; Broidy, 2001; Hay, 2003; Jang & Johnson, 2003; Manasse & Ganem, 2009; Mazerolle & Piquero, 1998; Warner & Fowler, 2003). Victimization (Baron, 2009; Carson, Sullivan, Cochran, & Lersch, 2009; Jang, 2007), family stress (Cheung, Ngai, & Ngai, 2007; Hollist, Hughes, & Schaible, 2009), physical and emotional abuse at school (Moon, Hays, & Blurton, 2009; Morash & Moon, 2007), and witnessing abuse (Maxwell, 2001) all seem to be causally related to deviance. GST's predictive ability does seem to be lower for nonviolent than violent offenses, but its greatest deficit is inconsistent support for the role of negative emotions and coping skills. There is mixed support for the hypothesis that strain operates through negative affect (see Brezina, 1998; Broidy, 2001, Hay, 2003; and alternatively, Kaufman, 2009; Mazerolle, Burton, Cullen, Evans, & Payne, 2000; Tittle, Broidy, & Gertz, 2008). No evidence is found supporting the idea that coping factors condition the effect of strain on deviance in several works (Aseltine et al., 2000; Johnson &

Morris, 2008; Stogner & Gibson, 2010; Tittle et al., 2008) with others finding limited support (Bao, Haas, & Pi, 2007; Carson et al., 2009; Hay & Evans, 2006).

It has been this incomplete ability of the theory to (1) accurately detail why some individuals who are exposed to strain act deviantly whereas others exposed to the same strains do not and (2) successfully delineate the way in which strain leads to deviance that have caused the theory's fall. While the ideas that strains operate through negative affect and are conditioned by coping skills such as self-esteem, constraint, religiosity, and social support are theoretically sound, the lack of consistent empirical support for these premises suggests that without modification GST will fare no better than its predecessors in the strain perspective. It may be that GST's inability to thoroughly connect strain and deviance is linked to its reliance on sociological constructs and exclusion of biological factors. An integrated biosocial perspective may help illuminate this relationship and aid in our understanding of deviance.

Gene × Stress Interactions

In introducing their seminal study, Caspi and colleagues (2002) question how child abuse and maltreatment so strongly affect the likelihood of adult deviance without all abused children becoming violent or antisocial adults. Put another way, arguably one of the most influential pieces in biosocial criminology poses a question not unlike that raised by Agnew's (2006) work. In each instance, the query revolves around explaining a paradox: stressors are linked to increasing the likelihood of negative behaviors, but those connections are far from universal. Agnew (2006) describes stresses more generally and applies the term *strain* whereas Caspi et al. (2002) specifically refer to one form of negative event, but each work suggests that the effect of a stress or stresses on behavior is moderated or conditioned by other factors. The focus of Caspi et al.'s (2002) work, parental abuse and maltreatment, is even one of the 13 strains that Agnew (2006) hypothesizes are most connected to deviance.

What separates these works is their evaluation of why these stresses affect deviant behavior in some instances and not others. While the sociologically trained Agnew focuses on environmental factors such as social support and opportunity and cognitive factors such as self-esteem, intelligence, and religiosity as moderators of stress's effect, Caspi et al. (2002) turn to genetics. They argue that as a result of genetic risk factors some individuals are more vulnerable to stress and more likely to react to stress negatively. It may be genetic risk, as opposed to those traditionally measured variables, that amplifies or diminishes the effect of stress on behavior.

Caspi et al.'s (2002) study demonstrated that severe child maltreatment interacted with the low activity allele of the MAOA gene polymorphism in males to affect four indicators of antisocial and violent behavior: adolescent conduct disorder, psychological disposition toward violence, reports of antisocial behavior, and convictions for violent crimes. The relationship between reported abuse and each of these outcomes was significantly more pronounced among those that possessed a low-activity allele. While some replications have failed to reach the same conclusion (Huizinga et al., 2006), the majority of studies and meta-analyses support the finding that the link between childhood victimization and both negative behavioral and psychological outcomes is conditioned by differences in the MAOA gene (Kim-Cohen et al., 2006; Kim-Cohen, & Gold, 2009; Widom & Brzustowicz, 2006).

Since Caspi et al.'s (2002) work, the stress-diathesis model has become central to research in the field. Stressful environments are often shown to be more likely to affect violence, substance use, mental health, and personal success when genetic risk factors are present. Alternatively, this could be viewed as genetic risk's effect on mental health and behavior being revealed when individuals are exposed to a stressful environment. Regardless of vantage point, the combination of genetic risk and environmental stress appears to be more influential than the additive effects of each (Moffitt, Caspi, & Rutter, 2006; Young-Wolff, Enoch, & Prescott, 2011). The majority of studies in this area explores individual gene × environment interactions (G×E) and refers to them as such. However, most of the environmental factors considered fall within the scope of Agnew's (1992) definition of strain, suggesting that the term *gene × strain interaction* could alternatively be used.

As it is likely that Agnew's definition of parental maltreatment is broader than the forms of parental behavior evaluated by Caspi et al. (2002) and those replicating the work, and as other genes may condition the effect, it is useful to examine additional findings related to this strain. A serotonin gene has been found to modify the relationship between childhood maltreatment and antisocial disorder but may only do so in certain ethnic groups (Douglas et al., 2011). The same polymorphic gene (5-HTTLPR) appears to interact with maltreatment to increase the likelihood of abuse alcohol (Kaufman et al., 2007). Additionally, the relationship between a specific form of maltreatment, sexual abuse, and negative outcomes also appears to be affected by genotype. Derringer, Krueger, Irons, and Iacono (2010) found evidence that childhood sexual victimization interacts with the MAOA gene to affect antisocial behavior and conduct disorder symptoms and Ducci et al. (2008) noted that this same interaction affected the likelihood of alcoholism. Cicchetti, Rogosch, and Sturge-Apple (2007) found that sexual abuse more strongly affected negative affect and behaviors for those with an S allele for the 5-HTTLPR gene. Another form of maltreatment, neglect, has been found to have a relationship with negative outcomes such as substance use that is conditioned by the 5-HTTLPR gene (Vaske, Newsome, & Wright, 2012), but not by the MAOA gene (Nikulina, Widom, & Brzustowicz, 2012).

In addition to parental abuse and neglect, many of the other strains specifically highlighted by Agnew (2006) have been shown to have effects conditioned by genetic factors. First, Agnew (2006) also stresses the relevance of abusive peers. Recent biosocial works suggest that the effect of peer victimization on female's emotions is moderated by the 5-HTTLPR gene (Benjet, Thompson, & Gotlib, 2010). Sugden et al. (2010) offer additional support for this connection, and Brendgen et al. (2008) similarly found that peer victimization had an effect on aggression that was conditioned by genetic risk. The effect of negative school experiences overall may also be tied to genetic risk. Brendgen et al. (2011) found that young children experiencing negative interactions with teachers were more likely to display aggression when a genetic vulnerability existed.

Though they use terminology distinct from Agnew's (2006) parental rejection, Feinberg, Button, Neiderhauser, Reiss, and Hetherington (2007) find that the effect of poor parent-child relationships on aggression is exacerbated by genetic factors. While a portion of this relationship may be the result of an rGE in which the conflict is tied to both the parent and child's genetic predisposition for aggression (Narusyte, Andershed, Neiderhiser, & Lichtenstein, 2007), additional research continues to demonstrate that poor parental relationships have an effect on deviance or factors connected to deviance that depends on genotype (Nilsson et al., 2010; Wright, Schnupp, Beaver, DeLisi, & Vaughn, 2012). Additionally, DeLisi, Beaver, Wright, and Vaughn (2008) found an interaction between the DRD2 and DRD4 polymorphisms and family environment. The risk alleles actually increased the age of onset for criminal behavior and age at first arrest in low-risk family environments.

Agnew does extend his focus on the family beyond poor relationships and severe abuse or neglect. He also notes that punishment that is harsh, overly severe, or erratic is one of the most important criminogenic strains (Agnew, 2006). Though Derringer et al. (2010) failed to find that MAOA genotype moderated the effect of harsh discipline, some research indicates that sensitivity to punishment is linked to serotonergic genes (see Carver, Johnson, & Joormann, 2008). Disciplinary practices are often collapsed with other stressors into scale measures, which have been shown to have a significant G×E. Foley et al. (2004) included inconsistent discipline in their measure of childhood adversity, which interacted with the MAOA gene to affect the likelihood of antisocial behavior, and Simons et al. (2011) included harsh parenting (slapping, grabbing, etc.) in their measure of an adverse social environment, which interacted with the 5-HTTLPR and DRD4 genes.

One of the strains that has received the most empirical attention in purely sociological tests of GST is victimization. It appears to have a consistent and direct effect on offending (Baron, 2009; Carson et al., 2009). Of course, victimization itself has been shown to be affected by gene × environment interactions (Beaver et al., 2007), but similar interactions may condition the effect of victimization on negative emotions and antisocial behavior. Scheid et al. (2007) discovered that depression was more likely for women who were violently victimized when they carried the short 5-HTTLPR allele. However, other studies have noted that a significant interaction between DRD2 and victimization only exists for African American females (Vaske, Makarios, Boisvert, Beaver, & Wright, 2009). Weder et al. (2009) additionally found that those children who possessed the low activity MAOA allele were significantly more likely to exhibit aggression after experiencing moderate levels of trauma.

Risk alleles for dopamine receptor genes (DRD2 and DRD4) were found to significantly affect violent behavior for those in impoverished neighborhoods, but not in average or strong neighborhoods. Barnes and Jacobs (2013) extended this work finding that both neighborhood disadvantage and community crime rates interacted with dopamine-related genetic risk (including DAT1 along with

DRD2 and DRD4). Additionally, neighborhood issues were another one of the four constructs included in Simons et al.'s (2011) adverse social environment measure that interacted with DRD4 and 5-HTTLPR.

It does not seem to be overly bold to hypothesize that each of the other strains central to Agnew's (2006) work will be found to have effects conditioned by genotype. For example, family material deprivation interacted with the MAOA gene to alter the likelihood of crime in one study (Fergusson, Boden, Horwood, Miller, & Kennedy, 2012), and racial discrimination was included in the aforementioned Simons et al. (2011) adverse environment measure. It is possible that measures of the other key strains are lacking in the large datasets with genomic information. For example, while measures of independent activities and pubertal development exist within the National Longitudinal Study of Adolescent Health (Add Health), no questions accurately assess respondents' present goals of autonomy or masculinity. Therefore, the dataset is unlikely to be useful in determining whether the potential effects of failure to achieve the desired goals of autonomy and masculinity are moderated by genetic factors. Similarly, genetic data is rarely collected from homeless youth.

Taken as a whole this research suggests that genetic variation *may* explain why some individuals exposed to stress cope deviantly while others do not, and further, it *may also* do so better than the constructs typically discussed as conditioning factors in GST. However, these statements come with a number of caveats. First, each of the studies previously mentioned focuses on one or a handful of stressors. While Agnew (2006) suggests GST is best evaluated without collapsing strains into a single measure, this does not mean that numerous strains cannot be evaluated at once. In fact, omitting additional strains and their interactions from models creates the possibility of model misspecification. It may, however, be argued that the inclusion of additional strains and controls can become problematic because they may be affected by, and thus correlated with, the same genes expected to moderate a strain's effect.

Second, many studies are undertaken without an overarching theoretical framework. This leads to studies evaluating numerous potential connections rather than testing a few theoretically driven propositions and opens the field to several biases. As significant results are more likely to be published, they are more likely to be to written about by academics. As criminological research does not maintain a record of results from unpublished analyses as may be done with clinical drug trials, we cannot be certain that we are exposed to complete information. Findings that have been replicated in multiple samples using varied analytic techniques (such as Caspi et al.'s [2002] study) can be assumed valid, but how should the field view findings limited to one sample? Do those significant interactions represent an actual moderating effect present in the population or were they a result of Type 1 errors? Did other studies find the opposite, but fail to ever reach completion and publication due to their nonsignificant findings?

These concerns must be at the forefront of research. Given that GST reached an untestable breadth without the restriction to the 13 theoretically most important strains prior to consideration of genetic influences (Jensen, 1995), it can be exponentially more unwieldy with their inclusion. Assuming that just 13 strains are evaluated using five candidate genes, both genders, four different racial groups, and the traditional α of .05, over 500 studies of potential interactions could be completed with one sample, but approximately 26 of those would suffer from a Type 1 error. With those in which the null hypothesis was not rejected being unlikely to be published, readers should be skeptical of unreplicated biosocial research in general and more specifically those articles not clearly driven by theory.

That being said, gene × strain interactions, whether labeled as such or not, do appear to be related to deviance and offer promise as a potential explanation of differential responses to strain. Those exploring GST from a biosocial viewpoint may wish to take a number of steps to avoid the previously mentioned potential issues. First, potential gene × strain interactions should be evaluated under a detailed, yet parsimonious theoretical framework. The framework must be testable, but not offer an unlimited number of tests. In other words, it must be falsifiable. This could be done by restricting the definition of "strain," focusing on overall stress/strain using a composite rather than individual measures, collapsing genetic risk into an index (see Belsky & Beaver, 2011), or using latent measures of genetic risk (Jaffee et al., 2005). Such decisions are left to those creating integrated theories. Second, correction factors for multiple analyses must be applied to each study. Appropriately modifying the α of each test would create a situation where a Type 1 error would occur approximately only once in 20 studies as opposed to once in 20 models. Third, the evaluation of gene × strain interactions should not be completed in ethnic group subsamples unless the gene or strain is expected to differentially affect races. If a gene solely affects processes not related to race, then running separate analyses for each racial group only serves to increase the likelihood of error and false positive results. Fourth, the roles that other environmental variables play in modifying reactions to strain should also be considered.

These concerns are not meant to dissuade the reader from attempts to develop and test an integrated biosocial theory that utilizes gene × strain interactions, but are merely intended to relate the complexity of that task. In fact, this author would argue that this is the most promising technique for merging strain theory and biosocial research. It may serve to strengthen both GST and genetic criminology. The concerns also represent the issues the author has been forced to consider in his own work, and he hopes that introducing them may aid the reader in preparing their future studies. Adherence to these recommendations will likely affect the utility of individual works, and may also affect the general acceptance of this field of study.

Hereditability of Antisocial Behaviors Through Stress

Numerous studies have estimated the heritability of violence, criminal offending, and other antisocial behaviors. Each represents an effort at determining what portion of a trait's variation within a population can be attributed to genetic factors (for a detailed review of behavioral genetics, see Beaver, 2009). Unlike the aforementioned genetic research, these behavioral genetics studies rarely specify which genes may be affecting behavior or through what processes. Prior to discussing heritability further, it should be noted that heritability estimates are not absolute. They vary by population, time, and environmental conditions (Bronfenbrenner & Ceci, 1994). To be clear, since certain traits are more likely to be expressed in some conditions but less likely in others, the degree to which a trait or behavior is heritable is linked to the extent to which it is allowed to vary (due to environmental restrictions) and the level to which it is nurtured in the population. A heritability coefficient only estimates the variation in the trait due to genetics in a particular population in a particular environment.

A large body of research has indicated that antisocial behavior is largely heritable in most social environments with even the more conservative heritability (h^2) estimates exceeding .32 (see the meta-analyses of Mason & Frick, 1994; Miles & Carey, 1997; Rhee & Waldman, 2002; Waldman & Rhee, 2006). This suggests that nearly one-third of the variation in antisocial behaviors within a population can be attributed to genetics. One of the most complete evaluations of the heritability of antisocial behavior, a meta-analysis of eight meta-analyses, suggested that the heritability of relevant behaviors such as deviance, drug use, depression, and anxiety was closer to 50% (Malouff, Rooke, & Schutte, 2008). Some studies have even estimated the heritability of antisocial behavior to be as high as .96 (Baker, Jacobson, Raine, Lozano, & Bezdjian, 2007).

Though some academics caution against overreliance on genetic studies for complex outcomes such as addiction (Buckland, 2008), a great deal of research has also explored the heritability of substance use, problematic substance use, and addiction. The extant research leads to the conclusion that the variation in both experimentation and heavy use has a genetic component for almost all substances (Prescott, Madden, & Stallings, 2006). It also appears that problematic use of a substance is more highly linked to heredity than to the general use of that substance (Young, Rhee, Stallings, Corley, & Hewitt, 2006). For example, heritability of cannabis use is estimated to be .31, cannabis craving .36 (Ehlers et al., 2010), and .51 to .59 for problem use (Verweij et al., 2010).

Interestingly, aggressive forms of delinquency have been shown to be more heritable than nonaggressive ones (Rodgers, Buster, & Rowe, 2001). The heritability of aggression, itself, also appears to vary by form. Social (nonphysical) aggression appears to be only minimally influenced by genetics, while physical aggression is strongly influenced (Brendgen et al., 2005). In sum, it appears that the more severe forms of antisocial behavior are more greatly influenced by genetics.

What behavioral genetic research leaves unanswered is how each form of antisocial behavior is influenced by genetic factors. The results from previously mentioned studies suggest that genetics influence antisocial behavior, but do not address how. Each behavior is likely affected by countless genes both distally through previously affected behaviors and environments and also factors more proximal to it in time. The most distal pathways, through which genetics influence early life situations which in turn influence a cascade of subsequent situations, are particularly complex. Many criminological theories and studies have attributed causal influence to variation in an environmental factor that was itself likely largely driven by genetic variation. In this situation, the environmental factor would be more appropriately labeled a partial mediator than a root cause. However, since not all the variation in social environment factors can be attributed to heredity, neither label is appropriate. Most are likely part root cause and part mediator of genetic influence. Identifying factors as partially mediating genetics' relationship with deviance, however, is equally important to exploring purely environmental influences. In each situation, an environmental intervention has the possibility of decreasing the likelihood of antisocial behavior.

Though we can be certain that biology underpins a significant portion of the variation in antisocial behaviors, we are unlikely to unravel each of the intricate pathways that alters the likelihood of each behavior. Yet identifying some key steps along a few of the most significant pathways seems possible and would create an opportunity for potentially modifying behaviors. One form of potential pathways is particularly relevant to general strain theory. It is possible that genetics affect crime largely through stress or strain. Put another way, some of the variation in antisocial behavior that is attributed to heredity may operate through genetic factors influencing stressful environments and perceptions of stress.

This may occur in multiple ways. First, variation in antisocial behavior linked to genetics may have a connection with individuals differentially selecting environments. Those distinct environments actively selected by individuals each influence overall exposure to stress and the specific stressors faced. Similarly, genetically driven traits are also likely to affect social environments in situations where individuals have minimal control. For example, learning disabilities can influence class placement, which may expose youth to more abusive peers, a more negative school environment, and academic frustration. Second, personal traits partially affected by heredity are likely to influence the way other members of society respond. As a result of genetic variation, individuals differentially elicit responses from others that may be interpreted as stress and incite negative reactions. Finally, subjective interpretations or perceptions of life stresses are likely to be partially affected by heredity. Perceiving a situation as relatively more stressful is likely to be linked to more negative reactions.

If arguments that stress or strain is a part of a process through which genetics' influence on antisocial behavior operates are to be viewed credibly, research must first establish that the experience of strain is heritable. The measures of stress utilized in extant behavior genetic research do not exactly match Agnew's (1992) definition of strain, but those studies do demonstrate that stresses are partially heritable. Kendler and Baker (2007) completed a meta-analysis of all studies exploring the genetic basis of stressful life events. They identified 10 relevant studies and calculated the weighted heritability estimate for the occurrence of stressful events to be .28 (Kendler & Baker, 2007). This means that, on average, the additive effect of genes accounted for 28% of the variation in stressful life events between individuals. They also calculated a .36 heritability estimate for traumatic events. More recent studies have noted similar results (Schnittker, 2010). The perceived experience of stress may be even more strongly influenced by genetics. Bogdan and Pizzagalli (2009) found that 54% of the variation of perceived stress could be linked to heredity.

These works suggest that variation in strain, as conceptualized by Agnew (1992), is likely significantly influenced by genetics, but future work should attempt to evaluate heritability of appropriately operationalized measures of strain. In his own research, this author has noted that seven of the key strains have heritability estimates ranging between .18 and .40 (Stogner, 2011), but like many other studies, these strain measures are based on existing items in large datasets and not ideally designed as indicators of strain. The operationalization of strain is highly consequential, because studies have noted that heritability estimates for stress can vary drastically dependent on how stress is measured (Federenko et al., 2006). Initial steps in studying genetics, strain, and antisocial behavior in this way include: theoretically determining whether objective stresses or subjective interpretations to them will be the focus (see Agnew, 2006), selecting valid measures of strain, collecting data (because measures in existing datasets are not adequate indicators of strain), and assessing their heritability.

After establishing that appropriately operationalized measures of strain are partially heritable, research may then turn to determining whether variation in strain and antisocial behavior share a common genetic basis. Put another way, it is not enough to simply demonstrate that both strain and antisocial behavior are affected by genetic influences. This form of theoretical integration requires demonstrating that strain and antisocial behavior have shared genetic effects. That is, the two must covary and a significant portion of that covariance must be due to genetic factors. This form of variance decomposition modeling is not uncommon in the field (Boardman, Alexander, & Stallings, 2011; Sartor et al., 2012), but this author is unaware of any study exploring shared genetic influences on any form of antisocial behavior and strain measures as theoretically conceptualized by Agnew (2006). Once again, this is likely due to major datasets that contain twins and sibling pairs not including adequate or complete strain measures. A recent study authored by Vaske, Boisvert, and Wright (2012) did show that correlation between one major form of strain, violent victimization, and delinquency is largely explained by shared genetic influences. Their work was not intended to be an evaluation of a biosocial strain theory and did not include other measures of strain, but can serve as an example for research in this area.

A number of other concerns must additionally be addressed to successfully integrate biosocial research and general strain theory. Among these is determining the time-ordering of events. If genetic influences on variation in antisocial behavior operate though strain, then variation in strain must precede variation in delinquency and violence. Given Agnew's (2006) arguments that delinquency is seen as a way to cope with stress and results from pressure to relieve strain, strains also should have a proximal impact on deviance. That is, changes in antisocial behavior should follow the presentation of new stresses, but the impact should be more immediate than remote.

This line of theoretical integration has great potential and would offer clear-cut and ethical policy implications if empirically supported. The focus of interventions could be preventing/alleviating strains, offering assistance for interpreting stressful situations in a positive way, or helping citizens develop positive coping skills. These, of course, are not unlike those recommended by GST.

The Relationship Between Stress, Injury, and Brain Development

While the previous sections largely highlight the psychological consequences of strain and how these may either be driven or modified by genetics, another route exists for connecting strain, biology, and deviance. Many strains, particularly those affecting children and adolescents, involve physical insult in some form. A quarter of the key strains Agnew (2006) stresses (i.e., violent victimization, parental maltreatment, harsh punishment, and abusive peers) are likely to involve some form of physical trauma. Similarly, several key strains such as neglect and poverty may be linked to malnutrition, and still others such as living in a disadvantaged neighborhood may increase exposure to toxins. Though Agnew's (1992, 2006) theory is structured around these strains creating psychological distress and pressure for resolution, it cannot be avoided that many key strains have the potential to lead to physiological injury and impair neurocognitive development. Their effect on deviance may not be solely through pressure for coping, but also through damage inflicted to the developing brain.

The relationship between physical trauma at a young age and cognitive development has been well established (Boll, 1983; Catroppa & Anderson, 2003). Similarly, those experiencing head trauma are more likely to be characterized as aggressive (Brower & Price, 2001). As a result, it is not surprising that those convicted of violent crimes often report traumatic head injuries (Lewis, Pincus, Feldman, Jackson, & Bard, 1986; Shiroma, Ferguson, & Pickelsimer, 2012). These reports exceed those of matched nonincarcerated samples, but some question whether this relationship is purely spurious due to factors such as low socioeconomic status affecting both (Perkes, Schofield, Butler, & Hollis, 2011). Regardless, there appears to be a connection between closed head injuries and antisocial behavior that warrants further investigation. If strains are found to partially operate through the long-term physical consequences of the events rather than simply through short-term pressures for coping, then the theory may become more powerful in that it would better explain why the impact of some strains are not immediate.

In much the same way, malnutrition during childhood affects cognitive development (Liu, Raine, Venables, Dalais, & Mednick, 2003; Martorell, 1999) as does exposure to toxins (Lanphear, Dietrich, Auinger, & Cox, 2000). These are additionally linked to aggression, impulsivity (Liu, Raine, Venables, & Mednick, 2004) and behavioral problems (Liu & Raine, 2006). Once again, we must consider that the relationship between these sources of strains and later delinquency might not operate through pressure to relieve strain, but on their long-term effects on the brain and cognition. Both prenatal and childhood aversive environments may have a greater effect through the resulting neural deficits than they do through stress.

Integrating strain theory and biosocial criminology in this way may be challenging because it would require clarifying both long-term physiological and short-term psychological effects of stress. Among others, Moffitt's (1993) work may be a useful foundation for this effort. Similarly, this form of integration would be challenging to test given that accurate longitudinal data on traumatic brain injuries, malnutrition, and toxins is rare and that each may be affected by recall bias or a lack of awareness (Maughan & Rutter, 1997). Still, such challenges can be overcome and a potentially more thorough integrated biosocial strain theory created and evaluated.

Previous Attempts at Theoretical Integration

In 2000, Walsh argued that our discipline needed to create and explore "biologically informed theories" (p. 1076) in order to truly advance. He demonstrated how biological factors might be tied to the works of Durkheim, Merton, and Agnew as an example of how the disciplines can be merged. He stopped short of providing a complete biosocially informed general strain theory or quantitatively testing propositions, but did include a call for a conceptual revival of criminological theory through the inclusion of biology. Despite his plea, very few attempts have been made to theoretically integrate biology and the strain perspective. The majority of works citing Walsh simply note that biology may play a role in modifying reactions to strain rather than offering a revised theory. Similarly, mentions of Agnew and GST are common in biosocial criminological works, but they are typically utilized to theoretically establish the connection between stress and deviance as opposed to being the foundation for a novel integrated theory. This is somewhat surprising in a field that draws curious and creative academics, but, as Bursik (2009) has suggested, we may be more practiced in reinvention than invention.

A Biosocially Informed General Strain Theory (BIGST)

In 2011, this author attempted to theoretically integrate modern strain theory with biosocial criminology in a framework labeled a "Biosocially Informed General Strain Theory" or BIGST (Stogner, 2011). The resulting theoretical framework included seven key components that were detailed in the work. Briefly, BIGST proposes that (1) that information from behavioral and molecular genetics can be added to GST without changing any of the theory's core concepts; (2) that genetics play a significant role in the strains to which people are exposed and also in how they interpret them; (3) that there is a genetic basis for the differences between people in their levels of negative emotions and their coping skills; (4) that genetic risk affects emotionality and temperament; (5) that genetic risk has minor, but significant direct effects on delinquency; (6) that genetic risk modifies emotional responses to strain; and (7) that it also modifies behavioral responses to strain. These components or principles were not presented as a final immutable product, but rather a foundation for the intertwining of biology and strain theory. They were intended to be fluid because early tests may suggest the modification of some of propositions and advances in the biological sciences may help refine them.

Put another way, this initial formulation should be viewed as the only foundation for BIGST just as Agnew's (1992) viewed his initial arguments as "the foundation" for a general strain theory.

To clarify, Agnew's (1992) GST forms the sociological core of BIGST, and its central tenets all remained unchanged (Principle 1). If, in empirical tests, the latter six arguments are found to be insignificant, then BIGST will be reduced to GST. The framework was created in this way because criminologists are more likely to accept renovations to theory that add to rather than alter traditional perspectives. BIGST additionally argues that the experience of strain is partially genetic in origin (Principle 2). Whereas GST's explanation of deviance leads to the question of why individuals experience different levels of strain, BIGST offers that differences in genetic makeup account for a significant portion of variation in both objective and subjective experiences of strain. Similarly, BIGST notes that the factors that may mediate, as well as those that may moderate, strains' effects are partially heritable (Principle 3). BIGST also suggests that genetic risk has a small, but significant direct effect on both negative affect (Principle 4) and antisocial behavior (Principle 5). However, BIGST's most important theoretical arguments are that genetic factors condition the effect of strain on both negative emotions (Principle 6) and deviant behavior (Principle 7). BIGST attempts to correct for one of GST's most glaring weaknesses, its inability to explain different reactions to strain, by suggesting that genetic factors modify these responses. Further, it is suggested that polymorphic genes may be more critical in conditioning reactions to genes than those sociological factors described in Agnew's (1992, 2006) works.

The seven key principles of BIGST:

1. GST is incorporated in whole.
2. Both the experience and differential perception of strains are partially hereditable.
3. Negative affect and conditioning factors are partially hereditable.
4. Genetic risk has a small, significant direct effect on negative affect controlling for strain.
5. Genetic risk has a small, significant direct effect on antisocial behavior controlling for strain.
6. Genetic factors condition strains' effect on the experience of negative emotions.
7. Genetic factors condition strains' effect on antisocial behaviors.

The initial evaluation of BIGST yielded positive results for all but one of the seven propositions (Stogner, 2011). However, these analyses suffered from measurement issues because the Add Health dataset was not designed to evaluate strain as conceptualized by theory and does not contain both objective and subjective measures of each form of strain. Nonetheless, the framework does appear to have utility and may serve to better our understanding of the relationship between stress and deviance.

Conclusions

With regard to the strain perspective on deviance, it appears that purely sociological theory may have taken the field as far as it can go. The incorporation of biology and genetics is essential for the future of criminological theory and allows for stronger, more detailed explanations of crime (Walsh & Beaver, 2009). In the preceding sections, three different avenues for theoretically intertwining biology and strain theory were explored. These three sections were presented not as theories but as recommendations for potential mechanisms of theoretical integration. It is this author's hope that readers explore these and other routes to connect general strain theory with biology. Finally, the author offered his own work as an example of how the two disciplines may be tied in a single unified theory. Regardless of whether BIGST serves as a foundation for future studies and theories, it demonstrates that a biosocial strain theory of deviance can be developed in a way that is parsimonious, logically consistent, and testable.

References

Agnew, R. (1992). Foundation for a general strain theory of crime and delinquency. *Criminology, 30*(1), 47–87.

Agnew, R. (2001). Building on the foundation of general strain theory: Specifying the types of strain most likely to lead to crime and delinquency. *Journal of Research in Crime & Delinquency, 38*(4), 319–362.

Agnew, R. (2006). *Pressured into crime: An overview of strain theory*. Los Angeles, CA: Roxbury.

Agnew, R., & White, H. R. (1992). An empirical test of general strain theory. *Criminology, 30*(4), 475–499.

Aseltine R. H., Jr., Gore, S., & Gordon, J. (2000). Life stress, anger and anxiety, and delinquency: An empirical test of general strain theory. *Journal of Health & Social Behavior, 41*(3), 256–275.

Baker, L. A., Jacobson, K. C., Raine, A., Lozano, D. I., & Bezdjian, S. (2007). Genetic and environmental bases of childhood antisocial behavior: A multi-informant twin study. *Journal of Abnormal Psychology, 116*(2), 219–235.

Bao, W., Haas, A., & Pi, Y. (2007). Life strain, coping, and delinquency in the People's Republic of China. *International Journal of Offender Therapy & Comparative Criminology, 51*, 9–24.

Barnes, J. C., & Jacobs, B. A. (2013). Genetic risk for violent behavior and environmental exposure to disadvantage and violent crime: The case for gene-environment interaction. *Journal of Interpersonal Violence, 18*(1), 92–120.

Baron, S. W. (2004). General strain, street youth and crime: A test of Agnew's revised theory. *Criminology, 42*(2), 457–483.

Baron, S. W. (2009). Street youths' violent responses to violent personal, vicarious, and anticipated strain. *Journal of Criminal Justice, 37*(5), 442–451.

Beaver, K. M. (2009). *Biosocial criminology: A primer*. Dubuque, IA: Kendall/Hunt.

Beaver, K. M., Wright, J. P., DeLisi, M., Daigle, L. E., Swatt, M. L., & Gibson, C. L. (2007). Evidence of a gene × environment interaction in the creation of victimization: Results from a longitudinal sample of adolescents. *International Journal of Offender Therapy and Comparative Criminology, 51*(6), 620–645.

Belsky, J., & Beaver, K. M. (2011). Cumulative-genetic plasticity, parenting and adolescent self-regulation. *Journal of Child Psychology & Psychiatry, 52*(5), 619–626.

Benjet, C., Thompson, R. J., & Gotlib, I. H. (2010). 5-HTTLPR moderates the effect of relational peer victimization on depressive symptoms in adolescent girls. *Journal of Child Psychology and Psychiatry, 51*(2), 173–179.

Boardman, J. D., Alexander, K. B., & Stallings, M. C. (2011). Stressful life events and depression among adolescent twin pairs. *Biodemography and Social Biology, 57*(1), 53–66.

Bogdan, R., & Pizzagalli, D. A. (2009). The heritability of hedonic capacity and perceived stress: A twin study evaluation of candidate depressive phenotypes. *Psychological Medicine, 39*(2), 211–218.

Boll, T. J. (1983). Minor head injury in children—out of sight but not out of mind. *Journal of Clinical Child & Adolescent Psychology, 12*(1), 74–80.

Brendgen, M., Boivin, M., Dionne, G., Barker, E. D., Vitaro, F., Girard, A., & Pérusse, D. (2011). Gene-environment processes linking aggression, peer victimization, and the teacher-child relationship. *Child Development, 82*(6), 2021–2036.

Brendgen, M., Boivin, M., Vitaro, F., Dionne, G., Girard, A., & Pérusse, D. (2008). Gene-environment interactions between peer victimization and child aggression. *Development and Psychopathology, 20*, 455–471.

Brendgen, M., Dionne, G., Girard, A., Boivin, M., Vitaro, F., & Pérusse, D. (2005). Examining genetic and environmental effects on social aggression: A study of 6-year-old twins. *Child Development, 76*(4), 930–946.

Brendgen, M., Vitaro, F., Barker, E. D., Girard, A., Dionne, G., Tremblay, R. E., & Boivin, M. (2011). Do other people's plights matter? A genetically informed twin study of the role of social context in the link between peer victimization and children's aggression and depression symptoms. *Developmental Psychology, 49*(2), 327–340.

Brezina, T. (1998). Adolescent maltreatment and delinquency: The question of intervening processes. *Journal of Research in Crime and Delinquency, 35,* 71–99.

Broidy, L. M. (2001). A test of general strain theory. *Criminology, 39*(1), 9–35.

Bronfenbrenner, U., & Ceci, S. J. (1994). Nature-nurture reconceptualized in developmental perspective: A bioecological model. *Psychological Review, 101*(4), 568–586.

Brower, M. C., & Price, B. H. (2001). Neuropsychiatry of frontal lobe dysfunction in violent and criminal behaviour: A critical review. *Journal of Neurology, Neurosurgery, & Psychiatry, 71*(6), 720–726.

Buckland, P. R. (2008). Will we ever find the genes for addiction? *Addiction, 103*(11), 1768–1776.

Bursik, R. J., Jr. (2009). The Dead Sea Scrolls and criminological knowledge: 2008 presidential address to the American Society of Criminology. *Criminology, 47*(1), 5–16.

Carson, D. C., Sullivan, C. J., Cochran, J. K., & Lersch, K. M. (2009). General strain theory and the relationship between early victimization and drug use. *Deviant Behavior, 30*(1), 54–88.

Carver, C. S., Johnson, S. L., & Joormann, J. (2008). Serotonergic function, two-mode models of self-regulation, and vulnerability to depression: What depression has in common with impulsive aggression. *Psychological Bulletin, 134*(6), 912–943.

Caspi, A., McClay, J., Moffitt, T. E., Mill, J., Martin, J., Craig, I. W., . . . Poulton, R. (2002). Role of genotype in the cycle of violence in maltreated children. *Science, 297*(5582), 851–854.

Catroppa, C., & Anderson, V. (2003). Children's attentional skills 2 years post-traumatic brain injury. *Developmental Neuropsychology, 23,* 359–373.

Cheung, C., Ngai, N., & Ngai, S. (2007). Family strain and adolescent delinquency in two Chinese cities, Guangzhou and Hong Kong. *Journal of Child & Family Studies, 16*(5), 626–641.

Cicchetti, D., Rogosch, F. A., & Sturge-Apple, M. L. (2007). Interactions of child maltreatment and serotonin transporter and monoamine oxidase A polymorphisms: Depressive symptomatology among adolescents from low socioeconomic status backgrounds. *Development and Psychopathology, 19,* 1161–1180.

DeLisi, M., Beaver, K. M., Wright, J. P., & Vaughn, M. G. (2008). The etiology of criminal onset: The enduring salience of nature *and* nurture. *Journal of Criminal Justice, 36*(3), 217–223.

Derringer, J., Krueger, R. F., Irons, D. E., & Iacono, W. G. (2010). Harsh discipline, childhood sexual assault, and MAOA genotype: An investigation of main and interactive effects on diverse clinical externalizing outcomes. *Behavior Genetics, 40*(5), 639–648.

Douglas, K., Chan, G., Gelernter, J., Arias, A. J., Anton, R. F., Poling, J., & Kranzler, H. R. (2011). 5-HTTLPR as a potential moderator of the effects of adverse childhood experiences on risk of antisocial personality disorder. *Psychiatric Genetics, 21*(5), 240–248.

Ducci, F., Enoch, M. A., Hodgkinson, C., Xu, K., Catena, M., Robin, R. W., & Goldman, D. (2008). Interaction between a functional MAOA locus and childhood sexual abuse predicts alcoholism and antisocial personality disorder in adult women. *Molecular Psychiatry, 13*(3), 334–347.

Ehlers, C. L., Gizer, I. R., Vieten, C., Gilder, D. A., Stouffer, G. M., Lau, P., & Wilhelmsen, K. C. (2010). Cannabis dependence in the San Francisco Family Study: Age of onset of use, DSM-IV symptoms, withdrawal, and heritability. *Addictive Behaviors, 35*(2), 102–110.

Ellis, L., & Walsh, A. (2004). Ideology: Criminology's Achilles' heel? *Quarterly Journal of Ideology: A Critique of Conventional Wisdom, 27*(1&2), 1–25.

Federenko, I. S., Schlotz, W., Kirschbaum, C., Bartels, M., Hellhammer, D. H., & Wust, S. (2006). The heritability of perceived stress. *Psychological Medicine, 36*(3), 375–385.

Feinberg, M. E., Button, T. M. M., Neiderhiser, J. M., Reiss, D., & Hetherington, E. M. (2007). Evidence of genotype × parenting environment interaction. *Archives of General Psychiatry, 64,* 457–465.

Fergusson, D. M., Boden, J. M., Horwood, L. J., Miller, A., & Kennedy, M. A. (2012). Moderating role of the MAOA genotype in antisocial behaviour. *British Journal of Psychiatry, 200*(2), 116–123.

Foley, D. L., Eaves, L. J., Wormley, B., Silberg, J. L., Maes, H. H., Kuhn, J., & Riley, B. (2004). Childhood adversity, monoamine oxidase a genotype, and risk for conduct disorder. *Archives of General Psychiatry, 61,* 738–744.

Hay, C. (2003). Family strain, gender, and delinquency. *Sociological Perspectives, 46,* 107–135.

Hay, C., & Evans, M. M. (2006). Violent victimization and involvement in delinquency: Examining predictions from general strain theory. *Journal of Criminal Justice, 34*(3), 261–274.

Hollist, D. R., Hughes, L. A., & Schaible, L. M. (2009). Adolescent maltreatment, negative emotion, and delinquency: An assessment of general strain theory and family-based strain. *Journal of Criminal Justice, 37*(4), 379–387.

Huizinga, D., Haberstick, B. C., Smolen, A., Menard, S., Young, S. E., Corley, R. P., . . . Hewitt, J. K. (2006). Childhood maltreatment, subsequent antisocial behavior, and the role of monoamine oxidase A genotype. *Biological Psychiatry, 60*(7), 677–683.

Jaffee, S. R., Caspi, A., Moffitt, T. E., Dodge, K. A., Rutter, M., Taylor, A., & Tully, L. A. (2005). Nature X nurture: Genetic vulnerabilities interact with physical maltreatment to promote conduct problems. *Development and Psychopathology, 17,* 67–84.

Jang, S. J. (2007). Gender differences in strain, negative emotions, and coping behaviors: A general strain theory approach. *Justice Quarterly, 24*(3), 523–553.

Jang, S. J., & Johnson, B. R. (2003). Strain, negative emotions, and deviant coping among African Americans: A test of general strain theory. *Journal of Quantitative Criminology, 19*(1), 79–105.

Jensen, G. F. (1995). Salvaging structure through strain: A theoretical and empirical critique. In F. Adler, W. S. Laufer, & R. Merton (Series Eds.), *Advances in Criminological Theory Series: Vol. 6. The legacy of anomie theory*. New Brunswick, NJ: Transaction.

Johnson, M. C., & Morris, R. G. (2008). The moderating effects of religiosity on the relationship between stressful life events and delinquent behavior. *Journal of Criminal Justice, 36*(6), 486–493.

Kaufman, J. M. (2009). Gendered responses to serious strain: The argument for a general strain theory of deviance. *Justice Quarterly, 26*(3), 410–444.

Kaufman, J., Yang, B. Z., Douglas-Palumberi, H., Crouse-Artus, M., Lipschitz, D., Krystal, J. H., & Gelernter, J. (2007). Genetic and environmental predictors of early alcohol use. *Biological Psychiatry, 61,* 1228–1234.

Kendler, K. S., & Baker, J. H. (2007). Genetic influences on measures of the environment: A systematic review. *Psychological Medicine, 37*(5), 615–626.

Kim-Cohen, J., Caspi, A., Taylor, A., Williams, B., Newcombe, R., Craig, I. W., & Moffitt, T. E. (2006). MAOA, maltreatment, and gene-environment interaction predicting children's mental health: New evidence and a meta-analysis. *Molecular Psychiatry, 11*(10), 903–913.

Kim-Cohen, J., & Gold, A. L. (2009). Measured gene-environment interactions and mechanisms promoting resilient development. *Current Directions in Psychological Science, 18*(3), 138–142.

Lanphear, B. P., Dietrich, K., Auinger, P., & Cox, C. (2000). Cognitive deficits associated with blood lead concentrations <10 microg/dL in US children and adolescents. *Public Health Reports, 115*(6), 521–529.

Lewis, D. O., Pincus, J. H., Feldman, M., Jackson, L., & Bard, B. (1986). Psychiatric, neurological, and psychoeducational characteristics of 15 death row inmates in the United States. *American Journal of Psychiatry, 143*(7), 838–845.

Liu, J., & Raine, A. (2006). The effect of childhood malnutrition on externalizing behavior. *Current Opinion in Pediatrics, 18*(5), 565–570.

Liu, J., Raine, A., Venables, P. H., Dalais, C., & Mednick, S. A. (2003). Malnutrition at age 3 years and lower cognitive ability at age 11 years: Independence from psychosocial adversity. *Archives of Pediatrics & Adolescent Medicine, 157*(6), 593–600.

Liu, J., Raine, A., Venables, P. H., & Mednick, S. A. (2004). Malnutrition at age 3 years and externalizing behavior problems at ages 8, 11, and 17 years. *American Journal of Psychiatry, 161*(11), 2005–2013.

Malouff, J., Rooke, S., & Schutte, N. (2008). The heritability of human behavior: Results of aggregating meta-analyses. *Current Psychology, 27*(3), 153–161.

Manasse, M. E., & Ganem, N. M. (2009). Victimization as a cause of delinquency: The role of depression and gender. *Journal of Criminal Justice, 37*(4), 371–378.

Martorell, R. (1999). The nature of child malnutrition and its long-term implications. *Food & Nutrition Bulletin, 20*(3), 288–292.

Mason, D. A., & Frick, P. J. (1994). The heritability of antisocial behavior: A meta-analysis of twin and adoption studies. *Journal of Psychopathology and Behavioral Assessment, 16,* 301–323.

Maughan, B., & Rutter, M. (1997). Retrospective reporting of childhood adversity: Issues in assessing long-term recall. *Journal of Personality Disorders, 11*(1), 19–33.

Maxwell, S. R. (2001). A focus on familial strain: Antisocial behavior and delinquency in Filipino society. *Sociological Inquiry, 71*(3), 265–292.

Mazerolle, P., Burton, V. S., Cullen, F. T., Evans, D., & Payne, G. L. (2000). Strain, anger, and delinquent adaptations: Specifying general strain theory. *Journal of Criminal Justice, 28,* 89–101.

Mazerolle, P., & Piquero, A. (1998). Linking exposure to strain with anger: An investigation of deviant adaptations. *Journal of Criminal Justice, 26*(3), 195–211.

Miles, D. R., & Carey, G. (1997). Genetic and environmental architecture of human aggression. *Journal of Personality & Social Psychology, 72*(1), 207–217.

Moffitt, T. E. (1993). Adolescence-limited and life-course-persistent antisocial behavior: A developmental taxonomy. *Psychological Review, 100*(4), 674–701.

Moffitt, T. E., Caspi, A., & Rutter, M. (2006). Measured gene-environment interactions in psychopathology concepts, research strategies, and implications for research, intervention, and public understanding of genetics. *Perspectives on Psychological Science, 1,* 5–27.

Moon, B., Hays, K., & Blurton, D. (2009). General strain theory, key strains, and deviance. *Journal of Criminal Justice, 37*(1), 98–106.

Morash, M., & Moon, B. (2007). Gender differences in the effects of strain on the delinquency of South Korean youth. *Youth & Society, 38*(3), 300–321.

Narusyte, J., Andershed, A. K., Neiderhiser, J. M., & Lichtenstein, P. (2007). Aggression as a mediator of genetic contributions to the association between negative parent-child relationships and adolescent antisocial behavior. *European Child & Adolescent Psychiatry, 16,* 128–137.

Nikulina, V., Widom, C. S., & Brzustowicz, L. M. (2012). Child abuse and neglect, MAOA, and mental health outcomes: A prospective examination. *Biological Psychiatry, 71*(4), 350–357.

Nilsson, K. W., Comasco, E., Åslund, C., Nordquist, N., Leppert, J., & Oreland, L. (2010). MAOA genotype, family relations and sexual abuse in relation to adolescent alcohol consumption. *Addiction Biology, 16*(2), 347–355.

Perkes, I., Schofield, P. W., Butler, T., & Hollis, S. J. (2011). Traumatic brain injury rates and sequelae: A comparison of prisoners with a matched community sample in Australia. *Brain Injury, 25*(2), 131–141.

Prescott, C. A., Madden, P. A. F., & Stallings, M. C. (2006). Challenges in genetic studies of the etiology of substance use and substance use disorders: Introduction to the special issue. *Behavior Genetics, 36*(4), 473–482.

Raine, A. (1993). *The psychopathology of crime: Criminal behavior as a clinical disorder.* San Diego, CA: Academic Press.

Ratchford, M., & Beaver, K. M. (2009). Neuropsychological deficits, low self-control, and delinquent involvement: Toward a biosocial explanation of delinquency. *Criminal Justice and Behavior, 36*(2), 147–162.

Rhee, S. H., & Waldman, I. D. (2002). Genetic and environmental influences on antisocial behavior: A meta-analysis of twin and adoption studies. *Psychological Bulletin, 128,* 490–529.

Rodgers, J. L., Buster, M., & Rowe, D. C. (2001). Genetic and environmental influences on delinquency: DF analysis of NLSY kinship data. *Journal of Quantitative Criminology, 17*(2), 145–168.

Sartor, C. E., Grant, J. D., Lynskey, M. T., McCutcheon, V. V., Waldron, M., Statham, D. J., . . . Nelson, E. C. (2012). Common heritable contributions to low-risk trauma, high-risk trauma, posttraumatic stress disorder, and major depression. *Archives of General Psychiatry, 69*(3), 293.

Scheid, J. M., Holzman, C. B., Jones, N., Friderici, K. H., Nummy, K. A., Symonds, L. L., . . . Fisher, R. (2007). Depressive symptoms in mid-pregnancy, lifetime stressors and the 5-HTTLPR genotype. *Genes, Brain, and Behavior, 6,* 453–464.

Schnittker, J. (2010). Gene-environment correlations in the stress-depression relationship. *Journal of Health and Social Behavior, 51*(3), 229–243.

Shiroma, E. J., Ferguson, P. L., & Pickelsimer, E. E. (2012). Prevalence of traumatic brain injury in an offender population: A meta-analysis. *Journal of Head Trauma Rehabilitation, 27*(3), E1--E10.

Simons, R. L., Lei, M. K., Beach, S. R., Brody, G. H., Philibert, R. A., & Gibbons, F. X. (2011). Social environment, genes, and aggression evidence supporting the differential susceptibility perspective. *American Sociological Review, 76*(6), 883–912.

Stogner, J. (2011). *A biosocially informed investigation of general strain theory*. (Unpublished doctoral dissertation). University of Florida.

Stogner, J., & Gibson, C. L. (2010). Healthy, wealthy, and wise: Incorporating health issues as a source of strain in Agnew's general strain theory. *Journal of Criminal Justice, 38*(6), 1150–1159.

Sugden, K., Arseneault, L., Harrington, H., Moffitt, T. E., Williams, B., & Caspi, A. (2010). Serotonin transporter gene moderates the development of emotional problems among children following bullying victimization. *Journal of the American Academy of Child & Adolescent Psychiatry, 49*(8), 830–840.

Tittle, C. R., Broidy, L. M., & Gertz, M. G. (2008). Strain, crime, and contingencies. *Justice Quarterly, 25*(2), 283–312.

Vaske, J., Boisvert, D., & Wright, J. P. (2012). Genetic and environmental contributions to the relationship between violent victimization and criminal behavior. *Journal of Interpersonal Violence, 27*(16), 3213–3235.

Vaske, J., Makarios, M., Boisvert, D., Beaver, K. M., & Wright, J. P. (2009). The interaction of DRD2 and violent victimization on depression: An analysis by gender and race. *Journal of Affective Disorders, 112*(1), 120–125.

Vaske, J., Newsome, J., & Wright, J. P. (2012). Interaction of serotonin transporter linked polymorphic region and childhood neglect on criminal behavior and substance use for males and females. *Development and Psychopathology, 24*(1), 181–193.

Verweij, K. J. H., Zietsch, B. P., Lynskey, M. T., Medland, S. E., Neale, M. C., Martin, N. G., . . . Vink, J. M. (2010). Genetic and environmental influences on cannabis use initiation and problematic use: A meta-analysis of twin studies. *Addiction, 105*(3), 417–430.

Waldman, I. D., & Rhee, S. H. (2006). Genetic and environmental influences on psychopathy and antisocial behavior. In C. J. Patrick (Ed.), *Handbook of psychopathy* (pp. 205–228). New York, NY: Guilford.

Walsh, A. (2000). Behavior genetics and anomie/strain theory. *Criminology, 38*(4), 1075–1107.

Walsh, A. (2009). *Biology and criminology: The biosocial synthesis.* New York, NY: Routledge.

Walsh, A., & Beaver, K. M. (2009). Introduction to biosocial criminology. In A. Walsh & K. M. Beaver (Eds.), *Biosocial criminology: New directions in theory and research.* New York, NY: Routledge.

Warner, B. D., & Fowler, S. K. (2003). Strain and violence: Testing a general strain theory model of community violence. *Journal of Criminal Justice, 31*(6), 511–521.

Weder, N., Yang, B. Z., Douglas-Palumberi, H., Massey, J., Krystal, J. H., Gelemter, J., & Kaufman, J. (2009). MAOA genotype, maltreatment, and aggressive behavior: The changing impact of genotype at various levels of trauma. *Biological Psychiatry, 65*(5), 417–424.

Widom, C. S., & Brzustowicz, L. M. (2006). MAOA and the "cycle of violence": Childhood abuse and neglect, MAOA genotype, and risk for violent and antisocial behavior. *Biological Psychiatry, 60*(7), 684–689.

Wright, J. P., & Beaver, K. M. (2005). Do parents matter in creating self-control in their children? A genetically informed test of Gottfredson and Hirschi's theory of low self-control. *Criminology, 43,* 1169–1202.

Wright, J. P., & Boisvert, D. (2009). What biosocial criminology offers criminology. *Criminal Justice and Behavior, 36*(11), 1228–1240.

Wright, J. P., Schnupp, R., Beaver, K. M., DeLisi, M., & Vaughn, M. (2012). Genes, maternal negativity, and self-control evidence of a gene × environment interaction. *Youth Violence and Juvenile Justice, 10*(3), 245–260.

Young, S. E., Rhee, S. H., Stallings, M. C., Corley, R. P., & Hewitt, J. K. (2006). Genetic and environmental vulnerabilities underlying adolescent substance use and problem use: General or specific? *Behavior Genetics, 36*(4), 603–615.

Young-Wolff, K. C., Enoch, M. A., & Prescott, C. A. (2011). The influence of gene-environment interactions on alcohol consumption and alcohol use disorders: A comprehensive review. *Clinical Psychology Review, 31,* 800–816.

Discussion Questions

CHAPTERS 11 AND 12

1. Sociologists and genetic researchers differ in their definitions and explanations of strain. Discuss the ways the two are different. For example, how would a sociologist explain why strain affects deviance? How would a genetic researcher explain why strain affects deviance?
2. General strain theory (GST) argues that coping skills will moderate the relationship between strain and deviance. Describe the ways genetic factors may also moderate the relationship between strain and deviance. Given the available evidence, are both moderators empirically supported?
3. Agnew's GST has the potential to gain advancement by integrating biosocial research into the theory. As addressed in Dr. Stogner's chapter, how may gene × strain interactions be used to integrate theory and research? Are there any caveats to this approach? What initial steps should be taken when studying genetics, strain, and antisocial behavior?
4. Researchers have argued that communities with high levels of economic deprivation and inequality will be the ones to experience the most strain. Describe how genetic factors may influence stressful environments. For example, is it possible that environments are actively selected by individuals? In turn, how do these selections influence overall exposure to stress and the specific stressors faced?
5. As noted in Dr. Agnew's chapter, one's reaction to strain is a function of how individuals are socialized. Discuss the ways neurocognitive deficits may compromise one's ability to cope with strain. In other words, how might the social environment interact with brain development and lead to deviance?
6. Describe how a biosocially informed general strain theory (BIGST) may be used to explain why individuals experience different levels of strain. How might BIGST be used to correct for GST's weaknesses?

13

Social Bonding and Crime

Ryan Schroeder

University of Louisville

Introduction

The *social bond*, broadly defined as integration of an individual into a social group, is one of the earliest sociological concepts thought to influence behavior. The notion of the social bond in sociology originated from the classic empirical assessment by Emile Durkheim (1951), a foundational sociologist credited with establishing the functionalist tradition in sociology. In his classic work *Suicide*, Durkheim links the degree of social integration to suicide, a highly personal action that can be related to social structure and social cohesiveness. Durkheim's emphasis, however, was not necessarily suicide; rather, Durkheim was concerned with uncovering the basis of social unity. In his classic work *Suicide*, Durkheim "viewed suicide as a manifestation of the lack of social cohesion and the suicide rate a convenient index of weak social bonds" (Berk, 2006, p. 60).

Durkheim's assessment of the social correlates of suicide identifies three distinct, but not mutually exclusive, categorical explanations of self-homicide based on the degree and trends in social integration associated with various historical, cultural, and social contexts. Egoistic suicide, for instance, results from a weak or nonexistent integration of an individual into society, exemplified by a lower rate of suicide among Catholics (a strong integration into the collective life) than Protestants (a more individualistic approach to religion). Egoistic suicide is also embodied by the lower rate of suicide among individuals in small and close families, and in nations undergoing great crises; in these social contexts, social integration and active participation in social life are necessary and egoism is muted.

Relatedly, anomic suicide also results from social circumstances that result in weak regulation of the individual by society. The difference between egoistic and anomic suicide, however, is that anomic suicide emphasizes contexts in which rapid changes in social life represent a shift from strong regulation of individual behaviors and aspirations to contexts characterized by weak regulation of the individual. For example, the sudden accumulation of wealth can weaken the impact of traditional societal rules and cause a state of anomie, or normlessness. Divorce also represents a rapid shift from strong societal integration and regulation to a relative state of anomie. The regulative influence of social structure is removed in both examples, which explains the higher rate of suicide among individuals who experience rapid increases in wealth or divorce.

Altruistic suicide, however, occurs in situations of overly strong societal integration, such as occurs in societies where social life is strictly dominated by custom and tradition; suicide results from appeal to higher authorities, such as religious sacrifice, political extremism, or a strong adherence to cultural traditions. Although somewhat contradictory to the social bond perspective that highlights the importance of social cohesion in reducing societal deviance, altruistic suicide nonetheless emphasizes that societal bonds influence individual decisions and actions.

The social bond perspective developed by Durkheim was originally formulated as a macro-level theory, because the original intent and accompanying analyses were designed to explain differences in suicide rates *between groups*, but current research and theorizing has largely focused on the micro-level implications of the social bond, or social control, on deviant behavior. Contemporary empirical and theoretical analyses of Durkheim's original conceptualization of the social bond has uncovered the incomplete specification of the theory (Lester, 1989; Pickering & Walford, 2000), criticized the methodological shortcomings of the original study, and questioned the micro-level implications of Durkheim's study (Berk, 2006; Pescosolido & Georgianna, 1989), but the notion that self-centered social desires can be controlled by a high degree of social integration remains a stalwart of sociological inquiry and forms the basis of the social bond tradition in criminological research.

Assumptions of the Social Bond Perspective in Criminology

Before outlining the classic and contemporary research on the effect of social bonds on criminal offending, it is important to first describe the fundamental assumptions of human behavior that form the basis of the social bond perspective in criminology. In contrast to other positivistic perspectives in criminology, which assume that individuals are naturally conformists and become criminals through some social force (e.g., strain, deviant peers), the social bond theory assumes that individuals are naturally inclined to deviance. In other words, the question addressed by the social bond perspective is different than the other major theories of criminality. Rather than ask "*why do people commit crime?*" the social bond theory asks the question "*why do people conform?*" As Hirschi (1969) explains, "The question remains, why *do* men obey the rules of society? Deviance is taken for granted; conformity must be explained" (p. 10).

The social bond perspective in criminology, therefore, assumes that crime will occur unless some social force, such as a social bond, controls this natural inclination (see M. Gottfredson & Hirschi, 1990; Hirschi, 1969). All theories that address social bonds focus on relationships and institutions that control criminal activity, but each theoretical approach varies in the degree to which external motivations for crime are accounted. For example, in an early conceptualization of social bond theory, Reckless (1967) integrated several crime-motivating factors, such as personality and social circumstances, into a theory that also accounts for how social bonds constrain these motivations to offending. Hirschi (1969) even recognized that the natural motivation to offending must be modified to account for social factors that motivate offending in addition to the social factors that restrain or control offending. Akers (2000) argues that social bond theories do not differ substantially from other criminological perspectives in the questions addressed:

> Consequently, there is really not much difference between control theory and other theories in the type of questions about crime that each tries to answer. Whatever their other differences, all theories of crime . . . ultimately propose to account for variations in criminal and delinquent behavior. . . . Conformity and crime are two sides of the same coin. It makes no meaningful difference which of the two a theory claims to explain, because to account for one accounts for the other. Theories vary in the extent to which they emphasize one side of the coin, whether it be the motivation of crime or the restrains on crime. . . . For this reason, it is difficult to divide explanations of crime into two mutually exclusive categories based on whether they try to explain either conformity or crime. (pp. 100–101)

In sum, social bond theories follow the assumption that all individuals are motivated toward crime and deviance, whether through natural tendencies or some other external social factor. The unique contribution of social bond perspectives is the focus on factors that constrain such motivations. For this reason, the rest of this chapter emphasizes the ways in which social bonds control or modify motivations toward criminal offending.

Early Theorizing on Social Bonds and Crime

Despite Durkheim's early conceptualization of social bonds, and his basic macro-level research establishing the importance of social bonds in reducing the likelihood of suicide, criminology did not incorporate the notion of social bonds as a dominant explanation for criminality until the 1950s. Albert J. Reiss's (1951) paper "Delinquency as the Failure of Personal and Social Controls" reinvigorated the concept of the social bond in criminological theory and helped set the stage for decades of research on social bonding and crime. In the paper, Reiss promotes the idea that delinquency occurs when personal and social controls are weak or absent. Personal controls are defined as personality components, similar to self-control (M. Gottfredson & Hirschi, 1990) and not directly related to social bonding. *Social controls*, defined as "the ability of social groups or institutions to make norms or rules effective" (Reiss, 1951, p. 196), result from socialization processes, including strong formal and informal sanctions resulting from deviant behavior. Especially important to Reiss's early theoretical advancement of social bonds, and the numerous sociological approaches to the social bond and crime, are the socialization processes promoted within the institutions of the family and the school.

Ivan F. Nye (1958) later refined Reiss's original conceptualization of social control to include three unique, albeit interrelated, forms of social control that influence delinquent behavior. The first category of social control is direct control, consisting of punishments (or threats of punishment) for deviant behavior and rewards for prosocial behavior from parents. Internal control, the second category of social control from this perspective, is a sense of guilt held by some youth that prevents delinquent engagement. The third category, and most related to the current view of social bonding, is indirect control that prevents youth misbehavior through the perceived fear that such acts will result in disappointment or pain for parents or others who have close relationships with the adolescents. The indirect control component, characterized by the anticipated negative reactions of others to criminal behavior, is central to contemporary theorizing and research on the social bond.

Reflecting the same external-internal dynamic promoted by Reiss (1951) and Nye (1958), the next major progression of the social bond perspective in criminology was advanced by Walter Reckless in a series of work on his containment theory of crime and delinquency (Reckless, 1961, 1967; Reckless, Dinitz, & Murray, 1956). The main contention of the containment theory is that individuals have internal and external constraints that buffer motivations to offend. Inner containment is again similar to the concept of self-control, but focuses less on personality and offers a stronger emphasis on "self-concepts" established through interactions within primary groups, most notably the family. Youth with "insulated" self-concepts are able to reject internal and external pressures to offend, whereas youth with "vulnerable" self-concepts more often give in to the pressures to offend. Self-concepts have implications for the development of other theoretical traditions in criminology, such as labeling theory and social learning theory. But self-concepts were also critical to establishing the social bond perspective in criminology, given Reckless's emphasis on family socialization processes in the development of self-concepts. Self-concepts, from this perspective, are essentially a proxy measure for social bonds.

More important to the social nature of the social bond is Reckless's (1961) conceptualization of outer containment. Outer containment encompasses a wide range of social experiences and relationships that establish high levels of supervision and discipline, and most important, strong group ties and moral beliefs. Similar to other early social bond theorists, Reckless emphasizes the imperative role of the family and schools in promoting outer containment as a control to deviant or delinquent behavior.

The last major early theoretical development contributing to the current social bond perspective in criminology is David Matza's (1957) counterfactual theoretical application—drift theory. Drift theory explains how youth who are already committed to conventional moral restraints utilize techniques of neutralization to temporarily "free" themselves from such restraints. Stated differently, otherwise strongly bonded individuals will implement techniques of neutralization, such as "denial of responsibility," to drift in and out of delinquency. The techniques of neutralization thus represent a weakening of social bonds (see Minor, 1981). In contrast to other early developments in social bonding or social control, drift theory thus assumes that all individuals have ties to, and therefore a stake in, conventional society, but enact a variety of strategies to temporarily counteract or diminish such bonds. Rather than focusing on the development of social bonds, drift theory emphasizes processes that work to weaken bonds, however temporarily. Nevertheless, drift theory clearly highlights the importance of social bonds in controlling crime and delinquency.

Taken together, the early conceptual and empirical work on factors that control delinquent and criminal behavior laid the foundation for what is now considered the social bond tradition in criminology. The main premise of all these early works is that family and other social relationships produce internal or external behavioral constraints that temper motivations and opportunities for offending.

Hirschi's Social Bond Theory

Although these early attempts at theorizing the role of social bonds in criminal behavior are recognized as important in establishing the framework for social bond theory, Hirschi's (1969) social bond theory is widely considered the preeminent explanation of the connection between social bonds and criminality. In *Causes of Delinquency*, Hirschi presents a complete theoretical development, conceptualization, operationalization, and empirical test of the theory. Hirschi's social control theory, also known as social bond theory, refines and combines the elements of the prior control theories into a singular, focused, and logically consistent theory replete with empirical measures of social bonds that is applicable to a wide range of behaviors. As Akers (2000) notes,

> In spite of its title, the book presented an internally consistent, logically coherent, and parsimonious theory that is applicable to any type of criminal or deviant behavior, not only delinquency. Hirschi formulated a control theory that brought together elements from all previous control theories and offered new ways to account for delinquent behavior. (p. 105)

Hirschi's (1969) theory has become the dominant control theory in criminology and remains widely cited to this day. Stitt and Giacopassi (1992) reported that the social bond theory was, at that time, the most frequently discussed and tested criminological theory, and a quick subject search of Sociological Abstracts for "social bonds" or "social control theory" reveals 1,667 peer-reviewed articles, far surpassing the article count for the other major criminological theories combined during that time period.

The main premise of the social bond theory is that individuals build a "stake in conformity" through social relationships and activities, which in turn deters such individuals from engaging in the natural tendency to deviate from social norms. Stated differently, a "stake in conformity" derived from valued social bonds prevents individuals from committing crimes. In a succinct summary of the primary proposition of the theory, Hirschi (1969) states, "delinquent acts occur when an individual's bond to society is weak or broken" (p. 16). The theory defines four non-mutually exclusive elements that constitute social bonds—attachment, commitment, involvement, and belief.

Attachment. Attachment refers to the affective identification between an individual and other individuals or institutions that comprise the dominant society. In essence, attachments are ties that one has to others, such as parents, teachers, coaches, religious leaders, or other role models, or institutions, including schools, athletics, community activities, or any other social institution. Central to the attachment component of Hirschi's social bond theory is the degree to which an individual has concern and respect for the reactions and opinions of others. If an individual has strong attachments to others or institutions, that individual will care about the reactions of those people, groups, or institutions might have in response to deviant acts. In other words, an attached individual will refrain from criminal offending because that individual does not want to elicit a negative reaction from others or put those valued relationships in jeopardy.

Commitment. Commitment refers to the value and investment individuals place on achieving future goals. Occupational and educational goals are often cited as key sources of commitment, because such goals necessarily entail a great deal of investment of time and energy to accomplish, and other goals such as building a family, becoming more religious, or any other personal goal can also be seen as indicative of commitment. The commitments an individual defines as important prevent criminal involvement because of the view that crime will impair the individual's ability to accomplish such goals. For example, if an individual is committed to graduating from college, it is unlikely that the individual will succumb to the natural inclination toward crime or deviance; criminal activity will likely impede the progress toward that goal and negate the investments the individual has made in the educational process.

Involvement. Consistent with the colloquial saying "Idle hands are the devil's workshop," the involvement component of the social bond suggests that being engaged in conventional activities reduces the time and energy required to commit criminal or deviant acts. Studying, playing sports, attending religious activities, spending time with family, and participating in school activities are examples of conventional activities that reduce the likelihood of offending by limiting the personal resources required for offending.

Belief. The belief component of the social bond refers to the degree of respect that an individual holds for societal rules and authority figures. If an individual endorses the conventional social values and norms, and believes that society's laws are fair and just, that individual is unlikely to evidence criminal behavior. Key to belief that a social bond is a factor that inhibits criminal offending is when individuals believe they have a moral obligation to follow societal rules. As Hirschi (1969) states, "[T]he less a person believes he should obey the rules, the more likely he is to violate them" (p. 26).

Taken together, attachment to conventional others or institutions, a commitment to future goals, involvement in conventional activities, and a belief in the moral validity of societal rules create a bond to society, or a "stake in conformity," that constrains impulses to commit criminal offenses or acts of deviance. The social bond theory has been tested repeatedly since it was first introduced in 1969. In general, support for the social bond theory has been strong, with some notable exceptions as described below. Furthermore, research has established that social bonds do not vary in importance or substance between males and females (Chapple, McQuillan, & Berdahl, 2004), by race (Cernkovich & Giordano, 1992), or by international context (Junger-Tas, 1992; Mak, 1991; Thyne & Schroeder, 2012).

In the following section, this author outlines the principal research findings related to social bonds in certain contexts and criminal offending, namely social bonds built through family interactions, school contexts, and religiosity. The author then details some of the lines of new research that show great promise in firmly establishing the salience of social bonds developed through social interactions and contexts as a predictor of crime and deviance.

Empirical Support for Social Bond Theory

FAMILY

The family is the primary agent of socialization in contemporary society and, therefore, is strongly implicated in patterns of criminal offending, especially from the social bond perspective (see Paulson & Sputa, 1996). The strength and warmth of the parent-child bond is critical in determining a variety of developmental outcomes among children (Amato & Keith, 1991), including delinquent and criminal offending (Glueck & Glueck, 1950; Sampson & Laub, 1993; Simons, Simons, Chen, Brody, & Lin, 2007). Numerous studies on the impact of parenting on adolescent outcomes have clearly established that children who are raised in a warm and loving home with parents who closely monitor their behavior show lower levels of criminal activity (Denham et al., 2000; Fagan & Najman, 2003; Patterson & Stouthamer-Loeber, 1984) and stronger attachments to their parents (Mason, Gonzales, Mari Cauce, & Hiraga, 1996; Simons & Robertson, 1989; Walker-Barnes & Mason, 2004). Parent-child bonds, therefore, are a reliable mediator in the relationship between parenting practices and offending.

Family structure. Family structure has also been implicated as a correlate of juvenile offending, with offending being significantly higher among youth from "broken" homes (Wells & Rankin, 1991). Stated differently, youth from one-parent, cohabiting, and blended homes show significantly higher levels of criminal behavior than youth from nuclear, two-biological-parent homes (see Apel & Kaukinen, 2008). Notably, however, research shows that, in addition to the economic problems faced by nonintact families, the weaker parent-child bonds in nonintact homes explain a significant portion of the broken home influence on delinquency (Cernkovich & Giordano, 1987; Laub & Sampson, 1988; Rankin & Wells, 1990). As Apel and Kaukinen (2008) note, "Parents in nonintact homes may be constrained in their ability to maintain this affective bond with their children as they deal with the day-to-day challenges and conflicts associated with separation and divorce" (p. 41).

Additionally, although children in broken homes are more delinquent, on average, than children from intact homes, research has established that the divorce process is not associated with significant increases in offending among youth (Schroeder, Osgood, & Oghia, 2008), likely due to the predivorce family dysfunctions (Cherlin, 1992). Remarriage, on the other hand, appears to exacerbate behavioral problems (Manning & Lamb, 2003), especially among families with poor pre-remarriage parental bonds (Schroeder et al., 2008). The remarriage effect on delinquent offending is especially instructive to the salience of parental bonding, because remarriage generally enhances family financial resources and parental supervision of children (Brown, 2004; Manning & Lamb, 2003), factors generally assumed to decrease offending (McLanahan & Sandefur, 1994; Patterson, Chamberlain, & Reid, 1982). Parental attachments, on the other hand, actually decrease in the transition from a one-parent family to a two-parent family (Schroeder et al., 2008), mainly due to the fact that the biological parent's time, energy, and attention are split between the child and the new spouse. The decreased parental bonds again mediate the impact of family structure transitions and delinquency.

Parenting style. Parenting style is the other primary family-related issue that highlights the importance of the family in establishing social bonds that deter criminal offending. Parenting style is defined by Darling and Steinberg (1993) as "the parents' perceivable attitudes toward the child" (p. 489). Two distinct parenting measures are used to operationalize parenting style: (1) parental demandingness, or control and supervision, and (2) parenting responsiveness, or caring and warmth (Baumrind, 1966; Schaffer, Clark, & Jeglic, 2009). Based on these parenting variables, Baumrind (2005) identifies four mutually exclusive parenting styles: (1) *authoritative parenting* is characterized by high demandingness and high responsiveness, (2) *authoritarian parenting* includes high demandingness but low responsiveness, (3) *permissive parenting* involves low demandingness but high responsiveness, and (4) *uninvolved parenting* is exemplified by low demandingness and low responsiveness. Of the four parenting styles, authoritative parenting is most strongly associated with parent-child bonds (Mason et al., 1996; Simons & Robertson, 1989). High levels of parental warmth and control create a family environment conducive to establishing strong social bonds between parents and children, whereas parenting styles deficient in warmth and/or control create a family context where bonding is more difficult (Walker-Barnes & Mason, 2004). Accordingly, children with authoritative parents show lower levels of juvenile delinquency than children with authoritarian, permissive, or uninvolved parents (Simons, Chao, Conger, & Elder, 2001). Furthermore, Schroeder, Bulanda, Giordano, and Cernkovich (2010) show that the controlling influence of authoritative parenting, relative to the other parenting styles, holds longitudinally, especially for Black youth.

Recent research examining the impact of parenting style shifts during adolescence further strengthens the importance of parental social bonds in adolescent offending processes. Schroeder and Mowen (in press) show that parenting style transitions during adolescence away from authoritative parenting are associated with increases in offending and decreases in maternal bonds, primarily the shift from authoritative to uninvolved parenting. Further, parenting style shifts to authoritative parenting from the other three parenting styles are generally associated with decreases in offending and increased maternal bonds. Notably, changes in maternal bonds partially mediate the impact of parenting style shifts on changes in delinquency. Similarly, G. E. Higgins, Jennings, and Mahoney (2010) show that decreases in parental bonds across adolescence are associated with a higher prevalence of delinquent offending. Taken together, social bonds established within the family are vitally important predictors of criminality in adolescence and beyond.

SCHOOL

Next to the family, the school is generally recognized as the second most important agent of socialization for children. After all, school is where children and adolescents spend the majority of their time while not with family and provides ample opportunities to develop attachments, build commitments, engage in conventional activities, and establish strong beliefs in school and societal rules. Therefore, social bonds developed within the institution of education are crucial determinants of offending within (D. C. Gottfredson, 2001; Jenkins, 1997; Stewart, 2003) and outside the school environment (Cernkovich & Giordano, 1992; Hagan & Simpson, 1978; Jenkins, 1995; McNeal, 1985; Thornberry, Moore, & Christenson, 1985).

Because of the central position of education in youth development, the most important advancements in research linking school social bonds and delinquency have focused on the intersections of school processes with family, neighborhood, peer, and socioeconomic factors, as well as a host of school organizational and culture variables (see Jenkins, 1997; Stewart, 2003). The multitude of school-based issues and individual background and social structural characteristics that influence bonds to education are too complex to adequately address in the current summary, but some general conclusions can be drawn from the vast array of research on the topic. First, parental involvement in education is associated with higher levels of academic performance (Astone & McLanahan, 1991), which in turn is associated with less antisocial or problem behaviors (Fehrman, Keith, & Reimers, 1987; D. C. Gottfredson, 2001), primarily because family involvement with education and academic ability directly influence school commitment and attachment (Jenkins, 1997).

Second, schools that foster positive working conditions for teachers create contextual conditions that improve teacher-student relationships (i.e., stronger attachments) and lower levels of delinquent behavior (D. C. Gottfredson, 2001). Of course, effective school functioning depends heavily on the social milieu of school, including background and demographic characteristics of the school staff and students (G. D. Gottfredson & Gottfredson, 1985) as well as the physical location of the school (D. C. Gottfredson, 2001). Schools in poor, urban, disorganized communities with high minority and low socioeconomic status populations tend to show more behavioral problems, mainly because such school environments do not readily nurture strong social bonds to the school (see Stewart, 2003).

Last, curriculum tracking has been shown to condition the effect of other sociologically relevant variables on offending, mainly by creating strong social bonds for students in the academic tracks and weakening social bonds for the lower-track/vocational students (Crosnoe, 2002). As students are likely to form friendships with others with similar backgrounds and those with whom they interact with most often (Homans, 1974), it is intuitive that schools generally, and curriculum tracks specifically, will structure friendship groupings and time spent socializing with such friends (Hallinan & Williams, 1989). Students in lower academic tracks tend to struggle academically and participate in fewer school activities, which in turn is associated with school disengagement (i.e., weak bonds to school); consequently, lower academic track students are at higher risk of deviant behavior (Gamoran & Berends, 1987). Compounding the impact of academic tracking on crime and delinquency is the fact that students in lower academic tracks are surrounded by other students with similarly weak social bonds (Hallinan & Tuma, 1978). Crosnoe (2002) assessed the intersection of academic track and delinquent peer groups, finding that students in high and low academic tracks are exposed to similar levels of delinquent peers. The lower track students, however, are more highly influenced by delinquent peers, suggesting that the weaker bonds to the school among the lower track students result in peers being of greater importance and influence to such students (Crosnoe, 2002).

The main point is that social bonds built through education are important determinants of criminal and delinquent offending, both within and outside the school. Many interpersonal and structural factors contribute to the development of school bonds, but it is clear that strong attachments, commitments, involvements, and beliefs associated with educational institutions constrain criminal behavior.

RELIGION

Religiosity is another commonly researched aspect of social life within the social bond tradition of criminology. Religiosity generally encompasses two interrelated features associated with religion: (1) the degree of religious belief, devotion, or spirituality; and (2) participation in religious services and other activities. Intuitively, the common assumption is that highly religious individuals should show lower levels of crime and deviance because of the interpersonal attachments conventional activities endemic to religion as an institution, as well as the commitment to future goals (i.e., afterlife) and moral teachings that cultivate beliefs in the legitimacy of social rules that define all major religions. In other words, religiosity should cultivate strong social bonds that discourage criminal behavior.

As discussed above, Durkheim first systematically examined the effect of religion, more precisely the degree of social integration associated with various religious denominations, on a deviant behavior—suicide. But Hirschi and Stark (1969) are generally credited with reinvigorating religion-crime research in criminology from a social bond perspective in the contemporary literature. In their paper "Hellfire and Delinquency," Hirschi and Stark hypothesized that adolescents who believe in an afterlife will be less delinquent than youth who do not, simply because youth who believe in an afterlife have a greater stake in conformity, hence a social bond that deters delinquent behavior. The analysis revealed, however, that the youth who believed in an afterlife offended at the same rate as youth who did not, therefore calling into question the legitimacy of religious beliefs as an indicator of social bonds and lower levels of offending. Subsequent research has supported Hirschi and Stark's findings of no relationship between religiosity and criminal offending (Benda & Corwyn, 1997; Evans, Cullen, Dunaway, & Burton, 1995; Krohn, Akers, Radosevich, & Lanza-Kaduce, 1982).

Other research, however, has shown a deterrent effect of religiosity on a range of criminal and deviant behaviors (Evans et al., 1995; P. C. Higgins & Albrecht, 1977; Jang & Johnson, 2001; Jensen & Erickson, 1979; Rohrbaugh & Jessor, 1975). The most widely accepted finding related to the deterrent effect of religiosity on offending is the "antiascetic" hypothesis first promoted by Burkett and White (1974). Burkett and White show that religiosity has a strong deterrent effect on offending, but only for behaviors that directly violate religious principles, such as drug and alcohol use. The reasoning offered is that dominant society condemns most forms of criminal offending, especially violence and property crimes, but religion uniquely and overtly prohibits some victimless and substance use behaviors (see Albrecht, Chadwick, & Alcorn, 1977; Burkett & White, 1974; Cochran & Akers, 1989). Religious teachings thus promote controls on behaviors that are less strongly condemned by the dominant culture in addition to reinforcing the dominant cultural denouncements of other criminal offenses.

In an effort to reconcile the contradictory findings in the literature regarding the impact of religious social bonds on criminal offending, Baier and Wright (2001) conducted a meta-analytic assessment of the literature addressing the connection between religiosity and offending. The study found that the overall effect of religiosity on offending across the 60 studies reviewed is negative and moderate in magnitude. Further reinforcing the antiascetic hypothesis, Baier and Wright also report that the effect of religiosity on criminal behavior is strongest for nonviolent crimes.

More recent research has further investigated the role of social bonds formed through religiosity on criminal offending by assessing the unique implications of nonbelievers. Drawing on social identity theory (see Tajfel & Turner, 1979), which includes a primary tenet that group identification promotes social bonding with other group members (Cameron, 2004), Schroeder, Bradley, and Parker (2012) contend that atheists and agnostics likely benefit from social bonds built through the nonbeliever group identification, similar to the benefits gained by religious believers through connections built within the religious community. The results of the study show that nonbelievers offend at the same level as religious believers across a variety of offenses, including drug and alcohol use; the respondents who are spiritual but not religious, believe in God about half the time, and those who believe in God but regularly have doubts offend at significantly higher rates than both the atheists/agnostics and the true believers (Schroeder et al., 2012). Further, once atheists and agnostics are removed from the sample, the relationship between religiosity and offending is significantly strengthened (Schroeder et al., 2012).

Overall, social bonds developed through religiosity have received a considerable amount of attention in the criminological literature over the past several decades. Although the results supporting the importance of religiosity on offending have been mixed, more recent research has defined the contexts in which religiosity deters crime and refined the analytical approaches to better specify the processes by which religiosity influences offending. Religiosity is once again increasingly being recognized as an important indicator of social bonding associated with lower levels of criminal offending.

LIFE COURSE THEORY

Perhaps the most convincing evidence in support of the sociological determinants of social bonds is promoted within the life course theory tradition in criminology. Broadly, the life course theory in sociology emphasizes that developmental and behavioral trajectories are altered by social events and historical contexts (Elder, 1998). Within criminology, the life course theory has focused primarily on shifts in the nature and strength of social bonds across time and specific social events and contexts.

In *Crime in the Making*, Sampson and Laub (1993) discuss three factors that highlight the importance of social bonds in the offending process from childhood to adulthood. First, the authors express that social bonding changes in form from childhood to adulthood, with social bonds primarily formed through family and school relationships in childhood; through school and friendship relationships in adolescence; and through school, romantic partner, and community relationships in adulthood. Second, the connection between juvenile delinquency in childhood and adolescence and adult criminal offending can be understood by the process of "cumulative continuity," whereby offending during childhood and adolescence "mortgage the future" by decreasing opportunities to form relationships with conventional others and institutions in adulthood. Third, criminal offending trajectories are potentially modified by changes in the strength of social bonds associated with life events (i.e., "turning points"), with increased social bonds increasing the odds of behavioral change in a prosocial direction.

Most research in the life course theory tradition of criminology has focused on marriage and stable employment as life course "turning points" that stimulate criminal desistance (Laub, Nagin, & Sampson, 1998; Laub & Sampson, 2003; Sampson & Laub, 1993). The logic follows that entering a strong and stable marriage or obtaining a stable and respectable job creates a strong increase in social bonds (in other words, a greater stake in conformity), which in turn limits motivations to offend. Empirical support for the marriage and employment effect on some criminal desistance has generally been strong, showing that marriage and employment significantly predict criminal desistance (Bersani, Laub, & Nieuwbeerta, 2009; Farrington & West, 1995; Laub & Sampson, 2003; Sampson & Laub, 1993; Sampson, Laub, & Wimer, 2006). It must be noted, however, that other studies have shown null effects for marriage and/or employment (Giordano, Cernkovich, & Rudolph, 2002; Horney, Osgood, & Marshall, 1995; King, Massoglia, & MacMillan, 2007; Uggen, 2000), and numerous factors condition the effect of such life events on offending trajectory shifts (see Maruna, 2001). Furthermore, the impact of marriage and employment on offending are gradual, evidencing an investment-quality of time within a marriage or a job (Laub et al., 1998; Nagin & Paternoster, 1994; Osgood, Wilson, O'Malley, Bachman, & Johnston, 1996).

Overall, marriage and employment do not inevitably or immediately reduce offending, but the gradual development of social bonds associated with such life events work to encourage desistance from criminal offending. The main contribution of life course criminology to the social bond literature is that social bonds are not entirely stable, and shifts in the strength and substance of social bonds often redirect criminal offending patterns toward more prosocial behavior.

Conclusions

Social bonds are a fundamental feature of sociological research on crime. From the earliest sociological theorizing and empirical assessments of social life, the idea that egoistic impulses can be controlled by a high degree of social integration has remained a defining feature of the discipline. Further, a wide body of research has firmly established that social bonds are developed through interactions with others and social institutions, and the interpersonal connections built through such interactions are negatively associated with criminal offending.

Social bond theory has received a considerable amount of empirical support across decades of research, but many important questions about the nature and effect of social bonds on criminal offending remain. Most important, although very few scholars question the negative relationship between social bonds and crime, the direction of the relationship is less clear. For instance, the relationship between negative parenting approaches and delinquency might be in the direction opposite to what is predicted by social bond theory; it is entirely possible that children with problematic behavior challenge even the most resourceful and loving parents (Moffitt, 1997; Patterson, 1982; Rutter, Giller, & Hagall, 1998).

Most research in the family-crime literature follows the *social mold model* of family socialization, where deficits in parental control or warmth negatively influence bonds between parents and children, which in turn increases the likelihood of delinquency (Hartup, 1978). The *reciprocal effects model*, however, proposes that parents influence misbehavior and misbehavior influences parenting in a mutual manner (Patterson, 1986). Despite the debate regarding possible reverse causal ordering in the connection between parenting practices and offending, however, the predominant finding within the literature is supportive of the social bond theory postulations; research has not established a direct link between adolescent delinquency and parental warmth or control (Schaffer et al., 2009; Simons & Robertson, 1989; Simons, Whitbeck, Conger, Conger, & Melby, 1990). Similar causal ordering debates have surrounded the relationship between school factors, school bonds, and delinquency, because it has been shown that delinquency, at least to a limited degree, causes negative school experiences and interactions (Thornberry, Krohn, Lizotte, Smith, & Tobin, 2003).

Another unresolved issue in the social bond theory literature is the possibility that the relationship between social bonds and offending is accounted for by a third variable (i.e., spuriousness). For example, negative parenting approaches are associated with factors such as low socioeconomic status, substance use, family structure changes, family size, and domestic violence (Conger, Conger, Elder, & Lorenz, 1992; Larzelere & Patterson, 1990). Stressful family contexts then might account for both poor parenting practices and delinquency. Many of the same issues also potentially explain the relationship between other social bonds and offending, such as economic, neighborhood, and family background factors potentially complicating school and religious experiences (D. C. Gottfredson, 2001; Krohn, Thornberry, Collins-Hall, & Lizotte, 1995). The question of possible third variables and causal ordering are valid, and research on these issues continues, but the general conclusion reached by longitudinal studies that control for a multitude of possible spurious influences is that social bonds have a modest causal effect on offending (Loeber, Farrington, Stouthamer-Loeber, & Van Kammen, 1998; Wright, Caspi, Moffitt, & Silva, 1999).

Last, there is still a question about the effect of forming bonds with nonconventional individuals from the social bond theory perspective. Especially problematic for the theory is the possibility of forming attachments or bonds with delinquent peers or criminal parents. Throughout his original conceptualization of the social bond theory in criminology, Hirschi (1969) repeatedly uses the phrase "attachment to conventional others" to stress that the normative orientation of others to whom one is bonded is important to the theory. But Hirschi also acknowledges the possibility that affective bonds can be formed with nonconventional others and stresses that those relationships can also control criminal behavior. In addressing the complications of delinquent peer bonds, he states that when the normative orientation of peers is held constant, "the more one respects or admires one's friends, the less likely one is to commit delinquent acts. We honor those we admire not by imitation, but by adherence to conventional standards" (Hirschi, 1969, p. 152).

The real issue of delinquent peers, according the Hirschi (1969), is that delinquents tend to be socially isolated and have difficulties forming true affective relationships with others; delinquents show weaker attachments to both delinquent and nondelinquent others than do nondelinquent youth. In short, the social bond theory postulates that bonds to delinquent or criminal others will control offending, but the likelihood of a delinquent forming an affective bond is low. This stance has, of course, stimulated a great deal of controversy and debate (see Akers, Krohn, Lanza-Kaduce, & Radosevich, 1979). Hirschi, rather than engaging in the debate about the influence of bonds formed with delinquents or criminals, restructured the delinquent peer debate to be about selection versus causation. From the social bond perspective, Hirschi claims that youth seek out friends who have similar social experiences and interests—the "birds of a feather flock together" hypothesis. Thus far, research has not firmly established whether the delinquent peer effect on offending is due to selection or causation, but the existing evidence points to a reciprocal relationship (Krohn, Lizotte, Thornberry, Smith, & McDowall, 1996).

The questions of causal ordering, spuriousness, and normative orientation notwithstanding, it is clear that the social bond theory is a dominant perspective in criminology. Research in the social bond tradition utilizing longitudinal data is beginning to resolve many of the questions that surround the theory, and the results provide further evidence about the vital importance of social bonds on criminal offending. Future work will continue to unravel the complexities of the theory, but the central tenets of social bond theory remain a central feature of criminology—strong and warm connections to others and a high degree of social integration built through such interpersonal relationships and participation in social institutions are unquestionably beneficial to healthy social functioning and prosocial behavioral outcomes.

References

Akers, R. L. (2000). *Criminological theories: Introduction, evaluation, and application* (3rd ed.). Los Angeles, CA: Roxbury.

Akers, R. L., Krohn, M. D., Lanza-Kaduce, L., & Radosevich, M. (1979). Social learning and deviant behavior: A specific test of a general theory. *American Sociological Review, 44*, 635–655.

Albrecht, S. L., Chadwick, B. A., & Alcorn, D. S. (1977). Religiosity and deviance: Application of an attitude-behavior contingent consistency model. *Journal for the Scientific Study of Religion, 16*, 263–274.

Amato, P., & Keith, B. (1991). Parental divorce and the well-being of children: A meta-analysis. *Psychological Bulletin, 110*, 26–46.

Apel, R., & Kaukinen, C. (2008). On the relationship between family structure and antisocial behavior: Parental cohabitation and blended households. *Criminology, 46*, 35–69.

Astone, N., & McLanahan, S. (1991). Family structure, parental practices and high school completion. *American Sociological Review, 56*, 309–320.

Baier, C. J., & Wright, B. R. E. (2001). If you love me, keep my commandments: A meta-analysis of the effect of religion on crime. *Journal of Research in Crime and Delinquency 38*, 3–21.

Baumrind, D. (1966). Effects of authoritative parental control on child behavior. *Child Development, 37*, 887–907.

Baumrind, D. (2005). Patterns of parental authority and adolescent autonomy. *New Directions for Child and Adolescent Development, 108*, 61–69.

Benda, B. B., & Corwyn, R. F. (1997). Religion and delinquency: The relationship after considering family and peer influences. *Journal for the Scientific Study of Religion, 36*, 81–92.

Berk, B. B. (2006). Macro-micro relationships in Durkheim's analysis as egoistic suicide. *Sociological Theory, 24*, 58–80.

Bersani, B., Laub, J., & Nieuwbeerta, P. (2009). Marriage and desistance from crime in the Netherlands: Do gender and socio-historical context matter? *Journal of Quantitative Criminology, 25*, 3–24.

Brown, S. L. (2004). Family structure and child well-being: The significance of parental cohabitation. *Journal of Marriage and Family, 66*, 351–367.

Burkett, S., & White, M. (1974). Hellfire and delinquency: Another look. *Journal for the Scientific Study of Religion, 13*, 455–462.

Cameron, J. E. (2004). A three-factor model of social identity. *Self and Identity, 3*, 239–262.

Cernkovich, S. A., & Giordano, P. C. (1987). Family relationships and delinquency. *Criminology 25*, 295–321.

Cernkovich, S. A., & Giordano, P. C. (1992). School bonding, race, and delinquency. *Criminology, 30*, 261–291.

Cherlin, A. J. (1992). *Marriage, divorce, remarriage*. Cambridge, MA: Harvard University Press.

Cochran, J. K., & Akers, R. L. (1989). Beyond hellfire: An exploration of the variable affects of religiosity on adolescent marijuana and alcohol use. *Journal of Research in Crime and Delinquency, 26*, 198–225.

Conger, R. D., Conger, K. J., Elder, G. H., & Lorenz, F. (1992). A family process model of economic hardship and adjustment of early adolescent boys. *Child Development, 63*, 526–541.

Crosnoe, R. (2002). High school curriculum track and adolescent association with delinquent friends. *Journal of Adolescent Research, 17*, 143–167.

Darling, N., & Steinberg, L. (1993). Parenting style as context: An integrative model. *Psychological Bulletin, 113*, 487–496.

Denham, S. A., Workman, E., Cole, P. M., Weissbrod, C., Kendziora, K. T., & Zahn-Waxler, C. (2000). Prediction of externalizing problems from early to middle childhood: The role of parental socialization and emotion expression. *Development and Psychology, 12*, 23–45.

Durkheim, E. (1951). *Suicide: A study in sociology*. Glencoe, IL: Free Press.

Elder, G. H. (1998). Life course theory and human development. *Sociological Analysis, 1*(2), 1–12.

Evans, D., Cullen, F. T., Dunaway, R. G., and Burton, V. (1995). Religion and crime reexamined: The impact of religion, secular controls, and social ecology on adult criminality. *Criminology, 33*, 195–224.

Fagan, A. A., & Najman, J. M. (2003). Sibling influences on adolescent delinquent behavior: An Australian longitudinal study. *Journal of Adolescence, 26*, 546–558.

Farrington, D. P., & West, D. J. (1995). Effects of marriage, separation, and children on offending by adult males. In Z. S. Blau & J. Hagan (Eds.), *Current perspectives on aging and the life cycle: Delinquency and disrepute in the life course* (pp. 249–281). Greenwich, CT: JAI Press.

Fehrman, P., Keith, T., & Reimers, T. (1987). Home influence on school learning: Direct and indirect effects of parental involvement on high school grades. *Journal of Educational Research, 80*, 330–337.

Gamoran, A., & Berends, M. (1987). The effects of stratification in secondary school: Synthesis of survey and ethnographic research. *Review of Research in Education, 57*, 415–435.

Giordano, P. C., Cernkovich, S. A., & Rudolph, J. L. (2002). Gender, crime, and desistance: Toward a theory of cognitive transformation. *American Journal of Sociology, 107*, 990–1064.

Glueck, S., & Glueck, E. (1950). *Unraveling juvenile delinquency*. Cambridge, MA: Harvard University Press.

Gottfredson, D. C. (2001). *Schools and delinquency*. New York, NY: Cambridge University Press.

Gottfredson, G. D., & Gottfredson, D. C. (1985). *Victimization in schools*. New York, NY: Plenum Press.

Gottfredson, M., & Hirschi, T. (1990). *A general theory of crime*. Palo Alto, CA: Stanford University Press.

Hagan, J., & Simpson, J. (1978). Ties that bind: Conformity and the social control of student discontent. *Sociology and Social Research, 61*, 530–536.

Hallinan, M., & Tuma, N. (1978). Classroom effects on change in children's friendships. *Sociology of Education, 51*, 270–282.

Hallinan, M., & Williams, R. (1989). Interracial friendship choice in secondary schools. *American Sociological Review, 54*, 67–78.

Hartup, W. W. (1978). Perspectives on child and family interaction: Past, present, and future. In R. M. Lerner & G. B. Spanier (Eds.), *Child influences on marital and family interaction: A life-span perspective* (pp. 23–46). San Francisco, CA: Academic Press.

Higgins, G. E., Jennings, W. G., & Mahoney, M. (2010). Developmental trajectories of maternal and paternal attachment and delinquency in adolescence. *Deviant Behavior, 31*, 655–677.

Higgins, P. C., & Albrecht, G. L. (1977). Hellfire and delinquency revisited. *Social Forces, 55*, 952–958.

Hirschi, T. (1969). *Causes of delinquency*. Berkeley: University of California Press.

Hirschi, T., & Stark, R. (1969). Hellfire and delinquency. *Social Problems, 17*, 202–213.

Homans, G. (1974). *Social behavior: Its elementary forms*. New York, NY: Harcourt, Brace, Jovanovich.

Horney, J., Osgood, D. W., & Marshall, I. H. (1995). Criminal careers in the short-term: Intra-individual variability in crime and its relation to local life circumstances. *American Sociological Review, 60*, 655–673.

Jang, S. J., & Johnson, B. R. (2001). Neighborhood disorder, individual religiosity and adolescent use of illicit drugs: A test of multilevel hypotheses. *Criminology, 39*, 109–144.

Jenkins, P. H. (1995). School delinquency and school commitment. *Sociology of Education, 68*, 221–239.

Jenkins, P. H. (1997). School delinquency and the school social bond. *Journal of Research in Crime and Delinquency, 34*, 337–367.

Jensen, G. F., & Erikson, M. L. (1979). The religious factor and delinquency: Another look at the hellfire hypothesis. In R. Wuthnow (Ed.), *The religious dimension: New directions in quantitative research* (pp. 157–177). New York, NY: Academic Press.

Junger-Tas, J. (1992). An empirical test of social control theory. *Journal of Quantitative Criminology, 8*, 9–28.

King, R. D., Massoglia, M., & Macmillan, R. (2007). The context of marriage and crime: Gender, the propensity to marry, and offending in early adulthood. *Criminology, 45*, 33–65.

Krohn, M. D., Akers, R., Radosevich, M. J., & Lanza-Kaduce, L. (1982). Norm qualities and adolescent drinking and drug behavior: The effects of norm quality and reference group on using and abusing alcohol and marijuana. *Journal of Drug Issues, 12*, 343–359.

Krohn, M. D., Lizotte, A. J., Thornberry, T. P., Smith, C., & McDowall, D. (1996). Reciprocal causal relationships among drug use, peers, and beliefs: A five-wave panel model. *Journal of Drug Issues, 26*, 405–428.

Krohn, M. D., Thornberry, T. P., Collins-Hall, L., & Lizotte, A. J. (1995). School dropout, delinquent behavior, and drug use. In H. B. Kaplan (Ed.), *Drugs, crime, and other deviant adaptations* (pp. 163–183). New York, NY: Plenum.

Larzelere, R. E., & Patterson, G. L. (1990). Parental management: Mediator of the effect of socioeconomic status on early delinquency. *Criminology, 28*, 301–324.

Laub, J. H., & Sampson, R. J. (1988). Unraveling families and delinquency: A reanalysis of the Gluecks' data. *Criminology, 26*, 355–380.

Laub, J. H., & Sampson, R. J. (2003). *Shared beginnings, divergent lives: Delinquent boys to age 70*. Cambridge, MA: Harvard University Press.

Laub, J. H., Nagin, D. S., & Sampson, R. J. (1998). Trajectories of change in criminal offending: Good marriages and the desistance process. *American Sociological Review, 63*, 225–238.

Lester, D. (1989). A test of Durkheim's theory of suicide using data from modern nations. *International Journal of Comparative Sociology 30*, 3–4.

Loeber, R., Farrington, D. P., Stouthamer-Loeber, M., & Van Kammen, W. B. (1998). The development of male offending: Key findings from the first decade of the Pittsburg Youth Study. *Studies on Crime and Crime Prevention, 7*, 141–171.

Mak, A. (1991). Psychological control characteristics of delinquents and nondelinquents. *Criminal Justice and Behavior, 18*, 287–303.

Manning, W. D., & Lamb, K. A. (2003). Adolescent well-being in cohabiting, married, and single-parent families. *Journal of Marriage and Family, 65*, 876–893.

Maruna, S. (2001). *Making good: How ex-convicts reform and rebuild their lives*. Washington, DC: American Psychological Association Books.

Mason, C., Gonzales, N., Mari Cauce, A., & Hiraga, Y. (1996). Neither too sweet nor too sour: Problem peers, maternal control, and problem behavior in African American adolescents. *Child Development, 67*, 2115–2130.

Matza, D. (1957). *Delinquency and drift*. New York, NY: Wiley.

McLanahan, S. S., & Sandefur, G. (1994). *Growing up with a single parent: What hurts, what helps?* Cambridge, MA: Harvard University Press.

McNeal, R. B. (1985). Extracurricular activities and high school dropouts. *Sociology of Education, 68*, 62–81.

Chapple, C. L., McQuillan, J., & Berdahl, T. A. Gender, social bonds, and delinquency: A comparison of boys' and girls' models. *Social Science Research, 34*(2), 357–383.

Minor, W. W. (1981). Techniques of neutralization: A reconceptualization and empirical examination. *Journal of Research in Crime and Delinquency, 18*, 295–318.

Moffitt, T. E. (1997). Adolescence-limited and life-course-persistent offending: A complementary pair of developmental theories. In T. P. Thornberry (Ed.), *Developmental theories of crime and delinquency: Advances in criminological theory* (pp. 11–54). New Brunswick, NJ: Transaction.

Nagin, D. S., & Paternoster, R. (1994). Personal capital and social control: The deterrence implications of a theory of individual differences in criminal offending. *Criminology, 16*, 581–606.

Nye, F. I. (1958). *Family relationships and delinquent behavior*. New York, NY: Wiley.

Osgood, D. W., Wilson, J. K., O'Malley, P. M., Bachman, J. G., & Johnston, L. D. (1996). Routine activities and individual deviant behavior. *American Sociological Review, 61*, 635–655.

Patterson, G. R. (1982). *Coercive family processes*. Eugene, OR: Castalia. Press.

Patterson, G. R. (1986). Performance models for antisocial boys. *American Psychologist, 44*, 432–444.

Patterson, G. R., Chamberlain, P., & Reid, J. (1982). A comparative evaluation of a parent training program. *Behavior Therapy, 13*, 638–650.

Patterson, G. R., & Stouthamer-Loeber, M. (1984). The correlation of family management practices and delinquency. *Child Development, 55*, 1299–1307.

Paulson, S., & Sputa, C. (1996). Patterns of parenting during adolescence: Perceptions of adolescents and parents. *Adolescence, 31*, 369–381.

Pescosolido, B. A., & Georgianna, S. (1989). Durkheim, suicide, and religion: Toward a network theory of suicide. *American Sociological Review 54*, 33–48.

Pickering, W. S. F., & Walford, G. (2000). *Durkheim's suicide: A century of research and debate*. London, UK: Routledge.

Rankin, J. H., & Wells, L. E. (1990). The effect of parental attachments and direct controls on delinquency. *Journal of Research in Crime and Delinquency, 27*, 140–165.

Reckless, W. C. (1961). A new theory of delinquency and crime. *Federal Probation, 25*, 42–46.

Reckless, W. C. (1967). *The crime problem*. New York, NY: Appleton-Century-Crofts.

Reckless, W. C., Dinitz, S., & Murray, E. (1956). Self concept as an insulator against delinquency. *American Sociological Review, 21*(6), 744–746.

Reiss, A. J. (1951). Delinquency as the failure of personal and social controls. *American Sociological Review, 21*, 196–207.

Rohrbaugh, J., & Jessor, R. (1975). Religiosity in youth: A personal control against deviant behavior? *Journal of Personality, 43*, 136–155.

Rutter, M., Giller, H., & Hagall, A. (1998). *Antisocial behavior by young people*. Cambridge, UK: Cambridge University Press.

Sampson, R. J., & Laub, J. R. (1993). *Crime in the making: Pathways and turning points through life*. Cambridge, MA: Harvard University Press.

Sampson, R. J., Laub, J. H., & Wimer, C. (2006). Does marriage reduce crime? A counterfactual approach to within-individual causal effects. *Criminology, 44*, 465–508.

Schaffer, M., Clark, D., & Jeglic, E. (2009). The role of empathy and parenting style in the development of antisocial behaviors. *Crime & Delinquency, 55*, 586–599.

Schroeder, R. D., Bradley, C., & Parker, R. (2012). *Atheism and crime*. Paper presented at the 2012 annual meeting of the American Society of Criminology, Chicago, IL.

Schroeder, R. D., Bulanda, R. E., Giordano, P. C., & Cernkovich, S. A. (2010). Parenting and adult criminality: An examination of direct and indirect effects. *Journal of Adolescent Research, 25*, 64–98.

Schroeder, R. D., & Mowen, T. J. (in press). Parenting style transitions and juvenile delinquency. *Youth & Society*. Advance online publication. doi:10.1177/0044118X12469041

Schroeder, R. D., Osgood, A. K., & Oghia, M. J. (2008). Family transitions and juvenile delinquency. *Sociological Inquiry, 80*, 579–604.

Simons, R., Chao, W., Conger, R., & Elder, G. (2001). Quality of parenting as mediator of the effect of childhood defiance on adolescent friendship choices and delinquency: A growth curve analysis. *Journal of Marriage and Family, 63*, 63–79.

Simons, R., & Robertson, J. (1989). The impact of parenting factors, deviant peers, and coping style upon adolescent drug use. *Family Relations, 38*, 273–281.

Simons, R., Simons, L., Chen, Y., Brody, G., & Lin, K. (2007). Identifying the psychological factors that mediate the association between parenting practices and delinquency. *Criminology, 45*, 481–517.

Simons, R., Whitbeck, L., Conger, R., Conger, D., & Melby, J. (1990). Husband and wife differences in determinants of parenting: A social learning and exchange model of parental behavior. *Journal of Marriage and the Family, 52*, 375–392.

Stewart, E. A. (2003). School social bonds, school climate, and school misbehavior: A multilevel analysis. *Justice Quarterly, 20*, 575–604.

Stitt, B. G., & Giacopassi, D. J. (1992). Trends in the connectivity of theory and research in criminology. *Criminologist, 17*, 3–6.

Tajfel, H., & Turner, J. C. (1979). An integrative theory of intergroup conflict. In W. G. Austin & S. Worchel (Eds.), *The social psychology of intergroup relations* (pp. 33–47). Monterey, CA: Brooks-Cole.

Thornberry, T. P., Krohn, M. D., Lizotte, A. J., Smith, C. A., & Tobin, K. (2003). Causes and consequences of delinquency: Findings from the Rochester Youth Development Survey. In T. P. Thornberry & M. D. Krohn (Eds.), *Taking stock of delinquency* (p. 11–46). New York, NY: Kluwer Academic/Plenum.

Thornberry, T. P, Moore, M., & Christenson, R. L. (1985). The effect of dropping out of high school on subsequent criminal behavior. *Criminology, 23*, 3–19.

Thyne, C. L., & Schroeder, R. D. (2012). Social constraints and civil war: Bridging the gap with criminological theory. *Journal of Politics, 74*(4), 1066–1078.

Uggen, C. (2000). Work as a turning point in the life course of criminals: A duration model of age, employment, and recidivism. *American Sociological Review, 65*, 529–546.

Walker-Barnes, C. J., & Mason, C. A. (2004). Delinquency and substance use among gang involved youth: The moderating role of parenting practices. *American Journal of Community Psychology, 34*, 235–250.

Wells, L. E., & Rankin, J. H. (1991). Families and delinquency: A meta-analysis of the impact of broken homes. *Social Problems, 38*, 71–93.

Wright, B. R. E., Caspi, A., Moffitt, T. E., & Silva, P. A. (1999). Low self-control, social bonds, and crime: Social causation, social selection, or both? *Criminology, 37*, 479–514.

14

A Biosocial View of Social Bond Theory

Danielle Boisvert
Sam Houston State University

Introduction

Hirschi (1969) introduced social bond theory over 40 years ago in his book *Causes of Delinquency*. Since then, there has been no shortage of empirical studies testing social bond theory (Kempf, 1993), and there is no doubt that Hirschi's theory will remain a permanent fixture in criminological literature for decades to come. A quick inspection of any modern-day criminological textbook will undoubtedly feature Hirschi's social bond theory, and the current text is no exception. Put briefly, Hirschi developed his theory as a way to account for people's conformity to prosocial behavior rather than try to explain why people engage in antisocial behavior. Rooted in control theory, Hirschi viewed humans as hedonistic and self-gratifying beings and argued that if people were left to their own devices they would all act toward maximizing pleasure. As such, people need to be restrained or controlled from pursuing their innate selfish desires. According to Hirschi, it is the social bonds between individuals and society that restrain people's natural instinct to commit deviant acts. These social bonds are categorized into four somewhat overlapping but distinct elements: attachment, commitment, involvement, and belief. Deviant and criminal behavior will emerge when individuals have weak or no social bonds to society.

A more detailed description of Hirschi's social bond theory along with a discussion of theoretical expansions from a sociological perspective is provided by

Schroeder in Chapter 13 of the current text. The purpose of this chapter is to take a completely different approach by presenting a biosocial discussion of Hirschi's social bond theory. The goal of this chapter is to challenge readers to rethink social bond theory by tackling two major aspects of the theory: (1) its main underlying assumption, and (2) its main components, namely the four social bonds.

Main Assumption of the Theory

The underlying assumption of social bond theory is that all people would exhibit antisocial behaviors if not otherwise controlled (Hirschi, 1969). As such, motivation to commit crime is considered a constant not requiring any explanation. This assumption has been criticized by others, particularly strain and social learning theorists who focus on answering the question, "why do people commit crime?" as opposed to control theorists who ask, "why don't people commit crime?" General strain theory, for example, would argue that people are motivated to commit crime due to negative emotions (particularly anger) that emerge as the result of negative relationships and experiences with others (Agnew, 1992). On the other hand, differential association and social learning theories would argue that motivation to commit crime comes from an individual's excess of definitions and attitudes favorable toward crime (Burgess & Akers, 1966; Sutherland, 1939). While pointing to distinctly different factors as the causes of criminal behavior, these opposing theories do agree on one thing: the motivation to commit crime is not constant across the population, but in fact, it varies.

A biosocial perspective is also well suited to add to the debate pertaining to the assumption underlying control theories. To say that *everyone* is born with the same motivations and desires is parallel to saying that everyone is born the same. A biosocial view takes a somewhat different approach by recognizing that genetic factors can account for variation in virtually every aspect of human behavior, traits, and temperament (Turkheimer, 2000). In other words, we are not all born the same, rather there is quite a bit of variation at the level of the genome that can help explain individual differences. The idea that people are born with varying genetic predispositions for a variety of behaviors, personality traits, and abilities is well established in the literature (Plomin, 1994; Turkheimer, 2000). Interestingly, parents are (probably unconsciously) aware of this fact if they have more than one child. For instance, parents may observe (sometimes drastic) behavioral differences between their children, where one child may aim to please his or her parents while the other seems to push the boundaries.

There is an important caveat to this discussion that needs to be addressed at this point. Although an individual may be genetically predisposed toward a particular behavior or trait, it does not mean that it is his or her "destiny." The environment is a key piece of the puzzle and can operate to either promote or buffer genetic predispositions. For example, someone may be genetically predisposed for higher intelligence but the level of intellectual achievement obtained will be influenced by the environmental conditions in which that person is raised. These environmental conditions can be at the community level (e.g., the state of the educational system the child is enrolled in), the familial level (e.g., parental guidance and encouragement to achieve academic success), and the individual level (e.g., time to dedicate to learning). It is obvious then that a genetic predisposition for higher intelligence does not automatically equate to a college degree, a prestigious career, or financial stability. The same is true in the discussion of genetic predispositions for antisocial and criminal behaviors—they are not guarantees. The environment may shape people, but it shapes people differently based on their genetic makeup. This process is referred to as *gene-environment interactions*, which is a topic that is discussed later in this chapter.

For now, take a moment to think of your own family. What are some characteristics, behaviors, or traits that seem to run in your family? Do you and your family members have similar religious affiliations? Do you share similar political viewpoints? Are you an affectionate family that cares about the well-being of each other and others? Are you a hot-tempered group that gets into heated discussions easily? How many of your family members have had encounters with the law? Now ask yourself, are these factors due solely to the environment that you and your family members share? The answer is no—well, not entirely. All these factors, including religiosity, temperament, attachment, political views, altruism, and criminal involvement are influenced by *both* genetic and environmental factors (Turkheimer, 2000).

When it comes to antisocial and criminal behaviors more specifically, the research is vast and conclusive—genetics matter. In fact, a meta-analysis of 51 twin and adoption studies conducted by Rhee and Waldman (2002) revealed that 41%, 16%, and 43% of the variance in antisocial behaviors was attributed to genetic, shared, and nonshared environmental factors, respectively, and a review by Moffitt (2005) estimated that about half the variance in antisocial behaviors was attributed to genetic factors. Moreover, studies examining altruistic and prosocial behaviors have also revealed significant genetic effects (Knafo, Zahn-Waxler, Van Hulle, Robinson, & Rhee, 2008; Rushton, Littlefield, & Lumsden, 1986). For instance, in observing 409 twin pairs aged 14 to 36 months on measures of empathy and prosocial behavior, Knafo and colleagues (2008) found that the genetic effects increased with age while the effects of the shared environment steadily decreased with age.

At this point, it is important to highlight the difference between shared and nonshared environments, because they serve two different functions. First, the shared environment serves to make siblings residing in the same home more similar to one another. These are environmental factors that do not vary across siblings in a home, such as neighborhood conditions, parental employment, and general parenting practices. In contrast, the nonshared environment functions to make siblings within a home different from one another. These environmental factors are considered unique to each individual child and can include differential parenting practices, unique peer groups, and different after-school activities (Plomin, 1990). The impact that both the shared and nonshared environments have on Hirschi's four social bonds is discussed in the next section of this chapter. For now, it is important to emphasize that of the two types of environments it is usually the non-shared experiences and events that tend to exert stronger effects on behaviors and traits, particularly in adolescence and adulthood (Plomin, 1994).

Let's return to the main assumption underlying social bond theory: everyone would commit crime if left to their own devices. As mentioned, such an assumption ignores individual differences in genetic predispositions for delinquent behavior (and its correlates). There is overwhelming evidence demonstrating that individual differences in behaviors, temperament, and traits previously thought to be environmentally caused are partly explained by genetic influences (Turkheimer, 2000). Of particular interest are the studies that have shown that individual differences emerge early on in the life course, even as early as 6 months of age (Wright, Tibbetts, & Daigle, 2008), as well as the research that has shown that antisocial behaviors tend to remain relatively stable across the life course (Campbell, Shaw, & Gilliom, 2000; Loeber, 1982; Olweus, 1979). Interestingly, this process of stability in antisocial behavior has also been attributed to genetic factors (Eley, Lichtenstein, & Moffitt, 2003; Reiss, Neiderhiser, Hetherington, & Plomin, 2000). This has important implications for Hirschi's social bond theory because it suggests that genetic predispositions coupled with the environment can place an individual on a trajectory toward criminal behavior at an early age and that understanding the complexities of behavior likely go beyond a sociological view of four social bonds.

Four Social Bonds

Having discussed the main assumption underlying social bond theory from a biosocial perspective now opens the door to further expanding our thinking about the theory's main variables: attachment, commitment, involvement, and belief. To date, Hirschi's social bonds have been discussed from a purely environmental perspective, which makes intuitive sense because it is a sociological theory of crime. But a glimpse into the behavioral and molecular genetic research has the potential to revitalize the way we think of Hirschi's social bonds and how they are related to antisocial behaviors. Many new and exciting techniques for understanding behavior have emerged since the introduction of social bond theory. Applying new methods and statistical techniques to an otherwise old theory may be exactly what social bond theory needs to regain popularity and interest among criminological scholars.

ATTACHMENT

The first social bond, attachment, is considered the affective component of the four bonds. *Attachment* refers to our close and personal relationships with others (e.g., parents, teachers, and peers). It is this process of caring about others that restrains individuals from engaging in delinquent acts. For this reason, attachment can be considered a form of indirect control over youth behavior. For example, adolescents who are attached to their parents are less likely to engage in delinquency because they do not want to disappoint their parents or lose their respect. Scholars have argued that the bond of attachment is highly intertwined with the other three bonds in that having strong attachments to others can also increase the strength of the bonds of commitment, involvement, and belief (Walsh, 2012).

There is a vast amount of research that has documented the impact attachment has on child development (Thompson, 2000). These studies are primarily from other disciplines, such as behavioral psychology, behavioral genetics, evolutionary psychology, and molecular genetics, yet are well suited to inform a biosocial view of attachment. For example, the field of psychology has long recognized and studied attachment theory and viewed attachment styles as an important construct related to child adjustment (Bowlby, 1969). One of the earliest techniques used in psychology to identify attachment styles in infants is the Strange Situation method. Put briefly, this is an experiment where a mother, infant, and stranger interact for approximately 20 minutes during which the mother leaves the room twice then returns to reunite with her child. The way the child behaves during the experiment, particularly on his or her mother's return, determines the child's classification into one of the three main categories of attachment: secure, insecure-avoidant, and insecure-resistant. Children are classified as securely attached if they greet their mother on her return and appear to be comforted by her presence. Children are classified as insecure-avoidant if they seem to avoid their mother on her return, particularly regarding physical contact. Last, infants are classified as insecure-resistant if they appear conflicted on their mother's return with a mixture of anger yet a need for contact. While these three strategies are referred to as *organized attachment styles*, Main and Solomon (1990) identified an additional dimension of attachment referred to as *disorganized attachment*, which refers to an infant's inability to resolve his or her anxiety during the Strange Situation assessment.

Research has shown that infants with insecure and disorganized attachment styles are significantly more likely to display behavioral problems later on in life (Lyons-Ruth & Jacobvitz, 1999; van IJzendoorn, Schuengel, & Bakermans-Kranenburg, 1999). Research on *why* infants behave the way they do during the Strange Situation experiment, however, has been debated in the literature. Two distinct sources of individual differences in attachment have been suggested. First, Ainsworth, Blehar, Waters, and Wall (1978) argue that it is the mother's behavior, particularly her level of sensitivity, that is the source of individual differences in infant attachment. That is to say, mothers who are more sensitively responsive to their child's signals and cues will produce more securely attached children compared to mothers who are less responsive (or respond inappropriately or not at all). Mothers with less sensitivity will in turn produce insecurely attached children (Pederson & Moran, 1995). In the end, a child's attachment strategy will then depend on his or her mother's level of sensitivity. From this perspective, the environment is most important to the development of attachment strategies in infants (Main, 1999).

Rothbart and Derryberry (1981), however, look beyond maternal sensitivity in explaining infant attachment by suggesting that there are important child factors to consider in the formation of attachment security. Specifically, they argue that individual differences in infants' temperament (and their reactions to stress) are the sources of variation in attachment. Research has found support for this claim by showing that a child's temperament is associated with his or her categorization of attachment (Belsky & Rovine, 1987; Goldsmith & Alansky, 1987). These divergent views on the etiology of attachment were pointed out by Ainsworth (1979) when she asked "to what extent is the pattern of attachment of a baby attributable to the mother's behavior throughout the first year, and to what extent is it attributable to the built-in differences in potential and temperament" (p. 933). Researchers seeking to answer this question have found support for both perspectives in that maternal behavior and child temperament have both main effects as well as interactive effects on attachment (Izard, Haynes, Chisholm, & Baak, 1991; Susman-Stillman, Kalkoske, Egeland, & Waldman, 1996).

A biosocial explanation of the sources of individual differences in attachment may further inform this discussion. Known as *evocative* or *reactive* gene-environment correlations, it is possible that a child's genetic predispositions (e.g., temperament) are influencing parenting behaviors, such as sensitivity (Plomin, 1994; Reiss et al., 2000). In other words, a child's negative temperament (which is influenced by genes) may lead parents to become less responsive toward their child. As such, the relationship between parental sensitivity, temperament, and child attachment may be partly due to the genetic predispositions of the child. It is also possible that *passive* gene-environment correlations are operating to explain this relationship. That is, parents not only pass down their genetic information to their child, but also provide the environment in which the child is raised. As such, the attachment style of the parents may be genetically transmitted to the child, who is ultimately placed in an environment that facilitates the expression of the attachment style. For example, parents who are insecurely attached may pass down those genes to their child, as well as provide an environment in which the child develops insecure attachments.

Several family studies have shown that attachment styles tend to run in the family. For example, a meta-analysis conducted by van IJzendoorn (1995) of 18 families revealed a concordance of 70% between parent and child attachment styles. Unfortunately, family studies are not well equipped to decipher the genetic and environmental effects on attachment because family members tend to share both their environments and their genes. As such, using samples of twins is preferable when attempting to uncover the genetic and environmental contributions to behaviors. Specifically, the similarity of behavior of monozygotic (MZ: identical) twins raised together can be compared to the similarity of dizygotic (DZ: fraternal) twin pairs raised together. If the within-twin similarity for attachment is greater among MZ twin pairs than DZ twin pairs, this would suggest that there are important genetic factors to consider in attachment styles. On the other hand, if there are no differences between MZ and DZ similarities for attachment, this would suggest that environmental factors are the only contributing factors influencing attachment.

A few studies on infant attachment and quality of bonding utilizing twins have been conducted (Brooks & Lewis, 1974; Cherro, 1992; Finkel, Wille, & Matheny, 1998; Goldberg, Perrotta, Minde, & Corter, 1986; Gottfried, Seay, & Leake, 1994; Lytton, 1980; Szajnberg, Skrinjaric, & Moore, 1989; Vandell, Owen, Wilson, & Henderson, 1988). Many of the early twin studies, however, were not applying the classical twin method as it is often used today. For example, the first twin study on child attachment conducted by Brooks and Lewis in 1974 was primarily interested in examining sex differences in the mother-infant bond. Their results showed significant differences in attachment behaviors with girls exhibiting more attachment (e.g., looked at and maintained closer proximity to their mother) compared to boys. While innovative for the time, the methodological issue of only including DZ twin pairs did not allow for the estimation of genetic influences on child attachment. Others have also neglected to report the separate concordance for attachment for MZ and DZ twin pairs (Cherro, 1992; Goldberg et al., 1986; Gottfried et al., 1994; Vandell et al., 1988), thereby making it impossible to estimate the genetic influence on attachment.

Recognizing this limitation, researchers began to compare the concordance rate of MZ and DZ twin pairs on measures of attachment to crudely estimate the level of genetic influence on attachment relationships. Most of these early studies, however, were plagued with small sample sizes. For example, an early study by Szajnberg et al. (1989) found that 3 out of 4 MZ twin pairs were concordant for attachment type compared to 2 out of 4 DZ twin pairs. Ricciuti (1993) sought to increase her sample size by combining three samples of twins. Despite these efforts, however, her sample size remained relatively small with a total of 29 MZ and 27 DZ same-sex twin pairs. She concluded that her study "does not provide strong evidence of a substantial genetic component for either the presence (secure/insecure) or degree of attachment security as assessed in the Strange Situation" (1993, pp. 67–68).

Using a modified Strange Situation procedure to measure attachment, Finkel et al. (1998) also examined whether genetic factors were contributing to attachment classification among a sample of 34 MZ and 26 DZ twin pairs aged 18 and 24 months. Their results revealed a significant difference in concordance (67.6% for MZ twins vs. 38.5% for DZ twins), suggesting a genetic contribution to attachment security. In 2000, Finkel and Matheny further examined the genetic and environmental influences on infant attachment security using a sample of 99 MZ twin pairs and 108 DZ twin pairs aged 24 months from the Louisville Twin Study. Their results revealed a concordance of 62.6% for MZ twins, which was significantly higher than the concordance of 44.4% for DZ twin pairs. Further analyses revealed that infant attachment security was 25% heritable with the remaining variance being attributed to the nonshared environment with no role for shared environmental influences.

Similar results were reported by O'Connor and Croft in 2001 in their analysis of 110 twin pairs (mean age of 43 months) using the Strange Situation method. More specifically, they found modest genetic effects (0.14) on attachment security as well as significant shared (0.32) and nonshared (0.54) environmental effects. Bokhorst,

Bakermans-Kranenburg, Fonagy, and Schuengel (2003) also found evidence for the environmental contributions to mother-infant attachment using two samples of twins from London ($N = 62$ twin pairs) and Leiden, the Netherlands ($N = 76$ twin pairs). For secure versus nonsecure attachment, they reported that 52% of the variance was attributed to shared environmental factors with the remaining variance being attributable to the nonshared environment, without any role reported for genetics. Furthermore, when comparing organized versus disorganized attachment, only nonshared environmental factors exerted a significant effect on disorganized attachment. This is interesting given that several molecular genetic studies have found that the dopamine receptor gene DRD4 is associated with disorganized attachment styles (Gervai et al., 2005; Lakatos et al., 2000; Lakatos et al., 2002).

The behavioral genetic studies mentioned above are specific to attachment styles in infants and toddlers. Unfortunately, the genetic influence on attachment styles in adolescence and adulthood has received little empirical attention. Although one study by Brussoni, Jang, Livesley, and Macbeth (2000) did report that genes accounted for 37%, 43%, and 25% of the variance in secure, fearful, and preoccupied adult attachment styles, respectively. The remaining variance in these adult attachment styles was attributed primarily to the nonshared environment. Nevertheless, the research is still mixed with regard to the role that genetic factors play in attachment styles. It is clear that additional studies with larger twin samples using more sophisticated statistical techniques are necessary before making any definite conclusions on the role of genetics on attachment throughout the life course.

This is an area of research that is wide open for criminologists to explore and incorporate into traditional views of attachment. For instance, a biosocial view of attachment would hypothesize that individuals who are genetically predisposed to attachment insecurities and who are raised in environments that lead to attachment issues would be at greatest risk for behavioral problems. This extended view of Hirschi's bond of attachment and how it relates to delinquency has not yet been empirically examined in the literature. A few studies have, however, looked at the parent-child conflict relationship and how it affects youth externalizing behaviors using behavioral genetic methodology (Burt, McGue, Krueger, & Iacono, 2005; Neiderhiser, Reiss, Hetherington, & Plomin, 1999). For example, Burt and associates (2005) found that the heritability of the mother-child conflict relationship was partly due to the child's externalizing behaviors, which were themselves partially heritable. Continuing along these lines of research has the potential to greatly advance Hirschi's social bond theory.

COMMITMENT AND INVOLVEMENT

The bonds of commitment and involvement described by Hirschi are best explained together. First, commitment represents our "stake in conformity" and is often thought of as the rational component of the four bonds. In other words, commitment represents the extent to which adolescents are invested in prosocial institutions and activities. As an example, adolescents who are committed to doing well in school have much more to lose by engaging in delinquency compared to adolescents who are uncommitted to their education. Thus, commitment to school can serve as a control on adolescent behavior. Next, involvement, which is considered the temporal component of the bonds, refers to how much of an adolescent's daily life is spent on conventional activities. The bond of involvement is closely related to the bond of commitment in that individuals who are heavily committed to prosocial activities have less time to engage in delinquent activities. For example, if an adolescent is involved in after-school sports, he or she will have less free time to get involved in crime and deviance after school.

A biosocial view of commitment and involvement would argue these two bonds are highly intertwined and are at least partially influenced by genetic factors. The question from a biosocial perspective is then why do some individuals spend their time and energy on prosocial activities while others do not. Also, the mechanism underlying the relationship between commitment and involvement and delinquency could arguably be one of self-selection. From this perspective, it is likely that individuals are selecting themselves, based on their genetic predispositions, into activities, such as sports, music, drama, dance, and reading clubs (Scarr, 1992). These same individuals may be considered at low genetic risk for delinquency and would be less likely to get involved in deviancy in the first place. The opposite is also true in that individuals who are considered at genetic risk for delinquency may select more deviant activities to pass the time such as delinquent peer associations rather than more prosocial activities. Considering individuals' level of genetic risk when assessing their level of commitment and involvement in various activities has been traditionally ignored in discussions of Hirschi's social bond theory.

Commitment is often operationalized in the literature using school-related items (Kempf, 1993). A variable of interest to the current discussion is school connectedness and the factors that are related to school connectedness. More specifically, research has shown that adolescents who are involved in extracurricular activities, who do not skip classes, and who perform well in their courses (exemplified by higher grades) tend to be more connected, attached, and committed to school (McNeely, Nonnemaker, & Blum, 2002). In turn, students who are connected and involved in their school and feel cared about by the people at their school are less likely to engage in a variety of antisocial acts, including substance use, early sexual activity, and violence (McNeely et al., 2002). Interestingly, research from the behavioral genetic literature suggests that school connectedness and the factors that increase the chances that adolescents will feel connected to their school (i.e., involvement in extracurricular activities, truancy, and school achievement) are all influenced by genetic factors.

For instance, Jacobson and Rowe (1999) explored the genetic and environmental influences on school connectedness using a sample of adolescent siblings from the National Longitudinal Study of Adolescent Health ($N = 2{,}302$). Their measure of school connectedness included eight questions pertaining to respondents' perceptions of their teachers, their own feelings of closeness to the people at their school, as well as their feelings of school safety. The results from their genetic analyses revealed significant genetic influences on school connectedness, which varied by gender. More specifically, genetic factors accounted for 45% of the variance in school connectedness for females yet accounted for only 17% of the variance in school connectedness for males. This suggests that genetic effects are stronger for females and environmental effects are stronger for males in explaining variation in school connectedness.

There remains a gap in our understanding about why some individuals are heavily involved in their education while others are not. As mentioned, some sociological factors known to affect school connectedness have been identified and include extracurricular involvement, truancy, and academic achievement. These same factors have also been studied from a behavioral genetic perspective, and a review of this literature is provided next. First, several studies have examined the genetic and environmental contributions to extracurricular activities, particularly sport participation, using various definitions that range in intensity, duration, and frequency of activity (Beunen & Thomis, 1999). Koopmans, van Doornan, and Boomsma (1994), for example, examined a sample of Dutch twins aged 13 to 22 years old and reported a heritability estimate of 0.48 for sport participation. Stubbe, Boomsma, and De Geus (2005) also examined a Dutch sample of twins ($N = 2{,}628$) between the ages of 13 and 20 years old and found that the effects of genes on sport participation increased with age. That is, environmental effects were strongest between 13 and 16 years old (78%–84%), but genetic effects began to emerge at the ages of 17 and 18 (36%) and played a large role after the age of 18 and up to 20 (85%). Maia, Thomis, and Beunen (2002) further examined whether the genetic and environmental influences on physical activity levels varied by gender. Using a sample of Portuguese twin pairs ($N = 411$), the authors reported significant genetic differences across the sexes for both measures of sport participation and leisure-time physical activity with heritability estimates ranging from 0.63 to 0.68 for males and 0.32 to 0.40 for females.

Overall, the research seems to suggest that commitment and involvement to the extracurricular activity of playing sports is partly dependent on someone's genetic makeup. Yet sport participation is only one example of a multitude of potential prosocial activities outlined by Hirschi. It is likely that a deeper exploration of the various prosocial activities that serve to strengthen the bonds of commitment and involvement would show a similar pattern of results. That is, it is a combination of both genetic and environmental factors that best explains variation in behaviors.

The second factor associated with school connectedness is truancy. Individuals who skip classes are less likely to commit or get involved in their educational experience (McNeely et al., 2002). Researchers have traditionally examined indicators of truancy within the broader context of nonaggressive types of antisocial behaviors (Eley, Lichtenstein, & Stevenson, 1999). A review of the behavioral genetic literature ($N = 34$ samples) shows that nonaggressive forms of antisocial behavior are influenced by genetic (48%), shared (18%), and nonshared (34%) environmental factors (Burt, 2009). To date, only one study has isolated truancy from the larger context of nonviolent offending to examine the genetic and environmental influences on this specific type of behavior. Using a sample of twin and nontwin siblings, van der Aa and colleagues (2009) found that 45% of the variance in truancy in adolescence was attributed to genetic factors, with the remaining variance being attributable to both the shared and nonshared environment (depending on the sample). This suggests that individuals may be genetically predisposed for antisocial behaviors, such as truancy, which may then further decrease their chances of committing to conventional activities.

Last, individuals who do not succeed academically are less likely to connect to prosocial institutions such as schools (McNeely et al., 2002). Yet academic achievement and intelligence more broadly are strongly affected by genes, with heritability estimates ranging between 0.60 and 0.80 (Plomin, 1990). Studies that have examined the mechanism underlying the relationship between intelligence and criminal behavior have pointed to an indirect linkage through school performance and attitudes toward school (Lynam, Moffitt, & Stouthamer-Loeber, 1993). More specifically, individuals with lower intelligence are more likely to perform poorly in school, which in turn affects their attitude toward school, which then influences their likelihood of delinquent involvement. From a social bond perspective, the bonds of attachment, commitment, and involvement are then implicated in the IQ-crime relationship. For example, a student who has a strong attachment with his or her teacher (or other school officials) will try to avoid disappointing that person. Individuals with strong bonds may also be more committed and involved in their educational experiences, thereby having more to lose by engaging in deviancy. Yet an individual's intellectual ability affects his or her performance in school, thereby making it more frustrating to succeed. This can weaken the individual's likelihood of forming attachments to teachers and school officials, as well as weaken his or her commitment and involvement in education, thereby increasing the chances of delinquency. As mentioned, intellectual ability has a strong genetic component, which may place an individual at risk for weaker bonds to school.

Overall, the factors that influence an adolescent's likelihood of committing to school (e.g., extracurricular activities, truancy, and academic achievement) have been shown to be influenced by both genetic and environmental factors. This discussion can be expanded to include additional variables pertaining to commitment and involvement that have traditionally been studied from a sociological perspective, but not yet fully explored from a biosocial perspective. These traditional measures of commitment and involvement include measures of achievement orientation, and educational aspirations and expectations as well as employment aspirations and expectations (Kempf, 1993). This is an ideal area for future researchers to incorporate both nature and nurture into our understanding of Hirschi's bonds of commitment and involvement, as well as the mechanism underlying the relationship between these bonds and delinquency.

BELIEF

The last bond presented by Hirschi is belief. This bond represents the extent to which individuals view the rules of society as legitimate, which Hirschi acknowledges varies significantly across individuals. Although delinquents know the value system, they see it as illegitimate; therefore belief does not control their behavior. Belief is considered the moral component of the bonds and is said to be highly dependent on the strength of attachment (Hirschi, 1969). The more a person believes he or she should obey the law, the less likely he or she will be to engage in criminal acts. Researchers have measured the concept of belief in various ways in the literature (Kempf, 1993). Religiosity, for example, could be used as a proxy for belief, particularly since research has shown that religiousness has a direct negative relationship on adolescents' belief about delinquent acts (Johnson, Jang, Larson, & De Li, 2001). That is, the more religious an individual the more likely he or she will view antisocial acts as illegitimate, which is at the heart of Hirschi's bond of belief. Furthermore, a review of the research ($N = 60$ studies) on the relationship between religiousness and criminal behavior has shown a significant, albeit somewhat weak, association with a mean effect of –0.12 (Baier & Wright, 2001). It is important to note, however, that some researchers have used measures of religiosity (e.g., church attendance) to test the bond of involvement rather than belief (Kempf, 1993). It is possible, however, that these elements are overlapping in that a strong belief and commitment to one's religion will translate into greater involvement in religious activities.

Social science research has traditionally viewed these concepts of morality and religiosity as primarily (if not completely) due to social-environmental influences, particularly within the family (Myers, 1996; Stark & Finke, 2000). Although a vast amount of research supports the argument that religious socialization occurs within the family, the problem then arises that family members share both their genes and their environment. In fact, there is a growing body of research that calls into question the assumption that religiosity is influenced primarily by environmental factors. Several studies using twins and adopted siblings have revealed significant genetic effects on measures of religiosity, including religious belief, religious values, spirituality, and service attendance (D'Onofrio, Eaves, Murrelle, Maes, & Spilka, 1999). The work by Koenig, McGue, Krueger, and Bouchard (2005), for example, showed that the heritability of religiousness increased with age with estimates ranging from 0.12 in childhood to 0.44 in adulthood. In a review of the literature, D'Onofrio and colleagues (1999) also showed that genetic factors accounted for 40% to 50% of the variance in measures of religiousness and 20% to 30% of the variance in measures of church attendance. Overall, the research on the heritability of religiousness in adulthood reveals estimates at around 0.40 (see Beer, Arnold, & Loehlin, 1998; Bouchard, Thomas, McGue, Lykken, & Tellegen, 1999). Shared environmental influences on religiousness are also important, particularly in childhood and adolescence (Koenig et al., 2005).

Not only is the bond of belief under genetic influence but its relationship with antisocial behaviors may also be explained from a biosocial perspective. As mentioned, research has demonstrated that religiosity can serve as a protective factor against delinquent and antisocial behaviors, including substance use in adolescence (Heath et al., 1999). The mechanism underlying this relationship from a social bond perspective is that it is the lack of (or weak) social bond that leads to antisocial behaviors. From a biosocial perspective, however, the relationship between religiosity and antisocial behaviors would arguably be due to shared genetic tendencies. Since both religiosity and criminal behavior are moderately heritable, it is possible that their association is due to shared genetic influences.

In fact, Maes, Neale, Martin, Heath, and Eaves (1999) reported that the majority of the covariance between church attendance and alcohol use in males was due to the same genes operating on both behaviors. For females, however, shared environmental factors explained the majority of the covariance between religiosity and alcohol use. Koenig, McGue, Krueger, and Bouchard (2007) also examined the relationship between religiousness and antisocial behaviors among a sample of adult male twin pairs ($N = 265$) from the Minnesota Twin Registry. Their analyses revealed that the inverse relationship between religiousness and antisocial behavior was due primarily to shared genetic and common environmental factors.

It has been argued that environmental conditions can also moderate the genetic effects on antisocial behaviors. For example, a social control model presented by Heath and colleagues (1999) states that certain environmental conditions can buffer the genetic liability for antisocial behaviors. Button, Hewitt, Rhee, Corley, and Stallings (2010) tested the moderating effect of religiosity on problem alcohol use in a sample of twin pairs ($N = 1{,}432$). Their results revealed that genetic effects on alcohol use decreased as religiosity increased in both male and female adolescents. Similar results have been reported by Koopmans, Slutske, Van Baal, and Boomsma, (1999), who reported heritability estimates of 39% to 40% for the initiation of alcohol use among individuals without a religious upbringing compared to 0% to 25% for individuals with a religious background.

From a biosocial perspective, it would be interesting to further examine Hirschi's conceptualization of belief by examining variables related to techniques of neutralization (e.g., most things that people call "delinquent" don't really hurt anyone), values relative to law and the legal system (e.g., respect for the local police), as well as fatalistic statements (e.g., what is going to happen to me will happen, no matter what I do). To date, no biosocial study has yet to examine these direct measures of belief as described by Hirschi. Based on the current trends in the literature, however, it is hypothesized that there would be a moderate genetic influence on one's view of the legal system.

Conclusion

For too long criminological explanations of behavior, including Hirschi's social bond theory, have ignored the influence of genes. Genetic and biological factors influence antisocial and criminal behaviors has been criticized by some (Walby & Carrier, 2010) perhaps because of the deep sociological hold that many criminologists maintain (Wright et al., 2008). This is unfortunate because taking a purely sociological approach to the study of criminal behavior is dismissing half the equation. Frankly, to focus solely on the environment at the expense of genetics is a gross error (as would be the reverse). The omission of genetic and biological factors in most criminological theories may help explain why theoretical advancements are slow-moving at best and why many of the policies that are derived from criminological theories are ineffective at lowering crime. This is not to say that there is no value in our current theories—to the contrary, many of our theories set the framework within which a biosocial perspective can operate, particularly Hirschi's social bond theory. In other words, a biosocial explanation to Hirschi's theory should not be viewed as competing with sociological interpretations. Rather, a biosocial approach to Hirschi's social bond theory has the ability to enhance our understanding by providing an integrative perspective that complements and advances the traditional sociological viewpoint.

References

Agnew, R. (1992). Foundation for a general strain theory of crime and delinquency. *Criminology, 30*(1), 47–88.

Ainsworth, M. D. (1979). Infant-mother attachment. *American Psychologist, 34*(10), 932–927.

Ainsworth, M. D., Blehar, M. C., Waters, E., & Wall, S. (1978). *Patterns of attachment: Assessed in the strange situation and at home.* Hillsdale, NJ: Erlbaum.

Baier, C. J., & Wright, B. R. (2001). "If you love me, keep my commandments": A meta-analysis of the effect of religion on crime. *Journal of Research in Crime and Delinquency, 38*(1), 3–21.

Beer, J. M., Arnold, R. D., & Loehlin, J. C. (1998). Genetic and environmental influences on MMPI factor scales: Joint model fitting to twin and adoption data. *Journal of Personality and Social Psychology, 74*(3), 818–827.

Belsky, J., & Rovine, M. (1987). Temperament and attachment security in the Strange Situation: An empirical rapprochement. *Child Development, 58*, 787–795.

Beunen, G., & Thomis, M. (1999). Genetic determinants of sports participation and daily physical activity. *International Journal of Obesity and Related Metabolic Disorders, 23*, S55–S63.

Bokhorst, C. L., Bakermans-Kranenburg, M. J., Fonagy, P., & Schuengel, C. (2003). The importance of shared environment in mother-infant attachment security: A behavioral genetic study. *Child Development, 74*(6), 1769–1782.

Bouchard, J., Thomas, J., McGue, M., Lykken, D., & Tellegen, A. (1999). Intrinsic and extrinsic religiousness: Genetic and environmental influences and personality correlates. *Twin Research, 2*(2), 88–98.

Bowlby, J. (1969). *Attachment and loss: Attachment* (Vol. 1). New York, NY: Basic Books.

Brooks, J., & Lewis, M. (1974). Attachment behavior in thirteen-month-old, opposite-sex twins. *Child Development, 45*, 243–247.

Brussoni, M. J., Jang, K. L., Livesley, W. J., Macbeth, T. M. (2000). Genetic and environmental influences on adult attachment styles. *Personal Relationships, 7*, 283–289.

Burgess, R. L., & Akers, R. L. (1966). A differential association-reinforcement theory of criminal behavior. *Social Problems, 14*(2), 128–147.

Burt, S. A. (2009). Are there meaningful etiological differences within antisocial behavior? Results of a meta-analysis. *Clinical Psychology Review, 29*(2), 163–178.

Burt, S. A., McGue, M., Krueger, R. F., & Iacono, W. G. (2005). How are parent-child conflict and childhood externalizing symptoms related over time? Results from a genetically informative cross-lagged study. *Development and Psychopathology, 17*(1), 145–165.

Button, T. M., Hewitt, J. K., Rhee, S. H., Corley, R. P., & Stallings, M. C. (2010). The moderating effect of religiosity on the genetic variance of problem alcohol use. *Alcoholism: Clinical and Experimental Research, 34*(9), 1619–1624.

Campbell, S. B., Shaw, D. S., & Gilliom, M. (2000). Early externalizing behavior problems: Toddlers and preschoolers at risk for later maladjustment. *Development and Psychopathology, 12*(3), 467–488.

Cherro, M. (1992). Quality of bonding and behavioral differences in twins. *Infant Mental Health Journal, 13*, 206–210.

D'Onofrio, B. M., Eaves, L. J., Murrelle, L., Maes, H. H., & Spilka, B. (1999). Understanding biological and social influences on religious affiliation, attitudes, and behaviors: A behavior genetic perspective. *Journal of Personality, 67*(6), 953–984.

Eley, T. C., Lichtenstein, P., & Moffitt, T. E. (2003). A longitudinal behavioral genetic analysis of the etiology of aggressive and nonaggressive antisocial behavior. *Development and Psychopathology, 15*(2), 383–402.

Eley, T. C., Lichtenstein, P., & Stevenson, J. (1999). Sex differences in the etiology of aggressive and nonaggressive antisocial behavior: Results from two twin studies. *Child Development, 70*(1), 155–168.

Finkel, D., & Matheny, A. P., Jr. (2000). Genetic and environmental influences on a measure of infant attachment security. *Twin Research, 3*(4), 242–250.

Finkel, D., Wille, D. E., & Matheny, A. P., Jr. (1998). Preliminary results from a twin study of infant-caregiver attachment. *Behavior Genetics, 28*(1), 1–8.

Gervai, J., Nemoda, Z., Lakatos, K., Ronai, Z., Toth, I., Ney, K., & Sasvari-Szekely, M. (2005). Transmission disequilibrium tests confirm the link between DRD4 gene polymorphism and infant attachment. *American Journal of Medical Genetics Part B: Neuropsychiatric Genetics, 132*(1), 126–130.

Goldberg, S., Perrotta, M., Minde, K., & Corter, C. (1986). Maternal behavior and attachment in low-birth-weight twins and singletons. *Child Development*, 57, 34–46.

Goldsmith, H. H., & Alansky, J. A. (1987). Maternal and infant temperamental predictors of attachment: A meta-analytic review. *Journal of Consulting and Clinical Psychology, 55*(6), 805–816.

Gottfried, N. W., Seay, B. M., & Leake, E. (1994). Attachment relationships in infant twins: The effect of co-twin presence during separation from mother. *Journal of Genetic Psychology, 155*(3), 273–281.

Heath, A. C., Madden, P. A. F., Grant, J. D., McLaughlin, T. L., Todorov, A. A., & Bucholz, K. K. (1999). Resiliency factors protecting against teenage alcohol use and smoking: Influences of religion, religious involvement and values, and ethnicity in the Missouri Adolescent Female Twin Study. *Twin Research, 2*(2), 145–155.

Hirschi, T. (1969). *Causes of delinquency*. Berkeley: University of California Press.

Izard, C. E., Haynes, O. M., Chisholm, G., & Baak, K. (1991). Emotional determinants of infant-mother attachment. *Child Development, 62*(5), 906–917.

Jacobson, K. C., & Rowe, D. C. (1999). Genetic and environmental influences on the relationships between family connectedness, school connectedness, and adolescent depressed mood: Sex differences. *Developmental Psychology, 35*(4), 926–939.

Johnson, B. R., Jang, S. J., Larson, D. B., & De Li, S. (2001). Does adolescent religious commitment matter? A reexamination of the effects of religiosity on delinquency. *Journal of Research in Crime and Delinquency, 38*(1), 22–44.

Kempf, K. (1993). The empirical status of Hirschi's control theory. In F. Adler & W. S. Laufer (Eds.), *New directions in criminological theory: Advances in criminological theory* (Vol. 4, pp. 143–185). New Brunswick, NJ: Transaction.

Knafo, A., Zahn-Waxler, C., Van Hulle, C., Robinson, J. L., & Rhee, S. H. (2008). The developmental origins of a disposition toward empathy: Genetic and environmental contributions. *Emotion, 8*(6), 737–752.

Koenig, L. B., McGue, M., Krueger, R. F., & Bouchard, T. J. (2005). Genetic and environmental influences on religiousness: Findings for retrospective and current religiousness ratings. *Journal of Personality, 73*(2), 471–488.

Koenig, L. B., McGue, M., Krueger, R. F., & Bouchard, T. J. (2007). Religiousness, antisocial behavior, and altruism: Genetic and environmental mediation. *Journal of Personality, 75*(2), 265–290.

Koopmans, J. R., Slutske, W. S., Van Baal, G. C. M., & Boomsma, D. I. (1999). The influence of religion on alcohol use initiation: Evidence for genotype × environment interaction. *Behavior Genetics, 29*(6), 445–453.

Koopmans J. R., van Doornen, L. J. P., & Boomsma, D. I. (1994). Smoking and sports participation. In U. Goldbourt & U. De Faire (Eds.), *Genetic factors in coronary heart disease* (Vol. 156, pp. 217–235). Dordrecht, the Netherlands: Kluwer Academic.

Lakatos, K., Nemoda, Z., Toth, I., Ronai, Z., Ney, K., Sasvari-Szekely, M., & Gervai, J. (2002). Further evidence for the role of the dopamine D4 receptor (DRD4) gene in attachment disorganization: Interaction of the exon III 48-bp repeat and the −521 C/T promoter polymorphisms. *Molecular Psychiatry, 7,* 27–31.

Lakatos, K., Toth, I., Nemoda, Z., Ney, K., Sasvari-Szekely, M., & Gervai, J. (2000). Dopamine D4 receptor (DRD4) gene polymorphism is associated with attachment disorganization in infants. *Molecular Psychiatry, 5*(6), 633–637.

Loeber, R. (1982). The stability of antisocial and delinquent child behavior: A review. *Child Development, 53*(6), 1431–1446.

Lynam, D., Moffitt, T. E., & Stouthamer-Loeber, M. (1993). Explaining the relation between IQ and delinquency: Class, race, test motivation, school failure, or self-control. *Journal of Abnormal Psychology, 102,* 187–296.

Lyons-Ruth, K., & Jacobvitz, D. (1999). Attachment disorganization: Unresolved loss, relational violence, and lapses in behavioral and attentional strategies. In J. Cassidy & P. R. Shaver (Eds.), *Handbook of attachment: Theory, research, and clinical applications* (pp. 520–554). New York, NY: Guilford Press.

Lytton, H. (1980). *Parent-child interaction: The socialization process observed in twin and singleton families*. New York, NY: Plenum.

Maes, H. H., Neale, M. C., Martin, N. G., Heath, A. H., & Eaves, L. J. (1999). Religious attendance and frequency of alcohol use: Same genes or same environments: A bivariate extended twin kinship model. *Twin Research, 2*(2), 169–179.

Maia, J. A., Thomis, M., & Beunen, G. (2002). Genetic factors in physical activity levels: A twin study. *American Journal of Preventive Medicine, 23*(2), 87–91.

Main, M. (1999). Attachment theory: Eighteen points with suggestions for future studies. In J. Cassidy & P. R. Shaver (Eds.), *Handbook of attachment: Theory, research, and clinical applications* (pp. 845–887). New York, NY: Guilford Press.

Main, M., & Solomon, J. (1990). Procedures for identifying infants as disorganized/disoriented during the Ainsworth Strange Situation. In M. T. Greenberg, D. Cicchetti, & E. M. Cummings (Eds.), *Attachment in the preschool years: Theory, research, and intervention* (pp. 121–160). Chicago, IL: University of Chicago Press.

McNeely, C. A., Nonnemaker, J. M., & Blum, R. W. (2002). Promoting school connectedness: Evidence from the National Longitudinal Study of Adolescent Health. *Journal of School Health, 72,* 138–146.

Moffitt, T. E. (2005). Genetic and environmental influences on antisocial behaviors: Evidence from behavioral-genetic research. *Advances in Genetics, 55,* 41–104.

Myers, S. M. (1996). An interactive model of religiosity inheritance: The importance of family context. *American Sociological Review, 61,* 858–866.

Neiderhiser, J. M., Reiss, D., Hetherington, E. M., & Plomin, R. (1999). Relationships between parenting and adolescent adjustment over time: Genetic and environmental contributions. *Developmental Psychology, 35*(3), 680–692.

O'Connor, T. G., & Croft, C. M. (2001). A twin study of attachment in preschool children. *Child Development, 72*(5), 1501–1511.

Olweus, D. (1979). Stability of aggressive reaction patterns in males: A review. *Psychological Bulletin, 86*(4), 852–875.

Pederson, D. R., & Moran, G. (1995). A categorical description of infant-mother relationships in the home and its relation to Q-sort measures of infant-mother interaction. *Monographs of the Society for Research in Child Development, 60*(2–3), 111–132.

Plomin, R. (1990). *Nature and nurture: An introduction to human behavioral genetics*. Pacific Grove, CA: Brooks/Cole.

Plomin, R. (1994). *Genetics and experience: The interplay between nature and nurture*. Thousand Oaks, CA: Sage.

Reiss, D., Neiderhiser, J. M., Hetherington, E. M., & Plomin, R. (2000). *The relationship code: Deciphering genetic and social influences on adolescent development*. Cambridge, MA: Harvard University Press.

Rhee, S. H., & Waldman, I. D. (2002). Genetic and environmental influences on antisocial behavior: A meta-analysis of twin and adoption studies. *Psychological Bulletin, 128,* 490–529.

Ricciuti, A. E. (1993). *Child-mother attachment: A twin study* (Doctoral dissertation). Available from ProQuest Information & Learning.

Rothbart, M. K., & Derryberry, D. (1981). Development of individual differences in temperament. *Advances in Developmental Psychology, 1,* 37–86.

Rushton, J. P., Littlefield, C. H., & Lumsden, C. J. (1986). Gene-culture coevolution of complex social behavior: Human altruism and mate choice. *Proceedings of the National Academy of Sciences, 83*(19), 7340–7343.

Scarr, S. (1992). Developmental theories for the 1990s: Development and individual differences. *Child Development, 63*(1), 1–19.

Stark, R., & Finke, R. (2000). *Acts of faith: Explaining the human side of religion*. Berkeley: University of California Press.

Stubbe, J. H., Boomsma, D. I., & De Geus, E. J. (2005). Sports participation during adolescence: A shift from environmental to genetic factors. *Medicine & Science in Sports Exercise, 37*(4), 563–570.

Susman-Stillman, A., Kalkoske, M., Egeland, B., & Waldman, I. (1996). Infant temperament and maternal sensitivity as predictors of attachment security. *Infant Behavior and Development, 19*(1), 33–47.

Sutherland, E. (1939). *Principles of criminology*. Philadelphia, PA: J. B. Lippincott.

Szajnberg, N. M., Skrinjaric, J., & Moore, A. (1989). Affect attunement, attachment, temperament, and zygosity: A twin study. *Journal of the American Academy of Child & Adolescent Psychiatry, 28*(2), 249–253.

Thompson, R. A. (2000). The legacy of early attachments. *Child Development, 71*(1), 145–152.

Turkheimer, E. (2000). Three laws of behavior genetics and what they mean. *Current Directions in Psychological Science, 9,* 160–164.

van der Aa, N., Rebollo-Mesa, I., Willemsen, G., Boomsma, D. I., & Bartels, M. (2009). Frequency of truancy at high school: evidence for genetic and twin specific shared environmental influences. *Journal of Adolescent Health, 45*(6), 579–586.

van IJzendoorn, M. (1995). Adult attachment representations, parental responsiveness, and infant attachment: A meta-analysis on the predictive validity of the Adult Attachment Interview. *Psychological Bulletin, 117*(3), 387–403.

Van IJzendoorn, M., Schuengel, C., & Bakermans-Kranenburg, M. J. (1999). Disorganized attachment in early childhood: Meta-analysis of precursors, concomitants, and sequelae. *Development and Psychopathology, 11*, 225–249.

Vandell, D. L., Owen, M. T., Wilson, K. S., & Henderson, V. K. (1988). Social development in infant twins: Peer and mother-child relationships. *Child Development, 59,* 168–177.

Walby, K., & Carrier, N. (2010). The rise of biocriminology: Capturing observable bodily economies of "criminal man." *Criminology and Criminal Justice, 10*(3), 261–285.

Walsh, A. (2012). *Criminology: The essentials*. Thousand Oaks, CA: Sage.

Wright, J. P., Beaver, K. M., DeLisi, M., Vaughn, M. G., Boisvert, D., & Vaske, J. (2008). Lombroso's legacy: The miseducation of criminologists. *Journal of Criminal Justice Education, 19*(3), 325–338.

Wright, J. P., Tibbetts, S. G., & Daigle, L. E. (2008). *Criminals in the making: Criminality across the life course*. Thousand Oaks, CA: Sage.

Discussion Questions

CHAPTERS 13 AND 14

1. Social bond theory assumes all individuals are naturally motivated toward committing crime. Does the biosocial view support the assumptions of social bond theory? What would biosocial researchers say about an individual's motivation to commit crime?
2. As noted in Dr. Schroeder's chapter, attachment is an important social bond in reducing criminal behavior. What does the available evidence indicate about attachment and its effects on deterring crime? In addition, how are attachments formed, and do they vary among individuals? Is there reason to believe attachment will deter crime for everyone?
3. The social bonds of commitment and involvement have traditionally been measured by achievements, aspirations, and expectations in various social contexts. How might the inclusion of genetic factors contribute to the understanding of the bonds of commitment and involvement? Furthermore, how might the social environment and genetic factors work together to influence these bonds?
4. Social scientists view concepts of morality and religiosity to be highly influenced by the social environment. Has the available research appropriately ruled out alternative influences on morality and religiosity? In other words, do genetic effects account for any variations in religiosity? How might genetic factors influence the relationship between the concept of belief and antisocial behavior?
5. Dr. Schroeder discusses how life course theory highlights the importance of social bonds from childhood to adulthood. How would biosocial research explain offending patterns across the life course? In your opinion, would biosocial research find social bonds to be important across the life course as well?
6. Discuss the limitations of taking a purely sociological approach to studying antisocial behavior. Beyond the ideas provided by Dr. Boisvert, how would the inclusion of genetic variables improve and advance social bond theory?

PART III

SPECIFIC TYPES OF ANTISOCIAL BEHAVIORS

15

When Violence Is the Norm

Sociological Perspectives on Intimate Partner Violence

Tasha A. Menaker

Sam Houston State University

Cortney A. Franklin

Sam Houston State University

Intimate partner violence (IPV) affects thousands of lives every year (Catalano, 2012). It wasn't until the mid-1970s, primarily through efforts from women's advocates working in conjunction with momentum spurred by the women's liberation movement, that attention was directed toward understanding the causes of this pervasive violence, and subsequent legislation and policy was focused on targeting perpetrators of woman battering (Lutze & Symons, 2003). Traditionally, scholars have tended to gravitate toward sociological explanations of intimate partner offending behaviors, naming poor parenting practices, including family-of-origin violence and corporal punishment, as causes, since these often violent or vicariously violent "behavior correction interventions" have traumatic impacts on those involved (Widom, 1989). This learning theory tradition has largely dominated the IPV literature. While the etiology of IPV has been sparsely populated with alternative biological explanations (e.g., hormone dysregulation), the majority of these early biological explanations have been poorly developed or have had dangerous implications for victims in violent home environments. Empirical scholarship has seen rapid development in recent years, with scientific advances in biosocial criminology (e.g., Wright & Boisvert, 2009), the neurobiology of trauma (e.g., Perry & Szalavitz, 2006), and behavior genetics (e.g., Beaver, Barnes, May, & Schwartz, 2011) providing a host of explanations from which to better understand the nature of interpersonal violence within intimate relationships. These sophisticated scientific explanations also provide the scaffolding for potentially more effective treatment and intervention to aid victims of relationship trauma and the offenders responsible for perpetrating such trauma.

That said, however, the purpose of this chapter is to provide the reader with an overview of the purely sociological explanations of intimate partner violence. As such, this chapter first discusses social learning theories of IPV, with particular focus on the intergenerational transmission of violence, including the effects of witnessing interparental violence and experiencing corporal punishment. Next, feminist explanations for intimate partner violence are detailed, with specific attention to the role of patriarchy, power, and control in facilitating gendered abuse. This is followed by a review of the social exchange and subculture of violence theories. Finally, conclusions and implications of sociological perspectives on intimate partner violence are discussed.

"I Learned It From You": The Social Learning Theories

Scholars have suggested that children learn behavior by watching and imitating their parents or guardians. Accordingly, most parents take great care to behave conventionally as positive role models for their offspring. Doing so has its payoffs, because sociological studies have demonstrated that children do learn behaviors, both good and "bad," from family members. The question is, then, whether exposure to violent parental behavior makes children more likely to use violence in adulthood. Social learning theorists have responded with a resounding yes.

Social learning theory suggests that individuals learn behavior as a result of external forces, such as life experiences and environments (Bandura, 1969, 1973). Most often, this learning takes place within the family-of-origin, where children gain techniques for interacting with others based on observations of interpersonal family dynamics. In other words, parents model behavior, children imitate what has been modeled, and, when reinforced, behavior either continues or desists. Specifically, when rewarded, behavior persists. When punished, children learn to discontinue whatever behavior elicited punishment.

The *intergenerational transmission of violence theory* incorporates the basic principles of social learning, and proposes that children who witness interparental violence (parents hitting, kicking, or slapping each other) or experience corporal punishment (getting hit, spanked, or slapped themselves) may grow up to view violence as a normal and appropriate conflict resolution strategy (Gosselin, 2005). In this case, children learn that it is appropriate to hit or physically harm those whom they are closest to. Adolescents whose problem-solving skills have been shaped by adverse or violent family-of-origin environments may gravitate toward similar peers, particularly because prosocial children have less tolerance for individuals lacking suitable social skills. Once peer networks have been formed, romantic partners are easily selected from a readily available pool of potential mates, all of whom may have deficits in interpersonal conflict resolution. It is these individuals who may be more likely to use violence in adult intimate partnerships. To be sure, social learning theories suggest a cycle of violence, in which parents who use violence condition children to use violence in an ongoing legacy of abuse. This perspective has long informed policy arguments trumpeting the need for effective domestic violence interventions that limit children's exposure to violent role models (Buzawa & Buzawa, 1996). These strategies suggest early intervention in family environments identified as violence-prone in order to teach alternative methods for prosocial parenting and conflict resolution. Doing so, advocates of this approach argue, will provide positive role modeling for children who will arguably see parents using mediation techniques for effective problem resolution without resorting to physical and/or violent intervention.

There is empirical support for the social learning and intergenerational transmission of violence theories. Research suggests that children have learned violent behavior by watching their parents (Doumas, Margolin, & John, 1994; McCord, 1988) and that family-of-origin violence is related to adult IPV perpetration (e.g., Kwong, Bartholomew, Henderson, & Trinke, 2003; Renner & Slack, 2006; Stith et al., 2000). Critiques of these theories, however, have underscored the heterogeneity of learning violent behavior (Kaufman & Zigler, 1987). Certainly, not everyone who witnesses family violence or experiences corporal punishment grows up to perpetrate violence. Consequently, explanations of IPV from the international transmission of violence framework have begun to account for factors that increase risk for perpetration among those individuals with violent family-of-origin histories. Studies have highlighted certain demographic characteristics (e.g., gender, age, race), attitudes, and behaviors that interact with family-of-origin violence to produce IPV perpetration.

It's All in the Family

Intergenerational transmission research has predominantly focused on the impact of witnessing interparental violence and experiencing corporal punishment on IPV. Children who witness interparental violence may learn aggression is an appropriate mechanism for resolving conflict within couples. Indeed, results have indicated that many adult IPV perpetrators witnessed interparental violence while they were children (Finkelhor, Hotaling, & Yllo, 1988; Sonkin, Martin, & Walker, 1985). One study, for example, found that 45% of male perpetrators of IPV had seen their fathers engage in domestic abuse targeting their mothers (Sonkin et al., 1985). Witnessing this kind of interparental violence has also been associated with a number of negative outcomes for men and women, including IPV perpetration and victimization (Brownridge, 2006; Franklin & Kercher, 2012), increased stress in a marriage (Mihalic & Elliott, 1997), and less overall relationship satisfaction (Mihalic & Elliott, 1997).

More recently, some studies have found a more indirect link between family-related variables, such as parent antisocial behavior and poor parenting practices, and the likelihood of children growing up to become IPV perpetrators as adults (Capaldi & Clark, 1998). In other words, those parents who more often used drugs and drank alcohol were less skillful parents—they spent less time with their children, monitored them less, and dispensed inconsistent discipline—and their children were more likely to use violence against intimate partners as adults.

Corporal Punishment: What's Love Got to Do With It?

While there is moderate support for the role of witnessing interparental violence on IPV, the relationship between corporal punishment and IPV is less clear. Although several studies have identified being the recipient of corporal punishment as a risk factor for later perpetration of IPV (Ehrensaft et al., 2003; Fang & Corso, 2008; Markowitz, 2001), some studies have found no significant effects (DeMaris, 1990; Mihalic & Elliot, 1997). Theoretically, children receiving corporal punishment may learn to associate violence with love. They may see their parents use forms of physical touch, in the form of violence or harm, as a method of communication and learn that conflict resolution is only possible through physical aggression. Indeed, social learning theories suggest violent punishment teaches children that violence is an acceptable response to anger or conflict, and there is some evidence to support this claim. Markowitz (2001) found, for example, that corporal punishment in the form of slapping or hitting was associated with children adopting attitudes condoning violence as adults, and subsequently using violence against their spouses. Other scholars have also found that severe physical punishment increased the likelihood that children engaged in psychological and physical intimate partner abuse as adults (Avakame, 1998; Ehrensaft et al., 2003; Fang & Corso, 2008).

Some findings suggest, however, that the link between corporal punishment and IPV is not so simple. Foshee, Ennett, Bauman, Benefield, and Suchindran (2005) reported there were additional factors impacting whether physical punishment predicted IPV. They found that the race and educational level of the disciplinarian (the parent or guardian enacting the punishment) influenced the degree to which violence was transmitted. Specifically, adult perpetration of IPV was more likely to occur when the disciplinarian was a Black female with less education than her peers. This suggests that more research is necessary to better understand the dynamics underlying the relationship between corporal punishment and later IPV. This is further substantiated by studies where no direct relationship between physical punishment and IPV was found (DeMaris, 1990; Mihalic & Elliot, 1997).

The Cumulative Effects of Violence

If violence does beget violence, then one might expect that multiple violent experiences in childhood would increase the probability of future IPV perpetration. Indeed, there is evidence to suggest this is the case. Although few studies have examined the cumulative effect of witnessing and experiencing familial violence (Franklin, Menaker, & Kercher, 2012; O'Keefe, 1998), results demonstrate that children exposed to interparental violence *and* corporal punishment are more likely to use IPV than children who have experienced only one form of family-of-origin violence (Franklin et al., 2012; O'Keefe, 1998). Findings have indicated, however, that the cumulative effects of violence may vary according to social and demographic factors, such as gender, community violence, and socioeconomic status.

O'Keefe (1998) found that, in a sample of adolescents who had witnessed interparental violence, receipt of physical punishment was partially responsible for distinguishing those who engaged in adolescent dating violence from nonviolent counterparts. Notably, this was only true for female participants. That is, female adolescents who had experienced both forms of family-of-origin violence were more likely to use violence in their dating relationships. For males, on the other hand, adolescent dating violence was more likely when exposure to interparental, school, and community violence was present, and corporal punishment had no significant effect. A subsequent study (Franklin et al., 2012) had similar results among a sample of adult men and women. Franklin and colleagues (2012) found that, overall, individuals who had experienced corporal punishment and witnessed interparental violence were more likely to use violence in adult intimate relationship when compared to those who had solely witnessed parental domestic abuse. Still, not all individuals with histories of family-of-origin violence engaged in IPV, suggesting that factors beyond witnessing and experiencing familial violence must be considered when trying to understand IPV using the social learning approach.

Risk and Resiliency Factors Associated With the Intergenerational Transmission of Violence and IPV

Collectively, the aforementioned studies suggest that social learning cannot be understood simply as a direct link between witnessing and experiencing family-of-origin violence and future IPV. To the contrary, there are several factors that may mediate the link between familial violence and IPV perpetration—that is, factors that may increase risk for IPV or protect against the development of such behavior. Indeed, studies have revealed a myriad of demographic characteristics, attitudes, contexts, and behaviors that may further explain the relationship between family-of-origin violence and IPV. The influence of some factors, such as education level, has been consistent across studies (individuals with higher education levels are less likely to perpetrate IPV), while findings about other factors, such as race, have been mixed and rather equivocal. Overall, the predominance of mixed findings related to factors that may mediate the relationship between family-of-origin violence and IPV speaks to the limitations of extant research in explaining the processes underlying this relationship.

Research has revealed few variables that tend to protect against IPV perpetration, including higher education level and employment (Caetano, Field, Ramisetty-Mikler, & McGrath, 2005; Chen & White, 2004; Coker et al., 2000; Ehrensaft et al., 2003; Fang & Corso, 2008; Hotaling & Sugarman, 1986). In addition, some studies have found that being married protects against IPV (e.g., Daigneault, Hébert, & McDuff, 2009; Franklin & Kercher, 2012), although others produced no significant effects (Caetano et al., 2005; Fang & Corso, 2008). Similarly, research on whether race/ethnicity has any effect on likelihood to perpetrate IPV has generated inconsistent findings. While some studies have reported that people of color are more likely to use IPV (Anderson, 1997; Caetano et al., 2005; Wareham, Boots, & Chavez, 2009), others have found IPV perpetration to be more common among White participants (Coker et al., 2000; Markowitz, 2001).

To date, risk factors for IPV perpetration have been more consistent. Younger individuals are more likely to use IPV (Anderson, 1997; Kwong et al., 2003), as are those with low self-esteem, posttraumatic stress disorder, poor school performance, and greater alcohol consumption or dependence (Bevan & Higgins, 2002; Dankoski et al., 2006; Guille, 2004; Whiting, Simmons, Havens, Smith, & Oka, 2009). Environmental factors may also increase risk for IPV perpetration, including low socioeconomic status and exposure to community and school violence (O'Keefe, 1998). Additionally, studies have shown certain attitudes predict the use of violence in intimate relationships. Consistent with the tenets of a social learning approach to IPV, research has demonstrated that family-of-origin violence increases the likelihood that men will have negative gender beliefs and condone the use of violence in intimate relationships (Delsol & Margolin, 2004; Jin, Eagle, & Yoshioka, 2007; Reitzel-Jaffe & Wolfe, 2001). Predictably, these men are more likely to perpetrate IPV. It is also important to consider, beyond individual characteristics and social influences, how relationship concerns and dynamics influence the use of IPV. To be sure, studies have shown that IPV is more likely to occur within couples reporting greater decision-making disagreement on household issues, such as money management; cooking, cleaning, and household duties; and sex/affection (Franklin et al., 2012). In sum, these findings suggest that individuals with adverse family-of-origin experiences cannot be considered a homogenous group. While family-of-origin violence increases risk for IPV perpetration, likelihood of perpetration cannot be adequately predicted with these variables alone. Individual beliefs, behaviors, and social and environmental constraints must be examined as they interact with familial violence, and ultimately increase or decrease risk for adult IPV.

Power and Control: The Feminist Theories

Feminist scholars were among the first to bring attention to the issue of intimate partner violence, particularly with regard to male-perpetrated IPV (Lutze & Simons, 2003). The feminist perspective suggests that IPV is a symptom of a patriarchal society—one that is male-dominated and male-centered, and where social, political, and economic structures serve to oppress women (Johnson, 2005). According to feminist theories, men have obtained and maintained status through access to resources, including occupational and educational statuses and financial wealth, resources that, until recently, were entirely unavailable to women. Moreover, legal and religious institutions have historically endorsed the husband's authority and legitimized or justified the use of violence to punish a "disobedient" wife (Buzawa & Buzawa, 1996). Accordingly, feminists focus on the role of power and gender inequality in explaining motivations for IPV (Dobash & Dobash, 1979; Walker, 1979). Simply put, the feminist perspective suggests that power structures that encourage male dominance and female subordination are replicated in the home, such that the division of power and authority is gendered. That is, while males have traditionally held the title of "head of the household" and had the associated financial control and decision-making power, women are seen as responsible for child-rearing and caretaking, as well as domestic duties such as housekeeping and cooking, even when working outside the home.

Feminist theories suggest that men use violence to control female partners, feel powerful, and regain power when their status or authority is threatened. For example, men with comparatively "low" statuses—those who lack economic or social resources—would be more likely to use violence as a way of asserting control and obtaining the feelings of power lacking in other aspects of their lives (Gelles, 1974). In a similar vein, men may also resort to IPV when their statuses are directly threatened by female partners acquiring more professional positions and greater resources. That is, within a patriarchy, male power is associated with financial and economic status. Female achievement of these statuses is a direct threat to patriarchal structures and, within couples, may result in male partners feeling inferior or less powerful. Thus, to regain power, men then rely on the most fundamental source of power available to them: physical strength and violence. Studies suggest, however, that only certain men will feel threatened by their female partner's achievements and resort to violence as a result (Steinmetz, 1980). Compared to males who do not use IPV, perpetrators of IPV are more likely to have low self-esteem, low self-control, and difficulty appropriately expressing their emotions.

Patriarchy, Power, and Violence Against Women

Early studies on violence against women tended to focus on the maladaptive cognitions and behaviors of individual perpetrators (e.g., Fischer & Rivlin, 1971; Rada, 1978). A portrayal of gender violence as a consequence of individual-level dysfunction among a subset of psychologically ill perpetrators may undermine the recognition of broader contextual factors that facilitate violence against women. Specifically, feminist scholars have argued that any consideration of gender violence must acknowledge the deep-seated roots of gender inequality enmeshed in the patriarchal social and cultural structures of society (Johnson, 2005; Ridgeway, 1997), including religions and ideologies that legitimize unequal gender hierarchies, laws that make the prosecution of abusive male partners more difficult (Lorber, 2001), and socialization processes and customs (e.g., gender roles, sex scripts, and rape myths) (Ben-David & Schneider, 2005; Check & Malamuth, 1983, 1985; Koss et al., 1994; Simonson & Subich, 1999).

Feminist theories suggest that structural factors, cultural components, and individual behaviors interact to produce negative outcomes for women, manifested at the individual behavioral level. Indeed, men and women are socialized to accept gender role ideologies regarding gender identity (masculine/feminine), appropriate roles for men and women (e.g., man as breadwinner and woman as homemaker), and distinct scripts with regard to heterosexual interactions. This socialization influences individual behavior so that when making decisions people most often choose the path of least resistance—the option with the least negative social consequences, or that which is aligned with patriarchal socialization and gender inequality. Figure 15.1 illustrates this dynamic relationship between patriarchal socialization influences, cultural ideology, and individual-level cognition/behavior (Franklin, 2008, p. 22).

Power and control are the forces that drive the perpetuation of a patriarchal culture (Johnson, 2005). The importance of control is particularly salient among men in a patriarchy, because control is perceived to be characteristic of masculinity and, therefore, is a powerful motivator in men's inner and social lives (Johnson, 2005). If greater power and control is central to the male identity, indicative of male worth, and associated with increased feelings of security among men, then it naturally becomes a sought-after male commodity (Johnson, 2005). In a social system that boasts male superiority and devalues the status and contributions of females, one of the ways in which male control manifests is through the subordination and exploitation of females (Brownmiller, 1975; Daly & Chesney-Lind, 1988). An unfortunate and inevitable outcome in a relationship of control is that the controller and controllee become disconnected and objectified so that, while controlling others, controllers can justify their behavior and discount the feelings of those they control (Johnson, 2005). The complex humanity of controllees, then, is minimized and ignored in order to maintain acts of control against them, such as intimate partner

Figure 15.1 Explaining Violence Against Women Through Patriarchal Socialization

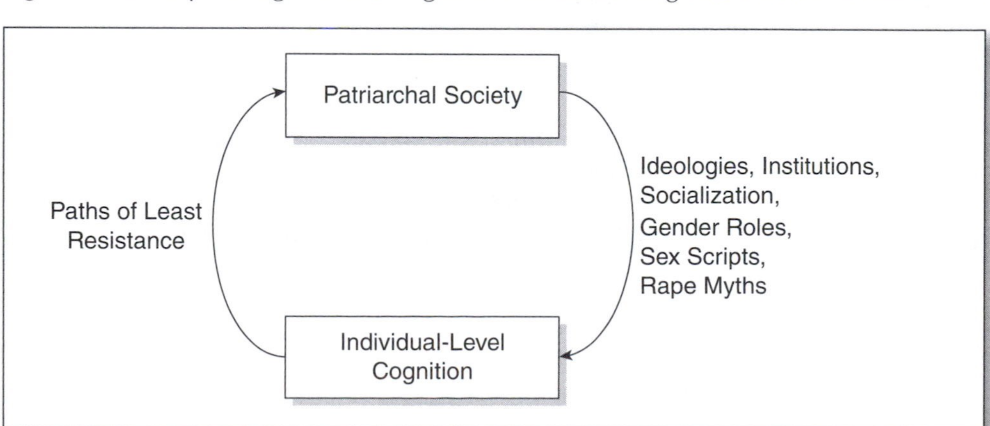

violence (Johnson, 2005). Therefore, according to feminist perspective, the power that a patriarchal system affords men allows them to aggress against women. Doing so creates a culture of fear, where women are immobilized by the risk of victimization and are further subordinated and victimized as a result (Franklin, 2008).

Who's in Charge Here?

According to feminist scholarship, men with statuses inconsistent with social norms or with their female intimate partner will be more likely to use IPV to regain power and status. In other words, men with comparatively low economic or social resources, or with fewer resources than their partner, are at risk for feelings of stress, fear, and inadequacy with regard to their masculinity, because within a patriarchal society, masculinity is measured by wealth, occupational status, and power (Lenton, 1995; Yick, 2001). Therefore, to dissipate feelings of inferiority, "low status" men may use IPV as a means of regaining power.

There is little research on the effect of within-couple status inconsistencies on IPV perpetration. Available literature has provided some support for this hypothesis. Macro-level studies (Yllo, 1983, 1984) have found higher rates of IPV in states with more traditional gender role ideologies and women in high status positions than those with more egalitarian gender role beliefs. Furthermore, micro-level examinations of couples where the female partner has greater social and financial resources as a result of employment, income, or education have revealed greater marital dissatisfaction among male partners, lower marital quality for female partners, and higher rates of divorce (Heckert, Nowak, & Snyder, 1998; Hornung & McCullough, 1981; Ono, 1998; Tichenor, 1999). Additional studies have reported that men were more likely to use IPV when their income was lower than that of their female partner (Anderson, 1997; Chung, Tucker, & Takeuchi, 2008), and when they perceived their female partner as having power (Claes & Rosenthal, 1990). On the other hand, findings related to the role of employment status on IPV have been mixed. MacMillan and MacMillan (1999) found that women were at greatest risk for IPV when they were employed and their male partners were not, while Franklin and Menaker (in press) reported that women in dual-income households were at greatest risk for male-perpetrated IPV. While these studies suggest that status-reversal couples (where the female partner has greater status) are at increased risk for male-perpetrated IPV, it is important to note that this body of literature is relatively small, and additional research is necessary to further disentangle this relationship.

"Everything in Its Place": Gender Role Socialization

One feminist explanation for the gender gap in IPV perpetration (the fact that males are more likely to be perpetrators and females to be victims) is gender role socialization. *Gender role socialization* is the process by which males and females are taught to conform to cultural gender roles based on notions of "masculinity" and "femininity." According to this perspective, males are encouraged to be competitive, unemotional, active, and aggressive, while females are socialized to be nurturing, emotionally expressive, passive, and weak (Johnson, 2005). Some feminist scholars suggest it is these gendered roles that increase male propensity for using violence in intimate partnerships (Miedzian, 1991). After all, men are instructed that aggression is acceptable behavior, and that physical domination enhances their masculinity (Mignon, Larson, & Holmes, 2002). Moreover, men are discouraged from showing or expressing their emotions and, as a result, may resort to violence out of frustration, or because they lack other means of communicating (Mignon et al., 2002).

Critics argue that a limitation of the gender role socialization framework is its failure to explain why, if males are socialized to accept and use aggression, only some males engage in IPV. Proponents of this explanation assert that, while historically males and females have been socialized in gender stereotypical ways, in recent decades some parents have encouraged more gender-neutral socialization for boys and girls. Thus, differences in propensity to perpetrate IPV among males are associated with the degree to which men endorse traditional gender role beliefs. The gender role socialization framework therefore implies that the risk for IPV is lower in relationships where both partners endorse egalitarian gender role beliefs, and the division of power is equitable. Indeed, studies show that, compared to men with more egalitarian gender ideologies, males who report traditional gender role beliefs are more likely to feel threatened when intimate partners gain occupational status, are more accepting of violence against women (Flood & Pease, 2009), and are more likely to engage in IPV due to status threat or perceptions of lost power (Atkinson, Greenstein, & Lang, 2005).

Risk and Reward: Social Exchange Theory

Social exchange theory posits that individuals rationally choose behaviors based on perceived costs or rewards (Gelles, 1983). Accordingly, people will behave in ways that provide the most positive rewards and avoid behaviors that result in negative sanction. Social exchange theorists suggest that individuals will engage in IPV when the perceived rewards of abuse outweigh the social costs. The rewards, in this sense, will be primarily psychological, such as reducing fear and strain, and increasing feelings of power. It can be reasonably argued that interpersonal discord and disagreement causes feelings of strain and powerlessness in both parties. Individuals with violent tendencies, or those unable to effectively communicate their feelings, are more likely to use IPV to diminish psychological distress.

It is important to note, however, that social exchange theory states that individuals will only use IPV if the rewards associated with its use are greater than potential sanctions. Thus, if the possibility of social sanctioning is salient in the mind of the would-be perpetrator, and the fear of sanctioning outweighs the anticipated relief, the person is unlikely to engage in IPV. "Costs" of intimate partner violence may include reciprocal violence by a partner, possible arrest or imprisonment, diminished status or reputation, or the dissolution of the family (Gelles & Cornell, 1990). Accordingly, scholars suggest that the frequency of IPV perpetration may be rooted in perceptions of IPV as a relatively "low-risk" crime because, historically, it has been treated as a "private" matter outside legal or social intervention (Buzawa & Buzawa, 1996). Proponents of this theory thus argue for harsher sanctioning for IPV perpetrators, increasing the costs of engaging in IPV and deterring potential offenders (Danis, 2003).

Possible rewards associated with IPV include decreased stress, anger, and powerlessness related to intimate partner conflict. Thus, social exchange theory suggests that the likelihood of IPV is negatively correlated with the number of nonviolent resources available for conflict resolution (Gelles & Straus, 1979). In other words, individuals with wealth and status can use the power associated with their position to enforce their will and do not need to resort to violence. Moreover, individuals who have prosocial strategies for addressing interpersonal conflict, such as self-esteem, adaptive coping strategies, and effective communication skills, will be less likely to use IPV, because they have other, less costly, methods for reducing feelings of relationship strain (Lazarus & Folkman, 1984). To be sure, studies have shown that couples lacking in effective coping and communication skills, that is, those individuals more likely to resort to anger, blaming, insults, or withdrawal, are at greater risk for IPV than couples who use nonconfrontational interaction styles (Bird, Stith, & Schladale, 1991). This provides evidence for the utility of family and couples counseling that strengthens individual psychological resources, such as anger management and effective communication strategies.

The Deviant Outgroup: Subculture of Violence Theory

Subculture of violence theory suggests that violent behavior results from cultural norms and values that condone violence for conflict resolution. This theory has been used to explain why certain geographical areas or groups have higher rates of violence than others. For example, one scholar (Sullivan, 1996) has suggested the prevalence of IPV among Black men and women may result from Black males commonly using demeaning epithets to describe Black women, such as calling them "bitches" and "ho's." Cultural acceptance of these disrespectful attitudes toward women, in conjunction with attitudes accepting the use of violence, might put Black women at increased risk for IPV victimization.

Official records have demonstrated that certain racial groups have greater levels of violence (Mignon et al., 2002). Evidence suggests, however, that the relationship between race and violence is mediated by several factors, including socioeconomic status and poverty, neighborhood disorganization, and lack of economic and political power (Farrington, Loeber, & Stouthamer-Loeber, 2003). With regard to intimate partner violence, findings related to the impact of race on likelihood of

IPV perpetration have been mixed. While some studies have found that people of color are more likely to use IPV, additional research has found greater IPV perpetration among White individuals (Anderson, 1997; Caetano et al., 2005; Coker et al., 2000; Markowitz, 2001). Thus, there is little evidence to suggest that the norms or values of certain ethnic or racial groups encourage violence to a greater extent than in other populations. Indeed, there is little research to suggest that, outside criminal street gangs, distinct violent subcultures exist (Mignon et al., 2002).

The subculture of violence theory has been criticized for facilitating an "us versus them" mentality. Since, within a subculture of violence framework, individuals who perpetrate violence are seen as part of a deviant subculture, it allows others to differentiate themselves from violent individuals by saying perpetrators are "different" or "other"—in other words, not like "us." Theories that encourage the creation of deviant outgroups minimize our common humanity and cultural origins, and potentially justify the differential treatment of transgressors. Critiques of subculture of violence theories argue these theories promote discriminatory biases and harsh punitive treatment of offenders, as opposed to the rehabilitative responses that are often more appropriate for IPV perpetrators and victims.

Conclusion

Although sociological theories give critical insights into the dynamic origins of intimate partner violence, it is important to recognize that sociological perspectives are not all-encompassing. While sociologists may argue for purely sociological explanations for behavior, prominent criminologists have suggested that failing to account for the impact of additional considerations, such as neurobiology, genetics, and biosocial factors, on explaining criminal behavior undermines the discipline of criminology (Wright & Cullen, 2012). This does not, however, imply strict determinism, or excuse abusive behavior as biological impulse. Moreover, the incorporation of biosocial explanations for intimate partner violence does not preclude interventions that target maladaptive ideologies and resulting dysfunctional behaviors. To the contrary, the implications of sociological approaches would only be enhanced by integration with more dynamic fields in the hard sciences.

To be sure, intimate partner research using sociological frameworks has provided important conclusions. First, evidence has suggested that family-of-origin violence is a significant contributor to later adult relationship conflict. Although not all children who witness interparental violence or experience corporal punishment go on to perpetrate intimate partner violence, studies have revealed risk and resiliency factors that mediate this relationship, including attitudes accepting the use of violence, alcohol consumption, and relationship factors such as decision-making agreement. These factors have implications for clinical practice and prevention strategies with potential perpetrators and victims, such as violence prevention programs for children who may be exposed to family-of-origin aggression. Moreover, the implementation of community parenting classes may decrease the incidence of physical abuse and maladaptive disciplinary techniques. Finally, findings have indicated that individual therapy for perpetrators of intimate partner violence would benefit from assessments identifying potential traumatic experiences in the family-of-origin such as witnessing interparental violence or experiencing abuse so that the cognitions and behaviors related to these events (e.g., low self-esteem, alcohol use) can be appropriately addressed.

Similarly, findings from studies using feminist approaches to understand intimate partner violence have implications for treatment with IPV perpetrators and highlight the importance of addressing both individual risk factors and sociocultural influences on IPV. Programming for youth exposed to interparental violence must address attitudes condoning the use of violence as a means to resolve conflict, as well as beliefs that violence against women is acceptable. Although many men do not use violence as a method of control in intimate partnerships, there is evidence that cognitive restructuring regarding patriarchal value endorsement and approval of gender stereotyping is critical for some male perpetrators of IPV.

Collectively, studies of intimate partner violence using sociological perspectives have suggested there is a need for continued research examining risk factors for IPV perpetration and victimization that incorporate psychological, biological, and sociological influences. Without doubt, a more comprehensive approach to intimate partner violence research will allow for more effective policy and social service provisions. While the impact of sociocultural factors on cognitions and behavior cannot be understated, human nature cannot be fully understood without considering the role of biology and our evolutionary origins.

References

Anderson, K. L. (1997). Gender, status, and domestic violence: An integration of feminist and family violence approaches. *Journal of Marriage and the Family, 59,* 655–669.

Atkinson, M. P., Greenstein, T. N., & Lang, M. M. (2005). For women, breadwinning can be dangerous: Gendered resource theory and wife abuse. *Journal of Marriage and Family, 67,* 1137–1148.

Avakame, E. (1998). Intergenerational transmission of violence, self-control, and conjugal violence: A comparative analysis of physical violence and psychological aggression. *Violence and Victims, 13,* 301–316.

Bandura, A. (1969). *Principles of behavior modification.* New York, NY: Holt, Rinehart & Winston.

Bandura, A. (1973). *Aggression: A social learning analysis.* Englewood Cliffs, NJ: Prentice Hall.

Beaver, K. M., Barnes, J. C., May, J. S., & Schwartz, J. A. (2011). Psychopathic personality traits, genetic risk, and gene-environment correlations. *Criminal Justice and Behavior, 38,* 896–912.

Ben-David, S., & Schneider, O. (2005). Rape perceptions, gender role attitudes, and victim-perpetrator acquaintance. *Sex Roles, 53,* 385–399.

Bevan, E., & Higgins, D. (2002). Is domestic violence learned? The contribution of five forms of child maltreatment to men's violence and adjustment. *Journal of Family Violence, 17,* 223–245.

Bird, G. W., Stith, S. M., & Schladale, J. (1991). Psychological resources, coping strategies, and negotiation styles as discriminators of violence in dating relationships. *Family Relations, 40,* 45–50.

Brownmiller, S. (1975). *Against our will: Men, women, and rape.* New York, NY: Simon & Schuster.

Brownridge, D. (2006). Intergenerational transmission and dating violence victimization: Evidence from a sample of female university students in Manitoba. *Canadian Journal of Community Mental Health, 25,* 75–93.

Buzawa, E. S., & Buzawa, C. G. (1996). *Domestic violence: The criminal justice response.* Thousand Oaks, CA: Sage.

Caetano, R., Field, C. A., Ramisetty-Mikler, S., & McGrath, C. (2005). The 5-year course of intimate partner violence among White, Black, and Hispanic couples in the United States. *Journal of Interpersonal Violence, 20,* 1039–1057.

Capaldi, D., & Clark, S. (1998). Prospective family predictors of aggression toward female partners for at-risk young men. *Developmental Psychology, 34,* 1175–1188.

Catalano, S. (2012). *Intimate partner violence, 1993–2010.* Washington, DC: U.S. Department of Justice, Bureau of Justice Statistics.

Check, J. V. P., & Malamuth, N. M. (1983). Sex role stereotyping and reactions to depictions of stranger vs. acquaintance rape. *Journal of Personality and Social Psychology, 45,* 344–356.

Check, J. V. P., & Malamuth, N. M. (1985). An empirical assessment of some feminist hypotheses about rape. *International Journal of Women's Studies, 8,* 414–423.

Chen, P., & White, H. R. (2004). Gender differences in adolescent and young adult predictors of later intimate partner violence. *Violence Against Women, 10,* 1283–1301.

Chung, G. H., Tucker, M. B., & Takeuchi, D. (2008). Wives' relative income production and household male dominance: Examining violence among Asian American enduring couples. *Family Relations, 57,* 227–238.

Claes, J. A., & Rosenthal, D. M. (1990). Men who batter women: A study in power. *Journal of Family Violence, 5,* 215–224.

Coker, A. L., McKeown, R. E., Sanderson, M., Davis, K. E., Valois, R. F., & Huebner, S. (2000). Severe dating violence and quality of life among South Carolina high school students. *American Journal of Preventative Medicine, 19,* 220–227.

Daigneault, I., Hébert, M., & McDuff, P. (2009). Men's and women's childhood sexual abuse and victimization in adult partner relationships: A study of risk factors. *Child Abuse & Neglect, 33,* 638–647.

Daly, K., & Chesney-Lind, M. (1988). Feminism and criminology. *Justice Quarterly, 5,* 101–143.

Danis, F. S. (2003). The criminalization of domestic violence: What social workers need to know. *Social Work, 48,* 237–246.

Dankoski, M., Keiley, M., Thomas, V., Choice, P., Lloyd, S., & Seery, B. (2006). Affect regulation and the cycle of violence against women: New directions for understanding the process. *Journal of Family Violence, 21,* 327–339.

Delsol, C., & Margolin, G. (2004). The role of family-of-origin violence in men's marital violence perpetration. *Clinical Psychology Review, 24,* 99–122.

DeMaris, A. (1990). The dynamics of generational transfer in courtship violence: A biracial exploration. *Journal of Marriage and the Family, 52,* 219–231.

Dobash, R.E., & Dobash, R.P. (1979). *Violence against wives.* New York, NY: Free Press.

Doumas, D., Margolin, G., & John, R. S. (1994). The intergenerational transmission of aggression across three generations. *Journal of Family Violence, 9,* 157–175.

Ehrensaft, M. K., Cohen, P., Brown, J., Smailes, E., Chen, H., & Johnson, J. G. (2003). Intergenerational transmission of partner violence: A 20-year prospective study. *Journal of Consulting and Clinical Psychology, 4,* 741–753.

Fang, X., & Corso, P. (2008). Gender differences in the connections between violence experienced as a child and perpetration of intimate partner violence in young adulthood. *Journal of Family Violence, 23,* 303–313.

Farrington, D. P., Loeber, R., & Stouthamer-Loeber, M. (2003). How can the relationship between race and violence be explained? In D. F. Hawkins (Ed.), *Violent crime: Assessing race and ethnic differences* (pp. 213–237). New York, NY: Cambridge University Press.

Finkelhor, D., Hotaling, G. T., & Yllo, K. (1988). *Stopping family violence: Research priorities for the coming decade.* Newbury Park, CA: Sage.

Fischer, G. J., & Rivlin, E. (1971). Psychological needs of rapists. *British Journal of Criminology, 11,* 182–185.

Flood, M., & Pease, B. (2009). Factors influencing attitudes to violence against women. *Trauma, Violence, & Abuse, 10,* 125–142.

Foshee, V. A., Ennett, S. T., Bauman, K. E., Benefield, T., & Suchindran, C. (2005). The association between family violence and adolescent dating violence onset: Does it vary by race, socioeconomic status, and family structure? *Journal of Early Adolescence, 25,* 317–344.

Franklin, C. A. (2008). *Sorority affiliation and rape-supportive environments: The institutionalization of sexual assault victimization through vulnerability-enhancing attitudes and behaviors* (Unpublished doctoral dissertation). Washington State University, Pullman, WA.

Franklin, C. A., & Kercher, G. A. (2012). The intergenerational transmission of intimate partner violence: Differentiating correlates in a random community sample. *Journal of Family Violence, 27,* 187–199.

Franklin, C. A., & Menaker, T. A. (in press). Feminism, status inconsistency, and women's intimate partner victimization in heterosexual relationships. *Violence Against Women.*

Franklin, C. A., Menaker, T. A., & Kercher, G. A. (2012). Risk and resiliency factors that mediate the effect of family-of-origin violence on adult intimate partner victimization and perpetration. *Victim & Offenders: An International Journal of Evidence-Based Research, Policy, and Practice, 7,* 121–142. dio: 10.1080/15564886.2012.657288

Gelles, R. J. (1974). *The violent home.* Beverly Hills, CA: Sage.

Gelles, R. J. (1983). An exchange/social control theory. In D. Finkelhor, R. J. Gelles, G. T. Hotaling, & M. A. Straus (Eds.), *The dark side of families: Current family violence research* (pp. 151–165). Beverly Hills, CA: Sage.

Gelles, R. J., & Cornell, C. P. (1990). *Intimate partner violence in families.* Newbury Park, CA: Sage.

Gelles, R. J., & Straus, M. A. (1979). Determinants of violence in the family: Toward a theoretical integration. In W. Burr, R. Hill, F. I. Nye, & I. Reiss (Eds.), *Contemporary theories about the family* (Vol. 1, pp. 549–581). New York, NY: Free Press.

Gosselin, D. K. (2005). *Heavy hands: An introduction to the crimes of family violence.* New Jersey, NJ: Pearson Education.

Guille, L. (2004). Men who batter and their children: An integrated review. *Aggression and Violent Behavior, 9,* 129–163.

Heckert, D. A., Nowak, T. C., & Snyder, K. A. (1998). The impact of husbands' and wives' relative earnings on marital disruption. *Journal of Marriage and the Family, 60,* 690–703.

Hornung, C. A., & McCullough, B. C. (1981). Status relationships in dual-employment marriages: Consequences for psychological well-being. *Journal of Marriage and the Family, 56,* 131–146.

Hotaling, G. T., & Sugarman, D. B. (1986). An analysis of risk markers in husband to wife violence: The current state of knowledge. *Violence and Victims, 1,* 101–124.

Jin, X., Eagle, M., & Yoshioka, M. (2007). Early exposure to violence in the family-of-origin and positive attitudes towards marital violence: Chinese immigrant male batterers vs. controls. *Journal of Family Violence, 22,* 211–222.

Johnson, A. G. (2005). *The gender knot: Unraveling our patriarchal legacy.* Philadelphia, PA: Temple University Press.

Kaufman, J., & Zigler, E. (1987). Do abused children become abusive parents? *American Journal of Orthopsychiatry, 57,* 186–192.

Koss, M. P., Goodman, L., Browne, A., Fitzgerald, L., Keita, G., & Russo, F. (1994). *No safe haven: Male violence against women at home, at work, and in the community.* Washington, DC: American Psychological Association.

Kwong, M. J., Bartholomew, K., Henderson, A. J. Z., & Trinke, S. J. (2003). The intergenerational transmission of relationship violence. *Journal of Family Psychology, 17,* 288–301.

Lazarus, R. S., & Folkman, S. (1984). *Stress, appraisal, and coping.* New York, NY: Springer.

Lenton, R. L. (1995). Power versus feminist theories of wife abuse. *Canadian Journal of Criminology, 37,* 305–330.

Lorber, J. (2001). *Gender inequality: Feminist theories and politics.* Los Angeles, CA: Roxbury.

Lutze, F. E., & Symons, M. L. (2003). The evolution of domestic violence policy through masculine institutions: From discipline to protection to collaborative empowerment. *Criminology and Public Policy, 2,* 319–328.

MacMillan, R., & MacMillan, R. G. (1999). When she brings home the bacon: Labor-force participation and the risk of spousal violence against women. *Journal of Marriage and Family, 61,* 947–958.

Markowitz, F. E. (2001). Attitudes and family violence: Linking intergenerational and cultural theories. *Journal of Family Violence, 16,* 205–218.

McCord, J. (1988). Parental behavior in the cycle of aggression. *Psychiatry, 51,* 14–23.

Miedzian, M. (1991). *Boys will be boys: Breaking the link between masculinity and violence.* New York, NY: Doubleday.

Mignon, S. I., Larson, C. J., & Holmes, W. M. (2002). *Family abuse: Consequences, theories, and responses.* Boston, MA: Allyn & Bacon.

Mihalic, S. W., & Elliott, D. (1997). A social learning theory of marital violence. *Journal of Family Violence, 12,* 21–47.

O'Keefe, M. (1998). Factors mediating the link between witnessing interparental violence and dating violence. *Journal of Family Violence, 13,* 39–57.

Ono, H. (1998). Husbands' and wives' resources and marital dissolution. *Journal of Marriage and the Family, 60,* 674–689.

Perry, B. D., & Szalavitz, M. (2006). *The boy who was raised as a dog: And other stories from a child psychiatrist's notebook: What traumatized children can teach us about loss, love, and healing.* New York, NY: Basic Books.

Rada, R.T. (1978). *Clinical aspects of the rapist.* New York, NY: Grune & Stratton.

Reitzel-Jaffe, D., & Wolfe, D. A. (2001). Predictors of relationship abuse among young men. *Journal of Interpersonal Violence, 16,* 99–115.

Renner, L. M., & Slack, K. S. (2006). Intimate partner violence and child maltreatment: Understanding intra- and intergenerational connections. *Child Abuse & Neglect, 30,* 599–617.

Ridgeway, C. L. (1997). Interaction and the conservation of gender inequality: Considering employment. *American Sociological Review, 62,* 218–235.

Simonson, K., & Subich, L. M. (1999). Rape perceptions as a function of gender-role traditionality and victim-perpetrator association. *Sex Roles, 40,* 617–634.

Sonkin, D., Martin, D., & Walker, L. E. (1985). *Group treatment for men who batter women.* New York, NY: Singer.

Steinmetz, S. K. (1980). Violence prone families. *Annals of the New York Academy of Sciences, 347,* 351–365.

Stith, S. M., Rosen, K. H., Middleton, K. A., Busch, A. L., Lundeberg, K., & Carlton, R. P. (2000). The intergenerational transmission of spouse abuse: A meta-analysis. *Journal of Marriage and Family, 62,* 640–654.

Sullivan, S. (1996). Domestic violence is a serious problem for Black women. In K. L. Swisher (Ed.), *Domestic violence* (pp. 37–40). San Diego, CA: Greenhaven Press.

Tichenor, V. J. (1999). Status and income as gendered resources: The case of marital power. *Journal of Marriage and Family, 61,* 638–650.

Walker, L. (1979). *Battered women.* New York, NY: Harper & Row.

Wareham, J., Boots, D. P., & Chavez, J. M. (2009). A test of social learning and intergenerational transmission among batterers. *Journal of Criminal Justice, 37,* 163–173.

Whiting, J. B., Simmons, L. A., Havens, J. R., Smith, D. B., & Oka, M. (2009). Intergenerational transmission of violence: The influence of self-appraisals, mental disorders, and substance use. *Journal of Family Violence, 24,* 639–648.

Widom, C. S. (1989). The cycle of violence. *Science, 244,* 160–166.

Wright, J. P., & Boisvert, D. (2009). What biosocial criminology offers criminology. *Criminal Justice and Behavior, 36,* 1228–1240.

Wright, J. P., & Cullen, F. T. (2012). The future of biosocial criminology: Beyond scholars' professional ideology. *Journal of Contemporary Criminal Justice, 28,* 237–253.

Yick, A. G. (2001). Feminist theory and status inconsistency theory: Application to domestic violence in Chinese immigrant families. *Violence Against Women, 7,* 545–562.

Yllo, K. (1983). Sexual equality and violence against wives in American states. *Journal of Comparative Family Studies, 14,* 67–86.

Yllo, K. (1984). The status of women, marital equality, and violence against wives. *Journal of Family Issues, 5,* 307–320.

16

Some Kind of Madness

The Biosocial Origins of Intimate Partner Violence

Brian B. Boutwell
Sam Houston State University
Richard Lewis
Sam Houston State University

Violent acts perpetrated toward loved ones—including intimate partners who share our homes, our lives, and our affections—represent an especially egregious form of aggression to contemplate. There is no shortage of scholars in the academy, fortunately, who are willing to devote considerable effort to probing the origins of intimate partner violence (IPV). Generally absent (in the field of criminology specifically), however, has been an attempt to fully consider the possibility that biology might partially underpin the behaviors so closely scrutinized by IPV researchers.[1] This is not wholly unexpected, though, given that to even mention biology in the context of IPV research can often mean inviting criticism, rebuke, and censure from one's colleagues (See Pinker's [2002] discussion of Thornhill & Palmer's [2000] work on the biology of rape).

Nonetheless, the argument we present—drawing heavily on work conducted across multiple disciplines—is that violence, including IPV, is a natural behavior rooted in human biology and an outcome that should be expected given the evolutionary history of our species (Pinker, 2002; Thornhill & Palmer, 2000). At no point, though, do we argue that because IPV is natural, that it also "good" or "inevitable" or anything of the sort (Pinker, 2002). As scientists, we are agnostic to the morality of outcomes in nature—it is our calling to be dispassionate observers, *not* moral activists. As human beings, however, no mountain of empirical evidence would ever be tall enough to ethically justify the abuse of one person by another (Pinker, 2002). With these very obvious points in mind, we move forward into a discussion of why IPV exists, what causes it, and how biology might offer us a platform for better understanding these deleterious experiences.

A final point that we wish the reader to remember is that research on the topic of IPV is highly nuanced, and we recognize that we simply cannot cover every detail of it in the space permitted here. Fortunately, we have the excellent chapter written by our compatriots in this section to accompany our own. We reiterate this point, however, only to say that we recognize the multifaceted nature of studying IPV, and we concede that we do not do full justice to the topic as a whole. Nonetheless, our purpose is to alert the reader to the potential limitations of omitting biological controls from the study of IPV. To that end, we are well equipped to supply the reader with some insight.

Individual Differences: Where Do They Come From?

One does not need conference of a university degree or years in the academy to arrive at the conclusion that human beings differ widely on a host of outcomes. Variation is part of life on this planet, not just in our species but in every species. Variation is what makes evolution possible, and without it there would be no "decent with modification," to borrow the words of Darwin (1859). Indeed, differences exist for outcomes ranging from disease susceptibility to personality traits (Buckholtz et al., 2007; Stead, Senner, Reddick, & Lofgren, 1990). Moreover, no one—academic or lay person—disputes the *existence* of individual differences. Indeed, we would wager that little convincing is required to sway the reader in favor of a belief that humans are different from one another (if doubt remains, we recommend momentarily setting this volume aside and walking out into the world—our thesis will be utterly vindicated at that point).

Having agreed on the universality of individual differences, let us wade into the topic that many researchers find far less palatable, which is the source of those differences. In the past, social scientists have clung tightly to what they perceive as a comforting idea: most of the differences that exist between humans are the product of social/environmental processes (Pinker, 2002). If humans differ because of their environments, or how they are socialized in their environments, then it becomes easier to envision how behaviors that are especially problematic might be remedied (Pinker, 2002). Should these differences emanate from something biological, however, where does that leave us? Indeed, the fear of all things biological has pervaded the social sciences for decades, and the consequences have not been benign (Pinker, 2002). Quite possibly, social science research has done more harm than good to our understanding of behaviors like IPV. The reason for this is that many researchers have stubbornly refused to explore the idea that biological factors might partially account for why some individuals abuse their romantic partners and others do not.

Just because most criminologists have ignored biological influences on individual differences, however, this does *not* mean that these influences are unimportant. The fact that most researchers in the area of IPV continue to omit genetic factors from their research designs simply illustrates the pervading ignorance regarding the actual sources of variation in human behavior. There are now no less than four independent meta-analyses (Ferguson, 2010; Mason & Frick, 1994; Miles & Carey, 1997; Rhee & Waldman, 2002) and numerous reviews (Moffitt, 2005; Turkheimer, 2000) clearly illustrating that genes account for a significant proportion of the variance in aggressive and antisocial behavior in humans. In other words, part (indeed, a considerable part) of the reason that humans differ in their proclivity to be antisocial, aggressive, and violent toward one another is accounted for by differences between the DNA sequences of individuals in the population (Ferguson, 2010; Rhee & Waldman, 2002).

The Heritability of Intimate Partner Violence

What does this mean for research in the area of intimate partner violence specifically? Has there been any research directly aimed at examining the heritability of IPV? To be sure, the sheer number of studies examining the heritability of violence toward a romantic partner is more limited compared to the body of research examining the heritability of behavior more broadly defined. Even so, there is emergent evidence in this area suggesting that IPV, like every other measurable human behavior, is heritable (Turkheimer, 2000). Hines and Saudino (2004), for instance, examined a sample of twin siblings to directly explore genetic sources of variance on a measure of IPV. Their analyses revealed a small to moderate heritability estimate for measures of IPV. In other words, at least some of the variance in their measure of IPV was accounted for by genetic factors (i.e., approximately 15% to 25%, depending on the measure used) (Hines & Saudino, 2004).

In a more recent analysis, Barnes, TenEyck, Boutwell, and Beaver (2012) extended the work of Hines and Saudino (2004) by examining the heritability of IPV in a larger sample of twins contained within the National Longitudinal Study of Adolescent Health (Add Health). For their analyses, Barnes and his colleagues examined three indicators of IPV: (1) hitting one's partner, (2) injuring one's partner, and (3) forcing sexual behavior on one's partner. The findings from analysis of the Add Health data revealed significant heritability estimates for each of the indicators of domestic violence. Genetic factors, in this case, accounted for 24%, 54%, and 51% of the variance in each of the outcomes, respectively (Barnes, TenEyck et al., 2012).

How or Why Would Genes Even Matter?

Our sociologically inclined readers are, at this point, most likely standing at the ready to punch holes in our argument that genetic factors might partially explain why some individuals abuse their mates and others do not. We feel capable, however, of anticipating what some of this attack will look like. How, exactly (gripes the critic) would a gene matter for IPV? Surely, there is not one gene that "makes" someone physically assault his or her significant other? Indeed, this is true, there is not a single gene that wields this preternatural power (but then again, there has *never* been a modern biosocial researcher who has ever suggested such a ludicrous idea). Instead, there are hundreds of genes that contribute to variation in personality traits (we already mentioned this above) (Turkheimer, 2000). In short, personality traits are one avenue for extending genetic influences on overt forms of IPV.

Ali and Naylor (2013) recently provided an excellent overview of the psychological and biological contributors to IPV. We direct readers with additional interest in the topic to the work of these scholars (and as a result, we do not delve too deeply into the topics covered in their review). We do, however, highlight several findings of note that have bearing on the issue of personality traits and IPV. As Ali and Naylor (2013) point out, personality outcomes such as borderline personality disorder (BPD) tend to be overrepresented in populations of male abusers (see Else, Wonderlich, Beatty, Christie, & Staton [1993] for the original finding and citation). Importantly, Distel and his colleagues (2008) reported evidence that heritability estimates for BPD hovered around .40. In other words, roughly 40% of the variance in BPD was accounted for by genetic factors.

Clearly, BPD would not be the only personality construct expected to correlate with IPV, and Ali and Naylor (2013) discuss many of the other traits that may also be important in this regard. The point is that to understand how genes might contribute to variation in IPV, one possible avenue worth exploring centers on the personality traits that are associated with partner abuse. It should not be overlooked, moreover, that there may also be genetic influences on IPV victimization. There is an amassing body of evidence suggesting that victimization outcomes are influenced by genetic factors (Barnes, Boutwell, & Fox, 2012; Beaver, Boutwell, Barnes, & Cooper, 2009; Beaver, Boutwell, Barnes, DeLisi, & Vaughn, 2013; Beaver et. al, 2007; Boutwell et al., 2013). To the extent that certain personality traits correlate with vulnerability to IPV victimization (Ali & Naylor, 2013), it would stand to reason that heritability estimates for IPV victimization should be greater than zero.

The Source of the Missing Variance . . .

We should probably pause at this point and reflect on several of the most important points that we have just discussed. First, we referenced vast amounts of research underscoring the heritability of human behavior (Turkheimer, 2000).

Second, antisocial and aggressive behavior, too, are influenced heavily by genetic factors (Rhee & Waldman, 2002). Third, there is also emerging evidence that IPV is a trait, like all other human traits, that is influenced by genetic factors. To this point, however, we have left unspoken one clear pattern of findings. Namely, genes do not account for all the variance (i.e., 100%) in any of the traits—IPV included—that we have discussed. Clearly, this suggests that the environment matters. But here is the key point to ponder when attempting to understand the origins of IPV (beyond what genes are doing): *which* environment matters?

This will undoubtedly strike some readers as an odd question. What do we mean: "which environment?" Behavioral genetic and biosocial researchers distinguish between different types of environments, and not all environmental influences are created equal, so to speak (Beaver, 2008). Specifically, biosocial scholars demarcate shared from nonshared environments (Beaver, 2008). You might think of it in this manner: shared environments exert influences that make two siblings raised in the same homes similar to one another, while nonshared environments are the uniquely experienced occurrences that make siblings raised in the same home different from one another (Plomin & Daniels, 1987). The problem with most social science research is that it leaves these two environments hopelessly confounded with one another, thus rendering the researcher incapable of understanding which environment might be accounting for more variance in human behavior (Harris, 1995).

Behavior genetic research overcomes this difficulty, thankfully, and the results are likely to threaten many of the closely guarded truisms in the social sciences (Pinker, 2002). That same mountain of evidence that we already mentioned regarding the heritability of human behavior also clearly pointed toward the nonshared environment as the primary *environmental* contributor to human variation (Rhee & Waldman, 2002; Turkheimer, 2000). What does this really mean for research into the topic of IPV? It means that the shared environment, the aspect of human life that encompasses parental socialization and that serves as the virtual bedrock of many theories regarding IPV (Jewkes, 2002), may be a "red herring" as a causal agent in the developmental origins of romantic partner abuse.

But what about IPV research specifically that has incorporated behavior genetic approaches to data analysis? After all, we just mentioned two studies (Barnes, TenEyck et al., 2012; Hines & Saudino, 2004) that examined the heritable underpinnings of IPV—what did these scholars find in regard to the shared and nonshared environment? Not surprisingly, neither study produced evidence of a significant shared environmental influence on intimate partner violence. This is an important finding, so it bears repeating. Neither study found any evidence that what happens inside the home explains any of the variance in the outcome measures of intimate partner violence. So where, exactly, does this leave us? Because, as our colleagues writing from the sociological perspective have illustrated, aspects of the home, of learning, and of shared environmental socialization are the *sine qua non* of IPV scholarship outside biosocial research. Perhaps it is time, however, for a deeply reflective reassessment among IPV researchers.

Which Environment?

We do grant that the body of behavior genetic evidence bearing directly on IPV is limited. However, if we take into account what has been done (Barnes, TenEyck et al., 2012; Hines & Saudino, 2004), along with the broader corpus of behavior genetic research pertaining to antisocial and aggressive behavior (Rhee & Waldman, 2002), the findings are stacking up in a clear direction. The shared environment is unlikely to yield much in the way of a deep understanding of the origins of IPV. That leaves us then with the nonshared environment. It appears that if we are to understand the environmental factors that predict IPV—net of what genetic factors are doing—then we need techniques capable of delving into the role of the nonshared environment. Thankfully, biosocial researchers have exactly those types of tools at their disposal (Beaver, 2008).

To illustrate, consider a study conducted by one of the editors of this volume, Kevin Beaver (2008). Beaver analyzed data drawn from the Add Health data in order to examine nonshared environmental influences on delinquency. To tease out the influence of nonshared environments, Beaver utilized a technique known as *MZ difference scores*. Essentially, the approach involves subtracting the score of one identical twin on a given variable from his or her co-twin on that same variable to create a difference score for the siblings. Because identical twins share virtually all of their genetic material, any differences that exist between them should (theoretically) be in place because of the environment.

We do not delve into the findings of Beaver (2008) here. However, the study is illustrative because it provides interested researchers with a technique (MZ difference scores) and a dataset (the Add Health) that can be used to probe the nonshared environmental influences of IPV. The point, more broadly defined, is that sociologically inclined researchers have *no* more excuses. The techniques are becoming widely known, and the data are available to employ a biosocial approach to the study of IPV. We anxiously wait to see if this actually transpires. Our suspicion is that research concerning the genetic and environmental predictors of IPV will continue to grow. We hope that criminologists will take part in contributing in this regard.

The Evolution of IPV

There is yet another lens from which biosocial researchers can (and should) view the topic of IPV, and that is through the lens of evolution (Buss & Duntley, 2011; Daly & Wilson, 1996; Wilson & Daly, 1998). Darwin's theory represents, arguably, the greatest scientific achievement ever (let us not forget Alfred Russell Wallace, either). This may seem superfluous, but consider that no phenotype, trait, or behavior for any animal would exist were it not for some natural process (we recognize that this statement might upset some readers of the volume who endorse magical thinking

[Kirkpatrick, 1999; Pinker, 1997; 2002]). The theory of evolution gave us the ability to understand the mechanisms—natural and sexual selection—that created all the diverse and wonderful variation that exists on our planet. Let us consider an additional point before wading off into an evolutionary explanation of IPV—a point made explicitly and cogently by Buss and Duntley (2011). The point is this: we take for granted that mating relationships are intended to be conflict free, generally speaking, *all the time* (Buss & Duntley, 2011). What if, however, this is just not realistic given the evolution of our species? What if conflict, to some degree, is inherent?

Evolutionary psychology is an effort to apply the tenets of evolution as a way of understanding the human mind (Pinker, 1997, 2002). Think of it in this way, the whole of the human experience—thoughts, emotions, behavior, morality, and so on—emanate from our brains (Pinker, 1997). Moreover, our minds—our conscious awareness—is the product of our brain (Dennett, 1984) (a reality so amazing that Francis Crick [1995] called it the "astonishing hypothesis"). Also, what should not be forgotten is that the brain is a physical organ and it was "designed" by natural selection (Buss, 1995; Pinker, 1997). So how do you look for design elements in the human psyche? Is that even possible? Indeed, it is possible, and it is how evolutionary psychologists make their living every day (Buss, 1995).

IPV in Nonhuman Animals

Before moving too much further ahead, let us first take a step back and discuss some nonhuman organisms. What we hope will become clear is that conflict between mates is not isolated only to our species. Indeed, it is a well-entrenched aspect of the natural world. This brings us to some examples of IPV or more accurately, *sexual conflict*, within nonhuman animals (Andersson, 1994). The first example worth mentioning concerns the behavior of a coercive live-bearing fish species known as *Gambusia affinis* (or more commonly, the western mosquito fish) (Deaton, 2008). Within this particular species, males—which are smaller in size than females—reproduce via the use of an anal fin that has been modified to serve as a reproductive organ (known as the gonopodia). The mating strategy of the males involves thrusting their gonopodia at the females' reproductive area (known as the gonopore) with the goal being fertilization and impregnation (Deaton, 2008). For females, this thrusting can result in physical damage to their bodies. Essentially, males and females are in a constant state of conflict, the goal of both being to satisfy the imperative to reproduce and spread their genetic material into the next generation (Deaton, 2008; Ptacek & Travis, 1997).

Moving on, we can discuss some closer relatives of humans: nonhuman primates (monkeys and apes). There are many examples of sexual conflict within primates, but one that is engaged in by both human and nonhuman primates alike is the practice of infanticide. Several species of primates from rhesus macaques (monkey), *Macaca mulatta*, to chimpanzees (ape), *Pan troglodytes* (Arcadi & Wrangham, 1999; Bloom, 1997) engage in the practice of killing their offspring on occasion. What is important to remember is that primate females will not enter estrus (or are less likely to do so) while nursing a newborn offspring (Bloom, 1997). When younger or subordinate primate males overthrow an alpha, it becomes to the males' advantage to mate and father their own offspring. Females, however, if they are nursing offspring from another male, will not enter estrus until they are no longer actively caring for newborns (Bloom, 1997). In this case, infanticide—perhaps even violence toward some of the females—could be advantageous for the male. We will see momentarily how, even in humans, stepchildren might be an evolutionary trigger for IPV and sexual conflict (Buss & Duntley, 2011).

Beyond sexual conflict and infanticide, is there any reason to suspect that IPV might have evolved to solve ancient problems in the human species, and what exactly would those problems consist of? Buss and Duntley (2011) propose, in an extremely cogent manner, that sexual conflict theory (Parker, 1979) may provide just the type of evolutionary framework necessary to understand the ultimate origins of IPV. As they note, *sexual conflict* refers to a scenario when the reproductive "goals," so to speak, of men and women are different and perhaps diametrically at odds with one another, in the same fashion as discussed in other nonhuman organisms above (Andersson, 1994). Indeed, as these scholars point out, conflict between mates can arise over a number of predictable scenarios. For instance, concerns over frequency of intercourse, allocation of resources, and amount of parental investment are all activities where the overall genetic fitness of men versus women could be at odds with one another.

There could be a scenario, for example, where a male would benefit from lower levels of parental investment and more sexual intercourse (Buss, 1995). In this way, the male expends fewer resources, while at the same time increasing his odds of conceiving multiple offspring who carry his genes. Females, on the other hand would not be subject to these same benefits due to impregnation and may also face the possibility that the male is gone by the time the offspring is born (Andersson, 1994). We direct the reader to the work of Buss and Duntley (2011) for a more in-depth discussion of sexual conflict (as well as other outstanding articles and books and the subject: Andersson, 1994; Buss, 1995; Kenrick, 2011).

For now though, we can return to the issue of which "problems" intimate partner violence might solve in the ancient past of human beings. Buss and Duntley (2011) suggest that there might be nine: (1) mate poachers, (2) sexual infidelity, (3) pregnancy with another man's child (cuckoldry), (4) resource infidelity, (5) resource scarcity, (6) mate value discrepancies, (7) stepchildren, (8) mating termination, and (9) mate reacquisition. We do not spend an inordinate amount of time discussing each point, primarily because Buss and Duntley (2011) do an excellent job of laying out their thoughts and rationale behind each topic (also because of space concerns). Even so, it would behoove us to spend a bit of time delving in to each of the nine problems, if for no other reason than to offer the reader unacquainted with evolutionary psychology a brief foray into this important field of inquiry.

Mate poaching is a relatively straightforward concept to understand. Essentially, it refers to the threat of losing a mate to the advances of another. Males and females are both vulnerable to this outcome, males might lose out to a higher status male with more resources (Buss & Duntley, 2011), or females might lose out to another female who is considered more physically attractive (Buss & Duntley, 2011). The possibility exists, regardless of the motivation, that someone might swoop in and steal your mate should you fail to be vigilant. Typically, and Buss and Duntley point this out, violence that might emanate in a situation concerning mate poaching would likely be directed toward the individual attempting to steal a mate. This is not always the case though, because male jealously over losing a partner could inspire violence toward the mate herself (Peters, Shackelford, & Buss, 2002). When one considers that it might be easier—in some cases and for some males—to retain a mate through force (or threat of force) (Husárová, 2005) than to fight off a rival, it would make sense that IPV could be a viable tool for solving the problem of mate poaching and mate retention.

The second and third problems are interwoven so we can discuss them both together. For males, sexual infidelity on the part of a mate (Problem 2) opens the door for cuckoldry (Problem 3). As we mentioned earlier, genetic cuckoldry is no small issue in the ancestral environment. If ancestral males failed to pass along their genes—more specifically, if they spent resources on offspring they assumed were theirs yet were not—then quite simply they didn't become ancestors. Females, too, might have reason to be concerned over sexual infidelity as Buss and Duntley (2011) point out. Females are always certain that their child is their own (they carried it for nine months, after all), yet a male who is sexually unfaithful might ultimately fall more deeply in love with his liaison. Should that happen, the male might begin funneling resources away from the original female and her offspring, which could harm their survival chances long-term (Buss, 1995). Importantly, there is evidence that both circumstances—sexual infidelity and suspicion of pregnancy—are linked to the experience of IPV (Burch & Gallup, 2004; Charles & Perreira, 2007). Buss and Duntley (2011) are careful to point out that the evidence in this regard is only preliminary, yet it certainly suggests that an evolutionary explanation of IPV needs more in-depth exploration.

Resource infidelity (Problem 4) and resource scarcity (Problem 5) are also interrelated so they can be discussed together—especially given that one might flow directly from the other. Discussion over the allocation of resources—any newlywed, for instance, is probably quite familiar with the stress that money can drum up—can often prime the pump for spousal conflict (Figueredo & McCloskey, 1993). In situations where both resource infidelity (perhaps one mate is spending unwisely) or resource scarcity (perhaps one mate has lost a job and income streams are waning), Buss and Duntley predict that there should be an increase in the odds of IPV. While there is some evidence in favor of this argument (Buss & Duntley, 2011), much more empirical scrutiny is needed.

The sixth problem—mate value discrepancy—is an interesting phenomenon. As Buss and Duntley (2011) point out, mating couples rarely form at random. Humans usually assort on certain characteristics when choosing a mate (Boutwell, Beaver, & Barnes, 2012; Geary, Vigil, & Byrd-Craven, 2004; Pawłwski & Dunbar, 1999). Interestingly, Boutwell, Beaver and Barnes (2012) found evidence that humans even assort on overt antisocial behaviors, a finding that accords with prior research as well (Krueger, Moffitt, Caspi, Bleske, & Silva, 1998). Buss and Duntley (2011) suggest that if there are discrepancies between the "value" of a given mate then IPV becomes more likely. While this is certainly possible, it may also be that assortative mating for antisocial behavior might serve as a viable (perhaps more proximal) explanation for violence in this type of situation. If, as prior research suggests, individuals actively choose mates who display similar levels of antisocial behavior and aggression—then it stands to reason that the odds of IPV may go up just as a product of having two aggressive individuals in close proximity to one another (Moffitt, Caspi, Rutter, & Silva, 2001).

We have already mentioned that male chimpanzees are known to perpetrate infanticide to facilitate reproductive opportunities. For a male entering a new relationship with a female who already has children, those offspring represent an expense (regarding resource investment) that has no payoff genetically speaking. For females, the children from a previous relationship may force a conflict of sorts regarding, as Buss and Duntley (2011; see also Daly & Wilson, 1996; Rohwer, Herron, & Daly, 1999) phrase it, "mating effort" versus "parental effort" (p. 416). Essentially, should the female invest energy in raising her offspring or in conceiving new offspring with her current partner? What might result is a decision to withhold sexual access to the new partner, or at least curtail the number of opportunities to reproduce (because the mother is focused more readily on parenting). Conflicts of interest such as the one just described could open the door to partner violence, yet more research is needed in this regard.

The final evolutionary scenarios that Buss and Duntley (2011) describe involve terminating a mateship and reacquiring a mate once a relationship has ended. Violence associated with the end of a relationship is documented in the literature in the form of stalking, threat making, and even violence toward the mate who walked away (Meloy, 2007). To the extent that violence, or the threat of violence, prompts a reproductive partner to stay (or return), such a behavior could be favored by natural selection because of its ability to increase the chances of the male to pass along genes into the next generation. Admittedly, some of the ideas suggested by Buss and Duntley (2011), as well as other evolutionary scholars (Wilson & Daly, 1998), are speculative, and all are in need of close empirical scrutiny.

As with any testable hypotheses, some evolutionarily informed predictions about IPV may hold up to empirical inquiry and others will not. Nonetheless, this does not obviate the need to explore the origins of IPV using the vantage point of evolution. The point, however, is that males and females in our species (and others as well) are not always striving toward the same goals (evolutionarily and reproductively speaking) (Buss, 1995). Moreover, moving beyond the romantic notion that all relationships should, when functioning "normally," be conflict free, may present avenues for research capable of yielding deeper insight regarding the ultimate origins of intimate partner violence and why it exists at all—not just in our species, but others as well.

Concluding Thoughts

This chapter, in a microcosm, captures the overarching goal of this edited volume. Specifically, we endeavored to probe the biosocial origins of a specific behavior—intimate partner violence—by using several academic disciplines (all biosocial in nature). On a larger plane, however, we also sought to demonstrate an overarching idea about the study of human behavior. Namely, that any explanation of behavior that excludes biological concepts, quite frankly, is empirically destitute. One simply cannot hope to offer a satisfactory and full explanation of animal behavior without an understanding of an organism's biology, environmental exposure, and social interactional styles. And never forget, humans are animals, too.

We are primates who walk on two legs, cure diseases, probe our evolutionary origins, and compile edited volumes attempting to understand our nature, but we are, nonetheless, animals. We are not above this fact so we should not automatically assume that our evolutionary past and biological makeup are irrelevant for a full understanding of our behavioral tendencies. Intimate partner violence, as abhorrent as it might be to contemplate, is not a behavior foreign in the animal kingdom. Other species also exhibit displays of sexual conflict. Importantly, our closely related primate cousins engage in a range of behaviors directly analogous to IPV (Smuts & Smuts, 1993). Abuse of romantic partners—both physical and emotional—moreover is a human universal appearing across cultures and societies the world over (Walker, 1999). In other words, IPV is not solely a Western phenomenon, a product of modernity, or some odd cultural artifact (Buss & Duntley, 2011).

The evidence outlined in this chapter is converging on several very important points regarding the origins of IPV. First, a significant portion of the answer to the question of "why is there variation in the tendency to commit IPV" involves genes (Barnes, TenEyck et al., 2012). Indeed, genetic factors accounted for an appreciable portion of the variance in multiple indicators of IPV using independent data sources (Barnes, TenEyck et al., 2012; Hines & Saudino, 2004). Although more research in this regard is needed, our very educated guess (centering on existing behavior genetic research) is that a similar pattern of findings will continue to emerge. Second, the shared environment does not appear to account for much of the variance in antisocial behavior in general, or IPV in particular (Barnes, TenEyck et al., 2012; Beaver, 2008). For scholars who maintain a dogged commitment to purely environmental theories of IPV (see the chapter by Menaker & Franklin for a review), it appears to be time for a reevaluation of research agendas. At best, these scholars are incapable of interpreting their findings because they lack appropriate controls for genetic factors (Beaver, 2009). At worst, findings gleaned from prior IPV research are completely misspecified due to unmeasured genetic factors.

Moving forward, it is our hope that scholars of IPV will see the current chapter, as well as the prior work mentioned herein, as a jumping off point. In truth, existing biosocial research does threaten some of the deeply held beliefs about why some individuals abuse their mates. That is the nature of science, though. Closely held hypotheses simply must be shed at certain intervals when new evidence emerges. To persist in the face of solid empirical data is almost perverse and completely antithetical to the enterprise of doing science. If the ultimate goal is to see the occurrence of IPV decline until it exists as a distance memory in our species, it would make sense to use every tool to understand the phenomenon (Thornhill & Palmer, 2000). Intimate partner violence is built into our biology, perhaps, but this does not mean that it is entirely intractable. There is much to be done, yet we are optimistic that biosocial research will do much to navigate the path forward. Moreover, we are confident (perhaps naïvely so) that the debate sparked with this volume will inspire a new generation of scientists to take up the challenge of understanding IPV through a biosocial lens.

Note

1. Certainly, important work in this area has been undertaken by scholars such as Margot Wilson, Martin Daly, Randy Thornhill, Craig Palmer, and others as well. However, we are referring to work conducted by classically trained criminologists, of which there is much less.

References

Ali, P. A., & Naylor, P. B. (2013). Intimate partner violence: A narrative review of the biological and psychological explanations for its causation. *Aggression and Violent Behavior, 18*(3), 373–382.

Andersson, M. B. (1994). *Sexual selection*. Princeton, NJ: Princeton University Press.

Arcadi, A. C., & Wrangham, R. W. (1999). Infanticide in chimpanzees: Review of cases and a new within-group observation from the Kanyawara study group in Kibale National Park. *Primates, 40*(2), 337–351.

Barnes, J. C., Boutwell, B. B., & Fox, K. A. (2012). The effect of gang membership on victimization: A behavioral genetic explanation. *Youth Violence and Juvenile Justice, 10*(3), 227–244.

Barnes, J. C., TenEyck, M., Boutwell, B. B., & Beaver, K. M. (2012). Indicators of domestic/intimate partner violence are structured by genetic and nonshared environmental influences. *Journal of Psychiatric Research, 47*(3), 371–376.

Beaver, K. M. (2008). Nonshared environmental influences on adolescent delinquent involvement and adult criminal behavior. *Criminology, 46*(2), 341–369.

Beaver, K. M. (2009). *Biosocial criminology: A primer*. Dubuque, IA: Kendall/Hunt.

Beaver, K. M., Boutwell, B. B., Barnes, J. C., & Cooper, J. (2009). The biosocial underpinnings to adolescent victimization: Results from a longitudinal sample of twins. *Youth Violence and Juvenile Justice, 7*, 223–228.

Beaver, K. M., Boutwell, B. B., Barnes, J. C., DeLisi, M., & Vaughn, M. G. (2013). Exploring the genetic origins of adolescent victimization in a longitudinal sample of adoptees. *Victims and Offenders, 8*(2), 148–163.

Beaver, K. M., Wright, J. P., DeLisi, M., Daigle, L. E., Swatt, M. L., & Gibson, C. L. (2007). Evidence of a gene × environment interaction in the creation of victimization: Results from a longitudinal sample of adolescents. *International Journal of Offender Therapy and Comparative Criminology, 51*, 620–645.

Bloom, H. K. (1997). *The Lucifer principle: A scientific expedition into the forces of history*. New York, NY: Atlantic Monthly.

Boutwell, B. B., Beaver, K. M., & Barnes, J. C. (2012). More alike than different: Assortative mating and antisocial propensity in adulthood. *Criminal Justice and Behavior, 39*(9), 1240–1254.

Boutwell, B. B., Franklin, C. A., Barnes, J. C., Tamplin, A. K., Beaver, K. M., & Petkovsek, M. (2013). Unraveling the covariation of low self-control and victimization: A behavior genetic approach. *Journal of Adolescence, 36*, 657–666.

Buckholtz, J. W., Callicott, J. H., Kolachana, B., Hariri, A. R., Goldberg, T. E., Genderson, M., . . . Meyer-Lindenberg, A. (2007). Genetic variation in MAOA modulates ventromedial prefrontal circuitry mediating individual differences in human personality. *Molecular Psychiatry, 13*(3), 313–324.

Burch, R. L., & Gallup, G. G., Jr. (2004). Pregnancy as a stimulus for domestic violence. *Journal of Family Violence, 19*(4), 243–247.

Buss, D. M. (1995). Evolutionary psychology: A new paradigm for psychological science. *Psychological Inquiry, 6*(1), 1–30.

Buss, D. M., & Duntley, J. D. (2011). The evolution of intimate partner violence. *Aggression and Violent Behavior, 16*(5), 411–419.

Charles, P., & Perreira, K. M. (2007). Intimate partner violence during pregnancy and 1-year post-partum. *Journal of Family Violence, 22*, 609–619.

Crick, F. (1995). *Astonishing hypothesis: The scientific search for the soul.* New York, NY: Scribner.

Daly, M., & Wilson, M. I. (1996). Violence against stepchildren. *Current Directions in Psychological Science, 5*(3), 77–81.

Darwin, C. (1859). *On the origin of the species by means of natural selection, or preservation of favored races in the struggle for life*. London, UK: Murray.

Deaton, R. (2008). Factors influencing male mating behaviour in Gambusia affinis (Baird & Girard) with a coercive mating system. *Journal of Fish Biology, 72*(7), 1607–1622.

Dennett, D. (1984). *Elbow room: The varieties of free will worth wanting*. New York, NY: Oxford Press.

Distel, M. A., Trull, T. J., Derom, C. A., Thiery, E. W., Grimmer, M. A., Martin, N. G., . . . Boomsma, D. I. (2008). Heritability of borderline personality disorder features is similar across three countries. *Psychological Medicine, 38*(09), 1219–1229.

Else, L., Wonderlich, S. A., Beatty, W. W., Christie, D. W., & Staton, R. D. (1993). Personality characteristics of men who physically abuse women. *Hospital and Community Psychiatry, 44*, 54–58.

Ferguson, C. J. (2010). A meta-analysis of normal and disordered personality across the life span. *Journal of Personality and Social Psychology, 98*(4), 659–667.

Figueredo, A. J., & McCloskey, L. A. (1993). Sex, money, and paternity: The evolutionary psychology of domestic violence. *Ethology and Sociobiology, 14*(6), 353–379.

Geary, D. C., Vigil, J., & Byrd-Craven, J. (2004). Evolution of human mate choice. *Journal of Sex Research, 41*(1), 27–42.

Harris, J. R. (1995). Where is the child's environment? A group socialization theory of development. *Psychological Review, 102*(3), 458–489.

Hines, D. A., & Saudino, K. J. (2004). Genetic and environmental influences on intimate partner aggression: A preliminary study. *Violence and Victims, 19*(6), 701–718.

Husárová, B. (2005). Adaptive mating strategies and the problem of mate retention. *Anthropologischer Anzeiger, 63*(3), 283–287.

Jewkes, R. (2002). Intimate partner violence: Causes and prevention. *Lancet, 359*(9315), 1423–1429.

Kenrick, D. T. (2011). *Sex, murder, and the meaning of life: A psychologist investigates how evolution, cognition, and complexity are revolutionizing our view of human nature*. New York, NY: Basic Books.

Kirkpatrick, L. A. (1999). Toward an evolutionary psychology of religion and personality. *Journal of Personality, 67*(6), 921–952.

Krueger, R. F., Moffitt, T. E., Caspi, A., Bleske, A., & Silva, P. A. (1998). Assortative mating for antisocial behavior: Developmental and methodological implications. *Behavior Genetics, 28*(3), 173–186.

Mason, D. A., & Frick, P. J. (1994). The heritability of antisocial behavior: A meta-analysis of twin and adoption studies. *Journal of Psychopathology and Behavioral Assessment, 16*(4), 301–323.

Meloy, J. R. (2007). Stalking: The state of the science. *Criminal Behavior and Mental Health, 17*, 1–7.

Miles, D. R., & Carey, G. (1997). Genetic and environmental architecture of human aggression. *Journal of Personality and Social Psychology, 72*, 207–217.

Moffitt, T. E. (2005). The new look of behavioral genetics in developmental psychopathology: Gene-environment interplay in antisocial behaviors. *Psychological Bulletin, 131*(4), 533.

Moffitt, T. E., Caspi, A., Rutter, M., & Silva, P. A. (2001). *Sex differences in antisocial behavior*. Cambridge, UK: Cambridge University Press.

Parker, G. A. (1979). Sexual selection and sexual conflict. In M. S. Blum & A. N. Blum (Eds.), *Sexual selection and reproductive competition among insects* (pp. 123–166). London, UK: Academic Press.

Pawłwski, B., & Dunbar, R. I. (1999). Impact of market value on human mate choice decisions. *Proceedings of the Royal Society of London. Series B: Biological Sciences, 266*(1416), 281–285.

Peters, J., Shackelford, T. K., & Buss, D. M. (2002). Understanding domestic violence against women: Using evolutionary psychology to extend the feminist functional analysis. *Violence and Victims, 17*(2), 255–264.

Pinker, S. (1997). *How the mind works*. New York, NY: W. W. Norton.

Pinker, S. (2002). *The blank slate: The modern denial of human nature*. New York, NY: Penguin.

Plomin, R., & Daniels, D. (1987). Why are children in the same family so different from one another? *Behavioral and Brain Sciences, 10*, 1–16.

Ptacek, M. B., & Travis, J. (1997). Mate choice in the sailfin molly, Poecilia latipinna. *Evolution, 51*(4), 1217–1231.

Rhee, S. H., & Waldman, I. D. (2002). Genetic and environmental influences on antisocial behavior: A meta-analysis of twin and adoption studies. *Psychological Bulletin, 128*(3), 490–529.

Rohwer, S., Herron, J. C., & Daly, M. (1999). Stepparental behavior as mating effort in birds and other animals. *Evolution and Human Behavior, 20*(6), 367–390.

Smuts, B. B., & Smuts, R. W. (1993). Male aggression and sexual coercion of females in nonhuman primates and other mammals: Evidence and theoretical implications. *Advances in the Study of Behavior, 22*, 1–63.

Stead, W. W., Senner, J. W., Reddick, W. T., & Lofgren, J. P. (1990). Racial differences in susceptibility to infection by Mycobacterium tuberculosis. *New England Journal of Medicine, 322*(7), 422–427.

Thornhill, R., & Palmer, C. T. (2000). *A natural history of rape: Biological bases of sexual coercion*. Cambridge, MA: MIT Press.

Turkheimer, E. (2000). Three laws of behavior genetics and what they mean. *Current Directions in Psychological Science, 9*(5), 160–164.

Walker, L. E. (1999). Psychology and domestic violence around the world. *American Psychologist, 54*, 21–29.

Wilson, M. I., & Daly, M. (1998). Lethal and nonlethal violence against wives and the evolutionary psychology of male sexual proprietariness. In R. E. Dobash & R. P. Dobash (Eds.), *Rethinking violence against women* (pp. 199–230). Thousand Oaks, CA: Sage.

Discussion Questions

CHAPTERS 15 AND 16

1. Researchers in the area of intimate partner violence (IPV) have continuously omitted genetic factors from their theoretical frameworks and research designs. What are the reasons for solely focusing on social environments when studying IPV? Are there any drawbacks to such an approach?
2. What does the available evidence indicate about the heritability of IPV? How could the study of personality traits be used to find genetic influences on overt forms of IPV?
3. Scholars often focus on home environments when deciphering the causes of IPV. Does behavioral genetic research find support for these types of environmental influences? Is there adequate evidence to believe that children learn to be violent from observing their parents? What other factors influence behavior?
4. Feminist theories argue that IPV is a symptom of a patriarchal society—where power structures encourage male dominance and female subordination. How would evolutionary psychology explain IPV? Likewise, what have nonhuman organisms taught us about IPV? How are the feminist perspective and the evolutionary perspective different?
5. The concept of "gender role socialization" has been used to explain the gender gap in IPV perpetration. However, as noted by Boutwell and Lewis, IPV has been used by both sexes to solve problems. Discuss some of the problems both sexes have faced in a mateship. Given the available evidence, how would we explain gender variations in IPV?
6. How does biosocial research threaten some of the deeply held beliefs about why some individuals abuse their mates? By understanding IPV through a biosocial lens, can researchers help reduce IPV in the future? Or would sociological explanations be more effective for reducing IPV?

17

Parents, Peers, and Socialization to Institutions in Childhood and Adolescence

Implications for Delinquent Behavior

Carter Rees

Arizona State University

Jacob T.N. Young

Arizona State University

Introduction

Few things provoke sociologists as easily or strongly as the perceivably improper invocation of "biology" as an explanatory device, especially when done on sociologists' own turf.

—Freese, Li, & Wade, 2003

While not official, disciplines often informally claim particular topics as their property. The violation of rules, and the social causes, is a key territory in the social sciences for which the property deed traces back nearly 400 years (e.g., Thomas Hobbes's *Leviathan*, 1668/1994). The leitmotif of a scientific understanding of crime and criminality in sociology has been the focus on the performance of social institutions. Institutions are "webs of interrelated rules and norms that govern social relationships" (Brinton & Nee, 1998, p. 8). They are "the humanly devised constraints that shape human interaction" and define "the structure of incentives in human exchange" (North, 1990, p. 3). By directing attention toward the functioning of institutions, sociologists seek to understand variation in crime and criminality as a consequence of how the family, peer groups, schools, and the criminal justice system are organized. An institutional perspective examines how laws and norms are generated and the conditions under which they are effective. This perspective is intrinsic to public responses to widely publicized criminal events. In such cases, individuals point to the failure of formal and informal organizations to protect citizens: the rise of out-of-wedlock children, overcrowding in schools, ineffective gun laws, broken mental health systems, distrust of police, and so on. From this perspective, crime and deviance are viewed as the outcome of weak institutions. Institutions are weakened when organizations, or "networks of actors performing a variety of tasks oriented toward a common purpose" (Messner & Rosenfeld, 2004, p. 91), lack sufficient control capacity (Hechter, 1987). Therefore, this framework distinguishes institutions from organizations:

> Most individuals do not experience the full extent of any one institution, but rather, experience only a subset of that institution. Thus the family can be considered an institution as the social norms and formal rules that define families, such as what constitutes a family, the purpose of family, and how they operate. However, most individuals are raised within one or a limited number of familial organization(s). An individual's understanding of the institution of family will be largely defined by their experiences within their own familial organization. (Lee, 2012, p. 12)

In this way, the primary intellectual contribution of a sociological approach is the analysis of social control by clear identification of the "machinery" regarding institutions that deal with crime and deviance.

As an illustration and device for conceptual clarity (see North, 1990, pp. 4–5), consider a group of children learning to play basketball. The actors involved are the players, coaches, and referees. These actors have goals that are defined by the rules of basketball. The players on one team try to score more points than the players on the other team. The coaches teach the players strategies for scoring points that comply with the behavioral rules of the game. The rules are those that describe what can and cannot be done in seeking to achieve these goals. For example, you have to dribble the ball rather than run with it in your hands, you cannot physically interfere with the movement of another player by tackling or pushing, after a point is scored the scoring team gives possession of the ball to the other team, and so on. The referees try to provide unbiased enforcement of these rules (i.e., monitoring and sanctioning).

Players who are observed violating the rules are sanctioned by forfeiture of possession and/or having a foul registered against them. In addition to these rules, coaches also teach norms that guide behavior on the court. Although you do not have to pass the ball to other players, passing is a more efficient strategy for scoring points than one individual being a "ball hog." Coaches transmit this information by encouragement of "playing as a team," and players develop an endogenous preference for following the norm if they are rewarded by the coach, by other players, and by winning.

This simple example illustrates the analytical lens through which an understanding of crime is viewed in sociological criminology. Institutions exist outside the individual (Durkheim, 1895/1938), representing a property of a collectivity (Messner & Rosenfeld, 2004). Therefore, understanding the social machinery that generates and sustains institutions is fundamental for an analysis of the formal and informal constraints that define institutions. Regardless of within-actor differences, though not independent of them, investigation of the mechanisms by which rules and norms are transmitted to and between actors is essential for an understanding of social control.

In addition, the basketball example illustrates an important conceptual distinction made in criminology leading to two separate research questions. We maintain the conceptual distinction emphasized by Gottfredson and Hirschi (1990) that crime is a behavioral act, and criminality is the propensity to engage in an act. This distinction is important because it allows analytic separation of the processes that lead to the sanctioning of particular behaviors and the processes that lead to variability in participation in such behaviors. Such a distinction has a long history in the sociological analysis of deviance between why individuals engage in deviant behavior and why behaviors are considered deviant (e.g., Durkheim, 1895, 1895/1938; Erikson, 1966; Goffman, 1959). Any explanation of phenomena must specify the variation it seeks to explain as well as the causal mechanism(s) that produces such variation. In other words, what is the explicandum and what are the explicans? Recognizing that crime and criminality are not conceptually identical is necessary for accurate identification of the variability that is to be explained by an argument. In the example above, we can ask why there are particular rules against behavior (i.e., questions about the properties of crime) and why some individuals are more likely to violate these rules (i.e. questions about the properties of criminality).

In this chapter, we argue that such an institutional perspective is an irreplaceable component for developing a coherent understanding of crime and criminality. We begin by describing the importance of socialization and agents of socialization. We finish by revisiting the distinction between questions about crime and questions about criminality and the utility of bridging an institutional perspective with a biosocial perspective for answering such questions. We provide a discussion of how the framing of crime and deviance through an institutional approach that focuses on socialization and agents of socialization provides a syntax that is compatible with the perspective in biosocial criminology. Rather than balkanize, we emphasize how recent developments in the empirical realm of biosocial criminology serve as a catalyst for establishing an intellectual commune of these two perspectives.

Transmission of Rules and Norms: Socialization

Sociological approaches to understanding deviant behavior and criminality often begin with socialization as a primary causal mechanism. Whether it is theories of insufficient socialization to prosocial behavior (e.g., Gottfredson & Hirschi, 1990; Hirschi, 1969; Nye, 1958; Reckless, 1967), or socialization to illegal or deviant behavior (Akers, 1998; Dishion, Spracklen, Andrews, & Patterson, 1996; Sutherland, 1924), or over-socialization to institutionally defined goals (Merton, 1938), the focus is clearly on the social processes that facilitate or impede socialization. However, in many cases, socialization is used as an explanatory device, yet it is often left unexplained or defined. In this section, we define socialization within an institutional framework.

All societies have formal (e.g., laws) and/or informal (e.g., social norms) rules that coordinate behavior to achieve particular goals. Socialization is the transmission of the rules and norms that define an institution to the actor. It is the process of teaching "naïve individuals skills, behaviors, values and motivations needed for competent functioning" (Maccoby, 2007, p. 13) within dyads and groups in which the child is growing up. We are all familiar with such rules: "don't take other peoples' things," "keep your hands to yourself," "treat others how you want to be treated." Agents of socialization are the conduit through which this transmission occurs (e.g., parents, teachers, coaches, peers, spouses, employers). The effectiveness of these rules as devices for socially preferable outcomes is highly dependent on the ability of actors to effectively transmit these rules. Generally, the goal is the internalization of social norms that remain relevant from generation to generation and offer guidance for appropriate and responsible behavior deemed acceptable in a wide variety of social contexts (Maccoby, 2007). In this way, socialization, or the transmission of rules and norms to other actors, facilitates social integration by "greasing the wheels" of social interaction.

In addition to effective within-institution socialization, the realization of socially defined goals is heavily dependent on the extent of overlap between institutions (see Goffman, 1982). For example, the rules to which children are socialized in the family (e.g., respect authority), are the same rules that help with integration and success as they enter school. This rule-isomorphism across arenas of social interaction means that socialization in one context will have consequences for behavior in separate contexts. This cohesiveness creates cumulative-advantage, or cumulative-disadvantage, embedding actors in particular configurations of rules and norms. The process of socialization, therefore, has important consequences for actors as they navigate key institutions throughout the life course.

Viewed through an institutional perspective, an understanding of variability in crime and criminality should focus on two properties of organizational performance. First is understanding the effectiveness of agents as devices for socializing individuals to the rules that characterize an institution. In the next section, we examine the empirical research indicating the properties of parenting that lead to effective socialization of children. Second, the overlap between institutions with respect to rules and goals is also important for understanding variability in crime and criminality. Following the section of parenting, we examine the role of peers as agents of socialization. This section discusses research suggesting how socialization by parents influences interaction with peers and susceptibility to negative peer influence.

Parents as Agents of Socialization

Parents are the first and primary agents of socialization during childhood and arguably into adolescence and young adulthood. Parents are the first to have the opportunity to protect, nurture, and express affection and warmth to offspring (Grusec & Davidov, 2007). Parents are also the first to offer guidance for life's more routine but socially demanded tasks of good hygiene, table manners, and other basic tasks. These familial bonds can never be formally severed like other relationships. As such, most Western cultures have formal and legally binding rules and regulations for parents regarding minimal care requirements of children in the home. Beyond broad legal codes, parents want to have appropriately socialized children simply because they live in close proximity to them and it makes life easier if both parties agree on suitable behavior (Grusec & Davidov, 2007).

But a primary purpose for the socialization of a child extends beyond the vertical, dyadic parent-child relationship. Being well socialized by definition prepares children to eventually move into more horizontal relationships with others, be able to recognize the needs of others, have empathy for them, and respond in an appropriate way. That is, children eventually move into relationships with others of equal status (e.g., peers), possibly placing the child in the position of nurturer instead of being nurtured. The ability to negotiate the rules of these relationships and cooperate is essential. Socialization, at least in Western cultures, is designed to hand off the child to be a socially responsible actor within society, alongside others, and to achieve some level of self-regulation. Parents are not just purveyors of information, they are "setting the stage for their children to become well-functioning members of the social group" (Grusec & Davidov, 2007, p. 284).

According to Grusec and Goodnow (1994), intergenerational transmission of norms depends on two things: the accuracy of the child's perception of the message, and the acceptance or rejection of the message. The goal is to have the child behave in a manner that is voluntary, not out of fear or coercion, and consistent with social conventions. How then, does a parent instill, guide, and prepare a child to be a well-functioning and socialized member of dyads and groups outside the family? What are the mechanisms by which culture, rules, and norms are transferred? The answers to these questions are complex. Mechanisms of parental socialization of children can be found in theoretical frameworks ranging from stimulus-response and social learning to psychoanalytics and self-regulation (see Bandura, 1977; Block & Block, 1980; Eisenberg, Smith, Sadovsky, & Spinrad, 2004; Maccoby, 2000; Patterson, 1982). However, much of what we know about parents and the socialization of children centers on the parenting style employed in the home and the quality of the dyadic relationship between these two actors.

The nature of the parent-child relationship has received and continues to receive much attention in academic literature (Steinberg, 2001). The study of the parent-child dyad has gone through methodological and technological advances along with shifts in theoretical viewpoints (Collins, Maccoby, Steinberg, Hetherington, & Bornstein, 2000; Maccoby, 2007). The theoretical and empirical depth of research on this singular relationship is expansive and rich. As such, Grusec and Davidov (2007) suggest a behavioral systems approach as an organizing tool, one that incorporates Bugental's (2000) domains of social life: protection and security, control, group identification, and mutual reciprocity (see also Bugental & Goodnow, 1998; Bugental & Grusec, 2006; Grusec & Davidov, 2010). The separation of the socialization process into each of these domains explicitly recognizes that "different mechanisms underlying socialization are operating and different practices are needed to achieve the desired goal of the domain" (Grusec & Davidov, 2007, p. 287). Again, the effective socialization of a child is a complex parental task but the common thread that binds these domains together is the quality of the relationship between the parent and the child. Of particular importance is the level of warmth, support, understanding, and sensitivity the parent shows the child while parenting.

PROTECTION AND SECURITY

Attachment theory (Bowlby, 1969/1982) focuses on an infant's obvious physical and emotional need for parental protection and security. Children under stress actively seek the parent (usually the mother) by crying or, if mobile, crawling or walking. Parents in turn offer protection from the stressor or negative environmental stimuli by holding, soothing, and generally comforting (Cassidy, 1999). Attachment is considered a normative behavior and therefore children will vary in their levels of attachment to the primary caregiver. Bowlby (1958) argued that the most important variable determining the level of attachment is "the extent to which the mother has permitted clinging and following, and all the behaviour associated with them, or has refused them" (p. 370). A child becomes securely attached if the mother is sensitive in her response to the distress, can accurately determine if the danger is no longer threatening the child, and successfully soothe and comfort. Insecure attachment is a result of inconsistencies in a mother's response to child distress or an outright failure to respond. That is, a child may minimize efforts to cry out or move closer in proximity to the mother or may remain upset when maternal attempts to soothe are made.

An important concept within Bowlby's attachment theory is that of the development of internal working models of a primary caregiver's type of response to the child's stress or overtures for proximity (Bretherton, 1997). Over time a child will develop a sense of how the caregiver responds, which is based on the caregiver's prior responses. That is, a child's expectation of the parent's responsiveness is based on the parent's performance history. A possible consequence of a poor early attachment history, if internalized, is a maladaptive working model of attachment carried forward, serving as a foundation for future relationships with different people. Sensitive protection leads to positive socialization and effective regulation of negative emotions thus making stressors less threatening (Bretherton, 1997; Bretherton, Golby, & Cho, 1997). The result of this type of socialization is that the child can modulate behavior better, develop empathy for others, and form a trusting bond with the parent.

CONTROL

It is important to emphasize that protection and security are only part of the parental socialization equation. According to Grusec and Davidov (2007), the positive socialization effect of parental protection and security is situational in nature, given during times of illness, physical danger, or emotional distress by providing a safe environment. But parents also assume a role of power and authority in the parent-child dyad. This makes them responsible for rule setting, enforcement, and discipline. In other words, parents occupy a position of control.

The control domain of socialization primarily consists of the type of parenting style used in the home. Maccoby (1992, 2007) reports this line of research has a long history, identifying different types of parenting styles. She states,

> The question underlying much modern parenting research, then, is not whether parents should exercise authority and children should comply, but rather how parental control can best be exercised so as to support children's growing competence and self-management. Thus it is increasingly understood that strong parent agency and strong child agency are not incompatible. Both can be maintained within a system of mutually understood realms of legitimate authority, though this understanding must be progressively renegotiated as children grow older. (Maccoby, 2007, pp. 36–37)

Steinberg (2001) strongly advocates the authoritative parenting style as the most effective in accomplishing positive socialization and therefore prosocial outcomes. This style emphasizes a warm and supportive relationship between parent and child but one that clarifies limits and keeps order. The balance of rule setting and discipline within a supportive context allows the child to be an active agent in decision-making processes. This style is in opposition to the punishment and power assertion style of the authoritarian parent. This parent is seen as inaccessible, infallible, and withdrawn (Baumrind, 1971). A child's feeling of powerlessness in the face of the authoritarian parent can lead to outbursts of anger and a general feeling of a lack of control of his or her environment. The authoritative parenting style promotes internalization through coparticipation in decision making, consistency in the enforcement and definition of behavior boundaries, within a supportive context. Authoritarian parenting is forceful, leaving the child feeling as if he or she has no choice in any decision-making process about behavioral standards. This can lead to a lack of empathy for others, inflexibility in rule negotiation in other relationships, and generally being poorly socialized.

MUTUAL RECIPROCITY

Effective parenting from an authoritative standpoint clearly defines the relationship of the parent-child dyad as being hierarchical in nature. Parents are in a position to control and guide a child's behavior in a manner that increases attachment and is in the best interests of the child. A key component of this parenting style is the allowance of the active voice of the child. This is not just a symbolic gesture. Effective socialization and internalization of norms requires parental action in response to a child's reasonable requests for attention and care. In other words, there must be a mutual reciprocity in calls for action between the parent and child (see Beaulieu & Bugental, 2007).

Simmel (1950) viewed the act of reciprocity as foundational to social cohesion and equilibrium: "All contacts among men rest on the schema of giving and returning the equivalents" (p. 387). Homans (1961) described exchange as social currency. Cialdini (2007) refers to reciprocation as a weapon of influence. The reciprocation rule is very basic; if you do something nice for me, I will do something nice for you. Both authoritative and authoritarian parents can exact compliance to rules and norms from their children. Authoritarian parents resort to displays of power, coercion, compulsion, and threatened or actual physical force to achieve the end goal of a child's compliance (Baumrind, 1996, 1997). However, the authoritative parent is in the advantageous position to receive willing compliance through the act of reciprocity (Maccoby & Martin, 1983; Martinez & Forgatch, 2001). This type of exchange is not only consistent with the authoritative style of sensitivity and warmth but also promotes positive socialization through cooperation. Reciprocal social and emotional exchanges with parents help children and adolescents develop important social skills (e.g., cooperation, values acquisition, and relational harmony) that can be applied in new settings and new relationships.

GROUP IDENTIFICATION

Humans are social animals (Spinoza, 1677/2005). There is a strong human need for social interactions (Baumeister & Leary, 1995); humans intentionally spend vast amounts of time in close proximity with each other. These relationships are crucial to survival. We rely on these relationships for goods and services, protection, knowledge, support, and guidance. Therefore, group identification is an important aspect of the human life course. A natural consequence is parents and family are the first group with which a child identifies and wants to be a part of in order to meet the innate human need for belongingness (see Allport, 1954).

The previously mentioned domains of socialization all share a common theme in that parents socialize by direct verbal or physical actions involving the child. Protective parents cuddle and soothe the stressed child, authoritative parents exercise control via communication exchanges with the child, and reciprocal verbal and physical exchanges between parents and children increase child compliance to rules and behavioral norms. However, within the group identification domain much of the socialization takes place by observational learning of principles. The type of learning that occurs within the group with which the child readily identifies with is closely tied with Bandura's (1977) social learning theory. Watching and learning routines and rituals through participation and observation with a trusted parent is a key mechanism to the socialization process and the acquisition of societal norms.

Observational learning by imitation and modeling is a less explicit form of socialization. The child observes and imitates or models the behaviors of those who are important to him or her to learn about routines and rituals. Socialization can happen between parent and child even during the most mundane everyday tasks that often are beneficial to the group as a whole. These tasks may simply be doing chores or housework. Grusec, Goodnow, and Cohen (1996) found that household tasks when done to benefit others predicted children's prosocial behaviors. Children see parents cleaning the house and therefore learn via observation and imitation, a socially conventional behavior. This type of social learning also aids in a child's cognitive development. For example, research shows children as young as 3 years old have an understanding of what it means to shop for groceries, having done so by observing parents (Farrar & Goodman, 1992; see also Hudson & Fivush, 1991). It is suggested that children have developed a script for what it means to do such an activity and the skills required for planning to do so (Guavain, 2001). Planning for an event such as this requires an organization of knowledge and a plan of action (e.g., what to buy and where to find it in the store). The social experience of seeing a parent shop for groceries increases the planning capabilities of the child. Learning by observation and imitation may not be the most powerful way for a child to internalize group or societal norms; however, it is important to the history of the relationship between the parent and child. Parents are fundamental in helping the child function appropriately in the social group because of their shared social identity (see Grusec, 2011).

Peers as Agents of Socialization

The prior section discussed research identifying the causal mechanisms by which parental socialization to institutional content occurs and linked them to research on childhood antisocial behavior and social interaction. In this section, we direct our attention toward adolescence and focus on peers as agents of socialization. This directed attention is important for several reasons. First, the sudden onset of delinquency in early adolescence has garnered substantial attention in criminological research, and the influence of peers has been at the center. A defining characteristic of developmental approaches in criminology (e.g., Thornberry, 1987; Weis & Hawkins, 1981) is that the magnitude of the effects of theoretically important constructs are dynamic over the life course, and developmental shifts explain the relationship between age and crime. Multiple studies find that the effect of peers differs across adolescence (e.g., Jang, 1999, 2002; Mears & Field, 2002; Thornberry, Lizotte, Krohn, Farnworth, & Jang, 1994; Warr 1993) suggesting that important dynamics are at play during this stage of development. Second, the properties of peer relationships are fundamentally different from those with parents due to differing role structures. Parents are an authority, whereas peer relationships are egalitarian and roles are negotiated. Moreover, peer relationships provide an aspect of agency that is absent from parental relationships. Simmel (1950) recognized this by stating that there are relationships that we cannot change and those that we intentionally seek, echoing the old adage "we cannot chose our family, but we can choose our friends." The emergence of agency is important, because a litany of research has debated the question of how adolescents select their friends and are, in turn, selected by others. We discuss this line of research by treating socialization by parents as the precursor for understanding the role of interactional- and cumulative-continuity in relationships.

The extent to which actors take the rules regarding social interaction into this context have ramifications for how they help construct and navigate this network and developmental period in the life course. We maintain our institutional perspective by examining two examples of how important it is to understand rule-isomorphism across institutions. First, we examine how the development of skills for forming and maintaining relationships with others influences friendship selection. In essence, how socialization in one context may have consequences for behavior in separate contexts. Then, we examine how ineffective or the weakening of parental socialization can make individuals susceptible to institutions that are not isomorphic with other institutions (e.g., family, school, criminal justice system). Particularly where there is a lack of overlap between the formal sanctions of the criminal justice system and the informal gestures of disapproval from peers. We argue that during this period, there is a punctuation in concern over acceptance from peers. This notion of susceptibility to influence is important because it recognizes that, while youth may be aware of the rules they were socialized to by their parents and reinforced by the school, goals may develop that conflict with the rules of parents and the school (norms, school codes, laws). Novelty may be the hallmark of adolescence because youth are exposed to new situations, people, and rules. Individuals meet persons from others schools, increasingly interact with the opposite sex, deal with physical development, and negotiate emerging adulthood. As adolescents interact without the presence of parents, the rules and norms of conduct may be less clear, or undefined. Moreover, rules and norms learned from parents may not be appropriate to the situation. Sexual behavior and substance use are well-researched behaviors for which incentive structures develop within peer groups to socialize individuals to such behavior. Such behaviors are rewarded, and as youth engage in the behavior and are rewarded for such behavior, this acts as a feedback mechanism because such individuals have a vested interest in maintaining such a system of rewards.

RELATIONSHIPS WITH PEERS

To the extent that rules governing social relationships learned from parents overlap with those that govern social interaction among peers, individuals will be better equipped to form sustained relationships in adolescence. This continuity is important because it suggests that earlier sequences have important implications for later outcomes. The social development model (Weis & Hawkins, 1981) posits that socialization to institutions occurs sequentially: children who do not have good familial bonds will have greater difficulty bonding to teachers and peers in school compared to those who are already bonded to parents. In their examination of continuity in maladaptive behavior of individuals over a 30-year period, Caspi, Elder, and Bem (1987) note that the way individuals interact with their environment is a necessary part of understanding such continuity. They first note that maladaptive behavior can select individuals into particular environments that elicit such behavior, a process referred to as cumulative-continuity. Second, Caspi et al. (1987) note that individuals may develop particular interactional styles that elicit particular responses in situations. Interactional-continuity occurs when individuals "learn a particular behavioral style that continues to 'work' in similar ways" (Caspi et al., 1987, p. 309). However, if behavioral styles of interaction (e.g., tantrums that are rewarded by parents) characterized by maladaptive behavior are carried into these situations, then they will conflict with interaction among peers. This continuity in the way an individual responds may produce cumulative-continuity in the types of relationships that individuals experience. As noted by Steinberg and Morris (2001), "adolescents bring many qualities to their peer relationships that develop early in life as a result of socialization experiences in the family" (p. 93). In this way, parental socialization plays the role of providing youth the skills to interact with their peers. This is important to emphasize because "peer groups" do not simply happen, but are constructed and reconstructed through social interaction, and this action is governed by informal rules.

The connection between parental socialization and consequences for later peer relationships can be seen in the research examining the quality of relationships among delinquent youth during adolescence. Perhaps one of the most important rules regarding relationships involves reciprocation and equity, or the rewarding of one's gestures (Gouldner, 1960). If actors differ on their ability to reciprocate, then particular structural configurations will develop. As Schaefer (2012) has shown, when "actors share a common definition of value and seek higher value partners, lower value actors will be excluded and ultimately turn to one another" (p. 1272). The connection here is to the argument that individuals who engage in delinquency lack requisite skills for reciprocating relationships.

The social disability model (see Hansell & Wiatrowski, 1981) holds that social skills among those who engage in delinquency are immature, leading to poor relations with others. The consequence is a lack of stable, mutual relationships. A review by Marcus (1996) noted that compared to those who do not engage in delinquency, delinquent youth have greater conflict and less cohesion with parents, greater conflict in friendship relationships, more impulsivity, lower social competency, and poorer social skills. Snijders and Baerveldt (2003) found that, compared to relationships between nondelinquent youth, relationships among those who engage in delinquency are made and broken faster. Similarity with respect to delinquency increases the chances that a tie will form, but these ties, once formed, dissolve faster. Baerveldt, Van Rossem, Vermande, and Weerman (2004) found that, though delinquents and nondelinquents tend to be nominated as friends the same number of times by delinquents as nondelinquents, they are less likely to nominate nondelinquents than delinquents. These findings are consistent with the notion that interactional continuity leads to particular responses from peers producing cumulative continuity in friendships.

Influence

SOCIALIZATION AND STATUS IN ADOLESCENCE

The importance of parental socialization in conjunction with cross-institution overlap in rules depends on the extent to which individuals are susceptible to peer influence. As Weis and Hawkins (1981) emphasize, "the more inadequate the [parental] socialization to conformity, the more likely to the socialization to nonconformity [by peers]" (p. 76). In other words, parental socialization acts as a buffer against negative peer influence. Early work on peer influence in criminology focused on socialization to subcultural values that confer status for engaging in delinquent behavior, particularly violence (e.g., Cohen, 1955; Wolfgang, 1958). These positions argued that those who engage in delinquency reject the goals of class-based institutions and develop their own rules endorsing delinquency, and sanction group members for noncompliance.

However, one of the most important findings in the literature on "subcultures" is that strong endorsement or internalization of violence and antisocial behavior values is lacking (e.g., Erlanger, 1974; Sampson & Bartusch, 1998). This is mainly due to the lack of structural properties necessary for groups to develop and enforce norms (see Hechter, 1987). Fine and Kleinman (1979, p. 3) emphasize this as confusion that subcultures are the same thing as subsocieties, and as a consequence the notion that individuals can "enter into" these delineated groups. Rather than viewing adolescence as a separate society with distinct values (e.g., Coleman, 1961), socialization by way of peers during this period has largely focused on learning the conditions in which particular rules apply or do not.

As Matza and Sykes (1961) argued, much of the behavior engaged in by delinquents from a moral- or rules-based position is consistent with adult society. As they state "rather than standing in opposition to conventional ideas of good conduct, the delinquent is likely to adhere to the dominant norms in belief but render them ineffective in practice by holding various attitudes and perceptions which serve to neutralize the norms as checks on behavior" (Matza & Sykes, 1961, pp. 712–713). This indicates that it is the conditional structure of rules, or the conditions under which they apply (see Diefenbach & Opp, 2007), that is the content of socialization. In other words, youth do not replace what they have been socialized to by their parents. Rather, they learn different conditions under which the rules apply.

An abundance of research has examined how adolescents are socialized to the ways in which status is attained among peers. Given that peers become more influential during adolescence (Krosnick & Judd, 1982), the role of status, or position in a hierarchy of relationships, during adolescence and the link to risky behaviors has received a great deal of attention. Scholars have drawn on Matza's (1964) notion of "drifting" into delinquency by linking this with the dynamics of popularity and status in adolescent friendship networks. For example, Hagan (1991) argued that some adolescent groups are characterized as a "party subculture" where risky behaviors (e.g., smoking, drinking) are normative and reinforced. Consistent with Matza and Sykes's (1961) argument above, these are not distinct values (i.e., risk), but are manifested in different behaviors. Several studies indicate that popularity is associated with higher alcohol use (Mayeux, Sandstrom, & Cillessen, 2008), onset and frequency of sexual activity (Mayeux et al., 2008; Prinstein, Meade, & Cohen, 2003), and marijuana use (Prinstein, Brechwald, & Cohen, 2011). More recent work (Kreager, Rulison, & Moody, 2011; Moody, Brynildsen, Osgood, Feinberg, & Gest, 2011; Prinstein et al., 2011) has begun to unravel the complicated relationship between social status, risky behaviors, and health-related outcomes. Overall, this work indicates that status is a critical link in the social influence process (see Prinstein et al., 2011, for a review).

Moffitt's (1993) dual taxonomy theory focuses specifically on social status with respect to delinquency. During adolescence, individuals who show a history of persistent antisocial behavior become focal actors in their social networks. The behavior of persistently antisocial individuals is then mimicked by those without a history of antisocial behavior. A large body of research indicates that children with behavior problems (e.g., aggression) are rejected and maintain peripheral positions in social networks during the early years of schooling (see Newcomb, Bukowski, & Pattee, 1993, for a review). However, as children enter adolescence these characteristics become less detrimental to social relationships and may actually be reinforced. In this way, the cumulative disadvantage in relations with peers may be knifed-off due to changes that are occurring in the status structure during adolescence.

It is important to emphasize that status is a "rival good" (see Kitts, 2006) because it has the property of subtractability. If I get some status, then there is less for you to get. As a consequence, rival goods will produce competition, particularly when such resources are scarce. This property helps explain why adolescent relationships can be so vicious and why individuals without a history of physical and relational aggression as interactional styles engage in such behavior during this period. This is an important example of how the context in which an individual is embedded is important for understanding variation in the person's behavior.

Integration With Biosocial Perspective

In this chapter, we have argued that an institutional perspective is an irreplaceable component for developing a coherent understanding of crime and criminality. Crimes are those behaviors that violate rules established and enforced by formal organizations. Criminality is variability among individuals in their involvement in these behaviors. Recognizing that crime and criminality are not conceptually identical is necessary for accurate identification of the variability that is to be explained by an argument. As we have emphasized throughout this chapter, understanding criminal behavior requires examination of how agents of socialization effectively transmit rules to actors and how the content of these rules overlap across institutions. In this way, the research questions are about how institutions operate. How are these rules transmitted (socialization)? To what extent are these rules consistent across institutions (isomorphism)? These are questions that are fundamentally different from those that examine variation in criminality.

For example, Beaver and Connolly (2013) have recently noted that multiple studies of twins suggest that about 50% of the variation in antisocial behavior is explained by genetic variability. The other 50% is nongenetic variation and has mainly been attributed to nonshared environment as opposed to shared environment (40% and 10%, respectively). It is important to emphasize that this claim involves the partitioning of variance into genetic and nongenetic causes. Shared and nonshared environment do not "explain" variability in a mechanistic sense, but simply account for the residual variability that is not due to genetics. In these models, "explained" is used in the statistical sense of accounting for residual variation. What we want to emphasize here is that "socialization" is asking a different question (focusing on different variation) than biosocial approaches. We stress this point because any perspective on a topic requires precision in identification of what is being explained. An argument cannot be criticized for not addressing a question it does not seek to answer. Biosocial arguments do not speak to the social machinery that operates in institutions because the question of interest is variability in criminality. However, an institutional perspective is not beyond reproach, because it cannot ignore significant research on the causes of criminality. To the extent that these perspectives focus on different manifestations of variability, the approaches in the discipline will not see eye to eye because they are looking at different things.

In this final section, we seek to coordinate this focus by examining two key areas by which a synthesis of institutional and biosocial perspectives is occurring. First, we examine how research in the biosocial approach has provided empirical evidence for theoretical assumptions made by institutional approaches. Second, we discuss how the blossoming area of research on susceptibility (gene × environment correlations and interactions) provides a micro-foundation for understanding why the effects of social contexts vary across persons.

Socialization arguments assume that humans have a preference for social approval, affiliation, and being included in the group. Parsons (1991) argued that this is "a need-disposition in the actor's own personality structure, relatively independently of any instrumentally significant consequences" (p. 37). Baumeister and Leary (1995) have argued that humans are fundamentally motivated to form interpersonal attachments: We "need to belong."

From an institutional approach, however, these notions of preferences for interaction have been assumed or inferred from behavioral evidence without precise identification of the causal mechanism(s) involved. Emerging research in neuroscience indicates that we have evolved structures for affiliation. There is compelling evidence to suggest that the reward structures of the human brain are specifically designed for social interaction. This is to say there is a neural basis by which social integration deters behavior. Smith and Stevens (2002) suggest that endogenous opioid systems in the human brain are regulated by social interaction: "[t]he pathways into the core brain systems controlling human comfort pass through social interaction . . . [E]volution has attached a neuro-sociological rudder to social interaction—one that steers behavior along a course constrained by the comfort of interactants" (p. 107). If social interaction influences the comfort levels of individuals, then reciprocated action is not entirely attributable to normative systems. Rather, evolution has designed the reward structure of the human brain to prefer cooperative action. We are essentially "addicted" to cooperative social interaction (see Panksepp, 1998). The idea here is that we have a drive for interaction, but we still have to understand the rules of the game if we are to interact.

A second area for synthesis involves the examination of differential susceptibility (see Simons & Lei, 2013, for a review). Though studies have partitioned the variability into genetic and nongenetic components, research utilizing genetic variables as predictors has yielded few main effects on behavior. Understanding the moderating role that genetics play is important. As Walsh and Ellis (2007) have noted, understanding the correlation between genes and the environment provides a way to "conceptualize the indirect way (there is no direct way) that genes help to determine what aspects of the environment will and will not be important to us" (p. 202). By definition, research on gene-by-environment interactions show that the effect of some context varies across individuals. This allows the researcher to identify a micro-foundation for explaining the nonuniform effects of context on individuals. In this way, the goal is to explain the dispersion of the effect. However, the central tendency of the effect, or why context matters in the first place, is outside the focus of this approach. This is where a synthesis with an institutional perspective is necessary. Contextual variability is hardly a novel concept, the importance of susceptibility was long ago recognized by Edwin Sutherland (1956) who argued that susceptibility is "a preliminary stage of behavior" and is "merely incomplete criminality" (p. 42). Sutherland went on to emphasize that engaging in the criminal event is a function of the interaction the actor has with his or her social environment. Susceptible individuals may be led to engage in crime because of exposure to a criminogenic environment. The point being that the explicandum lies in understanding why the contextual factors matter.

We conclude this section and the chapter by reminding the reader of the basketball game example used above to illustrate the language and focus of an institutional approach in criminology. Basketball is defined by particular rules that actors must follow, involves the transmission of norms and strategies for achieving goals, and the monitoring and sanctions of particular rule infractions. For the sake of argument, let us assume that a player's height is completely explained by his or her genes (i.e., no environmental influence). In such a framework, we can ask why taller players score more points and are more prevalent then shorter players (i.e., questions about criminality). We can also ask why certain norms emerge (e.g., the "don't be a ball hog" norm) and why certain rules may not be effectively monitored and enforced (i.e., questions about crime). However, as we have emphasized in this section, the intersection of these questions is a fruitful area for intellectual syntheses. We can ask whether taller players are more likely to be called for a foul or more likely to play a particular position (i.e., a gene × context interaction). The point here is that recognizing when analytical approaches diverge or intersect is necessary for evaluation, comparison, and synthesis.

References

Akers, R. L. (1998). *Social learning and social structure: A general theory of crime and deviance.* Boston, MA: Northeastern University Press.

Allport, G. (1954). *The nature of prejudice.* Reading, MA: Addison-Wesley.

Baerveldt, C., Van Rossem, R., Vermande, M., & Weerman, F. M. (2004). Students' delinquency and correlates with strong and weaker ties: A study of students' networks in Dutch high schools. *Connections, 26,* 11–28.

Bandura, A. (1977). *Social learning theory.* Englewood Cliffs, NJ: Prentice Hall.

Baumeister, R. F., & Leary, M. R. (1995). The need to belong: Desire for interpersonal attachments as a fundamental human motivation. *Psychological Bulletin, 117,* 497–529.

Baumrind, D. (1971). Current patterns of parental authority. *Developmental Psychology, 4,* 1–103.

Baumrind, D. (1996). The discipline controversy revisited. *Family Relations, 45,* 405–414.

Baumrind, D. (1997). The discipline encounter: Contemporary issues. *Aggression and Violent Behavior, 2,* 321–345.

Beaulieu, D. A., & Bugental, D. B. (2007). An evolutionary approach to socialization. In J. E. Grusec & P. D. Hastings (Eds.), *Handbook of socialization: Theory and research* (pp. 71–95). New York, NY: Guilford Press.

Beaver, K. M., & Connolly, E. J. (2013). Genetic and environmental influences on the development of childhood antisocial behavior: Current evidence and directions for future research. In C. L. Gibson & M. D. Krohn (Eds.), *Handbook of life-course criminology* (pp. 43–55). New York, NY: Springer.

Block, J. H., & Block, J. (1980). The role of ego-control and ego-resiliency in the organization of behavior. In W. A. Collins (Series ed.), *Minnesota Symposia on Child Psychology Series: Vol. 13. Development of cognition, affect, and social relations* (pp. 39–101). Hillsdale, NJ: Erlbaum.

Bowlby, J. (1958). The nature of the child's tie to his mother. *International Journal of Psychoanalysis, 39,* 350–371.

Bowlby, J. (1982). *Attachment and loss: Attachment* (Vol. 1). New York, NY: Basic Books. (Original work published 1969)

Bretherton, I. (1997). Bowlby's legacy to developmental psychology. *Child Psychiatry and Human Development, 28,* 33–43.

Bretherton, I., Golby, B., & Cho, E. (1997). Attachment and the transmission of values. In J. E. Grusec & L. Kuczynski (Eds.), *Parenting and children's internalization of values* (pp. 103–134). New York, NY: Wiley.

Brinton, M., & Nee, V. (Eds.). (1998). *The new institutionalism in sociology.* Stanford, CA: Stanford University Press.

Bugental, D. B. (2000). Acquisition of the algorithms of social life: A domain-based approach. *Psychological Bulletin, 26,* 187–209.

Bugental, D. B., & Goodnow, J. J. (1998). Socialization processes. In N. Eisenberg (Ed.), *Handbook of child psychology: Social, emotional, and personality development* (Vol. 3, pp. 389–462). New York, NY: Wiley.

Bugental, D. B., & Grusec, J. E. (2006). Socialization processes. In N. Eisenberg (Ed.), *Handbook of child psychology: Social, emotional, and personality development* (Vol. 3, pp. 366–428). New York, NY: Wiley.

Caspi, A, Elder, G. H., Jr., & Bem, D. (1987). Moving against the world: Life-course patterns of explosive children. *Developmental Psychology, 23,* 308–313.

Cassidy, J. (1999). The nature of the child's ties. In J. Cassidy & P. Shaver (Eds.), *The handbook of attachment* (pp. 3–20). New York, NY: Guilford Press.

Cialdini, R. B. (2007). *Influence: The psychology of persuasion.* New York, NY: Harper/Collins.

Cohen, A. K. (1955). The sociology of the deviant act: Anomie theory and beyond. *American Sociological Review, 30,* 5–14.

Coleman, J. S. (1961). *The adolescent society: The social life of the teenager and its impact on education.* New York, NY: Free Press.

Collins, W. A., Maccoby, E. E., Steinberg, L., Hetherington, E. M., & Bornstein, M. H. (2000). Contemporary research on parenting: The case for nature and nurture. *American Psychologist, 55,* 218–232.

Diefenbach, H., & Opp, K. D. (2007). When and why do people think there should be a divorce? An application of the factorial survey. *Rationality and Society, 19,* 485–517.

Dishion, T. J., Spracklen, K. M., Andrews, D. W., & Patterson, G. R. (1996). Deviancy training in male adolescent friendships. *Behavior Therapy, 27,* 373–390.

Durkheim, E. (1895). *The division of labor in society.* New York, NY: Free Press.

Durkheim, E. (1938). *The rules of sociological method.* (G. E. G. Catlin, Ed.). Chicago, IL: University of Chicago Press. (Original work published 1895).

Eisenberg, N., Smith, C. L., Sadovsky, A., & Spinrad, T. L. (2004). Effortful control: Relations with emotion regulation, adjustment, and socialization in childhood. In R. R. Baumeister & K. D. Vohs (Eds.), *Handbook of self-regulation: Research, theory, and applications* (pp. 259–282). New York, NY: Guilford Press.

Erikson, K. T. (1966). *Wayward puritans.* New York, NY: Wiley.

Erlanger, H. S. (1974). The empirical status of the subculture of violence thesis. *Social Problems, 22*(2), 280–292.

Farrar, M. J., & Goodman, G. S. (1992). Developmental changes in event memory. *Child Development, 63,* 173–187.

Fine, G. A., & Kleinman, S. (1979). Rethinking subculture: An interactionist analysis. *American Journal of Sociology, 85*(1), 1–20.

Freese, J., Li, J. C. A., & Wade, L. D. (2003). The potential relevances of biology to social inquiry. *Annual Review of Sociology, 29*(1), 233–256.

Goffman, E. (1959). *The presentation of self in everyday life*. New York, NY: Doubleday.

Goffman, E. (1982). *Interaction ritual: Essays on face-to-face behavior*. New York, NY: Doubleday.

Gottfredson, M., & Hirschi, T. (1990). *A general theory of crime*. Palo Alto, CA: Stanford University Press.

Gouldner, A. W. (1960). The norm of reciprocity: A preliminary statement. *American Sociological Review, 25*(2), 161–178.

Grusec, J. E. (2011). Socialization processes in the family: Social and emotional development. *Annual Review of Psychology, 62*, 243–269.

Grusec, J. E., & Davidov, M. (2007). Socialization in the family: The roles of parents. In J. E. Grusec & P. D. Hastings (Eds.), *Handbook of socialization: Theory and research* (pp. 284–308). New York, NY: Guilford Press.

Grusec, J. E., & Davidov, M. (2010). Integrating different perspectives on socialization theory and research: A domain-specific approach. *Child Development, 81*, 687–709.

Grusec, J. E., & Goodnow, J. J. (1994). The impact of parental discipline methods on the child's internalization of values: A reconceptualization of current points of view. *Developmental Psychology, 30*, 4–19.

Grusec, J. E., Goodnow, J. J., & Cohen, L. (1996). Household work and the development of concern for others. *Developmental Psychology, 32*, 999–1007.

Guavain, M. (2001). *The social context of cognitive development*. New York, NY: Guilford Press.

Hagan, J. (1991). Destiny and drift: Subcultural preferences, status attainments, and the risks and rewards of youth. *American Sociological Review, 56*, 567–582.

Hansell, S., & Wiatrowski, M. D. (1981). Competing conceptions of delinquent peer relations. In G. F. Jensen (Ed.), *Sociology of delinquency, current issues* (pp. 93–108). Beverly Hills, CA: Sage.

Hechter, M. (1987). The emergence of cooperative social institutions. In M. Hechter, K. D. Opp, & R. Wippler (Eds.), *Social institutions: Their emergence, maintenance, and effects* (pp. 13–33). Hawthorne, NY: Aldine de Gruyter.

Hirschi, T. (1969). *Causes of delinquency*. Berkeley: University of California Press.

Hobbes, T. (1994). *Leviathan*. Indianapolis, IN: Hackett Publishing Company. (Original work published 1668)

Homans, G. C. (1961). *Social behavior: Its elementary forms*. New York, NY: Harcourt Brace.

Hudson, J. A., & Fivush, R. (1991). Planning in the preschool years: The emergence of plans from general event knowledge. *Cognitive Development, 6*, 393–415.

Jang, S. J. (1999). Age-varying effects of family, school, and peers on delinquency: A multilevel modeling test of interactional theory. *Criminology, 37*(3), 643–685.

Jang, S. J. (2002). The effects of family, school, peers, and attitudes on adolescents' drug use: Do they vary with age? *Justice Quarterly, 19*(1), 97–126.

Kitts, J. A. (2006). Collective action, rival incentives, and the emergence of antisocial norms. *American Sociological Review, 71*(2), 235–259.

Kreager, D. A., Rulison, K., & Moody, J. (2011). Delinquency and the structure of adolescent peer groups. *Criminology, 49*, 95–127.

Krosnick, J. A., & Judd, C. M. (1982). Transitions in social influence at adolescence: Who induces cigarette smoking? *Developmental Psychology, 18*(3), 359–368.

Lee, J. S. (2012). An institutional framework for the study of the transition to adulthood. *Youth & Society*. doi:10.1177/0044118X12450643

Maccoby, E. E. (1992). The role of parents in the socialization of children: An historical overview. *Developmental Psychology, 28*, 1006–1017.

Maccoby, E. E. (2000). Parenting and its effects on children. *Annual Review of Psychology, 51*, 1–27.

Maccoby, E. E. (2007). Historical overview of socialization research and theory. In J. E. Grusec & P. D. Hastings (Eds.), *Handbook of socialization: Theory and research* (pp. 13–41). New York, NY: Guilford Press.

Maccoby, E. E., & Martin, J. A. (1983). Socialization in the context of the family: Parent-child interaction. In P. H. Mussen & E. M. Hetherington (Eds.), *Handbook of child psychology* (4th ed., pp. 1–102). New York, NY: Wiley.

Marcus, R. F. (1996). Friendships of delinquents. *Adolescence, 31*, 145–158.

Martinez, C. R., & Forgatch, M. S. (2001). Preventing problems with boys' noncompliance: Effects of a parent training intervention for divorcing mothers. *Journal of Consulting and Clinical Psychology, 69*, 416–428.

Matza, D. (1964). *Delinquency and drift: From the research program of the Center for the Study of Law and Society, University of California, Berkeley*. New York, NY: Wiley.

Matza, D., & Sykes, G. (1961). Juvenile delinquency and subterranean values. *American Sociological Review, 26*(5), 712–719.

Mayeux, L., Sandstrom, M. J., & Cillessen, A. H. N. (2008). Is being popular a risky proposition? *Journal of Research on Adolescence, 18*, 49–74.

Mears, D. P., & Field, S. H. (2002). A closer look at the age, peers, and delinquency relationship. *Criminology and Criminal Justice, 4*(1), 20–29.

Merton, R. K. (1938). Social structure and anomie. *American Sociological Review, 3*(5), 672–682.

Messner, S. F., & Rosenfeld, R. (2004). "Institutionalizing" criminological theory. In J. McCord (Ed.), *Institutions and intentions in the study of crime: Beyond empiricism* (pp. 83–106). New Brunswick, NJ: Transaction.

Moffitt, T. E. (1993). Adolescent-limited and life-course-persistent antisocial behavior: A developmental taxonomy. *Psychological Review, 100*, 674–701.

Moody, J., Brynildsen, W. D., Osgood, D. W., Feinberg, M. E., & Gest, S. (2011). Popularity trajectories and substance use in early adolescence. *Social Networks, 33*, 101–112

Newcomb, A. F., Bukowski, W. M., & Pattee, L. (1993). Children's peer relations: A meta-analytic review of popular, rejected, neglected, controversial, and average sociometric status. *Psychological Bulletin, 113*. 99–128.

North, D. (1990). *Institutions, institutional change and economic performance*. Cambridge, UK: Cambridge University Press.

Nye, F. I. (1958). *Family relationships and delinquent behavior*. Westport, CT: Greenwood Press.

Panksepp, J. (1998). *Affective neuroscience: The foundations of human and animal emotions*. New York, NY: Oxford University Press.

Parsons, T. (1991). *The social system*. New York, NY: Routledge.

Patterson, G. R. (1982). *Coercive family process*. Eugene, OR: Castalia Press.

Prinstein, M. J., Brechwald, W. A., & Cohen G. L. (2011). Susceptibility to peer influence: Using a performance-based measure to identify adolescent males at heightened risk for deviant peer socialization. *Developmental Psychology, 47,* 1167–1172.

Prinstein, M. J., Meade, C. S., & Cohen, G. L. (2003). Adolescent sexual behavior, peer popularity, and perceptions of best friends' sexual behavior. *Journal of Pediatric Psychology, 28,* 243–249.

Reckless, W. (1967). *The crime problem.* New York, NY: Appleton-Century-Crofts.

Sampson, R. J., & Bartusch, D. J. (1998). Legal cynicism and (subcultural?) tolerance of deviance: The neighborhood context of racial differences. *Law & Society Review, 32,* 777–804.

Schaefer, D. R. (2012). Homophily through nonreciprocity: Results of an experiment. *Social Forces, 90,* 1271–1295.

Simmel, G. (1950). *The sociology of Georg Simmel* (K. H. Wolff, Trans.). Glencoe, IL: Free Press.

Simons, R. L., & Lei, M. K. (2013). Enhanced susceptibility to context: A promising perspective on the interplay of genes and the social environment. In C. L. Gibson & M. D. Krohn (Eds.), *Handbook of life-course criminology* (pp. 43–55). New York, NY: Springer.

Smith, T. A., & Stevens, G. T. (2002). Hyperstructures and the biology of interpersonal dependence: Rethinking reciprocity and altruism. *Sociological Theory, 20*(1), 106–130.

Snijders, T., & Baerveldt, C. (2003). A multilevel network study of the effects of delinquent behavior on friendship evolution. *Journal of Mathematical Sociology, 27,* 123–151.

Spinoza, B. (2005). *Ethics.* London, UK: Penguin Group. (Original work published 1677)

Steinberg, L. (2001). We know some things: Parent-adolescent relationships in retrospect and prospect. *Journal of Research on Adolescence, 11*(1), 1–19.

Steinberg, L., & Morris, A. S. (2001). Adolescent development. *Annual Review of Psychology, 52,* 83–110.

Sutherland, E. H. (1924). *Principles of criminology.* Chicago, IL: University of Chicago Press.

Sutherland, E. H. (1956). *The Sutherland papers* (A. Cohen, A. Lindesmith, & K. Schuessler, Eds.). Bloomington: Indiana University Press.

Thornberry, T. P. (1987). Toward an interactional theory of delinquency. *Criminology, 25,* 863–892.

Thornberry, T. P., Lizotte, A. J., Krohn, M. D., Farnworth, M., & Jang, S. J. (1994). Delinquent peers, beliefs, and delinquent behavior: A longitudinal test of interactional theory. *Criminology, 32*(1), 47–83.

Walsh, A., & Ellis, L. (2007). *Criminology: An interdisciplinary approach.* Thousand Oaks, CA: Pine Forge Press.

Warr, M. (1993). Age, peers, and delinquency. *Criminology, 31*(1), 17–40.

Weis, J. G., & Hawkins, J. D. (1981). *The social development model. Preventing delinquency.* Washington, DC: Government Printing Office.

Wolfgang, M. E. (1958). *Patterns in criminal homicide.* Philadelphia: University of Pennsylvania Press.

18

A Biosocial Review on Childhood Antisocial Behavior

Chris L. Gibson
University of Florida

Elise T. Costa
University of Florida

Introduction

The emergence of early and persistent childhood conduct problems is arguably the largest "red flag" for antisocial behavior and violent offending in adulthood (see Moffitt, 1993). Not all children who exhibit behavioral problems in childhood grow up to become maladaptive adults, but it is often the case that maladaptive, antisocial, and violent behavior that continues into mid adulthood has its origins in early childhood. As the old saying goes, "past behavior is the best predictor of future behavior."

Research has consistently shown that roughly 10% of youth account for a disproportionate amount of antisocial and violent behavior (Moffitt, 1993; Wolfgang,

Figlio, & Sellin, 1972). Research has also shown that a large amount of violence and related behaviors tends to concentrate in a small percentage of families (Rowe & Farrington, 1997). Specifically, 10% of families account for roughly 50% of crime in a given community (Farrington, Jolliffe, Loeber, Stouthamer-Loeber, & Kalb, 2001). In both cases, these small groups of individuals and families often begin their involvement in antisocial behavior at early ages, typically below the age of 12, and this behavior gets transmitted to the next generation, likely due to a combination of biological, social, and cultural explanations. Ranging from caregiver socialization to genetics, various environmental and biosocial risk factors present in the first several years of life have been found to increase the likelihood of early childhood behavioral problems and disorders (Moffitt & Caspi, 2006; Raine, 2013), and studies show that the emergence of such behavior, especially when it is persistent throughout the first decade of life, predicts involvement in serious antisocial and criminal behaviors later in life (Broidy et al., 2003). Closely examining developmental processes occurring during infancy and early childhood for root causes of these behaviors will be most helpful for prevention and reducing costs to the criminal justice system and society (Cohen, Piquero, & Jennings, 2010). The goal of identifying root causes, however, is an ambitious one that will require a better understanding of how a developing biological organism (i.e., child) adapts or changes in response to its (i.e., his or her) local and changing environment (Ellis et al., 2012). One thing is for certain though; research that continues to assume that the emergence of childhood antisocial behavior is solely a function of changing environments will continue to mislead the academic community.

Our position is that a biosocial process explains why a relatively small percentage of children exhibit statistically abnormal and elevated levels of antisocial and externalizing behavior problems before the age of 12. First, our argument is grounded in an interdisciplinary body of research that reaches beyond the common onset measures examined by criminologists (e.g., age of first official contact with police or criminal justice system). We believe this is important because antisocial behavior trajectories start to take shape years before official intervention by the criminal justice system (Tremblay, 2013; Tremblay et al., 2004). A constellation of behaviors and disorders leading up to such reactive intervention can emerge as early as 3 to 6 years of age and can include externalizing problems such as serious physical aggression, oppositional and defiant behavior, conduct disorder, and attention deficit hyperactivity disorder (Zahn-Waxler, Shirtcliff, & Marceau, 2008). Second, we argue that research that excludes biological (or biologically related) correlates of childhood antisocial behavior will produce statistically biased estimates of environmental effects and may ultimately lead to misguided policy. Third, by providing examples from the extant literature using several biological factors, we offer strong evidence of a biosocial explanation for the emergence of serious forms of childhood antisocial behavior. In doing so, we turn much of our focus to genetic factors, but also summarize pre- and perinatal risk factors, as well as mention some intervening biological pathways that are partially responsible for the increasing risk for persistent childhood behavioral problems.

A Description of Early Childhood Antisocial Behavior

Criminologists have examined the onset of delinquent and offending behaviors by measuring the age at first contact with the criminal justice system (e.g., police contact, arrest, etc.) or self-reported age of first involvement in criminal acts (see Piquero, Farrington, & Blumstein, 2003). Generally, those who experience an onset before 12 years of age are classified as early onset offenders, but this cut-point has varied depending on the measures used (e.g., self-report, official records, etc.). Although this group consists of a small percentage of child offenders, understanding the etiology and prevention of their behavior is imperative because of the financial and social burdens they place on society and the criminal justice system later in life. This can be imagined by briefly summarizing later life offending outcomes for groups of children distinguished by early and late onset. Those who are classified as early onset offenders engage in crime more frequently over time, are more versatile in the offenses they commit, engage in more serious delinquent and violent behaviors, are at heightened risk for persisting in their antisocial trajectories into mid adulthood, and their criminal careers are typically longer (see Piquero et al., 2003). Research on early onset offenders and the developmental course of their behaviors has been useful for crafting developmentally sensitive prevention programs and has informed practitioners of the consequences that can stem from early involvement in crime.

Research from disciplines other than criminology shed even more light on the behavioral roots of early onset offending. Early onset offending often emerges from a constellation of behaviors and traits that can be observed earlier in a child's life course, sometimes even 2 or so years after birth, that have strong biosocial underpinnings (see Moffitt & Caspi, 2006; Tremblay, 2013; Zahn-Waxler et al., 2008). We broadly refer to these as *childhood antisocial behaviors* that include aggressive, oppositional, defiant, impulsive, and early onset conduct, which includes repeated violations of norms, rules, and the basic rights of others that persists over periods of time (for a review see Zahn-Waxler et al., 2008). This constellation of behaviors and behavior disorders resembles similar descriptive patterns among children that we commonly see among early onset offenders in the criminological literature. For instance, such behavior problems are often more prevalent in males, compared to females, and a small percentage of males actually exhibit these behaviors persistently during childhood. Further, many of these behaviors, especially if they are diagnosed as disorders, tend to be comorbid. That is, they tend to cluster within a child such that if he is diagnosed with conduct disorder it is very likely that he will also exhibit oppositional and defiant behaviors, as well as attention and impulsivity problems. We now turn to a discussion for why we think a biological component for understanding childhood behavior problems is needed in criminology.

Bad Parenting and Early Onset Antisocial Behavior: Building a Case for a Biosocial Perspective Using Genetic Research

In this section, we raise several key theoretical and methodological issues that lead us to question the validity of studies that have exclusively relied on one fundamental source of socialization as a driving force behind why some children engage in early onset antisocial behavior. Although we acknowledge research that examines other contexts of socialization (e.g., neighborhoods and peer groups), here we focus on parents or primary caregivers as a primary source of socialization that can influence antisocial behavior in childhood (e.g., Gottfredson & Hirschi, 1990). Specifically, we focus on "bad parenting," which is defined loosely and may manifest in moderate to severe forms. This spectrum may include erratic and harsh discipline, lack of warmth, hostility, weak supervision, and even more serious manifestations such as child maltreatment, abuse, and neglect. However, we do not spend time reviewing studies on these specific parenting indicators, because this can be found elsewhere and is not the overarching intent of our chapter. We should be clear that it is also not our goal to question whether such negative socialization efforts matter in understanding children's early onset antisocial behavior, because our interpretation of the research is that they do. However, we do question the degree to which such negative socialization affects childhood antisocial behavior and under what conditions it matters more. We shed light on how a biosocial process is important for understanding when bad parenting matters most and also how these forms of parenting may influence childhood antisocial behavior once genetic factors are considered.

To begin, we make two observations that call into question the magnitude of bad parenting's influence on childhood antisocial behavior. First, many developmental studies examining the influences of bad parenting have been carried out in the absence of controls for biological and genetic factors. Although several studies have assessed early onset antisocial behavior among children being raised in criminogenic environments who also have neurological deficiencies (see Moffitt & Caspi, 2006), less research has specifically tried to determine whether the influence of bad parenting on childhood antisocial behavior is confounded by genetic influences (Moffitt & Caspi, 2006). Second, criminological studies often neglect child-driven effects. That is, while studies frequently examine how bad parenting practices lead to increases in children's misbehavior, it is less often that we see criminological studies that examine this relationship while statistically controlling for the possibility that childhood antisocial behavior can lead to harsh disciplinary actions by parents (see Morris & Gibson, 2011). This implies that parenting may not have the strong direct effect on children that is so commonly argued. Taken together, these issues raise the specific concern of the degree to which bias is present in the estimation of the relationship between bad parenting and childhood antisocial behavior. Below we address these key points in more detail and provide research examples from various disciplines to support our argument.

For decades, the standard social science method (SSSM) has been used to explain why children, adolescents, and adults engage in violent and antisocial behavior. By design, this method assumes that the effect of biological and genetic factors on antisocial behavior is zero. With few exceptions (see Moffitt, 1993), this can also be observed in extant theories of crime and delinquency, where some even make explicit arguments against genetic and biological explanations (Gottfredson & Hirschi, 1990). However, recent empirical evidence from six independent, comprehensive meta-analyses confirms that this is not the case; the genetic influence on antisocial behaviors of children and adults is present, and this general finding spans multiple types of antisocial behavior across different developmental stages of the life course (Burt, 2009a, 2009b; Ferguson, 2010; Mason & Frick, 1994; Miles & Carey, 1997; Rhee & Waldman, 2002). Conclusions from these meta-analytic studies are drawn from hundreds of published twin studies, which by design allow for a genetic influence on antisocial behavior to be disentangled from environmental sources of variance. Nonetheless, a relatively large share of variance in antisocial behavior can be attributed to nonshared environments, or environments that siblings experience that are different from one another's. The main point is that these findings may have serious implications for evidence garnered from employing SSSM approaches suggesting that bad parenting is a strong underlying mechanism for why serious behavior problems emerge in childhood. But what do twin studies tell us specifically about the genetic influences on early childhood antisocial behavior?

Evidence from behavior genetic (i.e., twin studies) research provides evidence for both environmental and genetic influences on childhood externalizing behaviors, aggression, conduct problems, self-regulation, behavioral disorders (e.g., ADHD), and early onset/starter delinquency and substance use (see Arseneault et al., 2003; Baker, Jacobson, Raine, Lozano, & Bezdjian, 2007; Caspi et al., 2002; Legrand, McGue, & Iacono, 1999; Leve et al., 2010; Moffitt & Caspi 2006; Silberg, Maes, & Eaves, 2012; Taylor, Iacono, & McGue, 2000). Again, these designs not only allow for the decomposition of the variance of a trait or behavior into a genetic component, but they also broaden the examination of environmental influences by separating the percentage of variance explained by shared and nonshared environments (for a more extensive review, see Beaver, 2009).

Studies employing behavior genetic designs have also used multiple informant measurement approaches to examine early onset antisocial behavior (Arseneault et al., 2003; Baker et al., 2007; Legrand et al., 1999), which is beneficial because each informant or rater (e.g., teacher, parent, etc.) can provide a unique assessment of a child's behavior. When used together the different measurements provide a better-rounded, comprehensive assessment of a child's behavioral profile. Genetic effects have been found on childhood antisocial behavior regardless of the informant or rater reporting on a child's behavior. For example, using data from the Environmental Risk Longitudinal Twin Study, Arseneault and colleagues (2003) examined teacher, parent, examiner, and child reports and found support for a genetic influence on children's involvement in antisocial behavior. The genetic contribution ranged from 45% to 69% depending on the reporting source (informant) of the antisocial behavior, and the correlations from the cross-informants were in line with previous research. Baker and colleagues (2007) not only examined childhood antisocial behavior, but they also included aggression as an additional outcome measuring using three informants: children, teachers, and primary caregivers. Aggressive behavior was found to be highly heritable in the USC Twin Study of Risk Factors (Baker et al., 2007). Taken together, multiple informant studies demonstrate consistent and strong support that early onset externalizing behaviors, including aggression, are under some degree of genetic influence.

Additionally, behavior genetic studies of twins have garnered support for genetic influences on early onset substance use and delinquency (Legrand et al., 1999; Taylor et al., 2000). Examining 10- to 12-year-old boys in the Minnesota Twin Family Study, Taylor and colleagues (2000) found that early starters did not only exhibit persistent antisocial behavior, but their behavior was under a strong genetic influence, but only a moderate genetic effect was observed for late starters. The Minnesota Twin Family Study has also been used to examine early onset substance use (Legrand et al., 1999). When examining family (genetic) and environmental risk factors (e.g., negative peers, attitudes toward school, mother-son relationship), main effects were present for both types of risk. However, a gene × environment interaction demonstrated a pronounced influence on early onset substance use (Legrand et al., 1999). Using ACE models to estimate heritability and environmental effects, Legrand and colleagues showed that 39% of the variance in early onset substance was attributed to genetics. For the environment, shared environment explained roughly 20% of the variance, and the nonshared environment explained approximately 26% of the variance. Low environmental risk serves as a buffer against high familial/genetic risk; however, high environmental risk and high familial risk together have adverse consequences (Legrand et al., 1999).

Adoption studies also provide supportive evidence for genetic influences on early onset externalizing behaviors (Beaver, 2009). In such studies, 100% of the environment is shared with the adoptive parent(s) while 50% of the genetic information is shared with a biological parent. For an example, Leve and colleagues (2010) used an adoption study design that included biological parents, adoptive parents, and child when examining externalizing behaviors in infants during a frustration task. When adoptive mothers were above the mean for anxious or depressive symptoms (high-risk environment), the genetic risk was amplified and was associated with the birth mothers' externalizing behaviors. This finding supports the idea that low-environmental risk and genetic risk may not produce deleterious behavioral consequences, but high-risk environments paired with genetic risk may.

In summary, studies reviewed above show supporting evidence of a genetic influence on several antisocial behaviors that emerge in childhood, some even show evidence of a gene × environment interaction. What these studies also show is that genetic influence is only one piece of the puzzle for understanding antisocial behavior in childhood. Another piece gleaned from these studies is a child's environment. In most instances the environment accounts for a nontrivial share of the variance in childhood antisocial behavior. But how can we determine if bad parenting is an important aspect of a child's environment after accounting for genetic influences? This is an important question because genes could confound the relationship between bad parenting and a child's antisocial behavior for various reasons.

We know that children inherent genetic information from their biological parents. If bad parenting is a manifestation of parent's antisocial behavior that can be partially explained by their own genetics, then it could be the case that the relationship between bad parenting and a child's early onset antisocial behavior has a common genetic source. This could mean that the relationship is confounded by shared genetic influences that affect both bad parent and child behavior. To date, various studies have shown that variance in bad parenting is partially attributed to genetics and that the effect of bad parenting on at least some forms of early childhood antisocial behaviors (e.g., aggression) is explained by genetic influences. This of course could be due to various gene-by-environment correlation pathways, including passive evocative and active processes (Kendler & Baker, 2007), leading to the conclusion that the effect of bad parenting on childhood behavior problems will continue to be biased or inflated if genetic confounding is not taken seriously.

Child-Driven Effects: Does Childhood Antisocial Behavior Lead to Bad Parenting or Is It the Opposite?

A lurking possibility is that a child-driven effect may be responsible for the link between parent socialization efforts and the emergence of early antisocial behavior problems. After all, even the most loving parent is sometimes likely to react in an erratic and harsh way to a child's persistent antisocial and defiant behavior. As noted above, studies often empirically neglect this possibility and have proceeded by examining the less controversial path of how bad parenting leads to early problem behaviors among children. We argue that this is problematic because it can result in an incomplete picture of a more complex reality.

Assume that we have behavioral outcome measures tapping into the construct of serious externalizing behavior for a large cohort of toddlers measured at two time points with an interval of 6 months between observations. Also assume that we have measures for the construct of bad parenting practices also measured at each wave of data collection. It has often been the case that studies examine only the path that leads from Wave 1 bad parenting to Wave 2 childhood externalizing behavior to conclude that socialization explains the emergence of childhood antisocial behavior. However, another path is equally important, but often neglected, for understanding whether bad parenting leads to early childhood antisocial behavior problems. The path that leads from Wave 1 externalizing behavior to Wave 2 bad parenting practices is often neglected, instead of being simultaneously estimated as part of a causal process. Child-driven effect suggests that bad behavior of a child leads to reaction by a parent that results in bad parenting, opposed to the more common, reverse argument. Research that has neglected this issue cannot conclude that a measure of bad parenting is directly responsible for childhood externalizing behavior, and this becomes even more of a concern when genetic controls are not accounted for. Although less common in criminological studies, a cross-lagged model for understanding the emergence of early childhood behavior has the desirable properties of being able to simultaneously estimate parent influences and child-driven effects, stability in the parenting and behavior over time, and allows for the covariance between residuals.

Barnes, Boutwell, Beaver, and Gibson (2013) provide a recent example of this approach applied to differences in externalizing behaviors among young children. Using longitudinal data from the Early Childhood Longitudinal Study (ECLS)-Birth Cohort, they revisited two of the better-known predictors of early childhood externalizing behaviors (i.e., temper outbursts, physical aggression, hyperactivity, etc.): parent use of spanking and childhood self-regulation. One goal of the paper was to examine if the direct effect of parent disciplining on externalizing behaviors would persist after accounting for child-driven effects. Various statistical strategies were used, including biometric and cross-lagged models, to conclude that parent disciplining matters less for understanding childhood externalizing behaviors than what past studies have found. As it relates to the socialization hypothesis, a substantial portion of the covariance between parent spanking and young children's externalizing behaviors was explained by genetics and likely due to an evocative rGE explanation. More such studies are warranted in criminology to better understand the effects of bad parenting on early onset antisocial behaviors among children.

Molecular Genetics and Early Childhood Antisocial Behavior

Over the last decade, social science disciplines have witnessed an influx of molecular genetic studies that center on how specific gene variants correlate with human behaviors. These studies have capitalized on the fact that some genes are polymorphic, meaning that multiple copies of a gene are present in a population. Alleles are basically alternative forms of a gene. Given modern technology, the measurable genetic variability (i.e., allele) between individuals allows researchers to examine how certain gene variants are correlated with criminality, antisocial behavior, conduct disorder, and aggression beginning in childhood. This section provides a sample of studies to show how various genetic alleles, often in combination with environmental risk, predict antisocial outcomes in childhood.

Studies on childhood antisocial behaviors have examined genes related to the dopaminergic and serotonergic systems, as well as genes that play important roles in enzymatic breakdown. Dopaminergic genes that are examined include DAT1, DRD2, and DRD4. DeLisi, Beaver, Wright, and Vaughn (2008) examined the dopamine receptor genes DRD2 and DRD4 using one twin from each monozygotic twin dyad in the Add Health to predict criminal onset. They measured criminal onset in two ways: age of first police contact and age of first arrest. When examining age of first police contact, the DRD2 risk allele had a significant positive effect while the DRD4 risk allele did not. When dividing the sample by high-risk and low-risk families (environmental factors), the DRD2 risk alleles and DRD4 risk alleles were both significant predictors in the low family risk sample but did not reach statistical significance for the high family risk sample (DeLisi et al., 2008). The DAT1 dopamine receptor gene has been studied in children with ADHD to predict future conduct disorder (Lahey et al., 2011). A gene-environment interaction was supported for maternal parenting (both positive and negative) and DAT1 in predicting symptoms of conduct disorder 5 to 8 years later. Individuals with at least one copy of the 9-repeat allele showed more symptoms of conduct disorder.

Enzymatic breakdown genes, such as COMT and MAOA, have been linked to early onset conduct disorder, aggression, and antisocial behavior (Foley et al., 2004; Hirata, Zai, Nowrouzi, Beitchman, & Kennedy, 2013; Thapar et al., 2005). In an attempt to replicate Caspi et al. (2002), Foley and colleagues (2004) examined the interaction between MAOA with child adversity to predict conduct disorder. The low-activity MAOA allele did not show a main effect on conduct disorder; however, the interaction of childhood adversity and low activity MAOA alleles produced a statistically significant positive effect on conduct disorder. COMT has also been examined to predict both early onset antisocial behavior and aggression in children (Hirata et al., 2013; Thapar et al., 2005). Aggressive children who possessed two genetic markers of COMT (rs6269 & rs4818) had higher scores for callous-unemotional traits than children who possessed one of the two markers (Hirata et al., 2013). Hirata et al. (2013) also found a significant association between COMT and childhood onset aggression. The val/val genotype of COMT and low birth weight interacted to increase symptoms of conduct disorder in children (Thapar et al., 2005).

Other Biosocial Influences on Childhood Antisocial Behavior

Factors other than genetics have been found to be biologically related conditions or events early in life that can influence childhood onset antisocial behavior. Of these, some of the most consistently examined factors include those that are described as pre- and perinatal complications, including maternal cigarette smoking during pregnancy, maternal alcohol use, exposure to toxins such as lead, and low birth weight. On the whole, exposure to these conditions during the fetal stages, and perhaps even shortly after birth, have been argued as indirect indicators that a child may have subtle neurological deficiencies that impair verbal cognitive abilities, which are linked to early onset antisocial children (see Moffitt, 1993).

Maternal cigarette smoking has been linked to early onset offending and physical aggression (Gibson, Piquero, & Tibbetts, 2000; Gibson & Tibbetts, 2000; Huijbregts, Séguin, Zoccolillo, Boivin, & Tremblay, 2008). Significant main effects have repeatedly been found for maternal cigarette smoking on early onset antisocial and criminal behaviors (Gibson et al., 2000; Gibson & Tibbetts, 2000; Huijbregts et al., 2008), which include the age of first police contact (Gibson et al., 2000). Also, maternal cigarette smoking during pregnancy and a mother's involvement in antisocial behavior have been shown to interact to predict offspring's antisocial behaviors (Huijbregts et al., 2008). Gibson and Tibbetts (2000) ascertained that maternal cigarette smoking, in combination with the absence of a father or male figure in childhood, predicts early onset offending in a high-risk cohort of African American children.

Maternal cigarette smoking has exhibited significant effects on antisocial outcomes across various developmental stages. Because of this, Wakschlag, Pickett, Cook, Benowitz, and Leventhal (2002), as well as Pratt, McGlion, and Fearn (2006), provided extensive reviews and critical assessments of studies conducted on maternal cigarette smoking. Wakschlag and colleagues found moderate association between maternal cigarette smoking and severe antisocial behaviors; expressly, they calculated that youths who are exposed to maternal cigarette smoking are 1.5 to 4 times more likely to develop antisocial behaviors than youths who were not exposed to maternal cigarette smoking. Wakschlag and colleagues also offered alternative explanations for the consistent association of methodological and theoretical considerations in this body of research, but did not completely rule out the influence of maternal smoking; Pratt and colleagues found an overall statistically significant effect as well. Pratt and colleagues concluded "maternal cigarette smoking is a moderately important risk factor for criminal and deviant behavior of offspring" (p. 682).

Low birth weight and birth complications also have been linked to early childhood antisocial behaviors (Raine, Brennan, & Mednick, 1997; Thapar et al., 2005; Tibbetts & Piquero, 1999), some of which indicate low birth weight in combination with adverse family conditions in childhood. For instance, in a test of Moffitt's interactional hypothesis, Tibbetts and Piquero (1999) examined low birth weight by gender and disadvantaged environments to predict early onset offending. Effects were found to support that low birth weight is associated with early onset offending. As mentioned earlier, the val/val genotype of COMT in combination with low birth weight is associated with an increase in conduct disorder (Thapar et al., 2005). It is also possible that birth complications can contribute to neuropsychiatric deficits among offspring. These deficits may lead to maladaptive behaviors or early onset offending (Raine, Brennan, Mednick, 1994). Beaver and Wright (2005) emphasize that "complications at birth may thus set the stage for self-regulatory problems that emerge early in life and that remain stable over long periods of the life course" (p. 453). Raine and colleagues extended prior research on birth complications to test whether the presence of such complications in combination with early maternal rejection had effects offending behaviors and violence that extended to age 34. Biosocial interactions were observed for violent offenders but not for nonviolent offenders. Comparisons were also made for early versus late-onset offending; however, it is important to note that this study used less than 18 years old as the cutoff for early onset offending, while most studies use 14 years old as the cutoff age. A significant interaction between birth complications and maternal rejection predicted early onset offending (Raine et al., 1997). When more closely examining seven different complications, Beaver and Wright (2005) found that anoxia (absence of oxygen or oxygen starvation) was among the strongest predictors of low self-control behavior and remained significant when both parent and teacher reports were assessed (Beaver & Wright, 2005).

Previous research has supported the idea that exposure to lead increases the likelihood that children will engage in externalizing and violent behavior (see Wright et al., 2008). For instance, Wright and colleagues (2008) examined this further by observing participants at the prenatal stage and then continuing to monitor blood lead concentrations among children through the age of 6. Further, pre- and postnatal blood lead concentrations significantly predicted arrests in adulthood (Wright et al., 2008).

Early onset aggression has also been shown to be a function of an interaction between sociological and biological risk. For instance, Brennan, Hall, Bow, Najman, and Williams (2003) research was intended to examine two different developmental theories: Moffitt's life course and Patterson's coercion model. The biological risk factors examined were perinatal and birth complications. Perinatal and birth complications included many of the biosocial variables previously discussed such as birth weight, maternal cigarette smoking, and maternal alcohol consumption. If any participant had at least one of the perinatal or birth complications, the offspring was considered to have a biological risk factor (Brennan et al., 2003). Other biological variables were also measured, such as executive function and vocabulary scores. In line with previously discussed studies, children classified as high biological and social risk were the most likely to have early onset persistent aggression. These researchers concluded support for the notion that early social risks interact with biological risk to predict persistent aggression in boys, yet support was found for both theoretical models.

Similar to the evolving research on genetics and childhood antisocial behavior, studies discussed in this section have unfailingly demonstrated an interaction of biologically related variables with adverse social condition experienced by children, including both family and parenting variables. These studies only reconfirm our position that is necessary for research on early childhood antisocial behavior to include both social/environmental and biological factors to better understand the complete picture.

Conclusion

This review has made a strong case for the inclusion of a biosocial perspective for understanding multiple early childhood antisocial behaviors. In doing so, research from numerous disciplines and a variety of biological levels were examined to show not only that biology matters, but biology also is likely to matter most under certain stressful and adverse familial/environmental contexts that children experience. We believe that the evidence brought to bear in this chapter on a biosocial process should not be overlooked, especially among those who exclusively focus their efforts on understanding the social rearing environments of children. We believe that many of the biosocial processes and factors discussed in this chapter are certainly targetable and preventable. The more we come to know about the complex interactions between biological and social factors that produce early onset behavioral problems, the better our intervention efforts will be equipped to target factors giving rise to these behaviors that often result in devastating consequences in the life course of young people.

References

Arseneault, L., Moffitt, T. E., Caspi, A., Taylor, A., Rijsdijk, F. V., Jaffee, S. R., . . . Measelle, J. R. (2003). Strong genetic effects on cross-situational antisocial behavior among 5-year old children according to mothers, teachers, examiner-observers, and twins' self-reports. *Journal of Child Psychology and Psychiatry, 44*(6), 832–848.

Baker, L. A., Jacobson, K. C., Raine, A., Lozano, D. I., & Bezdjian, S. (2007). Genetic and environmental bases of childhood antisocial behavior: A multi-informant twin study. *Journal of Abnormal Psychology, 116*(2), 219–235.

Barnes, J. C., Boutwell, B. B., Beaver, K. M., & Gibson, C. L. (2013). Analyzing the origins of childhood externalizing behavioral problems. *Developmental Psychology, 49*(12), 2272–2284.

Beaver, K. M. (2009). *Biosocial criminology: A primer*. Dubuque, IA: Kendal/Hunt.

Beaver, K. M., & Wright, J. P. (2005). Evaluating the effects of birth complications on low self-control in a sample of twins. *International Journal of Offender Therapy and Comparative Criminology, 49*(4), 450–471.

Brennan, P. A., Hall, J., Bow, W., Najman, J. M., & Williams, G. (2003). Integrating biological and social processes in relation to early-onset persistent aggression in boys and girls. *Developmental Psychology, 29*(2), 309–323.

Broidy, L. M., Nagin, D. S., Tremblay, R. E., Bates, J. E., Brame, B., Dodge, K. A., . . . Vitaro, F. (2003). Developmental trajectories of childhood disruptive behaviors and adolescent delinquency: A six-site, cross-national study. *Developmental Psychology, 39*(2), 222–245.

Burt, S. A. (2009a). Are there meaningful etiological differences within antisocial behavior? Results from a meta-analysis. *Clinical Psychology Review, 29*, 163–178.

Burt, S. A. (2009b). Rethinking environmental contributions to child and adolescent psychopathology: A meta-analysis of shared environmental influences. *Psychological Bulletin, 135*, 608–637.

Caspi, A., McClay, J., Moffitt, T. E., Mill, J., Martin, J., Craig, I. W., . . . Poulton, R. (2002). Role of genotype in the cycle of violence in maltreated children. *Science, 297*(5582), 851–854.

Cohen, M. A., Piquero, A. R., & Jennings, W. (2010). Studying the costs of crime across offending trajectories. *Criminology & Public Policy, 9*, 275–305.

DeLisi, M., Beaver, K. M., Wright, J. P., & Vaughn, M. G. (2008). The etiology of criminal onset: The enduring salience of nature and nurture. *Journal of Criminal Justice, 36*(3), 217–233.

Ellis, B. J., Del Giudice, M., Dishion, T. J., Figueredo, A. J., Gray, P. Griskevicius, V., . . . Sloan, D. (2012). The evolutionary basis of risky adolescent behavior: Implications for science, policy, and practice. *Developmental Psychology, 48*(3), 598–623.

Farrington, D. P., Jolliffe, D., Loeber, R., Stouthamer-Loeber, M., & Kalb, L. M. (2001). The concentration of offenders in families, and family criminality in the prediction of boys' delinquency. *Journal of Adolescence, 24*, 579–596.

Ferguson, C. J. (2010). Genetic contributions to antisocial personality and behavior: A meta-analytic review from an evolutionary perspective. *Journal of Social Psychology, 150*, 160–180.

Foley, D. L., Eaves, L. J., Wormley, B., Silberg, J. L., Maes, H., Kuhn, J., & Riley, B. (2004). Childhood adversity, monoamine oxidase A genotype, and risk for conduct disorder. *Archives of General Psychiatry, 61*(7), 738–744.

Gibson, C. L., Piquero, A. R., & Tibbetts, S. G. (2000). Assessing the relationship between maternal cigarette smoking during pregnancy and age at first police contact. *Justice Quarterly, 17*(3), 519–542.

Gibson, C. L., & Tibbetts, S. G. (2000). A biosocial interaction of predicting early onset of offending. *Psychological Reports, 86*(2), 509–518.

Gottfredson, M. R., & Hirschi, T. (1990). *A general theory of crime*. Stanford, CA: Stanford University Press.

Hirata, Y., Zai, C. C., Nowrouzi, B., Beitchman, J. H., & Kennedy, J. L. (2013). Study of the catechol-o-methyltransferase (COMT) gene with high aggression in children. *Aggressive Behavior, 39*(1), 45–51.

Huijbregts, S. C. J., Séguin, J. R., Zoccolillo, M., Boivin, M., & Tremblay, R. E. (2008). Maternal prenatal smoking, parental antisocial behavior, and early childhood physical aggression. *Development and Psychopathology, 20*(2), 437–453.

Kendler, K. S., & Baker, J. H. (2007). Genetic influences on measures of the environment: A systematic review. *Psychological Medicine, 37*, 615–626.

Lahey, B. B., Rathouz, P. J., Lee, S. S., Chronis-Tuscano, A., Pelham, W. E., Waldman, I. D., & Cook, E. H. (2011). Interactions between early parenting and a polymorphism of the child's dopamine transporter gene in predicting future child conduct disorder symptoms. *Journal of Abnormal Psychology, 120*(1), 33–45.

Legrand, L. N., McGue, M., & Iacono, W. G. (1999). Searching for interactive effects in the etiology of early-onset substance use. *Behavior Genetics, 29*(6), 433–444.

Leve, L. D., Kerr, D. C., Shaw, D., Ge, X., Neiderhiser, J. M., Scaramella, L. V., . . . Conger, R. (2010). Infant pathways to externalizing behavior: Evidence of genotype × environment interaction. *Child Development, 81*(1), 340–356.

Mason, D. A., & Frick, P. J. (1994). The heritability of antisocial behavior: A meta-analysis of twin and adoption studies. *Journal of Psychopathology and Behavioral Assessment, 16,* 301–323.

Miles, D. R., & Carey, G. (1997). Genetic and environmental architecture of human aggression. *Journal of Personality and Social Psychology, 72,* 207–217.

Moffitt, T. E. (1993). Adolescence-limited and life-course-persistent antisocial behavior: A developmental taxonomy. *Psychological Review, 100*(4), 674–701.

Moffitt, T. E., & Caspi, A. (2006). Evidence from behavioral genetics for environmental contributions to antisocial conduct. In P. H. Wikström & R. J. Sampson (Eds.), *The explanation of crime* (pp. 108–152). Cambridge, MA: Cambridge University Press.

Morris, S. Z., & Gibson, C. L. (2011). Corporal punishment's influence on children's aggressive and delinquent behavior. *Criminal Justice and Behavior, 38*(8), 818–839.

Piquero, A. R., Farrington, D. P., & Blumstein, A. (2003). The criminal career paradigm. *Crime and Justice, 30,* 359–506.

Pratt, T. C., McGloin, J. M., & Fearn, N. E. (2006). Maternal cigarette smoking during pregnancy and criminal/deviant behavior: A meta-analysis. *International Journal of Offender Therapy and Comparative Criminology, 50*(6), 672–690.

Raine, A. (2013). *The anatomy of violence: The biological roots of crime.* New York, NY: Pantheon.

Raine, A., Brennan, P., & Mednick, S. A. (1994). Birth complications combined with early maternal rejection at age 1 year predispose to violent crime at age 18 years. *Archives of General Psychiatry, 51,* 984–988.

Raine, A., Brennan, P., & Mednick, S. A. (1997). Interaction between birth complications and early maternal rejection in predisposing individuals to adult violence: Specificity to serious, early-onset violence. *American Journal of Psychiatry, 154*(9), 1265–1271.

Rhee, S. H., & Waldman, I. D. (2002). Genetic and environmental influences on antisocial behavior: A meta-analysis of twin and adoption studies. *Psychological Bulletin, 128,* 490–529.

Rowe, D. C., & Farrington, D. P. (1997). The familial transmission of criminal convictions. *Criminology, 35*(1), 177–202.

Silberg, J. L., Maes, H., & Eaves, L. J. (2012). Unraveling the effect of genes and environment in the transmission of parental antisocial behavior to children's conduct disturbance, depression and hyperactivity. *Journal of Child Psychology and Psychiatry, 53*(6), 668–677.

Taylor, J., Iacono, W. G., & McGue, M. (2000). Evidence for a genetic etiology of early-onset delinquency. *Journal of Abnormal Psychology, 109*(4), 634–643.

Thapar, A., Langley, K., Fowler, T., Rice, F., Turic, D., Whittinger, N., . . . O'Donovan, M. (2005). Catechol-o-methyltransferase gene variant and birth weight predict early-onset antisocial behavior in children with attention-deficit/hyperactivity disorder. *Archives of General Psychiatry, 62*(11), 1275–1278.

Tibbetts, S. G., & Piquero, A. R. (1999). The influence of gender, low birth weight, and disadvantaged environment in predicting early onset of offending: A test of Moffitt's interactional hypothesis. *Criminology, 37*(4), 843–878.

Tremblay, R. E. (2013). Development of antisocial behavior during childhood. In C. L. Gibson & M. D. Krohn (Eds.), *Handbook of life-course criminology: Emerging trends and directions for future research* (pp. 3–19). New York, NY: Springer.

Tremblay, R. E., Nagin, D. S., Séguin, J. R., Zoccolillo, M., Zelazo, P. D., Boivin, M., . . . Japel, C. (2004). Physical aggression during early childhood: Trajectories and predictors. *Pediatrics, 114*(1), e43–e50.

Wakschlag, L. S., Pickett, K. E., Cook E., Jr., Benowitz, N. L., & Leventhal, B. L. (2002). Maternal smoking during pregnancy and severe antisocial behavior in offspring: A review. *American Journal of Public Health, 92*(6), 966–974.

Wolfgang, M. E., Figlio, R. M., & Selling, T. (1972). *Delinquency in a birth cohort.* Chicago, IL: University of Chicago Press.

Wright, J. P., Dietrich, K. N., Ris, M. D., Hornung, R. W., Wessel, S. D., Lanphear, B. P., . . . Rae, M. N. (2008). Association of prenatal and childhood blood lead concentrations with criminal arrests in early adulthood. *PLoS Medicine, 5*(5), e101.

Zahn-Waxler, C., Shirtcliff, E. A., & Marceau, K. (2008). Disorders of childhood and adolescence: Gender and psychopathology. *Annual Review of Clinical Psychology, 4,* 275–303.

Discussion Questions

CHAPTERS 17 AND 18

1. For sociologists, variation in crime and criminality is believed to be a consequence of how the family, peer groups, schools, and the criminal justice system are organized. A biosocial explanation proposes that antisocial behavior results from a confluence of factors related to biology and the environment. In your opinion, which of these two perspectives is better able to account for variation in antisocial behaviors?
2. Some scholars have argued that socialization is needed for children to become socially responsible and self-regulated members of society. Without properly controlling for biological and genetic factors, is it possible that research could be overestimating social influences? What does behavioral genetic research reveal about genetic and environmental influences on childhood behaviors?
3. Sociologists argue that parents are the first and primary agents of socialization, where the quality of socialization is contingent on the type of relationship between the parent and the child. However, how might child-driven effects influence the socialization process? Can we conclude bad parenting is directly responsible for childhood externalizing behavior?
4. Describe how genetic factors work in combination with environmental risk to predict antisocial outcomes in childhood. Can genetic risk alone predict antisocial outcomes? What do sociologists believe predicts antisocial outcomes?
5. Weak social bonds are often cited as important risk factors for developing antisocial behavior. What other environmental risk factors influence antisocial behaviors? For example, what type of risks are present in the prenatal environment?
6. How might sociological and biosocial perspectives be integrated to explain antisocial behavior? Moving forward, do you envision a change in the way scientists study and explain antisocial behaviors? Or, as noted by Drs. Rees and Young, are sociologists and biosocial researchers "looking at different things?"

19

Sociological Criminology and Drug Use

A Review of Leading Theories

J. Mitchell Miller
The University of Texas at San Antonio

Holly Ventura Miller
The University of Texas at San Antonio

Introduction

Whereas the fields of biology, medicine, and psychology engage drug etiology through focus on neurological and pharmacological factors predictive of and correlated with predisposition to use, sociological approaches are rooted in factors external to individual constitution such as environment, cultural outlook, and social interactional dynamics. After almost a century since early Chicago-school researchers began a line of inquiry examining urban ecological phenomena such as social disorganization, collective efficacy, and various related social problems, including substance abuse (Reckless, 1933/1969; Shaw & McKay, 1942), a distinct "sociology of drug use" has evolved largely around the central issue of drug use etiology.

The 1920s marked the beginning of the longstanding view that use is often harmful and that addictive substances should be regulated. Drug prohibition legislation followed and popularized views of users and addicts as criminal. Early sociological attention to drug use examined a range of issues, including the correlates of opiate addiction and the nature of drug crime trajectories (Dai, 1937), the pharmacology of addiction (Lindensmith, 1947), and comparative analysis of the objectives and implications of American punitive and British medical policy models (Schur, 1963). Collectively, these works swayed academic opinion that the social problem of drug abuse should be engaged per a humane treatment rather than criminal justice approach. The next wave of sociological drug research further entrenched liberal opposition to drug control policy and expanding narcotics enforcement through development of labeling and social stigmatization theories (Becker, 1963; Lemert, 1967; Wallace, 1968) that highlighted social inequality and the selective enforcement of lower-class and minority drug use. Within sociology, the majority view was that reaction to the drug problem had become a social problem itself and that the social response to drug use, particularly marijuana, was over-reactionary as soft drug users were portrayed as nonthreatening normal members of society (Becker, 1955).

Numerous subsequent theories reflecting various social science orientations and multidisciplinary approaches have been proffered reflecting thematic ideations of medicinal and recreational drug use (see Petraitis, Flay, & Miller, 1995, and the *Journal of Drug Issues* Spring 1996 special issue for detailed reviews of the drug etiology literature). Within contemporary sociology, drug research is far from monolithic because theoretical research programs are active across several areas of specialization including medical sociological epidemiology (patterns and extent of drug use), drug ethnography (symbolic meaning and social functions of use), and econometrics (societal implications of economic theory applied to licit and illicit substance exchange markets), as well as criminology (social origins, dynamics, and functions of use and regulation). Derived from the focal concern of crime, criminological drug research is more narrowly attentive to substance use specified as illegal, including both illicit drug use and the pharmaceutical diversion of medicine. *Social origins* and *social context* are leading themes within the sociology of drugs, evident across various research topics such as the history of drug prohibition; the manifest and latent functions of use, enforcement, and treatment; correlates of drug use and abuse; and cultural and environmentally determined drug use accelerants and barriers (Faupel, Horowitz, & Weaver, 2003; J. M. Miller & Selva, 1994).

Criminological theory is rooted in the three broader sociological paradigms that frame the meaning, functions, and appropriateness of drug use across social contexts (see Table 19.1). The structural-functionalist perspective is rooted in the social thought of Comte, Durkheim, and Parsons and takes a macro view of society as a multifaceted system comprised of complementary parts. Normative consensus promotes conformity to rules so that social solidarity and stability can be realized, but behavior breaching formal norms is thought to breed conflict, anomic conditions, and social dysfunction. Behavior is thus objectified as conventional or socially threatening. A second leading perspective, symbolic interactionism, provides a framework for sociological analysis of the subjective meanings people assign to things, others, behavior, and events (Blumer, 1986; Mead, 1967). This micro-meso-level perspective observes behavior as a function of subjective understanding of

Table 19.1 Theoretical Approaches to Drug Use

Theory	Sociological Perspective	Central Concepts	Level of Analysis
Learning	Symbolic Interactionism	Differential Association; Delinquent Peers; Reinforcement	Micro-Meso
Cultural Transmission	Symbolic Interactionism	Definitions; Values	Meso-Macro
Control	Functionalism/ Symbolic Interactionism	Social Bonds; Impulsivity	Micro
Strain	Functionalism/ Symbolic Interactionism	Anomie; Goals-Means Discrepancy; Negative Stimuli	Macro-Micro
Conflict	Conflict	Social Inequality; Stratification	Macro

assigned meaning instead of as objective reality. This social construction of society approach is particularly suited for deviance research foci such as drug subcultures and the social dynamics of use. While both functionalist and interactionist approaches recognize the importance of normative consensus, functionalism looks more to formal norms (i.e., law), while interactionism more broadly factors formal and informal norms derived from recognition of the legitimacy of law and solidification of shared values and beliefs regarding authority.

Last, the conflict perspective assumes social problems are a manifestation of conflict inseparable from social inequality (Marx, 1978). Inequality generated by disparities in wealth result in social class conflict wherein the ruling few enjoy power over the majority through control of social institutions aligned with their economic interests. This macro-level perspective assumes that the creation of criminal law generally, and especially the enforcement of morality law (like drug use), serve the purposes of social control and the manipulation of surplus labor.

Traditional Criminological Explanations of Drug Use

LEARNING AND CULTURAL TRANSMISSION THEORIES

Theories of learning and cultural transmission generally assume that criminal behavior is similar to other forms of human behavior in that crime is viewed as a product of social interaction. Social interaction offers both a context and process wherein learning occurs and behavior reflects the nature of what is learned through observation of one's environment and the socialization process facilitated by an individual's reference groups, generally, and role models, specifically. Within certain situations or environments, therefore, crime is normative behavior and to be expected.

Both criminal and noncriminal behaviors are thought to result from a combination of the socialization process, situational circumstances, and group values. According to the learning perspective, all human behavior, whether conforming or deviant, is learned in the same manner; the difference lies in the direction of influence. Criminality is not considered an innate human characteristic, but rather a product of interaction with others. Learning theories, such as differential association theory and social learning theory, emphasize the process in which criminal behavior is observed, learned, and engaged. Cultural transmission theories are similar to learning theories but focus instead on group values (which are shaped and perpetuated from one generation to the next by learning) that tolerate, condone, and even encourage crime and deviance.

Akers's (1998) social learning theory and its precursor, Sutherland's (1947) theory of differential association, are the most influential of the learning perspectives within criminology. These theories focus on socialization and view criminal behavior as the result of social learning processes; specifically, through differential association, the acquisition of criminal definitions and attitudes, imitation and modeling of criminal behavior, and the reinforcement of that behavior (Akers, 1998). Each of four main elements of social learning theory are important for the etiology of drug use. First, differential association with delinquent peers offers the context by which the other learning processes will operate. Individuals with peers who use drugs will likely have access to an environment where drugs are available and will be exposed to definitions favorable to the consumption of such substances. Association with drug-using peers also offers a means by which individuals will observe and thus have opportunity to imitate drug use.

Finally, the use of drugs carries with it considerable social and nonsocial reinforcements. Many individuals, especially adolescents and young adults, are willing to use drugs simply because they perceive their friends are favorably inclined to do the same. If adolescents perceive a favorable response from peers for drug use, then they are more likely to engage in such behavior. Interestingly, past research has shown that individuals need not even observe delinquency directly but rather perceive that the behavior will elicit peer approval (H. V. Miller, Jennings, Alvarez-Rivera, & Lanza-Kaduce, 2009). Further, recent research from the field of neuroscience indicates that in the presence of peers, adolescents demonstrate greater activation in reward-related brain regions, such as the orbitofrontal cortex (Steinberg, 2007, 2008), which offers physiological evidence for these social learning processes.

Differential association and social learning theories are some of the most widely tested by contemporary criminologists and have received a considerable amount of empirical support. Overall, research has indicated that differential association is a consistent predictor across a range of deviant behaviors including substance use

(Akers, Krohn, Lanza-Kaduce, & Radosevich, 1979; Hwang & Akers, 2003; McGee, 1992; H. V. Miller, Jennings, Alvarez-Rivera, & Miller, 2008). More specifically, social learning variables have been found to be associated with use of a wide range of licit and illicit substances such as alcohol, tobacco, marijuana, cocaine, and a variety of other drugs such as opiates, inhalants, barbiturates, and hallucinogens (Akers et al., 1979; Akers & Cochrane, 1985; H. V. Miller, 2011; J. M. Miller et al., 2008; J. M. Miller, Miller, Zapata, & Yin, 2008; Shedler & Block, 1990).

Cultural transmission, or subcultural, theories also view drug use as a learned behavior but focus instead on the values and definitions shared by social groups about acceptable behavior (E. Anderson, 1999; Cloward & Ohlin, 1960; Cohen, 1955; W. B. Miller, 1958). Simply put, in some social environments, using drugs is not viewed as deviant or delinquent but is instead a valued or condoned activity. Drug use serves the positive function of social acceptance necessary for group formation and continuation. Some subcultural theories have described such groups as class based while others have focused on youth culture as a driving force.

One of the earliest subcultural approaches to crime is Walter B. Miller's (1958) lower-class focal concerns theory. Miller argued that the lower classes place emphasis on certain values, or focal concerns, that engender deviant behavior such as drug use. He identified six focal concerns, which he argued explained why crime tended to concentrate among the lower classes: *trouble, toughness, smartness, excitement, fate,* and *autonomy.* Many of these focal concerns or values are related to drug use to varying degrees. For example, for the individual who values trouble and excitement, the use of drugs has the potential to satisfy both. The use of drugs can also be viewed through the prism of autonomy in that it represents a violation of the law to which few are held to account.

Cloward and Ohlin's (1960) differential opportunity theory also offers a subcultural explanation for drug use. This theory, which builds on the illegitimate opportunity structure construct described in Merton's (1938) strain theory, was presented as a theory of juvenile gangs. In this theory, Cloward and Ohlin offer a typology of three "ideal types" of juvenile gangs: criminal, conflict, and retreatist delinquent gangs. The last of these, the retreatist gang, has significance for understanding drug use among adolescents. Youth associated with retreatist gangs were neither violent (as in the case of the conflict gang) nor successful in criminal endeavors (as in the case of the criminal gang), and were thus viewed as double failures. That is to say, they could compete in neither the legitimate nor the illegitimate opportunity structure and, as a result, retreated from society into a world of drug use. Members of this kind of comparatively unorganized gang turn to drugs as an escape from status frustration that comes from falling short of both middle-class standards (legitimate) and those of others within their own social class (illegitimate).

More recently, E. Anderson's (1999) *Code of the Street* focused on the values of the modern urban underclass to explain crime, violence, and other problem behaviors in the inner city. While this theory focuses primarily on violence among young, African American males, it also informs understanding of high rates of drug use and abuse within America's inner cities. According to Anderson, the inner city is organized into two different types of families—street and decent, evaluative judgments made by the residents themselves that confer status in the inner city. Unlike "decent" families, "street" families embrace an oppositional culture characterized by a rejection of middle-class values. As Albert Cohen observed in the middle of the 20th century, the need for status and respect among the lower classes often involves the rejection of mainstream values (i.e., the middle-class measuring rod) and the creation of new standards of behavior. One particular standard of behavior in opposition to mainstream values is the tolerance, and even endorsement, of drug use. Drug use represents a focal concern for many in the inner city whose lives are characterized by violence, desperation, and disorganization. Drug use, abuse, and addiction, then, is a reaction to an environment plagued by profound feelings of despair, alienation, and hopelessness.

CONTROL THEORIES

Theories of social control are among the oldest sociological explanations for human behavior. Indeed, a central focus for Emile Durkheim, one the founding fathers of sociology, was the role of social control in maintaining order and solidarity in a diverse, organic society. Many observe that the field of sociology was in fact built on the concept of control, and many early criminological theories featured control prominently as a key construct (e.g., anomie, containment, social disorganization). For many who study crime and deviance, social control remains at the root of the phenomena.

Within the field of criminology, control theories enjoy a long history and influence in the understanding of crime, delinquency, and deviance. The 1950s and 1960s produced several early versions of control theory such as Reckless's (1961) containment theory and Reiss's (1951) theory of internal and external controls. Reckless's control theory hypothesized that two forms of control served to affect juvenile delinquency, which he termed inner and outer containments. *Inner containments* were defined as self-control, good self-concept, ego strength, a well-developed super-ego, high frustration tolerance, and a sense of responsibility. *Outer containments* were described as family and school reinforcement of social norms and values, effective supervision and discipline, and alternatives to deviance. Many of these ideas would also appear in later versions of control theories (e.g., social bond, self-control). Reiss and Nye also offered variants of these concepts, including personal (internal) and social (external) controls (Reiss, 1951) and direct, indirect, and internal controls (Nye, 1958). As with all control theories, these early approaches viewed deviance, including drug use, as a result of low levels of control, whether internal or external to the individual.

In 1969, Travis Hirschi introduced what is considered the seminal 20th century version of social control theory—social bond theory. Hirschi (1969) presented this theory in his book *Causes of Juvenile Delinquency* as a micro-level explanation for deviance among adolescents. Hirschi presents his theory somewhat differently from how most criminologists approached crime in that he did not aim to answer the question of why people commit crime. Instead, he asked why they do *not* offend. Crime, Hirschi reasoned, is attractive to people in their natural state because it offers benefits relatively easy to realize. Given this natural inclination to crime, then, the real issue was what prevented most people from offending? For Hirschi, the answer lay in social control; more specifically, the social bond.

The social bond is the key construct underlying Hirschi's social control theory. The social bond is hypothesized as the theoretical mechanism by which people are able to avoid deviant or problem behavior. Those who have strong bonds will be less likely to engage in crime, including drug use, while those with weak bonds are more likely to participate in such behavior. Hirschi conceptualized the social bond as possessing four distinct yet interrelated components: attachment, involvement, commitment, and belief.

Attachment, the first and arguably most important element of the social bond, is described as identification with peers and parents, emotional bonds with family and friends, and concern for the opinions of others. *Involvement* is defined as the amount of time-consuming activity spent in conventional activities (studying, working, extracurricular activities) as well as the amount of non-inactive leisure time. *Commitment* refers to the extent to which individuals are invested in conventionality or the conventions of society (e.g., education, career, family) and their aspirations and importance of their reputation. *Belief* is defined as a respect for authorities, an internalization of social norms, and an absence of neutralizations. Collectively, these elements comprise Hirschi's social bond and predict the likelihood of deviation from convention.

The causal link between social control and drug use is hypothesized in much the same manner as the mechanism underlying the former and crime: those who are more attached, involved, and committed will be less likely to use drugs (or commit any crime), while those lacking strong bonds will be more likely to use drugs. Individuals with a greater number of and stronger attachments to family, friends, and community will be less likely to use drugs because they have more to lose. Those who are less involved in conventional activities will also be more likely to use drugs, partially because they will have more time to do so. Involvement is a key component for juvenile delinquency in particular, because youth who are not occupied during nonschool hours or who are unsupervised will be more likely to use drugs or engage other forms of delinquency. The concept of commitment centers on the embrace of society's norms and concerns for one's reputation; as a result, those with greater commitment to conventionality are less likely to use drugs because they are concerned about reputation and their place in the conventional order. Finally, those who have internalized the normative standards of society will also be less likely to engage in drug use or any behavior contrary to these behavioral prescripts.

As with most other sociological theories, the social bond's effect on drug use is relative, and not absolute, which is to say those with stronger bonds are less likely to use drugs overall, while those with weak bonds will be more likely. However, this does not mean that those with strong bonds will abstain from using drugs, while those with weak bonds will necessarily use. And while attachment and commitment to conventional relationships and institutions may indeed impede drug use, attachment to unconventional, illegitimate, or delinquent relationships and institutions may increase the likelihood of use.

Overall, the extant literature has provided a fair amount of empirical support for the major tenets of Hirschi's social bond theory. Weak social bonds have been found to predict delinquency, generally (Krohn & Massey, 1980; H. V. Miller et al., 2009), and drug use, specifically (Hawkins, Catalano, & Miller, 1992; Marcos, Bahr, & Johnson, 1986). A number of studies have examined the relationship between social bonds and drug use and found that youth who are more attached, involved, and committed are significantly less likely to report the use of either licit or illicit substances (Akers & Lee, 1999; Hawkins et al., 1992; Hoffmann, 1995; Marcos et al., 1986). Collectively, these studies provide support for the role of social control in the etiology of drug use.

Self-control theory represents the most recent iteration of a control-based explanation of crime (Gottfredson & Hirschi, 1990). Unlike Hirschi's first version of control theory, self-control theory, authored with Michael Gottfredson (also termed "A General Theory of Crime"), centers on internal—as opposed to external—controls. While social bond theory saw control primarily as an external mechanism, self-control views internal mechanisms as key. This reformulated version of control theory views self-control in much the same way that Reckless (1961) viewed inner containments. Self-control is the ability to exercise control over one's impulses, to defer gratification, and to consider the consequences of one's actions. More specifically, Gottfredson and Hirschi present six elements of low self-control that they view as the underlying cause of crime and related problem behaviors, including drug use.

Gottfredson and Hirschi argue that self-control and involvement in deviant behavior have an inverse relationship such that those with relatively high levels of self-control will not succumb to the temptation of immediate gratification as easily as will those with relatively low levels of self-control. According to the theory, low self-control is a trait that consists of six dimensions: impulsivity, preference for simple over complex tasks, a high propensity for risk-seeking, preference for physical as opposed to mental activities, self-centeredness, and having a bad temper. Individuals possessing these traits, when given the opportunity, will be more likely to act on their impulses, deviant or otherwise. Those with low self-control will also engage in "analogous behaviors" that characterize their tendency "to pursue immediate pleasures that are not criminal: *they will tend to smoke, drink, use drugs,* gamble, have children out of wedlock, and engage in illicit sex" (Gottfredson & Hirschi, 1990, p. 90, emphasis added).

Gottfredson and Hirschi's (1990) general theory of crime frames the essential question for criminology in much the same way social bond theory does in that it asks why people refrain from crime. People with low self-control commit crime or use drugs because it is easy and because the opportunity presents itself. Those who are impulsive and short-sighted are more likely to use drugs when they are available because they act without consideration of the consequences of such behavior. Drug use is in many ways the quintessential behavior predicted by self-control theory—those who use are looking for immediate gratification through the psychotropic effects of the drugs on their brains, often with little regard for the long-term consequences. The ingestion of psychoactive chemicals is perhaps the most immediate of gratifications in both a physiological and, in many ways, social sense. By this we mean that drugs are often consumed in social settings in the presence of peers, which can also provide less biologically tangible social gratifications (or social reinforcements, to the learning theorists).

There have been few theories that have received the empirical attention afforded the general theory of crime. Like social bond theory, this version of control theory has also received strong support from prior studies examining the link between self-control and crime, generally, and drug use, specifically. Low self-control has been tied to the use of alcohol, tobacco, marijuana, cocaine, and a number of other serious drugs (Arneklev, Grasmick, Tittle, & Bursik, 1993; Baker, 2010; Ford & Blumenstein, 2013; Gibbs & Giever, 1995). Overall, the extant criminological literature offers considerable support for a link between self-control and drug use.

STRAIN THEORY

Similar to control perspectives, strain theories enjoy a long history in the sociology of crime and deviance (Durkheim, 1897; Merton, 1938). Strain theories, sometimes referred to as *anomie theories*, argue that deviant behaviors, including crime and drug use, are the result of some sort of societal or individual-level dysregulation that affects human behavior. Durkheim applied the concept of anomie/strain to suicide in the late 19th century, and Merton used strain as an explanation for crime in the early 20th century. Both of these early explanations for deviance were macro-level functionalist in their orientation in that they were attempting to explain how strain impacts rates of suicide and crime. The most recent version of strain theory, Agnew's (1992) general strain theory (GST) approaches the topic differently, instead focusing on individual-level motivations for crime and deviance. Both Merton's anomie/strain and Agnew's GST are discussed relative to drug use below.

Strain theory, in both of its major forms, contends that deviance, including drug use, is the result of negative stimuli that place stress on individuals (as in the case of GST) or certain segments of society (as in the case of Mertonian strain). The source of this strain, however, varies by theory. Merton's theory argues that strain arises from the discrepancy between the goals (values) and means (norms) legitimized by modern American society. The source of this discrepancy, according to Merton, is the economic system of capitalism that creates a situation wherein social inequality exists. Those who find themselves in the unfortunate position of being at the bottom of this economic system are faced with a quandary because they share in the legitimized goals of American society, which emphasize financial success and material acquisition, but lack the means to effectively realize these goals. According to anomie/strain theory, those faced with such a challenge will respond to this discrepancy through one of several *modes of adaptation*.

Merton offered five distinct models of adaptation, and all center around the concepts of goals and means. Most people, when faced with the understanding of society's legitimized goals and means, will confirm to these normative standards of behavior (termed *conformity*). These individuals accept the socially prescribed goals and means and, as a result, are unlikely to commit crime. Merton's second mode of adaptation, *innovation*, is defined as an acceptance of goals and rejection of means, a combination that results in criminal offending. These crimes are typically those that provide some sort of financial or economic benefit such as drug dealing, property crime, and fraudulent activities resulting in pecuniary gain. Note that innovation will not necessarily result in crimes such as the *use* of drugs.

Ritualism, the third mode of adaptation, is described as a rejection of goals and acceptance of means, while *retreatism* is defined as a rejection of both goals and means. The last mode of adaptation, *rebellion,* was defined as a combination of rejection of societal goals and means and a substitution of other goals and means. Both retreatism and rebellion have special significance for drug use in that they are best equipped to explain such behavior. Those who have retreated from society, who have no interest in either society's goals or means because they cannot or do not wish to compete, are more likely to use drugs because it enables them to retreat further into the shadows of society. Indeed, one of the major costs associated with drug use is the impact its chronic use can have on other aspects of an individual's life. If that individual has already given up on life, then this cost becomes immaterial to the calculation. The concept of retreatism was expanded on in the 1960s by Cloward and Ohlin (1960) in differential opportunity theory, which was conceived as an extension of Merton's illegitimate opportunity structure construct. Cloward and Ohlin presented a typology of ideal types of juvenile gangs, one of which was the retreatist gang. These delinquents were seen as double failures that could compete in neither the legitimate nor the illegitimate opportunity structure and, as a result, retreated from society into a world of drug use, abuse, and addiction. For this group, social interaction was limited to other drug using adults who were in a position to teach the ways of life as an addict.

Similarly, rebellion can also explain drug use in that its adherents are predisposed to challenge the conventional societal order. The prohibition of drug use is a cornerstone of modern American criminal justice (i.e., the "War on Drugs") and the violation of this norm, along with its symbolic representation of the 1960s counterculture, is a readymade opportunity for rebellion, particularly for youth. For those who value rebellion against conventionality, drug use is an opportunity to engage in behavior that has both actual and symbolic value.

The more recent of the strain explanations for crime, general strain theory, emphasizes a different source of strain than does Merton's version. GST presents strain as the result of one (or more) of the following three conditions: (1) removal of positive stimuli, (2) introduction of negative stimuli, or (3) failure to achieve positively valued goals. Any of these will produce strain that in turn will cause crime or deviant behavior. The general strain perspective is particularly useful for understanding drug use and abuse and is often utilized in studies of both licit (alcohol, tobacco) and illicit (marijuana, cocaine) drugs. In practice, treating those with alcohol and drug addiction requires an explicit focus on "triggering mechanisms," stimuli that occur in the addict's environment that trigger or cause the use of substances.

Agnew's theory does not predict that everyone will experience and react to strain in the same way, however. Indeed, all people are exposed to various stressors and strains, often on a daily basis, and certainly not all turn to drug use to alleviate this strain. Agnew argues that strain's impact is conditioned in part by individual behavioral coping mechanisms that will actually determine whether or not a person turns to problem behavior as a means of stress management. Those who utilize positive coping mechanisms such as minimizing negative outcomes and maximizing positive outcomes are less likely to use drugs to reduce strain. Conversely, those who utilize negative coping mechanisms such as externalizing, aggression, and problem behavior are more likely to use drugs to alleviate their strain.

Most of the research on strain and drug use has focused on testing the major hypotheses offered by Agnew's GST. A considerable amount of evidence supports the theory's main propositions and previous studies have found a significant relationship between the presence of strain and the use of a range of both licit and illicit substances (Agnew & White, 1992; Carson, Sullivan, Cochran, & Lersch, 2008; Hoffmann & Su, 1997; Moon, Morash, McCluskey, & Hwang, 2009). Strain has been linked to the use of alcohol (Moon et al., 2009; Stogner & Gibson, 2011), marijuana (Akers & Cochrane, 1985), cocaine (Stogner & Gibson, 2011), prescription drugs (Schroeder & Ford, 2012), and "hard drugs" such as heroin, PCP, and LSD (Stogner & Gibson, 2011). These studies have operationalized strain in a number of ways, including negative life events, health problems, economic stressors, gender discrimination, parental punishment, and family conflict. Overall, the extant literature suggests that strain-related variables account for a significant amount of the variation in drug use.

CONFLICT THEORY

Whereas most of the theories reviewed in this chapter observe the role of socioeconomic stratification in shaping environment, culture, and social interaction, conflict perspectives illustrate how by-products of inequality such as exploitation, shared alienation, and frustration manifest as social problems. Rooted in Marxist heritage (Marx, 1867/1978), this perspective contends that social order does not reflect the consensus model of society suggested by the structural-functionalist framework but that social institutions, including the criminal justice system, are defined by and attentive to uneven distribution of power and resources throughout society.

The emergence of critical criminology in the United States during the late 1960s and 1970s transpired during a period of great social unrest and change. The civil rights movement, the Vietnam War, and liberalization of the popular culture (i.e., the sexual revolution, feminism, and unprecedented recreational drug use) reflected widespread disenchantment with established traditions and the status quo. Challenges to authority were met with intensified social control responses, including the targeting of drug offenders whose use signaled defiance and challenge to authority. If anything, official efforts to abolish marijuana only heightened the symbolic significance of use and the intangible rewards of counter-culture identification. Though critical sociologists led the charge in disseminating the origins and discriminatory nature of drug policy through structural Marxist concepts, most criminological research focused on property and violent crimes committed by the lower class. Such focus serves to deflect attention away from drug legislation and selective enforcement practices disproportionately affecting the poor and racial minorities. To many, criminologists were simultaneously denouncing and contributing to the problem.

Social scientists, including criminologists, became increasingly opposed to class- and race-based discrimination by the criminal justice system and accentuated social justice themes in their work, characterizing responses to crime and delinquency as a function of offender social standing rather than objective differences in antisocial behaviors (Bonger, 1916/1969). In the countless events and protests during this era, open drug use (typically marijuana) became symbolically indicative of challenges to authority, autonomy, and self-expression—lasting themes that still attach to marijuana use in private and more public settings alike. Drug use transcended the simpler medicine-recreation dichotomy to represent a social common denominator, with use, jargon, and hippie fashion signifying subscription to drug subcultural values of self-expression, challenges to conventional authority, and realignment of economic opportunity.

The works of Tannenbaum (1938), Lemert (1951), and Becker (1963) observed that the *labeling* of criminal behavior was class-based and that the effects of labeling were frequently more consequential than the behavior itself. Labeling theory purports that legal construction often entails assignment of arbitrary designators to certain types of behavior that signal an individual's deviance and diminished social status (stigmatizing labels) largely apart from the objective inherent harm associated with the behavior. The theory also asserts that internalization of these negative assigned characterizations heavily shape self-esteem, image, and ultimately, future behavior. Acceptance of oneself as a "pothead," for example, would lead labeling theorists to predict that additional marijuana use should be expected as self-fulfilling prophecy.

Whereas marijuana use had become popular throughout society by the 1970s, intense narcotics enforcement of harder substance use concentrated in poor minority neighborhoods (heroin, cocaine, and later, crack) and often entailed racial profiling, which in turn deteriorated police-minority relations. Conflict theory is thus more applicable to heroin and crack use and trafficking than softer drugs, as theorists observe addiction to these drugs cluster around lower-class, predominately minority neighborhoods. Because more lower- and working-class residents, particularly in urban underclass settings, abuse hard drugs, enforcement is concentrated in lower-class neighborhoods where social disorganization and limited collective efficacy fuel and mask drug use and dealing. Little reduction in drug use and drug-crime-related violence, however, was realized, instead were deleterious results such as weakened police-community relations, reduced confidence in the police, and an enhanced symbolic significance of drug use as political resistance.

Integrated Theories of Drug Use and Abuse

The extension of traditional criminological theory to the topic of substance use suffers from both definitional limitations constituting theoretical asymmetry and reliance on theoretical singularity. Theories of crime causation address behavior defined as illegal and perceived as being associated with individual level victimization and public harm. As T. L. Anderson notes (1998), such an approach is problematic due to indiscriminate treatment of substance use and abuse. While recreational experimentation with marijuana is extensive throughout youth culture, most mature out of regular use if not altogether. A much smaller number of chronic habitual "hard" drug users should be the intended focus in drug etiological approaches, generally and given the import of delinquent peers and subcultural setting in the sociological criminology tradition, as this high offending drug dependent group is primarily responsible for most of the drugs-crime nexus. Though the multitude of arrests for the soft drug possession and distribution that constitute crime, more often than not they are not in an intrinsic and qualitative sense regarding property and safety threats. Accordingly, theoretical progression necessitates distinction between drug use and drug abuse and particularly when the explanatory focus is on drug-related or drug-driven crime. Addiction maintenance is a fundamental focal concern shaping addicts' primary life domain and criminal lifestyles. Future theorists should better target this population of interest in that all use is not abuse, and use is not necessarily criminal beyond moral code infraction.

Another limitation of extant criminological drug use theory is theoretical singularity. Learning, control, and conflict perspectives suffer from the common problem of purporting the causal nature of a sole or limited number of related factors rather than addressing their temporal alignment and interrelationships. Criminological theories of drug use have been characterized as complementary more than competitive, suggesting empirical support and theoretical variability across multiple concepts (Goode, 2011). More fundamentally, criminological theories, including integrated general perspectives, were not designed to explain drug use *per se*, and their application to use reinforces objective punitive philosophy. Perhaps greater integration of accepted drug use predictors and drivers into a more general theory will better recognize the need to measure across individual, interactional group, and societal factors specified across extant criminological theories. Though criminologists have pursued a general theory of crime far more than a general theory of drug abuse, explanations have been developed featuring both sequential integration (capturing the additive effects of multiple use correlates) and conceptual fusion (linking correlates across levels of analysis). A leading example of each integration strategy applied to drug use is illustrated below.

ELLIOTT'S INTEGRATED DELINQUENCY THEORY

Elliott, Ageton, and Canter (1979) integrated concepts from original strain theory (Merton 1938), social control theory (Hirschi 1969), and social learning and modeling theories (Akers et al., 1979; Bandura, 1962) in a delinquent peer bonding approach. As the foremost facilitator of initial and continued use, peers are necessary to acquire drugs, and the majority of use occurs in group contexts—particularly marijuana, the most commonly used illicit drug. Deviant peer bonding, then, is the driving causal concept resulting from nonconventional bonds with the mainstream school population, loose attachment to family members, and compensatory association with other delinquents.

Delinquent peers theories, such as Haynie's (2001) delinquent peer networks approach specifying delinquent group structural properties (centrality, density, and popularity of group members), are well suited to extend the Elliott et al. perspective given the solidifying function of meso-level drug use. While researchers observe that general social acceptance is a strong youth behavior motive conditioning initial use fairly common in contemporary society, chronic use associated with more serious crime and related social problems is conditioned by close associations with a small group of fellow drug subculture members. Though integrating distinct sociological constructs, Elliott's theory does not factor biosocial or psychological elements presumably relevant to friendship development and peer bonding processes. Additional shortcomings include equating use and abuse and the limited empirical distinction between delinquent peers, generally, and more consequential intimate drug subculture associations.

CULTURAL-IDENTITY THEORY

The cultural-identity theory of drug abuse (T. L. Anderson, 1998) provides perhaps the most robust contemporaneous explanation of drug etiology within the sociological criminology tradition. The notion of "drug-related identity change" is the central concept in this multifaceted theory that is unique in (1) focusing on drug abuse rather than drug use, (2) definitional appreciation of drug use as basic to abusers and substance-involved offenders' identities, (3) integration of subcultural and social disorganization effects on personal marginalization, and (4) the relevance of drug subculture participation. Beyond the explanatory scope of most theories of drug etiology, substance use and abuse is illustrated as an outcome of combined environmental, peer group, and societal influences. In short, the theory postulates that drug abuse is a function of a drug-driven identity change process incorporating explanatory factors across three levels of analysis.

Micro-level (*personal marginalization, ego identity discomfort,* and *lack of definitional control in identity development*), meso-level (*social marginalization* and *drug subculture immersion*), and macro-level (*economic opportunity, educational opportunity,* and *popular culture reinforcement*) concepts enable not only inclusion of a greater number of germane factors contributing to abuse, but also consideration of how environment and social dynamics frame structural conditions receptive to individual motives for substance abuse. Though there have been few empirical examinations of cultural-identity theory, several important contributions enhance the prospects of drug etiology advancement including: (1) generally, and especially for criminologists, use and abuse should not be treated interchangeably because the latter is more relevant to discussions of drug offending; (2) greater understanding of the nature of drug use and abuse through examination of causal factors across levels of analysis; (3) actual participation in a drug subculture and interaction with other subculture members as more consequential than peer group approval; and (4) drug subculture facilitates and reifies formation of an identity of which drug use is a defining characteristic (T. L. Anderson, 1998). While cultural-identity theory certainly is conceptually comprehensive and suitable for multi-level rigorous empirical testing far more so than other criminological explanations of drug use, it remains rooted in and draws largely on the sociological criminology literature.

Looking Beyond the False Dichotomy

As illustrated in this chapter, there are multiple "nurture" explanations within theoretical criminology that have been utilized to explain drug use. Virtually all are derived from larger sociological perspectives and contrast with substance use theories originating from biological factors. Historically, scholars have subscribed to either a nature or nurture theoretical approach and still have not posited a fully integrated etiological explanation. Acknowledgment that both biological and sociological factors are relevant suggests that policy and practice remain largely rooted in and driven by a false dichotomy. Sociological criminologists, as well as other social science drug researchers, are often rightly concerned with the quick and continuing rise of biosocial criminology. Researchers in some specialty areas are apt to lose theoretical ground, but drug research, from any disciplinary orientation, is inherently social.

For drug use to occur, it is requisite that two factors align in time and place: the desire to use and the availability of drugs. Neither the desire to use *sans* drug availability nor their presence with disinterested people will result in use. Biological and psychological theories of use, though often postulated with little empirical support, have been recently advanced with greater rigor to a point that few researchers challenge the existence of predisposition to drug use. Not all individuals predisposed to use, however, actually use or abuse drugs, and among those that do, there is considerable variability regarding the severity of use. Among virtually any sizeable population of drug users, researchers find that individual consumption patterns vary in regard to drug of choice, means of ingestion, and the social context of use. Even in urban underclass and impoverished rural areas riddled with substance abuse issues, the using percentage of the population, the frequency of use, and quantity consumed are negatively correlated with ascension of drug hardness.

The application of sociological theories of drug use entails the empirical discovery of risk and protective factors across prevention, intervention, and rehabilitation stages. The delivery of cognitive behavioral therapy (CBT) addressing patterns of thinking and underlying beliefs, attitudes, and values to substance abusing offenders in incarcerated settings examples both the relevance of and need for a more holistic treatment approach. Federal substance abuse prevention and reduction initiatives have been intensified through the United States Office of Justice Programs during the Obama administration (e.g., the Second Chance Act Reentry Program for Adult Offenders with Co-Occurring Substance Abuse and Mental Health Disorders and the Substance Abuse and Mental Health Services Administration Drug-Free Communities Mentoring Program) to complement the now nationally institutionalized Residential Substance Abuse Treatment Program sponsored through the United States Bureau of Justice Assistance (BJA). Most of these programs (1) apply the rehabilitation risk principle of targeting those most in need of treatment, such as the dually diagnosed; (2) deliver CBT modalities, such as moral reconation therapy; and (3) strive to identify social support to facilitate relapse avoidance and successful reentry.

Attempts to reconfigure criminal thinking and drug using patterns, bolster moral outlook, and repair severed social bonds presuppose that treatment participants engage in rehabilitation with an intelligence level and prosocial worldview that too often are missing. Identification of offenders unlikely to be responsive to CBT and better suited for alternative treatment strategies ostensibly would increase treatment success through the admission of program participants capable of engaging psycho-social change protocols. Through greater attention to biological (e.g., IQ and mental health issues) as well as sociological factors during general and inmate intake needs assessments, theoretically driven research can inform better targeting of needs and services.

The importance of incorporating biosocial insight into drug policy is also evident in the medicated therapy debate, especially opiate treatment and the different physiological effects of methadone, buprenorphine/naloxone (Suboxone), and lofexidine. Across the country, opiate addicts are "sweating it out" without medication or only homeopathic supplements. Regardless of whether the lack of appropriate medication is due to limited resources or punitive ideology, surely the physical and psychological pains of untreated withdrawal undermine rehabilitation goals. Somewhat ironically, applications of traditional criminological theory never intended to address drug use specifically, and generally the portrayal of use as abuse and users as criminals fortifies a punitive rather than holistic public policy orientation. Whereas early sociologists of drug use quickly recognized the often counterproductive nature of drug intervention, subsequent reliance on mainstream theoretical criminology has often validated it through the construction of "substance-involved offenders" and the linking of public safety to rehabilitation success.

The development of applied theoretical research programs executed through research-practitioner partnerships is needed to understand the relationships between deterministic factors and social mitigates of drug use and abuse to effectively inform substance abuse practice and policy. Accordingly, ongoing theoretical research programs should forgo replacement of theories based in sociological criminology with pure biosocial alternatives. While biosocial contributions enrich understanding of drug use, they should be considered as complementary rather than alternative explanations. Identification of genetic factors and related biological determinants of predisposition to use are separate from sociological factors impacting onset and predictive of continued use. As implied by Goode (2011), future drug use theorizing needs to address the vital elements of availability relative to opportunity to use. Theoretical advancement should look to the differential opportunities (i.e., access) to use drugs as conditioned by the conceptual overlap of individual tendencies, environmental factors, and interactional patterns. Instead of fostering theoretical competition between genetics theory and criminology, a more comprehensive understanding of drug use etiology can be realized through approaches effectively integrating the two paradigms.

References

Agnew, R. (1992). Foundation for a general strain theory of crime and delinquency. *Criminology, 30*, 47–87.

Agnew, R., & White, H. R. (1992). An empirical test of general strain theory. *Criminology, 30*, 475–499.

Akers, R. L. (1998). *Social learning and social structure: A general theory of crime and deviance.* Boston, MA: Northeastern University Press.

Akers, R. L., & Cochran, J. K. (1985). Adolescent marijuana use: A test of three theories of deviant behavior. *Deviant Behavior, 6*, 323–346.

Akers, R. L., Krohn, M., Lanza-Kaduce, L., & Radosevich, M. (1979). Social learning and deviant behavior: A specific test of a general theory. *American Sociological Review, 44*, 636–655.

Akers, R. L., & Lee, G. (1999). Age, social learning, and social bonding in adolescent substance use. *Deviant Behavior, 19*, 1–25.

Anderson, E. (1999). *Code of the street: Decency, violence and the moral life of the inner city.* New York, NY: W. W. Norton.

Anderson, T. L. (1998). A cultural-identity theory of drug abuse. In J. T. Ulmer (Ed.), *Sociology of crime, law, and deviance* (Vol.1, pp. 233–262). Greenwich, CT: JAI.

Arneklev, B., Grasmick H., Tittle C., & Bursik R. (1993). Low self-control and imprudent behavior. *Journal of Quantitative Criminology, 9*, 225–247.

Baker, J. O. (2010). The expression of low self-control as problematic drinking in adolescents: An integrated control perspective. *Journal of Criminal Justice, 38*, 237–244.

Bandura, A. (1962). *Social learning through interaction.* Lincoln: University of Nebraska Press.

Becker, H. S. (1955). Marihuana use and social control. *Social Problems, 3*(1), 35–44.

Becker, H. S. (1963). *Outsiders: Studies in the sociology of deviance.* New York, NY: Free Press.

Blumer, H. (1986). *Symbolic interactionism: Perspective and method.* Berkeley: University of California Press.

Bonger, W. (1969). *Crime and economic conditions.* Bloomington: Indiana University Press. (Original work published 1916)

Carson, D. C., Sullivan, C. J., Cochran, J. K., & Lersch, K. M. (2008). General strain theory and the relationship between early victimization and drug use. *Deviant Behavior, 30*, 54–88.

Cloward, R. A., & Ohlin, L. (1960). *Delinquency and opportunity: A theory of delinquent gangs.* New York, NY: Free Press.

Cohen, A. K. (1955). *Delinquent boys: The culture of the gang.* Glencoe, IL: Free Press.

Dai, B. (1970). *Patterson Smith Reprint Series in Criminology, Law Enforcement, and Social Problems No. 126: Opium addiction in Chicago.* Montclair, NJ: Patterson Smith. (Original work published 1937, Shanghai, China)

Durkheim, E. (1897). *Suicide.* New York, NY: Free Press.

Elliott, D. S., Ageton, S. S., & Canter, R. J. (1979). An integrated theoretical perspective on delinquent behavior. *Journal of Research in Crime and Delinquency, 16*(1), 3–27.

Faupel, C. E., Horowitz, A. M., & Weaver, G. (2003). *The sociology of American drug use.* New York, NY: McGraw-Hill Humanities/Social Sciences/Languages.

Ford, J. A., & Blumenstein, L. (2013). Self-control and substance use among college students. *Journal of Drug Issues, 43*, 56–68.

Gibbs, J., & Giever, D. (1995). Self-control and its manifestations among university students: An empirical test of Gottfredson and Hirschi's general theory. *Justice Quarterly, 12*, 231–256.

Goode, E. (2011). *The sociology of drug use: 21st century sociology.* Thousand Oaks, CA: Sage.

Gottfredson, M. R., & Hirschi, T. (1990). *A general theory of crime.* Stanford, CA: Stanford University Press.

Hawkins, J. D., Catalano, R. F., & Miller J. Y. (1992). Risk and protective factors for alcohol use and other drug problems in adolescence and early adulthood: Implications for substance use prevention. *Psychological Bulletin, 112*, 64–105.

Haynie, D. L. (2001). Delinquent peers revisited: Does network structure matter? *American Journal of Sociology, 106*(4), 1013–1057.

Hirschi, T. (1969). *Causes of delinquency.* Berkeley: University of California Press.

Hoffmann, J. P. (1995). The effects of family structure and family relations on adolescent marijuana use. *International Journal of the Addictions, 30*, 1207–1241.

Hoffmann, J. P., & Su, S. S. (1997). The conditional effects of stress on delinquency and drug use: A strain theory assessment of sex differences. *Journal of Research in Crime & Delinquency, 34*, 46–78.

Hwang, S., & Akers, R. L. (2003). Substance use by Korean adolescents: A cross-cultural test of social learning, social bonding, and self-control theories. In R. L. Akers & G. F. Jensen (Eds.), *Social learning theory and the explanation of crime: A guide for the new century* (pp. 39–64). New Brunswick, NJ: Transaction.

Krohn, M. D., & Massey, J. L. (1980). Social control and delinquent behavior: An examination of the elements of the social bond. *Sociological Quarterly, 21*, 529–543.

Lemert, E. M. (1951). *Social pathology; A systematic approach to the theory of sociopathic behavior.* New York, NY: McGraw Hill.

Lemert, E. M. (1967). *Human deviance, social problems, and social control*. Englewood Cliffs, NJ: Prentice-Hall.

Lindensmith, A. R. (1947). *Opiate addiction*. Bloomington, IN: Principa Press.

Marcos, A. C., Bahr, S. J., & Johnson, R. E. (1986). Test of a bonding/association theory of adolescent drug use. *Social Forces, 65*, 135–161.

Marx, K. (1978). Das Kapital. In R. C. Tucker (Ed.), *The Marx-Engels reader* (2nd ed.). New York, NY: W. W. Norton. (Original work published 1867.)

McGee, Z. T. (1992). Social class differences in parental and peer influence on adolescent drug use. *Deviant Behavior, 13*, 349–372.

Mead, G. H. (1967). *Mind, self, and society: From the standpoint of a social behaviorist* (Works of George Herbert Mead, Vol. 1). Chicago, IL: University of Chicago Press.

Merton, R. K. (1938). Social structure and anomie. *American Sociological Review, 54*(5), 597–611.

Miller, H. V. (2011). The social context of acculturation: Findings from a sample of Hispanic adolescents. *American Journal of Criminal Justice, 36*(2), 93–105.

Miller, H. V., Jennings, W. G., Alvarez-Rivera, L. L., & Lanza-Kaduce, L. (2009). Self-control, attachment, and deviance among Hispanic adolescents. *Journal of Criminal Justice, 37*, 77–84.

Miller, H. V., Jennings, W. G., Alvarez-Rivera, L., & Miller, J. M. (2008). Explaining substance use among Puerto Rican adolescents: A partial test of social learning theory. *Journal of Drug Issues, 38*(1), 261–284.

Miller, J. M., Miller, H. V., Zapata, J., & Yin, Z. (2008). Mexican-American youth drug use and acculturation: A note on the mitigating effects of contextual dynamics. *Journal of Drug Issues, 38*(1), 199–214.

Miller, J. M., & Selva, L. H. (1994). Drug enforcement's double-edged sword: An assessment of asset forfeiture programs. *Justice Quarterly, 11*(2), 313–335.

Miller, W. B. (1958). Lower-class culture as a generating milieu of gang delinquency. *Journal of Social Issues, 14*(3), 5–19.

Moon, B., Morash, M., McCluskey, C., & Hwang, H. W. (2009). Comprehensive test of general strain theory: Key strains, situational based emotions, trait based emotions and delinquency. *Journal of Research in Crime and Delinquency, 46*(2), 182–212.

Nye, F. I. (1958). *Family relationships and delinquent behaviors*. Englewood Cliffs, NJ: Prentice Hall.

Petraitis, J., Flay, B. R., & Miller, T. Q. (1995). Reviewing theories of adolescent substance use: Organizing pieces in the puzzle. *Psychological Bulletin, 117*(1), 67–86.

Reckless, W. C. (1961). A new theory of delinquency and crime. *Federal Probation, 25*, 42–46.

Reckless, W. C. (1969). *Vice in Chicago*. Glen Ridge, NJ: Patterson Smith (Original work published 1933).

Reiss, A. J. (1951). Delinquency as the failure of personal and social controls. *American Sociological Review, 16*, 196–207.

Schroeder, R. D., & Ford, J. A. (2012). Prescription drug misuse: A test of three competing criminological theories. *Journal of Drug Issues, 42*, 4–27.

Schur, E. M. (1963). *Narcotic addiction in Britain and America: The impact of public policy* (Vol. 7). Bloomington: Indiana University Press.

Shaw, C., & McKay, H. (1942). *Social factors in juvenile delinquency*. Washington, DC: Government Printing Office.

Shedler, J., & Block, J. (1990). Adolescent drug use and psychological health: A longitudinal inquiry. *American Psychologist, 45*(5), 612–630.

Steinberg, L. (2007). Risk taking in adolescence: New perspectives from brain and behavioral science. *Current Directions in Psychological Science, 16*, 55–59.

Steinberg, L. (2008). A social neuroscience perspective on adolescent risk-taking. *Developmental Review, 28*, 78–106.

Stogner, J., & Gibson, C. L. (2011). The influence of health strain on the initiation and frequency of substance use in a national sample of adolescents. *Journal of Drug Issues, 41*, 69–93.

Sutherland, E. (1947). *Principles of criminology* (4th ed.). Philadelphia, PA: J. B. Lippincott.

Tannenbaum, F. (1938). *Crime and community*. New York, NY: Ginn.

Wallace, S. E. (1968). The road to skid row. *Social Problems, 16*(1), 92–105.

20

Drug Abuse, Addiction, and Crime

A Cell to Society Perspective

Michael G. Vaughn
Saint Louis University

Christopher P. Salas-Wright
The University of Texas at Austin

Brandy R. Maynard
Saint Louis University

Introduction

There is no single cause of drug abuse and no single connection between drugs and crime. As Boyum, Caulkins, and Kleinman (2011) point out, simplistic notions about addiction causing crime are badly flawed. Some highly addictive substances such as heroin are related to crime but others like tobacco are not. The title of this chapter is fitting in that drug abuse, addiction, and crime cover so much biosocial terrain that a "cell to society" approach is necessary to coherently frame the many factors involved in this complex phenomenon. As such, we examine definitional issues, epidemiology, and prevailing frameworks before outlining the cell to society terrain in terms of etiology, correlates, and prevention and control.

WHAT IS DRUG ABUSE AND ADDICTION?

There are several definitional issues that require discussion. The first is what we mean by terms such as use, abuse, and addiction. *Use* refers simply to substance intake without the chronic life problems that abuse and addiction often entail. In this sense, use is the starting point. From a clinical-medical view, *abuse* is use of drugs even though it is having a negative impact on one's health and life situation. Although there are many clinical definitions of addiction, one definition that succinctly captures the essence of addiction has been put forth by George Koob and Michael LeMoal (2005), who defined *addiction* as follows: "Drug addiction, also known as substance dependence, is a chronically relapsing disorder characterized by (1) a compulsion to seek and take the drug, (2) loss of control in limiting intake, and (3) emergence of a negative emotional state (e.g., dysphoria, anxiety, irritability) when access to the drug is prevented (defined here as dependence)" (p. 25). Importantly, Koob and LeMoal's definition includes key features that result in or are connected to crime: compulsive drug-seeking behavior, lowered self-control, and negative emotions. Another factor is that abuse and dependence on substances often results in physiological tolerance where the body requires an increased amount to achieve desired effects. While it is abundantly clear that drug abuse and problem behavior have a strong biological basis, it is also clear that there are strong social and environmental elements that are intimately connected to these biological processes.

The Nature of Drug Abuse, Addiction, and Crime

EPIDEMIOLOGY OF DRUG USE

The use and abuse of illicit drugs and alcohol are widespread and constitute an important social and public health problem in the United States (Danaei et al., 2009) and beyond (Rehm, Taylor, & Room, 2006). Recent estimates from the National Survey on Drug Use and Health (NSDUH) suggest that roughly 22.5 million Americans, or approximately 9% of the total U.S. population aged 12 years or older, are current illicit drug users (Substance Abuse and Mental Health Services Administration [SAMHSA], 2012). The majority of these individuals are exclusively marijuana users (64.3%); however, important percentages also report use of cocaine, hallucinogens, inhalants, heroin, and, increasingly, prescription drugs such as opioid medications, sedatives, tranquilizers, and stimulants (McCabe, Cranford, & West, 2008). In terms of lifetime drug use, nearly half of all Americans (46%) report having tried illicit drugs at least once in their lifetime, with an average

age of drug use initiation of just over 18 years (SAMHSA, 2012). Similarly disconcerting numbers can be identified in terms of alcohol use. While roughly half of all Americans are nondrinkers (48.2%), nearly a quarter report recent binge alcohol use (22.6%), and an additional 6.2% report frequent binge drinking (SAMHSA, 2012). Given the widespread use of drugs and alcohol, it is perhaps unsurprising that the prevalence of substance use disorders in the United States is also noteworthy. For instance, Compton, Thomas, Stinson, and Grant (2007), drawing from the National Epidemiologic Survey on Alcohol and Related Conditions (NESARC), estimated that 1 in 10 American adults (10.3%) develops a drug use disorder during their lifetime (7.7% abuse, 2.6% dependence). These numbers cohere with findings from the NSDUH, which estimates that 8% of the U.S. population 12 years or older meets criteria for either alcohol (6.5%) or illicit drug (2.5%) abuse or dependence (SAMHSA, 2012).

Evidence suggests that substance use and abuse are particularly prevalent among young people in the United States. For instance, 1 in 5 (20.1%) American adolescents reports having tried illicit drugs by the 8th grade, a figure that steadily increases to approximately 2 in 5 (37.7%) by the 10th grade and roughly (49.9%) half of all adolescents by the 12th grade (Johnston, O'Malley, Bachman, & Schulenberg, 2012). As in the case of adults, marijuana is the most commonly used drug during adolescence (39.9%), followed by inhalants (11.4%), cocaine (6.8%), methamphetamine (3.8%), and heroin (2.9%) (Centers for Disease Control and Prevention, 2012). Alcohol use and abuse are also widespread during adolescence, while 1 in 5 teens (20.5%) reports using alcohol before the age of 13, nearly 3 in 4 (70.1%) report trying alcohol at some point during adolescence, and one quarter (25.0%) of all late adolescents report having been drunk during the previous month (Centers for Disease Control and Prevention, 2012; Johnston et al., 2012). Simply, during the critical developmental period of adolescence, a substantial proportion of Americans use and abuse a variety of illicit substances.

DRUG USE AND CRIME

Elevated rates of substance use during adolescence and throughout the life span are associated with involvement in crime and the criminal justice system. Indeed, compared to a rate of 8% to 10% in the general population (Compton et al., 2007; SAMHSA, 2012), it is estimated that roughly half of all local (55%), state (53%), and federal (46%) inmates meet criteria for drug abuse or dependence (Chandler, Fletcher, & Volkow, 2009). Criminal and antisocial behaviors associated with substance use/abuse include: drug selling (White, Loeber, & Farrington, 2008), violent and nonviolent crime (Krug, Mercy, Dahlberg, & Zwi, 2002; White, Tice, Loeber, & Stouthamer-Loeber, 2002), intimate partner violence (Moore et al., 2008), prostitution (Yacoubian, Urbach, Larsen, Johnson, & Peters, 2001), gang involvement (Hill, Howell, Hawkins, & Battin-Pearson, 1999), and delinquent behaviors such as status offenses (Maynard, Salas-Wright, Vaughn, & Peters, 2012), property crimes, drug crime, and interpersonal violence (D'Amico, Edelen, Miles, & Morral, 2008). Notably, however, despite the strong association between substance use and crime, person-centered analyses have highlighted the fact that many individuals nevertheless use illicit substances without becoming involved in criminal behavior and that some serious offenders report little or no substance use (Vaughn et al., 2011). In all, despite the aforementioned caveats, the overwhelming body of evidence clearly indicates that the use of a variety of illicit substances is strongly associated with a host of criminal behaviors ranging from shoplifting to armed robbery (Bennett, Holloway, & Farrington, 2008).

Prevailing Frameworks

ADDICTION AS A BRAIN DISEASE (BUT WITH CONTEXT)

In an influential commentary appearing in the prestigious journal, *Science*, Alan Leshner (1997), former director of the National Institute on Drug Abuse, declared that "Addiction Is a Brain Disease, and It Matters." Based on 20 years of scientific research on addiction, Leshner revealed that most of the neural circuits (mainly the reward pathway) affected by common drugs of abuse are fairly well established. Much of the best research has found that there indeed are major differences that can be found in the brains of addicted persons compared to nonaddicted persons. These differences are not minor. Leshner also recognized that context (i.e., the social environment) that drug abusers are nested in possesses an important role in the development and course of addiction and related behavior. Even today, few serious scientists of drug abuse disagree with the major points made by Leshner.

COMPULSIVE DRUG SEEKING

The main neural circuit impacted by drugs of abuse is commonly termed the *reward pathway*. Why is this so important? The reward pathway, or specifically the mesolimbic reward system, is of critical importance because survival depends upon it. The reward pathway is the area of the brain that provides the positive reinforcement for eating, drinking, sex, and other functions basic to survival. As such, the reward pathway is a major component of the evolutionary history of human beings. What happens to this area of the brain when drugs are ingested? The reward pathway becomes flooded with dopamine above and beyond the levels produced by food and other reinforcers to the extent that it becomes "hijacked." Depending on the person, the drug (e.g., heroin, methamphetamine), and the social context, sometimes compulsive drug seeking and craving follows due to the powerful pleasure and reinforcement effects. Of course, not everyone who ingests a major illicit drug falls into this pattern, because there is individual variation in the ability to exercise self-control. In drug dependent persons, these substances often powerfully overwhelm executive governance and affect the ability to plan and exercise judgment over one's actions and their environmental effects (Lubman, Yucel, & Pantelis, 2004). We know from extensive research that self-control is a potent predictor of crime and substance-related problems (DeLisi, 2011; DeLisi & Vaughn, 2008; Vaughn, Beaver, DeLisi, Perron, & Schelbe, 2009).

GOLDSTEIN'S TRIPARTITE FRAMEWORK

One of the most impactful frameworks on drugs and its connection to violence is Paul Goldstein's (1985) tripartite drugs-violence nexus conceptualization. Goldstein developed this typology inductively as he collected data in New York City on drug abuse and its behavioral effects. The first component in the tripartite framework is psychopharmacological violence, which is violence perpetrated due to the direct effects that drugs have on our biology. This type of violence is difficult to measure without controlling for an individuals' preexisting tendency toward violence. The second component of the drugs-violence nexus is economic-compulsive violence. This occurs when drug abusing persons engage in robberies to provide money to purchase substances that will sustain their reward pathway. Importantly, Goldstein points out that these persons are not motivated by violence; rather, their primary motivation is to obtain money to purchase drugs. The final component is systemic violence. This type of drug-related violence is a result of drug markets and the business of distributing illicit substances. Examples of this type of violence are disputes over territory, price, quality, nonpayment, takeovers, and enforcement of codes of the business. The first two components of Goldstein's framework are clearly biosocial due to physiological impact and brain-based compulsive drug seeking. From a cell to society perspective, the framework captures in simple and straight-forward terms violence and drug abuse across the bioenvironmental landscape. However, the specific mechanisms for understanding the landscape and greater attention to the many layers in which drugs and crime can be situated is in need of a larger conceptualization of human behavior.

A Cell to Society Viewpoint

Although these prevailing frameworks are considered seminal, a fuller multifactorial organizational understanding of drug use and crime is needed given the complexities involved. Taking a biosocial cell to society perspective (Vaughn, DeLisi, & Matto, 2013), the emphasis in this chapter is on the influence of genes, physiology, emotions, executive governance, temperament, social cognition, and proximal and distal environments. Below we provide an overview of the cell to society perspective as applied to drug abuse and crime.

GENES

Heritability studies indicate that substantial variance in the liability to drug abuse, addiction, and alcohol dependence is due to genes (Bouchard, 2004; Hicks, Krueger, Iacono, McGue, & Patrick, 2004). Explanations of addiction, as well as other behavioral disorders, in popular culture tend to suggest that there is a direct causal relationship between a gene and some behavioral outcome. This is clearly not the case with respect to drug abuse and crime. Substance use disorders and behaviors are not inherited in a direct Mendelian way. Complex behaviors such as compulsive drug seeking lack a "gene for" explanation (Chakravarti & Little, 2003; Meyer-Lindenberg & Weinberger, 2006). However, a number of genes have been found to play an important role. Recent work, for example, from the Collaborative Study on the Genetics of Alcoholism has found that GABRA2 (expressed more strongly in men) is associated with dependence on alcohol (Agrawal et al., 2006; Edenberg et al., 2004). Dick and colleagues (2009) have found support that GABRA2 may also underlie liability to drug dependence and acting out (externalizing) behaviors as well. Another gene, CHRM2, produced in the cholinergic system (a system that produces the excitatory neurotransmitters) has been associated (with replication) with alcohol and drug dependence (Dick & Agrawal, 2008). The low-activity alleles of the monoamine oxidase A (MAOA) have been found to confer an increased risk to developing a range of antisocial behaviors including alcoholism (Guo, Wilhelmsen, & Hamilton, 2007).

Many of the genes found to be associated with substance abuse and antisocial behavior are part of neurotransmitter systems that facilitate communication between neurons in the brain. Because of their basic importance to behavior and life itself, neurotransmitters are an important area of study with respect to drug abuse and addiction etiology. The dopamine system, which has a close relationship to the reward pathway, has led many researchers to study these. For example, based on brain-imaging investigations, low numbers of type 2 dopamine receptors (i.e., DRD2) have been found to be associated with heightened risk for addiction (Noble, 2000). Individuals with this risk allele have lower levels of dopamine in their brains. Another important neurotransmitter system, the serotonin system, helps regulate mood and aggression (Nelson & Chiavegatto, 2001). Although it is known that we inherit tendencies to behave in certain ways and genes play a role in many behaviors, additional "upstream" factors possess a clearer proximity to drug abuse and crime behaviors.

STRESS AND ADAPTATION

One of the major systems of the autonomic nervous system that is related to stress is the sympathetic nervous system. This system controls the reaction to stress and initiates the "fight or flight" response. Stress can be thought of as a challenge to an individual's sense of homeostasis. Stress is experienced physiologically and psychologically. Specific events, people, places, or situations that cause stress are termed *stressors*. There is much individual variation or susceptibility to the effects of stress. The inability to successfully adapt to stress can lead to dysfunctional maladaptations.

Stress is associated with drug use in various ways, including increased likelihood of drinking, smoking, and other substance use (Sinha, 2008). However, the mechanisms that explain these relationships are unresolved. One popular notion explaining the relationship between stress and drug abuse is self-medication as a maladaptive form of coping. Emotional distress is a hallmark of most mood disorders, and mood disorders are strongly associated with alcohol and drug use (Compton et al., 2007). There are several ways in which stress, drug abuse, and crime interact. Under stressful conditions, such as the urgency to gain a "fix," a drug abuser may make impulsive decisions such as stealing and robbing even when the likelihood of apprehension is high. Similarly, during an illicit drug transaction where the stakes are high, a weary drug dealer may react to threat or the slightest provocation with the use of violence. In both these scenarios, the sympathetic nervous system plays a central role. The ability to plan ahead and apply "brakes" under these conditions and override stress-induced reactions leads to the role of executive functions.

EXECUTIVE FUNCTIONS

Executive functions are involved in many behaviors from paying attention to maintaining focus, planning ahead, and following through. Executive functions are exceedingly important for understanding substance abuse and addiction (Berkman, Falk, & Lieberman, 2011) and antisocial behavior (Séguin, 2004). This is because conduct problems are implicated by deficits in the prefrontal areas of the brain that regulate emotional and reward drives. A meta-analysis of 126 studies conducted by Ogilvie, Stewart, Chan, and Shum (2011) found an overall medium effect size for associations between measures of executive functioning and antisocial behavior. Most individual-level theories of drug abuse and crime include constructs such as self-control, self-regulation, effortful control, inhibitory control, psychological regulation, impulsivity, and sensation seeking that is tied to executive functions.

There is substantial convergent evidence that the vulnerability toward chronic externalizing behavior involves prefrontal brain involvement (Gatzke-Kopp et al., 2009; Iacono, Malone, & McGue, 2008). A long history of clinical and systematic empirical testing has shown that individuals with frontal lobe damage behave in aggressive, violent, and impulsive ways and that there is a shared liability toward drug abuse and violence (Fishbein, 2000). Although knowledge on drug abuse and crime is enriched by the study of the role of executive functions, it is incomplete without attention to dimensions that move outward to the environmental inputs and contexts that shape its expression.

TEMPERAMENT AND PERSONALITY

Temperament and personality describe the fundamental "nature" of an individual's typical behavior and their usual way of interacting with others and the environment. Behavior genetic studies indicate that personality is strongly biosocial with a relatively even split between heritability and environment

(Bouchard, 2004). Certain temperament and personality traits are important factors in their relation to drug abuse and crime. For example, based on the Temperament and Character Inventory (TCI) conceptualization, antisocial personality is associated with low scores on traits of harm avoidance and reward dependence and high scores on novelty seeking (Cloninger, 2005). Interestingly, novelty seeking has much in common with other constructs shown to be related to both drug abuse and crime such as sensation seeking and low self-control, which, in turn, are related to behavior manifestations of psychopathy or psychopathic personality (Vaughn, 2007). Although most criminologists are quite familiar with the construct of self-control via the Gottfredson and Hirschi's (1990) *A General Theory of Crime*, substantially fewer have been exposed to the psychopathy construct. Psychopathy is an old construct with a long history in forensic psychology and psychiatry (Vaughn & Howard, 2005) that has been a valuable tool in the prediction of crime among adults and juveniles. Using the general TCI conceptualization of temperament and personality and breaking low self-control and psychopathy down into more intermediate trait-like phenotypes is revealing. Persons with low self-control can be described as low in harm avoidance and self-directedness and high on novelty seeking. Psychopaths are low on traits such as harm avoidance, cooperativeness, and self-directedness and high in novelty seeking. Antisocial personality disorder, low self-control, and psychopathy are highly convergent with one another and represent important individual-level constructs for understanding the drugs-crime nexus.

SOCIAL COGNITION AND LEARNING

Mainly due to being a point of contact between biology and environment, thinking and behaving in interaction with others are crucial aspects of drug abuse and crime. Social cognitive perspectives build on previously described domains. One reason why is expressed by Volkow (2003): "We are beginning to understand that drugs exert persistent neurobiological effects that extend beyond the midbrain centers of pleasure and reward to disrupt the brain's frontal cortex—the thinking region of the brain, where risks and benefits are weighed and decisions made" (p. 3). Thus, social cognitive and learning processes stand between our biology on one hand and environmental input on the other.

Two views stand out on the social cognition of drug abuse. According to McCusker (2001), these are social learning theory and cognitive neuropsychology. Social learning theories of drug abuse can be traced to the work of Bandura (1977) and assert that cognitive biases maintain drug abuse careers and that cognitive structuring is needed to break the cycle of habituated thoughts and behaviors associated with drug abuse and addiction. Cognitive neuropsychological approaches tend to focus more on emotion centers and frontal regions of the brain and assess these via performance-based measures. Social learning theories have much to offer and are not merely reflections of environmental input. After all, learning involves the human brain and associated neurobiological mechanisms involved in such key processes as memory. Constructs derived from social cognitive theorizing such as self-efficacy help explain many behaviors that are central to drug abuse and crime. For example, where self-efficacy is high there should be an associated increase in the ability to self-regulate and better govern one's behavior (e.g., think about the consequences on an action). Bandura considered self-efficacy as personal agency and not deterministic environmental behavior shaping (Scheier, 2010).

SOCIAL NETWORKS

Cognition and learning processes function not only in a neuro-network but also a social network. Peers, family, and community ties are major examples. Social network factors are involved in the development, maintenance, and desistance from a drug abuse career. Research has identified peer effects in being associated with substance misuse and delinquency (Haynie & Osgood, 2005; Poelen, Scholte, Willemsen, Boomsma, & Engels, 2007). Peer effects can be thought of as a contagion whereby vulnerable youth may become initiated on a pathway of drug abuse and delinquency. It is important to point out that individuals also select peers who are deviant.

There are several major ways families exert causal effects vis-à-vis drug abuse liability and addiction: genetics, modeling (e.g., family drinking and early initiation), and what parents do with respect to their children. Parenting behaviors associated with drug use include lack of supervision and monitoring and physical abuse (Castro, Brook, Brook, & Rubenstone, 2006; Tobler, Komro, & Maldonado-Molina, 2009). Although we know communities can exert influence over individuals that reside in them, the effects are likely indirect. Certainly, communities experiencing concentrated disadvantage and weak ties are related to a range of unhealthy outcomes including drug abuse (Lambert, Brown, Phillips, & Ialongo, 2004).

PHYSICAL ENVIRONMENT AND INSTITUTIONS

Social networks are nested in a larger context of institutions and physical environments. The abuse of drugs and resulting crime is influenced by laws and their enforcement and related policies. As Boyum et al. (2011) pointed out with respect to drug control and crime, "The single most important policy choice regarding a substance is whether it will be legal or prohibited" (p. 374). Either choice, however, entails a range of institutional involvement. The supply of illicit drugs is greatly influenced by the physical environment. Climate, transportation routes, and soils and vegetation are integral to the growth, manufacturing, and distribution of drugs. In simple terms, drug abuse does not exist without the substance. Illicit drugs such as heroin are derived from opium poppies, which thrive in particular habitats. Cocaine is also dependent on the biogeography of coca. At least in theoretical terms, the stability of institutions of countries where these plants flourish can likely impact their supply.

Figure 20.1 A Biosocial Cell to Society Perspective on Drug Abuse and Crime

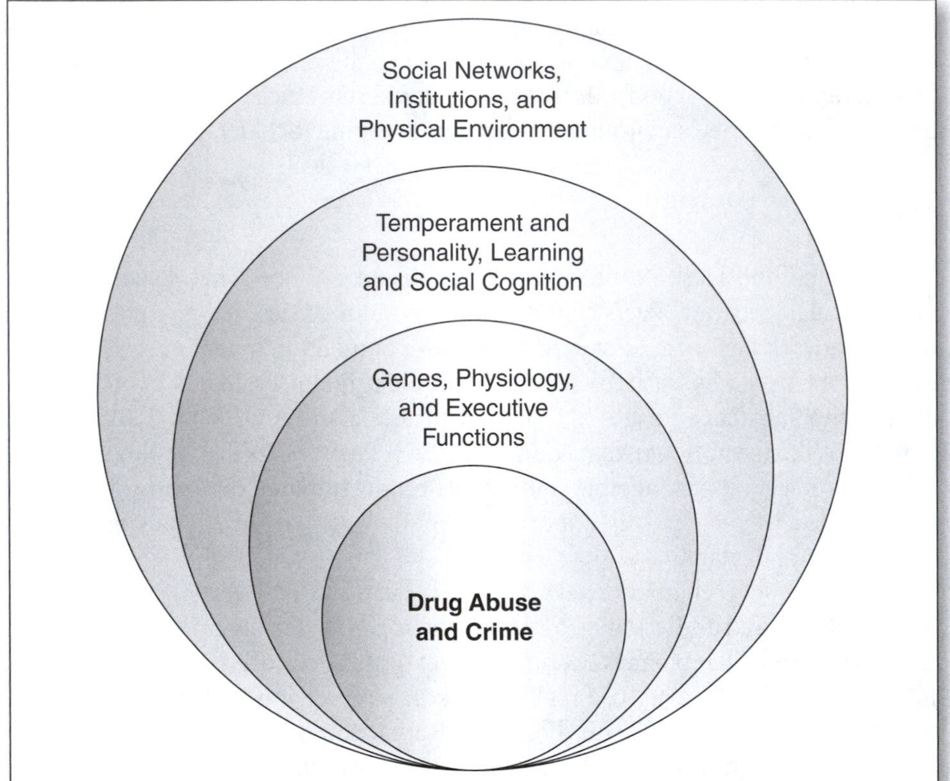

Cell to Society Based Prevention and Control

PREVENTION

Drug abuse prevention refers to the implementation of programs and preventative interventions designed to reduce the likelihood of either substance use initiation or the development of substance use disorders (Tarter, 1992). The manifold risk and protective factors identified in the scholarly literature not only span a variety of psychosocial domains (Donovan, 2004), but also include biosocial factors such as the interplay between genetic and environmental influences (Vaughn et al., 2009). Importantly, many of the key risk and protective factors associated with substance abuse have also been found to be predictive of involvement in delinquency, crime, and violence (Hawkins, Catalano, & Arthur, 2002). Given this substantive overlap, a number of prevention interventions have been designed to target underlying factors associated with both substance use and criminal behavior (SAMHSA, 2002; Welsh & Farrington, 2006).

As many of the antecedents of drug use disorders can typically be observed early in life (Kilpatrick et al., 2000), most substance use prevention programs are designed to target children, adolescents, and young adults (Faggiano et al., 2008). As such, the bulk of empirically tested prevention interventions are school-based (Faggiano et al., 2008), although others also have been designed for environments that might be more amenable to high-risk and criminally-involved youth, such as emergency rooms, institutions for juvenile offenders, and family or community contexts (Foxcroft, Ireland, Lowe, & Breen, 2002). While a variety of prevention approaches have been found to be effective in targeting substance use mediators and behaviors (Faggiano et al., 2008), meta-analytic evidence suggests that optimal programs target factors such as social influence, normative beliefs on substance use, and intentions and commitment not to use (Cuijpers, 2002).

TREATMENT

The high prevalence of comorbidity between substance use disorders and delinquent and criminal behavior, along with findings of higher recidivism rates among substance using offenders, has led to greater acknowledgment of the need to treat substance use in the criminal justice system (Bennett et al., 2008; Chandler et al., 2009). Because of the significant heterogeneity exhibited by substance using offenders, and an ever increasing body of research pointing to a myriad of biological, psychological, social, and environmental mechanisms at play, the treatment of substance use disorders within the juvenile and criminal justice systems covers a wide range of interventions targeting various biopsychosocial mechanisms.

Several community, residential, and incarceration-based programs have gained substantial empirical support to the point where they are considered evidence-based practices (Chandler et al., 2009; Marlowe, 2011). The treatments discussed herein affect brain-behavior interactions by altering activity of the brain in regions thought to be involved in substance use and criminal behavior (i.e., executive functions, sympathetic nervous system, emotion, and reward drives) to aid in the reduction, desistance, and prevention of relapse of substance use and/or criminal behavior in juvenile and adult offenders. Although there are differences between juvenile and adult offenders regarding development and treatment, most of the interventions discussed below have demonstrated effectiveness in both populations, with noted exceptions.

Interventions with substance using juvenile and adult offenders are delivered at all points of contact within the justice systems (i.e., sentencing, supervision, incarceration, and reentry) and range along the continuum emphasizing public health and rehabilitation objectives at one end and public safety and control objectives at the other end (Marlowe, 2011). Interventions with established empirical support targeting biosocial mechanisms include drug courts; behavioral, cognitive-behavioral, and motivational-based interventions; therapeutic communities; medication-assisted treatments for adult offenders; and family-based and multisystemic interventions for juvenile offenders.

Drug courts, one of the most widely adopted substance use treatment strategies within the criminal justice system, are problem-solving courts that provide a specialized docket to offenders who are drug involved. Over 2,300 adult drug courts are in active operation or planned (BJA Drug Court Clearinghouse Project, 2011), and over 458 juvenile drug courts are in existence across the United States (Office of Justice Programs, 2012). Drug courts are "presumed to affect an offender's drug use and criminal behavior through both the actions and influences of the court and the involvement of the offender in mandated drug and alcohol abuse treatment" (Wilson, Mitchell, & Mackenzie, 2006, p. 461). Drug courts sit at the median between the public health and public safety continuum, functioning as both a control function (i.e., alcohol treatment and random urine analysis are mandated by a judge and treatment compliance is monitored by the court), as well as a public health function (i.e., the drug or alcohol use problem is treated utilizing medical and/or psychosocial interventions by qualified substance use providers). Meta-analytic findings suggest that adult drug courts are more effective in reducing future drug use and criminal behavior than traditional correctional options; however, due to the weak nature of the included research designs, the findings were equivocal (Wilson et al., 2006). Evidence on juvenile drug courts is less robust and findings have been contradictory across studies; however, evaluations of juvenile drug court programs have demonstrated reduction in substance use and criminal behavior (Henggeler et al., 2006). Despite the lack of strong, randomized trials of adult and juvenile drug courts, they remain popular and are positively regarded by the court and participants.

Behavioral, cognitive behavioral, and motivational-based interventions are among the most commonly used and evaluated interventions to treat substance use with adult and juvenile offenders in both community and incarceration-based settings (Chandler et al., 2009). Behavioral interventions, including contingency management, and voucher-based reinforcement therapy, aim to reduce substance use and criminal behavior by rewarding specific desired behaviors (i.e., attendance, abstinence, drug-negative urines) directly with vouchers or other goods, services, or privileges (Prendergast, Podus, Finney, Greenwell, & Roll, 2006). Cognitive-behavioral interventions, including relapse prevention, target cognitive and affective determinants, address situational triggers, and provide training in coping, avoidance, and self-monitoring strategies to reduce substance use and prevent relapse (Mercer & Woody, 2007). Motivational-based interventions (i.e., motivational interviewing and motivation enhancement therapy) are client-centered and directive methods aimed to enhance "intrinsic motivation to change by exploring and resolving ambivalence" (Miller & Rollnick, 2002, p. 25). The effectiveness of behavioral and cognitive behavioral interventions for the treatment of substance use is well supported for adults (Dutra et al., 2008; Magill & Ray, 2009; Prendergast et al., 2006) and adolescents (Bender, Tripodi, Sarteschi, & Vaughn, 2011; Vaughn & Howard, 2004). Although the evidence for motivational-based interventions is not as strong as behavioral and cognitive-behavioral interventions, growing evidence supports motivational interventions in the treatment of substance use disorders with adults and adolescents (Jensen et al., 2011).

Therapeutic communities (TC), intensive and often longer-term residential programs based on the social learning model, demonstrate positive effects on reoffending and drug use with adults (Mitchell, Wilson, & MacKenzie, 2007). Therapeutic communities have been implemented across the criminal justice continuum; they have been utilized as front-end alternatives to incarceration, conducted in prisons, and implemented for parole-reentry programs. Although there is variability in TC programs, they share several components: they house participants in units distinct from the general population; provide a confrontational yet supportive atmosphere in which both staff and peers confront antisocial behavior and attitudes and reinforce and reward positive behaviors; and involve participants in running the TC and facilitate mentorship and camaraderie (Marlowe, 2011; Mitchell at al., 2007). Although therapeutic communities are used with juveniles and considered promising, evidence of the effects of TCs with juveniles is limited (Jainchill, Hawke, & Messina, 2005; Pealer, 2004).

Medication-assisted therapy (MAT), the use of pharmacotherapy in addition to other substance use interventions, has also been found to be effective in treating addiction with adult offenders. The use of agonist medications (i.e., buprenorphine or methadone) and antagonist medications (i.e., naltrexone) has demonstrated positive effects on substance use, treatment engagement, and offending/rearrest outcomes (Amato et al., 2005; Johnson, 2008). Despite positive and significant effects of MAT and being endorsed by leading scientific and practitioner organizations, MAT is underutilized due to stigma associated with medication treatment of substance use; various barriers related to regulations, availability, concerns of liability, and security; and the perception that they are inconsistent with the treatment philosophy of the criminal justice setting (Friedmann et al., 2012). Less is known about MAT with adolescents, because few controlled studies have assessed the effects of medications with adolescents, likely due to both practical and ethical reasons (Minozzi, Amato, & Davoli, 2009).

Conclusion

The relationship between drug abuse and crime is exceedingly complex. There are a host of biological, psychological, and environmental factors that play a role. We outlined one way to approach this complexity using a cell to society framework. The advantage of this framework is that it provides a blueprint from which to better organize findings on the drugs-crime relationship that have accrued across multiple fields. Although there remains much to be understood regarding the complex interactions between psychoactive substances and behavior and the ways in which laws and policies surrounding these substances act as antecedents and/or by-products of crime, it is clear that the etiology and prevention and control of drug abuse is multiply determined and biosocial at its core.

References

Agrawal, A., Edenberg, H. J., Foroud, T., Bierut, L. J., Dunne, G., Hinrichs, . . . Dick, D. M. (2006). Association of GABRA2 with drug dependence in the Collaborative Study of the Genetics of Alcoholism sample. *Behavior Genetics, 36*(5), 640–650.

Amato, L., Davoli, M., Perucci, C. A., Ferri, M., Faggiano, F., & Mattick, R. P. (2005). An overview of systematic reviews of the effectiveness of opiate maintenance therapies: Available evidence to inform clinical practice and research. *Journal of Substance Abuse Treatment, 28,* 321–329.

Bandura, A. (1977). *Social learning theory.* Englewood Cliffs, NJ: Prentice Hall.

Bender, K., Tripodi, S. J., Sarteschi, C., & Vaughn, M. G. (2011). A meta-analysis of interventions to reduce adolescent cannabis use. *Research on Social Work Practice, 21*(2), 153–164.

Bennett, T., Holloway, K., & Farrington, D. (2008). The statistical association between drug misuse and crime: A meta-analysis. *Aggression and Violent Behavior, 13,* 107–118.

Berkman, E. T., Falk, E. B., & Lieberman, M. D. (2011). In the trenches of real-world self-control: Neural correlates and breaking the link between craving and smoking. *Psychological Science, 22,* 498–506.

BJA Drug Court Clearinghouse Project. (2011). *Summary of drug court activity by state and county, February 2, 2011* (Tech. Rep.). Washington, DC: American University. Retrieved from http://www.american.edu/spa/jpo/customcf/get.cfm?doc=Summary%20of%20Drug%20Court%20Activity%20by%20State%20and%20County%202011

Bouchard, T. J., (2004). Genetics influence on human psychological traits: A survey. *Current Directions in Psychological Science, 13,* 148–151.

Boyum, D. A., Caulkins, J. P., & Kleinman, M. A. R. (2011). Drugs, crime, and public policy. In J. Q. Wilson & J. Petersilia (Eds.), *Crime and public policy* (2nd ed., pp. 368–402). New York, NY: Oxford University Press.

Castro, F. G., Brook, J. S., Brook, D. W., & Rubenstone, E. (2006). Paternal, perceived maternal, and youth risk factors as predictors of youth stage of substance use: A longitudinal study. *Journal of Addictive Diseases, 25,* 65–75.

Centers for Disease Control and Prevention. (2012). *Youth risk behavior surveillance system: Selected 2011 national health risk behaviors and health outcomes by race/ethnicity.* Retrieved from http://www.cdc.gov/healthyyouth/yrbs/factsheets/index.htm

Chakravarti, A., & Little, P. (2003). Nature, nurture and human disease. *Nature, 421,* 412–414.

Chandler, R. K., Fletcher, B. W., & Volkow, N. D. (2009). Treating drug abuse and addiction in the criminal justice system: Improving public health and safety. *Journal of the American Medical Association, 301*(2), 183–190.

Cloninger, C. R. (2005). Antisocial personality disorder: A review. In M. Maj, H. S. Akiskal, J. E. Mezzich, & A. Okasha (Eds.), *Personality disorders* (pp. 125–169). New York, NY: Wiley.

Compton, W. M., Thomas, Y. F., Stinson, F. S., & Grant, B. F. (2007). Prevalence, correlates, disability, and comorbidity of DSM-IV drug abuse and dependence in the United States. *Archives of General Psychiatry, 64,* 566–578.

Cuijpers, P. (2002). Effective ingredients of school-based drug prevention programs: A systematic review. *Addictive Behaviors, 27,* 1009–1023.

D'Amico, E. J., Edelen, M. O., Miles, J. N. V., & Morral, A. R. (2008). The longitudinal association between substance use and delinquency among high risk youth. *Drug and Alcohol Dependence, 93,* 85–92.

Danaei, G., Ding, E. L., Mozaffarian, D., Taylor, B., Rehm, J., Murray, C. J. L., & Ezzati, M. (2009). The preventable causes of death in the United States: Comparative risk assessment of dietary, lifestyle, and metabolic risk factors. *PLoS Medicine, 6*(4), e1000058.

DeLisi, M. (2011). Self-control theory: The *Tyrannosaurus rex* of criminology is poised to devour criminal justice. *Journal of Criminal Justice, 39,* 103–105.

DeLisi, M., & Vaughn, M. G. (2008). The Gottfredson-Hirschi critiques revisited: Reconciling self-control theory, criminal careers, and career criminals. *International Journal of Offender Therapy and Comparative Criminology, 52,* 520–537.

Dick, D. M., & Agrawal, A. (2008). Genetics of alcohol and other drug dependence. *Alcohol Research and Health, 31,* 111–118.

Dick, D. M., Latendresse, S. J., Lansford, J. E., Budde, J. P., Goate, A., Dodge, K. A., . . . Bates, J. E. (2009). Role of GABRA2 in trajectories of externalizing behavior across development and evidence of moderation by parental monitoring. *Archives of General Psychiatry, 66,* 649–657.

Donovan, J. E. (2004). Adolescent alcohol initiation: A review of psychosocial risk factors. *Journal of Adolescent Health, 35*(6), 529.e7–529.e18.

Dutra, L., Stathopoulou, G., Basden, S. L., Leyro, T. M., Powers, M. B., & Otto, M. W. (2008). A meta-analytic review of psychosocial interventions for substance use disorders. *American Journal of Psychiatry, 165,* 179–187.

Edenberg, H. J., Dick, D. M., Xuel, X., Tian, H., Almasy, L., Bauer, L. O., . . . Begleiter, H. (2004). Variations in GABRA2, encoding the alpha 2 subunit of the GABA(A) receptor, are associated with alcohol dependence and with brain oscillations. *American Journal of Human Genetics, 74*(4), 705–714.

Faggiano, F., Vigna-Taglianti, F. D., Versino, E., Zambon, A., Borraccino, A., & Lemma, P. (2008). School-based prevention for illicit drug use: A systematic review. *Preventive Medicine, 46,* 385–391.

Fishbein, D. (2000). Neuropsychological function, drug abuse, and violence: A conceptual framework. *Criminal Justice and Behavior, 27,* 139–159.

Foxcroft, D. R., Ireland, D., Lowe, G., & Breen. R. (2002). Primary prevention for alcohol misuse and young people. *Cochrane Database of Systematic Reviews, 3,* CD003024.

Friedmann, P. D., Hoskinson, R., Gordon, M., Schwartz, R., Kinlock, T., Knight, K., . . . for the M. A. T. W. G. o. C. J. D. A. T. (2012). Medication-assisted treatment in criminal justice agencies affiliated with the Criminal Justice—Drug Abuse Treatment Studies (CJ-DATS): Availability, barriers, and intentions. *Substance Abuse, 33*(1), 9–18.

Gatzke-Kopp, L. M., Beauchaine, T. P., Shannon, K. E., Chipman, J., Fleming, A. P., Crowell, S. E., . . . Johnson, L. C. (2009). Neurological correlates of reward responding in adolescents with and without externalizing behavior disorders. *Journal of Abnormal Psychology, 118,* 203–213.

Goldstein, P. J. (1985). The drugs/violence nexus: A tripartite conceptual framework. *Journal of Drug Issues, 15,* 493–506.

Gottfredson, M. R., & Hirschi, T. (1990). *A general theory of crime.* Stanford, CA: Stanford University Press.

Guo, G., Wilhelmsen, K., & Hamilton, N. (2007). Gene-life course interaction for alcohol consumption in adolescence and young adulthood: Five monoamine genes. *American Journal of Medical Genetics Part B (Neuropsychiatric Genetics), 144B,* 417–423.

Hawkins, J. D., Catalano, R. F., & Arthur, M. W. (2002). Promoting science-based prevention in communities. *Addictive Behaviors, 27,* 951–976.

Haynie, D. L., & Osgood, D. W. (2005). Reconsidering peers and delinquency: How do peers matter? *Social Forces, 84,* 1109–1130.

Henggeler, S. W., Halliday-Boykins, C. A., Cunningham, P. B., Randall, J., Shapiro, S. B., & Chapman, J. E. (2006). Juvenile drug court: Enhancing outcomes by integrating evidence-based treatments. *Journal of Consulting and Clinical Psychology, 74*(1), 42–54.

Hicks, B. M., Krueger, R. F., Iacono, W. G., McGue, M., & Patrick, C. J. (2004). Family transmission and heritability of externalizing disorders: A twin-family study. *Archives of General Psychiatry, 61,* 922–928.

Hill, K. G., Howell, J. C., Hawkins, J. D., & Battin-Pearson, S. R. (1999). Childhood risk factors for adolescent gang membership: Results from the Seattle Social Development Project. *Journal of Research in Crime and Delinquency, 36,* 300–322.

Iacono, W. M., Malone, S. M., & McGue, M. (2008). Behavioral disinhibition and the development of early-onset addiction: Common and specific influences. *Annual Review of Clinical Psychology, 4,* 325–348.

Jainchill, N., Hawke, J., & Messina, M. (2005). Post-treatment outcomes among adjudicated adolescent males and females in modified therapeutic community treatment. *Substance Use & Misuse, 40*(7), 975–996.

Jensen, C. D., Cushing, C. C., Aylward, B. S., Craig, J. T., Sorell, D. M., & Steele, R. G. (2011). Effectiveness of motivational interviewing interventions for adolescent substance use behavior change: A meta-analytic review. *Journal of Consulting and Clinical Psychology, 79*(4), 433–440.

Johnson, B. A. (2008). Update on neuropharmacological treatments for alcoholism: Scientific basis and clinical findings. *Biochemical Pharmacology, 75,* 34–56.

Johnston, L. D., O'Malley, P. M., Bachman, J. G., & Schulenberg, J. E. (2012). *Monitoring the Future national survey results on drug use, 1975–2011. Volume I: Secondary school students.* Ann Arbor: Institute for Social Research, The University of Michigan.

Kilpatrick, D. G., Acierno, R., Saunders, B., Resnick, H. S., Best, C. L., & Schnurr, P. P. (2000). Risk factors for adolescent substance abuse and dependence: Data from a national sample. *Journal of Consulting and Clinical Psychology, 68*(1), 19–30.

Koob, G. F., & Le Moal, M. (2005). *Neurobiology of addiction.* Burlington, MA: Academic Press.

Krug, E. G., Mercy, J. A., Dahlberg, L. L., & Zwi, A. B. (2002). A world report on violence and health. *Lancet, 360,* 1083–1088.

Lambert, S. F., Brown, T. L., Phillips, C. M., & Ialongo, N. S. (2004). The relationship between perceptions of neighborhood characteristics and substance use among urban African American adolescents. *American Journal of Community Psychology, 34,* 205–218.

Leshner, A. I. (1997). Addiction is a brain disease, and it matters. *Science, 278,* 45–47.

Lubman, D. I., Yucel, M., & Pantelis, C. (2004). Addiction, a condition of compulsive behaviour? Neuroimaging and neuropsychological evidence of inhibitory dysregulation. *Addiction, 99,* 1491–1502.

Magill, M., & Ray, L. A. (2009). Cognitive-behavioral treatment with adult alcohol and illicit drug users: A meta-analysis of randomized controlled trials. *Journal of Studies on Alcohol and Drugs, 70,* 516–527.

Marlowe, D. B. (2011). Evidence-based policies and practices for drug-involved offenders. *Prison Journal, 91*(3 Suppl.), 27S–47S.

Maynard, B. R., Salas-Wright, C. P., Vaughn, M. G., & Peters, K. E. (2012). Who are truant youth? Examining distinctive profiles of truant youth using latent profile analysis. *Journal of Youth and Adolescence, 41*(2), 1671–1684.

McCabe, S. E., Cranford, J. A., & West, B. T. (2008). Trends in prescription drug abuse and dependence, co-occurrence with other substance use disorders, and the treatment utilization: Results from two national surveys. *Addictive Behaviors, 33,* 1297–1305.

McCusker, C. G. (2001). Cognitive biases and addiction: An evolution in theory and method. *Addiction, 96,* 47–56.

Mercer, D., & Woody, G. E. (2007). Individual psychotherapy and counseling for addiction. In G. O. Gabbard, J. S. Beck, & J. Holmes (Eds.), *Oxford textbook of psychotherapy,* Oxford, UK: Oxford University Press.

Meyer-Lindenberg, A., & Weinberger, D. R. (2006). Intermediate phenotypes and genetic mechanisms of psychiatric disorders. *Nature Reviews Neuroscience, 7,* 818–827.

Miller, W. R., & Rollnick, S. (2002). *Motivational interviewing: Preparing people to change addictive behavior.* New York, NY: Guildford Press.

Minozzi, S., Amato, L., & Davoli, M. (2009). Maintenance treatments for opiate dependent adolescent. *Cochrane Library, 2,* 1–24.

Mitchell, O., Wilson, D. B., & MacKenzie, D. L. (2007). Does incarceration-based drug treatment reduce recidivism? A meta-analytic synthesis of the research. *Journal of Experimental Criminology, 3*(4), 353–375.

Moore, T. M., Stuart, G. L., Meehan, J. C., Rhatigan, D. L., Helmuth, J. C., & Keen, S. M. (2008). Drug abuse and aggression between intimate partners: A meta-analytic review. *Clinical Psychology Review, 28,* 247–274.

Nelson, R. J., & Chiavegatto, S. (2001). Molecular basis of aggression. *Trends in Neurosciences, 24*(12), 713–719.

Noble, E. P. (2000). The DRD2 gene in psychiatric and neurological disorders and its phenotypes. *Pharmacogenomics, 1,* 309–333.

Office of Justice Programs. (2012, May 15). *Drug courts.* Retrieved from http://www.nij.gov/topics/courts/drug-courts/welcome.htm

Ogilvie, J. M., Stewart, A. L., Chan, R. C. K., & Shum, D. H. K. (2011). Neuropsychological measures of executive function and antisocial behavior: A meta-analysis. *Criminology, 49,* 1063–1107.

Pealer, J. (2004). *A community of peers—promoting behavior change: The effectiveness of a therapeutic community for juvenile male offenders in reducing recidivism* (Doctoral dissertation). Retrieved from ProQuest Dissertations & Theses database. (UMI No. 3146517)

Poelen, E. A., Scholte, R. H., Willemsen, G., Boomsma, D. I., & Engels, C. M. (2007). Drinking by parents, siblings, and friends as predictors of regular alcohol use in adolescents and young adults: A longitudinal twin-family study. *Alcohol & Alcoholism, 42,* 362–369.

Prendergast, M., Podus, D., Finney, J., Greenwell, L., & Roll, J. (2006). Contingency management for treatment of substance use disorders: A meta-analysis. *Addiction, 101*(11), 1546–1560.

Rehm, J., Taylor, B., & Room, R. (2006). Global burden of disease from alcohol, illicit drugs and tobacco. *Drug and Alcohol Review, 25,* 503–513.

Scheier, L. M. (2010). Social-cognitive models of drug use etiology. In L. M. Scheier (Ed.), *Handbook of drug use etiology: Theory, methods, and empirical findings.* Washington, DC: American Psychological Association Press.

Séguin, J. R. (2004). Neurocognitive elements of antisocial behavior: Relevance of an orbitofrontal cortex account. *Brain and Cognition, 55,* 185–197.

Sinha, R. (2008). Chronic stress, drug use, and vulnerability to addiction. *Annals of the New York Academy of Science, 1141,* 105–130.

Substance Abuse and Mental Health Services Administration. (2002). *Science-based prevention programs and principles: Effective substance abuse and mental health programs for every community*. Rockville, MD: Center for Substance Abuse Prevention.

Substance Abuse and Mental Health Services Administration. (2012). *Results from the 2011 National Survey on Drug Use and Health: Summary of national findings*. Rockville, MD: Center for Substance Abuse Prevention.

Tarter, R. A. (1992). Prevention of drug abuse: Theory and application. *American Journal on Addictions, 1*(1), 2–20.

Tobler, A. L., Komro, K. A., & Maldonado-Molina, M. M. (2009). Relationship between neighborhood context, family management practices and alcohol use among urban, multi-ethnic, young adolescents. *Prevention Science, 10,* 313–324.

Vaughn, M. G. (2007). Biosocial dynamics: A transdisciplinary approach to violence. In M. DeLisi & P. J. Conis (Eds.), *Violent offenders: Theory, research, public policy, & practice* (pp. 63–77). Burlington, MA: Jones & Bartlett.

Vaughn, M. G., Beaver, K. M., DeLisi, M., Perron, B. E., & Schelbe, L. (2009). Gene-environment interplay and the importance of self-control in predicting polydrug use and substance-related problems. *Addictive Behaviors, 34,* 112–116.

Vaughn, M. G., DeLisi, M., Gunter, T., Fu, Q., Beaver, K. M., Perron, B. E., & Howard, M. O. (2011). The severe 5%: A latent class analysis of the externalizing spectrum in the United States. *Journal of Criminal Justice, 39,* 75–80.

Vaughn, M. G., DeLisi, M., & Matto, H. (2013). *Human behavior: A cell to society approach.* Hoboken, NJ: Wiley.

Vaughn, M. G., & Howard, M. O. (2004). Adolescent substance abuse treatment: A synthesis of controlled evaluations. *Research on Social Work Practice, 14*(5), 325–335.

Vaughn, M. G., & Howard, M. O. (2005). The construct of psychopathy and its role in contributing to the study of serious, violent, and chronic youth offending. *Youth Violence and Juvenile Justice, 3,* 235–252.

Volkow, N. D. (2003). The addicted brain: Why such poor decisions? *NIDA Notes, 18,* 1–15.

Welsh, B. C., & Farrington, D. P. (2006). *Evidence-based crime prevention. Preventing crime: What works for children, offenders, victims, and places.* New York, NY: Springer Science and Business Media.

White, H. R., Loeber, R., & Farrington, D. P. (2008). Substance use, drug dealing, gang membership, and the gun carrying and their predictive associations with serious violence and serious theft. In R. Loeber, D. P. Farrington, M. Stouthamer-Loeber, & H. R. White (Eds.), *Violence and serious theft: Development and prediction from childhood to adulthood* (pp. 137–166). New York, NY: Routledge.

White, H. R., Tice, P., Loeber, R., & Stouthamer-Loeber, M. (2002). Illegal acts committed by adolescents under the influence of alcohol and drugs. *Journal of Research in Crime and Delinquency, 39,* 131–152.

Wilson, D. B., Mitchell, O., & MacKenzie, D. L. (2006). A systematic review of drug court effects on recidivism. *Journal of Experimental Criminology, 2*(4), 459–487.

Yacoubian, G. S., Urbach, B. J., Larsen, K. L., Johnson, R. J., & Peters, R. J. (2001). A comparison of drug use between prostitutes and other female arrestees. *Journal of Alcohol and Drug Education, 46*(2), 12–26.

Discussion Questions

CHAPTERS 19 AND 20

1. For sociologists, the study of drug use is rooted within social contexts. What does brain research reveal about drug use? What is the "reward pathway," and why is it important for studying drug use? Can the etiology of drug use be solely explained by environmental factors?

2. A variety of traditional criminological theories have been used to explain drug use. Agnew's general strain theory argues that individuals who utilize negative coping mechanisms will be more likely to use drugs to alleviate strain. How does the sympathetic nervous system control reactions to stress/strain? Under what stressful conditions is drug use most likely to occur?

3. Discuss how self-control theory and the concept of executive functions can be integrated to explain drug use. For example, what types of behaviors are influenced by executive functions? Are these behaviors similar to the six dimensions of low self-control as described by Gottfredson and Hirschi?

4. As noted by Drs. Miller and Ventura Miller, social learning variables have been found to be associated with drug use. Describe how a social cognitive perspective can be used to explain drug use. How do social cognitive and learning processes link biology with the environment?

5. Many of the key risk and protective factors associated with substance abuse have also been found to be predictive of delinquency and crime. How could the knowledge of common risk and protective factors aid in prevention intervention design? In your opinion, do you believe these interventions will be effective in targeting substance use?

6. Traditionally, sociological approaches to understanding drug use have remained separate from biological approaches. Are there any advantages to integrating the two? Would our comprehensive understanding of drug use etiology improve if the two paradigms were united?

PART IV

TRENDS, CURRENT ISSUES, AND POLICY IMPLICATIONS

21

A Sociological Explanation of Crime Rates and Trends

Wesley G. Jennings
University of South Florida

Jennifer M. Reingle
The University of Texas School of Public Health, Dallas Regional Campus

Tracking crime over time is a complex process, because "crime" constitutes hundreds of heterogeneous behaviors that change in their definition and prevalence across persons, time, and space. What is a "crime"? Is using marijuana a crime? Clearly, the measurement of crime differs by jurisdiction, type of behavior, and social acceptability. For example, in the mid-2000s, a person who was apprehended in possession of a marijuana joint would be sent to jail. Today, that same person might present a medical marijuana card and be released without much question.

Marijuana use is a clear example to illustrate the difficulties in measuring crime over time. Official records of criminal behavior that measure trends of crime would have considered marijuana possession a "drug-related offense." Now, the same behavior is not considered a crime in many jurisdictions. Therefore, it may seem that drug use has gone down over time, when this observation is simply an artifact of a policy change. The behavior may have increased; however, it is no longer being reported as criminal activity. This word of caution is necessary to introduce our examination of crime trends and crime rates, because the recording of criminal behavior varies across law enforcement departments and agencies and changes rapidly due to public policy. In light of these issues, we describe in this chapter changes in crime trends and crime rates from a sociological perspective with a particular focus on community crime careers and factors that can influence crime trends and crime rates.

The Big Picture

The Federal Bureau of Investigation's Uniform Crime Reports (UCR) detail a consistent negative slope for crime over time. Specifically, in 2011, the population-adjusted violent crime rate was 3.8% lower than in 2010, and 15.4% lower than in 2007. These rates convert to an average of 386.3 violent crimes per 100,000 population in 2011 (USDOJ; United States Department of Justice, Federal Bureau of Investigation, 2012). Similarly, property crime decreased by 0.5% in 2011 compared to 2010 and was 8.3% lower than 2007. In 2011, this estimate corresponded to 2,908.7 property crimes per 100,000 persons living in the population. Overall, the crime trends and crime rates for both violent and property crime have consistently decreased over time.

Drug arrests, as discussed above, are much more complicated to evaluate trends. For example, in 2011, there were 1,531,251 arrests for drug abuse violations (USDOJ, 2012). In 2010, this number was 1,273,963 and 1,841,200 in 2007 (USDOJ, 2012). The trend of drug use was increasing from 1982 to 2007; however, these trends are not population-adjusted. Therefore, we cannot say that the rate of drug arrests changed over time; rather, we can assert that the *number* of drug arrests has consistently increased over time. Because the majority of arrests for drug use are marijuana-related (USDOJ, 2008), the fluctuations in arrests may be a function of differential policy enforcement. Therefore, surveys and self-reports are often used to examine drug use trends over time.

Crime trends and crime rates exist because variable sociological factors are at work to make crime more or less attractive to people. For instance, the economy, neighborhood context, and perceived normality of crime and drug use (often through media outlets) may affect crime trends and crime rates. Each of these factors is discussed in detail below.

Social Disorganization

Sociologists have long been interested in to what extent crime trends and crime rates vary and fluctuate across areas and places (or neighborhoods and communities). This rich theoretical and empirical tradition has its origins in the Chicago school and the work of Park and Burgess and later advanced by Shaw and McKay (1942). Relying on an etiological framework, Shaw and McKay began to note that crime and crime rates were noticeably larger near the central business district and were lower the farther the neighborhoods were from the core of the city. This observation soon led to the development of what is commonly known today as social disorganization theory.

Social disorganization as a theoretical framework asserts that crime and crime rates are disproportionately higher in certain areas because of a high level of poverty, racial/ethnic heterogeneity, and high levels of residential mobility. All these mechanisms affect informal social control or the residents' (un)willingness to come to the aid of their neighbor, watch over the neighbor's property, and/or report crime that is occurring to the police because the residents do not have a stake in the neighborhood. Or, in other words, once the residents are able to acquire some level of resources to move out of the neighborhood and into a better neighborhood, they will do so. Stults (2010) described the inverse of this situation as follows: "Neighborhoods with high levels of collective efficacy are characterized by mutual trust and shared expectations with regard to informal control and are better able to effectively mobilize to control criminal behavior among residents" (p. 247). There has been a considerable amount of support for the influence of social disorganization on crime and crime rates historically (Patterson, 1991; Sampson & Groves, 1989; Simcha-Fagan & Schwartz, 1986; Smith & Jarjoura, 1988) and more recently (Morenoff, Sampson, & Raudenbush, 2001; Sampson, Raudenbush, & Earls, 1997).

Research on Community Crime Trajectories

Beyond the more traditional approaches to examining the variation in crime and crime rates across areas or neighborhoods, there has been a recent trend in the sociological literature to investigate the "trajectories" of community crime rates or community crime careers (similar to individual-level examination of criminal careers; e.g., Piquero, Farrington, & Blumstein, 2003). Trajectories are often used to describe individual-level fluctuations in crime over time. For instance, we often call people "nonoffenders," "desistors" (if they discontinue their criminal behavior before adulthood), "escalators" (when their criminal career increases over time), and "chronic" offenders (when people continuously offend throughout the life course) (Jennings & Reingle, 2012). However, communities appear to have their own trajectories of criminal "behavior," as well.

This trajectory approach has a developmental influence from psychology and has largely been advanced through the application of trajectory analysis

(Nagin, 2005; Nagin & Land, 1993). In its most basic form, trajectory analysis involves the categorization of people (or places in the context of community-based crime rates) into a discrete number of groups who exhibit similar patterns of their crime trends and rates within a particular trajectory, yet their pattern of crime is distinct between/across the other identified trajectory groups. For instance, it is reasonable to assume that the crime rate for one city, such as Los Angeles, California, over a certain period of time is generally higher than the crime rate in Raleigh, North Carolina. Furthermore, the rate of crime in these two areas may not only differ regarding magnitude, but they may also differ in their trend (e.g., stable, increasing, or decreasing over time). Following this logic, there are potentially other cities that may exhibit similar trends to Los Angeles (e.g., New York, New York) and others that may resemble Raleigh (e.g., Greenville, South Carolina), but these other areas (Raleigh and Greenville) are different from one another with regard to their crime trends and rates. As such, an application of trajectory analysis to a large sample of cities across the United States may reveal that, while cities have distinct and identifiable community crime trajectories over time, their individual community crime trajectories may tend to approximate a distinct group-based trajectory of crime, representing a number of cities.

Griffiths and Chavez (2004) were one of the first to use trajectory modeling, as described above, to examine community-level homicide in Chicago. Specifically, they used Chicago homicide data of 831 census tracts over 15 years during 1980 through 1995, when crime in the United States was especially high. Similar to individual-level group trajectories, this analysis found that communities could be categorized into three specific groups: (1) nonviolent communities, (2) low-level violent communities, and (3) high-level violent communities. Approximately 53% (438 of 831 tracts) had few or no homicides during the years of study, and 40% (329 out of 831 tracts) had a slightly higher and relatively consistent homicide rate (approximately 1.5 to 2 homicides per 1,000 persons per year), and a minority of tracts (50 out of 831 or 6%) had the highest homicide rate consistently over time.

More recently, Stults (2010) conducted a similar study using the same dataset with an expanded time frame (1965 through 1995). As a result of using more data, Stults found seven distinct groups of communities. Three groups were characterized by very low levels of homicide in 1965 but diverged into stable (Group 1), moderately increasing (Group 2), and drastically increasing rates (Group 3). Groups 4 and 5 began at a moderate rate and split in opposite directions (high and low), while Group 6 started high and declined over time (desistor community). The final group had the highest homicide rate at each time point. Of the seven distinct groups, the most violent neighborhoods maintained a constant homicide rate of 53.6 deaths per 100,000 persons over the entire 30-year period and accounted for the largest percentage of tracts at 21.3%. In contrast, the only group that was consistently nonviolent throughout the 30-year time series included 11.7% of all census tracts evaluated during the course of the study.

Three notable "community crime career" studies have examined general criminal behavior (Schuerman & Kobrin, 1986; Weisburd, Bushway, Lum, & Yang, 2004) and juvenile crime (Weisburd, Morris, & Groff, 2009). In the early study of crime in communities, Schuerman and Kobrin (1986) found three different groups of communities based on their crime trends over time. Specifically, during an increase in crime from 1950 to 1970 in Los Angeles, they reported the following groups: (1) emerging neighborhoods (or communities that began with a very low crime rate in 1950 and increased in the level of crime over time); (2) transitional neighborhoods (e.g., neighborhoods that had moderate rates of crime, which also increased over time); and (3) enduring neighborhoods (which maintained a high, persistent rate of crime). Conclusions from this analysis suggest that the changes in crime rates were attributable to demographic shifts and transformations in land use (e.g., zoning for commercial or industrial vs. residential) in the earlier years of the study, although later changes were tied to social factors (increases in the level of community poverty).

The other two more recent studies of the social factors related to crime trends over time were conducted by Weisburd and his colleagues (2004; Weisburd et al., 2009). Specifically, Weisburd and colleagues (2004) used 14 years of offense data from Seattle, Washington, disaggregated into 29,849 micro street segments. This investigation found evidence of *18* unique groups, and 8 of the 18 trajectories (making up of 84% of the sample) were stable in their trends of crime over time. Three of the remaining 10 groups showed some increases in the rate of offending, while 7 community-level trajectory groups demonstrated substantial declines over time. Of the three trajectories that showed some increase in crime over time, two groups showed dramatic increases from the beginning of the study through the final follow-up. To illustrate the magnitude of change, one community increased fourfold from 5 annual incidents in 1989 to more than 20 in 2002. Another community more than doubled from 21 incidents each year to 44 incidents over a similar time frame. Of the declining trajectories, the group with highest crime rate began at a rate of almost 95 crime incidents each year and decreased to 75, while the second highest trajectory went from an initial estimate of more than 50 annual incidents to 25. Overall, Weisburd et al. found that the overall crime trend for the city of Seattle was driven primarily by the decrease in incidents in descending trajectories, which together only comprised 1.6% of total street segments. In other words, two small communities got much better and improved their crime rate substantially, and this made Seattle as a whole appear safer over time.

The second study by Weisburd et al. (2009) used similar data, but focused instead on arrests of juveniles for acts of delinquency. Findings suggested that there were eight unique groups of offending at the community level. The group characterized by the most frequent offending represented only 0.03% of the sample: 30 annual arrests in 1989, increased in 1996 to more than 45 arrests, and then decreased to less than 20 during 2002. Four groups were stable, and two groups decreased over time. Between these two studies, it is clear that communities themselves have a "criminal personality," and they vary substantially over time.

Urban Versus Rural Community Crime Trajectories

There is evidence that urban and rural communities behave differently in their crime trends and rates over time. For instance, Jennings and Piquero (2008) explored the differences in homicide rates between urban and rural settings. Using data from the FBI's Supplemental Homicide Reports between 1980 and 1999, this study found evidence of five distinct typologies (e.g., patterns) of nonintimate partner homicide at the county level, and these rates evinced the following three trends: (1) relatively low victimization rates and a steady downward decline over time (Groups 1 and 2); (2) noticeable declines in the early 1980s (Groups 3 and 4); and (3) an increase that began in the late 1980s and continued until the early 1990s followed by a decline (Groups 3, 4, and 5) (p. 441). Comparatively, although the majority of the counties (Groups 1 and 2) exhibited an observable 20-year downward trend in their intimate partner homicide rates over time, three groups (Groups 3, 4, and 5) looked very different regarding their trends. Furthermore, rurality was significantly associated with these three groups of intimate partner homicide, which all experienced periods of drastic increases in intimate partner homicide over a 20-year period. Therefore, we might conclude that urban neighborhoods, although densely populated and conventionally associated with violence, are not the only communities that are characterized by high-level violent activity, at least with respect to intimate partner homicide. Or, in other words, crime may spread through rural communities more rapidly than urban ones, in some circumstances.

The Economy and Crime

The fluctuating economic state that is commonplace today has a clear and consistent influence on criminal behavior. Sociological theories explaining the effects of economic strain on crime have traditionally focused on the pressures exerted on individuals. These societal pressures include the need to obtain prescribed, socially determined goals, and structural conditions that increase the separation between these goals and the legitimate means of attaining goals (Merton, 1968). This separation, which increases individual frustration with convention, fosters criminal activity.

In countries where material possessions and individual wealth define success, the relationship between the economy and crime is particularly salient (Messner & Rosenfeld, 1994). The economy dictates where citizens work, how much they make, and how secure employed individuals feel about their ability to provide for themselves and their families. Therefore, when fluctuations in the economy increase unemployment and underemployment, citizens may feel that they are unable to optimally survive in their present, less lavish, living conditions. When individuals feel that they are employed in an occupation that does not provide the status or level of financial security that they are accustomed to, this can create a sense of normlessness in dealing legitimately with the problem that is beyond their control, known as *anomie* (Merton, 1968).

From a sociological perspective, the expansion of the economy reduces the motivation for criminal behavior by increasing legitimate economic opportunities for citizens (Bernstein & Houston, 2000), because jobs are abundant, pay is adequate and meets individual needs for quality of life, and people are able to obtain the possessions they need through legitimate outlets (e.g., employment). According to Grogger (1998, 2000), when hourly wages increase, a quantifiable decrease in both property crime and violent crime rates is observed. The economic decline during the 1980s resulted in especially low wages. The economic boom in the 1990s coincided with a particularly large decrease in crime (Travis & Waul, 2002). Previously, Imrohoroglu, Merlo, and Rupert (2004) found that economic improvement was the second leading cause of decreased property crime between 1980 and 1996. In addition, both qualitative (Sherman, 1989) and quantitative (Laub & Sampson, 2003; Sampson & Laub, 1993) studies provided evidence for how legitimate employment provides the opportunity for abstention and desistance for previously delinquent individuals.

The effects of a poor economy on crime trends and crime rates are not entirely limited to unemployed populations, because the disproportionate increase in aggregate crime rates affects the population as a whole (Cantor & Land, 2001). Paternoster and Bushway (2001) have theorized that even the employed are at a greater risk of crime during high general unemployment because they may be underemployed, dissatisfied, or fearful of impending unemployment. As an illustration, Levitt (2001) found that a 1% change in the unemployment rate was typically found to increase property crime by 1% to 2%; however, unemployment often had no impact on violent criminal behavior.

Although it seems that unemployment does have an impact on crime, neighborhood-level contextual measures may confound this relationship. According to Piehl (1998), the influence of unemployment on property crime does not explain the high density of crime in low-income, urban neighborhoods. Further, Bushway and Reuter (2004) acknowledge that permanent job loss, particularly of well-paid, low-skill jobs, may spur high crime rates within some communities. However, the authors concede that introducing community job programs such as Community Development Block Grants or "Weed and Seed" cannot be the cure-all that removes the majority of social ills. In neglecting to account for pointedly localized neighborhood effects, analyses of the impact of economic change are incomplete. To provide a more complete description of the multitude of factors simultaneously influencing criminal activity, neighborhood and contextual effects that directly influence crime are detailed below.

Poverty, Crime, and Communities

The presence and prevalence of apparent criminal behavior are often used to characterize the quality and security of a community. Crime rates are not evenly distributed (Quetelet, 1831/1984), and ecological theories correlate crime with poverty rates, population transiency, and racial/ethnic heterogeneity (Sampson & Groves, 1989; Shaw & McKay, 1942). Community characteristics (e.g., unique structural characteristics of the community itself) seem to operate independently of individual-level decision-making processes. In other words, there is some evidence that the community you live in may change your behavior to make you more likely to be an offender, such as the presence of gangs or graffiti, homelessness, and high-density population (Sampson, 2006).

One of the strongest risk factors for criminality is community-level pervasiveness of poverty (Byrne & Sampson, 1986; Reiss, 1986; Sampson & Wilson, 1995). Control theories (Sampson et al., 1997; Sampson & Wilson, 1995) explain the link between poverty and crime through a lens of social disorganization (similar to how the process was reviewed above), which emphasizes that specific community characteristics such as poverty reduce the stability of a neighborhood. Over time, the social isolation and weakening social cohesion that is affected by poverty compromises informal social control (Sampson & Wilson, 1995). As a result, community members do nothing to control criminal behavior, gangs, graffiti, homelessness, and so on, because they are no longer invested in the community and seek to leave as soon as their personal economic circumstances allow. Or in other words, once they are able to move out of poverty, financially speaking, they literally move out of the neighborhood.

The Role of Opportunity and Exposure to Crime

As noted above, crime in the United States has been steady and slightly declining. There are several reasons why this may be explained through social phenomena. According to a review by Farrell, Tilley, Tseloni, and Mailley (2010), opportunity-related behaviors that may result in this crime-drop, nine specific hypotheses have been (and have not been) associated with reduced crime. These are reviewed below.

Associated with the crime rate:

1. ***Increase in the prison population***. Two studies (Langan & Farrington, 1998; Levitt, 2004) suggest that imprisonment of high-risk offenders may be related to (albeit a small) drop in the crime rate in the United States.

2. ***More police***. Marvell and Moody (1996) report that an increase in the number of police officers on patrol reduced the rate of crime. However, this finding is limited because it can only explain criminal behavior in the United States.

3. ***Changes in the drug market***. Levitt (2004) found that the reduction in crack cocaine usage was associated with decreased violence, homicide, and crime in general. Other studies have found drug availability and use inconclusively related to crime (Johnson, Golub, & Dunlap, 2000).

4. ***Increased abortion***. Donohue and Levitt (2001) found the increase in availability of legal abortions to be a strong factor in explaining the decrease in criminal behavior in the United States.

5. ***The economy***. The economy has been strongly related to the criminal justice system, as described above (Osborn, 2000; Pudney, Deadman, & Pyle, 2001), including detention rates, sentence severity, and unemployment. In addition to general economic effects of unemployment and low wages on crime, the exposure to crime and modeling of procriminal behavior may synergistically increase rates of crime when the economy is low. Further, the research is clear that those who are exposed to violence and criminal behavior are more likely to become offenders themselves (Farrell et al., 2010; Gorman-Smith & Tolan, 1998; Reingle, Jennings, Maldonado-Molina, Piquero, & Canino, 2011).
6. ***Lead exposure***. Wolpaw Reyes (2007) found that 59% of the drop in crime during the 1990s may be attributable to reductions in lead exposure from gasoline and air.

Not associated with the crime rate:

1. ***There has been a shift in the demographic composition of the United States***.
2. ***Better policing strategies***.
3. ***Gun control and concealed weapon laws***.

Conclusion and Directions for Future Research

Overall, this chapter has provided a summary of how communities themselves vary substantially in their crime trends and crime rates. This chapter began with a theoretical discussion of the fact that the variation in crime trends and crime rates across communities has historically been informed by social disorganization theory and the more recent advancements of Sampson et al. (1997), among others. Coinciding with this "revitalization" in sociological interest in communities and crime research has been the advancement of statistical tools such as trajectory analysis that has ushered in a wave of important research on community crime careers. Specific evidence from these applications was discussed. Furthermore, we also reviewed a number of factors including the economy and other changes in policy and criminal justice practice that can have an impact on individual-level criminal behavior and thus ultimately on aggregated levels of crime trends and crime rates.

Going forward, it is important for research on crime trends and crime rates from primarily a macro-level perspective to make an effort to continue to conduct longitudinal research. Unfortunately, the bulk of the research thus far has largely relied on cross-sectional data, although the application of trajectory analysis to study community crime careers represents a refreshing and beneficial addition to the larger literature on crime trends and crime rates. In this same vein, longitudinal research in this regard is essential for capturing and estimating how neighborhood structure and social processes change over time and how the changes in the neighborhood structure and social processes affect crime trends and crime rates over time.

Studying these dynamic influences rather than just merely focusing on a cross-sectional snapshot of these processes is critical for identifying points where policies may be targeted and implemented in an effort to reduce crime and crime rates. Ultimately, although sociological investigations into crime trends and crime rates have a long and rich tradition with nearly a century of valuable research, there is still a lot to be done to further flesh out the complexities of the causes of crime and crime rates and why these outcomes vary over time.

References

Bernstein, J., & Houston, E. (2000). *Crime and work: What we can learn from the low-wage labor market.* Washington DC: Economic Policy Institute.

Bushway, S. W., & Reuter, P. (2004). Labor markets and crime. In J. Q. Wilson & J. Petersilia (Eds.), *Crime: Public policies for crime control* (4th ed., pp. 191–224). Oakland, CA: Institute for Contemporary Studies Press.

Byrne, J. M., & Sampson, R. J. (1986). Key issues in the social ecology of crime. In J. M. Byrne & R. J. Sampson (Eds.), *The social ecology of crime* (pp. 1–22). New York, NY: Springer.

Cantor, D., & Land, K. C. (2001). Unemployment and crime rate fluctuation: A comment on Greenberg. *Journal of Quantitative Criminology, 17,* 329–342.

Donohue, J., & Levitt, S. (2001). The impact of legalized abortion on crime. *Quarterly Journal of Economics, 116,* 279–420.

Farrell, G., Tilley, N., Tseloni, A., & Mailley, J. (2010). Explaining and sustaining the crime drop: Clarifying the role of opportunity-related theories. *Crime Prevention and Community Safety, 12,* 24–41.

Gorman-Smith, D., & Tolan, P. (1998). The role of exposure to community violence and developmental problems among inner-city youth. *Development and Psychopathology, 10,* 101–116.

Griffiths, E., & Chavez, J. M. (2004). Communities, street guns, and homicide trajectories in Chicago, 1980–1995: Merging methods for examining homicide trends across space and time. *Criminology, 42,* 941–978.

Grogger, J. (1998). Market wages and youth crime. *Journal of Labor Economics, 16,* 756–791.

Grogger. J. (2000). An economic model of recent trends in violence. In A. Blumstein & J. Wallman (Eds.), *The crime drop in America* (pp. 266–287). New York, NY: Cambridge University Press.

Imrohoroglu, A., Merlo, A. M., & Rupert, P. (2004). What accounts for the decline in crime? *International Economic Review, 43,* 707–729.

Jennings, W. G., & Piquero, A. R. (2008). Trajectories of non-intimate partner and intimate partner homicides, 1980–1999: The importance of rurality. *Journal of Criminal Justice, 36,* 435–443.

Jennings, W. G., & Reingle, J. M. (2012). On the number and shape of developmental/life-course violence, aggression, and delinquency trajectories: A state-of-the-art review. *Journal of Criminal Justice, 40,* 472–489.

Johnson, B., Golub, A., & Dunlap, E. (2000). The rise and decline of hard drugs, drug markets, and violence in inner city New York. In A. Blumstein & J. Wallman (Eds.), *The crime drop in America* (pp. 164–206). New York, NY: Cambridge University Press.

Langan, P., & Farrington, D. (1998). *Crime and justice in the United States and in England and Wales, 1981–96.* Washington, DC: US Department of Justice Office of Justice Programs Bureau of Justice Statistics.

Laub, J. H., & Sampson, R. J. (2003). *Shared beginnings, divergent lives: Delinquent boys to age 70.* Cambridge, MA: Harvard University Press.

Levitt, S. D. (2001). Alternative strategies for identifying the link between unemployment and crime. *Journal of Quantitative Criminology, 17,* 377–390.

Levitt, S. D. (2004). Understanding why crime fell in the 1990s: Four factors that explain the decline and six that do not. *Journal of Economic Perspectives, 18,* 163–190.

Marvell, T., & Moody, C. (1996). Specification problems, police levels, and crime rates. *Criminology, 34,* 609–646.

Merton, R. (1968). Social structure and anomie. *American Sociological Review, 3,* 672–682.

Messner, S., & Rosenfeld, R. (1994). *Crime and the American Dream.* Belmont, CA: Wadsworth.

Morenoff, J. D., Sampson, R. J., & Raudenbush, S. W. (2001). Neighborhood inequality, collective efficacy, and the spatial dynamics of urban violence. *Criminology, 39,* 517–558.

Nagin, D. S. (2005). *Group-based modeling of development.* Cambridge, MA: Harvard University Press.

Nagin, D. S., & Land, K. C. (1993). Age, criminal careers, and population heterogeneity: Specification and estimation of a non-parametric, mixed Poisson model. *Criminology, 31,* 327–362.

Osborn, D. R. (2000). An investigation into quarterly crime and its relationship to the economy. In Z. MacDonald & D. Pyle (Eds.), *Illicit activity: The economics of crime, drugs and tax fraud* (pp. 75–101). Farnham, UK: Ashgate.

Paternoster, R., & Bushway, S. (2001). Theoretical and empirical work on the relationship between unemployment and crime. *Journal of Quantitative Criminology, 17,* 391–407.

Patterson, E. B. (1991). Poverty, income inequality, and community crime rates. *Criminology, 29,* 755–776.

Piehl, A. M. (1998). Economic conditions, work, and crime. In M. Tonry (Ed.), *The handbook of crime and punishment* (pp. 302–319). New York, NY: Oxford University Press.

Piquero, A. R., Farrington, D. P., & Blumstein, A. (2003). The criminal career paradigm. *Crime and Justice, 30,* 359–506.

Pudney, S., Deadman, D., & Pyle, D. (2001). The relationship between crime, punishment and economic conditions: Is reliable inference possible when crimes are under-recorded? *Journal of the Royal Statistical Society Series A—Statistics in Society, 163,* 81–97.

Quetelet, A. (1984). *Research on the propensity for crime at different ages* (S. F. Sylvester, Trans., Intro.). Cincinnati, OH: Anderson (Original work published 1831).

Reingle, J. M., Jennings, W. G., Maldonado-Molina, M. M., Piquero, A. R., & Canino, G. (2011). Investigating the role of gender and delinquency in exposure to violence among Puerto Rican youth. *Journal of Contemporary Criminal Justice, 27,* 361–377.

Reiss, A. J., Jr. (1986). Why are communities important in understanding crime? In A. J. Reiss, Jr., & M. Tonry (Eds.), *Communities and crime* (pp. 1–33). Chicago, IL: University of Chicago Press.

Sampson, R. J. (2006). How does community context matter? Social mechanisms and the explanation of crime. In P. H. Wikstrom & R. J. Sampson (Eds.), *The explanation of crime: Context, mechanisms, and development* (pp. 31–60). New York, NY: Cambridge University Press.

Sampson, R. J., & Groves, W. B. (1989). Community structure and crime: Testing social disorganization theory. *American Journal of Sociology, 94,* 744–802.

Sampson, R. J., & Laub, J. H. (1993). *Crime in the making: Pathways and turning points through life.* Cambridge, MA: Harvard University Press.

Sampson, R. J., Raudenbush, S. W., & Earls, F. (1997). Neighborhoods and violent crime: A multilevel study of collective efficacy. *Science, 227,* 918–924.

Sampson, R. J., & Wilson, W. J. (1995). Toward a theory of race, crime, and urban inequality. In J. Hagan & R. D. Peterson (Eds.), *Crime and inequality* (pp. 37–54). Stanford, CA: Stanford University Press.

Schuerman, L., & Kobrin, S. (1986). Community careers in crime. In A. J. Reiss, Jr., & M. Tonry (Eds.), *Communities and crime.* Chicago, IL: University of Chicago Press.

Shaw, C. R., & McKay, H. D. (1942). *Juvenile delinquency and urban areas.* Chicago, IL: University of Chicago Press.

Sherman, M. L. (1989). *"Getting paid": Youth crime and work in the inner city.* Ithaca, NY: Cornell University Press.

Simcha-Fagan, O., & Schwartz, J. E. (1986). Neighborhood and delinquency: An assessment of contextual effects. *Criminology, 24,* 667–699.

Smith, D. A., & Jarjoura, G. R. (1988). Social structure and criminal victimization. *Journal of Research in Crime and Delinquency, 25,* 27–52.

Stults, B. J. (2010). Determinants of Chicago neighborhood homicide trajectories: 1965–1995. *Homicide Studies, 14,* 244–267.

Travis, J., & Waul, M. (2002). *Reflections on the crime decline: Lessons for the future?* Washington, DC: Urban Institute.

United States Department of Justice, Federal Bureau of Investigation. (2008). *Crime in the United States, 2008.* Retrieved from http://www2.fbi.gov/ucr/cius2008/index.html

United States Department of Justice, Federal Bureau of Investigation. (2012). *Crime in the United States, 2011.* Retrieved from http://www.fbi.gov/about-us/cjis/ucr/crime-in-the-u.s/2011/crime-in-the-u.s.-2011/violent-crime/violent-crime

Weisburd, D., Bushway, S. W., Lum, C., & Yang, S. M. (2004). Trajectories of crime at places: A longitudinal study of street segments in the city of Seattle. *Criminology, 42,* 283–321.

Weisburd, D., Morris, N. A., & Groff, E. R. (2009). Hot spots of juvenile crime: A longitudinal study of arrest incidents at street segments in Seattle, Washington. *Journal of Quantitative Criminology, 25,* 443–467.

Wolpaw Reyes, J. (2007). *Environmental policy as social policy? The impact of childhood lead exposure on crime.* National Bureau of Economic Research, Working Paper 13097.

22

Darwin, Dawkins, Wright, Pinker, and the Reasons That Crime Declined

Brian B. Boutwell
Sam Houston State University

J.C. Barnes
The University of Texas at Dallas

Thus, from the war of nature, from famine and death, the most exalted object which we are capable of conceiving, namely, the production of the higher animals, directly follows. There is grandeur in this view of life, with its several powers, having been originally breathed by the Creator into a few forms or into one; and that, whilst this planet has gone circling on according to the fixed law of gravity, from so simple a beginning endless forms most beautiful and most wonderful have been, and are being evolved.

—Charles Darwin (*Origin of Species*, 1859, p. 507)

A remarkable event began in the late 1980s. Crime rates, for many reasons—some more apparent than others—began going down (Blumstein & Wallman, 2005). And scientists, being a curious lot rather than heed that old saying of never look a gift horse in the mouth began asking that age-old question of why? Why should crime rates go down? Over two decades have passed, and we are still pondering this very interesting question (Levitt, 2004). Given the unique nature of this volume—and the inherent debate built into it—our goal in this chapter is not to merely rehash old ideas about the crime drop. In many ways, we are conceding the debate—by now we probably have a reasonable understanding of the factors that could have contributed to declining crime (both property and violent), as well as those things that probably had little to do with diminishing rates (Levitt, 2004). Moreover, our sociological compatriot for this chapter will doubtless provide an exceedingly thorough overview of this issue.

For that, we are quite grateful because it frees us up to take a more circuitous route in discussing the topic at hand. Specifically, we wish to offer a rather radical idea, which will be underpinned by biosocial research. Namely, that the "crime drop," as well as more general declines in global violence (Pinker, 2012), was our "destiny" all along (Wright, 2000). We should confess outright that this is *not* our original idea. As is so often the case, other more influential thinkers have beat us to the punch. The work of Robert Wright (2000) and Steven Pinker (2012), especially, will undergird much of what is discussed herein. Even so, it is high time that these enthralling, and at times utterly brilliant, ideas are introduced to criminologists. Should the assertions of these individuals prove correct, they would be earth-shattering for scholars of crime (okay, not really, but a little hyperbole every now and then never hurt anyone).

So here are the basic premises from which we will operate. First, human nature was headed inexorably toward a more peaceful state (Wright, 2000). Yet this state would have never been achieved were it not for certain evolved mental faculties (Wright, 2000). Second, the idea that we are progressing to a higher moral plane and not digressing into the moral slums as many politicians, social scientists, and television evangelists would have us believe is probably a heretical idea (we could not possibly, however, care any less about committing this heresy) (Harris, 2010). Third, as Wright (2000) and Pinker (2012) suggest, this moral enhancement is the product of evolution—cultural and biological—and thus should naturally include declining crime rates. Fourth, criminologists may explain the crime drop, yet we suggest that without wrapping a larger theoretical framework around the subject renders any proximal explanation boring and pointless.

So where do we start? Let us immediately take a hard left turn and wade off into the waters of evolution. This little sojourn is necessary, though, if we are to have some grasp of why our "destiny" included a crime drop. We should alert the reader at this point to something. It takes us a bit to actually get to the meat of the argument, yet it does happen in due course. In this regard, we kindly ask for patience. We need to cover many millions of years in only a brief amount of page space, which will inevitably take a bit of digression. Moreover, this will undoubtedly mean that we gloss over many important and interesting details for the sake of brevity. But we promise to return to the issue at hand, and we also promise that the trip will be worth the destination (at least we hope). For now, let us start at the beginning (is it possible to start anywhere else, after all).

In the Beginning There Was . . . Darwin?

It may appear odd that Charles Darwin, that great naturalist and progenitor of the theory of evolution, should have the first word in a chapter intended to discuss the decline in crime. It is indeed fitting, though, that Darwin should offer us a starting point for our conversation here. Darwin, who, by most accounts, was a gentle man—meek and humble—was nevertheless well aware that nature could often house rather unpleasant characteristics (Wright, 1994). The quote taken from the final pages of *Origin of Species* speaks to the "war of nature" as well as the "famine and death" that often plague the natural world (Darwin, 1859). In the closing sentences of Darwin's masterpiece, however, he offered a nod to the amazing richness of life on our small planet. Fast-forward 150 years and perhaps now more than ever there is much that is deserving of marvel. In the lifetime of the authors, we have mapped the human genome (Collins, Lander, Rogers, Waterston, & Conso, 2004), coerced undifferentiated stem cells into performing truly remarkable tasks like generating new organs from scratch (Perin et al., 2007), and we are well on our way to eradicating diseases that generations ago were hopelessly intractable.

Darwin certainly might have anticipated the medical leaps that were to come and he would doubtless be in awe today were he witness to the advances of science and technology. Yet there is perhaps an achievement of modernity that Darwin might not have fully anticipated. Indeed, few in the general public seem to even be aware that it happened, and is happening, right in front of them. As Steven Pinker (2012) has pointed out, it certainly appears that modern man is living through, relatively speaking, a rather serene time period. On a historical scale, violence and atrocity have declined (Eisner, 2008; Pinker, 2012). Historical scales are often more difficult to conceptualize, but even on the more manageable scale of decades, crime and other forms of antisocial behavior have also gone down (Blumstein & Wallman, 2005). What do we make of this rather pleasing, if not unexpected, phenomenon? In a world where we concern ourselves with handgun laws, immigration regulation, global marketplaces, fiscal cliffs, bioethics, and religious zealotry, how is it that—despite ourselves—crime rates have dropped?

What will doubtless become apparent is that the explanation is not clear, it is not simple, and it is certainly not guaranteed to give itself up easily (causality is not known for being an accommodating mistress). Even so, we dive off into the problem using a biosocial approach, the goal being to muster everything in our arsenal to explain declining rates of violence and crime. There is a short caveat, though, that we should insert at this point before plowing ahead much farther. Before we can offer any type of adequate description regarding why crime might have declined, we need to first have a discussion about human nature. Certainly, if human behavior—including criminal behavior—in any way reflects our natural tendencies, then it might be good to know what those tendencies encompass.

To glean some pearl of wisdom regarding human nature, we need to peer back into history and try to understand how our nature would have evolved. Are we born in a way that makes us antisocial? Such views are not foreign to mainstream criminology (Gottfredson & Hirschi, 1990). Or is our nature inherently good? Again, prominent criminological theories have worked from this very assumption (Agnew, 1992). Ultimately, a better understanding of human nature may offer us a peephole from which to view the issue of declining violence and crime. So indulge us this brief venture into the past. We promise to bring the conversation back to a more criminological-sounding discourse; it just might take us a bit to get there.

Meet *Homo Sapiens*: The Proud Product of Evolution

A Cliff Notes version of Darwin's (1859) theory would, perhaps, read thusly: All the wonderful complexity in the natural world is the product of descent (with modification) from a common ancestor. Fast-forward billions of years, mix in a little natural and sexual selection and a painstaking migration out of Africa, and there you have it: modern humans. Clearly, we have over simplified, but we are sure the reader can see our point. To be clear, however, we are trying to illustrate a theme running throughout biosocial research. Human beings, just like every other living organism on the planet, have been shaped and molded by natural selection. The "design," so to speak, in our bodies is blazingly apparent (Dawkins, 1986).

The trial-and-error process of natural selection left us with a functional eye that we use to see the world, yet when one steps back it becomes obvious that parts of the eye were horribly assembled (see Dawkins [1986] for a more thorough discussion of design flaws, including the example of eyes). On perusal of human assemblage, it is clear that Dawkins's (1986) "blind watchmaker" has been on the scene cobbling together a functional organ with preexisting parts (in this case, a little light sensitive tissue to get the ball rolling and then you are off to the races). Eyes work reasonably well, but they often malfunction, requiring intervention (contact lenses, anyone?). But here is the kicker; the same process that designed your eye (and your heart, spleen, kidneys, etc.) also built your brain (Pinker, 1997).

Perhaps the most wonderfully complex piece of biological machinery in the entire universe resides in your skull weighing in at a whopping three pounds. More important, if we assume that the venerable Descartes got it wrong and that mind is *not* divisible from the brain, then we have a real issue on our hands with which we must contend (Pinker, 2002). See if you can follow the bouncing ball of logic. The brain is an organ designed by natural selection (Pinker, 1997). The mind is the product of brain function (Dennett, 1984). Our minds inform our daily decisions regarding what to have for lunch, whether we should pay our taxes (can you say overrated), who we should vote for (politics again?!), which grocery store to shop at, how to deal with our annoying coworker (you know who you are), and yes, our decisions whether or not to commit crime (Burnham & Phelan, 2000). It stands to reason, then, one might want to know "how the mind works" (to borrow from the title of Pinker's [1997] influential book) if one is to understand something about the crime drop (perhaps this seems like tortured logic, but hang in there, we are nearly to the good part).

I Don't *Mind* If You Don't

In his exceedingly important and influential book *How the Mind Works*, psychologist Steven Pinker (1997) presented a wonderfully spun theory regarding the vast complexities of mental life in humans. Unfortunately, we have promised to tell you why crime fell, so we do not have the space necessary to give Pinker's work on the mind true justice. Even so, the basic concepts in the book are relatively straightforward. Essentially, mental capacity in humans can be understood with the concept of "modules" (Buss, 2004; Pinker, 1997). Consider this; your Pleistocene ancestor (probably a very handsome sort, but in need of a razor) would have needed to overcome problems in daily life. Moreover, some of these problems were quite recurrent, such as how do I get a mate, who is angling to take something from me, how do I negotiate social life, is someone trying to steal my girlfriend—or something along similar lines. These recurrent problems may have resulted in mental modules that were designed by natural (and sexual) selection to get past these evolutionary imperatives—namely to survive and pass along your genes (Dawkins, 1976).

So what does all this mean for human nature? Consider the argument set forth by control theorists in criminology that human nature is inherently selfish (Gottfredson & Hirschi, 1990). When one assumes this, the obvious corollary is that we would all take advantage of one another were it not for some kind of "control" on our behavior (hence the name, control theory). Clearly, control theorists neglected to read their Robert Axelrod (1997). A purely selfish strategy is not evolutionarily tenable (see Dawkins, 1976, to illustrate the point beautifully). There is a need for something akin to self-interest. Yet the best strategy appears to be one where organisms in the population reciprocate with one another (Dawkins, 1976, 1982). In other words, you help me, I help you—as long as you don't cheat me (or me you)—everybody wins. A healthy dose of self-interest is good, but a pure population of cheaters would not work—they would all die off. Importantly, a pure population of utter dupes (completely *selfless* organisms) would not work either. Such a population would be vulnerable to evasion from cheaters (Dawkins, 1976).

Non-Zero-Sum: I Was Told There Would Be No Math!

So again, we return to this issue of mental modules, why would we need them? If you recall, there are many problems in life in need of solving (i.e., who do I mate with, who do I trust and cooperate with). Enter, from stage left, the eternally clever journalist Robert Wright. Wright has an amazing aptitude for taking rather banal subjects (like human cooperation) and transforming them into fascinating trips into the human psyche. For instance, in his book *The Moral Animal*, Wright (1994) lays out an argument for how human morality and goodness might have evolved. In what was an utterly brilliant example, Wright characterized the "modules" of human nature as more akin to radio knobs. Radios have several different options when it comes to knobs—you have your treble and bass, volume of course, as well as other fine tuning options. It may be the same with human nature.

Let us consider one possible example of a mental knob: cooperation. Cooperation clearly has a place in our behavioral repertoire, but the issue becomes who should you cooperate with? An easy place to start is with your kin—they share your genes (Hamilton, 1964). Given the overlap in the genome, by helping them you are actually helping yourself send similar copies of your genes into the next generation (Fowler, Settle, & Christakis, 2011). That is all well and good, but we help non-kin acquaintances all the time (see any celebrity telethon for direct evidence). Not to worry, the psychologist J. P. Rushton (1989) helped calm the concern surrounding this issue decades ago with his genetic similarity theory. Essentially, Rushton observed, very astutely, that humans do not pair off into peer groups at random. Just survey that treacherous savannah known as the human high school and observe the various groups of young humans roaming about it. It will become painfully obvious that peer groups resemble each other (just look for the flock of letterman jackets trundling along together for starters).

This is not magic, however. Friendship assortment involves sharing many things—one of which, perhaps, is personality traits (as well general interests, abilities, temperaments) (Fowler et al., 2011; Rushton, 1989). Follow closely because this is the key part: to the extent that genes influence each of the traits mentioned above—and they do (Rhee & Waldman, 2002; Turkheimer, 2000)—then biologically unrelated peers (i.e., nonsiblings) should resemble each other (at least somewhat) at the genetic level. The really interesting thing here is that there is some evidence that they do (Boardman, Domingue, & Fletcher, 2012; Fowler et al., 2011). Nonetheless, this leaves us back at a crossroad. If cooperation is a mental module that exists in humans, could this tell us something about the reason that crime (and overall violence) has declined?

Let us turn again to the work of Robert Wright (2000). In his important book, *Non-Zero*, Wright suggests that technology and globalization have inextricably linked the collective fortunes of humans across the planet. The idea of non-zero-sumness refers to the fact that multiple actors can succeed in life without compromising the success of others. Importantly, the idea of non-zero does not stipulate that we have to be completely altruistic—just the opposite; it recognizes that humans have a mental module for selfishness and aggression. The key, according to Wright, is that we have reached a point where the individually self-interested desires of humans covary along with each another. Thus, the success of one individual becomes necessarily tied to the success of others (Weyl, Frederickson, Douglas, & Pierce, 2010).

Bringing It Home: The Source of Declining Crime Rates

Okay, at this point we have toyed with the reader's expectations long enough. It is now time to actually consider the reasons why crime might have declined (cut us some slack, we just covered millennia in just a handful of pages). As we mentioned earlier, there are likely a multitude of reasons why crime fell, but generally any explanation can fall into one of two varieties: proximal and ultimate. By the nature of how the human mind works, the proximal causes are more easily contemplated than the ultimate contributors. As such, we begin by examining research pertaining to proximal contributions to declining crime trends (Farrell, Tilley, Tseloni, & Mailley, 2010). With that under our belts, we bring all the previous discussion to bear on uncovering the ultimate causes.

We should reiterate at this point that we are *not* offering a thorough overview of why crime declined. Our sociological counterpart herein offers outstanding guidance on the existing research—and we do not see biosocial ideas necessarily in conflict with this literature. Before the close of this chapter, however, what should become clear is that the only paradigm capable of uniting both proximal and ultimate factors is a biosocial approach. Without the biosocial paradigm, an understanding of proximal influences is facile. It offers only surface explanations for declining crime. To have something far more meaningful, we need a robust umbrella type theory. That is where the ideas of Wright (2000) and Pinker (2012) come into play; we are just not quite there yet. Stay tuned.

PROXIMAL EXPLANATIONS (INTERESTING, BUT WHAT IF THERE'S MORE TO IT . . .)

As the economist Steven Levitt (2004) has pointed out, there has been no dearth of theorizing about the why crime might have declined (Blumstein & Wallman, 2005). And it did decline; as Levitt mentioned, homicide rates plummeted over 40% from 1991 to 2001, which was followed closely by violent and property crime. The problem with armchair theorizing, however, is that it seldom produces anything worthwhile. There must have been something at the proximal level, though, that contributed to the vanishing crime rate. In statistical parlance, what variables might account for variance in the model? In laymen's terms, where the hell did all the crime go?

Remarkably, Levitt (2004) (the economist, mind you) is not convinced (nor are the authors) that the burgeoning economy of the 1990s had much to do with the drop in crime. Perhaps you might balk at this. Clearly, crime is linked to unemployment, thus make more jobs, put more people to work, and you should see crime decline. Let us put that to the acid test, however. America has recently (and indeed still is) navigated a pretty rough recession, yet crime rates have continued to decline (albeit not as steeply, but they surely have not spiked). Moreover, there has been no convincing evidence that employment does much to curb violent crime rates (Levitt, 2004).

As a brief aside, could we at least consider why employment might not play a large role in the crime drop? How about we get creative for a minute and consider the possibility that any correlation between unemployment and crime might be spurious. In other words, what if some variable predicted both an increase in the odds of being unemployed while also contributing to an increased probability of criminal involvement? Maybe one place to start is intelligence (Beaver & Wright, 2011). Evidence exists, for example, that IQ at the county level correlates negatively with crime rates as well as other social maladies—net of a number of important variables (including poverty and concentrated disadvantage) (Barnes, Beaver, & Boutwell, 2013; Beaver &Wright, 2011). Does this mean that increasing IQ levels contributed to declining crime rates (Pinker, 2012)? Perhaps; there is evidence that IQ is rising (see Flynn, 2012) yet there is also reason to be skeptical in this regard (Rushton, 1999). Even so, might we even consider the possibility that rising cognitive scores could have had some impact on declining crime at the proximal level (Pinker, 2012)? Perhaps that is a worthwhile mental activity.

Levitt (2004) does not stop there, though. Indeed, he presents five other factors that were most likely *unrelated* to the drop in crime. For the sake of much needed brevity, they are as follows: (1) changing demographics (i.e., incoming hoards of teenagers), (2) more effective policing strategies, (3) stricter gun control laws (if you listen closely, you can hear the NRA applauding), (4) concealed weapons permits (that applause has now transitioned to a standing ovation), and (5) increased use of the death penalty (sorry, Texas, but keep fighting the good fight). There have been more in-depth reviews of the topics just outlined (Lott, 2013; Radelet & Akers, 1996) so we humbly direct our readers to those to save space here. At this point, why be so pessimistic; let us turn to why Levitt thinks crime might have declined. In this regard, there are four factors at play: (1) increased numbers of police, (2) the rising prison population, (3) the declining crack problem, and (4) the legalization of abortion. Indeed, Levitt has argued that in combination, these factors can account for virtually all the declining crime rates.

Blumstein and Wallman (2006) have also presented thoughtful reviews concerning reasons that crime might have fallen. Their conclusion: it was likely an interactive model, with multiple factors playing a role, that would serve as the most appropriate explanation for declining crime rates. The idea works something like this: each of the factors (the economy, gun laws, increased policing, increased imprisonment, etc.) accounted for variance in declining crime rates—with some variables mattering more than others. All told, though, each of the variables would have contributed incrementally (and interactively) to diminishing rates of crime.

All this talk of proximal predictors of declining crime is interesting, but we would submit that it is rather banal when one actually considers several ideas. First, why should we necessarily restrict our analysis of declining crime to the last couple of decades? What would happen if we widened our lens to include the last century, or better yet, the last millennium (Pinker, 2012)? Would we find anything of interest? Second, it is one thing to talk about proximal influences of declining crime but it is quite another to wrap a coherent framework around these proximal factors and make them make sense. Could the declining crime rate have something to do with human nature, more broadly understood (Wright, 2000)? It certainly might, but most criminologists have failed to even consider the possibility.

ULTIMATE EXPLANATIONS (THE REALLY INTERESTING PART . . .)

Let us consider an interesting finding to emerge from the tomes of research recently combed through by the influential psychologist Steven Pinker (2012). Pinker started with a basic premise: figure out whether violence has been increasing or decreasing over the course of human history. Wading through numerous studies conducted by criminologists (Eisner, 2008), anthropologists (Schneider & Schneider, 2008), sociologists (Blumstein & Wallman, 2005), and others, Pinker suggested that violence—broadly defined—was going down. To be sure, the trend line is not smooth—it hiccups up and down, increasing and decreasing—but ultimately, the trend is toward that of diminishing violence worldwide.

Let us reiterate, it is not just crime over the last several decades that has been declining, it appears to be violence more broadly defined that is also going down (Pinker, 2012). This finding opens up a whole new spectrum of ideas that need to be considered. For one, the decline of crime in the 1990s may represent only a blip on the radar regarding the larger pattern of declining violence. If this is indeed the case, then we can compile all the proximal predictors that we like, but if we restrict them to modern day phenomena (the police, for example, haven't been around forever), then we are inevitably going to short ourselves in terms of a full explanation. Finally, when one considers the possibility that violence in general may have been going down, and this decline could have been under way for generations on generations, then our task becomes much larger than just accounting for why there was a noticeable dip in crime during the 1990s.

Human Destiny: The Ultimate Reason That Crime Declined?

At this point, we have probably managed to anger at least someone reading this chapter, but why stop now? Robert Wright (2000) suggested that human history has a direction—indeed, a logical destiny (how dare he?!). According to Wright, this destiny involves an ever growing and ever widening web of connectedness. Business has become more global, market economies in one country are tied to others (ever heard of a country called Greece) and the result is that humans have an ongoing non-zero-sum game with one another (Wright, 2000). That is all well and good, but how did we get to this point? Rewind back to our discussion about reciprocal altruism and friendship networks. If you imagine that it makes sense for family members to help one another because they share genes then we have a starting point. Now imagine that it also makes sense to help friends who share similar genes. How do you know that they share genes? Observe their personalities and behavior. If they overlap with your own, then there is a chance that they do (Fowler et al., 2011).

Now, if natural selection favored this kind of interdependence, then genes for reciprocating should have flourished (Trivers, 1971). Okay, so we have a lot of "helper" genes in the population, so what? What about the genes that might contribute to criminal offending (Barnes, Beaver, & Boutwell, 2011; Beaver et al., 2012)? Consider one of the unique findings to emerge in criminological research—namely, that a very small proportion of the population accounts for a large number of criminal acts (Moffitt, 1993). One can quibble over the name (i.e., life-course persister, career criminal, etc.), but it does not really matter. What matters is that these individuals account for a small proportion of the population and, importantly, genes play a large role in understanding why some individuals meet the definition of chronic offenders and others do not (Barnes et al., 2011). What if this is how selection pressures were operating the whole time; largely favoring genetically underpinned mental traits for reciprocation, yet failing to completely weed out genes that employ cheater and exploitative strategies (Boutwell, Barnes, Deaton, & Beaver, 2013; Buss, 2009)?

If this is correct, it suggests that the human condition should have been headed in a specific direction all along, toward a "non-zero-sumness" (to borrow from Wright [2000] again), which would drastically diminish the number of cheaters, or criminals if you like, within the population. But is there any evidence that this is how it actually happened? It would be nice to hop in our time machine and watch it all unfold over the deep time of evolution (the authors would also like to win the lottery) but this is just not likely. What do we have to base our speculation on then?

Well, ponder what life was like for ancient man as well as what it is currently like in prestate societies (Pinker, 2002). Beyond lacking the essential comforts of an iPod, iPad, eHarmony (for all those lonely nights), Twitter, Facebook, and ESPN (the last one is a personal bias), it was also quite dangerous. The murder rate of the !Kung San, for instance, is higher than that in the United States currently (Pinker, 2002). Moreover, rape, sexual jealousy, aggression, and other unpleasantries are well engrained aspects of life (Pinker, 2002). To the extent that modern prestate societies offer us a glimpse into our past, it suggests that hunter-gatherer life was rather treacherous (Keeley, 1996; Pinker, 2002).

Did it have to happen in such a way that humans evolved toward an ever more peaceful state? Perhaps not; as the famed biologist Stephan Jay Gould (2000) pointed out, one cannot necessarily rewind the videotape of life, hit play, and expect to get the exact same outcome. There is at least some evidence to the contrary, however, hinting that natural selection solves problems in very similar ways—even across species—and that a similar trend would have emerged were we to rewind the human game-tape and hit play all over again (Dobler, Dalla, Wagschal, & Agrawal, 2012). At this point, we have speculated enough to make our point, so we will leave it at that.

The Meaning of Life! (Or Maybe Just This Chapter . . .)

In concluding this chapter, we contemplated how best to summarize our arguments so that if the readers were so inclined, they could peruse these last few paragraphs and get a good sense of the previous discussion (which begs the question, if we could distill it down to a few paragraphs, then why not just write a paragraph to begin with). In our collective minds, here are the basics of what we suggest as a biosocial approach to understanding the declining crime rate. First, to consider only the crime drop of the 1990s is to widely underestimate what might have been happening in the human species for many centuries. Moreover, studying the crime drop outside the larger purview of human evolutionary history is largely misguided.

Second, to place the crime drop in its proper context, one must consider how evolution has shaped and molded our species over deep time. Third, such considerations inevitably bring human nature into play, so one must have an idea regarding what that nature looks like in a biosocial and evolutionary sense. Fourth, from our vantage point Wright (2000), and others (Pinker, 2002), got it right when they characterized human nature as being modular—with a portion devoted to reciprocal altruism. Fifth, as selection pressures further selected for reciprocal altruists, those genes would have flourished. Sixth, as "helper" genes flourished, genes that predisposed to antisocial (or cheating behavior) would have been kept in check (not disappearing entirely, though) (Boutwell et al., 2013; Buss, 2009). Seventh (and thankfully the last point), all these factors—combined with the more proximal level predictors (Levitt, 2004)—culminated in the overall declining crime rate that criminologists study so closely.

Our arguments herein are not perfect (nor are they originally ours, so thankfully we cannot be blamed entirely). For example, one might immediately accuse us of popping on our historical spectacles (or contacts) and employing the 20/20 vision afforded by hindsight. Guilty as charged. Nonetheless, this is a legitimate undertaking when one seeks merely to understand a body of facts and organize them in some coherent fashion. Additionally, one could contend that our argument would fall apart should crime rates begin to rise over the next few decades. They certainly could rise yet again (the crime rates, that is), but our argument would remain unscathed. Primarily this is because we are less concerned with minor fluctuations in the trend-line of violence over shorter periods of time, only that a trend is ultimately detectable.

So what is the meaning of life? We do not know. However, the meaning of this chapter is clear in that the decline in crime is nested within the broader history of the human lineage. We have accomplished some remarkable things (remember the whole "one small step for a man" thing) as a species. Yet we are governed by the same natural laws that lord over every other species on the planet. Scholars of human activities, then, simply must work within the organizing parameters of that framework. To do otherwise represents a doomed enterprise, one destined to fail—or at the very least offer diminishing and uninteresting returns. The incorporation of biosocial concepts, therefore, is the obvious remedy to the stagnation than can accumulate around a given topic.

The crime drop becomes all the more interesting—and even expected—when one stops to consider the broader (and by that we mean millions of years) scenario in which it occurred. The really fascinating question to ponder from here on out is just *how good* might things continue to become? Assuming, of course, that we do not find some new and inventive way of killing ourselves off (or if some large cosmic extinction event takes care of it for us) before we find out the answer. We can feel good about one thing at least: If you are reading this then it means that the Mayans got it wrong and the world did not end on December 21, 2012 (what did you expect, the Mayans were pre-Google). At least that is one hurdle cleared toward a more perfect existence for the human race.

References

Agnew, R. (1992). Foundation for a general strain theory of crime and delinquency. *Criminology, 30*(1), 47–88.

Axelrod, R. M. (1997). *The complexity of cooperation: Agent-based models of competition and collaboration*. Princeton, NJ: Princeton University Press.

Barnes, J. C., Beaver, K. M., & Boutwell, B. B. (2011). Examining the genetic underpinnings to Moffitt's developmental taxonomy: A behavioral genetic analysis. *Criminology, 49*(4), 923–954.

Barnes, J. C., Beaver, K. M., & Boutwell, B. B. (2013). Average county-level IQ predicts county-level disadvantage and several county-level mortality risk rates. *Intelligence, 41*(1), 59–66.

Beaver, K. M., & Wright, J. P. (2011). The association between county-level IQ and county-level crime rates. *Intelligence, 39*(1), 22–26.

Beaver, K. M., Wright, J. P., Boutwell, B. B., Barnes, J. C., DeLisi, M., & Vaughn, M. G. (2012). Exploring the association between the 2-repeat allele of the MAOA gene promoter polymorphism and psychopathic personality traits, arrests, incarceration, and lifetime antisocial behavior. *Personality and Individual Differences, 54*(2), 164–168.

Blumstein, A., & Wallman, J. (Eds.). (2005). *The crime drop in America*. New York, NY: Cambridge University Press.

Blumstein, A., & Wallman, J. (2006). The crime drop and beyond. *Annual Review of Law and Society, 2*, 125–146.

Boardman, J. D., Domingue, B. W., & Fletcher, J. M. (2012). How social and genetic factors predict friendship networks. *Proceedings of the National Academy of Sciences, 109*(43), 17377–17381.

Boutwell, B. B., Barnes, J. C., Deaton, R., & Beaver, K. M. (2013). On the evolutionary origins of life-course persistent offending: A theoretical scaffold for Moffitt's developmental taxonomy. *Journal of theoretical biology, 322*, 72–80.

Burnham, T., & Phelan, J. (2000). *Mean genes: From sex to money to food: Taming our primal instincts*. New York, NY: Basic Books.

Buss, D. M. (2004). *Evolutionary psychology*. Boston, MA: Allyn & Bacon.

Buss, D. M. (2009). An evolutionary formulation of person-situation interactions. *Journal of Research in Personality, 43*(2), 241–242.

Collins, F. S., Lander, E. S., Rogers, J., Waterston, R. H., & Conso, I. H. G. S. (2004). Finishing the euchromatic sequence of the human genome. *Nature, 431*(7011), 931–945.

Darwin, C. (1859). *The origin of species by means of natural selection*. London, UK: Murray.

Dawkins, R. (1976). *The selfish gene*. New York, NY: Oxford University Press.

Dawkins, R. (1982). *The extended phenotype: The long reach of the gene*. New York, NY: Oxford University Press.

Dawkins, R. (1986). *The blind watchmaker: Why the evidence of evolution reveals a universe without design*. New York, NY: W. W. Norton.

Dennett, D. (1984). *Elbow room: The varieties of free will worth wanting*. Cambridge, MA: MIT Press.

Dobler, S., Dalla, S., Wagschal, V., & Agrawal, A. A. (2012). Community-wide convergent evolution in insect adaptation to toxic cardenolides by substitutions in the Na,K-ATPase. *Proceedings of the National Academy of Sciences, 109*, 13040–13045.

Eisner, M. (2008). Modernity strikes back? A historical perspective on the latest increase in interpersonal violence (1960–1990). *International Journal of Conflict and Violence, 2*(2), 288–316.

Flynn, J. R. (2012). *Are we getting smarter?: Rising IQ in the twenty-first century*. New York, NY: Cambridge University Press.

Farrell, G., Tilley, N., Tseloni, A., & Mailley, J. (2010). Explaining and sustaining the crime drop: Clarifying the role of opportunity-related theories. *Crime Prevention and Community Safety, 12*, 24–41.

Fowler, J. H., Settle, J. E., & Christakis, N. A. (2011). Correlated genotypes in friendship networks. *Proceedings of the National Academy of Sciences, 108*, 1993–1997.

Gottfredson, M. R., & Hirschi, T. (1990). *A general theory of crime*. Palo Alto, CA: Stanford University Press.

Gould, S. J. (2000). *Wonderful life: The Burgess Shale and the nature of history*. New York, NY: Vintage Books.

Hamilton, W. D. (1964). The genetic evolution of social behaviour I and II. *Journal of Theoretical Biology, 7*, 1–16 & 17–52.

Harris, S. (2010). *The moral landscape: How science can determine human values*. New York, NY: Free Press.

Keeley, L. H. (1996). *War before civilization: The myth of the peaceful savage*. Oxford, UK: Oxford University Press.

Levitt, S. D. (2004). Understanding why crime fell in the 1990s: Four factors that explain the decline and six that do not. *Journal of Economic Perspectives, 1*, 163–190.

Lott, J. R. (2013). *More guns, less crime: Understanding crime and gun control laws*. Chicago, IL: University of Chicago Press.

Moffitt, T. E. (1993). Adolescence-limited and life-course-persistent antisocial behavior: A developmental taxonomy. *Psychological Review, 100*(4), 674.

Perin, L., Giuliani, S., Jin, D., Sedrakyan, S., Carraro, G., Habibian, R., . . . De Filippo, R. E. (2007). Renal differentiation of amniotic fluid stem cells. *Cell Proliferation, 40*, 936–948.

Pinker, S. (1997). *How the mind works*. New York, NY: W. W. Norton.

Pinker, S. (2002). *The blank slate: The modern denial of human nature*. New York, NY: Penguin.

Pinker, S. (2012). *The better angels of our nature: Why violence has declined*. New York, NY: Penguin.

Radelet, M. L., & Akers, R. L. (1996). Deterrence and the death penalty: The views of the experts. *Journal of Criminal Law and Criminology (1973-), 87*(1), 1–16.

Rhee, S. H., & Waldman, I. D. (2002). Genetic and environmental influences on antisocial behavior: A meta-analysis of twin and adoption studies. *Psychological Bulletin, 128*, 490–529.

Rushton, J. P. (1989). Genetic similarity, human altruism, and group selection. *Behavioral and Brain Sciences, 12*, 503–559.

Rushton, J. P. (1999). Secular gains in IQ not related to the *g* factor and inbreeding depression—unlike Black-White differences: A reply to Flynn. *Personality and Individual Differences, 26*, 381–389.

Schneider, J., & Schneider, P. (2008). The anthropology of crime and criminalization. *Annual Review of Anthropology, 37*, 351–373.

Trivers, R. L. (1971). The evolution of reciprocal altruism. *Quarterly Review of Biology, 46*, 35–57.

Turkheimer, E. (2000). Three laws of behavior genetics and what they mean. *Current Directions in Psychological Science, 9*(5), 160–164.

Weyl, E. G., Frederickson, M. E., Douglas, W. Y., & Pierce, N. E. (2010). Economic contract theory tests models of mutualism. *Proceedings of the National Academy of Sciences, 107*(36), 15712–15716.

Wright, R. (1994). *The moral animal: Why we are, the way we are: The new science of evolutionary psychology*. New York, NY: Pantheon.

Wright, R. (2000). *Non-zero*. New York, NY: Vintage.

Discussion Questions

CHAPTERS 21 AND 22

1. Sociologists argue that there are difficulties in measuring crime over time because the definition of crime has varied over time. Are there any limitations to this argument? How does evolution define antisocial behavior? Is there enough evidence to support the social etiology of crime?
2. What have community-level trajectories revealed about crime trends? What do we know about criminal offending in the population? For example, is there evidence to believe that a very small proportion of the population accounts for a large number of crime? Can this evidence be used to explain findings from community-level trajectories?
3. Describe the differences between proximal and ultimate explanations. Of the two explanation types, which do sociologists provide? How does a biosocial approach unite the two explanations?
4. Discuss the influences human cooperation has had on our ancestral environment. In other words, how does the idea of the "non-zero-sum" explain the decline in violence?
5. As noted by Drs. Boutwell and Barnes, employment has been found to have no effect on crime rates. What reason do the authors provide for this finding? How might IQ levels be used to predict crime rates?
6. Why would an evolutionary argument for crime rates remain intact even if crime rates began to rise and fall? Likewise, if crime rates began to rise, would sociological arguments have any clout?

23

The Age and Crime Relationship

Social Variation, Social Explanations

Jeffery T. Ulmer
The Pennsylvania State University

Darrell Steffensmeier
The Pennsylvania State University

The relationship between aging and criminal activity has been noted since the beginnings of criminology. For example, Adolphe Quetelet (1831/1984) found that the proportion of the population involved in crime tends to peak in adolescence or early adulthood and then decline with age. In contemporary times, the FBI's *Uniform Crime Report* (UCR) arrest data (1935–1997), particularly the Crime Index (homicide, robbery, rape, aggravated assault, burglary, larceny-theft, auto theft), document the consistency of the age effect on crime. They also reveal a long-term trend toward *younger* age-crime distributions in more modern times. Today, the peak age-crime involvement (the age group with the highest age-specific arrest rate) is younger than 25 for all crimes reported in the FBI's UCR program except gambling, and rates begin to decline in the late teenage years for more than half of the UCR crimes. Even the median age (50% of all arrests occurring among younger persons) is younger than 30 for most crimes. The *National Crime Victimization Survey* (NCVS), self-report studies of juvenile and adult criminality, and interview data from convicted felons also corroborate the robust effect of age on crime patterns (Elliott, Huizinga, & Morse, 1986; Rowe & Tittle, 1977). In fact, a significant portion of U.S. national crime rate trends over time can be explained by fluctuations in the proportion of the population in the crime-prone age group of 15- to 24-year-olds (Steffensmeier & Harer, 1987, 1999).

It is now a truism that age is one of the strongest factors associated with criminal behavior. In fact, some have claimed that the age-crime relationship is invariant, or universal across groups, societies, and times (Hirschi & Gottfredson, 1983), and that this invariance signals that the age-crime relationship is strongly biologically determined (Kanazawa & Still, 2000).

However, invariance in the age-crime relationship is a very bold claim, given that we have comparatively limited data. That is, we do not have an abundance of evidence about the age distribution of crime across countries, across time periods (especially times prior to the 1930s), and across population subgroups. Age-crime statistics covering the full range of ages across these comparisons are simply not available in many instances.

The claim of invariance in the age-crime relationship was contested soon after it was first articulated by Travis Hirschi and Michael Gottfredson in 1983 (see Greenberg, 1985; Steffensmeier, 1989). We also argue that a claim of invariance in the age-crime relationship is overstated, and that sociologically important variation exists across historical periods, societies, crime types, and groups in specific features of the age-crime relationship (e.g., peak age, median age, rate of decline from peak age). We note many social factors that are widely thought to shape and structure the patterns of criminal involvement in the life course.

It is also worth noting that consistencies in age differences in crime across space and time could indicate either that (a) differences have a biological basis, *or* (b) that age socialization and age-graded norms are remarkably constant across times and settings for reasons that are socially practical and only indirectly biological. For example, for any society to thrive, elder carriers of institutions must socialize youth to become productive members of the group that fills social structural roles, and must therefore ensure an adequate level of conformity among postyouth groups. One would expect that such socialization and pressures for conformity would inevitably be problematic and incomplete for some youth, but such pressures would increase with age.

More broadly, it is impossible to examine people, as social animals, apart from either their physical bodies or their social contexts. Our bodies are important instruments of action and social interaction. Obviously, there are biological dimensions to the age-crime relationship, since aging itself is a biological, neurological, psychological, and social process. Physical and neuropsychological development and aging over the life course (especially the early life course) set the parameters of possibility and limitation for behavior, including criminal behavior. The foundation of aging has long been seen as relevant to the age-crime connection by criminologists (Greenberg, 1985; Steffensmeier & Allan, 2000). In the early 21st century, evidence has amassed from neuropsychology that aspects of brain development relating to emotional maturity, decision making, and risk taking continue into the mid-20s (Farrington, Loeber, & Howell, 2012). It was once thought that brain development was more or less completed in the mid to late teens. "However, unlike logical-reasoning abilities, which appear to be more or less fully developed by age 15, psychosocial capacities that improve decision making and reduce risk taking—such as impulse control, emotion regulation, delay of gratification, and resistance to peer influence—continue to mature well into young adulthood" (Steinberg, 2007, p. 56). "Biological changes in the prefrontal cortex during adolescence and the early 20s lead to improvements in executive functioning, including reasoning, abstract thinking, planning, anticipating consequences, and impulse control (Farrington et al., 2012).

However, physical and neuropsychological aging do not precisely track the typical age-crime curve of contemporary times. This suggests that, contrary to claims by Kanazawa and Still (2000), biological aging is not the whole story behind the age-crime relationship. For example, the neuropsychological development and maturity noted above does not exactly track the age peaks of most street crimes. Farrington et al. (2012) note that higher executive functioning relevant to impulse control, planning, emotional control, and so on are not developed fully until age 25. However, most street crimes have peak age involvement well before age 25, and many peak before age 20, and begin sharply declining well before age 25.

There is also the intriguing and plausible idea that the link between age and criminal involvement is explained by physical development and aging. This is no doubt partially true. In a general sense, physical abilities, such as strength, speed, prowess, stamina, and aggression, are useful for successful commission of many crimes, for protection, for enforcing contracts, and for recruiting and managing reliable associates (for a review, see Steffensmeier, 1983). Although some crimes are more physically demanding than others, persistent involvement in crime is likely to entail a lifestyle that is physically demanding and dangerous. Declining physical strength and energy with age may make crime too dangerous or unsuccessful, especially where there are younger or stronger criminal competitors who will not be intimidated, and thus might help explain the very low involvement in crime of small children and the elderly. Certainly, beyond middle age, aging is associated with notable declines in energy and physical strength.

However, available evidence on biological aging reveals very little correspondence between physical aging and crime's decline in late adolescence. The research literature on biological aging (see review in Steffensmeier & Allan, 2000; see also Shock, 1984) suggests that peak functioning is typically reached between the ages of 25 and 30 for physical factors plausibly assumed to affect one's ability to commit crimes (strength, stamina, aerobic capacity, motor control, sensory perception, and speed of movement). Although decline sets in shortly after these peak years, decline is very gradual until the early 50s, when the decline becomes more pronounced. Chronological age and physiological change, as well as subjective awareness of aging, are related but separate phenomena (White, 1988). Although chronological age increases regularly and inexorably, physiological declines and/or changes may occur at a much more variable pace across individuals, cohorts, and population groups.

Other commonly mentioned physical variables like testosterone levels peak in early adulthood but then typically remain near peak levels until about the mid-40s (Shock, 1984; Yesalis, 2006). In contrast, the age curves for crimes like robbery and burglary that presuppose the need for physical abilities peak in mid to late adolescence and then decline very rapidly. Although biological and physiological factors may contribute toward an understanding of the rapid increase in delinquent behavior during adolescence, they cannot by themselves explain the abrupt decline in the age-crime curve following mid to late adolescence (see Steffensmeier & Allan, 2000).

One of the most popular biological explanations of the age-crime relationship centers on testosterone. The general argument is that variation in the amount of testosterone is an important cause of criminality and of violence in particular. Testosterone differences, it is argued, explain why men commit more crime than women, why some men commit more crime than other men, and most important for our purposes, why youth commit more crime than young adults to middle-aged adults. However, Archer, Graham-Kevan, and Davies (2005) conducted a review and meta-analysis of research on the link between testosterone and aggression, and their findings call the testosterone-aggression-violence links into question. They observed that there was much misinformation in many prior studies and reviews of literature, and that there often existed a slant toward a finding of strong associations between testosterone levels and aggression. Their meta-analysis found little overall support for claims that (a) testosterone was strongly associated with aggression; (b) testosterone declined with age, for example, that base levels are higher in adolescence than young adulthood (21–35); and (c) the rapidly rising testosterone levels at puberty increase the likelihood that young males between roughly 12 and 25 years of age would be the principal perpetrators of violence (see also Halpern, Udry, Campbell, & Suchindran, 1994).

Evidence of Variation in the Age-Crime Relationship

Hirschi and Gottfredson (1983) claimed that the age-crime relationship is invariant, or universal across groups, societies, and times, a claim that has been reiterated as grounds for focusing on biological or evolutionary explanations for the age-crime relationship (i.e., Kanazawa & Still, 2000). It is important to note that Hirschi and Gottfredson's argument was not that social factors or existing criminological theories that emphasized social factors were invalid or not relevant to the explanation of crime. Rather, their argument was that the age-crime relationship was a constant, and therefore it was not necessary for crime theories focusing on social factors to explain it. Social factors plausibly differentiated offenders from nonoffenders at all ages, explaining variation in criminal involvement within all segments of the age-crime curve. This also was their grounds for arguing that longitudinal studies of criminal behavior across the life course were unnecessary.

If invariance in the age-crime relationship is taken to mean that crime is proportionately higher among young people and then declines with age at some point in the life span, to where offending is rare among older people, then it is true that this pattern is commonly found across societies and time periods. Interestingly, there seem to be varying definitions of "young" or crime-prone young ages that are used in establishing the typical or invariant age-crime curve. Hirschi and Gottfredson have two somewhat different versions of the invariant age-crime parameters. In their initial and best known work (1983), they say that crime rises rapidly in early adolescence, *peaks in late adolescence, rapidly decreases throughout the 20s*, and levels off and declines slowly during the middle and older ages. Elsewhere, Gottfredson and Hirschi (1990) say that crime drops rapidly *in late adolescence and the early 20s*, then levels off and declines slowly. Kanazawa and Still (2000) expanded the boundaries of the crime-prone young ages further, by saying: "The proportion of *young men 15–34* in fact strongly predicts the incidence of murder, rape, assault, and robbery across all societies of the world" (p. 443, emphasis added). Of note here is, given the higher possibility of injury and death among active offenders, plus the realities of physical aging, that the realistic span of the age-crime curve is roughly ages 15 to 50. It is also notable that in past generations and still in some countries today, average life expectancy is only in the 40s or early 50s. Thus, if the realistic "at-risk" age span is roughly15 to 50, then Kanazwa and Still's 20-year span (15–34) makes up a sizable portion of the applicable life course concerning typical street crime.

Within the broad pattern of crime being typically committed by younger people and declining with increasing age, there are important dimensions of variation. Such variation is of great interest to social scientists, especially sociologists, and dimensions of variation in the age-crime relationship are likely shaped by structural, cultural, and historical factors. The biological facts of development and aging are obviously important, but they occur within social structures and cultures, which channel dispositions and characteristics in different ways, and define and give different forms to the patterning of criminal behavior across age groups. Even Hirschi and Gottfredson (1983) admitted that "Actually, in some social conditions, the effects of age [on crime] may be muted," and that the typical age effect on crime may be "obscured by countervailing social processes" (pp. 560–561).

Although crime tends to generally decline with age, substantial variation can be found in the parameters of the age-crime curve (such as peak age, median age, and rate of decline from peak age). "Flatter" age curves (i.e., those with an older peak age and/or a slower decline in offending rates among older age groups) are associated with at least three circumstances: (1) cultures and historical periods in which youth have greater access to legitimate opportunities and integration into adult society, (2) population groups for whom legitimate opportunities and integration into adult society do not markedly increase with age (i.e., during young adulthood), and (3) types of crime for which illegitimate opportunities increase rather than diminish with age.

HISTORICAL VARIATIONS

Unfortunately, reliable age statistics on criminal involvement are not available over extended historical periods. Nonetheless, we can compare age-crime distributions over the past 70 years or so in the United States and also compare these to

19th-century age-crime distributions reported in sources such as Quetelet's (1831/1984) pioneering study. Age-crime plots are shown in Figure 23.1 for U.S. homicide (the most reliable crime statistic) for 1940, 1980, and 2010.

The plots clearly show a trend toward younger age distributions and younger peak ages over the decades. That is, criminal involvement seems to have shifted to younger ages over time, into the late teens. The shift toward a greater concentration of offending among the young may be due partly to changes in law enforcement procedures and data collection. Nevertheless, the likelihood that real changes have in fact occurred is supported by the consistency of the changes from 1830 (reported by Quetelet, [1831/1984]) to 1940, 1980, and 2010. Cohen and Land (1987) also described a change in the age curve of homicide from the 1960s to the 1980s such that homicide involvement peaked earlier and offending rates for younger offenders increased relative to older offenders.

Greenberg (1985) reviewed research on historical and contemporary age-crime patterns across counties. This review found evidence for substantially older age peaks (into the early or mid-20s) for criminal involvement in the mid-1800s compared to the later 20th century in England, and a slower decline of criminal involvement with age in the 1800s than in the later 20th century. These historical differences, where criminal involvement peaked at later ages and declined more slowly with age in the past, were also evident in France, Norway, and the Netherlands (Greenberg, 1985).

Support for the conclusion that real change has taken place over the past century also is found in the age breakdown of U.S. prisoner statistics covering the years 1890 to 1980 (Steffensmeier, Allan, Harer, & Streifel, 1989; see also Steffensmeier & Streifel, 1991). As with the UCR statistics, the prison statistics show that age curves

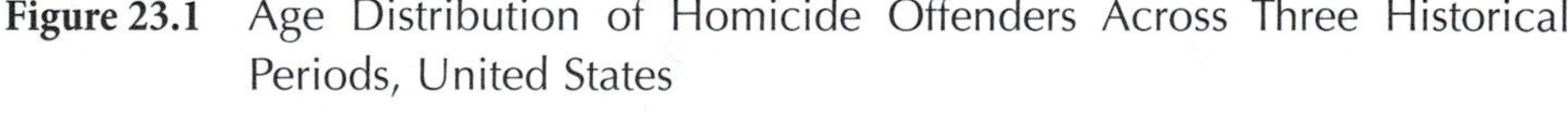

Figure 23.1 Age Distribution of Homicide Offenders Across Three Historical Periods, United States

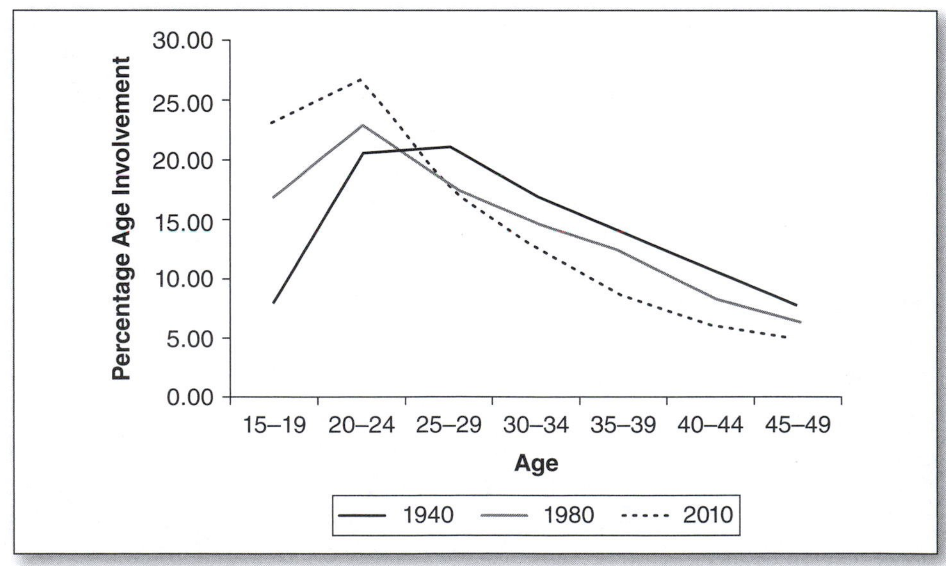

are more peaked today than a century ago. Moreover, research shows that more recent birth cohorts of juveniles are more violent than ones in the past (Shannon, 1988; Tracey, Wolfgang, & Figlio, 1990). Collectively, the research cited above suggests also that historical changes in the age-crime curve are likely gradual and can be detected only when a sufficiently large time frame is used.

There are several suggestive reasons that may explain why criminal involvement peaks at earlier ages in contemporary times, at least in Western industrialized countries, than in the past. In simple, nonindustrial societies, the passage to adult status is relatively simple and continuous. Formal "rites of passage" at relatively early ages avoid much of the status ambiguity and role conflict that torment modern adolescents in the developed world. Youths begin to assume responsible and economically productive roles well before they reach full physical maturity. It is not surprising, therefore, to find that such societies and time periods have significantly flatter and less skewed age-crime patterns (for a review, see Steffensmeier et al., 1989). Much the same is true for earlier periods in the history of the United States and other industrial nations, when farm youth were crucial for harvesting crops and working-class children were expected to leave school at an early age and do their part in helping support their families (Horan & Hargis, 1991).

By contrast, today teenagers typically live in a peer culture that emphasizes consumption, leisure, and peer status. If they work, they occupy marginal jobs that provide little self-pride or opportunities for adult mentorship, and instead segregate them into a separate peer culture. Although youth has always been seen as a turbulent time, social processes associated with the coming of industrialization and the postindustrial age have aggravated the stresses of adolescence, resulting in increased levels of juvenile criminality in recent decades than in the more distant past (Steffensmeier & Allan, 2000). The age status structure of modern societies, therefore, may foster crime and delinquency among the young because these societies "lack institutional procedures for moving people smoothly from protected childhood to autonomous adulthood" (Nettler, 1978, p. 241).

Together, these findings are consistent with the view that contemporary teenagers in industrialized nations are subject to greater status anxiety than in previous periods of history and that the transition from adolescence to adulthood is more turbulent now than in the past (Friday & Hage, 1976; Glaser, 1978; Greenberg, 1977, 1985). In comparison to earlier eras, contemporary youths have had less access to responsible family roles, valued economic activity, and participation in community affairs (Clausen, 1986). This generational isolation has fostered adolescent subcultures oriented toward consumption and hedonistic pursuits (Hagan, 1991; Hagan, Heffler, Classen, Boehnke, & Merkens, 1998). The weakened social bonds and reduced access to valued adult roles, along with accentuated peer-oriented youth culture influences, all combine to increase situationally induced pressures to obtain valued goods; display strength, daring, or loyalty to peers; or simply to engage in exciting and perhaps illicit leisure activities (Briar & Piliavin, 1965; Gold, 1970; Hagan et al., 1998).

Interestingly, recent arrest data by age for the time period from 1980 to 2010 shows slightly increasing (older) age peaks for all UCR index offending in 2000 and 2010 than in 1980. As in earlier time periods, there is also notable variation in age curves between specific offenses. Furthermore, there are varying degrees of change across the time period in age curves for specific offenses—some offense specific age curves change hardly at all from 1980 to 2010 (such as robbery, aggravated assault), some look rather different (such as murder, rape, burglary, auto theft). Readers can explore the interactive Bureau of Justice Statistics website (http://bjs .ojp.usdoj.gov/index.cfm?ty=datool&surl=/arrests/index.cfm#) and construct age-arrest curves over time, as well as examine age and crime data.

Hirschi and Gottfredson (1983) and Kanazawa and Still (2000), along with scholars who are adherents of the age-crime invariance position, dismiss such historical variation as "trivial" or "minor." However, according to Greenberg (1985),

> Although a decline in criminality at older ages is common to all these distributions, the parameters of the distributions are quite different. In the course of industrialization, the age distribution of crime has changed substantially. Although it may be a mere matter of preference whether a glass of water is described as half full or half empty, it is not so inconsequential whether the changes in the age distribution that we have seen in the past century or two are regarded as modest or major. In the former case, they are casually dismissed; in the latter, they are given full attention. (p. 13)

CROSS-NATIONAL VARIATION

International data can provide an intuitive and straightforward way to demonstrate the importance of social factors. If age differences in crime vary across countries, then this likely points to the importance of sociocultural factors. International variation also allows us to examine what kinds of countries have relatively larger or smaller age differences in crime, providing a sense of how macro-level societal factors influence the age-crime distribution. Again, this is not to say that biological factors are unimportant. International variation thus precludes a deterministic biological account, but may be compatible with social-biological interactions of various kinds.

Cross-national data on age and crime are mostly limited to homicide or total arrests. Global measures of arrests may be of suspect validity as indicators of serious crime, since they likely include minor offenses and because of considerable variability in reporting across jurisdictions or countries. Homicide statistics are likely a better (but far from perfect) measure, because it is the most reliable measure of crime. Notably, Kanazawa and Still (2000) argue that their evolutionary psychology theory of young male criminality applies most to serious and/or violent crime.

In his response to Hirschi and Gottfredson's (1983) invariance claim, Greenberg (1985) noted that in India in the 1980s, relatively few (3%) criminal arrests were of people under age 21, even though half the Indian population at that time was under 21. This contrasts sharply with the pattern in the United States and similar countries. An interesting example of recent evidence of cross-national variation in age-crime relationships comes from Japan. Figure 23.2 shows Japanese age disaggregated homicide rates and proportionate age involvement (PAI) in homicide for three decades, 1960, 1980, and 2000.

Figure 23.2 Age Disaggregated Homicide Rates and PAI in Homicide for Japan by Decade 1960, 1980, 2000

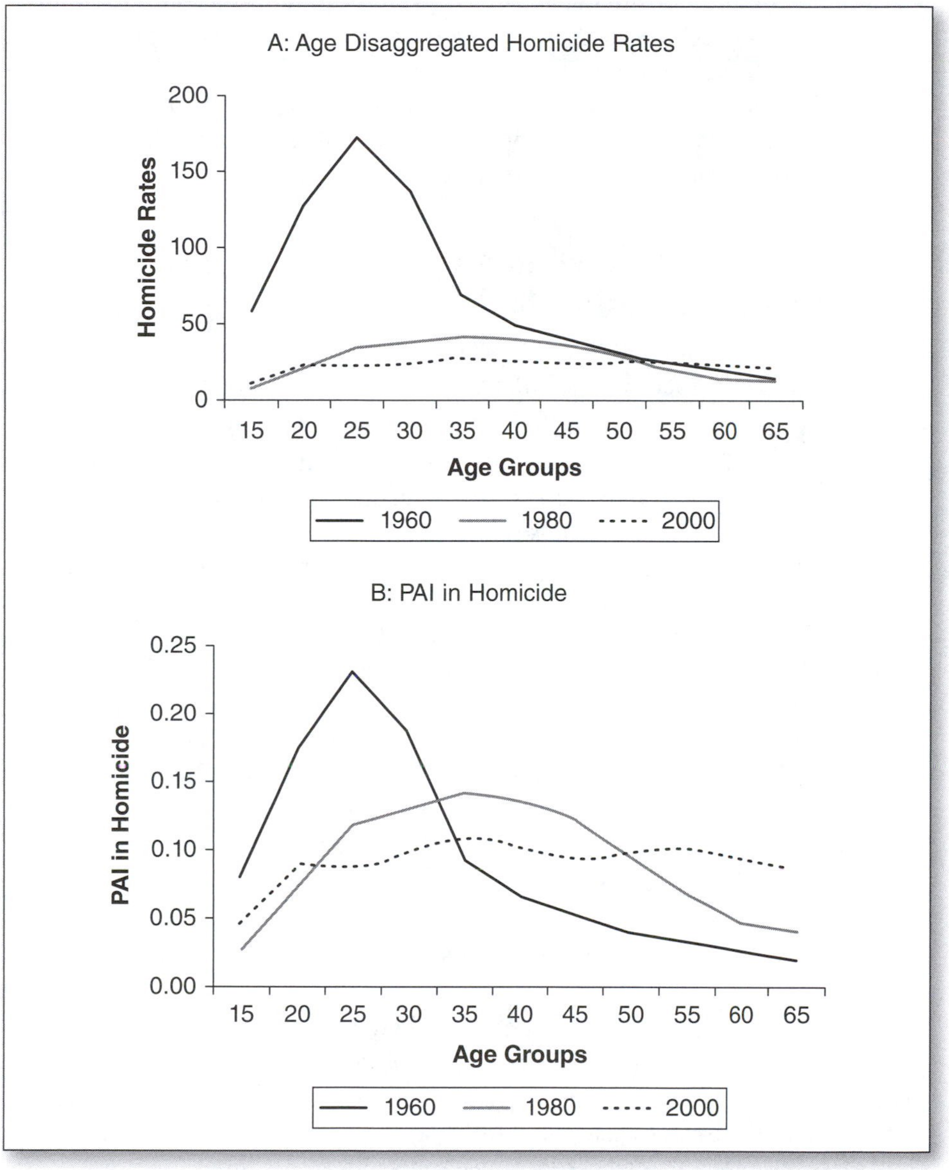

A: Age Disaggregated Homicide Rates

B: PAI in Homicide

Source: Hiraiwa-Hasegawa, M. (2005). Homicide by men in Japan and its relationship to age, resources, and risk taking. *Evolution and Human Behavior, 26,* 332–343.

Several features of these data are impressive. First, the age curves for homicide in Japan change shape dramatically from 1960 to 1980 and 2000, because homicide rates among men in their 20s decreased drastically since 1960, when Japanese society was still disrupted by the aftermath of World War II (Hiraiwa-Hasegawa, 2005). The 1960 age-homicide curve, especially shown by the PAI (PAI = percentage age involvement adjusting for age composition of Japan's population) figure, is much more sharply peaked, and much higher, than in the later decades. The age-homicide curves for 1980 and 2000 are much flatter, with more gradual increases, far shorter peaks, and slower declines compared to 1960. Second, in contrast to the recent U.S. pattern, none of the age-homicide curves peak in late adolescence or even in the early 20s. Rather, homicide peaked at 25 years of age in 1960 and around 35 in 1980 and 2000. Thus, Japanese homicide age curves not only show key differences with the United States, but differ within Japan across time.

Minority Differences in Dimensions of the Age-Crime Relationship[1]

For Black inner-city youths, the problems of youth described above are compounded by persistent racial discrimination and blocked conventional opportunity (W. J. Wilson, 1987, 1996). As inner-city Blacks move into young adulthood, they continue to experience limited access to high quality adult jobs and are more likely to associate primarily with same-sex peers. As UCR data show, adult offending levels among Blacks continue at higher levels than among Whites, and the proportion of total Black crime that is committed by Black adults is greater than the proportion of total White crime that is committed by White adults (Harris, Steffensmeier, Ulmer, & Painter-Davis, 2009; Steffensmeier & Allan, 2000).

Laub (1983) showed that the ratio of personal crimes in cities committed by White youth under 17 to those committed by Whites over 17 was 19.3, while this ratio for Blacks was 10.2. For rural areas, the ratio of personal crimes committed by White youth under 17 to Whites over 17 was 9.1, while for Blacks this ratio was 4.9. These findings also suggest a flatter age curve, and more criminal involvement at older ages, for African Americans.

VARIATION ACROSS CRIME TYPES

As mentioned above, there are notable differences in the age curves between specific offenses, such as the UCR index crime categories. Again, we refer readers to the interactive Bureau of Justice Statistics website (http://bjs.ojp.usdoj.gov/index.cfm?ty=datool&surl=/arrests/index.cfm#), where age curves can be interactively constructed for specific offenses for single years and across time.

Typically, the offenses that show the youngest peaks and sharpest declines are crimes that fit the low-yield, criminal mischief, "hell-raising" category: vandalism, petty theft, robbery, arson, auto theft, burglary, and liquor law and drug violations. Personal crimes like aggravated assault and homicide tend to have somewhat "older" age distributions (median ages in the late 20s), as do some of the public order offenses, public drunkenness, driving under the influence, and certain property crimes that juveniles have less opportunity to commit, like embezzlement, fraud, and gambling (median ages in late 20s or 30s). Furthermore, Laub and

Sampson (2003) find significantly differing age curves and peak ages for property (younger age peak), violent (age peaks in the mid-20s), and drug/alcohol (peak involvement in the mid-30s) crime types.

Those offenses with flatter age curves are often those for which the structure of illegitimate opportunities increases rather than disappears with age. For example, some opportunities for fraud exist for young people (such as falsification of identification to purchase alcohol or gain entry into "adult" establishments), but since they are too young to obtain credit, they lack the opportunities for common frauds such as passing bad checks, defrauding an innkeeper, or credit card forgery. Similarly, young people have more opportunities for some kinds of violence (e.g., street fights or gang violence) but less opportunity for other kinds of violence (e.g., spousal violence).

Older people may also shift to less visible criminal roles such as bookie, fence, or other criminal enterprise (Steffensmeier & Ulmer, 2005). Or as a spinoff of legitimate roles, they may commit surreptitious crimes, or crimes that, if discovered, are less likely to be reported to the authorities, such as workplace theft, embezzlement, stock fraud, bribery, or price-fixing. Unfortunately, we know relatively little about the age distribution of persons who commit these and related property crimes, but the fragmentary evidence that does exist suggests that they are likely to be in the 30s or older (Pennsylvania Crime Commission, 1991; Shapiro, 1984). Evidence also suggests that the age curves for lucrative crimes in the underworld like racketeering or loansharking not only peak much later but tend to decline more slowly with age (Steffensmeier & Allan, 2000; Steffensmeier & Ulmer, 2005). In addition, if offenders do not desist in early adulthood, they seem to be more likely to specialize in one category or niche of crimes.

Still less is known of the age distribution of "respectable" or upperworld offenders who commit lucrative business crimes, such as fraud, price-fixing, bribery, or official corruption. Data concerning these crimes are relatively scarce. However, data from *New York Times* articles on profitable business crimes (those involving gains of $25,000 or more) during the 1987–1990 period reveals a preponderance of middle-aged or older offenders, with a modal age between 40 and 50 (Steffensmeier & Allan, 2000). In addition, some research shows that white-collar offenders tend to begin offending and continue offending well into adulthood (see Benson, 2002; Steffensmeier, Schwartz, & Roche, 2013).

INDIVIDUAL VARIATION IN CRIMINAL INVOLVEMENT ACROSS AGES

The youthful peak and rapid drop-off in offending that constitutes the most common societal pattern for conventional crimes is actually but one of a number of patterns identified when criminal careers are tracked for individual offenders (see D'Unger, Land, McCall, & Nagin, 1998; Jolin & Gibbons, 1987; Nagin & Land, 1993). There is, in fact, a great deal of variability in criminal involvement over the life span (Laub & Sampson, 2003). In contrast to Hirschi and Gottfredson's claim of invariance in the age-crime relationship, Nagin and Land (1993) and Nagin and Paternoster (2000) demonstrate discrete groups of offenders with differing age-crime curves.

There is some convincing evidence of substantial individual-level variation in the relationship between age and criminal involvement. Several studies have conducted latent class analyses of criminal careers, effectively examining individual variation in the patterning of age and criminal activity. For example, D'Unger et al.'s (1998) latent class analyses of data from several well-known birth cohort studies from London, Philadelphia, and Racine, Wisconsin, demonstrated four age-crime trajectory patterns in the London cohort and five in the Philadelphia and Racine cohorts. While some groupings of individuals displayed the familiar pattern of early or late adolescence onset and peak involvement in crime, two other groupings are noteworthy for their deviation from this pattern. Some individuals began involvement in crime in adolescence but continued offending (some at low rates, some at relatively high rates) into early adulthood and up to age 30. Another interesting group, called "late onset chronic offenders," did not begin offending until the late teen years, and then offended at high rates through their 20s, with involvement peaking in the late 20s and remaining high beyond age 30.

Laub and Sampson also subjected their data from the famous Glueck sample of delinquent boys to a latent class analysis. They found six types of individual age-crime trajectories for total crime, and five for property, violent, and drug/alcohol crime (see Laub & Sampson, 2003, pp. 104–106). Of particular interest were the 30% of the total crime sample that made up the "low," "moderate," and "high rate chronic" offenders, who offended well into middle adulthood (the 30s to early 40s), thus contradicting the typical and allegedly invariant age-crime pattern. Laub and Sampson (2003) characterize their findings from their latent class analysis this way: "The ultimate conclusion to be derived from these figures is that the age-crime relationship is *not* invariant for all offenders and offense types" (p. 104, emphasis in original). Another example of a latent class analysis showing variation in age-crime trajectories and transitions to adulthood comes from Massoglia and Uggen (2010), who identified multifaceted, socioeconomic, and problematic transitions to adulthood and patterns of desistence from crime. Those individuals displaying the multifaceted and socioeconomic transitions to adulthood desisted from crime and delinquency as they attained educational credentials, gained employment, and/or got married and had children. The problematic transition group was much more likely to persist in delinquency past adolescence and early adulthood because they failed to attain markers of conventional adult social status.

Our knowledge of individual variations in age patterns of criminal involvement is still incomplete. In addition, a lot of criminological research has focused rather myopically on the adolescence-young adulthood period, to the exclusion of later adulthood (Cullen, 2011). Thus, our knowledge base regarding the breadth, variation, and scope of criminal behavior in later adulthood is insufficient. According to Laub and Sampson (2003): "It is remarkable . . . how little agreement there is regarding the variability of the age-crime relationship for individual offenders. Moreover, little is known about the age-crime relationship over the full life course" (p. 17).

Social Dimensions of the Life Course

As we have seen, there is reason to question the notion that the age-crime relationship is truly invariant, at least in its specifics. At the least, there seems to us to be important variation within the broad pattern of youth crime and older desistence; variation across time periods, countries, races, offense types, and individual criminal involvement trajectories. This suggests that social factors remain relevant to explaining the age-crime relationship. Taking a life course approach, the rise in crime in adolescence to the edge of young adulthood, and crime's decline with age thereafter reflects both the biological process of aging as well as the roles, norms, and socially constructed perspectives that accompany aging (Siennick & Osgood, 2008). Greenberg (1985) put the argument this way:

> [I]t is not to deny the possibility that nonsocial causes may contribute to some part of the age distribution; this possibility has been acknowledged explicitly in sociological theorizing about the age distribution of crime. . . . It is to assert that a substantial part of the variation can be explained by familiar sociological concepts and to deny only that nonsocial factors such as biology are entirely responsible for it. (pp. 17–18)

Understanding how and why age affects crime from a social perspective is a complex matter, involving several dimensions of the life course and important social transitions (Siennick & Osgood, 2008). There are three main age patterns of crime to explain: (1) The rise in adolescence from the early through late teens—the extent of the rise may vary across societies, time, and for specific offense types because of social-cultural variation and the social structuring of criminal opportunities and costs; (2) the *sharp* decline in late adolescence or the edge of early adulthood—whether this sharp decline occurs and at what magnitude may vary across space, time, and crime types because of social-cultural factors; and (3) for the gradual decline with advancing age (e.g., post-30s)—as we have mentioned earlier, the general, broad form of the age-crime curve (crime committed more so by young people, and declining among older people) may be near-universal, but the point at which the gradual decline begins and the extent of the decline may vary across space, time, and crime.

Social-cultural explanations provide accounts for each of these age patterns, but they leave room for considerable variation in the particular shape and parameters of the age-crime relationship because it is affected by social structural and cultural factors. A variety of social and cognitive factors can help explain the rapid rise in age-specific rates of offending around mid-adolescence. An important study by Rowe and Tittle (1977) found that social integration, moral commitment, fear of sanctions, and utility of crime substantially explained, or mediated, the age-crime relationship for individuals. Teenagers generally lack strong bonds to conventional adult institutions, such as work and family (Warr, 1998). At the same time, teens are faced with strong potential rewards for offending: money, status, power, autonomy, identity claims, strong sensate experiences stemming from sex, natural adrenaline highs or highs from illegal substances, and respect from similar peers (Steffensmeier et al., 1989; J. Q. Wilson & Herrenstein, 1985). Further, their dependent status as juveniles insulates teens from many of the social and legal costs of illegitimate activities, and their stage of cognitive development limits prudence concerning the consequences of their behavior. At the same time, they possess the physical prowess required to commit crimes. Finally, a certain amount of misbehavior is often seen as natural to youth and seen as simply a stage of growing up (Hagan et al., 1998; Jolin & Gibbons, 1987).

For those in late adolescence or early adulthood (roughly age 17–22, the age group showing the sharpest decline in arrest rates for many crimes), important changes occur in at least six spheres of life (see Greenberg, 1985; Laub & Sampson, 2003; Siennick & Osgood, 2008; Steffensmeier et al., 1989; Steffensmeier & Allan, 2000; Warr, 1998):

1. Greater access to legitimate sources of material goods and excitement: jobs, credit, alcohol, sex, and so on.
2. Patterns of illegitimate opportunities: with the assumption of adult roles, opportunities increase for crimes (e.g., gambling, fraud, and employee theft) that are less risky, more lucrative, or less likely to be reflected in official statistics.
3. Peer associations and lifestyle: reduced orientation to same-age/same-sex peers and increased orientation toward persons of the opposite sex or persons who are older or more mature.
4. Cognitive and analytical skill development leading to a gradual decline in egocentrism, hedonism, and sense of invincibility; becoming more concerned for others, more accepting of social values, more comfortable in social relations, and more concerned with the meaning of life and their place of things; and seeing their casual delinquencies of youth as childish or foolish.
5. Increased legal and social costs for deviant behavior.
6. Age-graded norms: externally, increased expectation of maturity and responsibility; internally, anticipation of assuming adult roles, coupled with reduced subjective acceptance of deviant roles and the threat they pose to entering adult status.

As young people move into adulthood or anticipate entering it, most find their bonds to conventional society strengthening, with expanded access to work or further education and increased interest in "settling down" and "acting like" or "being an adult" (Steffensmeier & Allan, 2000). Leaving high school, finding employment, going to college, enlisting in the military, and getting married all tend to increase informal social controls and integration into conventional society (Laub & Sampson, 2003). In addition, early adulthood typically involves a change in peer associations and lifestyle routines that diminish the opportunities for committing these offenses (Benson, 2002; Warr, 1998). Furthermore, at the same time when informal sanctions for law violation are increasing, potential legal sanctions increase substantially.

"AGING OUT" OF CRIME

In adulthood and especially with advancing age (e.g., late 30s into middle age), one would expect crime to diminish. The pressures for conformity are robust and likely increase across the life span. These pressures change and/or increase rather abruptly compared to adolescence as adulthood role transitions truly begin, and then become ongoing and continuous with age.

A large body of research shows that desistence from crime or exiting a criminal career is typically tied to the acquisition of meaningful bonds to conventional adult individuals and institutions, such as work, marriage and family, and community institutions (see Benson, 2002; Giordano, Cernkovich, & Rudolph, 2002; Laub & Sampson, 2003; Sampson & Laub, 1993; Uggen, 2000; Warr, 1998; see reviews by Massoglia & Uggen, 2010; Siennick & Osgood, 2008; Steffensmeier & Allan, 2000). This is commonly accomplished as part of the transition from youth to adulthood. One key tie to the conventional order is a job that seems to have the potential for advancement and that is seen as meaningful and economically rewarding. A good job may shift a criminal's attention from the present to the future and may provide a solid basis for the construction of a noncriminal identity to which to aspire (Silver & Ulmer, 2012). It also alters an individual's daily routine in ways that make crime less likely (Meisenhelder, 1977; Shover, 1983, 1996). Marriage is another key adult social bond that fosters desistence (Laub, Nagin, & Sampson, 1998; Warr, 1998). Other bonds that may lead people away from crime include involvement in religion (see Johnson & Jang, 2012), sports, hobbies, or other conventional activities (Goldman, 1970; Steffensmeier & Ulmer, 2005).

In brief, then, several factors combine to foster declining criminal involvement with age, with several of those below being especially prominent for those in their 30s and 40s (see, for example, Shover, 1996). It is important to note that these factors below are likely to be accompanied by biological and psychological processes of aging involving a decline in strength and energy, and changing decision making.

1. Offenders gradually may learn that crime does not "pay," that gains from crime are typically small and not worth the risk or effort. In addition, increasingly severe criminal justice penalties for recidivists may finally make crime insufficiently rewarding. Aging offenders are more likely to view incarceration and legal sanctions as more serious threats, because they have more to lose than youthful offenders, and as they more fully realize that time is a diminishing and increasingly valuable resource (see Shover, 1983, 1996).

2. Individuals experience age-graded expectations and norms to "settle down" and "act your age." As offenders age, antisocial peer pressure may also diminish and be replaced by social disapproval at not "growing up."

3. As they age, offenders may lose suitable co-offenders as partners or accomplices are incarcerated, die, or turn out to be unreliable associates (see Steffensmeier & Ulmer, 2005).

4. Diminishing physical capabilities as one gets older (especially beyond the 30s and 40s) make crime too dangerous or less likely to succeed. Also, for offenders, the "wear and tear" of involvement in crime and the criminal lifestyle likely take their physical toll (Akerstrom, 1985). In addition, offenders tend to live fast and dangerously, and therefore are at greater risk of dying young or becoming physically incapacitated.

5. Age may be accompanied by a tempering of aspirations and goals due to cumulative life experience and "hard knocks." In addition, it may be that adjusting and responding to life experiences tends to weaken the attraction of the major reinforcements for criminal behavior, such as money, sex, status among criminal peers, excitement, and so on. This would especially be the case if legitimate sources of reward are available, as often is the case as individuals age.

Some of the points above regarding offenders who persist into adulthood bear elaboration. The development of conventional social bonds may be coupled with burnout or a belated deterrent effect as offenders grow tired of the hassles of repeated involvement with the criminal justice system and the hardships of a life of crime. They may also have experienced a long prison sentence that jolts them into quitting or that entails the loss of street contacts that makes the successful continuation of a criminal career difficult. Or offenders may develop a fear of dying alone in prison, especially since repeated convictions yield longer sentences. Still other offenders may quit or "slow down" as they find their abilities and efficiency declining with increasing age, loss of "nerve," or sustained narcotics or alcohol use (Adler & Adler, 1983; Prus & Sharper, 1977; Shover, 1983, 1996; Steffensmeier, 1986: Steffensmeier & Ulmer, 2005).

LEARNING FROM OLDER OFFENDERS

Of course, some offenders persist into their 30s, middle age, or perhaps beyond. Older, "career" criminals (not counting those with mental disorders or deficits) may provide important information about social processes, opportunities, and crime (Steffensmeier & Ulmer, 2005). That is, older offenders may be key examples of social influences at work. A great deal of what we know about older offenders comes from ethnographic research.

Older offenders typically fall into two categories: (1) those whose first criminal involvement occurs relatively late in life (particularly in shoplifting, homicide, and alcohol-related offenses) and (2) those who started crime at an early age and continue their involvement into their 40s and 50s and beyond. What evidence is available on first-time older offenders suggests that situational stress and lack of alternative opportunities play a primary role. The unanticipated loss of one's job or other disruptions of social ties can push some individuals into their first law violation at any age (Agnew, 1992; Jolin & Gibbons, 1987). Laub and Sampson's (2003) quantitative and qualitative research on the later life courses of the men in the Glueck sample provides insight into the lives of later onset offenders as well as those who persist beyond young adulthood.

Older offenders who persist in crime are more likely to belong to the criminal underworld. These are individuals who are relatively successful in their criminal activities or who are extensively integrated into subcultural or family criminal enterprises. They seem to receive relational and psychic rewards (e.g., pride in their expertise) as well as monetary rewards from lawbreaking and consequently see no need to desist from lawbreaking (Klockars, 1974; Steffensmeier, 1986; Steffensmeier & Ulmer, 2005). Additionally, older persistent property offenders or those involved in the criminal underworld tend to be more criminally skilled than young offenders, tend to have greater criminal social capital, and tend to exhibit greater criminal specialization (Steffensmeier & Ulmer, 2005). Older offenders may be less likely to be caught when they break the law because they are more skilled than their younger counterparts and may be more likely to be in positions where they can commit crimes with greater "cover" or surreptitious crimes (such as switching from burglary to fencing and criminal enterprise: see Steffensmeier & Ulmer, 2005).

Alternatively, such offenders may "shift and oscillate" back and forth between conventionality and lawbreaking, depending on shifting life circumstances and situational inducements to offend (Adler, 1996; Adler & Adler, 1983; Akerstrom, 1985). These older offenders are also unlikely to see many meaningful opportunities for themselves in the conventional or law-abiding world. Consequently, "the straight life" may have little to offer successful criminals, who will be more likely to persist in their criminality for an extended period. But they, too, may slow down eventually as they grow tired of the cumulative aggravations and risks of criminal involvement, or as they encounter the diminishing capacities associated with the aging process.

Conclusion

Our approach in this chapter is *not* to define the age-crime issue as a simple dichotomy between genes and environment, nature and nurture, or biological and social processes. As sociologist Pierre Van den Bergh (1973) eloquently observed, human behavior is almost invariably the product of a complex interplay between at least three major classes of phenomena: our biology, our physical environment, and our social environment. Our biology is in good part genetically transmitted, but it is also modifiable through our physical and social environment. Our social environment is extraordinarily self-determined and modifiable compared to that of other species, but it is nevertheless subject to the constraints of both our biology and our physical environment (Van den Bergh, 1973).

Age is a consistent predictor of crime, both in the aggregate and for individuals. The most common finding across countries, groups, and historical periods shows that crime—especially "ordinary" or "street" crime—tends to be a young persons' activity. However, there is strong reason to question whether the age-crime relationship is truly invariant except in a very broad sense. In fact, the age-crime curve appears to vary in its specific features according to crime types, the structural position of groups, and historical and cultural contexts. In our view, we should not regard the invariance of the age-crime relationship as "settled law." Furthermore, relatively little is known about older offenders in general (Cullen, 2011). Clearly, the structure, dynamics, and contexts of offending among older individuals is a rich topic for future research.

In sum, the social structuring of age-graded roles, opportunities, and resources strongly shapes the age patterning of crime. Aging is a biological process, to be sure, but the life course is a key part of social structure. The life course structures and is structured by society. And crime is an important component of the social structure of aging and the life course. As Steffensmeier and Allan (2000) stated: "To a large extent, variation in societal age-crime patterns reflect patterns of age-stratified inequality. Age is a potent mediator of inequality in both the legitimate and illegitimate opportunity structures of society" (p. 106).

In addition, consistency in the age-crime relationship does not, by definition, point to biological causes alone. There are social reasons to expect consistency in the patterning of age and crime. We agree with David Greenberg (1985), who put it this way:

> That involvement in crime diminishes to some extent with age in all societies for which we have information does not contradict the claim that the age distribution has a social origin. . . . It is probably true in all societies that adults have more of the good things in life (possessions, social status) than their juniors and thus have less to gain and more to lose from crime than youths. Adults also have more experience from which to assess the probable consequences of crime for their own well-being and may be more heavily penalized than youth. (p. 14)

If we want to understand age effects on crime, we cannot ignore either the human organism or his or her environment, physical or social. Empirical behavior is nearly always a complex blend of physical/biological and social factors. The relative causal weight of each set of factors will depend on what specific aspects of behavior we seek to understand. In our treatment of age effects on crime, we recognize the importance of both the biological and the social, but our main thrust has been on the social realm.

Note

1. Sex Differences in the Age-Crime Relationship: Although age-crime parameters differ as described above, there appears to be considerable similarity in the age-crime relationship between males and females (Steffensmeier & Streifel, 1991). UCR arrest statistics from 1940–2000 show that the age curves of male and female offenders are very similar within any given period and across all offenses, with the exception of prostitution. To the extent that age differences between the sexes exist, the tendency is for somewhat lower peak ages of offending among females—apparently because of their earlier physical maturity and the likelihood that young adolescent females might date and associate with older delinquent

male peers. But overall, although male levels of offending are always higher than female levels at every age and for virtually all offenses, the female-to-male ratio remains fairly constant across the life span (Steffensmeier & Streifel, 1991). Also, the trend toward younger and more peaked age-crime distributions holds for both sexes.

References

Adler, P. (1996). *Wheeling and dealing: An ethnography of an upper level drug dealing and smuggling community.* New York, NY: Columbia University Press.

Adler, P., & Adler, P. (1983). Shifts and oscillations in deviant careers: The case of upper-level drug dealers and smugglers. *Social Problems, 31,* 195–207.

Agnew, R. (1992). Foundation for a general strain theory of crime and delinquency. *Criminology, 39*(1), 47–87.

Akerstrom, M. (1985). *Crooks and squares: Lifestyles of thieves and addicts in comparison to conventional people.* New Brunswick, NJ: Transaction.

Archer, J., Graham-Kevan, N., & Davies, M. (2005). Testosterone and aggression: A reanalysis of Book, Starzyk, and Quinsey's (2001) study. *Aggression and Violent Behavior, 10,* 241–261.

Benson, M. (2002). *Crime and the life course.* Los Angeles, CA: Roxbury.

Briar, S., & Piliavin, I. (1965). Delinquency, situational inducements, and commitment to conformity. *Social Problems, 13,* 35–45.

Clausen, J. A. (1986). *The life course.* Englewood Cliffs, NJ: Prentice Hall.

Cohen, L., & Land, K. (1987). Age structure and crime. *American Sociological Review, 52,* 170–183.

Cullen, F. T. (2011). Beyond adolescence-limited criminology: Choosing our future. *Criminology, 49*(2), 287–330.

D'Unger, A., Land, K., McCall, P., & Nagin, D. (1998). How many latent classes of criminal careers? Results from mixed Poisson regression analyses. *American Journal of Sociology, 103*(6), 1593–1630.

Elliott, D. S., Huizinga, D., & Morse, B. (1986). Self-reported violent offending: A descriptive analysis of juvenile violent offenders and their offending careers. *Journal of Interpersonal Violence, 1,* 472–514.

Farrington, D. P., Loeber, R., & Howell, J. C. (2012). Young adult offenders: The need for more effective legislative options and justice processing. *Criminology and Public Policy, 11*(4), 729–750.

Federal Bureau of Investigation. (1935–1997). *Uniform Crime Report.* Washington, DC: Government Printing Office.

Friday, P. C., & Hage, J. (1976). Youth crime in postindustrial societies: An integrated perspective. *Criminology, 14,* 347–368.

Giordano, P., Cernkovich, S., & Rudolph, J. (2002). Gender, crime, and desistence: Toward a theory of cognitive transformation. *American Journal of Sociology, 107*(4), 990–1064.

Glaser, D. (1978). *Crime in our changing society.* New York, NY: Holt, Rinehart & Winston.

Gold, M. (1970). *Delinquent behavior in an American city.* Belmont, CA: Brooks/Cole.

Goldman, I. J. (1970). *Characteristics associated with recidivism: A study of youths discharged from treatment centers of the New York State Division for Youth.* Rensselaer, NY: New York State Office of Children and Family Services.

Greenberg, D. F. (1977). Delinquency and the age structure of society. *Contemporary Crisis, 1,* 66–86.

Greenberg, D. F. (1985). Age, crime, and social explanation. *American Journal of Sociology, 91*(1), 1–21.

Hagan, J. (1991). Destiny and drift: Subcultural preferences, status attainments, and the risks and rewards of youth. *American Sociological Review, 56,* 567–581.

Hagan, J., Heffler, G., Classen, G., Boehnke, K., & Merkens, H. (1998). Subterranean sources of subcultural delinquency beyond the American Dream. *Criminology, 36,* 309–342.

Halpern, C. T., Udry, J. R., Campbell, B., & Suchindran, C. (1994). Relationships between aggression and pubertal increases in testosterone: A panel analysis of adolescent males. *Social Biology, 40,* 8–24.

Harris, C. T., Steffensmeier, D., Ulmer, J. T., & Painter-Davis, N. (2009). Are Blacks and Hispanics disproportionately incarcerated relative to their arrests? Racial and ethnic disproportionality between arrest and incarceration. *Race and Social Problems, 1,* 187–199.

Hiraiwa-Hasegawa, M. (2005). Homicide by men in Japan and its relationship to age, resources, and risk taking. *Evolution and Human Behavior, 26,* 332–343.

Hirschi, T., & Gottfredson, M. (1983). Age and the explanation of crime. *American Journal of Sociology, 89,* 522–584.

Hirschi, T., & Gottfredson, M. (1990). Substantive positivism and the idea of crime. *Rationality and Society, 2,* 412–428.

Horan, P. M., & Hargis, P. G. (1991). Children's work and schooling in the late nineteenth-century family economy. *American Sociological Review, 56,* 583–596.

Johnson, B. R., & Jang, S. J. (2012). Crime and religion: Assessing the role of the faith factor. In R. Rosenfeld, K. Quinet, & C. Garcia (Eds.), *Contemporary issues in criminological theory and research: The role of social institutions* (pp. 117–151). Belmont, CA: Cengage-Wadsworth.

Jolin, A., & Gibbons, D. (1987). Age patterns in criminal involvement. *International Journal of Offender Therapy and Comparative Criminology, 31,* 237–260.

Kanazawa, S., & Still, M. C. (2000). Why men commit crimes (and why they desist). *Sociological Theory, 18,* 434–447.

Klockars, C. B. (1974). *The professional fence.* New York, NY: Free Press.

Laub, J. H. (1983). Urbanism, race, and crime. *Journal of Research in Crime and Delinquency, 20,* 183–198.

Laub, J. H., Nagin, D., & Sampson, R. (1998). Trajectories of change in criminal offending: Good marriages and the desistence process. *American Sociological Review, 63,* 225–238.

Laub, J. H., & Sampson, R. (2003). *Shared beginnings, divergent lives: Delinquent boys to age 70.* Cambridge, MA: Harvard University Press.

Massoglia, M., & Uggen, C. (2010). Settling down and aging out: Toward an interactionist theory of desistence and the transition to adulthood. *American Journal of Sociology, 116*(2), 543–582.

Meisenhelder, T. (1977). An exploratory study of exiting from criminal careers. *Criminology, 15,* 319–334.

Nagin, D., & Land, K. (1993). Age, criminal careers, and population heterogeneity: Specification and estimation of a nonparametric, mixed Poisson model. *Criminology, 31,* 327–362.

Nagin, D., & Paternoster, R. (2000). Population heterogeneity and state dependence: State of the evidence and directions for future research. *Journal of Quantitative Criminology, 16,* 117–144.

Nettler, G. (1978). *Explaining crime.* New York, NY: McGraw-Hill.

Pennsylvania Crime Commission. (1991). *1990 report—organized crime in America: A decade of change.* Commonwealth of Pennsylvania.

Prus, R. C., & Sharper, C. R. D. (1977). *Road hustler: The career contingencies of professional card and dice hustlers.* Lexington, MA: Lexington Books.

Quetelet, A. (1984). *Research on the propensity for crime at different ages* (S. Sylvester, Trans.). Cincinnati, OH: Anderson (Original work published 1831).

Rowe, A. R., & Tittle, C. (1977). Life cycle changes and criminal propensity. *The Sociological Quarterly, 18,* 223–236.

Sampson, R., & Laub, J. H. (1993). *Crime in the making: Pathways and turning points through life.* Cambridge, MA: Harvard University Press.

Shannon, L. (1988). *Criminal career continuity: Its social context.* New York, NY: Human Sciences Press.

Shapiro, S. (1984). *Wayward capitalists: Target of the Securities and Exchange Commission.* New Haven, CT: Yale University Press.

Shock, N. (1984). *Normal human aging: The Baltimore Longitudinal Study of Aging.* Washington, DC: Government Printing Office.

Shover, N. (1983). The later stages of ordinary property offender careers. *Social Problems, 30,* 208–218.

Shover, N. (1996). *Great pretenders: Pursuits and careers of persistent thieves.* Boulder, CO: Westview.

Siennick, S., & Osgood, D. W. (2008). A review of research on the impact on crime of transitions to adult roles. In A. M. Liberman (Ed.), *The long view of crime: A synthesis of longitudinal research* (pp. 161–187). New York, NY: Springer.

Silver, E., & Ulmer, J. T. (2012). Future selves and self-control motivation: Toward a conceptualization of the "self" in self-control theory. *Deviant Behavior, 33*(9), 699–714.

Steffensmeier, D. J. (1983). Organization properties and sex-segregation in the underworld: Building a sociological theory of sex differences in crime. *Social Forces, 61,* 1010–1032.

Steffensmeier, D. (1986). *The fence: In the shadow of two worlds.* Totowa, NJ: Rowman & Littlefield.

Steffensmeier, D. (1989). On the causes of "white-collar" crime: An assessment of Hirschi and Gottfredson's claims. *Criminology, 27,* 345–358.

Steffensmeier, D. (1999). Making sense of recent U.S. crime trends, 1980–98: Age composition effects and other explanations. *Journal of Research in Crime & Delinquency, 36,* 235–274.

Steffensmeier, D., & Allan, E. (2000). Criminal behavior: Gender and age. In J. Sheley (Ed.), *Criminology: A contemporary handbook* (pp. 83–114). New York, NY: Wadsworth.

Steffensmeier, D., Allan, E., Harer, M., & Streifel, C. (1989). Age and the distribution of crime. *American Journal of Sociology, 94,* 803–831.

Steffensmeier, D., & Harer, M. (1987). Did crime rise or fall during the Reagan presidency? The effects of an "aging" U.S. population on the nation's crime rate. *Journal of Research in Crime and Delinquency, 28,* 330–359.

Steffensmeier, D., & Harer, M. D. (1999). Making sense of recent US crime trends, 1980 to 1996/1998: Age composition effects and other explanations. *Journal of Research in crime and Delinquency, 36,* 235–274.

Steffensmeier, D., Schwartz, J., & Roche, M. (2013). Gender and corporate crime: Female involvement and gender gap in Enron-era corporate financial frauds. *American Sociological Review, 78*(3), 448–476.

Steffensmeier, D., & Streifel, C. (1991). Age, gender, and crime across three historical periods: 1935, 1960, and 1985. *Social Forces, 69,* 869–894.

Steffensmeier, D., & Ulmer, J. (2005). *Confessions of a dying thief: Understanding criminal careers and criminal enterprise.* New Brunswick, NJ: Transaction.

Steinberg, L. (2007). Risk taking in adolescence: New perspectives from brain and behavioral science. *Current Directions in Psychological Science, 16,* 55–59.

Tracey, P., Wolfgang, M., & Figlio, R. (1990). *Delinquency careers in two birth cohorts.* New York, NY: Plenum.

Uggen, C. (2000). Work as a turning point in the life course of criminals: A duration model of age, employment, and recidivism. *American Sociological Review, 65,* 529–546.

Van den Berghe, P. (1973). *Age and sex in human societies: A biosocial perspective.* Belmont, CA: Wadsworth.

Warr, M. (1998). Life-course transitions and desistance from crime. *Criminology, 36,* 183–216.

White, L. (1988). Gender differences in awareness of aging among married adults ages 20 to 60. *Sociological Quarterly, 29,* 487–502.

Wilson, J. Q., & Herrnstein, R. (1985). *Crime and human nature.* New York, NY: Simon & Schuster.

Wilson, W. J. (1987). *The truly disadvantaged.* Chicago, IL: University of Chicago Press.

Wilson, W. J. (1996). *When work disappears: The new world of the urban poor.* New York, NY: Knopf.

Yesalis, C. (2006). *Can steroids enhance athletic performance?* [Interview by R. Szivos.]. Retrieved from http://live.psu.edu/index.php?sec=vs&story=18511&pf

24

The Puzzling Relationship Between Age and Criminal Behavior

A Biosocial Critique of the Criminological Status Quo

J.C. Barnes

The University of Texas at Dallas

Cody Jorgensen

The University of Texas at Dallas

Daniel Pacheco

The University of Texas at Dallas

Michael TenEyck

The University of Texas at Dallas

The age-crime curve is perhaps the best known yet least understood finding in the criminological literature (Shulman, Steinberg, & Piquero, 2013; Sweeten, Piquero, & Steinberg, 2013). The association has been a mainstay of criminological research for more than 200 years with the same general pattern emerging across both time and space (Farrington, 1986). Thus, some have been tempted to conclude that the relationship between age and crime is a just-so relationship; one that need not be explained but must otherwise be accounted for by researchers wishing to understand the etiology of crime (Hirschi & Gottfredson, 1983). Indeed, since at least the 1800s (Quetelet, 1831), the conclusions gleaned from the age-crime curve have been the same: Criminal activity rises with the onset of adolescence, peaks in late adolescence, and quickly plummets in young adulthood (see Figure 24.1).

Recent developments have attributed much of the rise and fall in crime over the life course to the weakening of social bonds in adolescence and the subsequent restrengthening of those bonds (albeit of a different type) in adulthood (Sampson & Laub, 1993; Sweeten et al., 2013). This line of research has, however, overlooked three curious pieces of information: (1) problem behavior—which is a well-known precursor of antisocial/delinquent behavior later in life—peaks within the first few years of childhood (around age 5 or so); (2) though it is normative, not all adolescents engage in delinquency, meaning that it may be possible to predict abstention and/or differential rates of involvement in adolescent delinquency; and (3) the aggregate age-crime curve peaks *well* before the aggregate age-marriage curve (the most celebrated of the adult social bonds that are hypothesized to predict the beginning of the desistance process), suggesting that

Figure 24.1 The Age-Crime Curve

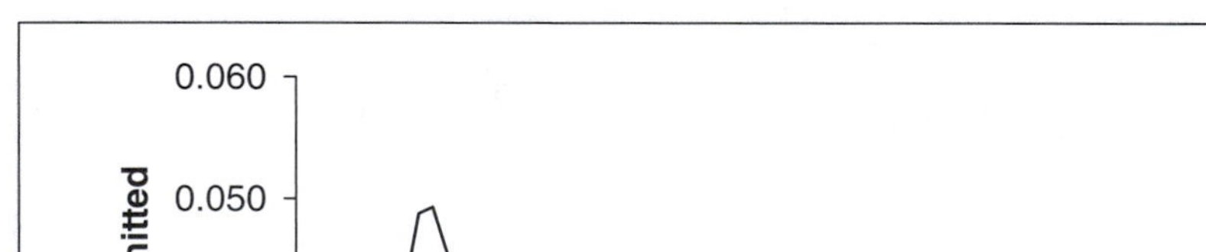

Source: Federal Bureau of Investigation. (2009). *Crime in the United States, 2008* (Table 38). Washington, DC: U.S. Department of Justice. Retrieved from http://www2.fbi.gov/ucr/cius2008/data/table_38.html

the assumed association between marriage and crime may be more complicated than has yet to be appreciated. This chapter considers each of these three points in detail. The shortcomings of the available criminological research into the etiology of the age-crime curve is discussed alongside potential inroads offered by biosocial criminology, developmental psychology, and other related disciplines. We conclude with a short summary and a brief discussion of the challenges facing 21st-century developmental/life course criminologists.

Onset of Problem Behavior

It is often claimed that the best predictor of future behavior is past behavior, and this is especially true when discussing criminality (Nagin & Paternoster, 2000; Robins, 1978). This empirical claim has been investigated, and research has shown that there exists a strong correlation between childhood, adolescent, and adulthood behavioral problems (Juon, Doherty, & Ensminger, 2006; Olweus, 1979). Interestingly, however, a paradox exists; almost all adult criminals exhibit some form of youthful behavior problems but the large majority of those who show behavior problems in childhood do *not* go on to become adult offenders (Robins, 1966). In short, it is far easier to *retro*spectively predict behavior problems than it is to *pro*spectively predict criminal behavior. This information naturally leads to an important etiological question: At what age can an individual be identified as having behavioral problems and how early is the die cast?

Traditional wisdom tells us to search for the causes of delinquency in the adolescence time period (Cullen, 2011). The age-crime curve consistently reveals that adolescence marks the beginning of the offending career (Moffitt, 1993; Quetelet, 1833), justifying criminologists' collective focus on this point of the life course. Unfortunately, as Cullen (2011) noted, an "adolescence-limited" focus neglects an enormous amount of variation in problematic behavior in childhood (see Tremblay et al., 1999); behavior that may serve as a harbinger for delinquency in the next few decades of life (Broidy et al., 2003; Piquero, Carriaga, Diamond, Kazemian, & Farrington, 2012; Tremblay et al., 1999).

Childhood problematic behavior has been operationalized in a variety of ways. A common, but not exhaustive, list of problematic behavior includes physical aggression, verbal aggression, competition, defiance, impulsivity, opposition, hyperactivity, and disruptive behaviors (Tremblay, 1991; Tremblay et al., 1991). However, some have argued that this approach is convoluted. Tremblay and colleagues (1999) suggested that the cacophony of behaviors used to operationalize problematic behavior should be broken into subcategories with physical aggression standing apart from nonphysical aggression (e.g., spreading rumors) and disruptive behaviors. The reasons were sixfold. First, physical aggression is more absolute and accurately measured than other forms of aggression. Second, there is consensus that physical aggression is harmful and undesirable. There is no such uniformity surrounding nonphysical aggression or other disruptive behaviors. Verbal aggression, aggressiveness in sports, competitiveness, and hyperactivity can be seen as a boon in some cases instead of being seen as problematic. Third, it is reasonable to expect that physical harm induces mental harm, but not vice versa. Fourth, the ability to cause physical harm precedes the ability to cause mental harm. Fifth, physical aggression is ubiquitous in society. Last, interventions for aggression require specifically designed efforts. For the aforementioned reasons, particularly the second, physical aggression is argued to be an optimal representation of problematic behavior early in the life course.

Having arrived at a conceptual definition of problematic behavior (physical aggression), the factors that predict its onset warrant discussion. As noted above, confining research efforts to adolescence ignores much variation in behavior leading up to adolescence. Several studies addressed this gap in the literature. Using a novel battery of items to specifically target physical aggression, Tremblay et al. (1999) found that physical aggression can onset in infants before their first birthday. Results from their study showed that almost all infants exhibited physically aggressive behaviors before the age of 2 with the sharpest increase in the age of onset occurring between the ages of 12 to 17 months. Tremblay (2006) has summarized these results (and other related findings) by noting that: "We need to take a second look at how we traditionally think about the development of youth violence and, consequently, how we attempt to prevent children and adolescents from 'becoming' violent" (p. 486).

Longitudinal studies have shown that aggression exhibited by children remains fairly stable throughout childhood and that these trajectories in aggressive behavior are nested within groups (recall the paradox mentioned earlier, however). Using a sample of North Carolina school children, Cairns and Cairns (1994) found four distinct group trajectories of aggressive behavior. Other studies have since replicated the group trajectory findings using samples drawn from all over the globe (Broidy et al., 2003; Nagin & Tremblay, 1999). Though it is important to emphasize that these groups should not be assumed to represent qualitatively distinct types of people in society (Sampson & Laub, 2005), it is informative to consider the different trajectories identifiable in the aggregate. First, a small portion of children can be identified as nonaggressors. These individuals rarely exhibit aggressive behavior throughout the first years of life and are expected to maintain a low level of aggression throughout the remainder of the life course. A second group, also consisting of a small portion of children, can be classified as high-stable aggressors. These individuals display the highest frequencies of aggression consistently over time. The remaining two groups will cover the vast majority of children in any sample. Both groups are identified as decreasing in their problem behavior over the first 10 years of life. Although the total number of aggressive acts committed can vary over time, the evidence suggests that membership in these trajectories remains relatively stable over large swaths of the life course (Piquero et al., 2012). Those who were high-rate aggressors in childhood have a higher *probability* of being identified as high-rate aggressors in adolescence and adulthood (see, generally, Moffitt, 1993).

Research has shown that physical aggressiveness during childhood is a salient predictor of both violent and nonviolent crime during adolescence and adulthood (see Broidy et al., 2003; Piquero et al., 2012). As such, acts of physical aggression in childhood may serve as developmental segues into more serious antisocial and delinquent behaviors in adolescence/adulthood. In other words, an adolescence-limited focus may mask important variation within the distribution of delinquent beginnings (Cairns & Cairns, 1994; Cullen, 2011), especially for offenders who follow a life-course-persistent pattern of problem behavior (Moffitt, 1993). Researchers have shown that life-course-persistent patterns of deviance begin earlier in the life course than the normal pattern of offending (Cairns & Cairns, 1994) and are typically demarcated by higher frequencies of offending and a later age of desistance (DeLisi, Neppl, Lohman, Vaughn, & Shook, 2013; DeLisi & Piquero, 2011). In short, life-course-persistent patterns of problem behavior appear to have roots early in the life course but more typical patterns of deviance follow a separate etiology, indicating the need for unique causal statements for each pattern of behavior. The most cogent explanation for the etiology of the different behavioral trajectories is Moffitt's (1993) developmental taxonomy. Moffitt's statement, along with evidence gleaned from the criminological literature, is discussed in the next section.

Adolescent Delinquency

Although physical aggression peaks in childhood (see previous section), it remains the case that delinquent/criminal activity peaks in late adolescence. As expected, criminologists have devoted much time to explaining the rise and fall of delinquency in the adolescent years. There are various theories that seek to explain this pattern of behavior, but Moffitt's (1993) developmental taxonomy provides several unique perspectives and explanations. Moffitt described two distinct trajectories of antisocial behavior that individuals may follow: life-course-persistent (LCP) offending and adolescence-limited (AL) offending. LCP offending is believed to emerge when a child with neuropsychological deficits is born into a criminogenic home environment. The interaction of these two forces drastically raises the probability that the child will develop behavior problems at an early age, will be involved in serious delinquency during adolescence, and will eventually become a violent offender in adulthood (Moffitt, 1993; Raine, Brennan, & Mednick, 1994). By definition, LCP offenders follow a different life trajectory (in many respects, but most important, regarding their offending) than is observed by the aggregate age-crime curve. There are many parallels between Moffitt's LCPs and the "high-stable aggressors" discussed above.

The second trajectory described by Moffitt (1993), the AL offenders, differs markedly from the LCP group. Unlike LCP offenders—whose problem behavior extends from childhood to adulthood—AL offenders are hypothesized to evince a normative level of problem behavior in childhood, they begin their foray into delinquency in adolescence but their offending is of the minor variety (e.g., minor property damage and low-level drug experimentation), and their offending career is limited to the adolescent years. Finally, for AL offenders, desistance is believed to take place in lockstep with the onset of adulthood and the ensuing responsibilities that follow the transition from adolescence to adulthood. In short, AL offenders are believed to limit their offending career to the decade or so spanning the adolescence time period. During that time, delinquent behavior is situational, often occurs in groups, and can be traced to the socioemotional dysphoria that accompanies the maturity gap.

ADOLESCENCE-LIMITED (AL) OFFENDING

Moffitt's (1993) explanation of AL offending entails three important processes. First, AL delinquency is motivated by the gap between biological maturity and social maturity that develops in adolescence as part of the natural aging process and the societal pressures that prevent one from fully achieving adult status until the adolescence period has passed. The *maturity gap* refers to the time period of life when an individual has reached biological maturity (i.e., he or she is capable of reproduction) but has not yet been afforded full social maturity (e.g., he or she cannot legally smoke cigarettes, drink alcohol, work a full-time job, or quit school). Second, Moffitt noted that delinquent behavior is learned and imitated by observing the delinquent behavior of one's peers, perhaps those who are life-course-persistent offenders. Behavior is learned according to the principles of operant conditioning (Skinner, 1937) such that behavior will be expected to remain stable as long as the individual receives positive reinforcement. The third, and most unique, element of Moffitt's theory of AL offending notes that the maturity gap will explain the onset *and* desistance from delinquency for AL offenders. Those caught in the maturity gap desire participation in adult-like behaviors such as having sex, using licit drugs, and exuding a certain air of independence. Yet society denies youth such privileges until they have reached their early to mid-20s. As a result, AL offenders will recognize the adult-like behavior of their LCP peers and, via the learning processes discussed above, will imitate delinquent behavior as a means of obtaining status and possessions that are otherwise off limits. In short, Moffitt's discussion highlights the importance of two factors in the etiology of AL offending: (1) peers and (2) the maturity gap.

The role of peers in the etiology of deviant behavior is one of the most robust findings in the criminological literature (Paternoster & Brame, 1997; Pratt et al., 2010). In a recent meta-analysis, Pratt and colleagues (2010) concluded that the effect size of the delinquent peer influence was large (relative to other micro-level predictors of human behavior) and consistent across various types of delinquent behavior. Specifically, the average correlation between peer delinquency and self-reported delinquency was found to be .27, revealing that adolescents who are exposed to friends who are more involved in delinquency (or a greater number of such friends) are more likely to report delinquent behavior themselves. This pattern of findings is consistent with the tenets of social learning theories (Akers, 2009; Sutherland, 1947) but important methodological/statistical limitations preclude one from claiming support for these theories (see generally Rebellon, 2012; Young, Barnes, Meldrum, & Weerman, 2011; Young, Rebellon, Barnes, & Weerman, in press).

Research has also examined the impact of the maturity gap on delinquency during adolescence. Recall that the maturity gap refers to the time period of the life course when one is biologically mature but has yet to be afforded social maturity in the larger sociopolitical environment. Consistent with Moffitt's hypothesis, Galambos, Barker, and Tilton-Weaver (2003) found that adolescents who scored above the mean on a measure of perceived maturity but below the mean on psychological maturity—those most likely to be caught in the maturity gap—reported the highest levels of problem behavior compared to other individuals in the sample. Piquero and Brezina (2001) examined the relationship between early maturity, autonomy, and delinquency. Using interviewer ratings of physical maturity and self-reported measures of autonomy and delinquency, the researchers found a significant interaction between maturity and behavioral autonomy on rebellious delinquency (e.g., arguing with teachers, skipping classes, and other school-related delinquent acts), but not aggressive delinquency (e.g., physical aggression and fighting). This is consistent with Moffitt's hypothesis in that physical maturity and autonomy are related to minor delinquent acts, but not serious delinquency.

Barnes and Beaver (2010) provided one of the first direct tests of Moffitt's maturity gap hypothesis (but see Galambos et al., 2003). Barnes and Beaver identified indicators of both biological maturity and social maturity in their dataset. By subtracting social maturity scores from biological maturity scores the authors were able to construct a measure of the maturity gap, allowing them to examine the impact of the maturity gap on both serious and minor delinquency. The findings were supportive of Moffitt's theory in that the maturity gap was a consistent predictor of minor delinquency and minor drug use for males even after controlling for known correlates such as association with delinquent peers and levels of self-control. Furthermore, the maturity gap was not associated with serious delinquency and serious drug use, as predicted by Moffitt's theory. More recent research by Barnes, Beaver, and Piquero (2011) employed the same maturity gap measure and found support for Moffitt's arguments concerning abstention from delinquency in adolescence.

As can be seen, there is a good deal of support for Moffitt's (1993) arguments within the criminological literature. Although Moffitt's theory has received a substantial amount of attention and support, it has been unable to fully explain the age-crime curve. Indeed, tests of Moffitt's maturity gap thesis have proven to be supportive, but the overall variance in deviance attributable to variance in the maturity gap is small. While this is not particularly surprising—given that individual-level research in criminology tends to explain less than 30% of the variance in delinquency (Weisburd & Piquero, 2008)—it does raise an important question: What else may account for the steep rise and fall of delinquency in the adolescent years? Recent evidence from developmental psychology may provide some clues.

THE DUAL SYSTEMS MODEL

Research indicates that young people are more likely than older adults to engage in risky, and often dangerous, behavior (Arnett, 1992). Moffitt's (1993) dual taxonomy suggests that antisocial behavior emerges during the formative years as a consequence of peer influences and exposure to the maturity gap. Under this paradigm, youth are perceived as acting impulsively in an effort to counterbalance the strains of the maturity gap and to send the message that they are capable of adult-like behavior. Interestingly, most criminological theorizing sees youth as acting without regard for future consequences; in other words youth are believed to succumb to low levels of self-control more readily than adults (Gottfredson & Hirschi, 1990). Recent evidence flowing from developmental neuroscience, however, suggests an alternative explanation. Specifically, this nascent line of research indicates that sensation-seeking and impulsivity are two developmentally and biologically separate but interrelated processes (Steinberg et al., 2008; see also Casey, Getz, & Galvan, 2008). As a consequence, Steinberg et al. (2008) proposed a dual systems model that is informative for the current focus.

Using 935 diverse respondents, self-reports, and behavioral measures, Steinberg et al. (2008) reported that impulsivity and risk-taking are unique processes with unique neurological substrates. Risk-taking (sensation-seeking) is the predilection for high sensory-arousal activities that tend to run counter to prosocial norms and values (Zuckerman, 1979). Reckless driving, driving after consuming alcohol or using drugs, and engaging in sexual activity are all considered risky or sensation-seeking behaviors. In contrast, impulsivity (i.e., deficient cognitive control) is characterized by an inability to control the desire for something with little, if any, cognitive resources devoted to the potential consequences such as consuming fast food without regard for the calories; using illegal drugs without regard for one's health, safety, or criminal prosecution; and purchasing something on credit without the means to pay.

Research by Steinberg et al. (2008) has helped identify and understand the underlying neurobiological mechanisms that demarcate sensation-seeking from impulsivity. These scholars noted an interesting relationship between age and sensation-seeking/impulsivity. Specifically, the age-sensation-seeking relationship was found to track very closely with the age-crime curve. For impulsivity, however, the relationship with age was found to be linear with a gradual decrease over the life course. Steinberg et al. noted that

> age differences in sensation seeking, which are linked to pubertal maturation, follow a curvilinear pattern, with sensation seeking increasing between 10 and 15 and declining or remaining stable thereafter. In contrast, age differences in impulsivity, which are unrelated to puberty, follow a linear pattern, with impulsivity declining steadily from age 10 on. (p. 1764)

Juxtaposed against one another, this pattern of results suggests that sensation-seeking and impulsivity are not only unique phenomena but that they may arise due to different brain maturational patterns (Casey et al., 2008; Galvan, Hare, Voss, Glover, & Casey, 2007; Steinberg et al., 2008). During adolescence, two major neurobiological systems undergo significant modifications that are often expressed as behavioral changes. The socioemotional system becomes extremely active during puberty and is particularly important for how youth interact with peers, while the cognitive control system is primarily responsible for behavioral regulation (Steinberg et al., 2008). Given that the socioemotional system is also associated with the reward network, during adolescence there is an elevated sensitivity to novel and highly arousing stimuli (i.e., sensation-seeking). In contrast, as the cognitive control system matures, individuals become better at regulating their responses and more skillful at inhibiting actions to their impulses. The dual systems model accounts for the differences between the two neurobiological systems—those governing the rise and fall in sensation-seeking during adolescence and those governing the long-term inhibition of impulsivity.

As noted above, the role of peers and peer-networks is one of the most consistent and theoretically central elements in the explanation of the etiology of adolescent delinquency. Unfortunately, the large majority of the criminological evidence is correlational in nature, limiting one's ability to speak to causal effects and to unpack the factors that explain the connection. Nonetheless, Gardner and Steinberg (2005) performed a simple study that allowed for the close examination of the effect of peers on adolescent behavior. Drawing on information gleaned from questionnaires completed by participants as well as a video game task tapping into respondents' decision making and behavior, various measures of risk preference and risk-taking were obtained. The analysis revealed that the younger age groups (13–16 and 18–22) were more likely to engage in risky behavior than their adult counterparts. Additionally, when in groups (compared to when alone), individuals took a greater number of risks, and the nature of the risk was more serious. These findings highlight the magnitude and valence that peer influence has on young people. Notably, however, these findings highlighted that the presence of peers increased sensation-seeking behaviors but not necessarily impulsivity. The fact that youth spend a great deal of time with their peers may place them at greater risk for engaging in maladaptive behavior, but not because it influences levels of impulsivity.

This section reviewed two distinct, but overlapping, paradigms for understanding the onset of delinquency in adolescence. First, Moffitt's (1993) theory of AL offenders was reviewed as was the available evidence that lends support to her hypotheses concerning the role of peers and the maturity gap. Second, the dual systems model of the development of sensation-seeking and impulsivity in adolescence and adulthood was discussed. Given the large conceptual overlap between sensation-seeking, impulsivity, and delinquency, we anticipate that the dual systems model can provide a useful framework for future theoretical and empirical developments in criminology.

Desistance From Crime in Adulthood

The previous sections of this chapter have covered the childhood precursors to deviance and the subsequent rise of delinquent behavior in adolescence. This section considers the factors that have been proffered as an explanation of the "fall," or desistance, in crime that appears in adulthood. In this respect, the effect of marriage on desistance from crime has received much attention (Sampson & Laub, 1993; Siennick & Osgood, 2008). Though there is some conflicting evidence, most studies indicate that marital status is inversely related to crime, especially for individuals who are attached to their spouse (Bersani, Laub, & Nieuwbeerta, 2009; King, Massoglia, & Macmillan, 2007; Laub, Nagin, & Sampson, 1998; Maume, Ousey, & Beaver, 2005; Piquero, MacDonald, & Parker, 2002; Sampson, Laub, & Wimer, 2006; Warr, 1998).

Research into the marriage effect has been motivated primarily by the theoretical writings of Sampson and Laub (1993; see also Laub & Sampson, 2003) and has utilized different samples and various statistical techniques. Although research into the marriage effect can be traced back for several decades, one of the most commonly cited studies in this area is Horney, Osgood, and Marshall's (1995). These authors estimated a multi-level model that allowed for the observation of within-individual changes in marriage and whether (and by how much) those changes affected changes in criminal behavior. The findings indicated that intraindividual changes in marital status—specifically, going from unmarried to married—were associated with decreased odds of committing an assault. There was no relationship between marital status and the odds of committing a property crime, or a drug crime, however, suggesting the marriage effect may not be as general as has been hypothesized.

Not all studies have supported the marriage effect. Some have found support but question the underlying causal processes (Barnes & Beaver, 2012; Barnes et al., in press; Giordano, Cernkovich, & Holland, 2003; Giordano, Cernkovich, & Rudolph, 2002; Warr, 1998), while others have reported results that are mixed or appear to stand in contrast to the marriage effect (Piquero, Brame, Mazerolle, & Haapenen, 2002; Simons, Stewart, Gordon, Conger, & Elder, 2002; Stouthamer-Loeber, Wei, Loeber, & Masten, 2004). Nevertheless, research into the marriage effect has exploded in recent decades. This extensive body of research appears to suggest that marriage reduces crime. But do adult social bonds have uniform effects across all individuals? The answer appears to be no. Adult social bonds have significant effects in some samples and under some circumstances but not in others. Researchers, however, have not adequately addressed some important issues; most notable is the issue of temporal ordering. For the effect of marriage on desistance to be a tenable explanation for the initiation of the desistance process, it is necessary for this adult social bond to occur *prior* to the beginning of the desistance process (Bushway, Piquero, Broidy, Cauffman, & Mazerolle, 2001). In short, marriage may well be correlated with deceleration or de-escalation of crime, but if these elements of the desistance process occur prior to the presence of an adult social bond, then the latter cannot cause the former.

Consider the age-crime curve (Figure 24.1). The curve peaks somewhere around 18 years of age. If desistance is understood as a process rather than a discrete event as many scholars have argued (Bushway et al., 2001; Bushway, Thornberry, & Krohn, 2003; Fagan, 1989; Laub & Sampson, 2003; Paternoster & Bushway, 2009), then the age-crime curve tells us that the desistance process begins in early adulthood (on average)—when the curve begins to turn downward. But when do adult social bonds typically set in? Obviously, an *adult* social bond must occur at some point in adulthood. Thus, the question becomes, when does adulthood occur? Of course, there is no hard-and-fast rule governing when a person is considered to have passed from adolescence into adulthood. However, if we accept the legal definition of adulthood as a proxy of this transition, then it would appear that adulthood does not begin until somewhere between ages 18 and 21. It should now be obvious that the timing of the transition from adolescence to adulthood almost perfectly matches the timing of the onset of desistance from crime as shown by the age-crime curve. This poses several complications for empirically discerning whether bonds cause desistance, whether desistance causes bonds, or whether a third variable causes both.

This brings us back to the original question of whether adult social bonds precede the beginning of the desistance process. If adulthood occurs at almost the exact same time in the life course as desistance, then it will be difficult to discern the temporal ordering of the events. Luckily, there is a small body of research that has investigated the timing of adult social bonds (Fussell & Furstenberg, 2005; Osgood & Lee, 1993). This research shows that many of the adult social bonds hypothesized to affect desistance actually appear *after* desistance processes are already in motion. Osgood and Lee (1993) showed that marriage and full-time employment probabilities (i.e., aggregate measures of the number of people that are married and employed full-time) do not peak until the late 20s to early 30s on average. For instance, the predicted probability of marriage for an 18-year-old is lower than .1, for a 23-year-old the predicted probability is less than .4, and the probability for a 28-year-old is .6. A similar trend is observed for the probability of full-time employment. Specifically, the predicted probability of full-time employment does not peak until the early 30s (Osgood & Lee, 1993).

More recent estimates from the U.S. Census Bureau (2010) tell the same story in regard to marriage. Specifically, as shown in Figure 24.2, the proportion of the population that is married remains well below 10% until the early 20s. To be sure, the portion of the population that is married between ages 18 and 19 (around the peak of the age-crime curve) is only 1.6. This number begins to grow steadily over the next few years: the portion married between ages 20 and 24 is 13.8, and the portion married between ages 25 and 29 is 38.1. By the end of early adulthood (i.e., the 20s) roughly half the population is married. Note, however, that the age-crime curve is well below its peak by the end of the 20s.

Figure 24.3 presents the age-crime curve along with the age-marriage curve. One point is immediately obvious: The age-crime curve peaks before marriage peaks. To be sure, the median age for first marriage was estimated to be 28 for males and 25 for females in 2009 (U.S. Census Bureau, 2009). It is also apparent that—in the aggregate—the two curves cross somewhere in the mid 20s. In short, crime is on the decline, meaning desistance processes have already begun, well before marriage is likely to occur.

If we accept the conventional argument of how marriage affects desistance—namely that it takes time and investment before marriage will influence behavior

Figure 24.2 The Age-Marriage Curve

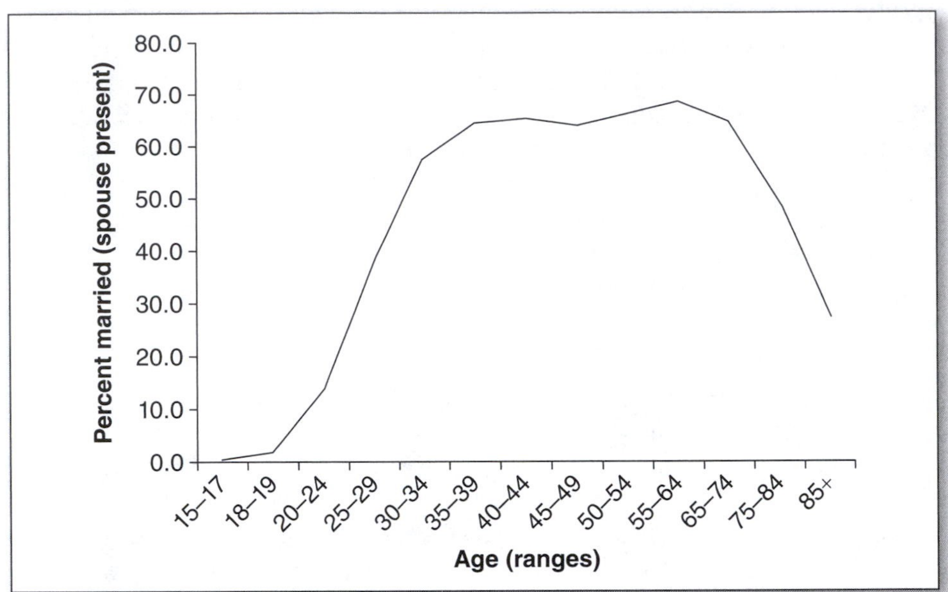

Source: U.S. Census Bureau. (2009). *Current population survey, annual social and economic supplements, 2009 and earlier.* Table A1. Washington, DC: Government Printing Office.

Figure 24.3 The Age-Crime Curve and the Age-Marriage Curve

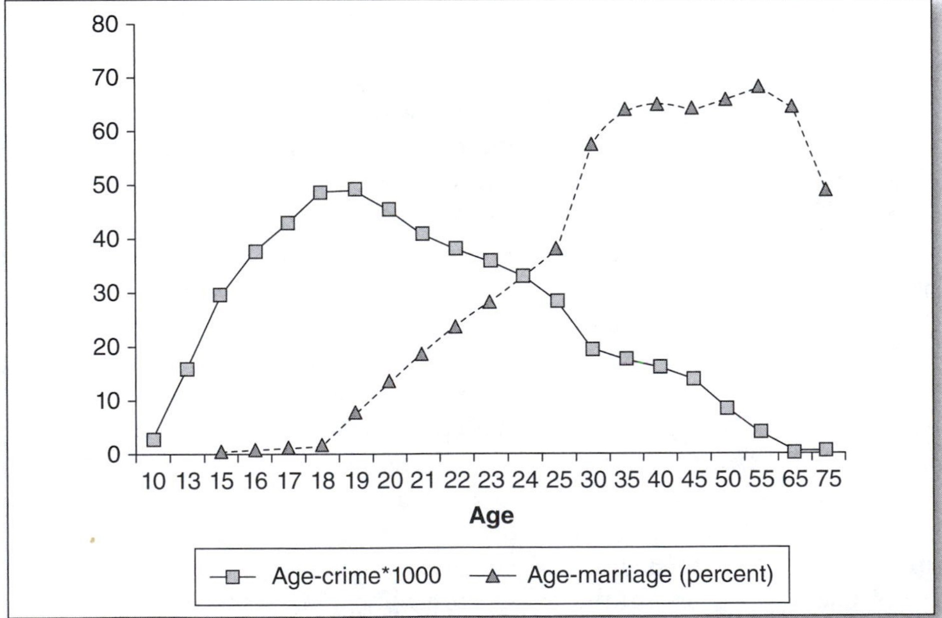

Notes: *The age-crime curve has been altered to reflect the proportion of the total offenses occurring within each age group, multiplied by 1,000 to put it on a similar measurement scale as the age-marriage curve. Also, the age-marriage data were presented for age ranges. Thus, linear interpolation was used to predict the percentage married at ages falling within each age range.

(Laub et al., 1998)—then the temporal ordering of events and direction of causality become even more problematic. In other words, if marriage takes time to influence a person's criminal career, the marriage effect would not appear until sometime after (currently an undefined time lag) marriage occurs. Marriage cannot explain the initial decline in crime and perhaps cannot explain much (if any) of the deceleration in crime in adulthood. It is important to point out, however, that these arguments are based on aggregate numbers of crime and marriage. It is possible to argue that different patterns of association should be expected between the individual- and aggregate-level variables.

In summary, it appears we have hit a crossroads regarding the link between marriage (and perhaps other social bonds) and desistance. As we see it, there are three options for moving forward. First, if we discard the understanding of desistance as a process, or if we change the argument to state that adult social bonds *accelerate* desistance processes (Le Blanc & Loeber, 1998), then perhaps adult social bonds can retain much of their theoretical import. It may turn out that the initial decline in crime observed in early adulthood has nothing to do with social bonds and is instead a normative developmental pattern (see the earlier sections of this chapter). If this were the case, social bonds would only matter for changes occurring later in the life course or for the discrete event of desistance (i.e., when the person "quits" crime).

A second way to reconcile the age-crime curve with the age-bond curve is that adult social bonds explain desistance, but only for more serious or frequent offenders. Sampson and Laub (1993) developed their theory based on the observation of the Glueck men. It is important to remember that 50% of their sample consisted of juvenile delinquents and that the majority of Sampson and Laub's analyses were performed exclusively on this delinquent subsample. It is possible Sampson and Laub's sample of delinquents followed a different trajectory of offending and desistance compared to the general population. This explanation accords well with the findings presented by Sampson et al. (2006, p. 486). Specifically, the age-crime curve and the age-bond curve are markedly different for the Glueck men than is found in the general population (compare Sampson et al. [2006] with the age-crime curve and the age-marriage curve presented here); the Glueck men desisted and married much later in life compared to the general population. These findings suggest that marriage may be influential for serious/persistent offenders, but not for normative offending patterns (see also Laub et al., 1998).

A third way to reconcile the age-crime curve with the age-bond curve is to argue that adult bonds reflect selection effects. In other words, it is possible that individuals most likely to desist are those most likely to get married, get a job, or join the military. If we look closely at the available literature, we begin to see evidence supportive of this argument. Specifically, in some studies (e.g., Blokland & Nieuwbeerta, 2005) social bonds are important for predicting crime, but only at the *between*-individual level. When analyses are extended to *within*-individual differences, the findings are less stable. Assuming that selection effects are operating, what might explain them? Could biosocial factors, such as genetic influences, play a role? Recent evidence suggests they might (see generally, Barnes & Beaver, 2012; Barnes et al., in press; Burt et al., 2010).

Discussion

The association between age and crime is compelling and has sparked many important discussions among social scientists. Few other relationships show such stability over time and across place (Hirschi & Gottfredson, 1983), suggesting that the etiology of the relationship might be easy to pin down. As this chapter has revealed, however, nothing is farther from the truth (e.g., Shulman et al., 2013; Sweeten et al., 2013). Despite many theoretical propositions seeking to explain the age-crime relationship, much remains unknown regarding the factors driving the rise and fall of delinquency in adolescence and adulthood. While the current efforts were not directed at answering all the questions surrounding the age-crime curve, we hope that scholars will gain insight into four points after having considered the above discussion. The first point of insight to be gained is that behavior problems emerge *much* earlier than the age-crime curve suggests. As revealed in the work of Tremblay and his colleagues (1999, 2004), physical aggression peaks during the first few years of life. This is extremely important given the relative stability that has been observed in physical aggression across temporal domains (e.g., Olweus, 1979; Robins, 1978; Sampson & Laub, 1993). In short, the criminological discipline cannot afford to ignore the origins of problem behavior in early childhood any longer; we must shed the "adolescence-limited" label (Cullen, 2011).

The second point to take away from the current discussion is that the age-crime curve represents an average association between aging and involvement in crime. Though it might be tempting to conclude that most people will follow a pattern similar to that which is seen in the aggregate, this conclusion is neither necessary from a theoretical standpoint nor from a mathematical standpoint. Thus, theoretical explanations of the age-crime curve that acknowledge the different trajectories of offending are likely to provide important clues for understanding the aggregate age-crime relationship (e.g., Moffitt, 1993). At a minimum, it appears that a distinction between life-course-persistent offending and adolescence-limited offending will be useful in reaching a clearer understanding of the emergent aggregate relationship between age and crime. This point provides a natural transition into our third key insight. Specifically, patterns of desistance appear to vary widely from person to person and perhaps even across different "types" of offending trajectories. Research into the factors that encourage desistance from crime has largely overlooked the possibility of heterogeneity in the impact of adult social bonds on criminal desistance (but see Blokland & Nieuwbeerta, 2005). As was shown, the impact of marriage on criminal desistance may be more complex than has been considered (though it is worth noting that our discussion relied on aggregate data, which is unlikely to reveal the nuances of the relationship, especially if the aggregate curves mask underlying heterogeneity as we argue here). Differentiating the impact of "selection" and "causation" will be difficult but vitally important to this line of scholarship.

Finally, it is our hope that this chapter will encourage scholars to consider the role of biological processes in the age-crime association. As was discussed in each section, biology appears to play a role in problem behavior. Specifically, it is likely that biological factors (e.g., genetic influences) play a role in early problem behavior (Barnes, 2013), that different biological factors (e.g., biological maturation and brain development patterns) predict the rise of delinquency in adolescence (Steinberg, 2007), and that still different biological influences underlie desistance from crime in adulthood (Barnes & Beaver, 2012; Burt et al., 2010). This does not mean that sociological/environmental factors are unimportant or that they are less important than biological factors. On the contrary, the truth probably lies somewhere in the middle where environmental factors interact with biological factors at each developmental stage. In essence, then, our position is that criminology will be more likely to unlock the secrets of the age-crime curve as biosocial research becomes more prevalent. Biosocial criminology must be thought of as a toolkit that can augment, not replace, the traditional instruments utilized by criminological researchers.

References

Akers, R. L. (2009). *Social learning and social structure: A general theory of crime and deviance*. New Brunswick, NJ: Transaction.

Arnett, J. (1992). Reckless behavior in adolescence: A developmental perspective. *Developmental Review, 12*, 339–373.

Barnes, J. C. (2013). Analyzing the origins of life-course persistent offending: A consideration of environmental and genetic influences. *Criminal Justice and Behavior, 40*, 519–541.

Barnes, J. C., & Beaver, K. M. (2010). An empirical examination of adolescence-limited offending: A direct test of Moffitt's maturity gap thesis. *Journal of Criminal Justice, 38*, 1176–1185.

Barnes, J. C., & Beaver, K. M. (2012). Marriage and desistance from crime: A consideration of gene-environment correlation. *Journal of Marriage and Family, 74*, 19–33.

Barnes, J. C., Beaver, K. M., & Piquero, A. R. (2011). A test of Moffitt's hypotheses of delinquency abstention. *Criminal Justice and Behavior, 38*, 690–709.

Barnes, J. C., Golden, K., Mancini, C., Boutwell, B. B., Beaver, K. M., & Diamond, B. (in press). Marriage and involvement in crime: A consideration of reciprocal effects in a nationally representative sample. *Justice Quarterly*.

Bersani, B. E., Laub, J. H., & Nieuwbeerta, P. (2009). Marriage and desistance from crime in the Netherlands: Do gender and socio-historical context matter? *Journal of Quantitative Criminology, 25*, 3–24.

Blokland, A. J., & Nieuwbeerta, P. (2005). The effects of life circumstances on longitudinal trajectories of offending. *Criminology, 43*, 1203–1240.

Broidy, L. M., Nagin, D. S., Tremblay, R. E., Bates, J. E., Brame, B., & Dodge, K. (2003). Developmental trajectories of childhood disruptive behaviours and adolescent delinquency: A six site, cross national study. *Developmental Psychology, 39*, 222–245.

Burt, S. A., Donnellan, M. B., Humbad, M. N., Hicks, B. M., McGue, M., & Iacono, W. G. (2010). Does marriage inhibit antisocial behavior? An examination of selection vs. causation via a longitudinal twin design. *Archives of General Psychiatry, 67*, 1309–1315.

Bushway, S. D., Piquero, A. R., Broidy, L. M., Cauffman, E., & Mazerolle, P. (2001). An empirical framework for studying desistance as a process. *Criminology, 39*, 491–516.

Bushway, S. D., Thornberry, T. P., & Krohn, M. D. (2003). Desistance as a developmental process: A comparison of static and dynamic approaches. *Journal of Quantitative Criminology, 19*, 129–153.

Cairns, R. B., & Cairns, B. D. (1994). *Life lines and risks: Pathways of youth in our time*. New York, NY: Cambridge University Press.

Casey, B. J., Getz, S., & Galvan, A. (2008). The adolescent brain. *Developmental Review, 28*, 62–77.

Cullen, F. T. (2011). Beyond adolescent-limited criminology: Choosing our future—The American Society of Criminology 2010 Sutherland Address. *Criminology, 49*, 287–330.

DeLisi, M., Neppl, T., Lohman, B., Vaughn, M., & Shook, J. (2013). Early starters: Which type of criminal onset matters most for delinquent careers? *Journal of Criminal Justice, 41*, 12–17.

DeLisi, M., & Piquero, A. R. (2011). New frontiers in criminal careers research, 2000–2011: A state of the art review. *Journal of Criminal Justice, 39*, 289–301.

Fagan, J. (1989). Cessation of family violence: Deterrence and dissuasion. *Crime and Justice, 11*, 377–425.

Farrington, D. P. (1986). Age and crime. *Crime and Justice, 7*, 189–250.

Fussell, E., & Furstenberg, F. F. (2005). The transition to adulthood during the twentieth century: Race, nativity, and gender.

In R. A. Settersten, F. F. Furstenberg, & R. G. Rumbaut (Eds.), *On the frontier of adulthood: Theory, research, and public policy* (pp. 29–75). Chicago, IL: University of Chicago Press.

Galambos, N. L., Barker, E. T., & Tilton-Weaver, L. C. (2003). Who gets caught in the maturity gap? A study of pseudomature, immature, and mature adolescents. *International Journal of Behavioral Development, 27*, 253–263.

Galvan, A., Hare, T., Voss, H., Glover, G., & Casey, B. J. (2007). Risk-taking and the adolescent brain: Who is at risk? *Developmental Science, 10*, 8–14.

Gardner, M., & Steinberg, L. (2005). Peer influence on risk taking, risk preference, and risky decision making in adolescence and adulthood: An experimental study. *Developmental Psychology, 41*, 625–635.

Giordano, P. C., Cernkovich, S. A., & Holland, D. D. (2003). Changes in friendship relations over the life course: Implications for desistance from crime. *Criminology, 41*, 293–327.

Giordano, P. C., Cernkovich, S. A., & Rudolph, J. L. (2002). Gender, crime, and desistance: Toward a theory of cognitive transformation. *American Journal of Sociology, 107*, 990–1064.

Gottfredson, M., & Hirschi, T. (1990). *A general theory of crime*. Stanford, CA: Stanford University Press.

Hirschi, T., & Gottfredson, M. (1983). Age and the explanation of crime. *American Journal of Sociology, 89*, 552–584.

Horney, J., Osgood, D. W., & Marshall, I. H. (1995). Criminal careers in the short-term: Intra-individual variability in crime and its relation to local life circumstances. *American Sociological Review, 60*, 655–73.

Juon, H. S., Doherty, E. E., & Ensminger, M. E. (2006). Childhood behavior and adult criminality: Cluster analysis in a prospective study of African-Americans. *Journal of Quantitative Criminology, 38*, 553–563.

King, R. D., Massoglia, M., & Macmillan, R. (2007). The context of marriage on crime: Gender, the propensity to marry, and offending in early adulthood. *Criminology, 45*, 33–65.

Laub, J. H., Nagin, D. S., & Sampson, R. J. (1998). Trajectories of change in criminal offending: Good marriages and the desistance process. *American Sociological Review, 63*, 225–238.

Laub, J. H., & Sampson, R. J. (2003). *Shared beginnings, divergent lives: Delinquent boys to age 70*. Cambridge, MA: Harvard University Press.

Le Blanc, M., & Loeber, R. (1998). Developmental criminology updated. *Crime and Justice, 23*, 115–198.

Maume, M. O., Ousey, G. C., & Beaver, K. M. (2005). Cutting the grass: A reexamination of the link between marital attachment, delinquent peers and desistance from marijuana use. *Journal of Quantitative Criminology, 21*, 27–53.

Moffitt, T. E. (1993). Adolescence-limited and life-course-persistent antisocial behavior: A developmental taxonomy. *Psychological Bulletin, 100*, 674–701.

Nagin, D. S., & Paternoster, R. (2000). Population heterogeneity and state dependence: State of the evidence and directions for future research. *Journal of Quantitative Criminology, 16*, 117–144.

Nagin, D. S., & Tremblay, R. E. (1999). Trajectories of boys' physical aggression, opposition, and hyperactivity on the path to physically violent and non-violent juvenile delinquency. *Child Development, 70*, 1181–1196.

Olweus, D. (1979). Stability of aggressive reaction patterns in males: A review. *Psychological Bulletin, 86*, 852–857.

Osgood, D. W., & Lee, H. (1993). Leisure activities, age, and adult roles across the lifespan. *Society and Leisure, 16*, 181–208.

Paternoster, R., & Brame, R. (1997). Multiple routes to delinquency? A test of developmental and general theories of crime. *Criminology, 35*, 49–80.

Paternoster, R., & Bushway, S. (2009). Desistance and the "feared self": Toward an identity theory of criminal desistance. *Journal of Criminal Law & Criminology, 99*, 1103–1156.

Piquero, A. R., Brame, R., Mazerolle, P., & Haapanen, R. (2002). Crime in emerging adulthood. *Criminology, 40*, 137–170.

Piquero, A. R., & Brezina, T. (2001). Testing Moffitt's account of adolescence-limited delinquency. *Criminology, 39*, 353–370.

Piquero, A. R., Carriaga, M. L., Diamond, B., Kazemian, L., & Farrington, D. P. (2012). Stability in aggression revisited. *Aggression and Violent Behavior, 17*, 365–372.

Piquero, A. R., MacDonald, J. M., & Parker, K. F. (2002). Race, local life circumstances, and criminal activity. *Social Science Quarterly, 83*, 654–670.

Pratt, T. C., Cullen, F. T., Sellers, C. S, Winfree, L. T., Madensen, T. D., Daigle, L. E., . . . Gau, J. M. (2010). The empirical status of social learning theory: A meta-analysis. *Justice Quarterly, 27*, 765–802.

Quetelet, A. (1833). La précision des résultats croit comme la racine carrée du nombre des observations. *Annales d'Hygiène Publique et de Médecine Légale, 9*, 308–336.

Raine, A., Brennan, P., & Mednick, S. (1994). Birth complications combined with early maternal rejection at age 1 year predispose to violent crime at age 18 years. *Archives of General Psychiatry, 51*, 984–988.

Rebellon, C. J. (2012). Differential association and substance use: Assessing the roles of discriminant validity, socialization, and selection in traditional empirical tests. *European Journal of Criminology, 9*, 74–97.

Robins, L. N. (1966). *Deviant children grown up: A sociological and psychiatric study of sociopathic personality*. Baltimore, MD: Williams & Wilkins.

Robins, L. N. (1978). Sturdy childhood predictors of adult antisocial behavior: Replications from longitudinal studies. *Psychological Medicine, 8*, 611–622.

Sampson, R. J., & Laub, J. H. (1993). *Crime in the making: Pathways and turning points through life*. Cambridge, MA: Harvard University Press.

Sampson, R. J., & Laub, J. H. (2005). Seductions of method: Rejoinder to Nagin and Trembley's "Developmental trajectory groups: Fact or fiction?" *Criminology, 43*, 905–913.

Sampson, R. J., Laub, J. H., & Wimer, C. (2006). Does marriage reduce crime? A counterfactual approach to within-individual causal effects. *Criminology, 44*, 465–508.

Shulman, L., Steinberg, L., & Piquero, A. R. (2013). The age-crime curve in adolescence and early adulthood is not due to age differences in economic status. *Journal of Youth and Adolescence, 42*, 848–860.

Siennick, S. E., & Osgood, D. W. (2008). A review of research on the impact on crime of transitions to adult roles. In A. M. Liberman (Ed.), *The long view of crime: A synthesis of longitudinal research* (pp. 161–187). New York, NY: Springer.

Simons, R. L., Stewart, E., Gordon, L. C., Conger, R. D., & Elder, G. H. (2002). A test of life-course explanations for stability and change in antisocial behavior from adolescence to young adulthood. *Criminology, 40*, 401–434.

Skinner, B. F. (1937). Two types of conditioned reflex: A reply to Knorski and Miller. *Journal of General Psychology, 16*, 272–279.

Steinberg, L. (2007). Risk taking in adolescence: New perspectives from brain and behavioral science. *Current Directions in Psychological Science, 16*, 55–59.

Steinberg, L., Albert, D., Cauffman, E., Banich, M., Graham, S., & Woolard, J. (2008). Age differences in sensation seeking and impulsivity as indexed by behavior and self-report: Evidence for a dual systems model. *Developmental Psychology, 44*, 1764–1778.

Stouthamer-Loeber, M., Wei, E., Loeber, R., & Masten, A.S. (2004). Desistance from persistent serious delinquency in the transition to adulthood. *Development and Psychopathology, 16*, 897–918.

Sutherland, E. H. (1947). *Principles of criminology*. Philadelphia, PA: J. B. Lippincott.

Sweeten, G., Piquero, A. R., & Steinberg, L. (2013). Age and the explanation of crime, revisited. *Journal of Youth and Adolescence, 42*(6), 921–938.

Tremblay, R. E. (1991). Aggression, prosocial behaviour and gender: Three magic words but no magic wand. In K. H. Rubin & D. J. Pepler (Eds.), *The development and treatment of aggression* (pp. 71–78). Hillsdale, NJ: Lawrence Erlbaum.

Tremblay, R. E. (2006). Prevention of youth violence: Why not start at the beginning? *Journal of Abnormal Child Psychology, 34*, 481–487.

Tremblay, R. E., Japel, C., Perusse, D., McDuff, P., Boivin, M., Zoccolillo, M., & Montplaisir, J. The search for the age of "onset"of physical aggression: Rousseau and Bandura revisited. *Criminal Behaviour and Mental Health, 9*(1), 8–23.

Tremblay, R. E., Loeber, R., Gagnon, C., Charlebois, P., Larivée, S., & LeBlanc, M. (1991). Disruptive boys with stable and unstable high fighting behaviour patterns during junior elementary school. *Journal of Abnormal Child Psychology, 19*, 285–300.

Tremblay, R. E., Nagin, D. S., Séguin, J. R., Zoccolillo, M., Zelazo, P., & Boivin, M. (2004). Physical aggression during early childhood: Trajectories and predictors. *Pediatrics, 114*, 43–50.

U.S. Census Bureau. (2009). *Current population survey, annual social and economic supplements, 2009 and earlier*. Washington, DC: Government Printing Office.

U.S. Census Bureau. (2010). *Current population survey, annual social and economic supplement, 2009*. Washington, DC: Government Printing Office.

Warr, M. (1998). Life-course transitions and desistance from crime. *Criminology, 36*, 183–216.

Weisburd, D., & Piquero, A. R. (2008). How well do criminologists explain crime? Statistical modeling in published studies. *Crime & Justice, 37*, 453–502.

Young, J. T. N., Barnes, J. C., Meldrum, R. C., & Weerman, F. M. (2011). Assessing and explaining misperceptions of peer delinquency. *Criminology, 49*, 599–630.

Young, J. T. N., Rebellon, C. J., Barnes, J. C., & Weerman, F. M. (in press). What do alternative measures of peer behavior tell us? Examining the discriminant validity of multiple methods of measuring peer deviance and the implications for etiological models. *Justice Quarterly*.

Zuckerman, M. (1979). *Sensation seeking: Beyond the optimal level of arousal*. Hillsdale, NJ: Erlbaum.

Discussion Questions

CHAPTERS 23 AND 24

1. What are some limitations to searching for the causes of delinquency exclusively during adolescence? In what ways can early childhood behavior inform researchers about the causes of antisocial behavior?
2. What does research tell us about individual age-crime trajectories? Is membership in these trajectories relatively stable over the life course? Or, is the age-crime relationship invariant for all offenders and offense types?
3. Discuss the differences between life-course-persistent (LCP) offending and adolescence-limited (AL) offending. Which type of offending peaks at an earlier age? Which type remains the most stable, and why?
4. Sociologists argue that criminal involvement has peaked at earlier ages due to the aggravated stresses from social processes of industrialization and the postindustrial age. Relate this argument to Moffitt's (1993) explanation of the AL offender. What influence does the gap between biological maturity and social maturity have on offending behaviors?
5. What does research reveal about the relationship between age and sensation-seeking/impulsivity? How are sensation-seeking and impulsivity different from one another?
6. How do life course theories explain the gradual decline of crime? What does the research reveal about the marriage effect? Is there enough evidence to indicate that social bonds truly affect desistance?

25

Policy Implications of Sociological Theories of Crime

Why Are They So Seldom Considered or Discussed?

Danielle J.S. Bailey

University of Nebraska at Omaha

Robert Lytle

University of Nebraska at Omaha

Lisa L. Sample

University of Nebraska at Omaha

Although criminal behavior is often associated with individual character traits, people do not live, think, or act in a vacuum. People make decisions within a sociological context that includes families, friends, schools, neighborhoods, towns, and cities. We, therefore, explored, developed, and tested sociological theories of crime. After years of testing these theories, and generally finding strong significant associations between several sociological factors and crime, these explanatory factors typically receive little media attention, rarely garner legislative consideration, and seldom find their way into policies meant to address crime. Why do the findings from sociological theory testing draw so little attention from scholars and policy makers when developing programs and laws to address crime? We posit that sociological theories of crime suggest factors for deviant behavior that are perceived to be beyond our reach to address.

When crimes occur, particularly those that draw widespread media attention, citizens want a "quick fix" to avoid such behaviors again (Garland, 2001). It is intellectually easier and clinically faster for citizens, criminal justice agents, and medical professionals to seek and find biological and/or psychological reasons for crimes. Once found, these factors can be quickly addressed through medication, therapy, or both. What is more difficult to address, however, is the degree to which individuals' friends, families, and/or local communities influenced their criminal behavior.

Sociological factors that can contribute to criminal behavior, such as learning through friends and family, parenting techniques, social attachments, and community structures, cannot be diagnosed quickly, addressed easily through medication or therapy, or "fixed" with a single crime policy. It would difficult at best to reorganize neighborhoods, redirect social learning to conventional norms, teach parenting skills, or legislate social bonding. If these things could be accomplished, it would take more time than policy makers and citizens would generally find acceptable (Garland, 2001). We argue that the policy implications of sociological theories are often overlooked by scholars and decision makers because the sociological factors that affect crime are too complicated and difficult to address, and they would take too long to "fix." To demonstrate our argument, the following reviews various individual- and aggregate-level sociological theories and discusses their policy implications. These sociological theories of criminal behavior are generally reviewed in terms of "families" of thought and are disaggregated into two categories: individual-level and aggregate-level theories.

Individual-Level Sociological Theories

Individual-level sociological theories focus on individuals and their behavior, social characteristics, and/or choices. Policies stemming from individual-level theories focus on changing the behavior of specific people. These theories can generally be grouped into control, strain, and social learning theories.

CONTROL THEORIES

One of the many families of sociological individual-level theories used to explain criminal behavior is control theories. Central to these theories is the belief that people are naturally oriented toward criminal behavior, and one's tendency toward crime is "controlled" by certain mechanisms present within the surrounding environment. These mechanisms, however, occasionally fail, freeing the individual to commit criminal behavior. Put simply, crime occurs when mechanisms of social control fail (Hirschi, 1969; Kornhauser, 1978; Sampson & Laub, 1993).

Specific control theories vary in the mechanisms identified as critical to dissuading criminal behavior, but generally they all suggest that informal relationships with family, friends, teachers, and other conventional role models provide social control of individual behavior. For example, Hirschi (1969) identified four social bonds (attachment, commitment, involvement, and belief) that, when maintained, serve to inhibit criminal behavior. Similarly, Gottfredson and Hirschi (1990) argue that the ability to control behavior is developed early in life, results from the ways in which children are parented, and remains stable thereafter.

Since control theories argue criminal behavior stems from a lack of social control, the policy implications of such seek to either strengthen existing controls (informal relationships) or add additional controls to offenders' lives (formal controls). Formal controls originate from a state or institution through legislation or policy. An example of formal control includes the use of community supervision officers to monitor released offenders' behaviors. However, citizens are never under state supervision at all times. Without round-the-clock surveillance, citizens still have opportunities to commit crime even when subject to multiple formal control mechanisms. This may explain why, even with additional supervision and control, offenders recidivate at high rates while under parole/probation supervision (Solomon, Kachnowski, & Bhati, 2005).

Another way to increase control over individuals is to strengthen informal social relationships and the social bonds people have with others. Any program or policy that increases the attachment, commitment, or involvement people have with conventional others would help reduce crime. For instance, mentoring programs, such as Big Brothers/Big Sisters (Catalano, Berglund, Ryan, Lonczak, & Hawkins, 2004; DuBois, Holloway, Valentine, & Cooper, 2002), try to provide children with an adult role model in cases where the children's own parents are not involved in their lives or are absent (DuBois & Silverthorn, 2005). These programs have been linked to decreased criminal behavior as well as increased academic achievement and emotional health (DuBois et al., 2002; DuBois & Silverthorn, 2005). The stronger the relationship between mentor and juvenile, the more substantial the decline in problematic behavior (DuBois & Silverthorn, 2005).

Other policies that would help encourage informal social relationships would include pro-marriage policies, pro-employment programs, laws financially supporting education, or any program or policy that provides children or adults the chance to bond with people who will help restrain their behavior through a series of punishments and rewards. For instance, if people are emotionally attached and committed to a spouse, coworker, employer, or teacher, their misbehavior would likely harm these relationships, which could be considered a form of punishment. Similarly, if people are committed to or involved in conventional activities that would end if caught committing criminal behavior, these activities would serve a social control function, and it would be considered a punishment to lose them. Individuals' conforming behavior, however, is rewarded by a strengthening of emotional bonds in existing informal social relationships, the addition of new ones, or the continuation of activities in which people have emotional investment.

In the same vein as above, Gottfredson and Hirschi (1990) suggest parenting is at the root of misbehavior. Juveniles with strong, supportive parenting develop strong self-control, which decreases their likelihood of engaging in criminal activity. Policy implications from this theory include parenting classes and mentoring programs that help people recognize, address, and consistently punish deviant behavior. Topics of parenting classes often include developing a positive parental role in a child's life (Jarvis, Graham, Hamilton, & Tyler, 2004), child development (Chang, Park, & Kim, 2009), appropriate styles of punishment (Campbell, 1992; Jarvis et al., 2004), and encouraging parent-child communication (Chang et al., 2009; Orchard, 2007; Schaefer, 2010).

Social control theories and their policy implications are closely associated with notions of deterrence theory and rational choice. Some criminological theories claim that crime is the result of a rational calculation of the benefits of some criminal act compared to the risk and costs of punishment (e.g., Beccaria, 1764/1963). If the result of this cost-benefit analysis indicates that the benefits of the crime outweigh its costs, individuals will commit the crime. However, if the risks of detection and costs of punishment outweigh the benefits of the act, individuals will be deterred.

Two basic tenets follow from the notion that criminal behavior is a rational choice. First, perceived costs of crime are naturally associated with perceptions of being caught and/or apprehended for deviant acts. Second, perceived costs and rewards of crime must be commensurate to what individuals value. To the degree that individuals value their informal social relationships and believe they could lose them if caught for deviant acts, they will choose to not commit crime (or will be controlled from committing crime). If, however, people do not believe their loved ones will learn of their misbehaviors, or they do not care if their informal social relationships are damaged or severed, they could choose to commit crime.

Although social control theories have some obvious policy implications for controlling criminal behavior, it is difficult and sometimes impractical to truly change people's informal social control network or judge what will be perceived as a "cost" of committing crime. To the degree that people's emotional investments vary across relationships, costs associated with crime will vary across people. It is then difficult to create crime control policies that will offer punishments that will be perceived as outweighing the rewards for committing crimes that will apply to all people equally. The punishments for crimes would need to be crafted individually based on the quality of people's informal social relationships and the degree to which they are controlled by such. The notion of individually assessing offenders' social networks has been embraced in policies such as presentence investigations, but by then the crime has occurred. It is simply not practical to determine which costs of crime would outweigh the rewards for all individuals before they commit an initial offense. These policies would then only address secondary criminal behavior and do little to prevent initial acts of crime.

Also, the ability of the state to create or strengthen individuals' social bonds is limited; people must be willing to change antisocial relationships and taught how to create bonds with conventional others. On conviction of a crime, formal social controls are easy to put into place, but this is a reactive policy response that does little to avoid initial offending. Also, scholars have found that informal controls appear to be stronger deterrents for criminal behavior than formal controls. Nevertheless, programs such as midnight basketball, athletic clubs, and social organizations in schools are consistent with notions of enhancing the involvement youth have in conventional activities and furthering informal social controls. Programs that help people find employment would accomplish the same type of involvement for adults. Control theories may also endorse social dating organizations and activities if they help people become attached and committed to others. Virtually any policy or program that helps individuals become attached, committed, and involved with others has the potential to further people's belief that the law applies to them and that they have too much to lose if they violate it.

INDIVIDUAL-LEVEL STRAIN THEORIES

Strain theories suggest that criminal behavior results from inconsistencies between what individuals expect or want and what they can reasonably achieve through legal means. For example, Merton (1968) viewed American society as maladaptive, encouraging unconditional pursuit of material wealth despite an uneven distribution of resources available to attain it. According to Merton, when living in a maladaptive culture, people are unable to obtain societally accepted goals using means considered to be legitimate, so these people will experience strain or *anomie*. Persons experiencing anomie will be driven to alleviate the strain, typically by reconsidering the nature of societal goals and legitimate means. For instance, Merton claimed that criminals are persons who accept cultural goals but are blocked from the legitimate means (jobs, schools, etc.) to achieve them, so they "innovate" or use illegitimate means to achieve goals. Agnew (1985, 1992) furthers these thoughts and considers criminal behavior to be a strategy for coping with four sources (actual or anticipated) of strain: (1) the failure to meet desired outcomes, (2) the loss of valued stimuli, (3) being provided with noxious stimuli, and (4) falling short of one's goals. Within this framework, crime and delinquency are responses to the negative emotions that result from actual, anticipated, or observed sources of strain (Agnew, 2001). Policy implications from this family of theories would then suggest that crime reductions result from decreases in factors that cause individual stress and strain.

One policy that embraced notions of strain as a cause of criminal behavior was the War on Poverty in the 1960s (Cullen & Agnew, 2011), when lawmakers implemented job training and educational programs directly aimed at improving the economic situation of impoverished individuals (Cahn & Cahn, 1964; Greenstone & Peterson, 1976). Economic improvements in jobs and training would allow the impoverished to continue to try to obtain material goods through legitimate jobs rather than obtaining goods through illegal means (theft, robbery, etc.) Unfortunately, the War on Poverty ultimately failed to increase the economic success of poverty-stricken individuals, nor did it solve the crime problem in poverty-stricken areas (Greenstone & Peterson, 1976). One problem strain-based policies face is that increasing legitimate opportunities is constrained by the willingness of citizens to take advantage of those opportunities. The existence of job training programs does not guarantee that citizens will enroll in them, or obtain and maintain steady employment. To be effective, policies must be able to increase legitimate opportunities as well as change individual attitudes toward criminal activity.

Reductions in strain are also constrained by the idea of relative deprivation, a recent addition to strain theory that suggests one citizen can feel inferior to another regardless of material wealth already achieved (Cullen & Agnew, 2011). Relative deprivation allows a cycle of strain to continue. As others in society gain material goods and wealth, individuals may feel strained to achieve more also, regardless of their own current success (Cullen & Agnew, 2011). Thus, there may be no way to completely end the strain individuals are under.

One policy implication of strain theories is to reduce crime through changes in cultural values and definitions of "success," which are not easily or quickly achieved. It would take years for parents, schools, and popular culture mediums to deliver messages that the societal goals of material wealth have been replaced by others. Since this is unlikely, we may then simply accept the goals of building material goods and wealth and find ways to provide these to individuals legally. We have enacted education and employment policies in the past to more equitably disperse legitimate resources, but they have failed to reduce crime for the reasons listed above. It is then understandable that scholars and policymakers have chosen to ignore aspects of individual strain in broad crime control policies. It is easier and quicker to medicate and treat individuals for psychological or biological deficits than to teach them to not want what others have and to simply be happy with what they have achieved.

SOCIAL LEARNING THEORIES

Social learning theories assert that criminal behavior can be directly or indirectly learned through interactions with others in broader social environments (Akers, 1985; Bandura, 1986; Burgess & Akers, 1968). For example, Edwin Sutherland (1947) stated that crime results when individuals have learned to ascribe more antisocial definitions to a situation than prosocial definitions. Essentially, Sutherland suggested that criminals learn to perceive certain situations as justifying criminal action directly from friends or family. As part of this process, individuals may also learn cognitive reframing techniques that may ease internal apprehensions about committing crime (Bandura, 1990; Sykes & Matza, 1957). These definitions are learned from persons whom we consider important to us. Indirectly, we may learn that "crime pays" if we observe or otherwise believe that others benefit from criminal enterprise without consequence (Burgess & Akers, 1968).

Policies based on social learning theories would need to address individuals' social learning environment. Usually, changes are accomplished by adjusting the peer environment of individuals in the hope that, by providing people with more prosocial peers, they will be exposed to and accept a greater number of favorable definitions to obeying the law. However, Sutherland (1947) never clearly defined antisocial and prosocial definitions of law violations, so it has been difficult to identify which actions should be taken to change peer environments. Additionally, even if we find a way to measure antisocial definitions, is it within the state's power to restrict the relationships of its citizens?

A literal interpretation of social learning theories would suggest a solution that forces at-risk individuals to socialize with conventional peers, or at the very least, limit the opportunities for youth to associate with criminals. Policies such as the "sight and sound" separation of detained juveniles from adult criminals have been enacted to limit learning opportunities, but scholars find it difficult to isolate the effects of this policy from others that co-occur, so it is not known if this separation actually reduces crime. There is also the possibility of changing the learning environment of individuals through counseling or therapy. Parents who send antisocial messages to children in the home may benefit from parenting classes focused on conventional behaviors. Programs such as Healthy Families America (HFA) provide weekly home visits for new parents deemed at risk for abuse or neglect of their child (Ericson, 2001). During these visits, which extend multiple years, providers give the new parents stress management techniques, parenting advice, and social assistance such as substance abuse counseling and/or domestic violence counseling to improve the parents' well-being (Daro & Harding, 1999; Ericson, 2001). Evaluations of HFA programs have found decreased parental stress, improved self-efficacy and attitudes, and increased parental skills such as play and discipline techniques (Daro & Harding, 1999; Harding, Galano, Martin, Huntington, & Schellenbach, 2007). While programs such as this change the familial learning environment, the impact of these interventions is limited without changing the youth's peer network, because researchers have found that peer networks also have an impact on delinquent behavior (Haynie, 2002; Haynie & Osgood, 2005; Weerman, 2011). Policies meant to address social learning factors that contribute to crime would have to find a way to reduce or eliminate informal social relationships with delinquent or criminal family members or friends. Although this may be manageable while an individual is incarcerated, it is unclear how this could be achieved when that individual is living in the community.

Aggregate-Level Theories

Aggregate-level sociological theories focus on broader cultural and structural conditions conducive to criminal behavior. These theories require solutions aimed not at individual people but at groups such as neighborhoods, communities, and entire societies.

ANOMIE THEORY

It is generally thought that some societies simply are more conducive to deviant and criminal behavior than others, which is often a result of anomie (Durkheim, 1893; Merton, 1968; Messner & Rosenfeld, 1994). Anomie generally describes a state of normlessness in society in which individuals are only loosely connected to each other and social institutions, leaving them free to deviate from conventional norms. These loose connections to broader social institutions, such as schools, churches, neighborhoods, and government agencies, create a situation in which people are not fully integrated in society or into groups that offer norms and values that constrain their behavior. For instance, Messner and Rosenfeld (1994) identified America's economy-driven society as a source for higher crime rates compared to other countries because the economy is emphasized in American culture above and beyond other social institutions, such as family and education, but the economy is the institution that offers the least restraint on behavior. Therefore, America has an anomic culture in that people are encouraged to be less integrated into the social institutions that teach conventional norms and values and more integrated into the one institution that teaches people to achieve goals "by any means necessary."

Anomie theories infer that entire societal or cultural norms need to change to reduce crime rates. Crime control policy should focus on shifting value across social institutions. For instance, policies that support families such as payment for child rearing, higher salaries for teachers and daycare workers, increased vacation time from work, and shorter work hours, would all suggest that families are more important than the economy and strengthen the bonds people have to the institution that is seen as responsible for socializing youth into law-abiding lifestyles. Policies that restrict property ownership, business operating hours, or offer flat wages would de-emphasize the value of the economy as a social institution, thereby allowing people to bond with social institutions that offer more constraint on behavior. In general, to the degree that anomie contributes to an environment ripe for crime, policies would need to work toward a society less ingrained in capitalistic thought, or promote other social institutions like education and the family within the capitalistic framework. Either route entails a lengthy process that would involve a multigenerational shift in attitudes and values. Perhaps the impracticality of these endeavors is why the policy implications of these theories so seldom find their way into crime control legislation.

SOCIAL DISORGANIZATION THEORY

Social disorganization theories explain why some neighborhoods or communities exhibit heavier concentrations of crime than others. In general, these theories predict that crime will be concentrated in areas with lower levels of informal social control. Shaw and McKay (1942) theorized that crime was focused in the inner city because of a pattern of disadvantage, including concentrated populations of extreme poverty, high rates of residential turnover, anonymity, and decreased informal social control in inner-city communities. Later revisions have reconceptualized informal social control to include the community's perceptions of influence over its own future (i.e., collective efficacy; Bursik, 1988; Bursik & Grasmick, 1993; Sampson & Groves, 1989; Sampson, Raudenbush, & Earls, 1997).

Social disorganization theories focus on at-risk areas, not specific at-risk populations, so policies based on social disorganization theories would focus on neighborhoods within some geographic boundaries. They would suggest strengthening neighborhood relationships among residents and broadening city services. The ways to accomplish this would occur by addressing poverty, residential mobility, and anonymity. Policies such as establishing free enterprise zones that encourage job growth in an area may help decrease the level of poverty within the community. Researchers have also supported reducing incarceration rates to increase informal social control within families, because the act of incarcerating an individual from the community reduces the level of community stability and increases the number of single-parent families and overall poverty (Rose & Clear, 1998).

Poverty is not the only factor leading to disorganization within communities; relationships between the members of the community are also important. Policies that increase the collective efficacy of the neighborhood would help unify the community. Block parties, neighborhood watches, or any activities that bring neighbors together could reduce anonymity and create higher levels of collective efficacy that result in stronger perceptions of control within the community (Kubrin & Weitzer, 2003; Sampson & Groves, 1989). The creation of neighborhood associations would facilitate dialogue between the neighborhood and local decision makers who manage city services, such as trash collection, sidewalk repair, and other cosmetic changes that make residents feel more invested in their communities (Wilson & Kelling, 1982).

The difficulty in organizing neighborhoods is that change takes time to occur. It takes time for neighbors to come to know each other and to feel integrated into the group—integration that is essential in increasing informal social controls over behavior. This is especially problematic in disorganized areas with high resident mobility, where the transient nature of residents creates anonymity and makes strong community relationships hard to maintain. It is difficult to regulate the behavior of residents if residents do not know who belongs in the neighborhood. Unless policies can restrict the number of residents moving into or out of neighborhoods, it will be difficult to reduce anonymity and create lasting social bonds among neighborhoods.

Another difficulty of reducing disorganization is that solutions require cooperation from the community. It takes the involvement of community residents and neighborhood businesses to combat social disorganization. The Chicago Area Project (CAP), developed in the 1930s, encouraged community leadership, provided educational and employment opportunities, and advocated services for community members. CAP, however, was deemed a failure at reducing crime rates in neighborhoods and was criticized for attempting to eliminate poverty within disorganized areas using methods and organizations from outside the neighborhood (Wright, 2007). Since the demise of CAP, few scholars or policy makers have discussed including social disorganization factors in crime control policies.

ROUTINE ACTIVITIES THEORY

Closely related to the tenets of social disorganization theories is routine activities theory (L. E. Cohen & Felson, 1979; Felson, 1995). According to this theory, some neighborhoods have higher crime rates than others because they possess more motivated offenders, more suitable targets, and fewer capable guardians to watch over the targets. This approach has inspired policies to prevent crime that are predominantly focused on situations (e.g., Situational Crime Prevention; Clarke, 1980, 1997).

Situational crime prevention techniques restructure an area's natural environment to make criminal activity more difficult or, at least, more visible (Clarke, 1997). Business managers serve as capable guardians in their own establishments by using crime prevention techniques when planning the location, layout, and activities within the establishment (Madensen & Eck, 2008). Situational crime prevention is also behind crime control strategies such as hot-spot policing and the use of surveillance cameras (Clarke, 1997). These policies have been found to have some success at reducing crime in one area, but have been criticized for simply displacing crimes to other areas. In the end, routine activities theory did provide policy suggestions that were relatively fast and cheap to adopt, but scholars, criminal justice agents, and citizens soon tired of the "whack-a-mole" style of crime control these policies offered.

SUBCULTURAL THEORIES

Some theorists have suggested that crime results from the creation of oppositional subcultures within a broader culture that encourage deviant and criminal acts (A. K. Cohen, 1955; Miller, 1958). According to subcultural theories of crime, disadvantaged populations respond to frequent obstacles to achieving conventionally defined goals by creating more achievable, deviant goals within a new subculture (Lilly, Cullen, & Ball, 2011). Further, when subcultures of deviance are present at the same time as opportunities for crime, children are more likely to engage in and continue delinquent and criminal acts (Cloward & Ohlin, 1960).

Relatedly, other subculture theories have focused on specific subcultures pertaining to violence. These theories have specified certain subcultures that endorse violence as a method for resolving problems (e.g., Wolfgang & Ferracuti, 1982). For example, Anderson (1999) identified violence as a critical element in "street culture" present in Philadelphia's inner city. In this street subculture, the use of violence is not only an accepted conflict-resolution technique, but it is also viewed as essential in that it deters future victimization.

If crime is encouraged by criminal subcultures, then policies should focus on removing subcultures or changing their views. To some degree, current gang policies such as police gang databases and gang intervention programs are an attempt at breaking apart deviant subcultures or redirecting their deviant views. Programs to address violence encouraged by subcultural views could include the teaching of anger management skills and ways to redirect anger into nonviolent activities, mediation for disputes, or techniques for settling disputes through boxing or other contact sports. Unfortunately, however, it is likely that the effects of such programs would be short lived unless time and resources were consistently invested in recruitment of participants and continual review of outcomes. Moreover, these types of policies and programs have been criticized in the past for simply moving gang subcultures from one neighborhood to another or increasing the likelihood of arresting minority youth, thus perpetuating differential treatment of people of color compared to White youth (Leyton, 2001).

Also, there has been a general lack of research into macro-level subcultural theories that suggest some regions of the country, or residents of some neighborhoods, hold different values than others (Cullen & Agnew, 2011). One difficulty is that most subcultures do not outright endorse criminal activity, but rather contribute to criminal behavior by condoning behaviors related to criminality like toughness, honor, or revenge (Cullen & Agnew, 2011). Therefore, to counteract crime, policies would have to address group-level attitudes toward criminal behaviors with the intention of indirectly decreasing crime rates. This would be difficult with the present state of the research, because little is known about how subcultures transmit views toward violence to new members. Without understanding the transmission process, we will find it difficult to aim policies at counteracting those subcultural messages.

LABELING THEORY

Labeling theories are broader structural theories that focus on how involvement in the criminal justice system encourages the continuation and amplification of criminal behavior (Lemert, 1951; Tannenbaum, 1938). Specifically, persons who enter the criminal justice system are labeled as deviants by members of their community. Once labeled, people are treated like deviants by others, which affects social bonding opportunities with conventional members of society, and conformity to conventional societal norms becomes difficult. Over time, labeled individuals begin to accept their new label (Becker, 1963) and pursue label-congruent actions, a process called *secondary deviance* (Lemert, 1951). As individuals internalize the "deviant" label, deviant behavior becomes more frequent and amplified, and "criminal" becomes part of self-identity.

Labeling theory promotes policies to reduce labels and the stigma of being involved with the criminal justice system; this in turn reduces the number of citizens labeled as deviant by the community so they can create or reestablish prosocial relationships. This is one of the reasons that the juvenile court system evolved as a rehabilitative rather than punishment-oriented system (Champion, 2001). Terms such as *adjudicated responsible* or *finding delinquent* are used rather than the standard "guilty" used in adult court, because these terms are meant to encourage responsibility over censure (Wizner & Keller, 1977). Labeling theory is also the driving force behind diversionary measures, moving people away from formal criminal or juvenile justice processing toward more informal, communal forms of surveillance. Mediation, as well as drug and gun courts, are all examples of diversionary measures to keep people from traditional justice processing. These measures seek to rehabilitate without creating the official label of delinquent or criminal (Osgood & Weichselbaum, 1984).

Labeling theory was also influential in the development of restorative justice programs. These programs use temporary, reintegrative shame rather than permanent, disintegrative shame (Braithwaite, 1989) as an attempt to restore the social bond between community members and offenders (Morse & Maxwell, 2001). One of the most common restorative justice programs is the victim-offender mediation process; this face-to-face meeting allows both parties to communicate and agree on an acceptable punishment for offenders (Morse & Maxwell, 2001; Van Ness & Strong, 2010). Mediation programs have been expanded into conferences, which consist of not only victims and offenders but also affected community members (Morse & Maxwell, 2001; Van Ness & Strong, 2010). These programs have been highly utilized across several countries, including the United States, New Zealand, Australia, Canada, England, and more (Morse & Maxwell, 2001). Although restorative justice has shown higher benefits when used for serious crimes compared to nonserious crimes (Sherman & Strang, 2007), many remain skeptical of the ability to apply restorative justice practices to more serious crimes such as murder or rape, and a majority of existing restorative justice programs focus exclusively on juvenile or nonserious offenses (Robinson, 2006).

Other than restorative justice programs, policies generally based on labeling theory have fallen out of favor over time. The inability of labeling theories to address the root cause of initial deviance, and the cyclical nature of the labeling process, has made it difficult to attest to the validity of this theory for explaining crime rates. There are few direct empirical tests of the ways in which the delinquent/criminal label is internalized and then affects behavior. Until this process can be more clearly delineated, it seems unlikely that policymakers or scholars will discuss or incorporate labeling factors into crime control policies.

CONFLICT THEORY

Within the paradigm of conflict theory, crime is the result of the unequal treatment of the powerless by the powerful. More specifically, some conflict theorists view law as a social control mechanism by which the elite maintain disproportionate amounts of power over marginalized populations (Turk, 1969). Consequently, crime can often be any action taken by marginalized people that the powerful deem as deviant or unlawful. The criminal justice system, then, becomes a means of enforcing the definitions of deviance held by the elite (Quinney, 1970; Quinney & Wildeman, 1991).

According to this perspective, the only way to avoid criminal activity is to decrease the power of the elite while promoting the inclusion of working-class values in legislation. This promotion could occur through the decrease in stigmatization of the criminal justice system, since the criminal justice system itself is biased toward the elite, in-power group. Currie (1997) calls for a compassionate capitalism, where intervention and treatment are valued above incarceration and isolation. This approach would allow for those in contact with the criminal justice system, most often part of the working class, to reintegrate into society without losing their voice.

One problem with policy suggestions from conflict theories is that they would do little to help us understand and address the variability in crime rates across similarly situated countries that all exhibit some form of capitalism. Aside from a few small, isolated cultures, most societies have a capitalist social structure, with a working class and an elite class. Therefore, it is almost impossible to determine if crime is the result of the capitalist structure, because we cannot observe the occurrence of criminal behaviors in noncapitalist societies. Without the ability to compare to a control group, there is limited use of policy pertaining to conflict theories.

FEMINIST THEORY

Feminist theories of crime typically consider criminal behavior to be predominantly masculine (Adler, 1975; Bernard, Snipes, & Gerould, 2010; Cullen & Agnew, 2011; Simon, 1975), "malestream" (Lanier & Henry, 2004, p. 293), or focusing on male criminality while overlooking alternative explanations more appropriate to female criminality (e.g., Chesney-Lind, 1989; Daly & Chesney-Lind, 1988; Messerschmidt, 1993). Males make the law in such a way to maintain control over females and their behaviors. Therefore, the traditional patriarchal society is organized to pay little attention to female behavior, and when it does, laws are made that favor the behavior of men over the protection of women (Brownmiller, 1975).

Like critical theories, feminist theories also call for a power change, increasing female voices in the criminal justice and legislative systems so they too can have a voice in the creation and application of law. Therefore, policies that focus on education and promotion of females within the criminal justice system and as policymakers, such as affirmative action used to promote women to higher ranks in the police and corrections subsystems, gender-specific education in schools that focus specifically on training women to be policy makers, or gender-specific programming for delinquent girls to ensure the reasons for their behaviors are addressed are all consistent with feminist theories. Unfortunately, however, we face the same problems with researching feminist theories as we do researching critical theories—the lack of comparable societies. Most capitalist societies are also patriarchal in nature, so comparing the outcomes of new policies or programs to other nonpatriarchal cultures is difficult if not impossible. Without the ability to test these theories, feminist theories will likely have little impact on current crime control policies.

Conclusion

Sociologists and criminologists have done well at identifying the sociological factors that influence criminal behavior. We have provided a social context for biological and psychological correlates of crime. Despite widespread testing and acknowledgment of sociological influences on crime, however, these factors rarely find their way into crime control policies. We argue that the reason for this is simple: Sociological factors are too difficult and time-consuming to address.

Above we briefly review individual- and aggregate-level sociological theories of crime and discuss their implications on crime control policy. What should be readily apparent is that it is difficult to assess parenting practices, social bonds, peer influences, neighborhood disorganization, and self-identity before people become engaged in the criminal justice system. Policies based on sociological theories of crime will then, by their very nature, always be seen as retroactive, addressing behavior that already occurred. Yet citizens clamor for proactive policies to prevent crime from initially occurring. To proactively affect change in sociological factors that contribute to crime would require us to clearly explain to citizens and lawmakers what needs to be done, which is difficult when we are still operationalizing the concepts, processes, and mechanisms that help retrain individual behavior.

Sociological concepts that may contribute to crime, such as "bad" parenting, antisocial learning, "weak" social bonds, neighborhood disorganization, and anomic societies are difficult to define and even harder to measure in isolation from one another. Moreover, even if we could define these concepts and isolate their individual influences, the policies suggested from such would require broad societal change that would likely not be in the interests of policy makers or welcomed by the general public. After all, what parents would like the state assessing their skills at rearing children? Further, to what standard should parents be held? Who wants the state to have a list of your friends, who should decide what friendships can or cannot exert control over your behavior, and which policy makers will want to tinker with a capitalist value system from which they most likely benefit? Once we operationalize the sociological concepts that contribute to crime and delineate the processes by which they occur, we will still be left with the task of ascribing values to these concepts, as "good" or "bad," "strong" or "weak," and it is doubtful there will be widespread consensus on who gets to ascribe these values or acceptance of what they are.

Scholars seldom spend time in their publications fully exploring the practical implications of their theory testing. The media rarely call on sociologists or criminologists to explain sensationalized crimes, and policy makers rarely ask us to testify about the social environment of sensational criminals. When public fear of crime is high, and demand for action is intense, few have the patience to listen to calls for changing our cultural value system, embracing policies that support parents, creating school policies to address deviant peers, or reducing the influence of patriarchy and capitalism on our value system. This has been evidenced time and again in policies passed to address terrorism, mass shootings, or serial sex crimes, because they inevitably include increased security measures and harsh punishments of individuals with no provisions to address family, peer, neighborhood, or state-level dysfunctions. Biological and psychological factors associated with crime are simply easier to identify and address than social causes. Until such time that people embrace the notion that the causes of crime are complex and they cannot be addressed overnight, it is likely that the policy implications of sociological theories will continue to be overlooked. This does not mean, however, that we should not identify them, highlight them in our publications, suggest them to policy makers, or introduce them to the general public. Sociological aspects of criminal behavior may never dominate crime control policies, but simply the mention of them may help people understand the complexities of criminal behavior and why crime control policies focused exclusively on individuals so often fail to prevent crime.

References

Adler, F. (1975). *Sisters in crime: The rise of the new female criminal*. New York, NY: McGraw-Hill.

Agnew, R. (1985). A revised strain theory of delinquency. *Social Forces, 64*, 151–167.

Agnew, R. (1992). Foundation of a general strain theory of crime and delinquency. *Criminology, 30*, 47–87.

Agnew, R. (2001). Building on the foundation of general strain theory: Specifying the types of strain most likely to lead to crime and delinquency. *Journal of Research in Crime and Delinquency, 38*, 319–361.

Akers, R. L. (1985). *Deviant behavior: A social learning approach*. Belmont, CA: Wadsworth.

Anderson, E. (1999). *Code of the street*. New York, NY: W. W. Norton.

Bandura, A. (1986). *Social foundations of thought and action: A social cognition theory*. Englewood Cliffs, NJ: Prentice Hall.

Bandura, A. (1990). Selective activation and disengagement of moral control. *Journal of Social Issues, 46*, 27–46.

Beccaria, C. (1963). *On crimes and punishments* (H. Paolucci, Trans). Indianapolis, IN: Bobbs-Merrill. (Original work published 1764)

Becker, H. S. (1963). *Outsiders: Studies in the sociology of deviance*. New York, NY: Free Press.

Bernard, T. J., Snipes, J. B., & Gerould, A. L. (2010). *Vold's theoretical criminology* (6th ed.). New York, NY: Oxford University Press.

Braithwaite, J. (1989). *Crime, shame and reintegration*. Cambridge, UK: Cambridge University Press.

Brownmiller, S. (1975). *Against our will: Men, women, and rape*. New York, NY: Simon and Schuster.

Burgess, R. L., & Akers, R. L. (1968). A differential association-reinforcement theory of criminal behavior. *Social Problems, 14*, 128–147.

Bursik, R. J., Jr. (1988). Social disorganization and theories of crime and delinquency. *Criminology, 26*, 519–551.

Bursik, R. J., Jr., & Grasmick, H. G. (1993). *Neighborhoods and crime: The dimensions of effective community control*. New York, NY: Lexington Books.

Cahn, S. E., & Cahn, J. C. (1964). The war on poverty: A civilian perspective. *The Yale Law Journal, 73*(8), 1327–1352.

Campbell, J. M. (1992). Parenting classes: Focus on discipline. *Journal of Community Health Nursing, 9*(4), 197-208.

Catalano, R. F., Berglund, M. L., Ryan, J. A. M., Lonczak, H. S., & Hawkins, J. D. (2004). Positive youth development in the United States: Research findings on evaluations of positive youth development programs. *Annals of the American Academy of Political and Social Science, 591*(1), 98–124.

Champion, D. J. (2001). *Juvenile justice system: Delinquency, processing, and the law* (3rd ed.). Upper Saddle River, NJ: Prentice Hall.

Chang, M., Park, B., & Kim, S. (2009). Parenting classes, parenting behavior, and child cognitive development in early Head Start: A longitudinal model. *School Community Journal, 19*(1), 155–174.

Chesney-Lind, M. (1989). Girls' crime and woman's place: Toward a feminist model of female delinquency. *Crime and Delinquency, 35*, 5–29.

Clarke, R. V. (1980). "Situational" crime prevention: Theory and practice. *British Journal of Criminology, 20*, 136–147.

Clarke, R. V. (1997). *Situational crime prevention: Successful case studies* (2nd ed.). Albany, NY: Harrow and Heston.

Cloward, R. A., & Ohlin, L. (1960). *Delinquency and opportunity: A theory of delinquent gangs*. New York, NY: Free Press.

Cohen, A. K. (1955). *Delinquent boys: The culture of the gang*. New York, NY: Free Press.

Cohen, L. E., & Felson, M. (1979). Social change and crime rate trends: A routine activity approach. *American Sociological Review, 44*, 588–607.

Cullen, F. T., & Agnew, R. (2011). *Criminological theory: Past to present* (4th ed.). New York: Oxford University Press.

Currie, E. (1997). Market, crime and community: Toward a mid-range theory of post-industrial violence. *Theoretical Criminology, 1*(2), pp. 147–172.

Daly, K., & Chesney-Lind, M. (1988). Feminism and criminology. *Justice Quarterly, 5*, 497–538.

Daro, D. A., & Harding, K. A. (1999). Healthy Families America: Using research to enhance practice. *Future of Children, 9*(1), 152–176.

DuBois, D. L., Holloway, B. E., Valentine, J. C., & Cooper, H. (2002). Effectiveness of mentoring programs for youth: A meta-analytic review. *American Journal of Community Psychology, 30*(2), 157–197.

DuBois, D. L., & Silverthorn, N. (2005). Natural mentoring relationships and adolescent health: Evidence from a national study. *American Journal of Public Health, 95*(3), 518-524.

Durkheim, É. (1893). *The division of labour in society*. New York, NY: Free Press

Ericson, N. (2001). *Healthy Families America fact sheet: Office of Juvenile Justice and Delinquency Prevention*. Washington, DC: U.S. Department of Justice.

Felson, M. (1995). Those who discourage crime. *Crime and Place, 4*, 53–66.

Garland, D. (2001). *The culture of control: Crime and social order in contemporary society*. Chicago, IL: University of Chicago Press.

Gottfredson, M. R., & Hirschi, T. (1990). *A general theory of crime*. Stanford, CA: Stanford University Press.

Greenstone, D., & Peterson, P. E. (1976). *Race and authority in urban politics: Community relations and the war on poverty*. Chicago: University of Chicago Press.

Harding, K., Galano, J., Martin, J., Huntington, L., & Schellenbach, C. J. (2007). Healthy Families America effectiveness: A comprehensive review of outcomes. *Journal of Prevention and Intervention in the Community, 34*(1-2), 149-179.

Haynie, D. L. (2002). Friendship networks and delinquency: The relative nature of peer delinquency. *Journal of Quantitative Criminology, 18*(2), 99–134.

Haynie, D. L., & Osgood, D. W. (2005). Reconsidering peers and delinquency: How do peers matter? *Social Forces, 84*(2), pp. 1109–1130.

Hirschi, T. (1969). *Causes of delinquency*. Berkeley: University of California Press.

Jarvis, J., Graham, S., Hamilton, P., & Tyler, D. (2004). The role of parenting classes for young fathers in prison: A case study. *Probation Journal, 51*(1), 21-33.

Kornhauser, R.R. (1978). *Social sources of delinquency: An appraisal of analytic models*. Chicago, IL: University of Chicago Press.

Kubrin, C. E., & Weitzer, R. (2003). New directions in social disorganization theory. *Journal of Research in Crime and Delinquency, 40*(4), 374–402.

Lanier, M. M., & Henry, S. (2004). *Essential criminology* (2nd ed.). Boulder, CO: Westview.

Lemert, E. M. (1951). *Social pathology: A systematic approach to the theory of sociopathic behavior*. New York, NY: McGraw-Hill.

Leyton, E. (2001). *Hunting humans: The rise of the modern multiple murderer*. New York, NY: Carroll & Graf.

Lilly, J. R., Cullen, F. T., & Ball, R. A. (2011). *Criminological theory: Context and consequences* (5th Ed.). Thousand Oaks, CA: Sage.

Madensen, T. D., & Eck, J. E. (2008). Violence in bars: Exploring the impact of place manager decision-making. *Crime Prevention and Community Safety, 10*, 111-125.

Merton, R. K. (1968). *Social theory and social structure*. New York, NY: Free Press.

Messerschmidt, J. W. (1993). *Masculinities and crime: Critique and reconceptualization of theory*. Lanham, MD: Rowman & Littlefield.

Messner, S. F., & Rosenfeld, R. (1994). *Crime and the American Dream*. Belmont, CA: Wadsworth.

Miller, W. B. (1958). Lower class culture as a generating milieu of gang delinquency. *Journal of Social Issues, 14*, 5–19.

Morse, A., & Maxwell, G. (2001). *Restorative justice for juveniles: Conferencing, mediation & circles*. Portland, OR: Hart Publishing.

Orchard, L. (2007). Evaluating parenting classes held at a secondary school. *Research in Post-Compulsory Education, 12*(1), 91-105.

Osgood, D. W., & Weichselbaum, H. F. (1984). Juvenile diversion: When practice matches theory. *Journal of Research in Crime and Delinquency, 21*(1), 33–56.

Quinney, R. (1970). *The social reality of crime*. Boston, MA: Little, Brown.

Quinney, R., & Wildeman, J. (1991). *The problem of crime: A peace and social justice perspective* (3rd ed.). London, UK: Mayfield.

Robinson, P. H. (2006). Restorative processes and doing justice. *University of St. Thomas Law Journal, 3*(3), 421–429.

Rose, D. R., & Clear, T. R. (1998). Incarceration, social capital, and crime: Implications for social disorganization theory. *Criminology, 36*(3), 441–480.

Sampson, R. J., & Groves, W. B. (1989). Community structure and crime: Testing social-disorganization theory. *American Journal of Sociology, 94*, 774–802.

Sampson, R. J., & Laub, J. H. (1993). *Crime in the making: Pathways and turning points through life*. Cambridge, MA: Harvard University Press.

Sampson, R. J., Raudenbush, S. W., & Earls, F. (1997). Neighborhoods and violent crime: A multilevel study of collective efficacy. *Science, 277*, 918–924.

Schaefer, T. (2010). Saving children or blaming parents? Lessons from mandated parenting classes. *Columbia Journal of Gender and Law, 19*(2), 491–537.

Shaw, C. R., & McKay, H. D. (1942). *Juvenile delinquency and urban areas*. Chicago, IL: University of Chicago Press.

Sherman, L. W., & Strang, H. (2007). *Restorative justice: The evidence*. London, UK: The Smith Institute.

Simon, R. J. (1975). *Women and crime*. Lexington, MA: Lexington Books.

Solomon, A. L., Kachnowski, V., & Bhati, A. (2005). *Does parole work: Analyzing the impact of postprison supervision on rearrest outcomes*. Washington, DC: Urban Institute.

Sutherland, E. H. (1947). Differential association theory. In F. P. Williams III & M. D. McShane (Eds.), *Criminology theory: Selected readings* (pp. 54–59). Saddle River, NJ: Pearson Education.

Sykes, G. M., & Matza, D. (1957). Techniques of neutralization. *American Sociological Review, 22*, 664–670.

Tannenbaum, F. (1938). *Crime and the community*. Boston, MA: Ginn.

Turk, A. T. (1969). *Criminality and the legal order*. Chicago, IL: Rand McNally.

Van Ness, D. W., & Strong, K. H. (2010). *Restoring justice: An introduction to restorative justice* (4th ed.). Cincinnati, OH: Matthew Bender.

Weerman, F. M. (2011). Delinquent peers in context: A longitudinal network analysis of selection and influence effects. *Criminology, 49*(1), 253–286.

Wilson, J. Q., & Kelling, G. (1982). The police and neighborhood safety: Broken windows. *Atlantic Monthly, 127*, 29–38.

Wizner, S., & Keller, M.F. (1977). The penal model of juvenile justice: Is juvenile court delinquency jurisdiction obsolete? *Juvenile Justice Standards, 52*(5), 1120–1135.

Wolfgang, M. E., & Ferracuti, F. (1982). *The subculture of violence: Towards an integrated theory in criminology*. Beverly Hills, CA: Sage.

Wright, A. N. (2007). *Civil rights, "unfinished business": Poverty, race, and the 1968 Poor People's Campaign*. Ann Arbor, MI: ProQuest Information and Learning Company.

26

Policy Implications of Biosocial Criminology

Crime Prevention and Offender Rehabilitation

Michael Rocque
Maine Department of Corrections

Brandon C. Welsh
Northeastern University

Adrian Raine
University of Pennsylvania

Introduction

A long-standing concern that many sociological criminologists have had with biological or biosocial theories has centered on the policy implications of this perspective. This is understandable given the history of criminology, which emerged from relatively undeveloped (and biased) biological understandings of behavior.

The misunderstanding of the role biology plays with respect to crime and other maladaptive behaviors, along with a strong dose of racism, led to policy implications that are considered unethical and morally repugnant by today's standards. In the late 19th and early 20th century, biological crime prevention emphasized the use of eugenics. For example, physician Charles V. Carrington (1909) wrote: "[n]o single measure for the prevention of crime would be more far-reaching in its deterrent effects, first, and prevention effects, second, than a law which provided for the sterilization of certain classes of criminals. Stop the breed is the whole proposition" (p. 129). Similar sentiments were echoed by crime researchers into the 1940s, when the use of eugenic arguments to justify Nazi atrocities served to turn the tide away from biology and crime prevention (Rafter, 1998, 2008a, 2008b; Vaske, Galyean, & Cullen, 2011).

In recent years, a new "biosocial" criminology has emerged that has attempted to understand human behavior as a construct of biological and social influences. Nonetheless, due in large part to the historical legacy of the biological theories and their implications, sociologically oriented criminologists have not warmed to this line of work. However, we agree with Wright et al.'s (2008) assessment that political ideology and "miseducation" have also contributed to the resistance of some criminologists to the biosocial view. Critics continue to speak of biological "determinism" (Rose, 2000). Popular criminological theory texts still discuss the implications of biological theories by beginning with medical treatments and notions that these theories suggest individuals "cannot be rehabilitated" (Akers & Sellers, 2009, p. 67). The policy implications of biosocial criminology remain perhaps the most important hurdle for its proponents. What, for example, can we do with the finding that low IQ is associated with crime? Isn't IQ a "fixed, immutable" trait? As one of us has argued, however, "[o]ne of the biggest and widely held myths in criminology research is that biology is destiny" (Raine, 2002, p. 71). We know this not to be the case; in fact, research has shown that even IQ—long thought to be fixed after childhood—changes substantially over time (Ramsden et al., 2011).

The purpose of this chapter is to discuss the policy implications of a biosocial approach to crime in a more balanced fashion than hitherto. We first discuss the general perspective that biosocial criminology takes toward the origins of criminal behavior. Next, we describe three major strategies of preventing and treating criminal offending from a biosocial perspective. The chapter ends with a discussion and some conclusions.

Overview of Biological Risk Factors

The recent emergence of scientifically rigorous work demonstrating the role of biology in behavior has pointed to a number of risk factors that increase the likelihood of criminal/antisocial acts (see Raine, 2002; Rocque, Welsh, & Raine, 2012; Walsh & Beaver, 2009). These risk factors center on four main areas: (1) genetics, (2) hormones, (3) physiology, and (4) cognitive development.

Perhaps the most controversial topic in biosocial criminology is the notion that crime is "inherited." Biological criminology has its roots in heredity as an explanation for criminality (e.g., Dugdale, 1877). However, this work was not informed by modern understandings of genetics and how genes influence behavior. We know that there is no "gene for crime," but genetic factors may increase the likelihood that individuals respond differently to environmental risk factors to crime. Evidence from twin studies, adoption studies, and adoptive twin studies all suggest there is something that is inherited that increases the risk of crime (Raine, 2013). Further, more recent work examining specific genetic correlates of crime, referred to as *molecular genetic studies* (Baker, Bezdjian, & Raine, 2006), has identified specific genes, such as the dopamine transporter gene (DAT1) and the dopamine D2 receptor gene (DRD2) (Beaver et al., 2007; Beaver, DeLisi, Vaughn, & Wright, 2010; Walsh & Beaver, 2009).

Other biosocial research has also indicated that particular physiological factors are related to an increased risk of criminal/antisocial behavior. This work has focused on the effect of abnormalities in the autonomic nervous system on behavior (Eysenck, 1964). Research has shown that those with low resting heart rate tend to have higher rates of risk taking and antisocial behavior (Farrington, 1997; Raine, 2002; Raine, Venables, & Mednick, 1997). Low resting heart rate has been hypothesized to be related to crime for a number of reasons, including an indication of "fearlessness" and underarousal (Raine & Portnoy, 2012). Electroencephalogram research, measuring electric activity of the brain, also shows underarousal for those engaged in crime (Hare, 1993; Lorber, 2004; Raine, 1996, 2002). These findings are generally attributed to the idea that people who take risks are often "underaroused" and seek stimulation at higher levels than others. That is, low arousal leads to fearlessness (Raine, 2002) or difficulty learning from negative consequences (Eysenck, 1964).

Finally, a wealth of neurological research has extended our knowledge on risk factors for criminal behavior. Due to recent advances in technology, researchers no longer have to guess at which areas of the brain are responsible for different functions. Thus, the age-old criticisms of phrenology—a favorite of biosocial critics—are no longer relevant. This work has shown that prefrontal and temporal lobe deficits characterize those who are most violent and have psychopathic tendencies (Raine, 2002). In an early study using PET technology to examine prefrontal cortex functioning for 22 serious offenders, Raine et al., Stanley, Lottenberg, Abel, & Stoddard (1994) compared violent offenders who pled not guilty by reason of insanity (NGBI) to a community comparison group ($N = 22$), matched on the basis of age and sex. They found significant differences across the two groups with respect to lateral and medial prefrontal cortex functioning, with the violent individuals demonstrating lower glucose levels in these regions (see also Raine, Buchsbaum, & Lacasse, 1997). Since this earlier work, a large number of studies using imaging technology have been carried out to examine brain abnormalities associated with violence. Yang and Raine (2009) meta-analyzed the results of 43 studies that used functional and structural imaging technology to examine antisocial and psychopathic individuals. Their findings indicated that brain impairment, generally localized to the right orbitofrontal cortex, right anterior cingulate cortex, and left dorsolateral prefrontal cortex, differentiated antisocial from "normal" individuals.

Healthy cognitive development is an essential protective factor against antisocial behavior. Several well-known correlates of crime, such as irritability, impulsivity, and neuropsychological, deficits are related to cognitive development, especially early in life (Rocque et al., 2012). Many factors seem to be related to healthy cognitive development, including physical activity and nutrition. Researchers have recently begun to recognize that cognitive or neurological development does not end in childhood, but extends throughout adolescence into early adulthood. This research on "brain maturation" indicates that changes in brain functioning contributes to elevated levels of risk taking in adolescence and to a decrease in such behavior by early adulthood (Giedd et al., 1999; Steinberg, 2008, 2010).

It is important to point out that the results of this biosocial work indicate that the body does indeed matter with respect to crime (Wright et al., 2008). Just as important regarding prevention and treatment or rehabilitation is that no serious biocriminologist argues that biological factors operate in a vacuum. In fact, the term *biosocial* indicates that this body of work is concerned not only with direct effects but also with the *interaction* between biological and social risk factors. Thus, prevention and treatment approaches can work to decrease crime from a biosocial perspective by focusing on "the psychosocial half of the biosocial equation" (Raine, 2002, p. 71), or by attempting to manipulate biological risk factors.

Early Developmental Crime Prevention

The developmental perspective holds that criminal offending in adolescence and adulthood is influenced by "behavioral and attitudinal patterns that have been learned during an individual's development" (Tremblay & Craig, 1995, p. 151). Early environmental factors and interaction are widely recognized as being crucial for healthy biological development. In fact, a new policy statement by the American Association of Pediatrics states that early adversity in life can lead to severe impediments to healthy brain development (see also Doyle, Harmon, Heckman, & Tremblay, 2009). Much of the work in this area has shown that intervening early (even before birth) can have positive effects on later development, cognitive functioning, and, consequently, reduced levels of criminal behavior.

HEALTH AND NUTRITION

Proper health and nutrition is recognized as an important factor in promoting normal development (Brown & Pollitt, 1996; Morley & Lucas, 1997; World Health Organization, 2000). Given this link, it follows that good nutrition early in life is related to later behavior. Several early developmental prevention programs incorporate nutrition (see Farrington & Welsh, 2007). A number of recent studies have also examined the contemporaneous effect of nutritional supplements—such as fish oil—on behavior. This work focuses on docosahexaenic acid (DHA) and eicosapentaenoic acid (EPA), which have been demonstrated to have a positive effect on neurite outgrowth and consequently, better cognitive functioning (Liu, Raine, Venebles, & Mednick, 2006; Raine, Rocque, & Welsh, 2013).

Using a variety of samples, several randomized controlled studies have shown that groups receiving fish oil supplements reduce aggression and anger compared to controls not receiving fish oil (Buydens-Branchey, Branchey, & Hibbeln, 2008; Gesch, Hammond, Hampson, Eves, & Crowder, 2002; Hallahan, Hibbeln, Davis, & Garland, 2007; Zaalberg, Nijman, Bulten, Stroosma, & van der Staak, 2010). In one example using an adult prisoner sample ($N = 211$), Gesch et al. (2002) found that a nutritional supplement including fish oil resulted in a significant reduction in antisocial acts. Importantly, Raine et al. (2013) argued that fish oil supplements have been shown to be most effective for "at-risk" samples, which may make it a more appropriate strategy for secondary prevention (reviewed below).

Related to cognitive or neurological deficits, researchers have found a relationship between mental health and antisocial behavior (De Coster & Heimer, 2001; Fazel, Gulati, Linsell, Geddes, & Grann, 2009). Certain programs have addressed serious mental illness, and reviews have shown that they can be effective in preventing such disorders. Cuijpers, Van Straten, and Smit (2005) meta-analyzed 13 studies related to preventing a range of disorders, including psychosis and anxiety. They found a combined relative risk of .73, which suggests the programs have the potential to prevent the onset of illnesses.

Programs that prevent mental illness should logically also prevent the onset of antisocial behavior. In a study by Raine, Liu, Venables, and Mednick (2003), 100 children (age 3) were given an "environmental enrichment" program in which nursery school teachers attempted to improve the health, physical activity, and education of the participants. The program lasted a total of 2 years. Compared to a "community control group," the intervention youth at age 17 had fewer behavioral problems and fewer signs of schizotypal personality. The authors noted that "it is conceivable that exercise by itself could account for a significant proportion of the observed effects. Exercise in animals is known to increase mRNA in the hippocampus and to have other beneficial effects on brain structure and function" (Raine et al., 2003, p. 1632). This finding has clear implications for crime prevention through a developmental approach. It seems evident that physical and nutritional health is important in reducing antisocial behavior.

HOME VISITATION PROGRAMS

Certain early intervention programs are based on the premise that providing assistance to new or expecting mothers, often in the form of visiting health nurses, can promote healthy development. These programs generally target parenting skills and other behaviors that improve the bond between the child and parent. Reviews of home visitation programs generally demonstrate a positive impact on child development (see Farrington & Welsh, 2007; Piquero, Farrington, Welsh, Tremblay, & Jennings, 2009; Tremblay & Craig, 1995; Tremblay & Japel, 2003). One way that home visitation programs may impact criminal behavior is through the prevention of neuropsychological or cognitive deficits along with a host of other risk factors (e.g., impulsivity, school failure). For example, teaching mothers to avoid the hazards of smoking or ingesting narcotics during pregnancy can reduce neuropsychological impairment of the infant (Beaver et al., 2010).

The Nurse-Family Partnership (NFP) program, created by David Olds in the 1970s and first tested in the 1980s in Elmira, New York, is one of the most widely known home visitation programs. The program has now been rolled out to many regions of the United States, including 400 counties and 32 separate states. It is becoming such an important program in the United States that a national office has been created to coordinate dissemination efforts.

In the original evaluation, Olds et al. (1998) enrolled women in their second trimester who were at risk for having children with developmental and/or behavioral problems (e.g., teenage mother, unmarried, or poor). The study randomly assigned women to either the treatment group or a control group. The program, which lasted for 2 years, brought nurses into the women's home to teach them about the benefits of healthy nutrition and proper childcare techniques. These techniques were meant to ensure proper physical (e.g., biological) development of the child/youth. Home visits occurred roughly 2 times a month during the course of treatment.

Olds, Henderson, Chamberlin, and Tatelbaum (1986) found that the children who had been assigned to the treatment group fared much better than those in the control group. For example, there were significantly fewer instances of child abuse or neglect (4% vs. 19%). A 15-year follow-up of the original families (Olds et al., 1998) showed that the children (now age 15) who received the program had significantly fewer arrests than the control group. These results were attributed to better overall development and improved environment, which the program helped create. For example, follow-ups of the women after the program showed that they were less likely to have engaged in child abuse and neglect (29% vs. 54%)—which are known to impede healthy child development (Olds et al., 1986; Olds et al., 1997). Further, studies have shown that children receiving the program have demonstrated "better language development" compared to untreated youth (Goodman, 2006, p. 14). This is indirect evidence that NFP may help prevent cognitive/neuropsychological deficits. Evaluations of the programs in other regions of the United States have similarly shown positive results long-term (Olds et al., 2007). However, in the most recent follow-up of the original Elmira sample (Eckenrode et al., 2010), results indicated that while treatment girls were still showing positive effects of treatment, the same was not true for boys. It is possible that the program effects are not as long lasting for boys as for girls.

Other home visitation programs that attempt to improve parenting skills begin antenatal—that is, after the child is born (Doyle et al., 2009; Farrington, 2003). Few programs begin with a crime prevention goal, however. For example, in a comprehensive review of 40 parenting programs, Tremblay and Japel (2003) found that many of these programs do not directly attempt to reduce antisocial behavior (or at least that is not their stated goal), but rather explicitly focus on the prevention of cognitive deficits through the strengthening of cognitive skills. These programs often show positive effects on later adjustment and behavior. This provides evidence of the important mechanisms linking biological or cognitive development and crime prevention. Other programs target what Tremblay and Craig (1995; see also Tremblay & Japel, 2003) term *socially disruptive behaviors*, including impulsivity and hyperactivity. The results of these programs have been mostly positive.

SCHOOL-BASED PROGRAMS

Certain primary prevention programs aim to intervene with children in school settings. These programs attempt to prevent the emergence of antisocial behavior among youth in high-risk settings (e.g., family poverty). Often, these programs attempt to address traditional "biological" characteristics, once thought to be fixed (e.g., intelligence, personality factors). Perhaps the best-known school-based program is the Perry Preschool Project, conducted in 1962 (Schweinhart & Weikart, 1997). This program recruited 123 low-income African American youth in Ypsilanti, Michigan, and through approximate random assignment provided preschool services to 58 of them. The intervention consisted of a program conducted at preschool supplemented with home visits (at age 3) meant to increase intellectual abilities and cognitive skills. The "plan-do-review" style program focused on intellectual enrichment to improve school outcomes. The results of several evaluations have consistently shown strong evidence that the program reduced delinquency/criminal behavior—from ages 13 to 40. For example, Schweinhart et al. (2005) in the latest follow-up at age 40 found that the treatment group compared to the control group had significantly fewer arrests (36% vs. 55% were arrested 5 or more times), higher levels of both school achievement and employment, and larger annual salaries.

Another school-based program that sought to tackle biological risk factors was the Johns Hopkins Research Center Project (Dolan et al., 1993). The program recruited children before individual risk factors emerged and used two basic interventions (the "good behavior game" and "mastery learning") to promote cognition and control of behavior. The results showed a positive impact on reading ability and depression. The program also reduced aggression but only for selected groups (Tremblay & Craig, 1995).

Finally, Second Step is a program that aims to reduce violence by teaching youth skills such as how to restrain immediate responses to provocations, how to effectively problem solve, and avoid aggression (Taub, 2001). The program has been designed for children as young as preschool. Results thus far have indicated that the program is effective in reducing aggression in schools as well as improving social competence (Institute of Education Science, 2008; Taub, 2001). Thus, the literature strongly suggests that school programs can have a positive impact on cognitive development, as well as improving problem behavior.

Interventions With At-Risk Children and Youth

Secondary crime prevention focuses on children and youth who have already evidenced risk factors for later delinquency (including antisocial behavior). These programs take place in a variety of settings, including the home, school, and clinics. Several secondary crime prevention programs are classified as parenting programs, and they often follow the same steps as those reviewed above. The difference between primary and secondary parenting programs is that the former are implemented prior to the emergence of childhood risk factors (e.g., behavioral problems). The studies we review below focus on addressing the environment to promote healthy biological development. They often target youth who have evinced what are thought to be biological risk factors (e.g., low birth weight, cognitive deficits, impulsivity).

CHILD-CENTERED PROGRAMS

Some programs target youth with nonbehavioral risk factors such as poor health. For example, the Infant Health and Development Program (Brooks-Gunn, Klebanov, Liaw, & Spiker, 1993) was developed to assist families with low birth weight children (a prominent biological risk factor for later crime and poorer overall outcomes—see McGloin, Pratt, & Piquero, 2006). This program provided child and parenting education as well as free medical and developmental services up to the third year of the child's life. The medical services included pediatric care as needed to ensure healthy development. Of the 1,028 infants enrolled, two groups were created, one comprising very low birth weight (< 2,000 grams) and one comprising those weighing slightly more (> 2,000 grams). Within each of these two groups, 33% were randomly assigned to the intervention and 77% to the control group (Brooks-Gunn & McCormick, 2009). Early evaluations showed that the program improved cognitive function and reduced problem behaviors (Brooks-Gunn et al., 1993; McCormick et al., 2006). Continued follow-ups, however, have suggested that the effect of the intervention may not have been long lasting (McCormick et al., 2006). This may point to the need for continued intervention throughout childhood rather than ending it in the toddler stage.

Another individual-centered program, titled Incredible Years, sought to intervene with children who had demonstrated conduct disorder or oppositional defiance disorder. These are traditionally thought of as psychological correlates with biological underpinnings. This program has been identified as a Blueprints program by the U.S. Office of Juvenile Justice and Delinquency Prevention. This indicates that there is strong evidence that the program is effective. While the program includes a parenting and teacher training component, it focuses on helping the child control his or her emotions and develop healthy relationships (Webster-Stratton & Reid, 2010). Several evaluations of the program indicate that it has a positive effect on the child's behavior, with some evaluations indicating a reduction of conduct disorder to subclinical levels (Reid, Webster-Stratton, & Hammond, 2003; Webster-Stratton, Kolpacoff, & Hollinsworth, 1988).

Certain prevention programs have taken place within clinical settings. Kendall, Reber, McLeer, Epps, and Ronan (1990) evaluated a program for conduct disordered children (age 10) in a psychiatric hospital. Children with this disorder are typically impulsive and hyperactive, risk factors thought to be biologically influenced (Rocque et al., 2012). Research suggests that intervening early in the lives of such children can prevent later serious delinquency or crime (Kendall et al., 1990). The program evaluated by Kendall et al. was based on cognitive behavioral therapy, used individual sessions to teach coping and problem-solving skills, and reinforced good behavior. This program was compared to a psychotherapy treatment. The results demonstrated slight improvements in behavior and impulsivity (see also Tremblay & Craig, 1995) attributed to the cognitive behavioral therapy program. Other programs designed for children referred to clinics for treatment have shown positive impacts on later behavior (see, for example, Scott, Spender, Doolan, Jacobs, & Aspland, 2001, who utilized the Webster-Stratton parenting video intervention).

PARENTING PROGRAMS

Parent management programs (Farrington & Welsh, 2007) sometimes begin after the emergence of antisocial behavior or conduct problems. These programs not only help reduce the *emergence* of biological risk factors for crime (e.g., cognitive deficits) but also attempt to interrupt the link between biological risk factors already present and later crime. For example, Kazdin (1997) states that parent management training programs seek to offer "treatment procedures in which parents are trained to alter their child's behavior at home" (p. 1349). Such programs target parents of children who have demonstrated risk factors for antisocial or delinquent behavior. Sometimes, these risk factors include delinquency itself. However, because the programs take place before the youth have become involved in the justice system, they qualify as secondary. The Incredible Years program, mentioned above, includes a parenting component delivered via video or in the home.

A prominent example of a secondary parenting program includes the work of Gerald Patterson at the Oregon Social Learning Center. Patterson's program targets families of children with risk factors for delinquency. This program teaches parents to better supervise and reinforce behavior so that the child learns to regulate his or her own conduct. Evaluations of the program over time have demonstrated that it reduces the risk of delinquency and criminal behavior. For example, Patterson, Chamberlain, and Reid (1982) conducted a study that randomly assigned a small number of families with children identified as aggressive (e.g., displayed temper tantrums, hitting, etc.) to either parenting training or a wait list control group. The results showed a significant impact on child antisocial behavior after completion of the parenting program. In general, the literature suggests that parenting/family programs for youth with biological or psychological risk factors can positively affect child behavior (see Farrington, 2007; Tremblay & Japel, 2003).

SCHOOL-BASED PROGRAMS

Several programs set within the school setting have been developed for youths for whom biological risk factors have already emerged. Conrod, Castellanos-Ryan and Strang (2010) reported on the results of a coping skills program targeting 13- to 16-year-olds identified as having personality traits such as impulsivity or sensation seeking. The study randomly assigned 732 students from 24 schools to treatment and control conditions. The program, which consisted of two 90-minute therapy sessions, showed positive results. Specifically, the treatment group experienced a reduction in problem behaviors such as drug use compared to their control group participants.

Shure and Spivack (1982) evaluated the Interpersonal Problem-Solving Intervention, a program designed to prevent the development of impulsivity and problem behavior. While one of the goals of the program was to prevent the emergence of impulsivity, it also targeted youths who had already been rated as impulsive. The intervention, implemented by teachers, was comprised of games, problem-solving lessons, and role-playing strategies. One-hundred and thirteen disadvantaged African American youth (ages 3 to 4) were given the treatment and compared to 106 control youth, though in a nonrandom fashion. The program, which took place over 2 years (from nursery school/daycare into kindergarten), demonstrated a positive impact on biological or biologically influenced factors such as IQ, behavior, and impulsivity. For example, at the end of the program, between 77% and 85% of the program children were rated as "adjusted" compared to just 30% of the controls.

In sum, individual, parenting, and school-based secondary prevention programs have shown significant promise in reducing antisocial behavior. Many of these programs target individuals with identified biological risk factors or operate by improving such factors (e.g., cognitive deficits). It seems reasonable to suggest that these programs indirectly affect antisocial behavior through these biological risk factors. For example, many of the programs noted above sought to strengthen problem-solving and interpersonal skills. These skills are essential in interacting, coping, and adjusting in today's world. Further, the programs address biological risk factors in a way that targets the environment, thus illustrating how a biosocial perspective informs policy without radically altering physiological characteristics.

Offender Rehabilitation

COGNITIVE BEHAVIORAL THERAPY

Perhaps the most broadly supported approach to offender rehabilitation is cognitive behavioral therapy (Andrews & Bonta, 2010). Cognitive behavioral therapy (CBT) emerged from the work of Beck (1963) and is a combination of cognitive and behavioral approaches. The basic idea is that changing attitudes or cognitions can be paired with changes in behavior (Milkman & Wanberg, 2007). CBT attempts to reinforce positive behavior and teach offenders how to recognize environments in which they are likely to be tempted to engage in antisocial acts (Vaske et al., 2011). Comprehensive reviews of CBT have indicated a substantial (22%) reduction in future criminal behavior and that the strategy is equally effective for juveniles as for adults (Landenberger & Lipsey, 2005).

Typically, CBT is seen as a psychological rather than biosocial approach. However, Vaske et al. (2011) argue that many of the cognitive functions that CBT targets (such as impulsivity, self-control, perspective, and agreeableness) have neurological underpinnings. It may be that CBT works to alter neurological functioning, thus enabling offenders to change their behavior. They suggest that "cognitive behavioral therapies for mental disorders may improve functioning in the frontal cortex, parietal cortex, cingulate cortex, hippocampus, and cerebellum" (Vaske et al., 2011, p. 96). Thus, CBT for offenders may have similar effects.

Casey, Day, Vess, and Ward (2013) agree with this assessment. In particular, they suggest that a variant of CBT, called dialectical behavior therapy (DBT), which was initially developed for those with borderline personality disorder, has the potential to be effective for offender rehabilitation. They argue that this may be due to DBT's focus on biologically based personality traits related to crime (e.g., impulsivity, aggression, temper, etc.). Finally, sexual offenders, a population widely thought to be affected by biological risk factors, respond best to CBT (Wormith et al., 2007). It seems clear that CBT has been demonstrated to address rehabilitation in a biosocially informed manner.

DRUG TREATMENT

Additionally, it has been well recognized that drug use and abuse plays a major role in a significant portion of offenses. Research has shown that roughly one third of state and federal prisoners were under the influence of drugs when they committed the offense for which they are incarcerated (Mumola & Karberg, 2006). Addiction to substances such as drugs or alcohol is a disorder that affects and is affected by the neurobiology of the brain (A. Goldstein, 2001). Neurological researchers posit that the process of moving from drug using to drug addiction takes place within the prefrontal cortex and striatum areas of the brain (Everitt & Robbins, 2005) and involves a change in brain functioning (Koob & Le Moal, 2005).

Perhaps not surprisingly, given the link between CBT and drug treatment (Magill & Ray, 2009), research has shown that drug treatment in an offender rehabilitation setting can be effective, not only in reducing drug use/dependence but also future offending. Studies of drug (or other substance) treatment for offenders have shown mixed results, ranging from modestly to highly effective. A systematic review conducted by the Campbell Collaboration (Mitchell, Wilson, & MacKenzie, 2012) found over 70 independent evaluations of drug treatment in prisons. The overall results indicated that incarceration-based drug treatment reduced the odds of future offending, and the effect was stronger for programs considered "therapeutic communities." A systematic review performed by Egli, Pina, Skovbo Christensen, Aebi, and Killias (2009) found that programs addressing drug use by replacement therapy (e.g., methadone) have the potential to significantly reduce future crime. Finally, drug treatment courts represent an alternative sanctioning approach that allows offenders to avoid criminal courts with successful completion of treatment. Randomized studies (see, e.g., Gottfredson, Najaka, & Kearley, 2003) as well as meta-analyses of rigorous evaluations suggest this strategy reduces future criminal offending (Mitchell, Wilson, Eggers, & MacKenzie, 2012).

PHYSICAL HEALTH

Few offender rehabilitation programs appear to target physical health as a risk factor for crime. One interesting and innovative program in the United Kingdom, called "Healthy Children, Safer Communities," improves physical health as a way to reduce antisocial acts (National Health Service, 2009). Specifically, the program seeks to ensure that youth who have come in contact with the justice system are given all the resources necessary to improve and maintain their health and well-being. Recent research is discovering strong links between offending and poor health over the life course (Piquero, Daigle, Gibson, Piquero, & Tibbetts, 2007; Piquero, Farrington, Nagin, & Moffitt, 2010). However, whether physical health is a direct risk factor for crime is not well established in the literature. Those involved in the U.K. program argue that improving physical health may also indirectly decrease problem behavior, perhaps through psychological mechanisms, such as self-esteem.

Discussion and Conclusions

The early critiques of biologically oriented crime control policies were not ill-conceived. Indeed, the lessons learned from the "misuse" of science to discriminate and perform atrocities against less powerful groups still serve as a warning that making the connection between biology and behavior can be a slippery slope (Rafter, 2008b; Rose, 2000). However, as we have made an effort to show in this chapter, the biosocial approaches in criminology are no longer born of prejudice or racism, but rather objective, value-free science (see Cullen, 2009; Rocque et al., 2012). In fact, advances in the biological sciences have exploded in the last 10 to 15 years, prompting some to argue that "the biological sciences have made more progress in advancing our understanding about behavior in the past 10 years than sociology has made in the past 50 years" (Robinson, 2004, p. 4) and that the 1990s was the "decade of the brain" (M. Goldstein, 1994).

Despite this history of antagonism between the sociological and biologically oriented criminologists, the new trend is toward a *biosocial* perspective, which recognizes that biology does not operate in a vacuum. Rather, human development (and behavior) involves the body and the environment. Consequently, the policy implications emerging from this perspective do as much, if not more, to change the environment of those at risk as they do to change biology (Raine, 2002). The examples from crime prevention and offender rehabilitation that we have detailed above demonstrate that the policy implications from biosocial criminology are amenable to sociological criminology. Further, the prevention strategies that align with biosocial criminology are among the most effective in reducing future offending.

Our aim in this chapter was not to show that the policy implications from a biosocial perspective are sufficient to declare a "winner" in the nature versus nurture debate. Rather, it was to demonstrate the compatibility between biosocial and social criminology. Blind allegiance to one side or the other is likely to stall scientific advancement, whereas a recognition of the validity of social and biological perspectives will help further our understanding of the causes of criminal offending—and the best methods to prevent it.

References

Akers, R. L., & Sellers, C. S. (2009). *Criminological theories: Introduction, evaluation, and application*. Los Angeles, CA: Roxbury.

Andrews, D. A., & Bonta, J. (2010). *The psychology of criminal conduct* (5th ed.). New Providence, NJ: Matthew Bender.

Baker, L. A., Bezdjian, S., & Raine, A. (2006). Behavioral genetics: The science of antisocial behavior. *Law and Contemporary Problems, 69*(1–2), 7–26.

Beaver, K. M., DeLisi, M., Vaughn, M. G., & Wright, J. P. (2010). The intersection of genes and neuropsychological deficits in the prediction of adolescent delinquency and low self-control. *International Journal of Offender Therapy and Comparative Criminology, 54*(1), 22–42.

Beaver, K. M., Wright, J. P., DeLisi, M., Walsh, A., Vaughn, M. G., Boisvert, D., & Vaske, J. (2007). A gene × gene interaction between DRD2 and DRD4 is associated with conduct disorder and antisocial behavior in males. *Behavioral and Brain Functions, 3*(30). doi:10.1186/1744-9081-3-30

Beck, A. T. (1963). Thinking and depression: I. Idiosyncratic content and cognitive distortions. *Archives of General Psychiatry, 9*(4), 324–333.

Brooks-Gunn, J., Klebanov, P. K., Liaw, F., & Spiker, D. (1993). Enhancing the development of low-birthweight, premature infants: Changes in cognition and behavior over the first three years. *Child Development, 64*(3), 736–753.

Brooks-Gunn, J., & McCormick, M. (2009). *Infant health and development program*. Retrieved from http://www.promisingpractices.net/program.asp?programid=136

Brown, J. L., & Pollitt, E. (1996). Malnutrition, poverty, and intellectual development. *Scientific American, 274*(2), 38–43.

Buydens-Branchey, L., Branchey, M., & Hibbeln, J. R. (2008). Associations between increases in plasma n-3 polyunsaturated fatty acids following supplementation and decreases in anger and anxiety in substance abusers. *Progress in Neuro-Psychopharmacology & Biological Psychiatry, 32*(2), 568–575.

Carrington, C. (1909). *Sterilization of habitual criminals. Transactions of the Fortieth Annual Session of the Medical Society of Virginia*. Richmond, VA: Everett Waddey Company.

Casey, S., Day, A., Vess, J., & Ward, T. (2013). *Foundations of offender rehabilitation*. New York, NY: Routledge.

Conrod, P. J., Castellanos-Ryan, N., & Strang, J. (2010). Brief, personality-targeted coping skills interventions and survival as a non-drug user over a 2-year period during adolescence. *Archives of General Psychiatry, 67*(1), 85–93.

Cuijpers, P., Van Straten, A., & Smit, F. (2005). Preventing the incidence of new cases of mental disorders: A meta-analytic review. *Journal of Nervous and Mental Disease, 193*(2), 119–125.

Cullen, F. T. (2009). Preface. In A. Walsh & K. M. Beaver (Eds.), *Biosocial criminology: New directions in theory and research* (pp. xv–xvii). New York, NY: Routledge.

De Coster, S., & Heimer, K. (2001). The relationship between law violation and depression: An interactions analysis. *Criminology, 39*(4), 799–836.

Dolan, L. J., Kellam, S. G., Brown, C. H., Werthamer-Larsson, L., Rebok, G. W., & Mayer, L. S., . . . Turkkan, J. S. (1993). The short-term impact of two classroom-based preventive interventions on aggressive and shy behaviors and poor achievement. *Journal of Applied Developmental Psychology, 14*(3), 317–345.

Doyle, O., Harmon, C. P., Heckman, J. J., & Tremblay, R. E. (2009). Investing in early human development: Timing and economic efficiency. *Economics and Human Biology, 7*, 1–6.

Dugdale, R. L. (1877). *The Jukes: A study in crime, pauperism, disease, and heredity, also further studies of criminals* (5th ed.). New York, NY: G. P. Putnam's.

Eckenrode, J., Campa, M., Luckey, D. W., Henderson, C. R., Cole, R., Kitzman, H., . . . Olds, D. (2010). Long-term effects of prenatal and infancy nurse home visitation on the life course of youths: 19-year follow-up of a randomized trial. *Archives of Pediatrics and Adolescent Medicine, 164*(1), 9–15.

Egli, N., Pina, M., Skovbo Christensen, P., Aebi, M., & Killias, M. (2009). Effects of drug substitution programs on offending among drug-addicts. *Campbell Collaboration*. doi:10.4073/csr.2009.3

Everitt, B. J., & Robbins, T. W. (2005). Neural systems of reinforcement for drug addiction: From actions to habits to compulsion. *Nature Neuroscience, 8*(11), 1481–1489.

Eysenck, H. J. (1964). *Crime and personality*. London, UK: Routledge and Kegan Paul.

Farrington, D. P. (1997). The relationship between low resting heart rate and violence. In A. Raine, P. A. Brennan, D. Farrington, & S. A. Mednick (Eds.), *Biosocial bases of violence* (pp. 89–105). New York, NY: Plenum.

Farrington, D. P. (2003). Advancing knowledge about the early prevention of adult antisocial behavior. In D. P. Farrington & J. Coid (Eds.), *Early prevention of adult antisocial behavior*. Cambridge, UK: Cambridge University Press.

Farrington, D. P. (2007). Developmental criminology and risk-focused prevention. In M. Maguire, R. Morgan, & R. Reiner (Eds.), *The Oxford handbook of criminology* (Vol. 4, pp. 657–701). Oxford, UK: Oxford University Press.

Farrington, D. P., & Welsh, B. C. (2007). *Saving children from a life of crime: Early risk factors and effective interventions.* New York, NY: Oxford University Press.

Fazel, S., Gulati, G., Linsell, L., Geddes, J. R., & Grann, M. (2009). Schizophrenia and violence: Systematic review and meta-analysis. *PLoS Medicine, 6*(8), e1000120. doi:10.1371/journal.pmed.1000120

Gesch, C. B., Hammond, S. M., Hampson, S. E., Eves, A., & Crowder, M. J. (2002). Influence of supplementary vitamins, minerals and essential fatty acids on the antisocial behaviour of young adult prisoners: Randomised, placebo-controlled trial. *British Journal of Psychiatry, 181*, 22–28.

Giedd, J. N., Blumenthal, J., Jeffries, N. O., Castellanos, F. X., Liu, H., Zijdenbos, A., . . . Rapoport, J. L. (1999). Brain development during childhood and adolescence: A longitudinal MRI study. *Nature Neuroscience, 2*(10), 861–862.

Goldstein, A. (2001). *Addiction: From biology to drug policy.* New York, NY: Oxford University Press.

Goldstein, M. (1994). Decade of the brain: An agenda for the nineties. *Western Journal of Medicine, 161*(3), 239–241.

Goodman, A. (2006). *The story of David Olds and the nurse home visiting program.* Princeton, NJ: Robert Wood Johnson Foundation.

Gottfredson, D. C., Najaka, S. S., & Kearley, B. (2003). Effectiveness of drug treatment courts: Evidence from a randomized trial. *Criminology & Public Policy, 2*(2), 171–196.

Hallahan, B., Hibbeln, J. R., Davis, J. M., & Garland, M. R. (2007). Omega-3 fatty acid supplementation in patients with recurrent self-harm: Single-centre double-blind randomised controlled trial. *British Journal of Psychiatry, 190*(2), 118–122.

Hare, R. D. (1993). *Without conscience: The disturbing world of the psychopaths among us.* New York, NY: The Pocket Press.

Institute of Education Science. (2008). *Reducing behavior problems in the elementary school classroom.* Washington, DC: U.S. Department of Education.

Kazdin, A. E. (1997). Parent management training: Evidence, outcomes, and issues. *Journal of the American Academy of Child and Adolescent Psychiatry, 36*(10), 1349–1356.

Kendall, P. C., Reber, M., McLeer, S., Epps, J., & Ronan, K. R. (1990). Cognitive-behavioral treatment of conduct-disordered children. *Cognitive Therapy and Research, 14*(3), 279–297.

Koob, G. F., & Le Moal, M. (2005). Plasticity of reward neurocircuitry and the "dark side" of drug addiction. *Nature Neuroscience, 8*(11), 1442–1444.

Landenberger, N. A., & Lipsey, M. W. (2005). The positive effects of cognitive-behavioral programs for offenders: A meta-analysis of factors associated with effective treatment. *Journal of Experimental Criminology, 1*(4), 451–476.

Liu, J., Raine, A., Venebles, P., & Mednick, S. A. (2006). Malnutrition, brain dysfunction, and antisocial criminal behavior. In A. Raine. (Ed.), *Crime and schizophrenia: Causes and cures.* New York, NY: Nova Science.

Lorber, M. F. (2004). Psychophysiology of aggression, psychopathy, and conduct problems: A meta-analysis. *Psychological Bulletin, 130*(4), 531–552.

Magill, M., & Ray, L. A. (2009). Cognitive-behavioral treatment with adult alcohol and illicit drug users: A meta-analysis of randomized controlled trials. *Journal of Studies on Alcohol and Drugs, 70*(4), 516–527.

McCormick, M. C., Brooks-Gunn, J., Buka, S. L., Goldman, J., Yu, J., & Salganik, M., . . . Casey, P. H. (2006). Early intervention in low birth weight premature infants: Results at 18 years of age for the Infant Health and Development Program. *Pediatrics, 117*(3), 771–780.

McGloin, J. M., Pratt, T. C., & Piquero, A. R. (2006). A life-course analysis of the criminogenic effects of maternal cigarette smoking during pregnancy: A research note on the mediating impact of neuropsychological deficit. *Journal of Research in Crime and Delinquency, 43*(4), 412–426.

Milkman, H. B., & Wanberg, K. W. (2007). *Cognitive-behavioral treatment: A review and discussion for corrections professionals.* Washington, DC: U.S. Department of Justice, National Institute of Corrections.

Mitchell, O., Wilson, D. B., Eggers, A., MacKenzie, D. L. (2012). Assessing the effectiveness of drug courts on recidivism: A meta-analytic review of traditional and non-traditional drug courts. *Journal of Criminal Justice, 40*(1). 60–71.

Mitchell, O., Wilson, D. B., & MacKenzie, D. L. (2012). The effectiveness of incarceration-based drug treatment on criminal behavior: A systematic review. *Campbell Collaboration.* doi:10.4073/csr.2012.18

Morley, R., & Lucas, A. (1997). Nutrition and cognitive development. *British Medical Bulletin, 53*(1), 123–134.

Mumola, C. J., & Karberg, J. C. (2006). *Drug use and dependence, state and federal prisoners, 2004.* Washington, DC: U.S. Department of Justice, Office of Justice Programs, Bureau of Justice Statistics.

National Health Service. (2009). *Healthy Children, Safer Communities: A strategy to promote the health and well-being of children and young people in contact with the youth justice system.* London, UK: HMSO.

Olds, D. L., Eckenrode, J., Henderson, C. R., Kitzman, H., Powers, J., Cole, R., . . . Luckey, D. (1997). Long-term effects of home visitation on maternal life course and child abuse and neglect. *Journal of the American Medical Association, 278*(8), 637–643.

Olds, D. L., Henderson, C. R., Chamberlin, R., & Tatelbaum, R. (1986). Preventing child abuse and neglect: A randomized trial of nurse home visitation. *Pediatrics, 78*(1), 65–78.

Olds, D., Henderson, C. R., Cole, R., Eckenrode, J., Kitzman, H., Luckey, D., . . . Powers, J. (1998). Long-term effects of nurse home visitation on children's criminal and antisocial behavior: 15-year follow-up of a randomized controlled trial. *Journal of the American Medical Association, 280*(14), 1238–1244.

Olds, D. L., Kitzman, H., Hanks, C., Cole, R., Anson, E., Sidora-Arcoleo, K., . . . Tutt, R. A. (2007). Effects of nurse home visiting on maternal and child functioning: Age-9 follow-up of a randomized trial. *Pediatrics, 120*(4), e832–e845.

Patterson, G. R., Chamberlain, P., & Reid, J. B. (1982). A comparative evaluation of a parent-training program. *Behavior Therapy, 13*(5), 638–650.

Piquero, A. R., Daigle, L. E., Gibson, C., Piquero, N. L., & Tibbetts, S. G. (2007). Research note: Are life-course-persistent offenders at risk for adverse health outcomes? *Journal of Research in Crime and Delinquency, 44*(2), 185–207.

Piquero, A. R., Farrington, D. P., Nagin, D. S., & Moffitt, T. E. (2010). Trajectories of offending and their relation to life failure in late middle age: Findings from the Cambridge Study in Delinquent Development. *Journal of Research in Crime and Delinquency, 47*(2), 151–173.

Piquero, A. R., Farrington, D. P., Welsh, B. C., Tremblay, R., & Jennings, W. G. (2009). Effects of early family/parent training programs on antisocial behavior and delinquency. *Journal of Experimental Criminology, 5*(2), 83–120.

Rafter, N. H. (1998). *Creating born criminals*. Champaign: University of Illinois Press.

Rafter, N. H. (2008a). *The criminal brain: Understanding biological theories of crime*. New York: New York University Press.

Rafter, N. H. (2008b). Criminology's darkest hour: Biocriminology in Nazi Germany. *Australian and New Zealand Journal of Criminology, 41*(2), 287–306.

Raine, A. (1996). Autonomic nervous system activity and violence. In D. M. Stoff & R. B. Cairns (Eds.), *Aggression and violence: Genetic, neurobiological, and biosocial perspectives* (pp. 145–168). Mahwah, NJ: Erlbaum.

Raine, A. (2002). The biological basis of crime. In J. Q. Wilson & J. Petersilia (Eds.), *Crime: Public policies for crime control* (2nd ed., pp. 43–74). Oakland, CA: ICS Press.

Raine A. (2013). *The anatomy of violence: The biological roots of crime*. New York, NY: Pantheon.

Raine, A., Buchsbaum, M., & Lacasse, L. (1997). Brain abnormalities in murderers indicated by positron emission tomography. *Biological Psychiatry, 42*(6), 495–508.

Raine, A., Buchsbaum, M. S., Stanley, J., Lottenberg, S., Abel, L., & Stoddard, J. (1994). Selective reductions in prefrontal glucose metabolism in murderers. *Biological Psychiatry, 36*(6), 365–373.

Raine, A., Liu, J., Venables, P., & Mednick, S. A. (2003). Preventing crime and schizophrenia using early environmental enrichment. In A. Raine (Ed.), *Crime and schizophrenia: Causes and cures*. New York, NY: Nova Sciences.

Raine, A., & Portnoy, J. (2012). Biology of crime: Past, present, and future perspectives. In R. Loeber & B. C. Welsh (Eds.), *The future of criminology*. New York, NY: Oxford University Press.

Raine, A., Rocque, M., & Welsh, B. C. (2013). Experimental neurocriminology: Etiology and treatment. In B. C. Welsh, A. A. Braga, & J. N. Gerben (Eds.), *Experimental criminology: Prospects for advancing science and public policy*. Cambridge, UK: Cambridge University Press.

Raine, A., Venables, P. H., & Mednick, S. A. (1997). Low resting heart rate at age 3 years predisposes to aggression at age 11 years: Evidence from the Mauritius Child Health Project. *Journal of the American Academy of Child and Adolescent Psychiatry, 36*(10), 1457–1464.

Ramsden, S., Richardson, F. M., Josse, G., Thomas, M. S. C., Ellis, C., Shakeshaft, C., . . . Price, C. J. (2011). Verbal and non-verbal intelligence changes in the teenage brain. *Nature, 479*, 113–116.

Reid, M. J., Webster-Stratton, C., & Hammond, M. (2003). Follow-up of children who received the Incredible Years intervention for oppositional-defiant disorder: Maintenance and prediction of 2-year outcome. *Behavior Therapy, 34*(4), 471–491.

Robinson, M. (2004). *Why crime? An integrated systems theory of antisocial behavior*. Upper Saddle River, NJ: Prentice Hall.

Rocque, M., Welsh, B. C., & Raine, A. (2012). Biosocial criminology and modern crime prevention. *Journal of Criminal Justice, 40*(3), 306–312.

Rose, N. (2000). The biology of culpability. *Theoretical Criminology, 4*(1), 5–34.

Schweinhart, L. J., Montie, J., Xiang, Z., Barnett, W. S., Belfield, C. R., & Nores, M. (2005). *Lifetime effects: The HighScope Perry Preschool study through age 40*. (Monographs of the HighScope Educational Research Foundation, 14). Ypsilanti, MI: HighScope Press.

Schweinhart, L. J., & Weikart, D. P. (1997). Lasting differences: The High/Scope preschool curriculum comparison study through age 23. *Early Childhood Research Quarterly, 12*(2), 117–143.

Scott, S., Spender, Q., Doolan, M., Jacobs, B., & Aspland, H. (2001). Multicentre controlled trial of parenting groups for childhood antisocial behaviour in clinical practice. *British Medical Journal, 323*, 194–197.

Shure, M. B., & Spivack, G. (1982). Interpersonal problem-solving in young children: A cognitive approach to prevention. *American Journal of Community Psychology, 10*(3), 341–356.

Steinberg, L. (2008). A social neuroscience perspective on adolescent risk-taking. *Developmental Review, 28*, 78–106.

Steinberg, L. (2010). Commentary: A behavioral scientist looks at the science of adolescent brain development. *Brain and Cognition, 72*(1), 160–164.

Taub, J. (2001). Evaluation of the second step violence prevention program at a rural elementary school. *School Psychology Review, 31*(2), 186–200.

Tremblay, R., E., & Craig, W. (1995). Developmental crime prevention. *Crime and Justice, 19*, 151–236.

Tremblay, R. E., & Japel, C. (2003). Prevention during pregnancy, infancy and the preschool years. In D. P. Farrington & J. W. Coid (Eds.), *Early prevention of adult antisocial behaviour* (pp. 205–242). Cambridge, UK: Cambridge University Press.

Vaske, J., Galyean, K., & Cullen, F. T. (2011). Toward a biosocial theory of offender rehabilitation: Why does cognitive-behavioral therapy work? *Journal of Criminal Justice, 39*(1), 90–102.

Walsh, A., & Beaver, K. M. (2009). *Biosocial criminology: New directions in theory and research*. New York, NY: Routledge.

Webster-Stratton, C., Kolpacoff, M., & Hollinsworth, T. (1988). Self-administered videotape therapy for families with conduct-problem children: Comparison with two cost-effective treatments and a control group. *Journal of Consulting and Clinical Psychology, 56*(4), 558–566.

Webster-Stratton, C., & Reid, M. J. (2010). The Incredible Years Parents, Teachers, and Children Training Series: A multifaceted treatment approach for young children. In J. Weisz & A. Kazdin (Eds.), *Evidence-based psychotherapies for children and adolescents* (2nd ed., pp. 194–210). New York, NY: Guilford Press.

World Health Organization. (2000). *Nutrition for health and development* (NHD). Progress report. Retrieved from http://whqlibdoc.who.int/hq/2000/WHO_NHD_00.6.pdf

Wormith, J. S., Althouse, R., Simpson, M., Reitzel, L. R., Fagan, T. J., & Morgan, R. D. (2007). The rehabilitation and reintegration of offenders: The current landscape and some future directions for correctional psychology. *Criminal Justice and Behavior, 34*(7), 879–892.

Wright, J. P., Beaver, K. M., DeLisi, M., Vaughn, M. G., Boisvert, D., & Vaske, J. (2008). Lombroso's legacy: The miseducation of criminologists. *Journal of Criminal Justice Education, 19*(3), 325–338.

Yang, Y., & Raine A. (2009). Prefrontal structural and functional brain imaging findings in antisocial, violent, and psychopathic individuals: A meta-analysis. *Psychiatry Research: Neuroimaging, 174*(2), 81–88.

Zaalberg, A., Nijman, H., Bulten, E., Stroosma, L., & van der Staak, C. (2010). Effects of nutritional supplements on aggression, rule-breaking, and psychopathology among young adult prisoners. *Aggressive Behavior, 36*(2), 117–126.

Discussion Questions

CHAPTERS 25 AND 26

1. Drs. Bailey, Lytle, and Sample note that biological factors associated with crime are easier to identify and address than social causes. However, the role of biology in crime prevention has been highly misunderstood. Why has this been the case? Do sociologists still express concerns with biological-based crime preventions?
2. Control theories that are used to inform prevention strategies often focus on improving social bonds between parents and children. Research reveals that intervening early (even before birth) can have positive effects on later development. Discuss some of the ways home visitation programs are able to influence early bonds between parents and children.
3. What has research revealed about the physiological factors related to criminal/antisocial behavior? In your opinion, how might this research inform prevention strategies?
4. Discuss the major differences between early crime prevention and secondary crime prevention. Are both types of prevention shown to be effective? Are there any drawbacks to implementing either one?
5. Explain how cognitive behavioral therapy (CBT) has been used to reduce antisocial behaviors in the offender population. Has this strategy been shown to be equally effective for both juvenile and adult offenders?
6. Traditionally, there has been antagonism between the sociological and biological orientations to crime prevention. However, a new trend is toward a "biosocial" perspective, where biology and the environment work interactively to reduce antisocial behavior. Moving forward, do you envision a change in the climate surrounding crime prevention?

Index

About the Editors

Kevin M. Beaver is a professor in the College of Criminology and Criminal Justice at Florida State University and a visiting distinguished professor in the Center for Social and Humanities Research at King Abdulaziz University. He is the past recipient of the American Society of Criminology's Ruth Shonle Cavan Young Scholar Award and the National Institute of Justice's Graduate Research Fellowship. He has published widely on the development of antisocial behaviors from a biosocial perspective, and his research on the genetic underpinnings to crime has been featured in major media outlets.

J.C. Barnes is an assistant professor in the Criminology Program at The University of Texas at Dallas. He is a biosocial criminologist whose research seeks to understand how genetic and environmental factors combine to impact criminological phenomena. Recent works have attempted to reconcile behavioral genetic findings with theoretical developments in criminology. He has published more than 70 papers and book chapters in outlets such as *Aggressive Behavior*, *Behavior Genetics*, *Criminology*, *Developmental Psychology*, *Intelligence*, *Journal of Marriage and Family*, *Justice Quarterly*, *Journal of Theoretical Biology*, and *PLoS ONE*.

Brian B. Boutwell is currently an assistant professor in the College of Criminal Justice at Sam Houston State University. His research interests span a variety of disciplines and include behavior genetics, developmental psychology, evolutionary psychology, as well as life course and theoretical criminology. His work has appeared in such journals as *Developmental Psychology*, *Behavior Genetics*, *Theoretical Biology*, *Criminology*, *Journal of Research in Crime and Delinquency*, and *Aggressive Behavior*, among others.